la Biennale di Venezia

49. ESPOSIZIONE INTERNAZIONALE D'ARTE·PLATEA DELL'UMANITA'·PLATEAU OF HUMANKIND·PLATEAU DER MENSCHHEIT·PLATEAU DE L'HUMANITE

Electa

la Biennale di Venezia

LA BIENNALE DI VENEZIA

49. Esposizione Internazionale d'Arte
Venice - Giardini di Castello, Arsenale
June 10 - November 4 2001

Director
Harald Szeemann

Assistant to the Director
Cecilia Liveriero Lavelli

International Jury

Ery Càmara

Carolyn Christov-Bakargiev

Manray Hsu

Hans Ulrich Obrist

Virginia Pérez-Ratton

Leoni d'oro for lifetime achievement

Richard Serra

Cy Twombly

Organizational Coordination and Support
Dario Ventimiglia
Chiara Bernardi
Angela Cicolini
Gianpaolo Cimarosti
Maria Cristina Cinti
Amyel Garnaoui
AnnaMaria Porazzini
Roberto Rosolen
Paolo Scibelli

Installation
Manuela Luca Dazio
Jérôme Szeemann
Matteo Ballarin
Christian Dominguez
Alvise Draghi
Ivano Gandin
Kees Hensen
Lucio Ramelli
Una Szeemann
Christoph Zurcher

Pina Maugeri (*site restoration*)
Maria Elena Cazzaro
Arianna Laurenzi
Francesca Mamprin

Transport and Insurance
Josy Kraft
Claudia De Zordo
Rita Musacco
Luigi Ricciari
Alessandra Versace

Communication and Public Relation
Flavia Fossa Margutti
Silvio Sircana
Alexia Boro
Elisabetta Scantamburlo

Paolo Lughi
Barbara Del Greco
Chiara Farnea
Diego Giacomini
Michela Lazzarin
Donato Mendolia
Maddalena Pietragnoli
Fiorella Tagliapietra
Donatella Venturini

Guerino Delfino (*web site*)
Giovanni Alberti

Marketing, Visitor Services, Sponsors
Fabio Achilli
Dario Merighi
Alessandra Miraglia
Laura Revelli Beaumont

publicity
Eugenia Fiorin
Cristina Graziussi
Michela Mason

General Services

Secretariat and General Affairs
Daniela Barcaro
Nicola Bon
Roberta Savoldello
Cinzia Tibolla

Giusi Conti
Cristina Abele
Patrizia Andres
Marta Pellizzato

Technical - logistic Unit
Angelo Bacci
Aldo Roberto Beltrame
Cinzia Bernardi
Marina Bertaggia
Andrea Bonaldo
Paolo Casarotto
Alessandra Durand de la Penne
Marco Garofalo
Silvia Gatto
Stefania Guerra
Tiziano Inguanotto
Silvia Marchetto
Nicola Rizzo
Lucia Scarabottolo
Giuseppe Simeoni
Guido Vianello

Legal Services
Debora Rossi
Isabella Cecchini

Hospitality
Antonia Possamai
Nella Bertelli
Barbara Carpenedo
Sabina Mabilia
Jasna Zoranovic

Human Resources
Sandro Vettor
Silvia Bruni
Federica Camali
Graziano Carrer
Giovanni Drudi
Mariano Folin
Antonella Sfriso
Alessia Viviani

Auditing
Valentina Borsato

Administration
Daniela Venturini
Bruna Gabbiato
Martina Fiori
Maria Cristina Lion
Manuela Pellicciolli
Giorgio Vergombello
Sara Vianello
Leandro Zennaro

Documentation Project curated by ASAC
Gabriella Cecchin
Erica De Luigi
Roberta Fontanin
Michele Mangione
Oriana Rispoli
Francesca Sardi
Adriana Rosaria Scalise
Michela Stancescu
Evelina Piera Zanon
Giorgio Zucchiatti

Inter-sector projects within the 49. Esposizione Internazionale d'Arti Visive

Cinema
Alberto Barbera
Michael Tarantino
The Cinema Department Staff

Dance, Music, Theatre
Bruno Canino
Carolyn Carlson
Giorgio Barberio Corsetti
The DMT Department Staff

Acknowledgements

Ministero per i Beni
e le Attività Culturali

Ministero della Difesa,
Marina Militare di Venezia,
Ammiraglio Paolo Pagnotella

Ministero delle Finanze,
Agenzia del demanio,
sede di Venezia

Sindaco di Venezia, Paolo Costa

Soprintendenza per i Beni
Ambientali e Architettonici
di Venezia

Istituto di Cultura Italiano a Berlino

Istituto di Cultura Italiano a Londra

Istituto di Cultura Italiano a Parigi

MUSEI
CIVICI
VENEZIANI

KataWeb
kwArt

Club
la Repubblica

Rai Sat Art

ACTV Venezia

AMAV Venezia

APT Venezia

SAVE
Aeroporto di Venezia Marco Polo Spa

Venezia Tronchetto Parking s.p.a.

VELA Venezia

OTIM

Special acknowledgements
for supporting the Exhibition

Main sponsors

TELECOM
ITALIA
www.telecomitalia.it

(the interactive "Cloud" installation in
the Giardini di Castello was produced by
Studio Azzurro)

Microsoft

Posteitaliane

Thanks to GUCCI
for sponsoring the work of
Richard Serra
and special thanks to
Artis, François Pinault Group

Technical sponsors

GRAPHICREPORT.

The technical apparatus in the press
room was generously provided by

hp
invent

FONDAZIONE P.I.
"Domenico Chiesa"

Media sponsor

SITCOM

Acknowledgements

In the making of the "Plateau of Humankind", this first exhibition of the "post-Postmodern", I could count on the help and support of many people.

First of all I would like to thank the artists, the only ones who make possible a Biennale by their works and their engagement. They are the very ones who keep the promise of a Plateau of Humankind and have contributed to the realisation of the exhibition by providing new solutions to the cut in means and funds: Hence, they allow Venice to present once again a great event. Many of them have also created new works for the Biennale, tight schedule, as usual, notwithstanding.

I am grateful to the President of the Biennale Paolo Baratta, for the confidence he placed in me by trusting me with the last Biennale of the 20th century and the first of this new millennium. He has done all he could to make available new spaces at the Arsenale, thus emphasising the fact that the importance of the Biennale also depends on the acquisition of new exhibition structures. I also want to express my thanks to the members of the Board of Directors, who have supported his choice: Laura Barbiani, Paolo Costa, Giorgio Orsoni, Giorgio van Straten.

My sincere thanks for the precious suggestions they gave me goes to: Zdenka Baldovinac, Saskia Bos, Mario Cristiani, Melle Daamen, Lorenzo Fiaschi, Bernhard Fibicher, Alanna Heiss, Stephan Huber, Udo Kittelmann, Kati Kivinen, Kaspar König, Rosa Martínez, Dominique Païni, Thomas Pfister, Silvia Pichini, Maurizio Rigillo, Maaike Ritsema, Osvaldo Sanchez, Hugo and Irina Schär, Marketta Seppälä, Uli and Rita Sigg, Frank Thiel, Michael Tarantino, Yushi Yakimato, Otto Zitko and many others, whose contribution helped me in defining the general vision of the exhibition.

I want to mention with special gratitude the enthusiasm, perseverance, optimism and energy of my assistant Cecilia Liveriero Lavelli in the preparation of both the exhibition and the catalogue. I'm also grateful to Lara Facco for her generous collaboration.

In thanking the General Coordinator Massimo Coda, I whish to express to all the collaborators of the Società di Cultura my most heartfelt thanks. First of all to the Managing Director of the Institute Activities Dario Ventimiglia — responsible of the Exhibition Activities Department and of all pertained the making of the exhibition and the difficult problems connected to it — but also to the members of the Department: Anna Maria Porazzini, Gianpaolo Cimarosti, Roberto Rosolen, Paolo Scibelli, with the assistance of Chiara Bernardi, Angela Cicolini, Maria Cristina Cinti, Amyel Garnaoui, Luigi Ricciari, who have taken charge of an enormous amount of administrative and technical work. Not to forget Angelo Bacci and the technicians, Lucio Ramelli and his co-workers; and obviously my thanks go as well to the people in charge for the exhibition logistics and installation, transport and insurance, Claudia De Zordo, Alvise Draghi, Manuela Lucà Dazio and Rita Musacco, who have collaborated with my crew, namely Christian Dominguez, Josy Kraft, Jérôme Szeemann, Una Szeemann e Christoph Zürcher: without them this huge undertaking would have never been possible. They have worked in close connection with Michele Tosetto, who has helped greatly even when it was not included in the terms of his contract. Finally, we will not forget to mention the helpful spirits of Fabbrica: Cornelia Faist, Ivana Falconi, Juliette Duca Fierz.

Many thanks also to Daniela Venturini for the Administration, to Antonia Possamai and her assistants for the Hospitality, Sandro Vettor and his staff of Human Resourses, Fabio Achilli and assistants for the Services to the Public and, last but not least, the smiling Flavia Fossa Margutti who tenaciously strives for Communication and Image, with the help of Alexia Boro and of the central Press Office coordinated by Paolo Lughi on one side and of Jenny Fiorin and her team for the Advertising on the other.

There are no exhibitions without lenders.

Among Museums and Institutions we remember

Kunsthaus Zürich (Joseph Beuys); Stedelijk van Abbe Museum, Eindhoven (Joseph Beuys); Staatliche Museen zu Berlin, Nationalgalerie, Sammlung Marx / Eigentum des Landes Berlin (Joseph Beuys); Fondazione Sandretto Re Rebaudengo, Torino (Marko Lehanka); Kunstmuseum Wolfsburg (Neo Rauch); Solomon R. Guggenheim Museum, New York (Neo Rauch); The Museum of Fine Arts, Houston (Gerhard Richter); Ville de Genève, Musée d'Art et d'Histoire, Genève (Auguste Rodin); Musée Rodin, Paris (Auguste Rodin); Museo di Capodimonte, Napoli (Gerd Rohling); Stedelijk Museum, Amsterdam (Fiona Tan)

Among the Galleries

Galerie Peter Kilchmann (Francis Alÿs, Santiago Sierra); Lisson Gallery (per Francis Alÿs, Pierre Bismuth, Roderick Buchanan, Egoyan/Sarmento); Massimo Minini (Vanessa Beecroft), Brescia; Lia Rumma, Napoli (Vanessa Beecroft); Anthony Reynolds Gallery, Londra (Richard Billingham, Paul Graham, Marin Karmitz, Keityh Tyson); Alfonso Artiaco, Napoli (Botto e Bruno); Alberto Peola, Torino (Botto e Bruno); Le Case d'Arte, Milano (Botto e Bruno); Liebman Magnan Gallery, New York (Tania Bruguera); Galleria Continua, San Gimignano (Loris Cecchini); Galerie Barbara Thumm, Berlin (Com&Com); Anthony d'Offay Gallery, London (Chris Cunningham, Rineke Dijkstra); Sixpackfilm, Vienna (Josef Dabernig); Susan Hobbs Gallery (Max Dean – Raffaello d'Andrea); m Fotografie Bochum (Lucinda Devlin); Sean Kelly Gallery, New York (Egoyan/Sarmento); Galerie Nächst St. Stephan, Vienna (Helmut Federle); VU' Galerie, Paris (Cristina Garcia Rodero); Photo & Contemporary, Torino (Luis González Palma); Galerie Bob van Orsouw, Zürich (Paul Graham); Lawrence Rubin Greenberg Van Doren, New York (Paul Graham); Donald Young Gallery, Chicago (Gary Hill); Galería Camargo Vilaça, São Paulo (Yishai Jusidman); Galeria OMR, Mexico (Yishai Jusidman, Manuel Ocampo); Jeffery Deitch Projects, New York (Matthieu Laurette, Nick Waplington); Salvatore Ala, Milano (Christiane Löhr); Zeno X Gallery, Antwerp (Mark Manders); Galleria S.A.L.E.S., Roma (Eva Marisaldi); Jack Shainman Gallery, New York (Manuel Ocampo); Beetz & Kemfert Kunstberatung, Frankfurt (Arnold Odermatt); Springer Winkler Galerie, Berlin (Arnold Odermatt); Galerie Neu, Berlin (Manfred Pernice); Gio Marconi, Milano (Paul Pfeiffer); The Project New York / Los Angeles (Paul Pfeiffer); Nicole Klagsbrun Gallery, New York (John Pilson); Galleria Raucci/Santamaria, Napoli (John Pilson); Galerie Six Friedrich Lisa Ungar, München (Alexander Ranner); Galerie Eigen+Art, Berlin/Leipsig (Neo Rauch); Galerie Hauser & Wirth, Zürich (Neo Rauch, Nedko Solakov); The Goodman Gallery, Johannesburg (Tracey Rose); Galleria Fabjbasaglia, Rimini (Mimmo Rotella); Galerie Rüdiger Schöttle / Galerie Johnen + Schöttle (Anri Sala); Gagosian Gallery, New York (Richard Serra, Cy Twombly); Galeria Enrique Guerrero, Mexico (Santiago Sierra); Sommer Contemporary Art, Tel Aviv (Eliezer Sonnenschein); Pinksummer, Genova (Georgina Starr); Emily Tsingou Gallery, Londra (Georgina Starr); Lehmann Maupin Gallery, New York (Do-Ho Suh); Galerie Paul Andriesse (Fiona Tan);Serge Ziegler Galerie, Zürich (Javier Téllez); White Cube (Gavin Turk); Anthony Meier Fine Arts, San Francisco, CA (Richard Tuttle); Sperone Westwater, New York (Richard Tuttle, Not Vital); De Pury & Luxembourg, Zürich; Agnes B. (Massimo Vitali); Arndt & Partner, Berlin (Massimo Vitali); Crown Gallery, Bruxelles (Massimo Vitali); Galerie Rüdiger Schöttle, München/Köln (Jeff Wall); Marian Goodman Gallery, New York (Jeff Wall); Antenna (Magnus Wallin); Galerie Meyer Kainer, Wien (Heimo Zobernig); Novel Art, Männedorf

Private lenders are also present

Saba Saba Collection, Verona & Giorgio Bazzani (Sunday Jack Akpan, Seni Camara, Ousmane Ndiaye, John Goba, Cheff Mwai, Jean Baptiste Ngnetchopa, Peter Wanjau, scultore Giriama); Werner Khon, Bergisch-Gladbach (Erich Bödeker, Gilberto de le Nuez, Hans Schmitt); Uli Sigg, Mauensee (Hai Bo, Xiao Yu); Renato e Sonia Jelmorini (Ettore Jelmorini); Brondesbury Holdings LTD, Tortola, B.Y.I., Private Collection (Yishai Jusidman); Gisy Klot, Frankfurt am Main (Marko Lehanka); Andreas Schülter, Napoli (Marko Lehanka); Erika Hoffmann-Koenige und Rolf Hoffmann, Berlin (Ron Mueck); Mr and Ms Keith L. Sachs, Rydal (Ron Mueck); Collection Ron and Anne Dees (Manuel Ocampo); Dimitri Daskalopoulos (Paul Pfeiffer); Susan & Michael Hort (Neo Rauch); Collezione Renata Novarese, Moransengo (Alessandra Tesi); Herr und Frau M. Studer-Walsh, Rüschlikon (Richard Tuttle); Collection Vandermeulen, Stekene, Belgio (Eulalia Valldosera)

Many loans were made by the artists themselves

Tiong Ang & Lumen Travo, Amsterdam;

Richard Billingham; Pierre Bismuth; Tania Bruguera; Max Dean; Stan Douglas; João Onofre; Paul Pfeiffer; Do-Ho Suh; Fiona Tan; Alessandra Tesi; Keitrh Tyson; Eulalia Valldosera; Minnette Vári; Bill Viola; Nick Waplington

Many of these projects would not have been possible if not for the support of sponsoring Institutions or private enterprises
Afaa, Association Française pour l'Action Artistique (Pierre Bismuth, Matthieu Laurette); Christian Aid, Guatemala (per Regina Galindo); Amanco, Costa Rica (per Priscilla Monge); British Council, Londra (Chris Cunningham); Bundesamt für Kultur Bern (Com&Com, Helmut Federle, Ingeborg Lüscher, Chantal Michel, Arnold Odermatt, Niele Toroni, Not Vital); Ca' del Sol (per Susan Kleinberg); Canadian Art Foundation, the Canada Council for the Arts and the Ontario Arts Council (Max Dean – Raffaello D'Andrea); Canadian Embassy and League of Human Rights (Ken Lum); C.I.M. Cardificio Italiano S.p.A., Verano Cremasco, (Priscilla Monge); Cinemagnetics (Susan Kleinberg); CONACULTA – Consejo Nacional para la Cultura y las Artes (Yishai Jusidman); Contexto Arte Contempóraneo, Guatemala (per A1-53167, Galindo, Gonzalez-Palma); Giancarlo Danieli – Commercio metalli, Vicenza (Barry McGee, Stephen Powers, Todd James); Deitch Projects, New York (Vanessa Beecroft; Barry McGee, Stephen Powers, Todd James); Anthony d'Offay Gallery, Londra (Chris Cunningham, Rineke Dijkstra, Ron Mueck, Gerhard Richter, Francesco Vezzoli, Bill Viola, Jeff Wall), Epson Italia, Milano (Alessandra Tesi); FC Grashoppers / FC San Gallo (Ingeborg Lüscher); Film i Skåne (Magnus Wallin); Fondazione per l'Arte Nicola Trussardi, Milano (Ingeborg Lüscher); FRAME – Finnish Fund for Art Exchange, Helsinki (Veli Granö, Laura Horelli, Tuomo Manninen, Heli Rekula, Charles Sandison, Salla Tykkä, Maaria Wirkkala); Fundação Luso-Americana para o Desenvolvimento (FLAD) (Egoyan-Sarmento); Fundação Luso-Americana para o Desenvolvimento (FLAD) (Egoyan-Sarmento); Fundação Calouste Gulbenkian (Egoyan-Sarmento); Fundacion Paiz, Guatemala (Aníbal López, A1- 53167); Galleria Continua, San Gimignano (Ilya e Emilia Kabakov);

Gagosian Gallery, New York (Richard Serra); Governo messicano (Gustavo Artigas, Yishiai Jusidman); Gruppo Teseco per l'Arte (Botto e Bruno); Gucci (Serra); Näf Holybau, Kessvil (Com&Com); Patasch und Hans Guggenheim, St. Gallen (Com&Com); Hauser & Wirth, St. Gallen (Nedko Solakov); IASPIS (Lars Siltberg, Magnus Wallin); Ifa, Institut für Auslandsbeziehungen, Stuttgart (Marko Lehanka, Carsten Nicolai, Olaf Nicolai, Neo Rauch, Gerd Rohling); INBA — Instituto Nacional de Bellas Artes (Yishai Jusidman); Instituto de Arte Contemporânea / Ministério da Cultura (Egoyan-Sarmento); Christian Lacroix, Paris (Tania Ostoi); Lista, Schweiz (Com&Com); Madema (Susan Kleinberg); Susan & Lewis Manilow, Chicago (Nedko Solakov); MK2 / Galerie de France (Abbas Kiarostami); Mountain DV Solution, Zürich (Com&Com); Ministerio de Asuntos Exteriores, Secretaría de Estado para la Cooperación Internacional y para Iberoamérica, Madrid (Cristina Garcia Rodero, Eulalia Valldosera, Santiago Sierra); Mondriaan Stichting, Amsterdam (Tiong Ang, Atelier van Lieshout, Rineke Dijkstra, Mark Manders, Fiona Tan); Pinault (Serra); Pro Helvetia – Arts Council of Switzerland / Cultural Exchange East -West (Nedko Solakov); Ringier TV (Ingeborg Lüscher); Samsung (Susan Kleinberg); Hugo und Irina Schär-Tkachenko (Viktor Maruščenko); Schwarzkopf Professional, Milano (Santiago Sierra); Settore Cinema della Biennale di Venezia (Chantal Akerman, Samuel Beckett/Marin Karimtz, Atom Egoyan & Julião Sarmento, Yervant Gianikian & Angela Ricci Lucchi, Abbas Kiarostami); SRE — Secretaría de Relaciones Exteriores (Yishai Jusidman);TEOR/ética, Costa Rica (A1-53167, Galindo, González-Palma, Herrero, Monge, Tischler); Donald Young Gallery, Chicago (Gary Hill); Serge Ziegler Galerie, Zürich (Minnette Vári); Zwirner, New York (Stan Douglas)

The artists thank
Pierre Bismuth: Lisa Rosendhal, Orsola de Castro, Stella Cattana, Thilo Hoffman, Margherita Castellani, Viktoras Bismutas, Uberta Camerana.
Com&Com: Can Asan, Tobia Bezzola, Gilgi Guggenheim, Tabea Guhl, HR Giger, Kunsthaus Zürich, Angelika Richter, Georg Rutishauser, Barbara Thumm

Max Dean – Raffaello D'Andrea: Electro-Mechanical Designer (Colin Harry), Design Sponsor and Fabrication (Matt Donovan and Alex Laverick), Additional Software Development (Thibet Ringratkitiyot and Dennis Polic)
Yervant Gianikian & Angela Ricci Lucchi: Dominique Païni, Danièle Hibon, Chrisitan Longchamp, Claudine Kaufmann (Cinèmathèque Française)
Luis Gonzalez Palma: Sagrario Perez-Soto, Rodolfo Jimenez Borbon, Glenn Jampol
Federico Herreo: Sagrario Perez-Soto, Rodolfo Jimenez Borbon, Glenn Jampol, Flor Fallas
Ilya & Emilio Kabakov: Galleria Continua, San Gimignano; Galeria Lia Rumma, Napoli; Thaddaeus Ropac Gallery, Paris/Salzburg; Chiara Bertola; Guntis Brands; Adelina von Fürstenberg
Susan Kleinberg: Ms R. Ziegler
Marko Lehanka: Barbara Weiss, Berlin; Leo Koenig, Inc, New York; Martina Detterer, Frankfurt am Main; Galerie Art Attitudes, Hervé Bize, F-Nancy; Museum für Moderne Kunst, MMK, Frankfurt am Main; Dr. Andreas Bee, Frankfurt; Horst Hadergasser, Frankfurt; Domberger Gruppe, München; Caroline Krause, Frankfurt; Prof. Dr. Marcel Baumgartner, Giessen; Alexander Demuth, Frankfurt
Eva Marisaldi: Enrico Maria Serotti per la realizzazione
Priscilla Monge: Sagrario Perez-Soto, Rodolfo Jimenez Borbon, Glenn Jampol
Gerd Rohling: Progetto realizzato in collaborazione con la Soprintendenza Archeologica di Napoli e Caserta, Servizi educativi (Michele Iodice e Marco de Gennis)
Alessandra Tesi: Moyens Aériens, Securité Civile France; Carla Conca & Alessandro de Pasquale (Epson Italia); Comandante Jean-Luc Chivot, Brigade de Sapeurs-Pompiers de Paris
Jaime David Tischler: Sagrario Perez-Soto, Rodolfo Jimenez Borbon, Glenn Jampol

A special thanks to the artists' collaborators and assistants, like
Pilar Corrias (Francis Alÿs); Otto Hubacek (Joseph Beuys); Kathy Lucas (Chris Burden); Lucio Zotti (Maurizio Cattelan); the five collaborators of Max Dean e Raffaello D'Andrea; Chiara Bersi Serlini (Rineke Dijkstra, Francesco Vezzoli and Bill Viola); Peter Raich (Helmut Federle); Colin Griffiths (Stan Douglas); Yu Shuyuan (Hai Bo); Chiara Zabatta (Ilya & Emilia Kabakov); Urs

Odermatt (Arnold Odermatt); Stuart Elster, Andrea Mason, Miguel Clark, Zwi Wasserstein (John Pilson); Alison de Lima Greene (Gerhard Richter); Ernst Fuchs (Richard Serra); Andy Avini & Gary Rough (Cy Twombly); Luca Corbetta (Francesco Vezzoli); Kimberli Meyer (Bill Viola).

A feature caracterizes the Biennale long tradition: in addition to Partecipating Countries with their Pavilions in the Giardini, there has been an increasing number of other countries partecipating to the exhibition in external spaces, as well as individual artists and institutions with initiatives in parallel to the main exhibition. In here I would like to give heartfelt thanks to all the artists, curators and collaborators, to the organizations and ministries which worked with renewed commitment in making — whether in conjunction with us or not — their contributions.

To confirm its leadership in the field of Visual Arts, the Biennale di Venezia needed
a new impulse with a wide-ranging, authoritative broadening of its scope and through
the implementation of new, extraordinary developments.
In particular, it was a matter of increasing our capacity for reception and representation
in recognisable sites that have a precise identity, and not only just for current exhibitions
but as a valid way forward. A strategic choice, therefore, during a phase in which we are asked
not so much and not only to present artistic schools and movements as a priority, as we are
to highlight the varied artistic individualities operating around the world (and with these also any
evocations of the recent past) in various distinct ways. In other words, in the new globalisation
that involves us all, to reveal what artists of the moment are working upon,
their trends, their stresses, their gestures, and to represent (without creating hierarchies)
"the other truth": the truth of artists, without a knowledge of which an understanding of our
times would be incomplete. In this sense, the International Exhibition of Art is not addressed
simply to specialists and art-lovers, but to anyone wishing to enrich his awareness and hence his
belonging to the present. Our commitment to the young also takes this as its objective: special
didactic programmes will be implemented from September in collaboration with schools. In this
sense, there is new value in the presence of the "pavilions" of other nations that have accepted
the Biennale's innovation, and which have responded with enthusiasm and interest (and not only
in the field of visual arts, but also in other sectors, especially that of Dance, Music and Theatre,
which has in the meantime been reorganised).
The 49ᵗʰ Exhibition marks the largest participation of countries in the history of the Biennale (64).
This is an interesting phenomenon because the role of the pavilions is evolving little by little:
from "representations" to "original exhibitions", promoted directly by the countries with their
own curators.
The white walls of the Padiglione Italia and the plastic spaces of the monumental Venetian
Arsenale, which were already open over the past two years and are strongly characterised
by the Venetian architecture of the late 16ᵗʰ century, will be joined by two new spaces which are
currently undergoing work in the Tese delle Vergini, after the so-called Gaggiandre: these are
rather more severe locations, appearing like two real "camerae obscurae" from which it will be
possible to reach the green of the Giardino delle Vergini. From surprise to surprise.
The new spaces made over to Dance, Music and Theatre have also in the meantime been further
improved and integrated with the exhibition spaces. The continuity of our work could not but help
include greater inter-sectorial collaboration. Other sectors will expressly dedicate
to the Exhibition some productions from their programme. Such is the case, for example,
of Dance. Also present at the 49ᵗʰ Exhibition will be film directors especially invited to produce
a work. Likewise, poetry will also be presented as a work.
With the realisation of these new widened spaces, the Biennale offers the directors new,
interconnected possibilities. All the directors have responded to the challenge in a positive manner.
In perfect tune with this broadening of scope, using this new platform Szeeman first managed
to implement his "dAPERTutto" in 1999 and now the "Plateau of Humankind".
This sense of agreement could not fail to appear in a curator who, thanks to his nature
and cultural background, loves far more to discover artists world-wide in their creativity
than to classify them as a critic.
We wish to thank all the collaborators for the incredible enthusiasm they dedicate
to this extraordinary undertaking, the Biennale di Venezia.

Paolo Baratta
President of the Biennale di Venezia

Catalogue edited by
Harald Szeemann
Cecilia Liveriero Lavelli
Lara Facco (assistant)

with the collaboration of
Chiara Barbieri
Elena Cinenti
Claudia De Zordo
Alessia Facco
Rose Porter
Chiara Zabatta

Graphic Design
Dario Tagliabue (catalogue)
Tapiro Venezia, Enrico Camplani,
Pierluigi Pescolderung,
(cover and official image)
Carlo Maria Biadene
(page layout)

General editor
Rosanna Alberti

Translations
Marina Baruffaldi
Richard G. Carlsson
Tina Cawthra
Laura Dal Carlo
Roberta Lazzaro
James Manley
Anthony Marasco
Andrew May
Nicholas Mayow
William Murphy
Katarzyna Niementowska
Stefano Polesello
Luigina Romor
Giuliana Schiavi
Monica Sonck
Carla Toffolo
Susan Wise

Catalogue production
Electa, Milano
Elemond Editori Associati

Contents

Bazon Brock

The Plateau of Friendship – Critique of Truth! Problems unite more

The citizens of Athens called the plateau *Acropolis*, the Diadochians succeeding Alexander called it the *Summit of Haimon;* the early Humanists, following in the footsteps of Petrarch, climbed *Mount Ventoux;* in the absolutist age the plateau resembled a burial mound; for the founder heroes of our modern civilisation in the eighteenth century it took on the form of a small temple in every English park. Goethe established the *towers* ("born to be seen, demanding attention") as the guardian of high points of view. In the nineteenth century the plateau assumed the form of a capital for monuments and works of art whereas in the twentieth century the plateau assumed the form of the leader's chancel or the display gondola of the Zeppelins.

The plateau has therefore always been a feature that permits an overall view by means of a general view, of observation as *theory* and *supervision.* Whoever wishes to lead, to make revelations or inspire has to prove himself or herself a visionary. But he cannot just stubbornly stare ahead; he has to comprehend the panorama of the world in its unity and a whole. He has to become a *super visionary.* It is the panoramic view that guarantees the continuity of the view, only the distinct model of a whole that directs it towards futuristic and utopian dimensions. Only those who are able to view things simply, achieve a *synopsis* by creating a theory, and can see beyond the horizon of visibility to include what is imaginable.

A thousand times and more the "Plateau of Mankind" has symbolised points of view, fixed points, references as its focus or centre. This polycentrality in the relationships of humans with each other does justice only to one type of

social bond: friendship. It is not without reason that sociologists and media-scientists, artists and social protagonists are currently discussing with such passion the meaning of the bonds of friendship for the extremely problematic cultural development beyond the twenty-first century. For example, the world-famous cultural scientist, Neil Postman, with his latest book "The second solution, a bridge into the twenty-first century". A further good example is that of the artist, Nan Goldin, with her strategy of identifying photographic work as the structure of a bond of friendship. The friendship between Kippenberger, Öhlen and Büttner was legendary as was that of the artists from the Michael Weiner Gallery: Lüpertz, Immendorff, Baselitz, Penck. They and many others were naturally referring to Joseph Beuys' *Social Sculpture* through the bond of friendship and the Free University and its many predecessors in the history of the *elective affinities.*

In the field of design and the applied arts, campaigns such as those by Benetton (United Colours), for example the campaign "We are family" for department stores or the now accepted belief that research groups formed a "research family", are based on the historical motives of friendship bonds as romantic groups of common suffering or optimistic brotherhood groups. But unlike the conspiratorial combat groups of *Fight Clubs*, the SS units, the mafia or the groups of religious martyrs, friendship does not exactly demand agreement in the obligatory declaration and submission to the higher instance of divine revelation or dictatorial patronage.

Friendship becomes the dominant type of bond in social relationships because it only becomes effective when all the other common factors

from religious and political membership, race and nation, gender roles and behavioural attitudes have been resolved. And that currently seems to be the case – no matter how hard one tries to awake the bloody impression that the parties are adamant in their beliefs – in religious wars (Northern Ireland), wars of nationality (Basque), cultural wars (Ex-Yugoslavia). Not even the characters of the art scene that have claimed to be enlightened spirits since the 18th century believe in the unshakeability of their convictions and opinions. They have experienced that one can only produce something New and Different if one is well aware of one's prejudices and is able to annul them. Only those who are willing to question their convictions and opinions and do not exclude themselves from radical doubts will be productive.

Anyway, considering the bloody consequences that inevitably follow excessive convictions, it should be clear that the surest way to avoid murder and manslaughter is to give up dogmatic convictions; in their place one develops a lasting awareness of the problem, its provisional character, the restrictedness of all opinions, even if they can be justified as "true".

If, therefore, in the future, people still want to have something in common that encourages and protects them, then it is not religious convictions, cultural identities or preferences of style or taste (always a reason for a fight). Rather, it is the common orientation towards problems, in particular malevolent problems, that is, mainly problems that cannot be solved, that creates the feeling of togetherness: precisely that of friendship. The different to the love relationship, the parents-child relationship, the teacher-pupil relationship or the employer-employee relations is that friendship opens up acceptance and orientation, since one entrusts one's girlfriend or boyfriend blindly with the very mention of one's owns doubts, shortcomings, fears of failure and general deficits. The bond of friendship has proved to be one of the most stable in a world in which there is no longer any certainty and in which one must expect malevolent and uncontrollable problems.

The oldest strategy and the self-image of the artists who saw themselves as *avant-gardes* still remain in the 21st century. Their self-assurance came from their ability to turn all certainties into problems. They were masters in finding problems – even where scientists and businessmen saw none. Since the Renaissance, artists have shown that problems cannot be solved; one can only learn how to deal with them – which is why engineers and business-men smile down upon artists as negative and

someone who fouls his own nest. In the mean-time they have all realised that problems can only be solved if new ones are created. Accordingly, as creators of problems, artists have always been of significance, whereas a pupil who claimed that practice and perfection would overcome the shortcomings of his teacher would only be laughed at. And the activists of the art scene have always been geniuses of friendship; their stimulators were called *curators*, or *publishers* or *collectors* or *negotiators.*. It is significant that such a genius of friendship, which has been on the Plateau of Supervision for 35 years to great effect, and has thereby redefined the type of curator, pro-ducer, negotiator, has chosen to use the con-cept of *Plateau* for the 2001 Biennial. It is the only notion we can trust, going right back to the 18th century and the history of modernity, without wanting to force a following of inspi-ration through mere speculation or through reward and punishment. Whoever reproaches

Harry Szeemann for only wanted to present friends to the public community in larger exhi-bitions has not yet understood that one gets involved with the arts and artists because one can always depend on their awareness of problems that links them to us all. Friends are people who can be depended on, precisely because they do accept the exemplary nature of our shortcomings, our failures and our embarrassing restrictedness. It is only with friends that I can be my true self and nowhere else where only power, fame and money that matter. It is friends who experience their effect and value over the impotence of power, of the inflation of the 15-minute of fame, the loss of money won and the reduction of our creative potential through the realization as capital.

It is for this that the unforgettable Piero Manzoni has created this wonderful Plateau of a *Socle du Mond:* friendship carries the world rather than staging it with a crown.

ime The timeless, grand narration of human existence in its time The

Harald Szeemann

The timeless, grand narration of human existence in its time

The two questions, that are constantly asked in connection with the Biennale or biennial exhibitions and events like *documenta* are: "Do such large exhibitions still make sense?" and "Is art still topical?" The first question is easy to answer. "It depends solely on who organises them". The answer to the second could be "Art is a language, and whoever takes the time to read it will always find it topical". And with this, we find ourselves at the heart of Venice 2001.

I have always maintained that "Plateau der Menscheit" (The Plateau of Humankind) is not a theme but rather a dimension. Let us take a wider view.

In 1969, with "When Attitudes become Form", I was given the chance to unite the revolutionary strength of the 20th century Fine Arts through the medium of the exhibition, thus giving a new dimension to cultural space and the institution, as well as to the role of curator. In my active participation at the Biennale of Venice, I have always sought the expansion of these borders in this direction and therefore the adventure of creating, via the form of the exhibition, a temporarily valid world, anchored in the spirit of the times and linked to the intuition of what is to come. In 1975 it was the energy streams in the form of a closed circuit, fed by the obsessive impulse of creative man, whether reflected or experienced, which culminated in the challenge: more eroticism and less procreation. Schizophrenia, capitalism, birth-control, the sudden jump from *I* to *We* were the motivations that the "Bachelor machines/ Macchine celibi" (and not *nubili*) were based on.

In 1980 the additional exhibition "Aperto" was created in the Magazzini del Sale under the assigned theme "Gli anni settanta". I was only able to curate it by threatening to resign and on the condition that I was able to work alongside Achille Bonito Oliva. "Aperto" expressed the wish to go beyond the avant-garde of the late Sixties and which from an evolutionary point of view had already assumed a historical character, and to enrich the re-elaboration of the avant-garde with the current situation around 1980 in the Padiglione Italia. The choice in that case was not minimally influenced by the age and sex of the artists, or by chosen medium. Unfortunately, "Aperto" later became a bureaucratic appendix, linked to proposals of curators and reserved for artists under 35 years of age, physically separated from the main exhibition, as if the age of the artist was a decisive factor for the youth of his work. These considerations led to the 1999 "dAPERTutto" event, to the breaking of the Biennale's self-imposed rules, to the presentation of the Italian section as a virtual but not spatially defined unit in the setting of the international exhibition. The central element was represented by the refusal of the eternal representation of art on art, and thereby to distance the abbonées of former Biennales, and to break down age boundaries and national ghettos. This made it possible to integrate a considerable number of Chinese artists and to present their works as autonomous and not "exotic" artistic expressions, giving voice to a subversive desire for change.

Desire for change was also the goal of the 1995 exhibition "Illusion <–> Emotion <–> Realität". Die siebente Kunst auf der Suche nach den sechs anderen: 100 Jahre Kino" (Illusion <–> Emotion <–> Reality. The seventh art in search of the six others: "100 Years of Cinema"), conceived on the occasion of the Biennale centenary, which unfortunately due to different reasons could not take place in Venice and was then shown in Zürich and Vienna. That was a pity, as such a project was complementary in nature with respect to the official Biennale exhibition of the same year, entitled "Identità/Alterità", taking as its subject the illusion machine of motion pictures showing destinies. The sections selected at that time built out of sequences from films were: The public as introduction, stars, pioneers, the great epic poems, heroes and heroines, antiheroes and antiheroines, catastrophies, taboo breaking, comedy, fear, the bold camera: editing and rhythm, experiments, the demonic screen, realism in social reality, propaganda, war, science-fiction: mutants and travel, eros, violence, music, dance, text, light, authors, New American Cinema, artists and images, architecture, advertising, confrontation between the end of the commercial account in cinema and sculptural gesture in the art video, which includes failure.

If I have brought this last project not shown in Venice to mind, it is not to awaken regret, rather to stress the continuity of the ambition. The Biennale of Venice is one of the most important exhibitions in the world, it is in direct competition to "documenta" in Kassel, many other exhibitions have been modelled upon it, and together with São Paolo, it brings national and global viewpoints together as polarities. This reality is always to be kept in mind considering the greatness of Venice, which however means also a curtailment of accessibility. As one who is convinced that everything is interconnected, this year's exhibition is strongly linked, also from the thematic point of view, with "Illusion—Emotion—Realität", conceived in this case from the viewpoint of figurative arts, but nearer to that which is referred to as film editing in its articulation and what the press in 1999 individuated as a stylistic feature of "dAPERTutto". This structural element is considered most suitable for the expansion of the exhibition in the new edition. This year Biennale will present itself as "Plateau der Menschheit, Platea dell umanità, Plateau of Humankind, Plateau de l'humanité" as a place which one looks at and from which one will be seen, a place in which the public onlooker is the protagonist and the measure of things, a place of encounter between artist, work, and spectator.

"Plateau of Humankind" is, as mentioned, not a theme, rather a dimension. No thematic criterion decided the selections of the artist. The artists themselves were the factors which determined the dimension. After "dAPERTutto", "Plateau". The idea contains many ideas: it is plateau, basis, foundation, platform. The Biennale as mirror and platform of humankind. But other considerations also led to "Plateau of Humankind". In 1995 Jean Clair dedicated the main exhibition of the Biennale to the hundredth anniversary of the identity card, naming it "Identità/Alterità" and took advantage of the occasion for a new interpretation of modern art from the point of view of figuration. This led to a hateful conflict above all in France: figuration versus abstraction. For me such discussions are superfluous. In my work towards spiritual activity at the service of the possible visualisation of a museum of obsessions there is only one art history of intensity, in which "figurative" or "abstract" are not opposing images. Intensity is the basis. Intensity finds its expressive form and the medium in natural ways. We do not find ourselves facing new art revolutions like at the end of the Sixties, but in a cli-

mate of increasing interest in human behaviour, in human existence. Paraphrasing the title of the time, one could say, "Quando le attitudini diventano forma", instead of "Quando le forme diventano comportamenti ed esistenze"—"La platea per la presentazione delle esistenze umane". Inherent to this concept is a subversive—revolutionary trend, that in the near future will certainly lead to an explosive eruption in Art, which we can only hint at here. Art today however also searches for the dissolution of borders, which is the characteristic of the "trend towards global artwork". "Plateau of Humankind" is ready to host the other arts too. The encounter between them could nourish the illusion that we find ourselves in front of global artwork. This however remains a utopia. Every art has its own laws, conditions, its own way of making use of space reception. The great space of the Arsenale, which the president Paolo Baratta far-sightedly opened up to the Biennale, offers numerous spaces inside which may hold surprises for the future, already houses within its reserved spheres the arts of theatre, dance and music and architecture alternating with the figurative arts. For this reason, not only an attempt but also a temptation was proposed, to give space to two arts that otherwise are missing in these rooms: cinema and poetry. Traditionally, the Film Festival takes place in autumn, while poetry was completely absent until now, if not for the fact that some Biennales or artists could be considered poets.

With my exhibition "Die siebente Kunst auf der Suche nach den sechs anderen", film was the point of departure. Biennale focuses on the creativity of he who creates. And so "alcuni cineasti invitati a dare un contributo." Film has its own time. In order to live the experi-

ence of a film, one needs a dark room, the cinema, the *fauteuil*. On the contrary, the exhibition is to be experienced walking. For it *Chantal Akerman*, *Atom Egoyan* working together with the painter *Julião Sarmento*, the Gianikians: *Yervant Gianikian* and *Angela Ricci Lucchi*, *Marin Karmitz* (1966 with *Samuel Beckett*), *Abbas Kiarostami* have put together short contributions. The encounter of these film-makers with figurative artists like *Stan Douglas*, who are moving ever-closer to film, will be deeply exciting.

The second enlargement of the exhibition is about Poetry, to which the area dividing the exhibition from the Marina Militare is dedicated. Two years ago this metal fence disturbed me, because it brought back too many memories. Now it belongs to poetry. Already 700 poets of all styles, from all continents have sent poems written on different media, which adorn and cover the bunker fence as a starting point. As a visual event it recalls the Encyclopaedia in the Forest of Armand Schulthess, which was exhibited in 1975 in "Junggesellenmaschinen" (Bachelor Machines). In form it comes close to the Omikushi/Fortune strips phenomenon in the trees and hedges of the Japanese temple areas. This "Progetto Bunker" will be carried out by *Marco Nereo Rotelli*. The temporal sequence of the poetical insertions constitutes a homage to Pier Paolo Pasolini and his rebellion against institutions.

The fact that it is the first exhibition in the third millenium and of the 21st century, combined with the greatness of the Biennale of Venice—in contrast to all the most recent biennial exhibitions in the world—allows and suggests a look back on the 20th century and also to propose a selective selection of its artists. From the beginning I had the notion of opening the Biennale with the exhibition of Antonin Artaud, the most radical poet and artist in search of a new concept of the body and to continue with *Beuys*, with his work "Das Ende des 20. Jahrhunderts" (The End of the 20th Century). Given the poor condition of his drawings, and in view of the humidity of Venice, I gave up the idea of exhibiting Artaud's work. The starting point is therefore the positive, utopian spirituality of Beuys. Three important works by him are on display, not at the beginning of the exhibition in the Padiglione d'Italia, but in the heart of the Artiglieria: "Voglio vedere le mie montagne" ("i miei" in Beuys original title)—the last words of Segantini, who let his deathbed be moved to the window—"Olivestone"—the most important of the works realised in Italy, five stone vats for the decantation of olive oil, which Beuys himself filled with limestone blocks, forming a union of feminine and masculine principals which were ever more united, transformed into acid by the oil, fusion through destruction—and suddenly "The End of the 20th Century". The work consists of man-sized basalt stones with eyes the size of flowerpots carved out, laying on the floor like pre-historic fish. Beuys conceived this variation as the only starting point for the "Trend towards Global Artwork". Pieces of wood lay under the stones and a trolley forms a reference to the operation of transport. Beuys conceived this sculpture as an appeal to ourselves. Through our human warmth we should bring inorganic material back to life—at the end of the 20th century. Further artists of this 20th century are: *Cy Twombly*, who through his gesticulated painting again revitalizes the grand narration of the ancient myths and dra-

mas, *Gerhard Richter*, who risked an abstract evocation of the mysteries with his series of predominantly red paintings for the cathedral of the beatified Padre Pio, which was however refused by the Vatican, *Niele Toroni*, who since the Sixties has placed his brush strokes, *Marisa Merz* with her delicate little heads, who, detached from their environment, lift their eyes upwards to the heavens, *Richard Tuttle* with his delicate projections, *Helmut Federle* with his impressive and solid new images, *Bill Viola*, who in slow-motion modifies a group picture, its configuration, and with it the interpersonal relationships, *Mimmo Rotella*, the over eighty year old representative of Nouveau Réalisme, who draws constantly new impulses and images from the world of posters, *Jeff Wall* with his still-life which realises the modern *arte povera*.

The exhibition ends in the rooms of the Tese delle Vergini, inaccessible until today, with two opposing installations: *Richard Serra* with a sculpture created especially for the Biennale, composed of two parts and characterised by a dynamism in a seldom seen until today, born from steel curvatures that jut outwards and bend inwards, and *Ilya* and *Emilia Kabakov* who pose question of vital importance to the artist not only Russian: is it better to appreciate the contemporary or to work with the objective of a journey on the train of the future? Or has the latter already departed? Between the Artiglierie and the Tese to *Chris Burden*'s "Flying Steamroller", a flying 15 ton American Navy steamroller, painted yellow, a military vehicle, taken from the context of its original use. Pacificism and/or imagined and realized experiment, which at the time of the writing of these lines, was still a victim of this year's budget cuts.

In the main space of the Padiglione Italia, there are no longer monumental rats, as in 1999, presenting their enforced solidarity in kingly union, but rather a "Platform of Thinking" will be erected. "Le Penseur" of *Auguste Rodin* sits there, thoughtful, surrounded by works from African artists, by sculptures by naïv sculptors, by Indian and Chinese statues. And nearby, ahead of its time, is "L'Homme qui marche" from Rodin, which was exhibited in Venice exactly one hundred years ago. And for all those who still criticize the idea of "Platea dell'Umanità", *Pierre Bismuth* has listed a series of thoughts and ideas on the walls, illustrating the subsequent dimensions experienced by humankind on its journey to art. And a wall-projection from the young South African artist *Minnette Vari* shows the flag of her country in a constantly disappearing and re-appearing image, while on the façade of the Padiglione Italia, proudly bearing the word "Italia", shimmer 192 country flags painted by *Marco Neri*. Façade and "The Platform of Thought" should be in harmony with our action: with the "Plateau of Humankind" we don't wish to illustrate a style, a theme, but to offer a possible opening: to give a connotation, to susbstain freedom against barriers erected by styles, nationalities and nationalisms, by the idea of age limits. To be intensity ouside ideologies and stock exchange. *L'imagination au pouvoir*—to quote a motto from '68. To celebrate fragility again.

Carsten Nicolai's vibrators which shake weights leaving the surface of the water, the liquid, flat, stand for the reversal of values.

There are various possibilities or problematic approaches to try and put a little order into such a diversified offer of the "Plateau of Humankind": the course of human life, man and his behaviour, his relationship with his surrounding environment. It is logical that some overlapping is also present.

Birth control, along with the nuclear arms race, the air-pollution desired by U.S. presidents and the hunger crisis is one of today's biggest problems. *AVL (Atelier van Lieshout)* working together with the Dutch women's group "Women on Waves", exhibits a project in the form of a hospital ship for women from countries where abortion is outlawed to allow them to have abortions. The operation will take place in international waters, where abortion is not punishable. The shocking number of victims (175,000 per year) of mis-handled illegal abortions only serves to underline the urgency of the initiative.

Doctor *Michael Schmitz* conceived the project "Kinderbaum" (Children's Tree) with the aim of helping children. He is planning a world helicopter trip to find sponsors for a children's home with an occupational school in the country most afflicted with AIDS in the world, South Africa.

In both of these cases the instrument of help is presented: the hospital container and the helicopter.

The video work from *Tiong Ang* shows Indian school children. In silence, seated at their desks, they seem to dream with open eyes. Abruptly they are taken from their thinking, as the teacher enters the classroom and drives stupidly repetitive material into their heads. After she leaves silence rules, and the children are again in their inner worlds.

Endangerments to the health of children is shown in an endless loop by *Fiona Tan* with her two smoking "Javaanses Jongs" with the little brother forced into the role of passive smoker. The artist uses "ethnographic" archive material in an arranged slapstick.

Georgina Starr conjures Halloween scenes. Small kids in police costumes march through the city, gun in hand, enter into the hall of a fashion show and shoot the models in a blood bath on the catwalk.

Realistic three-dimensionality for the age of the male sex. Between the "Baby" and the old man "Shaved Head" *Ron Mueck* shows the "Boy" as extremely large. In a squat, dressed in only a slip, he strikes each onlooker upon entry into the Corderia with a tender and penetrating questioning glance. Earlier, when men still possessed control, the Sphinx was feminine. Today given the explosion of female creativity and energy the Sphinx is masculine. The stigmata on the hands is not only held up for Christ and Saint Francis, but also for girls in puberty. Unheroically they bear their wounds, enduring the pain.

Heli Rekula places two feminine figures in a timeless contraction of the shattering of men's power craze in the metaphor of the capsized "American Star".

Priscilla Monge evokes the purity and streams of menstrual blood, covering a white room with snow-white sanitary napkins. And in white marble the truths of masculine genius are engraved, in the form of pieces from the "Tempest" by Shakespeare.

The bodily fluids of men and women are the starting point for the installation "Ciao Bella" by *Tracey Rose*.

A feminine being, both girl and young woman goes jogging, she stops before a closed bungalow style house, crosses the garden to the window, her gaze is full of curiosity, tenderness and expectancy. Through the slats of the blind one can see an expressionless youth, jumping a lasso in the bourgeois interior. With a crack the lasso hits the floor. Tears appear in the girl's eyes. She draws back from the window and the camera pulls back to show the suburban landscape. The end of a tender drama expressing Strindbergian power. "Lasso", a silent film from *Salla Tykkä*.

Kept in the house by the bond with her son and husband, and driven by the desire to live a nomadic life, greater independence and disorder, *Eulalia Valldosera* makes everyday objects move and travel in a room.

In a strangely detached manner, a young woman, her head closely-cropped, hangs and shoots herself in desperation. But the stool returns under her feet, the bullet returns to the revolver, and she goes back to the table to read. A rewind-roulette between life and death by *Ene-Liis Semper*.

Mother, nourishment, life, death. The key words to define the people of reference, the necessities, the inevitable, which move relentlessly in the space of *Charles Sandison*.

The empress Elisabeth, Sissi from Austria, cared for her body; she was one of the first female body builders. Her wasp waist is legendary, just like her tragic life and fate. To know that she was always the most beautiful in the land, she created an album with the most beautiful women from other countries. Special ambassadors took care to provide her with their photos. *Francesco Vezzoli* also establishes such collections, the faces of beautiful people from films, theatre, fashion, society. On their pictures he intervenes with superimposed tears and eye make-up, as homage to Beauty, as a dream-like antidote for its transitory nature.

In small plaster boards *Eva Marisaldi* portrays all of the contacts, the transitoriness and the sturdiness between two bodies. There are no faces to distract the viewer's attention in this still catalogue of nearness, metopes of modernity.

The healthy man does sports. After a decades long stasis of the image of the athlete—who still remembers the spear and discus throwers in the nimble declension of ancient images on the grass before the administrative buildings of sports organizations and ministries for culture and sport, or the museum for the Olympic games?—sport, as a metaphor for the race, for competition and for the cult of the body is once more of great topical interest in art. The topic of reference is no longer the construction of a tough body in overblown projections of sweaty muscle-bound bodies working out on fitness machines. Sport is used as a representation of pursuit of higher goals.

As a new variant of the "Unending Column", *Roderick Buchanan* puts forth the brutal and fine faces of Football and Rugby players during the singing of the national anthem, as they survey us horizontal and mute. Heavy cushions are used to represent the body weights of famous boxers in sculptural form. *Gustavo Artigas* protests as a Mexican against the borderline, erected from waste material of the Gulf War between his country and the United States. He puts two sports together: Football (Mexico) and Basketball (USA). The two teams play simultaneously on the same combined field. In the work "Fusion", *Ingeborg Lüscher* depicts a football game between two teams in Trussardi suits, as a metaphor for the emotion of competition, sport and business. This fusion is caused by the jubilation and scrum of men after the goal.

Against the urban backdrop of a desolate eastern European city, *Josef Dabernig* shows the phlegmatic and calm, typically Austrian scene of football team coaches experiencing the emotions of an invisible football game on benches similar to bus stop shelters, but recounted at high volume and in many languages. The great staged appearance of the two under the grandstand is in contrast, as are the parting handshakes with several functionaries. But even: there are no onlookers, the stands are empty, only the ritual, played out in its misery survives, despite the solemn exit through the passageway. "Wisla" is the parable of the emptiness inherent in the worldliness of sport.

Paul Pfeiffer compresses sports reporting into little scenes, which repeat endlessly, rising simultaneously to the level of static images and expanding the absurd and tragic effect of "figures at the base of a Crucifixion" through serial reproduction. In the exhibition, this artist is represented by the work "Self-portrait as a Fountain".*Lars Siltberg* binds spheres to the hands and feet of his well-made judo fighter, who then attempts to stand up and remain standing in water on a smooth icy surface against an air stream. He has so formed the Beauty of Failure, which as a dimension in art breaks into something wonderful. Courage, tenacity, strength and endurance. How difficult it is without life experiences to speak convincing words, to give them meaning and weight. *João Onofre* lets the young participants of the modelling course come before the camera alone and speak this simple sentence from Roberto Rossellini's "Stromboli" (1959): "Che io abbia la forza, la convinzione e il coraggio!". *John Pilson* leads us behind the scenes of today's office life. In a slapstick manner he explains the inefficiency of a law firm which should be efficient, recounting a deal lost as a result. These images are contrasted with the moving scene of a singing child, drawing figures on the steamed up window in front of the opposing skyscraper.

Nedko Solakov also speaks of the profound meaning of the senselessness of human actions. For five months he let two painters, one after the other, paint over the work of the other. White cancels black, black cancels white. No one can say that at the Biennale there isn't enough painting: "A Life (Black and White)".

The rising costs of health care premiums, the explosion of hospital costs, the agreements of the chemical giants over the price of medicines. The newspapers are full such news. The affected are usually only used as examples: The sick, the invalid person.

Cancer threatens and destroys the lives of those living around the Chernobyl atomic power plant, hit by the nuclear disaster. *Viktor Maruščenko's* photographs show the normality of the threatened life in the area, the daily acceptance of the poisoning, and living with death. Maruščenko has shown this "stalker" area so effectively, that, although his reportage was commissioned, he was forced to disappear.

The Ukraine is a poor land, life is miserable. Switzerland on the other hand is one of the richest lands in the world, where it is tempting to turn away from misfortune and death. The retired vice-commander of police *Arnold Odermatt* has photographed accidents for years as an official duty, and from these—leaving aside the bloody toll—has made several images of considerable aesthetic impact.

Tatsumi Orimoto has for years cared for his mother, who suffers from Alzheimer's. So she has become the object of his art, she along with her friends who communicate with each other in a strange way with auto tyres around their necks. The mother is extremely small; the artist wishes that she were bigger. He built her big green shoes and placed her on a cast-iron pothole cover of the city works, inspiring images such as " Small Mama, Big Shoes".

Martin Bruch suffers from Multiple Sclerosis. Before he obtained a safety wheelchair he fell down a countless number of times, and he has documented the consequences of his disease with self-irony, contributing to a reappraisal of his illness. The snapshots of his "Bruchlandungen" (Breaklandings) reach the respectable length of 67 meters.

Javier Téllez visited a fishing community on Maracaibo Lake in Venezuela, where many inhabitants have fallen prey to Huntington's disease. The main symptom of this condition is the uncontrollable movements which can be fatal. Téllez has united four projections in his octagonal installation: two different portraits of St. Vitus' dance sufferers, a film realised by a doctor about the disease and a spider that is weaving its web. He bombards these moving pictures with tennis ball machines; he wants to meet the disease with vehemence.

And age? The population is growing old; the decline in birth rates is endangering the relationship between generations to ensure old age insurance benefits. In "Uomoduomo", *Anri Sala* observes a "poverello" in the cathedral of Milan, his sleeping head always listing to one side.

The pope is the most famous old man in Christianity and in the world. Because they are infallible, his decisions are binding for the inhabitants of poor and rich areas of the first, second and third world. Celibacy, contraception, birth control, sexuality only for the purpose of procreation on the one hand, the hier-archic or democratic ecclesiastical organisation on the other, are difficult decisions to take. They must be taken alone. *Maurizio Cattelan* shows us the old pope met with meteorites ("La Nona Ora"), the cross upheld in the middle of oil tanks. Oil still bubbles forth, but not for long in the Islamic lands that the pope recently visited. The "Islam" décollage by *Mimmo Rotella* refers to this very aspect.

"Theological Dispute" is the title of the work by *Vadim Zakharov*, who in the dress of a Russian orthodox priest struggles against Sumo wrestlers and loses. The contestants are depicted as conciliatory, with the loser in their arms in the final image. *Maaria Wirkkala* appeals to reconciliation and the reflection of opposing positions in an evocative table scene, with both the Bible and the Koran open on the two ends, with animals either on the way into or on the way out of Noah's ark in ("Found a Mental Connection").

Magnus Wallin is an invalid. In his film "Exit" invalids attempt, crippled in the labyrinth of the city, to escape from a fire, an inferno for the figures, that could come out of a painting from Bosch and for most of whom, despite the presence of a helicopter, there is no salvation. In the second work "Skyline", athletically built people throw themselves into the deep, attached to an elastic cord and return upwards into the sky, against which they are smashed, because it is only a mirrored skyscraper wall.

After Thanatos, Eros. The creation of man and woman, advancement, desire of the flesh, union, release, struggle of the sexes, brutality, tenderness, the film from *Chris Cunningham* is based on the saga of the pair relationship between cosmic greatness and earthly banality. We also owe one of the best music clips to Cunningham: "Björk", the creation and appreciation of the robot men and their feeling for each other.

The photographic records of *Jaime David Tischler* propose a crescendo from the shy approach towards the body of the other in places where one undresses to bathe up to the recognition and representation of one's own homosexuality. "White Murmuring" is the title of the self-portrait of the attractive Chantal Michel as the flesh for men's fantasies and desires for innocence and repressed depravity. "Rainbow" is for *Xu Zhen* the result of a punishment inflicted on a naked back. The blows are not visible, only audible, what is visible is only the changing of the colour of the skin.

Atom Egoyan together with *Julião Sarmento* propose a highly elaborated game of Dominatrix-Slave. The foot care is applied with an agonising slowness. The nail clipper cuts the toenails that fall into the mouth of a lying woman, who freely or forcedly takes the hornlike "nourishment" with difficulty. The projection can only be experienced through a corridor one metre wide, in a close-up view. The whole picture is never given; the spectator must make do with body fragments.

Maaria Wirkkala offers also soft voyeurism with the projection on black stone of the nape of a man 's neck, which he cannot see for himself ("Dream Screen-Prime Time").

Society punishes the law-breaker with prison or death. *Loris Cecchini* has made the death judgement into an isolated pneumatic sculpture. And *Lucinda Devlin* delivers a shocking documentary, cold and hygienic, where the condemned are put to death by rope, electric chair, firing squad and lethal injection. With this she brings into question the death penalty, by showing what men can do to men.

The unavoidable, man's death is omnipresent, but is rendered concrete by absence. *Hai Bo* finds old photos, young men on a bridge, a school photo, in the military. Years later he looks for the photographed, to put themselves into the same position again. Whoever is missing, lives no more.

Man is a social animal, and therefore group pictures are well-loved subject. *Tuomo Manninen* surprises with photos from Finland and Kathmandu, in which he depicts people who do the same jobs. Over-population is a fact. In the space by *Do-Ho Suh*, the onlooker finds himself facing a mass of people. Thousands of small atlases support the transparent floor on which he treads, millions of tiny heads look at him from the walls.

Man is an obsessive being; he has the collector's nature. *Veli Granö* collects especially adroit specimens of this type in her "Collector of Collectors". There was in the past period—especially since the "Les magiciens de la terre" exhibition—an enormous expansion and contemporaneous integration of the idea of the exotic in the sphere of shared concepts. The meeting of the whites with the aboriginal populations is signalled in *Fiona Tan's* "Facing Forward", and *Yervant Gianikian and Angela Ricci Lucchi* demonstrate the evolution of the black man in "La marche de l'homme". Both films use archive material.

Luis González Palma photographs the faces of the indigenous of Guatemala and with landscape and symbols gives them back their own history and identity, freeing them from the realm of the exotic.

Cristina Garcia Rodero after her suggestive work on the occult in Spain in the spirit of the Bunuel film "Los Hurdes", has now photographed the voodoo rituals in Haiti, ecstasy,

the exorcisms, unity, the enticement, the concentrations of the black population.

A white, who wishes skin-close contact with the local population, is *Sarenco l'Africano*. In the group of sculptured figures he, the white, lets the blacks tell him about the MauMau movement, the freedom struggle against the English colonial power, the atrocities from both sides and, finally the independence with the new president Kenyatta.

And *Santiago Sierra* evokes the problem of the foreigners to the European community, by calling two hundred of them, and paying them to let their hair be coloured yellow, thereby easily recognized, and in a certain sense putting them at the centre of the target.

Ernesto Neto has installed in oversized dimensions stockings of spice from his homeland of Brazil, the production of which, along with the presence of gold, was the reason for the colonization of the continent. His installation appeals to our sense of smell, but is also a kind of revenge in the form of seduction. The bonds with their countries occupy many artists. *Tania Bruguera* was inspired by the poem "La Isla en peso" by Virgilio Pin expressing with sparing gestures of her face the times of day, "in order to evoke the chaos and the exquisite agony of Cuba, which still resounds and is even a little prophetic". *Minnette Vári* deals with her homeland, South Africa, in a very efficient way. Like a female Chronos who devours her own children, swallows and vomits the history of her country in a sort of transformation of history and politics. As well as in "Oracle", she uses the same procedure in sleep and dreams in her second work, "REM". *A1-53167* (Aníbal Asdrubal López Juárez), on the occasion of the national holiday of the 30th of June, protests with

street manifestations against the masked death squads and the State terror, that reduces any opposition to ashes so as not to leave any trace behind. The artist spreads coal dust in front of the parade, which is however immediately swept away. In the same country, *Regina Galindo*, poetical activist and opponent of the regime—dressed in white and hanging from a balcony—reads poems and lets them flutter towards the people in the street. In other works she protests against the violence against women. A protest against the Austrian government elected in the year 2000 was staged in Vienna by the *Secession*, which led to a poster action organised by Austrian and international artists. Even the Vienna *Museum in Progress* has protested against the government with daily inserts in the "Standard" and has entrusted *Ken Lum* with the project to realise a series of posters against xenophobia. *Human Condition* has translated the bitter experiences in Bosnia-Herzegovina into an aggressive, ironic, cynical design. And how much the military service in crisis areas can leave scars on young men is shown in a very efficient way in the photographic portraits by *Rineke Dijkstra* from Israel, who took the pictures shooting the subjects first as civilians and then in military uniform.

Alexander Roitburd attempts to evoke the end of ideologies and the motivation and responsibilities of their birth. The Ukrainian artist projects his own psychodrama starting from the scene of the Odessa staircase of Eisenstein ("The Battleship Potemkin") onto a painting in the style of socialist realism. Two different types of heroicness, which are combined and which both necessarily lead to disaster.

"Fear Not" by *Susan Kleinberg* also has a

political connotation, consisting of a question posed by the artist to famous people, which can be chosen by the spectators. Among those interviewed there are: Susanna Agnelli, Silvio Berlusconi, Bill Clinton, Chuck Close, Spalding Grey, General Schwarzkopf, and Gore Vidal. "Wall Piece" by *Gary Hill* is dedicated to language, to words, linked to a physical effort. Man likes leaving traces of perfume in public places as in "Paintings" by *Paul Graham*.

The large photographic installation by *Botto and Bruno* with squalid suburban architecture, practically deserted, evokes the social environment.

In his photos in black and white and his less well-known videos, *Richard Billingham* documents the desolate life of his family in an English industrial town in a merciless but sympathetic manner.

Stan Douglas' latest film "Le Détroit" is a true masterpiece. A black woman gets out of her car and with a flashlight inspects an abandoned house in Detroit, the city of cars which has been particularly stricken by the crisis in the automobile sector. The film brings together very efficiently great social criticism, the woman's search for her own memories, her curiosity, nostalgia and resignation, and offers tension and twists in the tail like a film by Hitchcock.

The lack of a way out, the feeling of being imprisoned are typical sensations of a situation in which existential and physical aspects are combined and which emerge if we explore the relationship between three different figures of man, wife and lover, as happens in the film "Play" (1966) by *Samuel Beckett*, which he filmed with *Marin Karmitz*, absent from last year's Beckett retrospective in Venice.

Thinking. At the entrance of the Padiglione d'Italia sits the "Penseur" by *Auguste Rodin*. *Keith Tyson* offers the modern "Thinker", a

metal column inside of which a series of computers is at work not visible to the eye. Outside there are notes for the comprehension of the incomprehensible.

The world of the WWW still seems to be free. But where do the confines of this freedom lie? *Nick Waplington* goes in search of theses limits through bizarre, invented sites.

Laura Horelli shows us a map of the world in white, a continent waiting to be discovered with the exception of the few places where the president is a woman, which are highlighted in colour.

Cy Twombly revitalises ancient myths. In contrast to the guest directors of the exhibition and the painters *Com & Com* with their trailer about the saga of Wilhelm Tell propose the glamour of Hollywood and its Studios once again at the end of the exhibition.

And cloning? *Xiao Yu* composes new beings using human and animal material.

After all these artists' contributions and desires for change, someone may want to abandon himself to consumeristic urges; to those the "Streetmarket" is recommended, which *Barry Mc Gee, Stephan Powers and Todd James* have constructed at the end of the Corderie. While *Matthieu Laurette* nearby suggests to buyers and sellers how to eat for free and manage the family budget making a first investment buying articles with the inscription "first purchase, money back". Not far away is *Gavin Turk's* garbage bag. There are also special sections: *Gerd Rohling* presents his remarkable precious objects looking like glass, which, recovered by the artist from the trash of the major cities and displayed in Venice, have a particular appeal. *Alexandra Ranner* realizes a room that calls for the pres-

ence of man. The table conceived by *Max Dean* must be approached with care, for it is an object that communicates with man, speaks to him, follows, and oppresses him. What does the pet store offer? Great tortoises of the *Cracking Art Group* in the gardens, that warn us about presumption when we think about their lifespan—up to a thousand years—in comparison with our average life expectancy. The camels of *Not Vital* are lined up in the water, visible only at low tide. Upon seeing them one wishes to exclaim: "And so Moses crossed the desert and the camels followed him". And who is the big man, who leads the peacocks—a metaphor *par excellence* for the artist, who at the Biennale willingly spreads his tail? This is *Francis Alÿs*. Furthermore we recommend a diversion into the calendar section. *Vanessa Beecroft's* monthly pictures are absolutely sensational, showing always the same model, her sister clad as Olympia–Maya.

And who, after so many encounters and possibilities of acquaintance still seeks new ones and at the same time desires rest, can find them at the "Pic Nic" in the Tuileries, on the beach and in a belgian swimming pool, photographed by *Massimo Vitali*. *Eliezer Sonnenschein*, in his narration chooses the artist's life as his subject, from school to the academy, the nervousness at his first exhibition, fame, the museum, immortality.

Art today is characterised by an extraordinary, and impressive variety, it is self-awareness and concentration also during play.

The expressive medium of painting, for example, in the works of Alessandra Tesi and of Heimo Zobernig experiences an amazing expansion of its own possibilities in video.

Alessandra Tesi loves water, the river, the sea, and the use of water jets of firemen and civil protection. Thanks to the invention of a screen consisting of small spheres of glass and with the help of a strong light projection, she is able to perform daylight projections, transforming footage into paintings.

One mass of water after another transform themselves into a painting with the nuances of a landscape with nymphs in contrast to the more solid objects like the helmet and the helicopter.

Heimo Zobernig struggles and twists in his painting made of cloth in continuously changing colours. Performance art with the base colours becomes thus a painting constellation of variable compositions.

Federico Herrero intervenes with a painting in the public space, beautifying social structures and paints in the form of a synthesis of *sgraffitto*, taking of fingerprints, and amorphous forms.

Manuel Ocampo tackles auto-imposed taboos and strongly rooted convictions in an anarchic and coarse manner painting with irony and humour. With his brush he extrapolates elements of wisdom, which have become absurd on the pedestal of presumption.

Yishai Jusidman gives us portraits of artists, Sumo wrestling, realistic to the point of combining them with a formal geometrical language and penetrating close-ups of patients treated in psychiatric hospitals in the painting style of the old masters.

Olaf Nicolai reduces a Flemish flagellation of Christ to blood drops, which become the pattern of wallpaper, in such a way as to grasp the symbolic element through the multiplication of the signs of contraction. The great "Maze" in the Giardino delle Vergini is further testimony of the extension of the concept of painting in the environment.

Surreal elements in the form of over-sized mushrooms, solid figures from the most recent past, flaunted and dreamlike elements are brought together by *Neo Rauch* in powerful, constructed figurative paintings, stories of events, which from marginal, the misery of the life of workers and farmers in the past, change into something positive. The position of the artist and the evolution of painting after Baselitz, Lüperts and Polke is comparable to that of the Belgian Magritte with relation to the surrealist painting of Paris linked to André Breton.

Despite the pessimistic forecasts, painting is rich in its variety and is represented in all its possible forms by artists like *Twombly, Rotella, Toroni, Richter, Wall, Graham, Tuttle* and the last mentioned ones. Even the "Black Square" of Casimir Malevich is present, the new icon of the beginning of the 20th century, not open to the public but translated proudly by Tanja Ostojic in the form of pubic hair cut in a squared shape.

Sculpture and plastic arts are in no way inferior to painting: *Rodin, Beuys, Serra, Marisa Merz, Ilya and Emilia Kabakov, Neto, Turk, Do-Ho Suh*, and furthermore the *art brut* figures of *Erich Bödeker* and *Hans Schmitt*, the Madonna of *Ettore Jelmorini* released by stone, the African idols of *Seni Camara, John Goba, Cheff Mwai, Jean Baptiste Ngentchopa, Peter Wanjau*, the sitting figure of the chieftain by *Sunday Jack Akpan*, the Buddha statues from India. To these works we must add the sculptural meeting place, formed by small containers, flexible, variable, which are packing and structure elements at the same time, by *Manfred Pernice*. *Mark Manders* enchants with a still-life scene full of mystery realised in precious stone.

Christiane Löhr constructs delicate towers with seeds. *Marko Lehanka* presents a discourse about monuments. The pedestal, brutally rejected and despised for a long time, comes back into the field of sculpture, pleased and amused with its new role as an element which elevates a small miraculous spring, as the support for a monument to the Peasant's Revolt inspired by Dürer, as a column for a surprising version of the "Brandenburg Gate".

From Richard Serra to Marko Lehanka, an extraordinary leap of thirty years. The "Refreshing" project promises institutional continuity. The dAPERTutto artists, *Massimo Bartolini, Cai Guo-Qiang, Olafur Eliasson, Rirkrit Tiravanija* together with *Tobias Rehberger* will take care of the physical well being of the visitors. It's small homage to honour the memory of *Chen Zhen*, who passed away prematurely last year.

Like every one of you, I too am curious to see how all of these diverse elements will unite in the "Plateau of Humankind", bringing the exhibition, a temporary world, to life. Will the visitors in their humanity appreciate this return to man, or will they be looking forward to a return to abstraction? Certainly, the Biennale is not always an exquisite offering, but if the Biennale of Venice doesn't break with the exterior gleam of biennial exhibitions, who will?

Welcome onto, into, under, next to the Plateau! Discover the wonders as you walk from surprise to surprise. And excuse my LMRF!*

*Last Minute Roman Fleuve!

The Platform of Thought Piattaforma del pensiero Platform

Bonjour Madame Humanité

Who isn't familiar with the meeting in a nice place between artist and collecter in a closed circle of company , where the collecter rings out to the artist with a "Bonjour Monsieur Courbet?" And who isn't familiar with the paintings of this restless artist spirit, who for his social dream had to go into exile: "L'origine du monde" and "L'Atelier". In the last painting the artist sits at his easel, assisted in the spirit by the naked Muse and by the Child, by Beauty and Innocence. On his left side are grouped together townspeople, beggars, mothers, children, clochards, Jews, on his right side the intelligentsia of the time, above all Charles Baudelaire, the composer of "Fleurs du Mal", the poet of the "Correspondances", the praiser of words and the analyzer of the great geniuses and of the vivacity of "modern life". In "L'Atelier" the artist is the center, the swinging door to the imagination of all classes and their members. Everyone is born from the womb, the vagina as "L'origine du monde". Only much

the fall and of the emptiness didn't persist with holy statues, but rather, transgressed. In parantheses *L'Homme qui marche*, which was exhibited at the 1901 Biennale, is to be added here. Old times, new times. The *Thinker* is surrounded by man's exhibitions and his way of behaving has renewed today's artist generation from different cultures, which have moved from their exile. This without a complete aspiration in either elements or in the continents, neither in the evocation of a great inauguration. All of it is as a rememberance of the *Commedia del dapertutto* and as a release for this *Plateau of Mankind*, gives dimension to this first Biennale of the new millenium.

Harald Szeemann

The Platform of Thought Piattaforma del pensiero Platform

later can the ribs as bones from monkeys be swirled into dirigibles in the air, into rockets, into space surveyors. In a closer sense "L'origine du monde" has given the investigation into the origin of mankind, his physique, his psyche, his ever growing dreams, a linear and vertical viewpoint and models of explanation for history and the world through the potential feeling of the magnetic field.

The painter no longer sits at the center of our one-way plateau but, rather, the *Thinker*. And Auguste Rodin has provided the key and the final form to *Hell's Gate* along with the thoughtless and helpless man, who as an advance on his statue, notwithstanding the danger of

Erich Bödeker
Seni Camara
Gilberto De La Nuez
Jhon Goba
Ettore Jelmorini
Cheff Mwai
Jean Baptiste Ngnetchopa
Auguste Rodin
Hans Schmitt
Peter Wanjau

Giriama Sculptor
Standing regal Bodhisvatta
Buddah: large-sized gilded-head
Two standing Cāmaradhāriṇī in piedi
Mithuna, Tantric yoga exercices
Eigh-armed Narasiṅha (temple relief)
Śiva Naṭarāja
Tirthaṅkara Pārśvanātha
Ball Mask
African figure
U.S. Navy Diving Helmet

Seni Camara
Untitled
1998
Terra-cotta, h 30 cm

John Goba
Untitled
1997
Painted wood and
porcupine prickles,
h 125 cm

Ousmane Ndiaye Dago
La femme-terre
1998
Photograph on
plastic canvas,
140 × 200 cm

Peter Wanjau
*One man can fill
the world*
1998
Painted wood,
h 54 cm

Gilberto De La Nuez
Los No Alineados
1979
Oil on canvas,
95 × 131 cm

Peter Wanjau
Aids Killing
1998
h 63 cm

Ettore Jelmorini
Mazzo di fiori
1960
Granite,
37 × 35 × 13 cm

Hans Schmitt
Adam and Eva
1975
Painted wood, fabric, tow
Adam: 163 × 58 × 53 cm;
Eva: 157 × 52 × 56 cm

Erich Bödeker
Schwarze Stürzende
1969
Concrete on boards,
painting,
128 × 70 × 40 cm

Anonymous
Standing Cāmarādhariṇī
Gujarat, Pratihara
X–XI century
Stone sculpture,
94 × 41 × 33 cm

Erich Bödeker
Apollo 0
(birds drinking trough)
1970
Concrete, painting,
metal handle,
87 × 39 × 40 cm

Anonymous
Templar Erotic Frieze
(man with six women)
Tanjore, District
XVII–XVIII century
Wood frieze,
54 × 25 × 10 cm

Erich Bödeker
Saint Barbara
1970
Wood (mine stamp),
wood piece, painting
miner lamp,
190 × 28 cm

Anonymous
Standing Cāmarādhariṇī
Gujarat, Pratihara
X–XI century
Stone sculpture,
95 × 40 × 32 cm

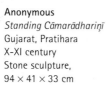

Anonymous
Tirthañkara Pārśavanātha
(Large-sized Stele with
78 Jina and 32 figures)
North India, Gujarat
XI-XIII century
Bronze,
73 × 39 × 13 cm

Anonymous
Śiva Naṭarāja

Mysore, Hassan District
(Belur Region)
XII century
Black basalt,
70 × 51 × 19 cm

Anonymous
Buddah: larged-sized
gilded-head
Siam
XIV century
Bronze,
s42 × 32 × 31 cm

Artists Artisti

rtisti Artists Artisti Artists Artisti Artists

Samuel Beckett
Mimmo Rotella
Joseph Beuys
Marisa Merz
Arnold Odermatt
Cy Twombly
Gerhard Richter
Ilya & Emilia Kabakov
Ingeborg Lüscher
Niele Toroni
Marin Karmitz
Richard Serra
Sunday Jack Akpan
Abbas Kiarostami
Richard Tuttle
Yervant Gianikian - Angela Ricci Lucchi
Helmut Federle
Massimo Vitali
Sarenco l'Africano
Chris Burden
Viktor Maruščenko
Tatsumi Orimoto
Gerd Rohling
Jeff Wall
Cracking Art Group
Lucinda Devlin
Not Vital
Max Dean - Raffaello D'Andrea
Cristina Garcia Rodero
Susan Kleinberg
Chantal Akerman
Gary Hill
Bill Viola
Maaria Wirkkala
Josef Dabering
Paul Graham
Luis González Palma
Nedko Solakov
Ron Mueck
Heimo Zoberning
Francis Alÿs
Rineke Dijkstra
Vadim Zakharov
Maurizio Cattelan
Stan Douglas
Atom Egoyan - Julião Sarmento
Veli Granö
Neo Rauch
Jaime David Tischler
Tiong Ang
Martin Bruch
Marko Lehanka
Alexander Roitburd
Hai Bo

Georgina Starr
Do–Ho Suh
Atelier Van Lieshout
Botto & Bruno
Yishai Jusidman
Manfred Pernice
Heli Rekula
Eulalia Valldosera
A1–53167
Pierre Bismuth
Ernesto Neto
Roderick Buchanan
Christiane Löhr
Carsten Nicolai
Manuel Ocampo
Magnus Wallin
Nick Waplington
Xiao Yu
Eva Marisaldi
Barry McGee – Stephen Powers – Todd James
Paul Pfeiffer
Santiago Sierra
Fiona Tan
Alexandra Ranner
Eliezer Sonnenschein
Gavin Turk
Tania Bruguera
Mark Manders
Chantal Michel
Priscilla Monge
Marco Neri
John Pilson
Lars Siltberg
Minnette Vári
Vanessa Beecroft
Loris Cecchini
Charles Sandison
Ene–Liis Semper
Javier Téllez
Alessandra Tesi
Keith Tyson
Gustavo Artigas
Richard Billingham
Chris Cunningham
Matthieu Laurette
COM & COM
Francesco Vezzoli
Tanja Ostojić
Salla Tykkä
Regina Galindo
Tracey Rose
Anri Sala
Laura Horelli
João Onofre
Xu Zhen
Federico Herrero

Play (*Comédie*), one of the works Beckett wrote for the theatre (written in 1963 and performed for the first time in German at the Ulmer Theatre, Ulm-Donau, on June 14 1963), is a highly original work that takes up themes first dealt with after the classical parenthesis of *Waiting for Godot* and *Endgame* and continues along the path of a conscious linguistic disintegration, taking the text to the limits of expression.

Beckett has always been aware of the technical means of the theatrical medium, and he progressively refined and stylised these, eventually honing them and bringing them to bear on the individuation and ever more complete and total laying bare of the situations and attitudes of his works.

This progressive formation of a critical conscience in reference to the techniques to be used led the Irish author to use each and every means at his disposal (in fact, Beckett tried his hand at theatre, radio, television and cinema), not so much, or at least not only, to experiment with more or less novel and authentic solutions, but rather to extend these expressive possibilities and make them serve a complexity and totality of meanings that could never have been borne by a simple and summary choice of formal props.

Here in *Comédie*, and above all in the English version, we have a series of technical-practical director's suggestions on lighting and the construction of the jars that are to contain the characters—these are very specific instructions.

(as represented by the single beam).

In fact, the entire mechanics of the work is played out in this slow movement of the beam that moves from one face to another; this light opens a breach and takes us into their character and their expressive shadows. It seems as though the same function of the alarm clock in *Happy Day!* has been taken over by the beam, which renders the need for verbal communication between individuals material.

The characters in *Comédie*, in fact, also represent a part, and are freed by the "comedy" of separate words proffered to the beam that illuminates them one at a time; during the first movement, the "truth" (light) slides and moves like a fitting on a plane, leading us to believe that what will later be contradicted in the second movement is in fact certain, but constituting, in a sort of often unstable archipelago of configuration, the three insular and mobile witnesses caught in a banal triangle: a woman, a lover and a man.

These three characters, "unnameable" and anonymous (Beckett simply calls them First Woman, Second Woman and First Man) enclosed in their jars, reduced to an expressionless face, each of them lost in the final mumblings of their own thoughts, speak with expressionless voice and participate anxiously as they relate their story. They have been extracted from their nothingness by this luminous "investigating authority" or "inquisitor" who extorts their words and reanimates them only to hurl them back into their nothingness.

Comédie into a void that is deeper than in Beckett's earlier works, much more desolate than the hell of *Huis Clos*: there is nothing after the comedy of life except for an even more solitary foundering than Winnie's—even more monotonous than the silence of the void. The comedy of life consists in speaking or inevitably lying; the past then surges into the present (which in turn evokes the past), like the prototype itself of lying in so far as it rightly demanded to grasp truth.

The man's words thus negate the truth of the story on behalf of a truth that must always come according to the words that are pronounced, and that constitutes the great utopia of the Beckettian character when he forgets his conviction.

It is precisely this affirmation that leads him back to his hell—the future-in-the-past is full of teachings: it is not possible to think of the present as the past of a future that is already devouring it; there is almost the fear of a meaning that is being made fun of via the anticipatory movement towards the infinite.

We can thus understand, as the beam that both threatens and frees the characters is lowered, why the characters should feel threatened by a sense of disquiet, and specifically that of not being listened to any longer.

We are thus faced with an extreme form of the confession; extreme because *Comédie* is the radicalisation of the being seen, of the being said, just as the *Unnameable* and *Texts for Nothing* were the radicalisation of *being said*.

Samuel Beckett 1906-1989

uel Beckett Samuel Beckett Samu

There is to be only one light source, and it must not be placed outside the ideal space (the stage) occupied by its victims.

The optimal position for the beam is at the centre of the forestage so that the faces can be lit from as close as possible and from below. When three beams have to be used in order to light three faces at the same time, they must configure a single beam that breaks up into three; for the rest, a single mobile beam has to be used that turns on a pivot as quickly as possible so as to move from one face to another; the method that consists in giving each face its own distinct beam is not satisfactory because it is less expressive of the idea of there being only one investigating authority

The reconstruction of the story is simple enough in that it is the traditional theme of a love triangle: a man and two women—his wife and his lover.

The wife thinks that her husband is cheating on her and has him followed by a private detective; the lover fears for the man's safety and urges him to leave his wife, but his wife forgives him, as he has professed his love for her. The man, however, goes to visit his lover, who tries to convince him that they should run off together. When the wife thinks she has refound her husband and the lover thinks that she has conquered him, the man disappears.

The meaning lies entirely in the bitter initial realisation that Man, in his simplicity, drags

Beckett's theatrical research led him to a circumnavigation of man and to rendering man visible and listened to by external space after having made him speak from the depths of his internality. This circumnavigation of man is provided through Winnie's monologue, under the beam of light and addressed in the form of mumblings, to an almost absent character.

Comédie is also extreme because it concentrates within a brief unit of time and space all the elements of what might be called a semiology of the jar syndrome. The incarceration of the body, the anonymity of the character, the paralysis of the face/mask and the endless gasping for breath indicate that everything has been closed off, walled (like the jars that

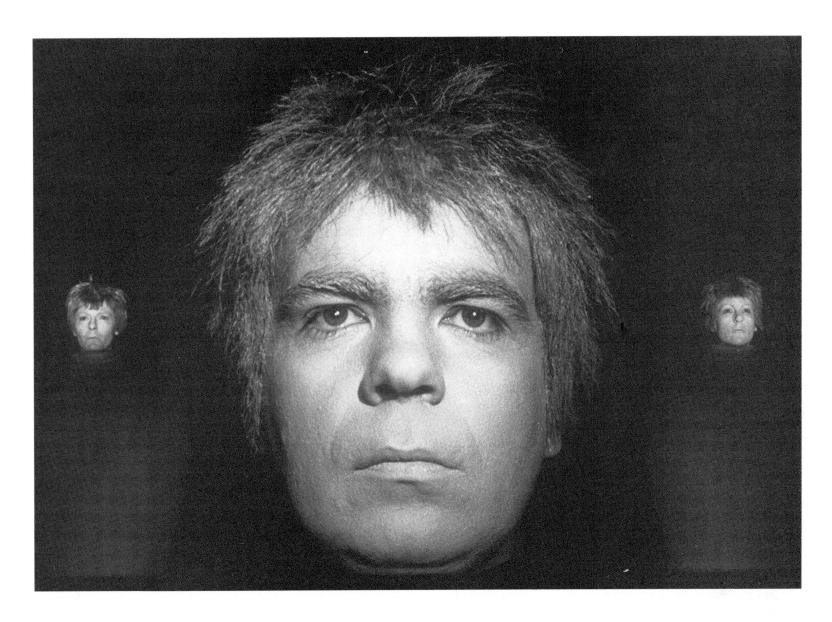

encapsulate the bodies of the three characters), reduced to a single word through which we search for the proof of an impossible truth. These faces gasp, continue, start up again: they constitute this other extremity, which is the repetition of their three-fold confession while, in the second movement, the word "comedy" is made to assume its real meaning. It is no longer in the order of fragmentary truth, reconstituted and then shattered again, that the separation of beings appears; but in the order of the word itself that, as has often been noted, brings itself into question and denounces itself as soon as it is proffered.

Light assumes a meaning with its acute and subtle *transferences* that incessantly persecute these faces; in fact, the continual, sharp light slamming into their faces, a medium through which the characters meditate at the same time as they relate their separate disorders, has no reason bar as a responsible impulse from which all of

Beckett's adventure ensue: the speech impulse.

If *Comédie* presents itself twice and precisely doubles itself in a manner that is almost similar and identical (Beckett offers some notes regarding possible variations) it is because it is impossible to escape from the hell of words, and this duplication has the clear outline of a bait for an easily-interpreted multiplication: while the tale reaches its end, an image, a silence, an identical word are needed to make the play see-saw into an eternal repetition.

Comédie again represents an extreme experience in that the forceps is, in this play, the beam: you must be plumbed and fathomed by this inquisition in order to be born into the world from the "blackness" within yourself; in order to relate yourself you must have this violent mechanism, this analogical operation the writer has set himself to, and not without the cruel participation of the audience.

The beam of light, like the light of exteriorised

consciousness in the anxiousness to make people speak, extracts you from your silence and throws back in your face three separate speeches: this is the common desire for confession, but *outside* and *compressing*, in order to have greater force and greater depth, dividing so as to extract singularity, reuniting so as to bring forth separation within confusion (illuminated at the same time, the three faces speak together); it is the light of intention, the decision/constriction to be-speak according to oneself, an experience regarding the existential measure of the human being brought back to the matrix of language.

Dario Ventimiglia

Comédie
1966
35 mm film, 18' 43",
film still

There is a reckless way of living art that transform itself into the wisdom of the art of living, and this is something that Rotella is also a master at—that means, at lacerations that induce knowledge.

It is therefore not surprising that his *décollages* attract large numbers of young people who look towards communication and art.

The most obvious reason is that his work, which is extraordinarily ahead of its time, is in tune with the evolution of mural messages in an era of metropolitan graffiti. The deepest attraction, which marks its uniqueness, lies in the exemplary exchange between transgression and passion and between the individual and the masses—this is what the artist has been proposing for half a century. Rotella's art has for fifty years been a manifesto of eternal youth. Each new canvas, each exhibition during his lengthy career has constituted a victory over time. Today, newspapers all say that Rotella's art "appeals to the young," and, obviously, Rotella takes immense pleasure in this.

attention so as to remove yesterday's gaze from the new day. Thus his works have presented the proliferation of material compositions of the *Retro-d'affiche* and the iconography of cinema myths; then the printing of photo-reports onto enamelled canvas and the superimposition of Artypòs that were discarded by printing houses; then Blanks from advertising posters covered after they were put up and various paint jobs undertaken over posters—like just as many branches of a single tree or an immense sheet (millenarian painting) well and truly rooted in mass communication more than within the realm of private expression. No *décollage*-ist, no contemporary painter, has branched out more than Rotella from the figural skin of the world to cultivate his revelatory action. For European Informalism, a canvas did not represent anything—it simply presented itself; it was a thing, in and of itself, comparable to nature, like a substitute for a wall or a mirror on a wall: hence Rotella's "wall poetics." The Rotella *décollage* was particularly fostered in its incubation period by the recollection of the

him. On the walls of Rome he saw materials that were already set for an art that was not only painting, but also action: a gesture, a performance. After a happy sojourn in America, he thought about composing and making public the coloured strips of paper he was collecting or ripping from walls at night around Piazza del Popolo; and that had now gone beyond the geometric weave of Concrete canvases. His new form, based on the ripping of advertising posters, is what he called *décollage* because—or so it has been said—*collage*, which it also integrates, had already been invented by Picasso and Braque. The temporal sequence of the two techniques is of little importance, to be honest. Much more important is the depriving sense of the prefix *dé-*, the deconstruction of the real and set of symbols (a poster being the carrier of symbols and myths), the abstention from the habit of art based on painting—*décollage* was Franciscan. Rotella gave continuity within change to the ramification of *décollage* when, in 1960, he joined the then fledgling Nouveau-Réalisme, which was to constitute Europe's main chal-

Mimmo Rotella 1918

What is less obvious is how he finds the time to play with his little daughter Asya. His precocious début in the world of the experimental avant-garde in 1949 (with a series of astounding phonetic poems) and, above all, his early adherence to the policy of ripping posters from city walls (with the result that simple news reporting helped in the evolution of the history of art) were not simply linguistic records. Going beyond the feted invention of an innovative language—Rotella's *décollage*—these early forays became a model for a daily choice and were propounded as a means of continuous renewal. What is a *décollage*, first of all, and what is it for those who do it every day? It's a way of paying detached

passions cultivated by Futurism for the artifices of the city, transgressive evenings, poetry made up of onomatopoeic sounds and the music of noise. Amongst the first, along with Lucio Fontana, to recuperate Futurist teachings, the young Rotella débuted with a dry painting based on Geometric Abstraction, tying it in with his interest for photography and, above all, the invention of the "epistaltic poems" he recited. Rotella exhibited his first *décollages* in Rome in 1954. He had already discovered the expressive potential of posters ripped from walls some time before thanks to his special observational skills—that of always being present with himself and grasping the "here and now" of the phenomena all around

lenge to American Pop Art. This would be a long sodality, lived for the most part in Paris, at the beginning of which it was to receive from Pierre Restany (one of the group's founders, along with Yves Klein, Arman César and a few other *décollage*-ists) the most articulated theoretical pieces on *décollage* ever written. He contributed to the history of Nouveau-Réalisme in 1963 when he created mec-art, by which photography was brought onto the canvas. From the outset you could feel his sense of the eternity of matter within the very precariousness of form. At the turn of the millennium, his ephemeral is like a calendar of the eternal.

Tommaso Trini

Islam
1999
Decollages and painting,
200 × 235 cm

Biennale 2001 begins with a homage to the artists, to whom the last revolution in the twentieth century owes its gratitude. Joseph Beuys, the tragic atist in the Kassel documentary, has also been in Venice many times: with *Strassenbahnhaltestelle* 1976 in the German pavillion, in 1978 with *Feuerstaette I*, in 1980 with *Das Kapital Raum* 1970-1977. Now in 2001 there are *Voglio vedere le mie montagne* (1950-71), *Das Ende des 20. Jahrhunderts* (1983), and *Olivestone* (1984), the most important work happening in Italy. Beuys' originality is not to be found in the appropriation of large contents, but rather in their surprisingly provocative reactiveness without following the beat of the aesthetical realm. Beuys lived and worked for the conviction that a greated spirit, renewed strength and revolutionary energy are only to be advanced from the future. Christianity and Humanism were the western ideas that came along with the past. The post-capitalistic and post-communistic "new society of the real socialism" based upon the principals of freedom, equality, solidarity, a freedom from authority, the unity of diversity with a self-governing culture and economy is the greatest "evolutionary alternative", the "Social Plastic", upon which the "Man as Artist" is formed. Every person will be engaged. Everything can be a vehicle to appeal to the individual freedom impulse. This "expanded art concept" must also reactivate the potential that lays in the "conveyed ideas" of the past, in order to accelerate the trans-

that self-consciousness is formed becomes a world changing action. His pushing point is the future. And with the pushes man realizes what type of god he is".

Man is a creature of nature, a social creature, as a spiritual creature he is a creative celebration and also a god. Because of this he can and must compare and assosciate himself with other gods, to work together to create a future societal order. In this process the evolutionary power of art, with all its possibilities of expression and exchanges, is the transmitter of a complex unity.

he three installations exhibited here represent this and his process of calling out images and appeals, for his dilated association with time, for the scenic, appealing manifest to plastic art and the enlarging of the principle of plastic art in the social realm. For Beuys plastic art is the "inner organic image", it contains "more polarities, possibilities" in itself. One can "hear plastic before one sees it", while sculpture corresponds more to the old sense of the sculpting art.

"Voglio vedere i miei montagne" are reputed to have been the last words of the painter Giovanni Segantini (1858-99), who after the experience of the city and social misery chose solitude in the mountains. Beuys formed a barren interior with objects, which by their Celtic and Rhaeto-romanic inscriptions are associated with the Barnina mountain landscape: "Val", "Vadret" = Valley, through the recedence of the glacial mass the "Felsen", "Cime", "Penin",

cism of materialism. And it should not be forgotten that, Beuys first opposed in the places loved by Segantini, the institutionalized rule of man over men, and the "Dictatorship of the Party". "La rivoluzione siamo noi" set against, his humanitarian anarchism.

Olivestone was formed of five tubs of lime bearing sandstone into which olive oil was poured. They came from the Palazzo Durini in Bolognano and were placed at Beuys' disposal for his piece at the opening of the Castello di Rivoli. The artist had the tubs, the vessel of a feminine nature, filled with stone blocks, the masculine nature. As a unifying fluidity he poured the oil over the "Two-sex Block." A chemical analysis proves that Beuys wanted to disaffirm the principles: the oil seeping into the stone became part of the sculpture and corroded the stone. The ideal condition of "Androgyny" as a unified conception destroyed in a slow process the metaphor, the material, the plastic.

Das Ende des 20. Jahrhunderts was presented for the first time in my 1983 exhibition *Der Hang zum Gesamtkunstwerk* in the Düsseldorf Kunsthalle together with the works of Rudolf Steiner and the provocative picture *Deutschlands Geisteshelden* by Anselm Kiefer. It was formed of 21 basalt sculptures, which layed individually in the room on wood and pallets with a forklift underneath the last transported stone . There are many forms of this piece, but this is the starting point. In every sculpture there is an pressed out open-

Joseph Beuys 1921-1986

formation. Beuys affirmed this in a discourse with Hagen Lieberknecht: "I don't want to put forth the ancient myths and imagine a picture of the past. We are really at another place in development. This place, this position demands... that something completely new be discovered about "how" we are connected to the past. To gain a consciousness of the methodology of the connection means not only this dressing of the unconsciousness through the built up historical process into consciousness as individual analysis, societal analysis, and thus an analysis of an unfinished past—that is the psychoanalysis of the unknown and the not-so-well-known—rather,

"Scira", and the "Walsun" became valleys. About this Doris Leutgeb writes: "To make clear Beuys' established solidification of rational ways of thinking, the placement of crystal elements and structures was preferred... instead of the principal organic components. These for him imply the mineral strength of the mountain... the potential renewal of the materials. In a deeply psychological aspect "Mountain" signifies a high level of self-consciousness... and if I make the environment "Voglio vedere..." I intend the archetypical idea of the mountain, "The Mountain of the Self". In sharp contrast to this the writing on the weapon says: "Think". Beuys put it there as an archetype of his criti-

ing the size of a flower-pot, the piece of which was then laid upon the stone as a cone. They have the effect of eyes and lend the stones a pre-historical life aspect, and gives an enrgy-field to the whole being. Beuys said when talking about this plastic art, that is given to us, to awaken this inorganical material through our warm qualities at the end of the 20th century. "The Warmth quality. This dimension is really another dimension, one that has nothing to do with the Space-and-Time relation..." Naturally, the ideal exit product for the first exhibition in the 21st century and third millenium with the dimensions of a "Plastic art of Humanity".

Harald Szeemann

**Voglio vedere
i miei montagne
(Ich will meine Berge
sehen)**
1950-71
Space installation
of 29 elements,
4,2 × 5,8 × 7,82 m

La fine del 20° secolo
(Das Ende des 20.
Jahrhunderts)
1983
21 basaltstones in
different sizes, felt, clay,
wheel-barrow, squared
wood, installation,
4,7 × 12 × 9 m

Olivestones
1984
Limestone, olive oil,
installation, variable size

Seldom are there aspects in modern art in which timelessness is to be found, those in which generations of life and sorrows, distance and interest have been so impressed as on Marisa Merz's little heads.

Tenderness in the being, transitoriness in the material, composure as demeanor, a shifting of the gaze upwards. Abandoning at the beginning of the 80's the sombre allusion to spaces delicately occupied, these heads develop an upwards gaze, removing themselves from the idea of time as custom; they reach a multiplicity of significance in the atemporal dimension already turned to sculpture. The iconography of upwards gazes not immediately alluding to heavenly apparitions is not easily found.

Merz's little heads distance themselves from the devotional sphere, representing instead the awarness of delicacy. They are silent, and in their silence, eloquent. Born from a wealth of experience, in their existence these heads leave behind the consistency of Being.

They evoke the ephemeral and at the same time, withdrawing in themselves, they deny it. The heads carry within the appeal to present inquietude about the past. They represent the appreciation of suffering, and are eloquent because deprived of the features of a protrait, while imbued of a silence absorbing in itself love and revolt.

They know very well what evil man can inflict, but their sensitivity reaches beyond the shock, and they live on emotional surcharge.

Marisa Merz 1925

And so their colorfulness is also based upon the realm of primary attraction, on war-paint and nostalgia. Visual contact relies on notches and relieves, the physiognomies are simplified, the neck becomes an elongate support. The corporality is lapidary and ineffable. The upwards gaze turns inwardly.

Seldom in modern art one encounters faces in which timelessness can be read with such intensity.

Harald Szeemann

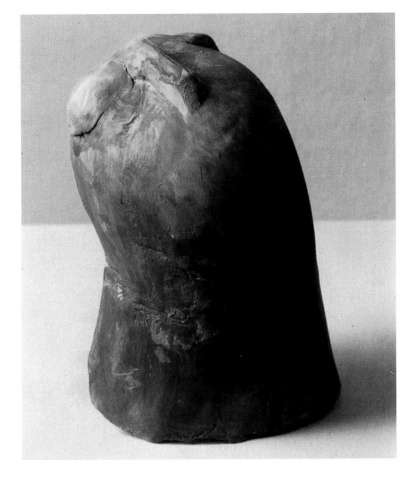

Testa rosa
1989
Polychrome argil

Testa
1983
Polychrome argil

Carambole

It was a bright Sunday morning even though it had been a cold night. Six of us set off for the mountains—four adults and two children, all crammed into a Fiat 1400. I was five years old. Suddenly, a series of zigzagging curves and countersteering manoeuvres were followed by a loud bang as we crashed into a garden wall. Then I heard someone say: "Don't go near the car if you've got any metal under your shoes—the gasoline's leaking." My sister and I were crushed under all the others; the car had turned over onto its side. Later we found ourselves, shivering and tending to our cuts and scratches, sitting in a farmhouse kitchen. We were bruised, our lips were cracked, and one of us had a broken cheekbone.

For the next thirty years, my mother would break out in a cold sweat whenever she got into a car. Luckily nobody was knocked down that time—in fact, the Mass had already started, and the sidewalk was empty. "Thank God!" was the comment.

Let's imagine that Odermatt had photographed our accident peovoked by ice on the bridge as well: it would have been possible from a temporal point of view. Odermatt the "policeman" would have got onto the roof of his little VW van, and with his Rolleiflex in hand he would have aimed at the overturned car and then the skid-marks leading up to the garden wall, underlined by chalk. But from a logistical point of view, this wouldn't have been possible—we were going

There are two types of distinguishing photos in *Carambole*: landscape photos and sculpture-photos. The former show us typical Swiss landscapes, with lawns, flowers, lakes and that atmosphere which is always rather redolent of Sundays. The landscape involuntarily becomes a stage: in its tranquillity and quiet a specific point is focused on, and then bang! there's a car crash; or it's partly covered by a strange scratch, a sort of skid-mark; and in one extremity there's a car smashed up against a tree, a wall or a crush barrier. Or hurled against a post, or half immersed in a lake. The otherwise undisturbed peace is suddenly shattered, as if someone had basely thrown fresh paint over an already-finished canvas. An accident in the midst of orderliness. An accident of orderliness, cleaned up and put right, but only up to a certain point.

The second type of photo concentrates on a more restricted field, and focuses on cars. These photos are more sculpted: they are close-ups of cars scrunched up into each other, crumpled mudguards, car hoods transformed into contorted metal sheets and broken windows. The volume rises before us, its skin peeled off, thus involuntarily formulating an impact between the integral and the mangled, between open and closed form. From these oh-so-neutral, neat and clean photos is born a sort of "involuntary sculpture."

"The truth of art lies in the breaking down of the monopoly of reality, just as is in fact exerted within society. With the aesthetic form that derives from this rupture, the fictional world of

Arnold Odermatt 1925

towards the Flumser skiing district, and not the Nidwalden canton, which was his battleground. The bodies piled up on top of each other, the careful but hurried slide out of the car, the fear while drinking tea and the cold sweat—none of this would be seen in an Odermatt photo. This sort of story isn't one of his themes, nor is he interested in it. His photos are extremely neat and clean, except for the vehicle he photographs. He takes his photos after the accident, sometimes well after, when the tale of the accident proper has already faded. One photo, for example, shows a child lying on the ground, probably after having been run over: but the situation effects us precisely because it is represented just like that, "without bloodshed."

art becomes the real reality." Thus writes Herbert Marcuse at the same time as these photos were taken. His observations could also be applied to Odermatt's photos. The accident "dysfunctionalises" the car, abruptly transforming it into fiction, into a contemporary dinosaur. The "accidentalist" surrealism of day-to-day life. And despite the violence of the crash and the destruction, what dominates the scene is more a comic than a tragic sense. When Freud said that the grandiosity of humour lies in the triumph of narcissism and a belief in the inviolability of the ego, he could not have known that his words would one day have also made sense for the ego of the new form of mobility—the AUTO-EGO.

Urs Stahel

Buochs
1965
Black and white
photograph, 40 × 50 cm

The Triumphs and even the tyrannies of history endure for only a moment; it is their ruins which are eternal. Tempting to say that in the battle of Lepanto, where Cervantes lost an eye, Twombly recovered a vision. Such paradoxes are the justice of art: to children, to foreigners (and in history we are all foreigners), such syllables as *Guernica* or *Anghiara* are alien indeed, yet we live on terms of intimacy, of understanding, with an artist's response to the wreckage they signify. Was it not Picasso who once called a painting the sum of its destructions?

For Twombly, the Mediterranean *pathos* has always been an invoked phenomenon. Somewhere on his giant canvases, among glowing or effaced marks and signs, the glorious names are scrawled like so much scornful graffiti: Apollo, Virgil, Troy... When I put together a program of poems alluded to in Twombly's work, I had a veritable anthology of the classical world, from Homer to Cavafy. His response to an envisioned past which American genius has most characteristically found unvisitable (is not Whitman more characteristic of that genius than Eliot, Melville than Pound?) is passionately singular, though it is scarcely an ordered one, as Pound's and Eliot's sought to be. Twombly's variations on the classical world, the classical past, are like jazz compositions–loose structures which "go" on their nerve, their necessary discoveries of a

Cy Twombly 1928

man's desire which lead to what he learns, by inspired guesses, of the weather of history, the climate of time.

There were, of course, particular manifestations along the way. For decades this artist—especially in his sculpture—has been concerned with the making of boats, recognizable *solar barques* like the kind ancient Egyptians buried in their tombs, vessels to conduct the soul to a transcendent condition. There has always been a kind of archaic splendor—primitive, delicate—

about these little ships of Twombly's; they have reminded me many times of those late obsessive sequences by D.H. Lawrence, *The Ship of Death*, in which the self is abjured to prepare in a traditional yet home-made style the vessels that would carry across, would go over, would depart... In *Lepanto* a work of 12 canvases offering a heroic series of variations on a Mediterranean theme of triumph and death, the boats are burned, of course (it is the destruction of the Turkish fleet by combined European forces under Venetian leadership); there is a mystery about what I am calling the splendor and the triumph, for they are often reduced (if that can be the word to use in such transactions, such events) to skeletal remains, to the elemental rudiments of what has been a terrible destruction. It is as if, for Twombly, the dozen panels of the tremendous sea-fight, which represented the rescue of Europe from Ottoman invasion in the 16th Century, were a meditation on the destiny of the soul in terms of that vulnerable and fragile barque Twombly has so obsessively produced.

In the maritime museum of Barcelona, the star exhibition is the gallery of Don John of Austria, from which the victory of Lepanto was commanded. The vessel is astonishingly decked out with teak carvings and what Shakespeare calls gold adornings, yet for all its glamorous embellishments it is one of the very ships which, in decorative tapestries and frescos representing naval victories in all the palaces of

Europe, represented the astonishment of Lepanto. There is no question, as we look at Don John's flagship, of the risk of the enterprise, of the value to the West of victory and the disgrace to the Ottomans of defeat. Twombly's canvases are concerned with precisely these issues—the showy glory of the ships on fire is what represents that victory, and the unscathed crudity of the linear (stick-figure!) European ships indicate the elusive triumph of the aggressor. Twombly has arranged his dozen panels to begin and end with the

conflagration, which appears in such scarlet and gold splendor on every fourth panel, a sort of over-all splendor, which signifies defeat. The second, fifth and ninth panels describe actual combat—the last in which hand-to-hand or ship-to-ship fighting occurred: from now on battles at sea would be won or lost by artillery and sail. A certain human prowess and brutality is registered here, though no human form is shown amid the elements of fire and water in their paradoxical opposition, just as the desert sand swallows the solar barques in pyramid interments.

It is always dangerous for a maker to employ in a single project the entire range of his art—his whole armory, one might say. There is a kind of tombstone effect in the affair; as one feels about the elegiac mastery of Monet's water-lily panels at the Orangerie; where the whole project of the splendors and miseries of brushed vision is conducted to its end. What if the artist—as in Monet's case—has something more to devise, further invention? As we move along the swarming gamut of Twombly's sea-fight, there is something of this anthology of creative invention—the spontaneous development of painterly possibility, all-out and all-over. Yet the sheer exuberance of the 12 panels, and the decisive rhythm which this registration of the ambivalence of victory and defeat subserves, makes this work a much less totalizing enterprise than the anticipated spectacle of "the old man's toys." Always grim

and sometimes uproarious as the panels are, their cumulative effect, as we move among them, or step back to take in the whole sequence as a single image, is one of luminous intensity, a proposition of the striving imagination of victory which is defeat, of destruction which is escape, historical evidence through a personal meditation on tragedy. Certainly *Lepanto* is an accounting, but not a final summing up. We are still, with Twombly in 2001, in the thick of the fight.

Richard Howard

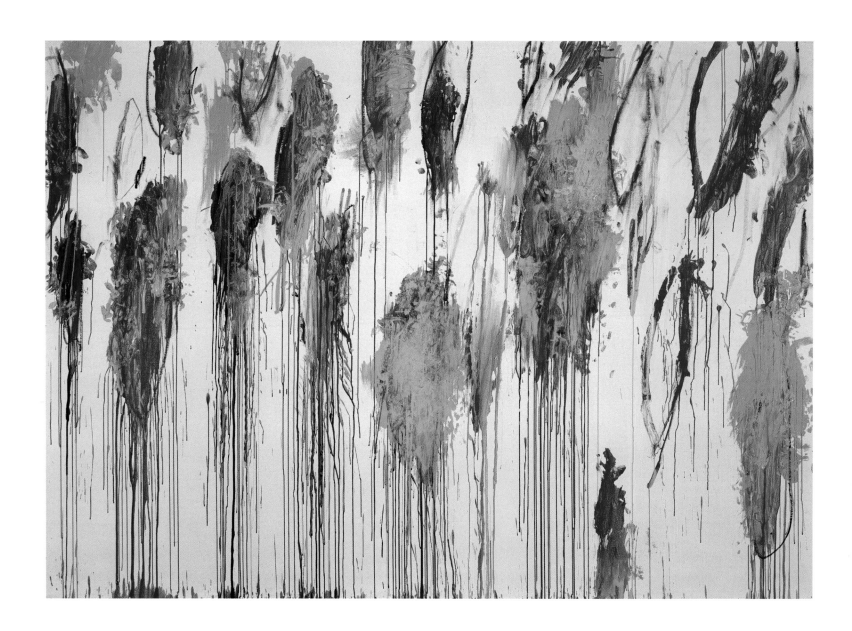

Lepanto
2001
Acrilic on canvas,
216,5 × 334,5 cm

Lepanto
2001
Acrilic on canvas,
216,5 × 333,5 cm

Gerhard Richter's *Abstract Paintings (Rhombus)* series is at once formally brilliant and conceptually provocative. Installed together, the dramatic sweep of the five smaller paintings and the keystone larger work elicits the power of the great mural cycles of the Renaissance and Baroque: the canvases are both an ensemble and a sequence of independent entities. The rhombic shape, slightly greater in width than height, draws the viewer's eye from one painting to the next, an effect given greater impetus by the unity of palette and the horizontal swipes of pigment. At the same time, the scraped surfaces, the arresting tenor of the crimson and orange tones, and the implication of concealed imagery and inner light are immediately engaging, focusing attention on the particular features of each composition.

The rhombus, while a familiar format for such artists as Ellsworth Kelly and Kenneth Noland, is not merely a formal device in Richter's hands, and the shape was in part determined by the unusual history of these works. As Martin Hentschel observed on the occasion of the 1998 exhibition of these paintings at the Anthony d'Offay Gallery in London: "The external form, unprecedented in Richter's work, must not be misread as a 'shaped canvas'. [There is] a remote and highly discreet allusion to the pictorial type of a standing human figure with outstretched arms. It is no accident that Richter has chosen this form, for his commission was to depict the Stigmatization of St. Francis of Assisi."[1]

These paintings were originally conceived for of rhombic photographs. Then I began to paint on these six canvases. And after many phases with different abstract images they got to the final state: red and reddish orange, almost monochrome. So, one day suddenly they were finished—and that was hard to believe."[2]

What Richter chose not to discuss in this statement, however, is the precise relationship of the Crucifixion to the miracle of St. Francis receiving the stigmata: the five wounds of Christ were transferred by rays of light directly onto the saint's body as he envisioned Jesus on the Cross. So too did Padre Pio receive the stigmata during his lifetime. While Christian iconography does not assign a particular shape to stigmata—and it would be absurd to reduce the Rhombus paintings to mere representations of the wounds—the number of the five smaller canvases and their throbbingly vibrant palette provide an analogue to Christian tradition. The single larger composition, which is more densely worked, can be regarded as the palimpsest that both opens and concludes the cycle.

Themes of death, punishment and redemption have been discerned in Richter's work across his career. Always critically aware of the power of conviction that can be invested in images, in 1988 he wrote: "Art is the pure realization of religious feeling, capacity for faith, longing for God... The ability to believe is our outstanding quality, and only art translates it into reality. But when we assuage our need for faith, we court disaster."[3] Excluded from their intended context, the *Rhombus*

Gerhard Richter 1932

Gerhard Richter Gerha

Renzo Piano's Aula Liturgica di Padre Pio, the Franciscan church currently under construction near Foggia, Italy. Yet when the cycle was completed, the commissioning body of the church rejected these works as too abstract, an unparalleled irony in light of the paintings' rich frame of reference. Richter has recounted: "I do not know why I chose that diamond-shaped format, which reminds me always of a cross. I can only repeat the circumstances.

Two years ago I received Renzo Piano's request to create a mural in his new large pilgrimage church in Italy in honor of Saint Francis. My first idea was that rhombic shape, which I had never used before. I started with photographs of abstract images and made a smaller series paintings remain Richter's most succinct exploration of spiritual passion. St. Francis's mystic and ecstatic moment of transcendence was also deeply visceral in nature; appropriately, Richter conceives the sacred from the mundane in these uncompromisingly contemporary and deeply beautiful paintings.

Alison de Lima Greene

[1] Martin Hentschel, "On Shifting Terrain: Looking at Richter's Abstract Paintings," *Gerhard Richter 1998* (Anthony d'Offay Gallery, London 1998), p. 16.
[2] Gerhard Richter, letter to the author, 14 June 1999.
[3] Gerhard Richter, "Notes, 1988", *Gerhard Richter: The Daily Practice of Painting*, London, Thames and Hudson Ltd. and Anthony d'Offay Gallery, 1995, p. 170.

**Abstract painting
(Rhombus) (851-2)**
1998
Oil on canvas,
186 × 209 cm

This installation is dedicated to the problematic that is very topical for the situation in the contemporary art world today: What will happen to artists and their works in the very near, and not so near, future? How will they be accepted and understood by the new viewer of the future, the new art critic, the new collector, the new curator? In our mind, this problem today is masked by the dominant reality, the demand to be "contemporary" no matter what! The demand "to exist today" overwhelms the question: What will happen to these works tomorrow? This is a personal problem for every artist: What is more important, to have his works understood and accepted today, or to wish for them to live into "tomorrow," and what is the difference? Description of the Installation: The viewer, upon entering the space, encounters a fence and a bridge. In order to be able to see what is behind this fence, he has to go and walk onto the bridge. From the bridge he sees, in the center, a fragment of *The Last Train Car*, which is "leaving" from two wooden platforms (trucks). Paintings and rolls of drawings are on one of these platforms. The same kinds of paintings are also lying scattered on the ground. On the train car we see a running electronic text (in red, in Jenny Holtzer's style) that reads: "Not everyone will be taken into the future." The text, running from left to right, is repeated in different languages: English, Italian. 1. The viewer's point of view from the bridge is that of a bird in flight, i.e., it is a view from "another space," from the future,

Not Everyone Will Be Taken Into the Future

You can't even describe Malevich: a great artist; an inspirer of awe; a great master, said the headmaster of our school, a stern formidable man, as the end of the spring term approached: "Only those who have deserved it will go to the school's Young Pioneer camp for the summer; the others will remain here." Everything broke apart inside me. Everything depended on the master: what he could do I could not do; what he knew, I did not know. We had many masters at school: headmaster Karrenberg, head of studies Sukiayan, the poet Pushkin, head of military studies Petrov, the artists Repin and Surikov, the composers Bach, Mozart, Tchaikovsky... if you didn't obey them, if you did not do what they said or recommended, you were told, "you will remain here". Not everyone will be taken into the future. This chilling sentence signifies a primordial division of all people into three categories, like children:
1. Those who are the takers
2. Those who are taken
3. Those who will not be taken
... I shall not be taken.
... A great, epoch-making picture appears in my imagination: 1913. Europe. A high mountain. Not even a mountain, but a kind of plateau. A small gathering of grim leaders is standing at the very edge of the plateau, where it falls away like a sliced-off of cheese. Before them, right at their feet, where the land, going downhill, breaks off, a sea of mist is spread out. How are

of being. He is totally gripped by this new spirit, of which he himself is the embodiment. At this great moment the horizon openes up for him in both directions. The future is clear and so, therefore, is the past. He has completely mastered the old existence and knows it; he has squeezed it in his fist. There it lies, fallen, quiet, wrinkled, a small square on his broad palm. There will be no repeat. Ahead is only the "Other". A small group of people will accompany him into this new, precipitous world. They will live in the future, closely united around their teacher, given wings by his spirit, his ideas. How to join this select company? How to buy a ticket for the departing train? There is a system of tests for this, to determine your preparedness for spiritual flight. For those left behind, a square is simply a square and five colored rectangles are five rectangles. For those who have grasped, and entered into, the new spirit, these squares and rectangles are signs of a new spiritual domain; they are like gates beyond which lies the new land; they are like *koan* (the paradoxical puzzles of Zen Buddhism) whose solution leads to a new, unprecedented plane. Those in touch with this new life will work to transform the old world into the new, re-conceiving their clothing, their furniture and everyday objects under the sign of Suprematism, imbuing everything with energy so that nothing on this earth or in the surrounding cosmos shall remain without the vivifying force of supreme consciousness. But what would happen to the "unpromising" citizens who are left behind? One more recollection from my

because the train has already left. 2. The paintings and the images on them belong to the authors of the installation. There is "no critical escapade aimed at anyone in particular." This is the problem of the authors themselves.

Ilya and Emilia Kabakov

they to go forward? Frightened, huddled humanity stands at a respectful distance, not daring to interfere with this conference. What will the leaders decide? Silence. A great historical moment. If, trembling all over, you draw close to this small, elevated meeting, there, among the other great helmsmen, you can see Malevich: calm, self-controlled, fully prepared for the immense responsibility that has fallen upon him. He reccomends that they go on, straight towards the sky. He regards the edge of the precipice at his feet as the end of the past. The entire past history of mankind, all of its affairs, its art, has ended right here and now. The end of the old country is in sight; ahead is the new land, the breath of the cosmos, a new state

schooldays. I lived in a dormitory at school. When the headmaster said, at the assembly I mentioned earlier, that not everybody would go to the Young Pioneer camp, but only the best, one of the pupils asked quietly whether he could stay in the dormitory for the summer. "No", the headmaster replied. "The dormitory will be closed all summer for repairs and it will be forbidden to stay there".
In conclusion: The way ahead is with Malevich alone, but only a few will be taken—the best; those whom the headmaster chooses—only he knows which ones. It is also impossible to remain; everything will be shut up and sealed after *les suprèmes* fly away into the future.

Ilya Kabakov

General view of
the installation
Общий вид
инсталляции

"NOT EVERYONE WILL BE TAKEN IN
THE FUTURE"

И.К. 2001

Of two squares
Two squares fly to the earth
And they see that it is black and troubled there.
A blow. Everything is scattered.
The blackness is covered with redness, brightness.
It's finished here. Go forward.
(El Lissitzky, *A-Z*, Paris 1982, 1998² pp. 34-35).

Not everyone will be
taken into the future
2001
General view
of the installation
Water painting, pencil,
charcoal pencil

**Not everyone will be
taken into the future**
2001
The view from the bridge
Water painting, pencil,
charcoal pencil

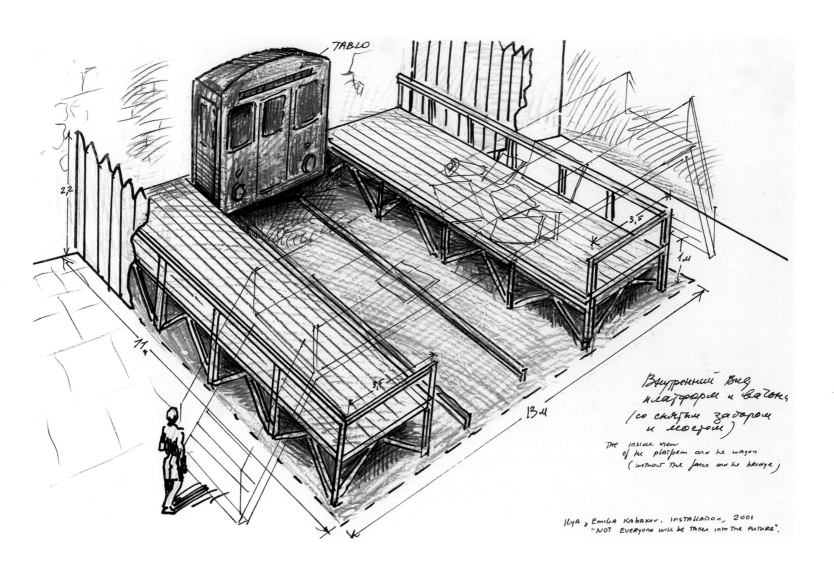

TABLO

Внутренний вид
платформ и вагона
(со снятым забором
и мостом)

The inside view
of the platform and the wagon
(without the fence and the bridge)

ILYA & EMILA KABAKOV, INSTALLATION, 2001
"NOT EVERYONE WILL BE TAKEN INTO THE FUTURE".

**Not everyone will be
taken into the future**
2001
The inside view of the
platform and the wagon
(without the fence
and the bridge)
Water painting, pencil,
charcoal pencil

Mergerism

"Thank goodness I know nothing about football, so I have more time..." for something better, obviously!

This is what I said to someone shortly before I began spending all my time on this sport and the other connected activities for one year and a half.

As it is so often the case, it all began by chance: I came home after a trip, put down my suitcase and noticed the television that was on even though nobody was watching it, mainly because of the sound of incredible rejoicing. Then I saw how a bunch of men were embracing each other, bodies against bodies, jumping, hopping up and down, rubbing, pushing, jerking, arms flying upwards—complete bliss and thousands of people were watching—the joy of having scored a goal.

That was the moment when sperm and egg cell met—at least in my mind—experiencing the joy of scoring a goal. Only that we are just as used to this sight as we are to that of a man who controls, hides, transforms or sublimates his emotions of sensuality and bliss. The normal man.

In the video *FUSION* footballers are playing in elegant business suits, the ball becomes an instrument of the business world, a laptop, a financial newspaper; mobiles and briefcases fly through the air and in some of the scenes of the game there is another image, the one going through the manager's mind while still maintaining the appearance of fair-play.

closed. He rattles and pushes, it finally opens a little bit and he can look through the crack. He sees a strange figure. First he notices the long tail, the horse-like foot, and when he finally sees the little horns on its head he cries out "But I'm Mr. X, I should be in heaven!" The demon replies: "Oh, Sir, haven't you noticed that we, too, have merged."

Ingeborg Lüscher

Ingeborg Lüscher 1936

The managers as players, the players as managers.

Hard training, discipline, strength, staying the course, the aggressive wish to win, the willingness to make sacrifices in order to win, fantasy, tactics, bluffs, tricks, being willing to take risks, popularity, idolism, politics, money and power—which qualities belong in which categories of actions?

A friend recently said to me: "Have you heard, that Mr. X has died?", and he tells me the name of a well-known banker. My reaction was not exactly regret, more surprise because I hadn't heard about it. "Yes," he continued, "and then Mr. X found himself on a little cloud, an enormous door before him, but

Fusion
2001
Video, 6', still from video

For Toroni repetition is not an issue, since a cast is never identical, its configuration depending largely on wrist movement, quantity of paint permeating the brush, fatigue resulting from the repetition of the same gesture gone over a number of times. A method rather than a system, the cast's repetition guarantees the infinite possible variations of the task/painting. The absence of explanations, the artist's voluntary withdrawal and non-identification with the work, his taking the viewer into account, leave Toroni's painting complete latitude to come about in a given place, to be receptive and accessible. The strength of the work lies in that everthing-is-possible, in that "vacuum" left open to the apparition and the experience of painting, allowing them to always be different and singular, neither didactic nor dogmatic. Toroni lets us be masters of our vision and our grasp of reality, while urging us to perceive it differently. So we come back to learning-how-to see, as already mentioned.

The rule of repetitive casts effectively dismiss-

ing on many accounts. With a strict method, a rigorous economy of means, consideration of the intrinsic characteristics of a given space, every time Toroni's painting refreshes our perception of the chosen place by revealing its plasticity and originality, showing us what we usually ignore or fail to see.

The absence of a demonstrative and theoretical finality, a resolute anchoring in the present, freedom left to the "Other," allow Toroni's task / painting to outmoded claims about the disappearance of the practice of painting. Instead, with simplicity and great modesty, rejecting the spectacular and the monumental, it asserts its vitality and necessity, giving meaning to time, to wonder, urging us to question, perhaps, what lies beyond the visible, a quest that lies at the root of many works of art. As Alessandro Delco so aptly put it : "Besides, how can we deny that in all likelihood the invisible has been since its origins the main stake of painting?" By his implicit search for the non-visible, we might compare Toroni to a zen monk. Is there not indeed a

Niele Toroni 1937

ele Toroni Niele Toroni

es the notion of novelty, inseparable from art history, making it obsolete. Gone also are concepts of evolution and maturity of style, classifications and judgements by periods, chronology and the notion of retrospective, and so on. Each work contains its origin and its end, each work is a beginning and a completion. But this return to the genesis of the pictorial practice is not able, however, to suppress the idea of beauty, often inseparable from art, at least in its traditional conception. There again we run into one of the paradoxes of this work, surpris-

definite likeness between them, in their self-detachment, the desire to allow things to happen without the intervention of will, revealing their hidden meaning. They both know that being receptive is a difficult exercise; demanding and without concessions. In full awareness they persevere; repetition is not an issue. Existence is at that cost...

Béatrice Parent

Extract from *Un Apprentissage de la Vision*, 2000.

Pour Rimbaud
1999
Installation, acrilic/paper,
imprints of paint-brush
n° 50 at regular space
intervals (30 cm)

Intervention on
Schweizer Rück
Zürich, Adliswil
1998
Imprints of paint-brush
n°50 at regular space
intervals (30 cm)

Miroir Argus
Imprints of paint-brush
n°50 at regular space
intervals (30 cm)

Comédie: Marin Karmitz and Samuel Beckett

The film *Comédie*[1] was realised following the meeting between Samuel Beckett and Marin Karmitz who at that time was a very young film maker (he had only made one short film previously, *Nuits Noires*, with Marguérite Duras). After seeing a theatre production of *Comédie*, Karmitz proposed to Beckett that they should work together. It seemed to him that the questions raised in the theatre piece were so much in tune with his own ideas as a film maker. *Nuits Noires* had already demonstrated his great skills in rendering extremes of black, white and grey and his heightened sensitivity to concurrences of visual and verbal language. Beckett and Karmitz developed a profound rapport and spent a year together, a period of intense discussion and research, before making the film. Beckett was involved at every stage.

The result is a masterpiece which, however, was not well received when premiered at the Venice Film Festival of 1966. The work seemed

work of Beckett has been of seminal importance for many contemporary artists so the nature in which Karmitz has deployed the medium of film has an astonishing resonance in the context of current artist film and video. On the lighting the authors worked with Pierre L'homme who enabled them to realise the appearances and disappearances in tune with the sound; the more light there is, the less the spoken word is comprehensible and vice versa. The extraordinary qualities of the greys made it impossible at the time for the film to be screened on television and this remained critical for the authors, as it does for Karmitz today. The soundtrack was repeated twice and added after the edit. The actors were dubbed and the soundtrack was accelerated. Beckett and Karmitz used a machine developed in the lab of Pierre Scheffer and they were able to manipulate the recording in a way which had never been used before. The process allowed the recorded sound to be speeded up without altering the tonality of the voices.

Marin Karmitz 1938

to put into question all cinematic convention. There was a total rejection of the work. Even the title sequence conceived by Talon was a challenge to the linear conventions of film credits at the time.

Only last year was the film revived and introduced to a new and different audience.

It is not surprising that *Comédie* has been recognised and acclaimed on its reemergence in the context of contemporary art. Just as the

The experience of *Comédie* lies outside language, narrative, understanding and ventures into abstraction in the play between light and dark. The characters in their "despair" occupy a zone of total solitude, an existentialism that seems utterly contemporary.

Caroline Bourgeois

[1] *Comédie* was presented for the first time since the Venice Film Festival (1966) in the exhibition *Voilà*, Musée d'Art Moderne de la Ville de Paris, 15/6 - 29/10/2000

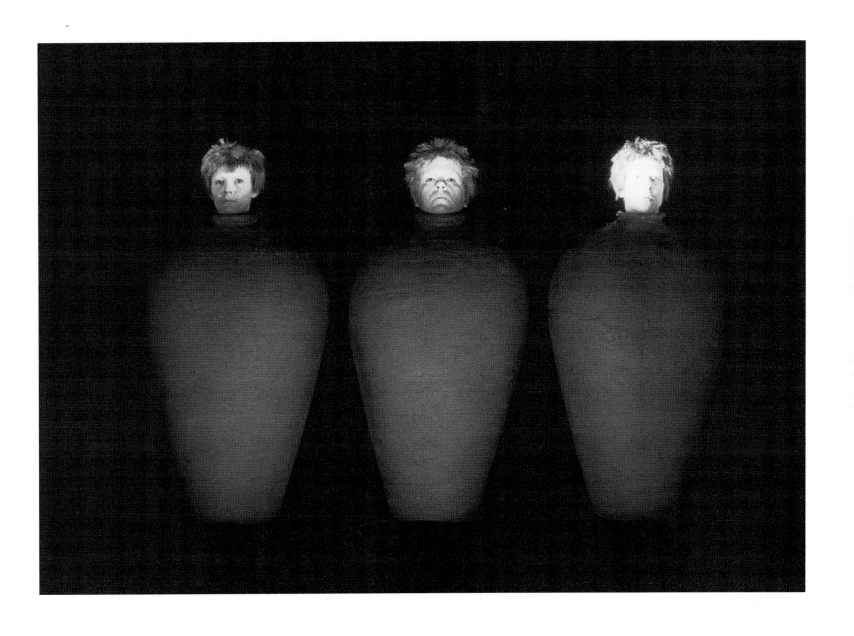

One of the basic functions of art is to enable us to acknowledge thought and perception in ways that other things do not. To engage thought does not mean that the thought is contained solely within the work itself, it means that the thought is contained within the dialogue that the work engenders in relation to its place.

I consider space to be a material. The articulation of space has come to take precedence over other concerns. I attempt to use sculptural form to make space distinct. Part and parcel of making space distinct is to ground the spectator in the reality of the context. For me, the emphasis is on the work's ability to achieve this in sculptural terms. My response to a context is to use sculptural means that both reveal and are relevant to the connotative specifics of the context.

Thought often arises from the physical conditions of a given context; in effect, places engender thoughts. Thoughts and ideas that derive from the experience of a specific context are different from concepts that don't derive from the particularities of a place; you have to make connections while evaluating your experience within the specifics of the context: thinking on your feet so to speak.

Richard Serra

Richard Serra 1939

Richard Serra's sculpture is about sculpture: about the weight, the extension, the density and the opacity of matter, and about the promise of the sculptural project to break through that opacity with systems which will make the work's structure both transparent to itself and to the viewer who looks on from the outside... Again and again, Serra's sculpture makes a viewer realize that the hidden meanings he reads into the corporate body of the world are his own projections and that interiority he had thought belonged to the sculpture are in fact his own interiority—the manifestation from the still point of his point of view.

Rosilind Krauss

"A View on Modernism," *Artforum*, September 1972, p. 48 ff.

THANKS TO GUCCI
FOR SPONSORING THE WORK
OF RICHARD SERRA
and special thanks to ARTIS,
GROUP OF FRANÇOIS PINAULT

In/Out/Left/Right
2001
Watherproof steel,
outer spiral:
$4 \times 12 \times 9$ m c.
inner spiral:
$4 \times 9 \times 7,5$ m c.

In/Out/Left/Right
2001 (top)
Four
2001 (middle)
Left/Right
2001 (bottom)

Four
2001 (above)
Waterproof steel
outer spiral:
4 × 12 × 10,8 m c.
inner spiral:
4 × 9 × 6 m c.
In/Out/Left/Right
2001 (below)
Waterproof steel
outer spiral:
4 × 12 × 9 m c.
inner spiral:
4 × 9 × 7,5 m c.

Richard Serra

An artist such as Sunday Jack Akpan works both on and within tradition, a tradition that permitted making art concerning the vicoissitudes of live and death. As with Kane Kwei and his nephew Paa Joe, it is again in the extreme mourning that originates a simple and paradoxical art, one that is all the more convincing because of its unavoidable reality. But Akpan does not create strange coffins adapted to all tastes and all myths, from fish to Mercedes cars. He creates statues with the physical and symbolic attributes of the dead. He uses cement which, though not a very traditional material, arrived in Africa between the two world wars and was widely known. This material is simple, malleable, and costs little. Differently to wood, it is easy to handle and renders detail more precisely. And this is apparent in Akpan's work. He usually depicts Chiefs, though perhaps because only they can afford to commission him. He works from photos, which give the best idea of the appearance of the deceased person and then he sculpts more or less life-size, almost as though the figures were casts. He also became an artist as a result of a revelation that came to him in a dream, and because a god suggested it with the complicity of Hypnos.

In fact he is a Natural Authentic Sculptor, as is written on his visiting card, and we have to believe it. Like a renaissance artist his studio is full of models which his patron can choose from. Everyone can decide which image to use, just as he pleases. The sculptor too can do as

Sunday Jack Akpan 1940

Sunday Jack Akpan Sunday Jack Akpa

he pleases with respect to funerary images, sculpting figures that he enjoys most without feeling himself limited in any way. And if he runs out of cement—well, then he uses sand or an iron framework: he is a professional who mixes tradition with renewal, tribal with modernity.

Valerio Dehò

Chief
2001
Concrete, acrylic paints
and flatting

How can the exercise of photography inform the way one directs film and vice versa?

A simple and immobile mise en scène is in fact like photography. When it involves something more complex with a camera that moves, it is still photography, but in movement. The viewfinder functions like a simple camera. To look in order to find a framing is a permanent exercise, which, in the end, aids the directing of a film. I'll make a confession: I wish I was born with rectangular bars attached to my pupils so that I would have the habit of looking at everything through this sacred frame...

Your landscapes reveal very concerted compositions: five-sixths field + one-sixth sky, or a quarter landscape below + a quarter mountains + a quarter blue sky + a quarter clouds... Do you look for order and geometry in nature?

Geometry and the art of proportion has always

these images is up to the spectator. In the photographs in which the sky occupies five-sixths of the space, we can notice the emptiness of the sky, and trhe earth thereby becomes the center of existence. Spectators can have diverse interpretations.

Snow plays a more important role in your photographs than in your films. Is this a new interest in the whiteness of landscape?

I have always wanted to do a movie that takes place in winter. A winter film would be a nice gift for the spectator comfortably seated in a movie theater. I have always been nostalgic about snow. It is associated with my childhood. I have the impression that it used to snow more, to the point that we had to close down schools. Maybe that's why we were happy when it snowed, or perhaps snow itself simply makes people happy? Even children who weren't old enough to go to school were happy when it snowed. I think children are more sensitive to the presence of snow than adults. In any case, they are more enthusiastic.

the snow no longer resembles a car, but rather, a modern statue. It's like a Fontana painting. In winter, nature, normally in color, tranforms itself into a nature in black-and-white. Maybe that's why we imagined that the clothes of children had brighter colors in winter. I won't speak anymore about the whiteness and cleanness of snow. It's a vast topic.

Text by Michel Ciment excerpt from the catalogue *Abbas Kiarostami Photographies, Photographs, Fotografie...*, Hazan 1999.

Abbas Kiarostami 1940

existed in nature, even things that appear disproportional. One must simply discover it and understand its meaning or at least know how to interpret it. A proportion of 1:6 between earth and sky in a photographic composition is an aesthetic proportion and, in my opinion, it did not come about by chance.
The world itself is thus proportioned. In photographs, when we see sky, it is purely and simple about sky. The dark and light clouds are in the proportions of 5:1 or 4:2 with the sky. Yet, we can link the proportion fo the sky to the earth, to a secret or a meaning. The relationship and architecture of 5:1 sky to earth can pull our attention to a meaning that goes further. This a choice and the interpretation of

Winter starts with snow and Christmas is enriched by it. The other seasons arrive at slower tempo. Snow, on the other hand, can entirely change a landscape in one fell swoop. It is a *coup d'état* of whiteness leading toward cleanless and prosperity. Despite all this, I avoid shooting during winter. This beautiful creature, snow, is very fragile and it disappears with the first ray of sunlight, which makes things difficult when one has a long shooting session to complete. Landscapes lose their details when they are covered with snow and find a new beauty. It is a minimalist beauty.
The white volumes, thanks to the gray nuances, take on new forms that are no longer functional. A Volkswagen Beetle buried under

This selection of work for the Venice Biennale (2001) extends from 1996 (*Waferboards*) until 2000 (*Pyramids*). Included are several *New Mexico, New York* works from 1998. All these works use wood as a background for painting, although their precise installation invokes a sculptural space.

The *Waferboards* are made of Aspenite (chips of Aspen wood compressed in glue), are painted many colors, and are meant to be hung on a light grey wall. The *New Mexico, New York* works are made of two pieces of fir plywood, so that the upper half is double thickness. They are subtitled *Conjunction of Color*, for each is a study of how two colors meet. The adsorptive quality of the wood mimics the saturation capacity of the paint, and the graining migrates color into color, mimicking that conjunction. The *Pyramids*, also of fir plywood, extend this and stop it; they create a stopped "motion", which the eye can take in at once. The *Pyramids* consists of ten elements and can be arranged in any sequence as long as the pyramid configuration is maintained and the height of the topmost element remains constant.

Richard Tuttle

Ten, C
2000
Acrylic on fit ply wood,
10 panels,
each 25,4 × 25,4 cm,
overall 101,6 × 101,6 cm

Richard **Tuttle** **1941**

Walking and Editing

"Slow movement is essentially majestic" Honoré de Balzac wrote in his *Théorie de la démarche* in 1833. This could almost sum up the figurative principles of Yervant Gianikian and Angela Ricci Lucchi's films.

For the first time ever, these filmartists are exhibiting a confrontation between two types of movement. On the one hand, the succession of photograms along with the reproduction of a certain rythm of fulfilment of body trajectories. On the other hand, the walk of the "spectator stroller" whose wandering allows a visual discovery and creates a reading, an interpretation. Balzac also wrote: "Isn't there good reason to think about the as yet unknown conditions of our inner nature? Couldn't we ardently seek the very laws that govern both our intellectual and motor systems in order to discover the precise point at which the movement is beneficial and the point where and when it becomes fatal? " Indeed, one must think about this. 170 years later, a certain number of artists still experiment in order to try and understand these laws.

The World Fairs gave opportunities for certain encounters with exotic faraway worlds which is to a certain extent the topic of the artists' propositions. Etienne-Jules Marey filmed or rather, chronophotographed, from a distance, from a respectful distance and in profile since man's movement is ideally represented in profile. A frontal view is not suitable to represent pedestrian evolution. Thus perspective was taken over by the recording of movement at the end of the nineteenth century.

Merleau-Ponty attributed to Bishop Berkeley the following argument in an attempt to define perspective: "What is commonly called depth would only make sense for a spectator who would consider it from the side and as it were, in profile."

Distance, profile, and respect. In Marey's work, distant horizons remain an images in the background on the canvas.

Chronophotography is thus still painting.

2

But the walking spectator plunged into the century and the film maker did not hold his

3

Walking and watching can no longer be dissociated. There is even less and less distance, and less respect. In order to be shown, bodies now have to be naked, bought and prostituted. Just like a stroller who is irremediably drawn towards the consumption of bodies, acting as a substitute for their representation. This is without doubt the most obvious process of a colonizing century.

When the Gianikians propose a form of editing, they do not impose it in a rigid duration in accordance with filmic devices. They spread the editing work in a walkable space in which the spectator imposes his linking rhythm and his speed. An act of vision and an act of memory. A reminiscence of movement as physical action in that contemporary installation of virtual journeys. But the return is poetic: the spectator is that walking man again. Walking, watching and thinking.

Dominique Païni
Danièle Hibon

Yervant Gianikian 1942 - Angela Ricci Lucchi 1942

1

Very early on, the first recordings of time were made from physiological observation of human's walking. It is no doubt the main outline from which most mechanisms of rhythmical or continuous, repetitious linear movement were conceived in the nineteenth century. The walking man is most probably the main motif which Muybridge and Marey tirelessly used to represent time. And with the walking man now represented, time has become a malleable and therefore variable material, visually, as they say.

Gianikians' works remind us of that origin of representation which specifies the twentieth century.

place at a reasonable distance from his motif. The film maker then went in search of distant bodies not only visually but effectively: he started travelling. He no longer needed the World Fairs to offer him faraway countries within camerashot. He conquered and entered triumphantly the space of representation the way a hunter proudly places his foot on the mortal remains of the slaughtered animal. The film maker has become a hunter as well by intervening on bodies and their movements, by transforming these faraway anonymous humans into actors against their will. It is no more the recorded movement only which captivates the film maker, but the very bodies upon which he acts.

La marcia dell'uomo
2001
4 water painting
on paper

On the Creation of the World in the Image
For R.S.

Dealing with the world as the world *per se* is difficult. But what do people do when the World has made them especially sensitive? Are they to abandon all hope in this world, should they try to explain this world, should they let this world destroy them just to keep from attracting attention, or should they take their own first-person stand *vis-à-vis* this world?
Traveling helps, helps allow a person to put himself in the shoes of another and let go of the solid ground beneath his own feet; one gains the recognition of others. But is the Mannerist view of the inclined plane that distorts perspectives permitted, or are we to adopt the view of the pilot who, like Beuys, liberates from above, or as Gerhard Hoehme once put it, from the fallacy of perspective? Has the invention of the Eiffel Tower, the new precipitous rush, had the effect that artists are withdrawing from the seen reality into a felt world in which intuition and impressions are

It is trite to call to mind now, when I see Helmut Federle's painting in all its conclusiveness and consistency, that we ourselves are constantly questioning our lives, that the good of today will be the bad of tomorrow, that the views of then will be declared abnormal tomorrow, that what was abnormal yesterday will be legitimate tomorrow, that our society is in a process of constant progression, which the conservatives want to stop; the utopians, on the other hand, are unable to explain because the visions of society have gotten lost.
But it is precisely these visions for a society that inspire artists as well as painters. Today the artists are the last ones who being outside of sects, which are always bound by tradition, and freed from these pasts are able to formulate tomorrow. It is a tomorrow different from what society envisions and is at the same time necessary if society still wishes to envision anything at all.
Never has it been as important as now to listen to these subtle, tensely powerful, microstructural products of art; to watch and

Kunstmuseum Bonn, *Death of a Black Snake* (1999, 320 × 480 cm), permanent loan of the Mondstudio collection. These paintings destroy prejudgments as well as definitive judgments. They do not confirm prejudices, but instead provoke common ways of viewing. *El Omrane* is a quarter in Tunis. In 1967 Federle interrupted his studies to go abroad, not to Paris but to Tunisia, in order to become familiar with the foreign.
El Omrane reduces the speed of experience to a minimum. The painting is directed against the acceleration trap, against high speeds in the tunnel. It shows the triumph of the tortoise: the slow pace of the broadening view. It isn't directed against history in the sense of the destructive avant-garde and the economist Schumpeter's theory of creative destruction. Instead it refers directly to the responsibility of history, pointing out that rapid change is inhuman. It is inhuman in the sense of the capacity of mental comprehension, it is unreal in the sense of societal conduct, it is possible in the virtual picture, but not when it comes to

Helmut Federle 1944

more important than visual constatations?
Federle's paintings confirm questions many artists are concerned with. They set forth without the need for theorizing the reflections of philosophy. They don't construct using technology or new media; they invent in the matrix of their feelings and their collective experiences as artists' new image forms, image codes, which, like an ancient epics, like *Gilgamesh* or the *Edda*, stand looming gigantic before us. They emanate an extreme inner power of persuasion because they speak a graphic logic that rouses, calls for a fresh start, for a new way of thinking, for a different way of behaving. The World once again becomes an image: Genesis, the artist as the ancient *deus*.

feel them and to discuss them as a whole if the seismographic energies that allow our society to experience the demands of the future are to be preserved.
But society—Helmut Federle's paintings are eminently political—has chosen to lower its standards; it creates one crisis after another, is itself dependent on the tectonic activity of the Earth, loses and wins, destroys and annihilates; does so not as a natural phenomenon, but as a product of Nature as well as of the mind and the intellect. But society is against the creation of images.
Helmut Federle's answer to this is paintings such as *El Omrane* (2000, acrylic on canvas, 290 × 435 cm), or the parallel painting in the

the reality of the abstraction of a constant, perpetuating picture with no beginning or end. Helmut Federle is not a dialectic painter. He produces with immediacy and directness. But he is a painter of immense personal experience, of great knowledge gleaned from study, of high standards through technical examinations, of expert skill through his striving to better himself. The asceticism of the painting does not correspond to the asceticism of being, but to the knowledge of how one lives. Helmut Federle's world view of being. The picture effortlessly eludes the conditionings of both texts and history because it is dominated by a graphic autarky.

Dieter Ronte

El Omrane
2000
Acrylic on canvas,
290 × 435 cm

Massimo Vitali's photographs of the rites and rituals of modern leisure represent a dominant theme of modernity—the fantasy of escape from social and economic restrictions in the libidinal spaces of "nature" conceived as the site for spontaneous sociality: the spaces that map the affinities and contradictions of the nature/culture divide in ways which have done much to define our modern and post-modern sensibilities. These large-scale colour format prints in their descriptive clarity relate to the genre of "landscape with figures" but without investing the scene with the symbolic values usually associated with this Western pictorial tradition. In fact, the individuals and family groups populating the sea, the pool and the park represent the bricolage of "everyday life", that quotidian realm of the concrete and the specific interrupted by the arbitrary and occasional pleasures of segmented leisure time.

Vitali's images apply a topographical clarity and wealth of detail to these paradigmatic representations of the social imaginary, a heightening and flattening of visual plenitude that produces an image whose status hovers between the spatial metaphors of "closeness" and "distance." The photograph maintains an ambivalence between its evidentiary status—what Roland Barthes termed the "effect of the real"—and the distancing or estranging consequence of the viewer reading the visual text against the grain of normative representation, that is, for the contradictory signs that mark the alterity of the image, its resistance to the

an area of the land seen as if it were a picture, to the whole of nature as potentially scenographic and symbolically invested. With the rise of mass tourism, landscape became a spectacle, a social and cultural construction for the pursuit of certain forms of leisure, and as the "other" to the repetitive monotony of urban living. As an increasingly mobile population travelled beyond the town and the city to the country and the seaside, and then further afield to experience the "foreign" in the resorts of the Mediterranean, so the need for souvenirs of travel produced the holiday snap as the family album's memorialization of tourist experience.

And well before mass tourism and the development of leisure time, photography provided, for the working class family, the vicarious experience of travel in studio portraits posed against a painted backdrop of the natural world (an experience reproduced in its postmodern form in the exoticised bathing pool, replete with abundant vegetation and simulated wave effects). This touristic gaze is characterised by the distinctiveness of the visual—of the everyday resituated in a context that signifiies the strange, the "exotic", a time and place for imaginative play free from the regimentation of work and domesticity.

Formally, the photographic picture plane is divided into foreground, middleground and horizon, but these spatial zones are unequally distributed with a high horizon line and enlarged foreground. Partly this is a result of

and the narrative cross-referencing that repetitions of dress, pose and interaction suggest, makes them agents rather than objects of the gaze. Oscillating between panorama and detail, the images are simultaneously large-scale and intimate, landscape and portraiture. In these scenes, the distribution of figures and their legibility creates a spatial trajectory both into and across the field of vision which, rather than escape perspectival representation, tends to reveal its irrationality. The multiplicity of focal points, the wealth of visual interest produced from bodies suspended in water, or congregated on the beach or the grass, suggest spaces simultaneously dreamlike and naturalistic. Both the scale and the lucidity of these images produces an effect somewhere between stereography and cinematography: a concentration of the gaze and minute attention to detail as the eye imaginatively projects the body into the spatial and temporal realm of the image. This produces spaces best described as "liminal"—spaces of ambiguity and ambivalence. Liminal space falls between the social spheres of the public and the private—in anthropological terms, the spaces for ritual and rites of passage which depend upon the suspension of social codes and conventions for the exchange of meanings. Water has, for many cultures, carried ritualistic and symbolic connotations, the beach implies the possibility of transgressing normative behaviour patterns, and the picnic has its roots in the disruptive celebration of the carnival.

Massimo Vitali 1944

consuming look. Perhaps it is Vitali's experience of working in both the mediums of photography and film that produces this mixture of recognition and unfamiliarity that shift the image from documentary realism towards the surreal.

These images have their historical referent in late nineteenth century paintings of modern life (themselves heavily influenced by the compositional and aesthetic concerns of the mechanicaly reproduced image): the representation of new sites of leisure and consumption as an emergent social class explored the potential of city life and the pleasures to be had from nature. The historical meaning of landscape developed from the designation of

the positioning of the camera—mounted on an eighteen-foot tripod—which distances the lens/viewer, a scopic relation that could easily be voyeuristic, particularly given the content of some of the images (the proliferation of semi-naked bodies), but constantly founders on our fascination with the hallucinatory wealth of detail which acts to draw the viewer both optically and physically into the image. In addition, the equal concentration of points of interest and the detail and clarity of the visual field, brings both peripheral and central vision into play in the viewer's relation to the image. We are sufficiently removed from the immediate presence of the figures to read the picture as a totality, but their self-absorption

The actions and interactions spread laterally across the scene as the viewer makes narrative connections, imposing order and design out of the arbitrariness of the everyday, and this performative patterning becomes an endless and fascinating process of meaning production giving to the viewer an authority over the indiscrimate groupings, a kind of knowledge that is both intimate and disturbing for these people at play are singularly self-contained. A certain loss of self is the aim here. Apparently unaware of the camera's gaze, the figures do not signify the significant moments or arrested actions of documentary realism—the more we search the image for meaning, the more meaning slips away into surrealist absurdity.

What games and social exchanges are being enacted in the water, on the beach or at a picnic in the park?

Massimo Vitali's colour-prints trace the patterns of a certain kind of urban activity—the experience of sensual embodiment offered by the combinations of water, sun, sand and nature. In so doing they reveal the resistant strata within everyday life, the *uncanny* that Freud perceived in the unconscious encounters with something *déjà vu*, for there is also a familiarity to these images, a hedonistic quality that touches upon the collective experience, however temporary and hard-won, of bodily pleasure and an erotic of display.

Jon Bird

De Haan – Kiss – # 0756
2001
Color Print on plexiglass,
aluminium frame, edition
1/3, 370 × 150 × 2 cm

Riccione Diptych
1997
Color Print on plexiglass,
aluminium frame, edition
4/9, 150 × 180 × 2 cm

The disruption of logical-discursive communication has led poetry to overstep and break out beyond the frame of the page, towards a berthing in a form that signifies the visual representation of the spatial-temporal dimension, taken as the *locus* and moment of the poetic event.

The consequence is that poetry now founds a time of perception and contemplation of itself which is not dissimilar to that of painting, which was once unitary and relied on simultaneity and instantaneousness, a unitary dimension that no longer provides for a temporality that trickles down along the vertical dimension of verse but, if anything, contracts within the moment of horizontal dispersion within three-dimensional space.

Hence poetry has recaptured its own body with the medieval pleasure of composition, with a taste for simplicity and didactics that seems to belong to the contamination of the Gothic, to a bestiary that is able to hold within itself the image of elevated and lowly, abstract and concrete references which are nonetheless full of density and matter. Finally, poetry has rediscovered the energetic force of a new elementary grammar where each element has been rendered "physical" and made evident.

During its evolution, Sarenco's visual poetry has developed a progressive strategy that has finally managed to found its own plastic dimension, a sort of unwonted three-dimensionality. This is possible in that the construction of the poetic event *qua* physical occurrence implies a series of deferments that go from typographical

been filled by any sign or word by the written, painted or sculpted image.

Thus Sarenco's visual poetry assumes all the linguistic problems that belong to the formulation and formalisation of the image, with an autonomy deriving from its own tradition, which tradition in its turn belongs to it, straining towards abstraction, and a reference to the problems of the figurative representation of the word which dilate the possible expressiveness of poetry. The overstepping towards a total dimension of art produces a broadening of plastic representation, a breaking down of the sectorial and specific production of the image.

The effect is the total word, able not only to relate itself but also to force itself to be observed, become architecture and visual construction, sound and figurative echo of a poetic tension that uses the materials of many specific traditions in order to arrive at an image that can be perceived as will and representation of a culturally "other" universe—the African universe of Kenya.

Sarenco's work is inhabited in its producing itself as a total sign by a drive of domination and overstepping, by an attitude that we can find in all the most important currents in contemporary culture which are based on the need for values which are autonomous and internal to their own operating. In this, visual poetry goes beyond the evolutionary concerns of the neo-avant-gardes in that it places itself beyond the rigid technicist Darwinism that directed the transformations of art in the

ble, taken together, of giving a vital rush to poetic expression and a creative pragmatism that has challenged avant-garde fads against a skeletalised, purely cerebral proposition. Simultaneity, instantaneousness and totality are the characteristics of the new image that is presented as a concrete epiphany, a global apparition able to epitomise the interweaving of a vision of art that corresponds to an equally complex vision of the world.

The word goes beyond the limits of its proverbial abstraction, of that character which, bordering on indeterminacy, designates conventional poetry, invests a tactile dimension that plays between architecture and figurative dimension: visual poetry is "constructed literature": wood, painting, collage, canvas, an anthology taken from the African materials of Sarenco's texts from 1963 and from his creative sodality with Kenyan craftsmen and artists.

Poetry, playing on the semantic cross-referencing of the word, puts itself forward as designated literature in that the design for definition always harks back to a more corporeal linguistic event. Here visual poetry immediately constructs that which literature only promises via its postponement: a concrete image that is able to challenge the depth of real things. The total word, therefore, is the realisation of the construction of a poetic universe through the use of autonomous characters which are not specular but symmetrical in terms of internal functional laws that move according to principles that are no different to

Sarenco l'Africano 1945

experimentation to the introduction of codes, and even includes installations.

In this sense, the poetic word conquers the entire expressive space, occupying all the interstices that go from the code of intersocial communication to the ineffability of the subject's drives. The page becomes not only a support, but also the field of an event that plays not only with the *said* of the word but also with the *non-elect* of space which has not

post-World War II period. It has operated beyond all mechanical specificities, opting instead to move towards a linguistic confluence that invests Western culture in specific historical moments and that, in any case, finds its *raison d'être* in a definition of total art that always designates a strong *Sturm und Drang*.

The movement through the secular Futuristic and Dadaist charge has allowed Sarenco to rediscover a playful spirit and hedonism, capa-

those governing the dynamics of reality.

In Sarenco, finally, visual poetry as total word and total sign designates the need for art to reach for an expression of presence and no longer of a lent-like expression of absence, of constructive affirmation and not destructuring negation, within the dynamics of creation which is always in conflict with the world—and as such is politics.

Achille Bonito Oliva

Sarenco l'Africano,
installation detail
1990-2001
Painting drawings,
painting canvas, painting
and cut wood,
installation, variable size

The Flying Steamroller, 1996

The Flying Steamroller is a huge sculpture which consists of a twelve-ton steamroller that is attached to a pivoting arm with a counter balance weight. The steamroller is driven in a circle until its maximum speed is reached. At the same time, the counter weight is moved away from the central pivot point, causing the steamroller to lift off the ground. Because the combined weight of the steamroller and the counter balance, which is approximately 48 tons, the steamroller, once lifted off the ground, continues to spin, i.e. "fly", for several minutes. As the steamroller nears the end of its circular motion, or when the spinning momentum is exhausted, the counter balance is slowly moved back toward its central pivot point and the steamroller slowly "lands."

Chris Burden

Chris Burden 1946

The Flying Steamroller
1996
Steel, concrete, 1968
Huber road grader

Chernobyl. The dream of a peaceful use for atomic energy was rudely shattered. As early as the 1950s, after the repercussions of Hiroshima and Nagasaki, scientists have tried to dominate atomic energy. Along with politicians, they fooled themselves into believing they could build cathedrals in the desert by using this apparently inexhaustible and multipurpose source of energy. Their aim was to reach even the remotest corners of the world and finally free man from the constraints imposed by ever-diminishing oil and coal resources. Despite differing ideologies, neither East nor West was able to maintain the promise of widespread wellbeing for all.

On April 26, 1986, because of a technical error one of the four nuclear reactors exploded in Chernobyl, in the north-west of the Ukraine. Strong winds carried toxic clouds into the heart of Europe. The then Soviet power, headed by Gorbachev, tried on the old tactic of silence, minimisation and denial. In the meantime they sent 800,000 "liquidators" to the site—800,000 firemen and soldiers without adequate protection who were being sent to

and distressed. They took everything they could with them as they left for destinies unknown. They left behind them empty cities, deserted villages and a nuclear wreck locked up in a cement sarcophagus. Only a few hundred mainly elderly people have returned. For them, nuclear radiation is a lesser evil than life in an anonymous block of flats.

The photos are not sensationalist; they do not exploit the national tragedy or the suffering of the individual. Maruščenko, refusing to use any special technical effect, profoundly shares in the direct gaze of the people he photographs. It is thus possible for us to understand, without any overly-dramatic effect, what these impotent people cannot grasp—that after the disaster, nothing is as it was before. The past is lost, and, for many, the future has been destroyed by the poisonous effects of radiation. The present itself is immersed in a silent mourning that not even home-distilled vodka can mitigate.

"You can photograph in many different ways: by shouting or whispering, by using the force of a short sharp shock or by swearing; but

Viktor Maruščenko 1946

or Maruščenko Viktor Maruščenko

an almost certain death due to radiation poisoning. Only seven days later did the Kremlin admit that there had been "what is probably the greatest incident" and had the entire area evacuated. 400,000 people had to abandon their homeland, which had become radioactive forever. A stretch of land within 30 kilometres of the site was declared off-limits.

The Ukrainian photographer Maruščenko has spent the 15 years since the "incident" chronicling a tragedy that has destroyed the reality of the inhabitants of this contaminated area.

A few days after the incident, on May 8, 1986, Maruščenko left for Chernobyl. He thus began to take a series of photos that describe the destiny and mood of the locals, who feel lost

daily human dialogue is made up of simple sentences, delivered in a calm, controlled voice. This is how people talk when they talk about something important." And this is the premise Maruščenko uses to create a document of our times that goes beyond artistic quality, testifying to one of the greatest industrial catastrophes of our time.

Millions of people are still living on land that has been contaminated by radiation. Just how many are sick or have died we do not know. There is only one thing we do know for sure: even after the Chernobyl nuclear plant was closed down, on December 16, 2000, not all the victims of the super-GAU were born yet.

Astrid Kohl

ЗАПРЕТНАЯ
ЗОНА

Чорнобильська зона, 1991р.

Bewachung der Zone
1991
The spot light on the
lower part of the photo
is result of radiation on
the film material,
25 × 36 cm

Values change– symbols hang on

I say: "The bread is yellow." And he says: "The bread is to eat." I ask: "Why? What is the difference between bread, fixed around the head of a man or served on a plate?"

This was reported by Tatsumi Orimoto as part of a conversation between him and a member of the audience at his performance, in which he appeared as his alter ego *Bread-Man.*

His head wrapped into loafs of bread and French baguette, Orimoto has been seen worldwide appearing in public places like streets, squares, museums, trains, train stations, restaurants and cafes. Seeking contact with all kinds of people in their professional or daily routine, he faces diverse reactions like amusement, doubt, surprise, rejection, aggression and joy.

The variety of reactions show, that it is always a question of beliefs and cultural background or attitude and taste, which make people from various parts of the world enjoy or feel disgusted by *Bread-Man.*[1] The conflict between the decision either to feed their stomach or their brain spontaneously structures their aesthetic judgement on bread and their attitude towards *Bread-Man.*

Solidity and expansion

On the photograph *Heavy Clothes on my Mother's Head*, taken in 1998 at Midorioka Reien Cemetery in Kawasaki, Orimoto can be seen holding a bunch of clothes over his little

ication. Orimoto´s activities and events, which he calls *Communication-Art,* are partially able to bridge this handicap. The photographs, which have been taken in Orimoto´s house or in the neighbourhood at Kawasaki city, which they pass through frequently, show the sometimes absurd-looking situation from an artistic point of view, thus giving their everyday life a twist of performance and playfulness.

There are two facts which attract our attention. First one notices that Orimoto fixed material on or over his head and one can see that he held objects over his mother's head. The second feature is the use of foamlike material, which characteristically expands a minimum of substance over a maximum of space. Being originally solid substances like dough, Styrol, or fabric, expanding fast and effectively when they come into contact with air which is generated inside, foams have become the metaphor for the "bubble econony". It addresses the explosive growth of the Japanese industry in the '80s and '90s, the era in which Orimoto created *Bread-Man* and his *Art-Mama* series.

Bubbled matter is a "body without organs" (Deleuze/Guattari) which has a skin or a crust enclosing an amorphic interior. It may explode, implode; it can be soaked, and contain fluids or air from the environment. Also, each bubble can be regarded as an organ, which is unspecific, simple and only effective to take in but has no capacity to transform or transport the matter inside. It is passive like bread, which

Tatsumi Orimoto 1946

mother's head. Both are standing in front of her husband's and his father's grave, where they went to trim the bushes and bring new flowers. The worn clothes above her head recall memories of the past.

When in the same year Orimoto places blocks of Styrofoam above his mother's head, echoing the previous gesture in front of the carport of the local fire brigade, the son's gesture might seem enigmatic if one were not to interpret the Styrofoam as the visualisation of a brain affected by Alzheimer's. In fact the artist's decision, to take care of his old mother has changed his whole life, as he has to look for ways to communicate with her, since she is almost deaf because of antidrepressive med-

can soak up gravy but does not digest it. Soaked it is only good if it is eaten fresh; but it is spoiled when it is stored. This is a fact, which life, art and bread have in common. To keep it enjoyable, constant repetition and production are required.

Johannes Lothar Schröder

[1] For reference of the religious, cultural, and sculptural implications of dough and bread see the essay "Out of the shoes of inheritance" of the author, in the monographic catalogue of Tatsumi Orimoto at the Centre for Contemporary Graphic Arts and Tyler Graphics Archive Collection (CCGA) at Sukagawa-shi, Fukushima, Japan 2001

Tire tube
communication
1996
Color print, 300 × 250 cm

Bring a glass of mead! Raise your cups! Collect the glasses! Enjoy the abundance of their forms! Admire their transparency! Note their engraving! Praise the glass blower! Pump the bellows! Compare the cut! Be amazed at the abundance of their forms! Succumb to their *enchantement!* And then take a closer look at what Gerd Rohling has magically produced in the city of glass!

It was more than exultation when the artist dedicated his work to the canister in 1987 and painted it with bitumen and acetone varnish, decorated it as a line of ancestors, treated it with irony, even though they are all industrially made goods. Rubbish, the chemical component in PVC that does not decompose in the consumer society's throw-away goods as well as a deep fascination with rubbish, led Gerd Rohling to refine things he found on the beach and create precious imitation glasses. The spiral of progress generated the spiral of rubbish. The artist intervenes in this process of produc-

Gerd Rohling 1946

tion and consumption, as a figure returning what has been rejected as a unique object, in the field of what is precious. Recycling as an obsession, creation of beauty from the piles and chaos of things and fragments that have been relinquished, the ancient world, Alexandria, Hellenism, Renaissance, Baroque, Rococo, founders of the northern and southern design of the cup of hemlock, of the tankard, the vase, the Triton's horn become the simultaneous evocation of archaeology, collecting mania, interference with procedures, intervention on the beautiful semblance of what is not congruent. The mass of glasses is waiting for the amazement of cultural history.

Harald Szeemann

Wasser und Wein
1984–2001
Sculpture PVC, 30 cm

Wasser und Wein
1984–2001
Sculptures PVC,
different sizes

Two points are habitually made regarding Jeff Wall's large-scale cibachrome transparencies, backlit and ensconced in aluminium display cases. Firstly, observers note that they are carefully staged, so that every grimace, gesture or prop is significant; secondly, that Wall's principal references are to French painting of the nineteenth century, hinging on the end of the Academy and the birth of Modernism. There is, of course, something paradoxical about this: Manet (for example), to whom Wall's iconography frequently refers, is characteristically considered to have finally put to rest the tradition of eloquence in painting and to have ushered in a radical muteness, resistant to the rhetorical codes of the past. Wall assumes the paradox openly. Indeed, it defines his specific position as an artist emerging after the age of Modernism—which is not to say Postmodernist, in any immediately recognisable way.

Wall's more recent works continue, in the main, to show street scenes and interiors in which some trivial and/or violent drama of

way of interpreting the refusal of eloquence in the visual arts after Manet). Rather, the lack of expression in Wall's figures empties his scenes of any suggestion of even repressed resentment; these people have the impassivity of characters seized by an unspoken event.

Even in the abstract, time and events are cruel. If there are events, this is only because there is time; and awareness of time is awareness of mortality. Gilles Deleuze suggests that it is difficult to respond to the pure event which takes hold of us, that is, to accept the role of actor in an event as it befalls (i.e., literally falls on us). Look, however, at the faces of Wall's insomniac, of the man witnessing a fight on the sidewalk—even of the figures in the gigantic, gory tableaux of dead soldiers or vampires at a picnic. Perhaps it is because Wall does indeed use actors in his work, but these faces do not question what is happening, do not protest at what has overtaken them. In this sense, even if they are caught up in an argument or overtaken by some conflict, they are not quarrelsome.

there, in the shadows. Any attempt at narrative reconstruction of a before and an after is therefore not pertinent: the impassivity and the smile are both modes of acceptance of the event. The blood is evidence of the cruelty with which it hits one; the smile and the absence, of a visible psychological (i.e., reactive) imprint, of the openness to occurrence which Wall's work characteristically communicates. Working against the grain of photographic instantaneity, Jeff Wall avoids the pitfall of pathos which haunts the photograph as index. Paradoxically, his carefully constructed scenes register the openness of the instant more radically than many spontaneous snapshots.

In certain of Wall's recent works, the characters stand with equal impassivity in relation to objects which—blankly, mysteriously, lightly...—incarnate the event. Thus, Kafka's *Odradek*, the spilled Jello, the hat and papers carried on the wind, a pile of rope, etc., are figures of non-determination: that is, of the non-reducible complexity of entanglement or scat-

Jeff Wall 1946

Wall Jeff Wall Jeff Wall Jeff Wall Jeff Wall

everyday life is eloquently frozen: a street brawl, papers and a hat being whisked away by a gust of wind, a spilt bowl of Jello, an insomniac stretched out on the kitchen floor, a man with a bloodied face and coat, etc. Doubtless all these scenes speak of domestic or social dramas which add up to a gloomy picture of the miseries of modern life. However, what has stood out since the very beginning in Wall's work is the consistent lack of expression in so many of his human figures. This distinguishes his production from the carefully coded dumb show of academic painting. However, it does not appear appropriate to take such muteness as a symptom of anomie (which remains one

Wall's figures allow themselves to be seized by the event, however difficult to articulate, or even imagine, this may be. If Stoicism (as Deleuze again suggests) constitutes a poetics of life, then Wall's bloodied Man in the Street exemplifies such an attitude. At first sight, something seems to have happened between the left-hand panel, on which he is seen seated smiling on a bench, and the right hand panel where, sober-faced, he walks down the street. However, one realises on closer inspection that whatever violence may have struck him occurred before he sat down, since the bloodstains on his face and coat are already

tering which is the event. The same is true of the works which only feature objects, such as an entangled octopus or scattered beans. Although there are no human figures here to register the entwining or the dissemination, thin pieces of wood have been inserted under the legs of the two tables featured in each of these works, in order to ensure a stable surface. This detail confirms that they are not so much still lives as poised moments, avoiding the pathos of the *momento mori* associated with early still lives. Once again, his work stands beyond the melancholy with which it has so often been assimilated.

Yves Abriouxî

S.O.S. World

The slowness and wisdom of millenary chelonians from prehistory pit themselves against the vacuity and indolence of man.

Cracking Art Group

Omar Ronda, founder of the group, was born on 1947. With Renzo Nucara, Marco Veronese, Alex Angi, Carlo Rizzetti, Kikko and Alessandro Pianca found Cracking Art Group on 1997 in Biella.

Turtles in Venice
S.O.S. World
2001
Recicled and gold
painting turtles

The Omega Suites

Lucinda Devlin's images are meant to upset the viewer. At first sight we are struck by their formal beauty, their austere composition and color. The artist photographically frames rooms that are defined first of all by their architecture and color. They are so clean, neat, nearly aseptic they look like operating rooms in a hospital. Lit by artificial lighting that erases nearly every shadow, these rooms, with their pale colors, practically seem transparent. By concentration and reduction the artist focuses vision on the center of the picture, where most of the time the only visible furniture is placed: wooden electric chairs or cots with leather straps and buckles form a counterpoint to the luminousness of the spaces, giving the photographs a martial air. Lucinda Devlin's theme is the "Death Row" of American jails, a suite of thirty works created in the '90s.

The dread felt by anyone looking at this work springs from the violation of a taboo. The formal elements making up the composition of the image clash with the content of the theme represented. And that is not all. Since Devlin does not refer to traditional photographic reporting and so does not appeal to our sensibility and outrage at the sight of the condemned person's pain, grief and death, she leaves us by ourselves with our power of imagination by just showing us the spaces, the row of rooms that will be the sentenced

death sentence, but instead analyzes the space surrounding it at the moment it takes place, she forces whoever looks at it to expand his or her own personal opinion to a more general reflection. Through the principle of the suite, that is, the repetition of the typologies of rooms, the artist wishes to present an architectural and formal type of "death row" that multiplies like a prototype beyond local or temporal prerogatives.

For the State dead, a corresponding space exists, localized in the very architecture of the jail.

In Devlin's work we can observe its American documentary-photographic origin whose roots lie in Walker Evans' works, and elements of German conceptual art of the '70s. The principle of serial works, with representations very like one another, particularly connects her works with the industrial typologies of the couple of artists Bernd and Hilla Becher, but her vision that segments, without concealing any details, also recalls historical German photography (see August Sanders' portraits at the time of the Weimar Republic). In her work Devlin's theme is not just the place of the death sentence in society, but she also critically demands that the spectator take a stand. Not only is he there in the empty chairs and armchairs in the witnesses' room, but his voyeurism is heightened by the photographs. Hardly any of the photos are without a frame, "the picture in the picture" (so deeply rooted in traditional art history), figured by curtains and windows cutting the plane of the image.

Lucinda Devlin 1947

person's last passage.

We look at the death cell, we go through the room where the execution will take place, we cross the postmortem room and at the end will take a look at the room for the witnesses, that is, the family and friends, either of the victim or of the sentenced person, wishing to attend the execution.

Devlin's works show the background; it is up to our imagination to reconstruct what actually happens. The images go beyond their documentary content while refusing to be mere photographic reproduction. Since Devlin does not openly take a stand for or against the

Here, too, the artist violates a taboo, since she shows something ordinary people are not allowed to see. Public performance of the execution, shown us in historical, documentary films and that we always watch with a certain horror, is displayed here in a subtle manner leaving the spectator to a naked voyeurism.

A style so accurate is useful to the work's unfolding, but the artist puts herself in the role of a simple documentary-maker, avoiding presenting herself aggressively. So the observer, who is not given a precise interpretative key, is cast back upon himself.

Inka Graeve

Electric chair,
Greensville correctional
facility, Jarrat, Virginia
1999
Chromogenic print
48,5 × 48,5 cm

Camel heads on sixty-metre-long poles.
Not Vital's surrealistic monument swimming in water

Ebb and flow, mountain and valley, north and south, life and death—these are the cultural and climatic extremes that Not Vital unites in a short circuit. His *World Animal, Wheel Animal* and *Pole Animal* marked the beginning in 1982. These continental, symbolic sculptures could be seen in the New Yorker East Village Galleries. A dinosaur figure carried a mountain path made of nails and wire on its back; a small animal torso was on each wheel and on a high pole. Over a period of almost twenty years there have been sculptures with horns, eyes, ears and noses. Sometimes sensory organs hung down like bronze fruits from branches made of plaster or they were to be found in marble caverns. Again and again, not only in the seventy camel heads in the Venice Biennial, Vital's work fastens life to high poles. They remind one of the stakes and signposts in the mountains. Now a very such work is standing in the sea.

Moments freeze that we could call blue hours. The fragility and vulnerability of the body is put on show, just like after a hunt. Moments of slaughter and the pictures of sudden death vanish however, and instead of grief and even terror, a comic effect and the beginnings of a Dionysian celebration become clear. The organs and animals, signs for feelings and pain, become laughing monuments in Vital's

Alps in Sent. His camel heads have coupled ideas of heat and endless desert sand with snow and hints of winter sports in not only in galleries, but also in the open air. Now the camels find themselves in water as an elevated caravan of aluminium heads—on poles in a row in front of a wall. Every six hours when it is high tide, they drown before our very eyes; afterwards they tower up for the same length of time as shining figures that gradually become Totems encrusted with salt.

We see them as surrealistic allegories of the tides and as Nietzsche's shepherds of Being. Perhaps one day geologists will find the caravan with the heads deep down at the bottom of the lagoon with us humans. They'll laugh out loud.

Thomas Kellein

Not Vital 1948

work and from their stake-like form, humour comes gushing out like champagne.

In 1990 he created a *Golden Calf* with his first large remuneration and personally hammered the gold foil and twisted it with all his might. As a child he had been told that the people from Sent, his birthplace, were donkeys. In his own sculpture park that he has been designing for several years in Unterengadin, he recently built a long two-piece bridge with donkeys' heads on rails. Only the more courageous cross it because it goes over a six-meter-deep glen. The first bronze camel head motive on poles was created in eight pieces in 1990 and in 1995 Vital created plaster camels which he placed on eight-meter high poles below the

70 camel's head
2001
Sculpture, 60 m long

The Table: Childhood, 1984-2001

In *The Table: Childhood*, 1984-2001, a fully autonomous robotic table selects a viewer to attempt a relationship with that person. The table will not interact with everyone who comes into the room; it will choose only one viewer. As long as that visitor stays, he or she will be the object of the table's attention.

For dAPERTutto of 1999, I exhibited a robotic work, "As Yet Untitled", 1992-95. This interactive work sets up a situation in which visitors can intervene to stop the shredding of found family photographs. There is no "save" button and no "shred" button. The robotic arm shreds photos relentlessly unless a viewer stops the process. The viewer could simply watch, or walk away, allowing the photographs to be destroyed. The robot's cycle of picking up, presenting and shredding photographs puts the viewer in a position of choice in the fate of family photos. Even doing nothing is a decision. Whatever one does is a public act. For the current exhibition, I am showing a work that reverses this process of choice.

The Table switches the roles of viewer and object. The artwork and not the viewer is in the position of choice. My work has often addressed the museum—the choices of what is included, what is rejected and who chooses. In *As Yet Untitled*, a selection process is inherent. One cannot save everything and choices must be made about what is looked at, what is ignored, what is kept and what is discarded. The viewer chooses whether or not to participate. In *The Table* I am empowering the object and giving it the responsibility for making selections of viewers. This focuses the attention of other viewers on one particular visitor, making that person the "object" of attention. My earlier work, *The Telephone Piece*, (1982, rebuilt in 2000) also places attention on the viewer. *The Telephone Piece*, a pavilion encircled by lines of audio tape, invites viewers to contact friends outside the museum. What is important is the relationship between participants. Like *The Table*, the artwork falls away as an object, becoming transparent. Once viewers enter *The Telephone Piece* and choose to phone friends outside the museum, the dynamics of the conversations of people describing where they are and what they're doing supersedes the sculptural context.

The Table continues my interest in highlighting the behaviour of viewers. They soon become absorbed in their interaction with the table, anticipating what it might do and how to respond to its advances. Why has or hasn't it moved? Why is one person picked and not another? If a selected viewer wishes, a conversation with this table is possible. While the table discovers the body language of the visitor, that person, in turn, can learn to interpret the table's behaviour and have an engaging relationship with this machine, while others watch. *The Table: Childhood* is an early issue of a developing robot that will soon acquire increasingly complex capabilities. Regardless of its youth, it is fully autonomous and unpredictable, operating on its own, reacting to its environment, and to the behaviour of visitors who enter its space, responding with gestures of courtship. It will soon mature into adolescence, and with more experiences, to adulthood. The table is not only mobile, with an extensive catalogue of complex behaviours, but even at this early stage, its character is beginning to evolve, shaped by my collaborator, Raffaello D'Andrea, a pioneer in the development of modern control systems. Raff has created the code for the table's behaviours, and continues to develop its repertoire of abilities, enabling it to not only track objects of its affection and respond in various ways to the viewer's movements, but also to accomplish this with masterful co-ordination, making its movements fluid and graceful, as if alive.

The table has a vocabulary based loosely on the subtleties of how people meet. First it tries to catch the eye of the person it selected by drawing attention to itself, as if to say, "Excuse me? Hello? I'd like to meet you!" suggested by a wiggle, or slight motion from side to side. It attempts to show the selected viewer that he or she has been chosen. What follows is a salutation. Each viewer is treated differently; there is a library of salutations, as varied and sophisticated as human introductions. Depending on the selected viewer's motions, speed of movements, responses to the table's behaviour, and general conditions in the room, the table might try to get closer.

Throughout the encounter, the table monitors the chosen visitor's physical reactions. If that person is unresponsive, *The Table* tries harder: it might initiate an action enticing the viewer to copy it; it might dance by itself, turning on its axis with an elegant pirouette; it might decide to chase—or even to flee. Once some kind of relationship is established, depending on the actions of the viewer, the table determines how to handle the situation, whether lyrically or aggressively. If there is a crowd in the room, preventing it from interacting with any one single person, it may wander around as if at a cocktail party, searching for someone with whom to relate. Like people meeting for the first time, sometimes the table will connect and sometimes not. But once the table picks someone, it is loyal, making every attempt to stay with that person. Indeed, if there are people between the table and its choice, the table will try to circumvent them to get to its chosen viewer. While the table has a range of performances, it is the selected person's reactions to the courtship that is the focus of the audience. Leaving *As Yet Untitled*, was troubling for some viewers, because it led to the loss of family photos. Similarly, the departure of the chosen visitor may leave the table struggling to follow. But it can't. The sculpture is trapped in the museum, with a doorway too narrow for exit. One question which might occur to viewers is, "Does the table move when there is no one in the room?" (It does.)

Max Dean

Max Dean **1949** - Raffaello D'Andrea **1967**

The Table: Generation A
1984–2001
Interactive installation

For Cristina Garcia Rodero, the photo-documentary has long been, and still is, a privileged way of communicating with life, of looking at it head on and being completely caught up in it. For over thirty years she has trekked across the globe, her camera slung over her shoulder, capturing scenes of human events, of the dramas, wretchedness and beauty dwelling in the most recondite. Despite the solitude and harshness of her work, she still holds that, for her, the most important thing is to feel free, to seek out what interests her and to not feel dominated.

This existential, creative independence has rendered her work extraordinarily powerful. An essential example is provided by the images of popular festivals and religious ceremonies she shot over a fifteen-year period and brought together under the global title of Hidden Spain. They reveal features of a recondite Spain where, even in the 20th century, ancestral rituals coexist with the needs of day-to-day survival, and where the wealth of the symbolic merges with the precariousness of things material the force of magic and the harshness of the real. Cristina Garcia Rodero is currently immersed in a new body of work entitled *Between Heaven and Earth*. This designation takes in a series of reportages on several countries, from Georgia to Haiti, from Ethiopia to the United States and from Cuba to India. In all of them she talks of the body and spirit, of the religious and pagan, of war and peace, of life and death; in other words of all the coexisting opposites.

and shadow) blend to communicate the full semantic gravity and aesthetic potential of an instant. For their intensity and beauty, these pictures are anthropological tesimonials that transcend the mere transposition of visual information, shattering the boundaries between documentation and Art.

While taking photographs, there is a moment when Cristina Garcia Rodero becomes invisible, her camera ceases to intimidate her subjects and she melts into the setting, as if she were yet another of the ceremonies she portrays. At other times she sets up an emotional empathy through which her subjects unabashedly exhibit the best of themselves in front of the camera, or again take up their places, unconcerned about the gaze of eyes that are no longer alien to them. These images are not the fruit of stage-settings arranged in the safety of the studio. They well up from the very flux of life, from direct interaction with it. They are the outcome of respect and love. They are also the harvest of a long relationship with the history of painting and of knowledge of the laws of figurative representation. Thus, they provide the spectator with double pleasure: that of traversing time and space to view life's contradictions, and that of delighting in the wisdom of a generous, emotive and deeply human vision; a vision which is also a mirror for each of us to reassess our rightful place between heaven and earth.

Rosa Martinez

Cristina Garcia Rodero 1949

The series made in Haiti reveals the power of religion as a refuge for anguish and as a source of meaning for an oppressed, forsaken people. There, the Catholic religion imposed by settlers has been amalgamated
with the African cults brought by slaves, generating, through a complex process of acculturation and trans-culturation, a fascinating syncretism and the fearfulness of voodoo. As in the rest of her work, black-and-white is used to accentuate contrasts and distil messages to an essence, with images cast in the rich tradition of photojournalism.

The choice of subject and the intelligent articulation of different elements of photographic code (framing, composition, interplay of light

Haiti, Rites vaudous
2000

Fear Not - Non Temere

What is courage? Susan Kleinberg has posed this question to dozens of people from the arts, politics, science and the street. The responses, elicited in conversation with the artist, are each singular and unexpected. From the most famous American General discussing episodes of chance and extreme peril, to an astronaut's measured thoughts on risk, to the most important man in Italian politics saying that ultimately courage is perhaps an act of love.

The voices are heard through headphones hanging from the wall in an organic tangle—along one wall in English and the other in Italian. Flat screens embedded in the walls identify each person as they speak by name and image. The images, in most cases photographs taken by the artist after the interview, provide not only visual reference and augmentation, but a landscape of context. Overhead, a weaving DNA-like canopy of light filament connects us to the rope-making history of the Corderie as well as to the weave of texture and substance in the progression of the interviews.

The interviews run in seriously considered sequence on a continuous loop. Each exists individually, but grows or is challenged by the next. The result is operatic, a collective epic, a document of our times.

The question, "What is Courage?", functions as a key to a further realm of interaction between the interviewee and Ms Kleinberg. What we

Fear Not

Chuck Close, artist
General Norman Schwarzkopf
Gore Vidal, author
John Lewis, congressman
Sally Ride, astronaut and astrophysicist
Mike Meyer, journalist
Four Firemen, speaking anonymously
Santa Isaacs, domestic worker
John Podesta, Clinton Chief of Staff
Spalding Gray, actor
Sidney Lumet, director
George McGovern, Ambassador
Simon Verity, artist
Dr. Holly Anderson, cardiologist

Non Temere

Susanna Agnelli
Herve Scule, Albanian student
Silvio Berlusconi
Luigi Sfriso, fishmonger
G. Marzi, G. Salvadori,
U. Bressanello, P. Beniamin, gondoliers
Omar Buracco, greengrocer
Othello Ghigi, electrician
Attilio Codognato, jeweller, collector
Leon de Santillana, student
Rabbin Abraham Pietelli, Roma
Graziella Buontempo
Adriana Buontempo
Elisa Floride
Luciano Zanon, florist
Papa Giovanni Paolo II (addr)
Sergio Bottiston, greengrocer

Susan Kleinberg 1949

hear is the result of an assault, a gentle assault, but an assault nonetheless on social convention, restriction, exposure.

It is a piece about perception—not only how we perceive, but that we perceive. The technology involved exists only to serve this purpose. It is material, as in Ms Kleinberg's paintings, forming a work stripped of irony or obfuscation, a straight shot at a core investigation.

Each interview is an essential portrait. We come to know the interviewees, locate ourselves in relation to them. Through each conversation, thought after thought, in her choices, Ms. Kleinberg reveals herself. Ultimately we come to a portrait of the artist.

Angela Vettese

General N. Schwarzkopf

Fear Not, Non Temere
General Norman
Schwarzkopf
2001
Mixed media
installation,
still from video

"For a long time, I could not deal with *Jeanne Dielman*. It's the kind of film you do at the end of your life and I made it when I was twenty-four."

"It is a film about space and time... and about how you organize your life in order to have no free time at all so that you don't let anxiety and the feeling of death come in to submerge you." Chantal Akerman, quotes from *Bordering on Fiction: D'Est*, published by the Walker Art Center, 1995.

Woman Sitting After Killing is a mosaic of fragments taken from the last shot of Chantal Akerman's *Jeanne Dielman, 23 quai du Commerce, 1080 Bruxelles* (1975). The original film defies categories. Even its title, which includes the address of the heroine, is a way of anchoring the fiction within the real. It is, like all of Akerman's films, somewhere between fiction and documentary, between capturing life and creating it. It is about the impossibility of boundaries.

Jeanne is a prostitute. In the course of the film's 200 minutes, we watch her going through the day's ordinary, banal activities: having meals with her son, doing the dishes, taking a bath, etc. Each activity seems to take the amount of time on screen as it does in "real life". That, of course, is due to the director's manipulation of "space and time", of erasing the seams between what we are witnessing and what we are experiencing.

At the end of the film, a client comes to see Jeanne. They have sex. She lies on the bed, as if she is asleep, as if she is dead. And then she kills him. The last sequence of the film finds her sit-

Chantal Akerman 1950

ting, breathing, in and out. The narrative is reduced to its most basic expression.

Woman Sitting After Killing makes this activity its subject. As Jeanne inhales, she takes in air, takes in courage for the act she has just committed. She is affirming life, in her own, inexorable way. When she exhales, she releases herself, expels the killing, hopes to integrate it into the fabric of the day that she has just experienced. Breathing, and the fragmentation of breathing, like the waves of the sea crashing on the shore and pulling back, represents the restoration of balance. A fragile balance, but a balance, nevertheless. Anxiety and death have made an appearance in Jeanne's life. She is trying to find a way not to be submerged by them.

Michael Tarantino

Women sitting
after killing
2001
Beta sp + 7 monitors +
sound & magnetoscope
player MPEG,
stills from film

Chantal Akerman

89

I am supersonic and alien. I have the feeling of being a fuselage. Am I walking? Dreaming? Sitting in a chair? Killing? Eating? Could it not be any of these—any and all simultaneously? Where am I? I can't remember at will. It can only be described as holy for fear of something completely other. Parts come back not quite like what was before but the connection is certain. A few switches flipped—that's it. The wherewithal generator is next to close by— happening right before my hands. I'm synthe- sized. Thought—that tree that won't let go brings to mind the terrifying possibility—its only words that separate things. I feel aban- doned by the real, leaving what's left. I'm going. I'm watching myself go. Everything's changing speed—backing into itself. The effect mesmerizes. Movement eludes me. I'm para- lyzed. Waiting awaits what's left. It's doing exactly what it says. No question. No ques- tions. Circumstance is at a standstill. Things have exited. If I go everything will have already followed. I know it. It knows it. There is nothing to leave—nothing. Difference exists only through sound; a wall of sound. Can I go through it? Can I go through with it? Where is *it* now, Where does *it* reside? What does it feed on? Why does it flicker? Nothing approximates its speed. It's something from the outside. Way outside. I didn't think this. This is not me. I'm not accountable. It wasn't thought out. It has no relation to thought. This is that hole that everything must pass through. I'm going now before it comes. Will I know when it comes?

Gary Hill 1951

Will it approach with signals? Will there be a moment of recognition? Is that when I am it? Am I simply tapping myself on the shoulder? What *is* the point? It's always there; on again; on again. It waits without pathos. Waiting is human. This point wants to show me some- thing inhuman. It wants to bring me to my knees. It wants me to pray, it wants me to see through seeing, it wants me to act like knowl- edge. It wants acknowledgment. It wants me completely at the edge. It burrows itself in, blows up and begins again. Plural. Points. Cells.

Gary Hill

Excerpt of spoken text from *Wall Piece*, 2000.

Wall Piece
2000
Single channel
video/sound installation,
stills from video

Bill Viola's art consists in showing us bison as mountains or shifting dunes, the eyes of exotic birds as the "origin of life" (Courbet), somewhere between *nature morte* and *tableau vivant*. The snail-shell in a little boat, hung with jewelry, looks like a Dutch still life; some time later the snail creeps out of its shell, leaving the boat and the field of vision. Yet what is dead? What is alive? *Nature morte/nature vivante?*

Insects eat their way into an animal carcass reduced to no more than a head. Before our eyes, people in a trance state let their cheeks, lips, arms, and backs be pierced by small metal rods; in order to overcome death they walk across a red-hot carpet of ash. A chick breaks out of its eggshell in order to escape death and, lying on its back, kicks itself into life. Late at night an elephant's truck seizes the artist's inspiring teacup and enters his studio, as in a dream—menacing, real, soothing. The camera

and birds fall upon it. Before long it merges with the forest floor. The videotape begins with drops of water. The water has been dripping for millions of years, forming stalactite caves. Forms appear as in an opened body—bloody, veined, slippery. Creeping insects feed on the precious liquid.

Bill Viola does not simulate anything. Through the telephoto lens the images begin to dissolve, to fluctuate, to break up into a sea of colors, then become suddenly precise; they plunge into the water and are reflected in the water, in the eyes of the animals; they become painting, art history, a document, pitiless reality, dream and reality.

What is shown is never an end itself: it is as though history, determined by fate, were bound to come to an end, yet this never happens, because everything repeatedly starts all over again. Death is transition. A perpetual beginning and ending, violence and beauty. In Bill

Bill Viola 1951

moves under water. The fish becomes a bird in the form of a helicopter. The flight leads from the Fiji Islands to the far north of Canada. The fish is carried like a metal insignium through mountain valleys and forests. The helicopter—which one never sees during the flight—lands in a clearing. The fish, deposited in the clearing, turns out to be a real fish. Instantly insects

Viola's cyclic thinking there is no place for brutality, because it is a deformation of violence. His work deals with life, with survival, with the will to live, and hence also with death.

An extract from the introduction by Jean-Christophe Ammann to Bill Viola's *Reasons for Knocking at an Empty House.*

The Quintet
of the unseen
2000
Video installation,
still from video

Dream screen/prime time
2000
Mixed media installation,
50 × 70 cm

Two fundamental forces coalesce in the work of Maaria Wirkkala—the desire to illuminate shadows and the need to establish new relationships between people, places and things. Maaria Wirkkala sets out from a given situation and explores its complexity in order to uncover its poetic potential or charge it with new meanings. Some items in her vocabulary (chairs, screens, fields of light) feature in different works, creating an associative continuum of emotions and reflections which on each occasion take on new meaning.

Maaria Wirkkala is unveiling two works at the 2001 Venice Biennial: *Found a Mental Connection II* and *Dream Screen/Prime Time*. In both works there is a strange contrast between stillness and movement, and both of them are the continuation of worries and obsessions that were present in her previous pieces. In *Found a Mental Connection II*, an iron bridge 8 m long and 80 cm wide is suspended in the middle of space. At both ends of the bridge, a Koran and a Bible lie open. Different groups of animals walk from each end of the bridge in a strange exodus. They cross in different directions and, despite sharing the same space, never actually meet.

Elephants, zebras, giraffes, lambs, wolves, kangaroos, dromedaries, crocodiles, hyenas and bears walk with an absent gaze at times, and a menacing one at others. While quite different in its formal resolution, this work has its direct, conceptual precedent in the site-specific project which the artist staged at the Maiden's

ates a disturbing interplay of mirrors, while the durability associated with stone contrasts with the fleeting appearance and disappearance of the images. For the artist, *Dream Screen-Prime Time* refers to the power of video art: while in the past it was a dream to be inmortalised in stone now it is enough to be seen on TV. This piece further develops the intuitions formalised in a previous one—*Dream Screen*—blowed by breathing black coal dust on the wall. Here, the blackness acted directly as a symbol of the unconscious, and spectators projected their own invisible dreams onto that surface.

Maaria Wirkkala conceptualises her works as a space for encountering either oneself or others. Her creations are force fields for us to project our individual or collective phantoms in. They make us feel that art is still a valid instrument for generating emotional, meaningful transferences, as well as for coming to grips with the stranger that dwells without, which at times may well be ourselves.

Rosa Martinez

Maaria Wirkkala 1954

Tower in Istanbul in 1997. In that instance, Maaria Wirkkala's purpose was to connect the two banks of the Bosphorus by shining huge light beams from the small island where the Tower is located. The distance between the continents, and differences between cultures, were shortened by the ethereal path of light set up on the waters. Now, the iron bridge emerges as a symbol of transits, but the metaphor of encounter remains disquietingly suspended.

Dream Screen/Prime Time consists of a black stone screen. The stone is polished and serves as a projection field where, thanks to a video camera, the spectator can see the back of his or her own head on-line. Being confronted by the only part of oneself that one usually cannot see cre-

Found a mental connection
1998
Installation, variable size

Josef Dabernig's *Wisla* starts with the image of a fragment of architecture. The tower shaped building in the rigidly neo-classical style leads one to think of totalitarian Fascict architecture or about the Stalinist system. From here the camera swivels along the horizon and moves over several modern living blocks and comes to a sudden stop at the image of yet another neo-classical colonnade. In this first sequence two separate worlds seem to come together. The normality of the utilitarian buildings, in which the life of anyone whosoever takes place is framed by the pathos of a monumental architecture, whose purpose in general is to demonstrate the presence of a higher order.

In the next sequence, the two men in suit and tie who are seriously and decidedly walking through a passage way, seem to be agents in such an instance. As they move into the open,

game. The mimicry of the professionals doesn't even change as the cheering of the fans turns to hisses and cat-calls. The same setting, that for some is one type of place, a place to step out of their ordinary lives and to project themselves and possibly identify with something, for others is only an ordinary workplace. In *Wisla*, Josef Dabernig watches the coaches body language with the same exact concentrated attentiveness that the actors in the film bring to the invisible game. From the repertoire of such a body language one could easily take slapstick material or one could take it out to be typically male behaviour.

Wisla is equally distant from both of them. The film is neither comical nor openly critical. Its primary quality lies in the convincing representation of a specific habitus and the evocation of the context respective, without further

Josef Dabernig 1956

pf Dabernig Josepf Dabernig Jose

it becomes apparent that they are in a stadium, and we can recognize them as "football coaches" who sit down on a bench. Although the stadium is rather empty and somewhat desolate, the sound begins to grow to a level like that before the start of a game. Again there is a discrepancy between the profane emptiness and ritualised fullness. The concentrated attention of the "coaches" is in contrast to the collectively produced and experienced spectacle of an invisible game, in which the masses invest emotions and in turn receive meaning. Their gestures and movements, which are exactly modelled on the repertoire of real coachers, let neither their emotions be known, nor belie the imaginary outcome of the

illustrating it. But the film takes a lot from its discrepancies, from the empty stands and the roaring noise, from the Polish stadium and the Italian recording.

As the coaches leave the stadium and the camera once again swivels over the houses, the stadium announcer is reading the Standings. With this a certain order is again set in place, which for one round had been dissolved. And the individuals, who in that moment of dissolution had formed the masses, return once again to their ordinary lives. The coaches, however, as representatives of a mellow professionality receive congratulations on the grand stand.

Christian Kravagna

Wisla
1996
16 mm film/DVD, black
and white, 8', still from
film

Colour Fields

Hard edged, monochromatic, each work singular yet a component of a series, Paul Graham's *Paintings* take their place in a historical genealogy which may be traced from the Suprematists' utopian abstractions to the new objectivity of Moholy Nagy or Renger Patsch; from Mark Rothko's colour fields to Donald Judd's specific objects. Graham presents flat planes of gunmetal grey, flesh pink, pea green or shiny black in large horizontal rectangles. Some of these monochromes have been rationalised, with the overlay of a grid, or through the bifurcation of a vertical "zip" edging to the left or right of the picture frame. Others are more expressively modulated: subtle variations of tone progress in chromatic scales from light to dark; washes of colour appear to be poured one over another. These works are in fact photographs but not pictures, surfaces which at first refuse to become images. Yet the purity of Graham's apparently resolute formalism is corrupted, its exquisite surface scratched, leached through with the impurities of despairing psychobabble, wild profanity and stutterings of rage.

Paul Graham works in series, which in turn evolve around locations. His subjects range from the micro to the macro—he has moved between the interiors of social security offices to the landscapes of Northern Ireland, from sitting rooms to continents, from the private domain of individual consciousness to the

incised or embellished with scrawled words and drawings, with obscene graffiti. Graham documents the grotesque yet oddly banal profanities which routinely sprout across the walls of public conveniences from lavatories to bus shelters. Despite the best efforts of management the pathology of transgression defeats the abrasives and cleaning fluids. Some go further into the realm of the taboo; where descriptions of sex acts or drawings of genitalia are not enough, they smear or jerk actual bodily fluids onto these communal canvases.

In a small book of these works, Graham reproduces a letter written to the *New York Times* in 1943, by Mark Rothko, Barnett Newman and Adolph Gottlieb; they assert the use of flat form as a way of destroying illusion and revealing truth; they call for a subject matter that is tragic and timeless; they stress their spiritual kinship with primitive and archaic art; and they reject "pictures for the home [...] for the Whitney Museum..." Like these artists, Graham also uses scale and colour to articulate perception as phenomenology; the attraction of these images is both retinal and physical. He too reveals a truth—of the return of the repressed, itself a timeless, primeval drive that will always find its way to the surface, to transgress social facades. These photographs refuse accommodation as interior decor or institutional trophy. But the graphic assertions of the body, often found alongside expressions of racist and sexist hatred, of fear of the other, are not authored by the heroic artist. They are

Paul Graham 1956

public sphere of history and politics. This series converges and inverts private and public space. The *Paintings* function only as flat planes, offering no horizon, no space of perspective; these momentarily sublime expanses of colour and texture offer no way out. In fact they image abjection, elevated to the public realm through the public/private surface of the toilet wall.

Like some perverse doppelganger of a Cy Twombly canvas, each colour field is either

anonymous articulations of a collective imaginary. Scratching their way through the abstraction that once seemed to offer a universal, trans-social language of transcendence, they constitute an anti-social expression of an almost unbearable sense of being. The grotesque profanities of the graffitied wall reveal the frustration, anger and alienation of everyday life, transformed here into an abject beauty.

Iwona Blazwick

Untitled n° 2
1999
From the series **Paintings**
Fujiflex archive print,
75,6 × 99,5 cm,
edition of 6

Untitled n° 8
1999
From the series **Paintings**
Fujiflex archive print,
99,5 × 130 cm,
edition of 6

Untitled n° 11
1999
From the series **Paintings**
Fujiflex archive print,
75,6 × 99,5 cm
edition of 6

To gaze is to discover the world as much as to show oneself to others. In the eyes crops up the interior in the form of expression. Therefore, the portrait captures the psychology and the soul the body hold, thus turning into model of symbols. The gaze is the site of expression, but it is always a silent expression. Luis González Palma has modeled his own gaze through the gaze of his sitters, because he shares with them a conscience and a sensibility based on silence, on the fear and pain of the body and the forms. These are precisely the sites of confluence for personal histories and traditions of a culture of exclusion characteristic of Guatemala that since the conquest still remain irresolute, engaged in the brief postwar period of a war (more dirty than clean—a war is never clean) so long that it has lasted more than thirty years.

In his work, when he tackles perceptive and psychological issues centered on the gaze such as silence, the difficulty of expression, pain, or the symbols of representation and their transgression, he sums up and abstracts (almost without seeking or trying) the tragedy—silent—of the Guatemalan history through personal experience with models symbolic of beauty and exclusion.

Past and history fuse with the present through allegory, fable and fiction that in the shape of permanently renovated palimpsest formulates the question not so much of iden-

and conceals through guilt. His images often transform into means that restore the gaze to those to whom not only history but existence was seized: those who do not bear the gaze that shows and discovers are excluded from their own history. In the transparent eyes of the characters of his portraits, the gaze is recuperated through a symbolic interpretation of history, allegories and metaphors of the narratives, and the words that the eyes are capable of formulating.

González Palma's gazes do not dwell on the exotic image of the indigenous people; they do not pretend to establish the conditions of a non-existent, lost arcadia. They value the entity of empty figures, figures who have been emptied of entity and dignity by history, weighing the value of reestablishing *other ways of looking* as an antidote to frustration incited by pain: the gaze turns them into subjects, and all of them observe as they show themselves. Restoration of a gaze, reconstruction of a subject for history from the symbols that time has accumulated on layers of words, forms and narratives.

The baroque tone of his images is a point of departure, a symbolic language, an allegory. The baroque represents the theatrical tradition where the fable fits; entwined narratives allow double readings, but, above all, to be able to see in a freer, fuller way. The baroque is the language that permits fusion and excess, it is a dramatization where metaphor liberates itself with ingenuity and fantasy in order that

González Palma's images, tend to be a bridge of atonement and reconstruction endowing the gaze with new meaning.

Touch is always present. But like a forbidden desire, like a spectacle prohibited to hands and bodies: in the fabrics and damasks that form some of the diptychs; in the pages of ancient books superimposed on faces; in the skins and brocades that cover them... touch is like a temptation. It is offered to the eyes and denied to the body, it is the punishment inflicted on perception. There is no idea of sensuality because its mock appearance through the (forbidden) illusion of touch does not imply carnality. Touch is reserved only to sight: maybe for that reason the gaze penetrates only from the short-lived sparkle of internal expression. Maybe for that reason pain is so evident. Sorrowful gazes, gazes that express abandonment. There is no drama because tragedy hides in the interior that crops up only lightly through symbol and allegory—so profoundly baroque—that nourish the silent narrative, lightly mute. They are also new gazes stripped of the exotic, freed from having to mirror the stereotype of the sanctioning gaze of the others: gazes aware of their sorrow and of the unfair burden of a history. This new gaze assumes the language of its own forms like a poetic affirmation, like the beginning of reconstruction of its own existence in the countenance of the subject.

Santiago B. Olmo

Luis González Palma **1957**

tity as of that which brings forth the drama of excision and which entails dis-identification. To gaze to discover and explore fusions and tears; to gaze to show the impossibility of expressing what is seen. The silence of the gaze (that is the title of one of his books) is a way of describing the paralysis of understanding and reason, examining the absurd (not of Goya's monsters) but of a sensibility successively stimulated then curtailed or punished. In referring to the character of Guatemalan thought, Luis González Palma speaks of an *emotional veiling* and of a *veiled gaze,* the gestural ways that people's eyes adopt to discover the world and disclose themselves to others. The weight of the past is what veils

its fragments be crushed by the weight of what is immense. Opposites unite and separate to project the idea of a "limited" infinity. Symbols are codes that build models. From the transgression of those models history traces another profile capable of cherishing, from the conscience of pain, hopes for a new dignity.

The poetry of Francisco Nájera (friend and speaker) expresses a coincidental standstill, a paralysis of gesture and expression that transforms into pain, "in a reality always lacking, in an experience always absent". Nájera speaks in his prose poetry of an aesthetic of lack, of a silence that extends voraciously as if aspiring to disintegrate, of absence, of loneliness. But his words, just as much as

Entre raíces y aire
1997
Hand printed gelatin
silver print, Kodalith,
100 × 200 cm

What strange sensation does this piece evoke? What awkward allusion lurks beneath the surface of Nedko Solakov's work *A Life (Black & White)* of 1999? What third discourse, as it were, imbues this work with a halo of signifiers which undermines the descriptive hold of the obvious technical reference to installation and performance art? Might it be film, we wonder, drawn towards this association by the simple visual analogy of both the painters/actors and the black and white, the two colours/non-colours, which are the defining parameters of the work; an analogy that draws us back into a reverie about the pre-technicolor age, the age of silent movies and their simplified decor of narration devoid of any false promise of livelihood, mimesis and empirical sensation? Why is it that we think of Buster Keaton, Charlie Chaplin, or, somewhat later, Samuel Beckett when confronted with *A Life (Black & White)*?

The setting of *A Life (Black & White)* is as clear as it is simple: A painter starts from the left hand side of a singled-out room, painting the walls black clockwise. (The possible location has been tentatively prefigured by the artist as "a project room", "a cell within a bigger space", "an office space" etc., in other words: any more or less closed space which retains a human dimension, as if the space itself should protect the visitor from spatial alienation...) This first painter will be followed, at some distance, by a second painter,

essential to the course of life, and man is a malleable entity. In this perspective, so writes Milosz, one can easily imagine that maybe everyone will, at some point, walk on all fours and carry, placed right on top of his or her ass, a little tower with colourful flowers. It is noteworthy that the industrialised countries try to do away with such signs of instability, covering them up with the glittering facade of powerful economics, with the impenetrable surfaces of mass media and mass entertainment and smoothly operating political operations, in order to produce a natural order of things—as if nothing could ever change. And yet, the history of the 20th century has amply testified to the contrary: the catastrophe can always erupt from underneath.

A Life (Black & White) with its sleight-of-hand touch, its coquettish quality of potentially not being identified as work of art, is restrained on commenting upon the above topics, although it lets them shine through like the black colour that shines through the white over-paint, topics such as politics, power structures, the suppression of the uncontrollable and the absurd. But its reserve and caution can be likened to the one single and powerless gesture of Buster Keaton trying desperately, and desperately funny, not to lose hold of the clock hand of a public watch towering high above the deadly emptiness of the urban space below—a small gesture enlarged by the cinematic apparatus, thus becoming an allegory of life—our tenderly fragile and yet rudely unforgiving life.

Daniel Kurjakovic

Nedko Solakov 1957

painting the walls white, again clockwise, ensuing a double-layered process of painting and re-painting, going on during the overall time span of the opening hours. It will have the the air of a never-ending undertaking, transforming a profane gesture into an allegory of the abysmal, Sisyphus-like futility of human action (one layer of paint will be, this much is sure, covered by the next, differently coloured layer of paint).

In a collection of essays published in the fifties, Polish noble prize winner Czeslaw Milosz reminded the then-readers in the West, that the eastern European thinks in sociological and historical terms, that his notion of life is less rigorously relying on the idea of permanence. Inconstancy and incessant change are what is

A life (black & white)
1999-2001
Black and white paint;
2 workwers/painters
constantly repainting
in black and white the
space walls for the entire
duration of the
exhibition, day after day
(following each other);
dimensions variable,
installation view

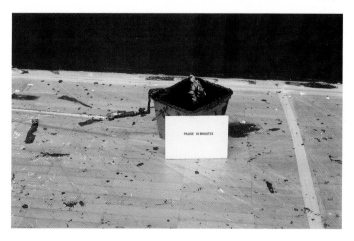

Sensation: Young British Artists from the Saatchi Collection, which opened at the Royal Academy of Arts in London in 1997, was a remarkable exhibition for several reasons. For a display of contemporary art, the amount of mainstream media coverage and popular interest which it generated was unprecedented. It initiated fierce debate over the quality of work included, the moral stance of its creators, and the influence of their common patron. However, most of the artists featured were already familiar names.

Australian-born Ron Mueck was a notable exception in that this was the first occasion on which he was shown as an artist in his own right. His haunting contribution was *Dead Dad* (1996-7), a *trompe l'oeil* sculpture of the artist's father as a three-foot long naked corpse. It was widely acknowledged as one of the most affecting pieces in the exhibition; the work of a virtuoso talent.

Mueck has no formal art training beyond high school, but was inspired by the fantastic make-believe universe of *Star Wars* to pursue a career in model-making. He began with children's television, graduating to motion picture special effects and finally advertising. Over a period of twenty years, he built up a fluency with materials which allows him to transform with confidence raw silicon into skin that feels alive; simple resin into eyes possessed of an eerie intelligence. His late entry into the art world allowed him to escape the frustration of having to realize other people's ideas rather than explore his

at Anthony d'Offay Gallery in London. On both occasions he showed small but intense selections of new work, confirming a reputation for perfectionism. *Ghost* (1998) is a sculpture of an awkward-looking adolescent girl, dressed in a saggy blue swimsuit. Her skin is pale and blotchy, her arms flecked with dark hairs. Gauche and gawky, she is getting on for seven feet tall, though she obviously wishes that she could disappear from view. Under scrutiny, her self-consciousness and insecurity become ever more painful, the look she returns from the corner of her eye seems increasingly hunted. By contrast, the subject of *Untitled (Man in Blankets)* (2000), a model of a middle-aged man nestled in a soft womb of bedding, has been reduced to the size of a new-born baby. As always, the degree of verisimilitude is compelling, transcending mere surface likeness to signify a genuine engagement with mental and emotional states. *Untitled (Big Man)* (2000) belongs to the same grouping. Sitting in a corner as if it were a punishment, this bald and bloated nude exudes vulnerability despite his bulk.

Untitled (Boy) (1999) is one of the Biennale's most prominent works. A gargantuan model of a hunched and crouching pubescent figure, it constitutes a monumentally imposing, if somewhat ominous, welcome to the Corderie. Like Pinocchio, there is more than a hint of rascality about him, but the overall mood of the piece is darker. *Untitled (Boy)* is perhaps Mueck's most powerfully successful attempt

Ron Mueck 1958

own. In 1996, his mother-in-law Paula Rego asked him to become her very own Geppetto by commissioning a model of Pinocchio. Rego admired the result so much that she exhibited it alongside her canvases in *Spellbound* at the Hayward Gallery. *Pinocchio* represents a small boy in white underpants, with tousled hair and a subtly mischievous expression. Like *Dead Dad*, its naturalism is uncanny. The childish anatomy, the expectant posture, the sidelong glance; all are utterly, unnervingly human. The interest in Mueck's practice generated by this exposure soon prompted a quantum leap, from artisan to artist.

In 1998 and 2000, Mueck had solo exhibitions

yet to engender psychological tension through an alteration of our physical relationship with readily identifiable character types. The boy's expression—uncertain, defensive, resentful—is brought into intimate focus, yet his extraordinary size makes him alien too.

This is where Mueck's project differs from that of American super-realist sculptor Duane Hanson, who works to accurate life-size. While Hanson's portraits of suburbanites and tourists, cops and cleaners are, even when contextually displaced, always part of our everyday world, Mueck's seem increasingly isolated within their own.

Michael Wilson

Untitled (boy)
1999
Mixed media,
4,9 × 4,9 × 2,4 m

Untitled (Shaved Head)
1998
Silicon, polyurethene
foam, acrylic fibre,
49,5 × 36,7 × 83,8 cm

Untitled (baby)
2000
Mixed media,
26 × 12,1 × 5,3 cm

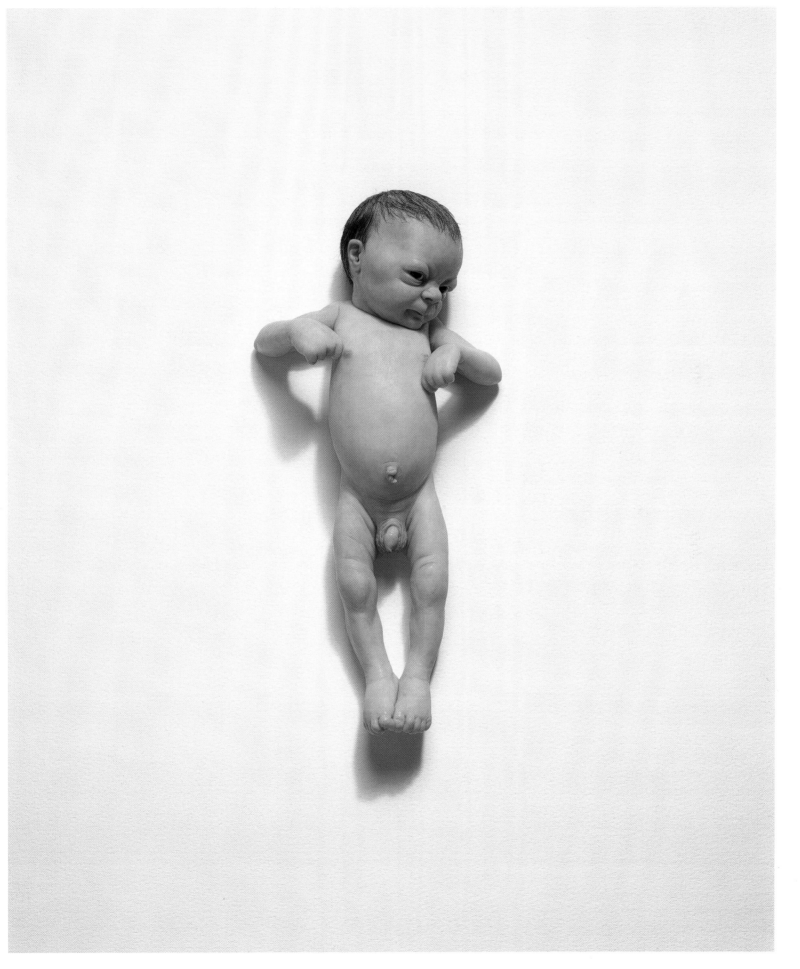

Video, or the Art of painting invisibile pictures. On Heimo Zobernig's "Nr. 18, 2000, 13 min., Loop without sound"

The theory of colours, in comparison to the *Topos* of the white wall, in addition to the naked artist subject performing a special form of painting—all in the medium video. Heimo Zobernig's *Nr. 18* starts where video becomes painting, painting performance, preformance video. Here the loop closes—not, however, without having made central issues of the modern understanding of art clear these media passages. Or to have revealed a paradox subject in the multi-superimposition of the different methods: that of the invisible picture.

The set-up is simple. The naked artist, that inevitably reminds one of a mixture of *Ecce Homo* and Body Painting, is rummaging in continuation through a pile of remnants. He goes through lengths of material and drapes them around himself. This constantly changing half abstract picture, that its agile arranger covers to varying degrees, changes its colours every minute. Blue-white-red becomes red-white-green which then becomes green-white-blue, red-white-green, and so on. The changing forms and their tireless creator never seem to get to the end and repeatedly have to start again from scratch. Sisyphus meets Modern Painting, or rather, he always has to paint the same picture. The blue box helps him.

The "picture" with the colourful remnants follows a simple code: the four colour tones used are the standard colours of today's video-technology (bluebox, video blue, video red and green box) that can be faded in or out altogether in any combination. In *Nr. 18* these colours are used in alternation and in each setting one of them is replaced with white, while at the same time the white spaces are faded out by one of the four colours and a further colour remains unchanged. This colour scheme is especially interesting because it consists in only "invisible values", that is, in stand-ins that can be filled in any way you choose. The supposed basic values of a certain technology (video) in themselves are insubstantial and, as Zobernig has already shown in many of his previous videoworks, can be linked to the world arbitrarily. The apparant system (that is the basis of modern art) is just as open to the world, as is, the other way round, the apparently open, invisible and thus replaceable, recognisable as a non-neutral component of the system.

The endless dying and bleaching, covering and uncovering, winding and smoothing has a further dimension: the *Topos* of the white screen/wall. The white wall represents the apparant neutrality and transparency as a fundamental aspect of modern architecture and later as the starting point of modern painting. It actually represents a specific type of disguise ("a white wash in a political sense" according to the architect theorist Mark Wigley). The video presents a modern version of this modern dialectic. Far from simply filling an empty white space, it becomes clear that it is precisely the emptiness of this background or the purity of the screen that will always remain a biased structure. Zobernig struggles, literally physically, to present what is arbitrary and replaceable as non-neutral, independent quantities. Invisibility goes visible.

This dialectic finally touches the artist-subject itself: he appears naked but covers himself in the "invisible" elements of the medium (video). He plunges into the instable areas of the picture he has formed, and then reappears in new layers. A moving *tableau* of increasing de-subjectivisation becomes visible rather than the simple revelation of a subject that was the starting point of his production. Or could this body be more than a disappearing part in a mostly invisible screen?

Christian Höller

Heimo Zobernig 1958

Nr. 18
2000
Video installation, site
specific, mixed media,
still from video

Nr. 18
2000
Video installation, site
specific, mixed media,
still from video

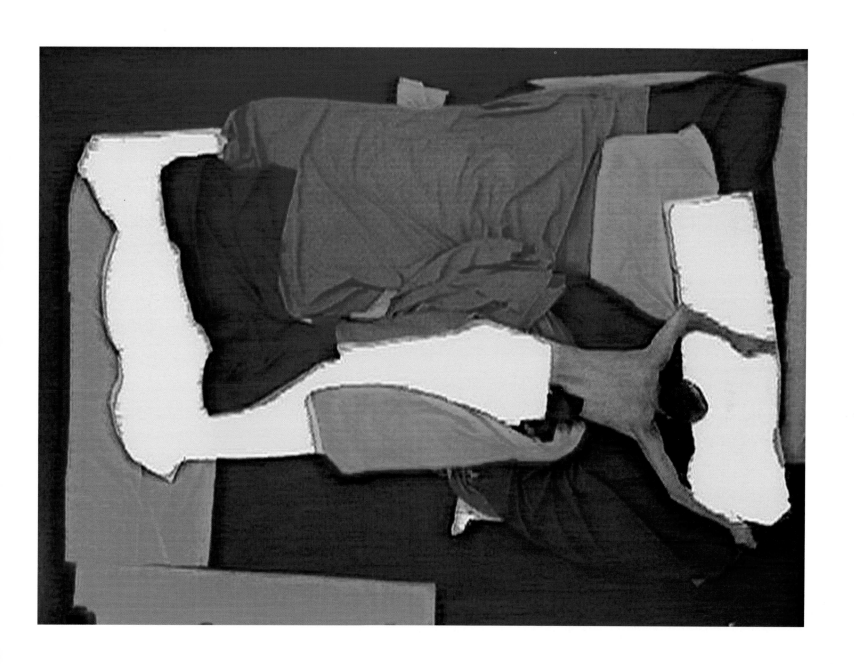

Nr. 18
2000
Video installation, site
specific, mixed media
still from video

For while the highly rational societies of the Renaissance felt the need to create Utopias, we of our times, must create fables.

Francis Alÿs 1998

For Francis Alÿs, the invention of a field of practice took place in the fall of 1991, when in a common machine workshop he carried out the task of constructing an animal made of magnetized metal, similar in form to a multitude of sculpted figures, all made of cubic sections, with which he tried to evoke the effigy of every species of mammal. Entitled *The Collector*, the piece was part of a series of schematic animals through which Alÿs had explored a diversity of poetic/material associations.

Among these early attempts to challenge the inert condition of the artistic object, the magnetic *The Collector* marked the opening of a new direction.

Rather than the traditional contemplation of the relations of mass, volume, weight, and form proposed by the modern vision of sculpture, *The Collector* took form as a tool to be activated, as an instrument of exploration. Alÿs sought to submerge artistic action in urban mythology, subjecting it to the circulation (and creative distortion) of rumour. Walking the work in order to develop it created a narrative structure whereby he aspired to inscribe himself in a territory

would replace the iconic and formalistic concept of sculpture by an interaction with the urban, an interaction destined to weave narratives around alternative, underground, embryonic or dissident forms of social flow.

All these interests would return in Alÿs's work over the years. But above all, *The Collector* established Alÿs's discipline of walking as an artistic action. Alÿs has used strolling as a method both to affect the urban imaginary and to appear within it. Thus the polyvalence of Alÿs's actions: each of his walks would be the origin of a story, the impulse for a sociological exhibition, and an instrument for political intervention.

Walking, for Alÿs, is equivalent to emulating/ interacting/observing/diverting the microscopic resistance that the fabric of the city and its inhabitants offer to the uniformizing project of modernity. Thus his interventions tend to place themselves in relationships of tension, or outright transgression, with respect to the modernist structures of control, transparency, and efficiency, including curatorial power and the ideal order of artistic events. They are best seen as anti-functional forms of thinking.

His walks are above all a means of emulating the friction between the new authoritarianism of efficiency and the open or subterranean forms of sabotage that accompany it. This is why a

Francis Alÿs 1959

where he was a foreigner. Every day Alÿs took his mascot, equipped with wheels like a toy, for a walk on the streets of Mexico City in order to attract nails, pieces of tin and wire, bottle caps, or any other kind of metal fragments which would stick to it to form an epidermis of scrap and detritus. Its skin of rusty scales gathered from the pavement emulated the opportunistic existence of the street dogs and rodents that abound in urban centres like Mexico City. *The Collector* formulated a poetics of the social interstice. It suggested a symbolic practice that

great deal of his work consists in the exploration of redundancies, tautological cycles, and wasteful actions, the execution of fables/actions involving the breakdown of systematic and instrumental thinking. It is an attempt at emulating the labyrinthine, subterranean and undeclared model whereby the common citizen outwits the projects of power. Thus their inbuilt reluctance to the structures of prestige of the artworld. His fables are, in that sense, productive diversions from the curatorial machine.

Cuauhtémoc Medina

Mr. Peacock will
represent Mr Alÿs at the
49. Venice Biennale
2 peacocks, 2 guardians,
postcards, peacocks
owner: Marisa Albertini,
Lanuvio

Rineke Dijkstra practices an art of quiet, engaged observation. Since she began exhibiting her photographic work in 1993, she has developed an international reputation as one of the most visible and highly regarded Dutch artists of her generation. Dijkstra's flat, frontal, color portraits of individuals alone and in small groups are characterized by a remarkable formal classicism, conceptual rigor, and psychological depth. Like many contemporary photographic portrait artists, Dijkstra records people who are at once specific and generalized, familiar but anonymous. According to her, "Both my videos and photographs are based on a documentary moment, but at the same time, I isolate them so they become a certain icon or symbol". For the viewer, the almost immediate accessibility of Dijkstra's images is always balanced by the sense that the artist has come to know a person but has chosen to present the resulting image as a type.

Over the course of the last decade, Dijkstra has used her camera as a passport to enter widely divergent social and cultural environments around the world. In each place, her raw curiosity and innate sensitivity have enabled her to identify with particular faces

For several years, Dijkstra worked as a successful commercial photographer making portraits of writers, artists, musicians, and businessmen for newspapers, magazines, and corporate annual reports. However, after a serious bicycle accident in 1990, Dijkstra stopped working for nearly a year and began an intense regimen of physical therapy that included swimming regularly. Freed from the demands of photojournalism, Dijkstra created her first (and last, she claims) self-portrait immediately after a strenuous workout. Dijkstra recalls, "[In my commercial work] I used certain poses again and again, and, after seven years, I wanted to create something for myself, something more substantial. I made a portrait of myself after swimming thirty lengths, too tired to think about which pose to strike that moment when you just stand".

In her best work, Dijkstra returns to the essential elements of vulnerability and fatigue manifest in this early self-portrait. First, she focused on the emotional content of the picture, particularly the insecurity commonly associated with partial undress, by asking friends in Holland (whom she had previously photographed in their homes) to pose in their

tographing individuals during moments of duress or exhaustion: Dutch mothers holding their newborn babies, Portuguese matadors immediately after bullfights, and English and Dutch teenagers in nightclubs in the early-morning hours. Too tired or too distracted to be inhibited, these individuals allowed momentary glimpses into their lives that, under ordinary circumstances, they might not have been willing or able to share.

During the last two years, Dijkstra's work with young soldiers both in the Israeli army and in the French Foreign Legion provided a vehicle for the artist to continue her examination of the poetic resonances of similarly transitional moments in individual lives. In particular these images demonstrate the artist's interest in the ways that the military serves as a rite of passage either by choice or obligation between adolescence and a more complicated notion of adult citizenship. The artist photographed a disparate cross-section of young Israelis with a particular emphasis on soldiers during the induction process, training sessions, active duty, and at home on leave in the early months of their conscription. The first artist ever allowed such full access to military bases and field training facilities of the Israeli army,

Rineke Dijkstra 1959

and moments in time that seem at once common and extraordinary. The clarity and honesty that mark Dijkstra's images are the result of the artist's consistent ability to structure moments of sincere emotional connection with the individuals she photographs. She has said, "For me it is essential to understand that everyone is alone. Not in the sense of loneliness, but rather in the sense that no one can completely understand someone else. I know very well what Diane Arbus means when she [said] that one cannot crawl into someone else's skin, but there is always an urge to do so anyway. I want to awaken definite sympathies for the person I have photographed".

bathing suits on nearby beaches. But because she was working with people she knew well, Dijkstra discovered that her collaborators were too self-conscious to permit candid or sufficiently abstract photographs. This realization led her to beaches in Belgium, Croatia, England, Poland, the Ukraine and the United States in search of children and adolescents who were willing to pose. Despite differences in posture, complexion and swimwear, the individuals represented in this early, widely praised series constitute a collective portrait of the existential insecurity and awkward beauty of youth that transcends national boundaries. Dijkstra later expanded upon the physical aspects of her self-portrait by pho-

Dijkstra has emerged from this unique, and at times challenging, experience with a highly charged, profoundly accomplished series of photographs.

In Israel the role of the armed forces is in many ways central to the collective, national experience. The Israeli Defence Forces (idf) were born in the chaos of the country's 1948 War of Independence. Since its formation, the draft policy of the idf, or Tsahal, has held that nearly every able-bodied man and woman must serve. The army conscripts eighteen-year-old men for three years of service and women (who until just recently served for two years) for twenty months. Throughout the nation's modern history, with

long-standing strategic concerns in an unstable region, the armed services have been one of the country's dominant social institutions; for most the military is the principal point of transition from childhood to young adulthood.

In 1998 Dijkstra gained access, with the sponsorship and assistance of the Herzliya Museum of Israeli Art and Sculpture Garden, to a variety of military sites throughout the country. Through museum contacts and the assistance of local residents in the city of Herzliya, she began photographing men and women during their first days of service. Three-quarter-length portraits depict young women, wearing ill-fitting uniforms and blank expressions, at the Tel-Hashomer Induction Center, while life-sized images portray individual male soldiers from the Orev Unit of the Golni Brigade immediately after basic weapons training. Outfitted in battle fatigues and seemingly oversized automatic rifles, each of these young men is photographed in the same verdant, hilly landscape and responds to the artist with varying degrees of poise, comfort, or self-consciousness. Dijkstra also made portraits of some soldiers in civilian dress at home, taking special note of changes in hairstyle, fashion, posture, and attitude that accompany their temporary return to lives as average teenagers.

Since early 2000, images of Israeli soldiers are once again a staple of the daily news. In December 2000, Dijkstra returned, after several month's absence, to a country that appeared on the verge of war. Although she concluded the project under intense circumstances, Dijkstra is reluctant to allow the specific geopolitical realities of Israel to overwhelm an understanding of this new body of work. In this presentation, only the cautiously documentary titles reveal the location of these portrait subjects. As always, the artist confronts the viewer with the larger, near-universal wonder of images that inspire an understanding of difference, as well as a profound sense of personal recognition.

James Rondeau

Golni Brigade, Orev
(Raven) Unit, Elyacim,
Israel
May 26, 1999
C-print, 180 × 150 cm

Maya, induction center,
Tel-Hashomer, Israel
April 12, 1999
C-print, 126 × 107 cm

Maya, Herzliya, Israel
November 21, 1999
C-print, 126x107 cm

The piece presented at the Venice Biennale is called *Theologische Gespräche*. It is based upon the project *Lustige und traurige Abenteur des Dummen Pastors* . In the context of the above mentioned project an action was performed in 1996: Pastor (Vadim Zakharov) fought against a Sumo wrestler and lost. At that time a video-recording of the action was taken. Later on I extracted a videostill from it, but only after a while I discovered in it a detail worth spending a few words about.

It has to do with a young woman. Small, wearing a white blouse, she emerged from behind the figures of the struggling contestants with her camera. I'll say it without delay, I knew this woman. She had helped me with my project in Japan; now, however, her present whereabout is uncertain. She disappeared. After my return to Cologne I was told that apparently the woman had a drowned on the island of Okinawa some 10 days after the performance took place.

As I showed the piece *Theologische Gespräche* to friends and acquaintances, I kept drawing the attention on the silhouette of the woman telling her story. Over time I found myself talking more and more about the small silhouette with the camera, instead of the piece itself. This silhouette gained more and more space, progressively replacing the main subject, the clarity of the concept, the irony, the humor. This is what is happening now: I no longer see a foreground, as if there isn't any. My eyes run to the white spot, the tender figure, the cam-

the onlooker towards a biblical subject—the struggle between Jacob and the Angel—as well as to a drunken monologue. Wherever is casted, the glance will meet scenes of sheer madness. And therefor, let us be funny and laugh. Hopefully Kazimoto, the tender japanese girl, will laugh too, if ever she will see these photos of her on display at the 49. Venice Biennale.

Vadim Zakharov

Vadim Zakharov 1959

era lens, difficult to detect, apparently focused on me, rather than on the wrestler. The young woman photographs me everytime I look at her. I know this. Maybe it's the same for everyone who notices her. But then there's another aspect—the photographer chooses her own objects to be recorded. The onlooker has no chance to notice the small silhouette, to follow the profundity in the banality, unless the girl herself discovers in the onlooker a correspondance, or peculiar characteristics.

A final remark: on the horizon of our perception stand two struggling figures. This eternal pair informs our projection of the world and produces commentaries, endless associations, difficult instructions and analogies, leading

Theology Conversation
1996-2000
Mixed media installation,
variable size

There are no facts, only interpretations.

F.N.

*In the past year, I diligently collected
thirty interviews with Maurizio Cattelan.
I transcribed the first and the last paragraph
from each interview. I pasted them
in random order*

Massimiliano Gioni

Most of my works bear a singular relation to narrative. Theatre, like art, is a biological function. I don't care about narratives: I like to get straight to the point. Theatre bores me. People have too many expectations from artists. We are all alone. I am thinking of a collaborative conception of art. I always liked Alighiero, but never could stand Boetti. I'm hypnotized by ambitious artworks: art is by definition a finite product. The theme of art works that were never made often recurs in my work.

I like art works that escape physical presence. Art works you can carry in your mind or in your pockets. The best art works are complete objects, with an unbearable weight. I don't like to work with other people. I do everything with other people. I do everything alone. If you want to work with other people, you have to give yourself away completely, with no fear.

I've never had ideas. Artists don't have ideas. I get my ideas mostly in the morning. Ideas are born out of a continuing practice. Ideas are dialectical short circuits.

I work with images, trying to reflect the schizophrenia of reality. My images are univocal: they are a barrier against the schizophrenia of the real. Your pope sparked off an actual revolution. Last December I exhibited *La Nona Ora* in a show commemorating the centenary of the Warsaw Gallery of Modern Art.

I changed my mind a thousand times, every day. I was afraid: it's an image of terrible pain. I never change my mind. When I have an image in mind, I just go all the way. I'm never afraid.

Let's start off with a very direct and simple question, could you tell us a little about *La Nona Ora?*

Since the times of Ancient Rome, wax has had a direct relationship with death: extended as a shroud on the faces of corpses, wax preserves the features for ever, bestowing on the dead the consolation of celebrity, the mirage of immortality.

Many art works conceal an interesting story about their creation, their inception. The art works I like the best don't have any story to tell: they are speechless. There are just there. They never speak about their inception. Art works need to function very quickly, no matter how complex and varied they are: it's art or war. Art

Maurizio Cattelan 1960

I never studied to be an artist. I'm trying to build a structure for my work, an idea: I'm not really an artist. If you need something, you have to write it down. I stopped asking myself if I'm an artist. I've become a partisan. I studied art at the Academy in Nice. I always felt I was an artist. When I was a kid, I wanted to become an artist.

I'm attracted by time, by geological time. Art can work as an accelerator: it concentrates life in an image, and that makes life faster, lighter maybe, simply bearable. Art is a matter of coincidence and slowness, just like life itself. My works are there to be tested, discussed and interpreted. My work refuses the idea of discussion.

is slow, by definition. Otherwise, it becomes fashion. We are all living a schizophrenia.

Reactions transform art works, they change their shape and reception. Objects are nothing but projections of desire, images of a struggle. My art doesn't change, no matter who's looking at it. Art works have a precise meaning. It's not important who they are talking to.

Messages are for advertising, not for art. Art doesn't need explanations. Art should lie. Art tells the truth, by definition. When an artist is lying, it's over. I have nothing against art. I hate art. Art is life with the dull bits cut out. Art must be dull, just like life itself.

La rivoluzione siamo noi
2000
Polyester resin figure,
felt suit, metal coat rack,
puppet:
124,9 × 32,8 × 23 cm;
wardrobe rack:
188,8 × 46,9 × 52 cm

Le Détroit

Douglas's *Le Détroit* is a six-minute-long 35 mm black-and-white film comprising two loops that are projected on a "dual-vision" screen: an image is seen on one side of the screen, while its negative counterpart is shown on the other side. The interaction of the two images produces frequent after-images, shadowy forms that seem to blend into one another. This unsettling superimposition renders a fragile surface of image that appears to flake off the screen like silvery fish scales, heightening the work's sense of indeterminacy and creating a lurking threat which pervades the film. In the gallery, a wide screen divides the space into two equal halves. The film's protagonist, a black woman named Eleanore, sits pensively in a parked white Chevrolet Caprice[1], its engine still running as if it has just arrived on the scene. The woman's furrowed brow displays a certain premonition. Slowly, she steps out of the car and places a powerful searchlight on the left corner of the hood, near the bottom edge of the windshield, illuminating an abandoned, overgrown house [...]

As if returning to the scene of a crime or a traumatic event, Eleanore has come to this place in search of something unknown, at least to us. She walks up the driveway; flashlight in hand and boots crunching broken glass on the pavement, and enters the house through the front door; where she discovers a single, fresh shoe print in the accumulated dirt

the house's former occupants, while drops of water from a slow leak in the roof keep pace with Eleanore's investigation. Slowly closing the closet door, she walks through a hole in the wall into a room that appears to have been the study. Amid carefully arranged objects and furniture, Eleanore picks a piece of paper up off the floor and places it on a desk.

Although the worried look on Eleanore's face betrays neither empathy for nor full recognition of the place, her methodical exploration creates the feeling that this is a setting she knows intimately.

Details of the interiors and once-fashionable furniture suggest that this home may have been inhabited by a middle-class family or one with such aspirations.

Eleanore walks upstairs and proceeds to search for something left behind, or perhaps even purposefully hidden. As she pokes behind a wall, the searchlight mounted atop her vehicle dies out, and a sudden gust of wind slams the car door shut. She glances out the window and heads back to the car hurriedly. Making her way through the house, Eleanore passes all of the rooms and objects she encountered earlier. The film seems to run in reverse: the piece of paper she picked up slowly falls back to the floor, the closet doors she closed swing open, and so forth. Outside, she grabs the burned-out searchlight, gets into the car, and shifts into gear. At this crucial juncture, the film begins again, blurring the distinction between Eleanore's arrival at and departure from the scene. [...]

by its loss of social cohesion and its corrosion through urban neglect, poverty, and economic degradation. [...]

Today, Detroit seems hollow and emptied, a ghost of its former image as prosperous city of the nation's industrial belt. But how, Douglas seems to ask, does one fully apprehend the social impact of a city's demise? Often this has been explained as one of the ways modernism failed to organise social space along functionalist lines. Douglas's Detroit photographs are partly a response to this sceptical view of modernist urban planning. However, these images, rather than simply providing a view of a failed utopia, also signal ruin, obsolescence and decay. The photographs seek, in a dispassionate fashion [...], to present images of modern ideology, with their pretensions of progress, and the reality of that ideology's undoing.

Le Détroit continues the quest running through all of Douglas's work to analyse how time-based images are constituted and in which fields of inquiry, phenomenological or ontological, they acquire their proper meaning. Following Eleanore in her investigation, one asks: What does she see and what has Douglas set up for the camera (and us) to see? [...]

Throughout *Le Détroit*, our attention is called time and again to this very mechanism. The horizontal frame created by the camera forms part of the repertory of how what is seen in the film assumes the viewer's own unconscious subjectivity, implying that we need not necessarily see from the point of view of the camera but from

and dust. Cautiously, she bends down, wipes the print with her fingers, and then proceeds on her excursion, wherever it may lead.

Here, the films begins to assume aspects of a gothic drama. As Eleanore proceeds from one space to the next, horizontal camera pans reveal, slow view of desolate rooms, peeling paint, and knocked-out walls. Piled in one corner of a room are broken furniture, crockery, an old television set, clothing, and milk crates, all of which lend a melancholic disquietude to the scene. In another room, a small picture hangs above an old, nineteenth-century-style sofa with brocade upholstery. Discarded shoes in the corner and a woman's clothes, visible through an open closet door; bear witness to

Douglas used two books to establish the setting for *Le Détroit* and its engagement with the disjunctions of time and space, history and memory: Shirley Jackson's 1959 novel *The Haunting of Hill House* provides the narrative trope of the horror/thriller genre (this connections is underscored by the fact that the main character of Jackson's novel is also named Eleanore), while historian Marie Hamlin's 1884 chronicle *Legends of Le Détroit* creates, as the artist put it, "a repertoire of peculiar objects."[2] [...]

In 1997 Douglas began traveling to Detroit to photograph blighted areas of this distressed city's urban fabric. These images provided the foundation for *Le Détroit* and its view of today's Detroit: the psychic trauma produced

that of the protagonist. In other words, we see from Eleanore's perspective as she scans the rooms with her flashlight. Herman Gardens, where the film was made, comes to stand then as the symbolic unconscious of Detroit's trauma, while Eleanore's presence and her search restore the black social order that disappeared with the city's urban decline.

Okwui Enwezor

Excerpt from "Stan Douglas, Le Détroit", *Focus*, The Art Institut of Chicago, 2000-2001.

[1] Stan Douglas refers to the fact that the most common police car models in the United States and Canada are the Chevrolet Caprice and the Ford Crown Victoria and that an unmarked police car, similar to the one Eleanore drives, is called a "ghost car" in slang.

[2] Stan Douglas, *Le Détroit (project draft)*, 1999.

Le Détroit
1999–2000
35 mm film installation
for two 35 mm film
projectors, looping
device, anamorphic lens,
one screen, stills
from video

Close (Atom Egoyan / Julião Sarmento)

"The installation will be a meditation on projection. The act of receiving the projection becomes a graphic and physical activity that involves the viewer to spatially organize himself. The actual image that is being projected will involve a scene that is almost unimaginable."
Atom Egoyan, Notes on *Close*.

"I am not interested in pornography *per se* but rather in the sensations that rise from it or are associated with it. I don't care about the specifics of sex, although, thank god, everything has sex in it. What matters to me is the physical contact: violent, intimate, sexual, whatever."
Juliao Sarmento, interview with Kevin Powers. *Catalogue* published by Galeria Joan Prats, Barcelona, 2001.

The viewer is in a corridor. A screen stretches from floor to ceiling. There is only a short distance between the viewer and the screen. He/she looks up. There is a temptation to touch it, to run one's hands over to surface to verify

Atom Egoyan and Juliao Sarmento's *Close* is not only a "meditation on projection". It is an attempt to represent, physically and emotionally, the phenomenon of voyeurism. This is, of course, at the very heart of cinema, and the seduction of the viewer is central to its success. Like the boy in Jean-Luc Godard's *Les Carabiniers* (1963), who runs up onto the stage of the cinema in order to examine the image more closely, or Buster Keaton's *Sherlock Jr.* (1924), who goes from the projectionist's booth into the film itself, film has always played on the relationship between a suspension of belief and a desire to know the image (or apparatus) more intimately. *Close* seems to provide us with the opportunity to solve the riddle. And then frustrates that very same desire. Is this not the nature of voyeurism? To promise the impossible? To fantasize the real?

In a sense, Egoyan's films and Sarmento's paintings both represent the trace of an action, of an event, of a memory, of a fantasy. The white, tactile space of the painting that "frames" the disassociated image. The cinematic space that is

Atom Egoyan 1960 - Julião Sarmento 1948

that it is real. To somehow read the image. A voice narrates a series of stories on the soundtrack. Water drips. There is another sound as well. We're not sure what it is. We look up at the image. It is a blur of forms and movement. We try to step back and crash into the wall.

devoid of characters, in which objects or sounds connote the memory of what has just happened. In each case, there is the erotic which informs our attempt to make sense of things. Forget about the specifics. "Everything has sex in it."

Michael Tarantino

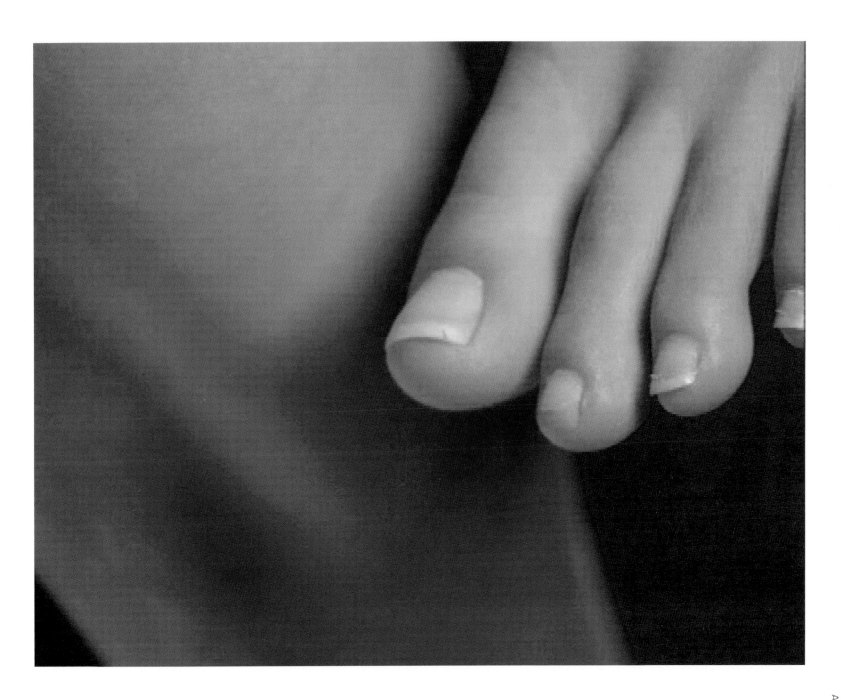

Close
2000-2001
DVD projection,
11' loop, still from video

More than just ordinary art

Veli Granö is basically a curious person. For years he has tried to figure out what motivates people who want to create an alternative world for themselves.

Granö has photographed folk artists, those backyard sculptors and do-it-yourselfers who enjoy making things with their own hands as much as making at least some impression on their environment. (*A Trip to Paradise*, 1986, *DIY Lives*, 2000.) He has photographed collectors engulfed by vast numbers of objects (*Tangible Cosmologies*, 1997) and filmed the story of a man who dreams of a better life somewhere in outer space (*Strange Message from Another Star*, 1998). His latest installation and film project (*The Stardweller*, 2000) again respects people's strangest desires. It tells the story of a woman who dreams of going to Sirius.

Granö's pictures seem to be documentary, at least until we start wondering what they are about. In fact, he has arranged other people's spontaneous creations of reality into captivating *natures mortes*.

Granö's photographs also ask: What makes 'a real artist, not long ago folk artists used chainsaws to carve bears out of blocks of wood—now they build scale models. What counts in the models, as in Granö's pictures, is the detail. They tell of the extra mental dimensions gained by tinkering with details. Folk artists, collectors and model builders care little for problems specific to the art world. And neither does Granö. In his work since the 1980s the factitious borders between art and "folk art" have melted. Granö is a professional who makes art for other people, for his audience, despite his role as a collector of collectors.

He makes other people's stories and realities visible. People are industrious. They want to leave their mark and to give their lives meaning by creating "tangible cosmologies". Granö portrays vernacular history in a way that radiates both warmth and strangeness. Except that it is impossible to document other people's thoughts and memories accurately. We can feel them or be amazed, that's all.

His installations scrutinise the fragmented world that folk artists, collectors and scale-model builders have tried to reconcile. Yet his focus has always been on light. This can be materialised in silk screens, video images, photographs or film, either as material or as an image recorded on it. Light brings culture to the darkness, but it also makes us visible. Random TV programmes scatter living blue light around installations with culturised light slowly becoming imaginary and primitive again.

The people in Granö's photographs are often in a state of absent-minded, unintentional muteness, i.e. they are lost in their own thoughts, or they are busy doing something that apparently totally absorbs them, so they are not on the alert. If they are posing for the photographer, there is something reserved about their gestures. As spectators we imagine we can get more information about reality through these photos. In fact, Granö's pictures are only bits of stories, "paths to reality", as he wrote in 1997. Sometimes he conceals or reveals parts of the photographs in his installations. We are used to taking photography for real. Granö investigates the concept of reality in photographs by showing that there are only things in different kinds of light.

The spectator wants to know more although s/he senses that further detail would add nothing to the story. Granö depicts tales and stories, the charm of which is in repetition, in familiarity. Once upon a time... again.

Helena Sederholm

Granö Veli Granö Veli Granö Veli

Veli Granö 1960

Vejio Rönkkönen
(jogapark)
From serie Onnela –
A Trip to Paradise
1986
Colorprint, 50 × 60 cm

This artist with an unusual name from Leipzig is in the process of influencing also internationally the conditions of perception of recent painting. Since the mid-nineties, he has been creating with incredible imagination complex narrative pictures that were initially considered strange during the discussions of that time, while today they are interpreted as the incarnation of deeper lying needs. Everything that was considered obsolete could be found in them: the isolation of a self-referential work against an oppressive world, the demand for an elaborate figuration, even the narrative gesture itself that the sculptural sin of narration grants absolution that was no longer thought possible. So many anachronisms that seem to have grown from a peripheral background and continual distance; today, they suggest opposing forces that were more effective: personal quality and temporal experience. Since it has now become evident that these pictures are anything but divorced from reality. The contaminated myth of what is modern primes them as do the military-planning manoeuvres of the leading characters involved. The memories of lives of different generations become a web of interweaving planes and perspectives which can help develop a wider view of the mass of what has been and can also light the paths of prophecy. The scenes and installations presented may be named or known, but alienate themselves in the aura of

same time one should remember to take the painting in as a whole initially, as a highly organised inter-play of colours and shapes, areas and rooms, composition and empty spaces: it is only in this way that the true rhythm of the picture narratives becomes clear. This is particularly useful with works such as *Tank* that does without the figurative carrier of a plot and relies completely on the evidence of simultaneous set pieces. The picture space is layered: analogue to the operations of remembering and dreaming there is sequence after sequence, the opening of the format to zigzagged bin bags—again with three motives and constructed letters above. The loss of balance creates the air of something plunging, something sinking to the ground from days long gone. It is from there that the inner pictures are conjured up, pictures that were closed in the visible reductions of the factory, the petrol pump, closed behind steel doors. The desolation of an industrial plant gone to waste, long silent, is caught in the pink coloured sculpture from which diesel, fuel and energy are pumped, the ingredients of the supposed progress that fed the utopia of reconstruction, an alternative for society with a counter project. It is all a long time ago, sealed off and kept behind the steel doors of an age that has ended, covered with the thicket of being forgotten: this is what a picture of the 60's in the East could have been like and Neo Rauch has painted it, recalling the conditions of his childhood.

large switchbox and the model of a transformer field appear to supply the *tableau* with energy in the normal way. Platform elements in the background suggest plans already underway, but the word on the front brick wall becomes the writing on the wall of confusion. Is Neo Rauch working off his own paralysis in his painting? Is he the warrior in the rank of general who is following the (blind) mascot with his eyes closed, exhausted and without any inspiration, now only accompanied by two wooden domestics? It is possible that there really are such phases of weakness and despair. What, however, is fascinating, is how Neo Rauch overcomes himself and is always able to offer resistance with the flying sparks of his imagination, lighting up our memory of pictures for ever like a flash of lightning.

Harald Kunde

Neo Rauch 1960

paralysis that seals each work to an allegoric happening of exemplary significance. Above all, these panels are characterised by the mastery with which Neo Rauch unites western and eastern paradigms in painting, with which he staggers picture spaces, domestic trading, visual barriers and snatches of conversation. In short, the way he successfully manages to bind the elements through reflective loading in a final and complex outlook.

If one remembers these characteristics while considering works shown at the Venice Biennial, it will be noted how a strong iconographic wake leads the visitors' attention and enables clear lines of understanding. At the

On the other hand, one of the latest works *Tabu* deals with something from the artist's present surroundings. In an almost theatrical construction a scene is presented that persists in the typical tension between picture movement and the powerlessness to act. It is dominated by two large vertical lines: the unusual mannequin with its feet and head in coloured buckets wanders through the left half of the picture, and the tired giant on the right, who is led to the field supported by two extras. While the colours red, yellow and blue in the pots clearly refer to programmatic fields of painting, warming them up on the stove in the area at the back as well as the flashing of the explosives of the exhausted giant is puzzling. The

Regel
2000
Oil on paper, Ø 300 cm

Übung
1999
Oil on canvas,
180 × 300 cm

Nerv
2001
Oil on paper,
248 × 198 cm

Between Time and Desire

Ithaca has given you a beautiful voyage
Without her you would have never taken
the road.

But she has nothing more to give you
Kostantino Cavafis

There is no other destination than the journey itself; that is what Jaime-David Tischler's photographs seem to suggest with candor and impiety at the same time. The work of this Costa Rican artist could not have referred to anything else but displacement as he tries to put Desire in the spotlight.

Thus, a brief survey of his artistic production from 1994 to the present suggests a positive sense of time, which goes by from the past to the future implying much more complex temporalities during the process. This way, in the series *Descent into Heaven* (1994) desire is manifested as yearning. There the nostalgic gaze seems to be attached to a certain sense of timelessness, based on indefinite resources close to pictorialism. As in recollection, those images are offered to us in a diffused fashion.

On the contrary, *Fragments of a Mendicant Desire* (1994-95) attempts to register not delayed time, but a temporary course, an occurrence which refers to desire because of its constant mobility, emigrating from one place to another. Furthermore, by recording movement and resorting to infrared film, the desire

us as a subtle confirmation of our temporality. Thus the joint presence of glowing and toning-down on the image tell us about a transience that threatens to be persistent.

Now, this voyage by Tischler can also be described as the artist's progressive approach to his own desire and sexuality. Thus, if at the beginning he looked for romantic places, he then shifted to the dancing of bodies and their erotic relationships to finally exhibit his own intimacy. So, by including himself in the scene, the artist intends to abolish that distance separating him from the object, thus offering himself as a point of reference.

"Photographing is appropriating what is photographed," states Susan Sontag. And somehow, the photographer's greatest closeness becomes the culmination of that magic value entailed by photography. This way, if what characterizes magic is the effectiveness of the significance—the moment when saying is doing—then Tischler's pictures are offered here as the desire and, at the same time, its satisfaction. In this fashion, a new temporality is incorporated into that recording of desire: anticipation. According to it, the event should follow its magic representation.

Yet for Tischler love is essential; it precedes the act of photographing. The physical bond necessarily established by the picture to its point of reference is here, also, a link that goes through affection: "Choosing desire as a subject always puts you in a vulnerable position. Nothing valuable can be created without having loved it

La Sagrada Familia
From serie **Bajar al Cielo**
1994
Gold toned gelatin silver
print, 22 × 34 cm
(40 × 50 cm with frame)

Jaime David Tischler 1960

Jaime David Tisc

would be involved in the magnificence emanating from the bodies, from their energy and not only from their physical presence.

However, on their journey, those aura-filled bodies ended up in the mud. In *Feet of Clay* (1996), the theme of desire refers to its most earthly dimension. Here, the gold toning emphasizes the chromatic value of mud while introducing a certain sacredness. The mud implies a dual symbolic reference: to the fertile and vital, but also to what becomes degraded, as well as to death itself.

In fact, the series *Threads of Desire* (1998) completes a cycle where the relationships to death are addressed. As much as they intend to portray fletting instants, these pictures appear to

intensely," has said the artist. Perhaps that is why there are so many attempts of image indefiniteness, as well as a resistance to display through the use of several technical procedures and decisions aimed at making the reference disappear, so that no fixation whatsoever is possible.

The impossibility of fixing the desire is, likewise, photography's fatality upon retaining an image that—as Barthes insists—*has already been*. In Tischler, there is an emphasis on the imaginary more than on reality. At the end of the day, defeated by the fantasy of a feasible goal, he postpones the return to a remote Ithaca to take pleasure in the road.

Tamara Díaz Bringas

School

As soon as I sat down in the back of the classroom
I realised it was the wrong position to be in.
I tried to be ignored but it was useless.
My entrance had spoilt the situation, although
the children were having excellent fun.
Not one of them was able to look in another
direction.
I swung the camera back and forth, but didn't
know what to aim at.
I felt hopelessly out of place, I felt trapped and
annoyed by my indecisiveness.
The teacher, a woman in her fifties, didn't budge.
She was carelessly waving her fan, her eyes
fixed on the paintings behind me.
After some desperate moments I stood up
from my corner, and just before leaving the
room I managed to gather my last bit of
courage and, only for a few seconds, aimed the
lens at the class straight in front of me.

Tiong Ang

Tiong Ang 1961

School
1999
Videoprojection,
still from video

Crash Landings - Bruchlandungen
The Subjective photography immediately after the fall

My great grandfather August Riepenhausen, who was a landscape photographer, produced many postcards of Halle and its surroundings. Thus art hung above my bed from my early diaper years on.

My interest in this medium was awakened through the exhibition *Photography as Art/Art as Photography* which curator Peter Weiermair organised in the Tiroler Landesmuseum Ferdinandeum with the help of my mother in 1979. At the time I was 18 and was allowed to carry some of the photographs which were being shown up to the third floor where the exhibition rooms were. Here I saw all the top photographers from all over the world as well as from history of the photography. It became clear to me that I did not need to photograph anything because all the photos in the world already existed. In 1992 the Lomography Society was founded and one didn't look through the viewfinder anymore but shot from the hip instead. My cousin Clemens Bruch gave me his Lomo and I began to lomograph. I have a drawer full of Lomos which are all unfocused, and no one can tell who it was or where it was. Out of 1250 pictures only 50 are worth anything. I began, however, to like the 7 c 10 cm format, which cost 90 *groschen* at *Billa-heute*, and since eight photos fit on to one A4 page, the binders filled up in proper archival manner.

that sometimes the falls came one after the other and then sometimes there was a long pause between them. I began in May, 1996, to take a photo, if possible, with every fall. Since then I've had 307 falls. In 1996 I fell 99 times; in 1997 133 times; in 1998 54 times; in 1999 12 times and this year 3 times.

Originally I called the falls *Fritzelacke*, which was named after the logo of the O Fritz Paint Company: the apprentice Fritz is depicted in a full pratfall next to a toppled can of paint. The term *einen Fritzelack reißen*, is used colloquially in Vienna. I heard it for the first time from the actor Hanno Pöschl when I met him in a curve after a descent from *Vollererhof* near Salzburg with the mountain bike at the relatively high speed of 65 kilometers per hour. That was 1989 during the shooting of *Illona and Kurti*, directed by Reinhard Schwabenitzky. From that moment on, I have used this phrase with great pleasure although not everyone understands me, not even some of the Viennese

This book should actually have been called *Fritzelacke*, but thanks to Gabi Orac's idea *Bruchlandungen (Crashlandings)*, I have finally given my name the honour it deserves.

The photos were always taken directly after the falls, so usually there was no time to choose a frame while lying on the ground trying to explain as succinctly as possible to my friendly fellow humans who were trying to help me up. Almost everyone got out of the photos, except for friends who knew and they were mostly laughing. Thus all the photos are equally valu-

Martin Bruch 1961

Since the Lomos were unfocused, I chose the one-way Fun-Gold from Kodak with flash. It was sturdy, small, light and 99.5% recycleable. I simply always carry this camera in my shoulder bag wherever I go.

The fact that from around 1995 on I landed on the ground more and more often whenever I came to a stop with my scooter, created a certain excitement which I documented with a photo. As a result of the progressive spread of my multiple sclerosis (in a wheelchair since May, 1997), I was not spared further falls. I noted down place, date and time. By observing the time and date more exactly, one can see

able, whether more or less successful. On some occasions there was no possibility to shoot a photo, for example, on an escalator or in the entrance to the *Zur Goldenen Glocke Inn*, where I was lying at the feet of the half blind architect Margarete Schütte-Lihotzky and couldn't manage to get the camera out of the shoulder bag before two nervous waiters quickly righted me and the wheelchair. In such a case, the words "Without a Photo" are written after the description of the place and a black space stands in for the missing picture. I am alive and life is beautiful!

Martin Bruch

Wien, Mariahilferstraße
89/36
10.02.97, 21:23
C-print

Wien, Margaretestraße
108/15, store-room
07.08.98, 09:43
C-Print

Summit in Venice: Lehanka meets Dürer and Mishelanshelo

Per favore PRENDERE PLAZA: The invitation with which the artist greets the audience from his wooden benches that appear to be rigged together out of roof laths, rather than constructed. He artfully adapts the high standard of the 49. Biennale—*Platea dell'umanità / Plateau of Humankind / Plateau der Menschheit / Plateau de l'humanité* to a level he feels more at ease with (and is probably more digestable for the visitor). This attitude is typical of the sociable and communicative qualities of Marko Lehanka's art. However, his extremely free "translation" of the German expression "Bitte Platz nehmen" into Italian shows a perfidy that perhaps not in life, but in art, one can say nothing against and which should always be kept in mind where Marko Lehanka's work is concerned.

Of course it would have been easier for him to look up the correct Italian expression—*si accomodi!*—in the dictionary. Doing so would be completely alien to Marko Lehankas' idiosyncrasy for any aspect of what is considered *correct*. The ensuing frictions bring about the same sparks that can always be seen in his eyes; we can detect accurate and precise calculations in most of his work that initially appears casual or created by chance; it is the same process of the so-called "luck" of the fisherman, whose great catches don't resulte from sheer chance but are the more than deserved prize resulting from a mix of perseverance and the membership in some club of "Friends of radical Fishing Ltd." Although it cannot be completely excluded that he is only pretending to be a fish-lover and is, in reality, an extremely crafty and perfidious person who loves to stir up all the once-clear waters around him.

Si accomodi: Whether by chance or not, it would be really difficult to find an expression more provocatively contraddicting the core of Marko Lehanka's work. Because his art is not *comoda*—comfortable—; and *accomodarsi*—feel at home (in it)—is only temporarily possible, if at all. And anyone who not only reads correctly the writing on Lehanka's signs, but also understands the graphical choice of colors, typical of warning signs, will soon suspect that the friendly greeting, "Take a seat", might hide a certain insidiousness. Not: *si accomodi,* but: *Per favore PRENDERE PLAZA*—and *subito!* Or even shorter: *Sit!*

Platz, Plaza, Basta. Marko Lehanka has recently had considerable experience with squares, lately known as *Plazas,* and expecially with their builders, in important German cities such as Frankfurt (and soon if not now, in Offenback or in Muehlheim an der Ruhr). His design of the *Telephone box fountain* for the Frankfurter *Main-Plaza* won a prize in a competition but remained on paper because it did not correspond to the "man-of-the-world" concepts of those "man-of-the-world" clients. As Andrea Bee sarcastically but accurately remarked, rather than the Telephone box model 1953 flooded with water, they would have preferred a "beautiful fountain coated with precious materials by Albrecht Dürer; if necessary, Michelangelo would have done too."

It would almost seem that Lehanka draw his conclusions from these thoughts that, at first glance, seem unrealistic. In any case, in Venice he is the patron of an artistic summit of a special type. From the top of a tower, comparable to the "*Gezeugs*" that Albrecht Dürer had recommended to those who "wanted victory over the rebelling farmers" (in: "Underweysung der Messung mit dem Zirckel und Richtscheyt", 1525), a farmer is smoking a cigarette, "apparently lost in thought and self-satisfied" (Andreas Bee), enjoying his "privileged view" of the totally drunk *Bacchus.* In 1993 Lehanka built the sculpture while staying in the Florentine Villa Romana, much to the horror of a fellow sculptor also staying in Florence: beginning from the feet, than modelling the legs, slowly bending under the increasing weight of the body.

Conceiving and creating the statue of a human figure not as a volume developing from the inside out—from the skeleton to the skin, passing throught muscles—but rather as a mass of papier maché building up from the sole to the head, is a notion conceivable either by somebody who is completely ignorant about, or by someone who knows exactly what meaning materials and means play in the visual arts. But nobody can teach anything on this reguard to Marko Lehanka, a professional "handy-man".

In his famous study on "Wild Thinking", 1962, the French ethnologist and cultural anthropologist Claude Lévi-Strauss defined "handy-man" (French: *bricoleur*) someone "who uses his hands with materials that are alternative in comparison to those used by an expert"—just as deviating, in the eyes of somebody reasoning in conformity with the categories of modern sciences, as the methods of that mythical "Science of the concreteness", defined by Lévi-Strauss as "the first" rather than "the primitive one". Precisely his "wild thinking"—a line of thought that has not yet lost its contact to the power of imagination and intuition and that he describes as "a manner of intellectual creativeness (*bricolage)."*

According to Lévis-Strauss, the *bricoleur* (who differs from an engineer in that he makes do with whatever heterogeneous raw materials and instruments he has available) is not an artist. However, what happens when someone cheekily comes along and has this "*bricoleur*-type [...] dialogue with material and the means of creation" (Lévi-Strauss) simply as *Art...?* This can be seen in the case of Marko Lehanka. Then is it possible that this "rubbish" (only partially "there by chance", it made its way into the Atelier mostly because one "might" be able to "do something with it"—and now is handy) may not only become Dürer's *Bauernsaeule,* but possibly an *Eiersauele* (after Brancusi? Or the homage to the colleague Piero di Cosimo, who according to Vasari, "was so in love with Art that he heeded no comfort" and limited himself to eating hard eggs that he "boiled while making glue to save fire... and not just six or eight at a time, but nearer fifty?"). Therefore even the mad but nonetheless clear provocation constituted by an "unsuccessful" Michelangelo copy, juxtaposed to a *High Voltage Stag,* whose synthetic skin lies over a skeleton of roof laths "bones" nailed together, can offer an example of what meaning can have today—still or also—the definition of "sculpture".

Marcel Baumgartner

Marko Lehanka 1961

1:1 Model von Platz
Plaza Basta
2001
Mixed media, detail
(Bacchus, Wilderer,
Highvoltage Stag)
9,20 × 15,60 m

Psychedelic invasion of the Battleship "Potemkin" into Sergei Eisenstein's tautological hallucinations by Alexander Roitburd

In 1925 Maxim Shtraukh, who was entrusted by Sergei Eisenstein to collect historical materials about the events of 1905 which had to be used for the epic movie about the first Russian revolution showed to his boss an issue of French magazine *Illustration* with an expressive drawing depicting the massacre of the Odessa revolutionaries on the historic Potemkin steps. The drawing was the work of imagination of some French magazine illustrator who was commissioned to depict the bloody crimes of the czarist regime. The artisan producing drawings for the press, which during those remote days still hadn't switched to photography, could hardly imagine what kind of impact on the history of modernist cinema his horrific depiction of the events he never saw could have.

Eisenstein was not interested in the true depiction of historic events. He was interested in the power of images. A page from the illustrated French magazine gave birth to one of the most important movies of the 20th century and to one of the most expressive scenes of violence created by world cinematography.

Eisenstein recreated history, and the history produced by him became more important, more convincing and truer that the real events. His mythology of the Potemkin steps, of the pram, jumping from step to step among the dead bodies, of the bullets smashing the glasses of a screaming woman stayed with us

and completely replaced the reality of the year 1905, which was ugly and bloody, but different. There is no historical proof of any butchery on the famous steps, despite the fact that bullets were flying around Odessa that year and many people later remembered the heavy sound of the shots of the cannons from the rebellious battleship.

Other Soviet avant-garde movies of the period of *Battleship Potemkin* were trying to undertake very similar task. If Eisenstein was recreating, or actually creating history, such film directors as Lev Kuleshov or Dziga Vertov were creating new reality.

The main tool for such manipulation was the method of montage discovered by Kuleshov, who in his famous movie sketches united in different order the same steals thus engendered totally different meanings. Kuleshov discovered the philosophers' stone not only of 20th century cinema, but of art in general. It is possible to say that his method became the foundation of propaganda, this new church of the politicized world. Montage was the first step to the discovery of virtual reality. It was possible to create it only after the death of the meaning achieved through the widespread application of montage. An artist received the power to produce any meaning using any kind of material, just by reshuffling the images. The only criterion of this new world was the power of the image itself.

It is simply logical that Alexander Roitburd used as the raw material for his video installation the legendary film by Eisenstein. Roitburd grew up in Odessa and spent nearly 40 years of

his life in the set of the Eisenstein movie walking practically every day up the famous steps. So the jumping pram became a part of the artist's personal hallucinations. Rotburd's remake of Eisenstein is a sharp parody on the method of montage. The artist is anatomizing the scene on the steps, transforming Eisenstein's picturesque violence into the endless denseness in the discotheque of history. However Roitburd is not satisfied with the simple execution of an exercise *à la Kuleshov*, proving that any meaning is just an illusion. He is adding his own touch to the film. Shorts of youngsters on skate boards jumping down the steps are competing with the legendary pram. Among the victims of the czarist bullets are not only revolutionary workers, but some creatures which came to the Potemkin steps directly from *Star Wars*. It is not even clear if the butchers belonged to the czarist army, or to our days—we are offered a line of Ukrainian riot police at the top of the steps.

The dialogue of Eisenstein and Roitburd, the Soviet avant-garde and contemporary art didn't exhaust all the layers of meanings of the work. The artist created it not just as a video work, but as a video installation. The first time the work was shown at the Odessa art museum, where the Eisenstein-Roitburd movie was projected onto the 1950s socialist realist painting depicting the uprising on the battleship "Potemkin". The baroque images of the huge Stalinist painting were reduced to the role of a screen for the projection of Eisenstein's ballet of violence choreographed by Roitburd.

Konstantin Akinsha

Alexander Roitburd 1961

Psychedelic invasion
of the battleship
"Potëmkin" into Sergey
Eisestein's tautological
hallucinations
1998
Video installation,
view of installation

The inspiration for Hai Bo's "photographic couples" is the plentiful documentation of souvenir-photos taken during the Great Cultural Revolution, surfacing from old drawers in every Chinese family. Seeing, years later, the snapshots taken about thirty years ago (most of them date from the '70s) arouses a feeling that is not merely an agonizing nostalgia. It is not just a game of recognizing yourself and remembering your schoolmates of bygone years like for us looking at old schooltime pictures. It is a whole era, a world, a shared credo, that are recalled in the black and white of these well-composed shots. The people are placed in order, in rows, so that they all have the same importance and nobody prevails over the others. The clothes are the blue-gray ones a number of Westerners still like to imagine the Chinese wearing, all with the same cut and identical close-fitting collar. Even the girls' hairstyles follow the standards of the period: short bobs or thick braids that the vainer ones display full length, while the others wear them hanging down their backs.

Starting from a person of the group, an acquaintance, Hai Bo undertook the long, interesting process of the "recovery" of others in their present lives, scattered in various cities, each one with a different reality and a personal experience. In China when two people Hai Bo's age (the 1962 contingent) meet, they need but a few sentences relating to their parents' experience during the years fol-

is a strong sense of homologation. The lengthy task of connection, made of phone-calls, encounters, negotiations, reassurances, that leads Hai Bo to the final moment when all the members of the original group photograph are assembled and rearranged in the same order to take a new picture that seals the present, "conserving it for the future", appears to hold in reserve some unforseen results.

As mere viewers of the final snapshot, which we see next to the original one, we can but imagine the intensity of emotions experienced by the persons who were brought together after such a long time, and wonder if they still have anything in common, if they will find a way to communicate and recognize one another, after their paths have parted for so long. We would expect that in the China of today, where everybody can dress and wear their hair the way they want, where you can also live without *danwei* (work unit) and *liangpiao* (vouchers for cereals), single personalities would forcefully stand out, styles differ, people finally be themselves. A careful examination of the two pictures leads us to think that instead it is not so; expressions, postures appear for the most part unchanged, if you exclude the inevitable physical marks left by time. The choice of the artist to strictly stick to the original poses allows us to concentrate precisely on the faces, on those mirrors of the soul that material well-being does not seem to have modified in substance.

Hai Bo 1962

lowing the "Liberation" (1949) and the decade of the Cultural Revolution (1966-76 circa) to get a clear picture and discover eventual analogies and common acquaintances. This prelude takes place at each new encounter. Actually even now what strikes the Chinese when, re-arranging drawers, they are suddenly confronted with the images of those days,

On the other hand there is perhaps the desire—although unconscious—in the portrayed persons to erase in a flash the lapse of time between one snapshot and the other, and start all over from today with a fresh enthusiasm, freed of the cynicism that life and time had left in their souls.

Monica Dematté

They n° 3
1998–2000
Photograph, 78 × 200 cm

Bridge
1998–2000
Photograph, 127 × 360 cm

Tuomo Manninen's photographic series of *Nepal* (1995) manifests a silent protest against mainstream Third World imaging.

For this series, Manninen chose not to depict destitution and poverty as such, but to carry on shooting the same thoughtfully arranged, carefully-lit group portraits he shot back on home ground.

In all of this work, Manninen seeks out not the exotic but the everyday; not the different but the common. Thus in his Kathmandu series we are not presented with human objects repressed by traditions of documentary or pretensions of piety, the "others" forcibly removed from their own environment and transplanted into the Western mediascape. On the contrary, we find lorry drivers, girl scouts and the elephant keepers of the Jawalakhel Zoo radiating human dignity and pride—entirely on their own terms.

It is within the framework of the group that we may find a person at his/her best. Here the individual is stronger than he/she would be alone; at the same time, however, he/she is not yet obscured in the mass, is still a distinctive personal voice as, indeed, in a choir.

A community or group is something we can locate somewhere between the "free" individual imagined by market forces and the "common" society construed by politics. A space where individuals are willing to surrender their own

these close communities, many of which in fact are older than the state. They remind us of an era when a vulnerable individual would have to seek the protection of a clan or a guild, of a brotherhood.

Innocent as the enthusiasm of committed amateurs may seem at first glance, do not be fooled—there is something sullen, even threatening, hidden in these images. What happens if the midwives go on strike? And in the event of the city slipping into the sea, it would certainly be good to know a few members of the Ice Swimmers Club.

The nation state, the concept of which is barely 200 years old, has been in place in Finland for a mere three generations. This new, artificial identity embodies an older, more emotional mode of association—the inner circles of secret rituals, codes and uniforms, vows and pledges of eternal loyalty among the initiated. At their core, these groups are subversive. By this we refer not to the Hell's Angels MC, but the seemingly more inconspicuous groupings of the Taxidermists and the Association of Wives of Professors.

The inner circle may well be the only space of true loyalty, *ethnos*, to which we must eventually return once our present magic wears off. Once the prosperous and omnipotent "free", market-coined Überconsumer turns out, in the light of reality, to be just a drunk salesman crying alone, the door of the empty mini-bar swinging noisily in the wintry wind, far away from home. Once the utopia of our common

Tuomo Manninen 1962

will for a greater good, since it is they who still define and benefit from the outcome.

In countries where no pervasive state structures exist or that are crippled by a crisis, people still have to rely on the extended family, an inner circle of trusted friends and colleagues. Some of these associations are traditional (the thousand-year-old Buddhist monastery), some are products of modernisation (the kindergarten and the school) and some, even, of post-modernisation (the garage rock band).

Industrialised Western societies too are held together by tiny, invisible strings comprised of

Europe boils down to mere collective fights against procurement fraud and diseased cattle epidemics.

The inner circle is the one unit we can define without irony, with pride even, as "We".

Self-containing, restricted and restricting as a group identity may be, it is, as we discover, universal. Tuomo Manninen, being the methodical humanist that he is, shows us the local globally.

When our "we" and the "we" of others confront each other, the result is genuinely *glocal*.

Timo Harakka

**Pashupati school scouts
(Kathmandu)**
1995
Chromogenic color print
(photograph),
102 × 102 cm

Association of wives
of professors (Helsinki)
2000
Chromogenic color print
(photograph),
102 × 102 cm

Ice-swimmer club
(Helsinki)
1996
Chromogenic color print
(photograph),
102 × 102 cm

A mere copier of nature can never produce anything good.

(Sir Joshua Reynolds)

(In answer to a lady who said that a landscape reminded her of his work) *Yes Madam nature is creeping in.*

(James McNeill Whistler)

Olaf Nicolai's work has to do with the complexity and ambiguity of relationships between individuals and society, as well as the interspaces that arise between the binary combinations whereby we try to schematize reality, natural/artificial, original/reproduced, ethical/aesthetic. A particularly complex investigation at this date when the overwhelming acceleration of means of communication, the global market, the increasing gap between industrial countries and the rest of the world, scientific discoveries in genetics, are challenging traditional representation processes and resistence to power systems, and further fragmenting the map of possibilities. Instead of a direct, didactic analysis, Nicolai creates a short-circuit by provoking parallel situations within the very system, altering pre-existing, functioning situations to reveal their contradictions and potentials, and by using a broad range of media tools and cultural, scientific disciplines, including the web and botany, design and social science, fashion and the leisure industry. In his installation *Interieur/Landschaft. Ein Kabinett* (1996-1997) at Documenta X, Nicolai presented five minia-

on wallpaper that reproduced, in improbable shades of brown, repetitive stylized plants, an "invented", "arranged" nature to be endlessly reproduced for the "naturalization" of the spaces we live and work in. Coming full circle, on that same occasion at Kassel, the artist had a computer screensaver designed, active during the exhibition, with the same wallpaper pattern and a sound-tape reproducing forest birdsongs, delocating the same operation into our contemporary tool for work, entertainment and archiving data *par excellence*. In another work, *Modul* (1998), he transfers inside the exhibition area the real-scale module of a New York urban design article, a bench built around a flowerbed with little trees, creating an incongruous situation illustrating the interchangeability between inside and outside by "staging" a "natural" space. In *...fading in, fading out, fading away...* (2000), Nicolai "re-arranged" and re-contextualized works of art belonging to the Westfälischer Kunstverein of Münster, where he had been invited to exhibit. In order to reconstruct the historical changes in the concept of collecting and archiving images over the past two centuries, the artist compared the institution's collection with the archive of an online company specializing in cartoons. The artist isolated and reproduced *ad infinitum* on posters or wallpaper details of works belonging to the Kunstverein, say a drop of blood spilled from Christ's flagellated body in a sixteenth-century painting by Jan Baegert.

Mario Codognato

Olaf Nicolai 1962

ture landscapes in the same number of sculptures that he called "biological", made of volcanic rock upon which tiny plants were made to grow. Thus an open system was formed, characterized by the formal unpredictability of the growth of the plants—live elements—all during the exhibition, and the exercisable control on every other aspect of the landscape, touching on the issue of dichotomy and the dialectic of natural/artificial, outside (natural territory) and inside (human territory, where nature is artificially reproduced). That proposal was further repeated by the other elements forming the installation, a series of photographs on luminous panels realistically featuring, like open windows, a luxuriant vegetation, in turn hung

Nach der Natur I
1997
Lightbox (documenta X),
100 × 154 cm,
edition of 3

Portrait of the Artist
as a Weeping Narcissus
2000
Polyester,
90 × 156 × 268 cm

Following pages

**Bubblegram – A Street
Surfing Painting**
1999
Street marking paint
on bitumen, 2,5 × 4 m

Dresden 68
2000
Lamp made of 16
polyhedral elements,
200 × 200 × 200 cm

Untitled (Blutstropfen)
2000
Dimensions variable

**MAZE (The Dukes
of Hazzard)**
2001
Mixed media (Concrete,
Painted concrete), length
24 m, width 17 m,
height 30 cm

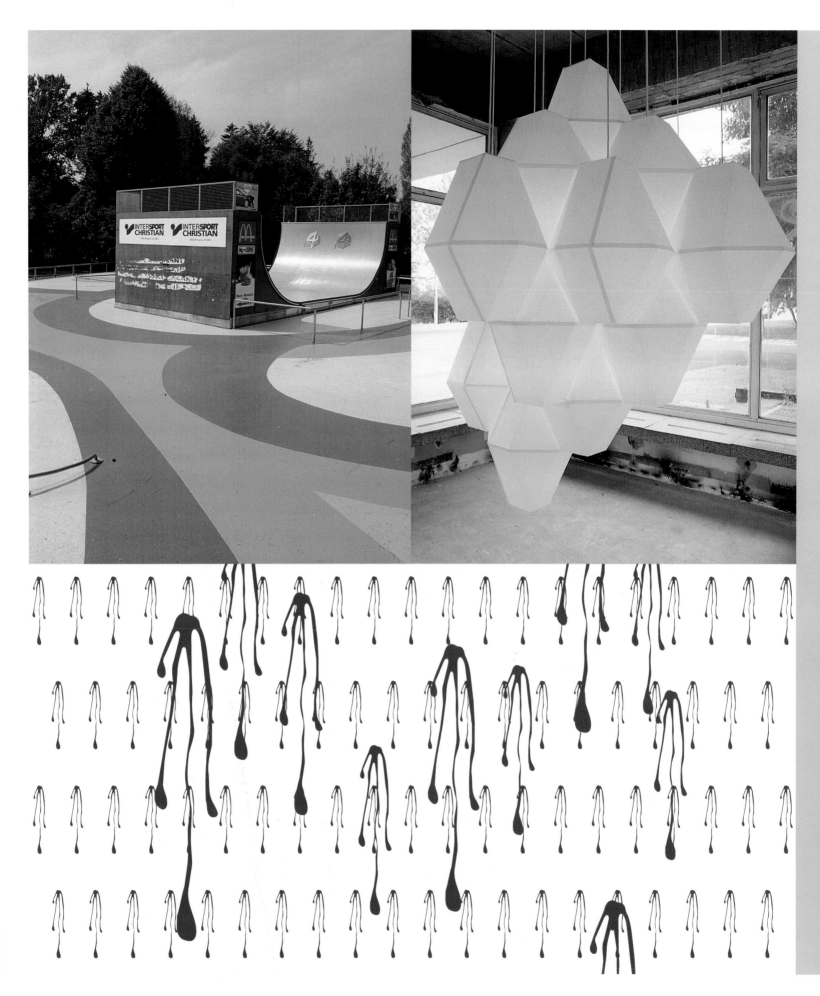

Olaf Nicolai

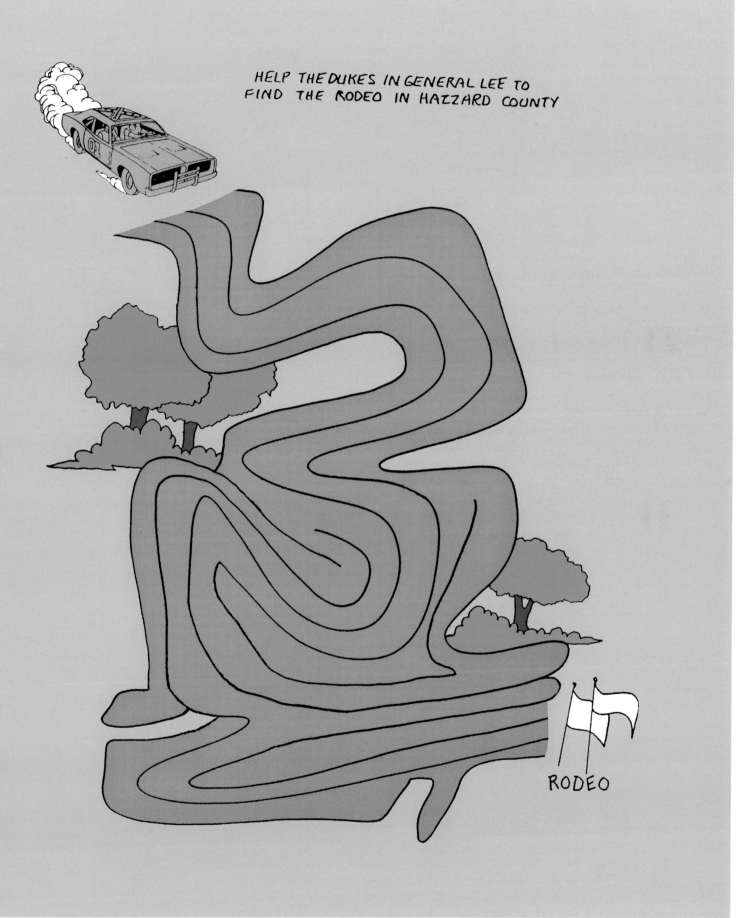

The Bunny Lake
Collection
2000
Mixed media installation
and DVD video projection

Even before Pop, art with more than a glancing interest in popular culture has been accused of moral infirmity, aesthetic impoverishment and cultural opportunism. During the 1990s, in Britain, when young art was under constant suspicion for its love affair with the media, no artist got more flak than Georgina Starr for her alleged bubblegum sensibility. Starr has proved, however, that her exploration of identity through the products of popular culture doesn't have to discard sweetness and bright colours in order to be bruising and eerie.

Starr's new work has not abandoned the lures of popcorn culture for more serious pursuits; soreness and distress always lurked within her restaging and reinvention of mainstream culture. The Bunny Lakes series, set off at Anthony Reynolds Gallery, London, in September 2000 with *The Bunny Lakes Are Coming*, is not only Starr's most elaborate and large-scale project to date, it is also her most heartbreaking. Bunny Lake is an emblem of the mournful anger that fell across the UK last year following the abduction, assault and murder of the angelic, little Sarah Payne. *Bunny Lake is Missing* is the title of Otto Preminger's 1965 movie about a girl who never returns home from her first day at school. There are no records of Bunny at the school and nobody remembers seeing her there. Bunny Lake never appears in the movie that takes her name, and for most of the time her absence is evidence that the 'mother' is a fantasist. Starr's extended reworking of the

When a keyhole top's erotic promise becomes a formalised sign of attack, every hem is a scar; every buttonhole a wound. A model struts across the catwalk with her head wrapped in a hood without an opening: an image of fashion's cutting edge blends with asphyxiation and disposal. When a model emerges with the remains of a bush around her neck, the game is up, you might think. But the theme never fully settles.

Bunny Lake is neither an emblem of the resistance to fashion's political unconscious, nor of ironic submission. If anything, she is a casualty of her own virtue. It is the purity and goodness of these suffering children that singles them out for ritual corruption. Bunny Lake is a kind of martyr—which is just another way of saying that her private and very lonely hell stands in for a general trauma and why Starr converts Bunny Lake into the plural right from the start. When Starr reanimates Bunny as a mob of cute vigilantes, we endorse their aggression because it corresponds to our anguish. In *The Bunny Lakes Are Coming*, the gang attack the occupants of cars at a Drive-In; for *The Bunny Lake Collection*, they burst in at end of the catwalk show and gun down the models. Infant *Charlie's Angels* would be on the side of law and order; the Bunny Lakes are not.

In the video of the events prior to the catwalk massacre, one of the Bunny Lakes dashes across the road, peers down a lane and beckons the others on. It is a stock scene from TV

Georgina Starr 1962

Bunny Lake motif is a heart-rending study of the betrayal of innocence and the uncontainable retribution it provokes.

The Bunny Lake Collection, the second of the series, was first shown as a live catwalk event at Pink Summer Gallery, Genoa, in October 2000. Themes developed in *The Bunny Lakes Are Coming* installation, of a young girl's victimisation and an incipient narrative of avenging violence, are criss-crossed with the craving and glamour of haute-couture. Tailored slits and holes often decorate the surfaces of fashion, so the *Bunny Lake Collection* can disguise its butchery with chic virtuosity. As the traces of violence accumulate, though, the facade of fashion's innocuousness tears into shreds.

and film. The gesture connotes action and danger. At the same time, of course, we are being beckoned, too: we are *with them*. We are still with them when they cut down the models with their pistols. Blood-splattered dresses on a pile of catwalk models might protest against the fashion industry but the bloodstains are too decorative for that. So, the avoidance of pat political answers has an aesthetic correlate in this violent scene: do the bloodstains ruin the dresses or complete them? The Bunny Lakes escape analysis and then escape. And with the sorry state of our society, no field of human activity can safely say it is not in line for the Bunny Lakes' wrath.

Dave Beech

154

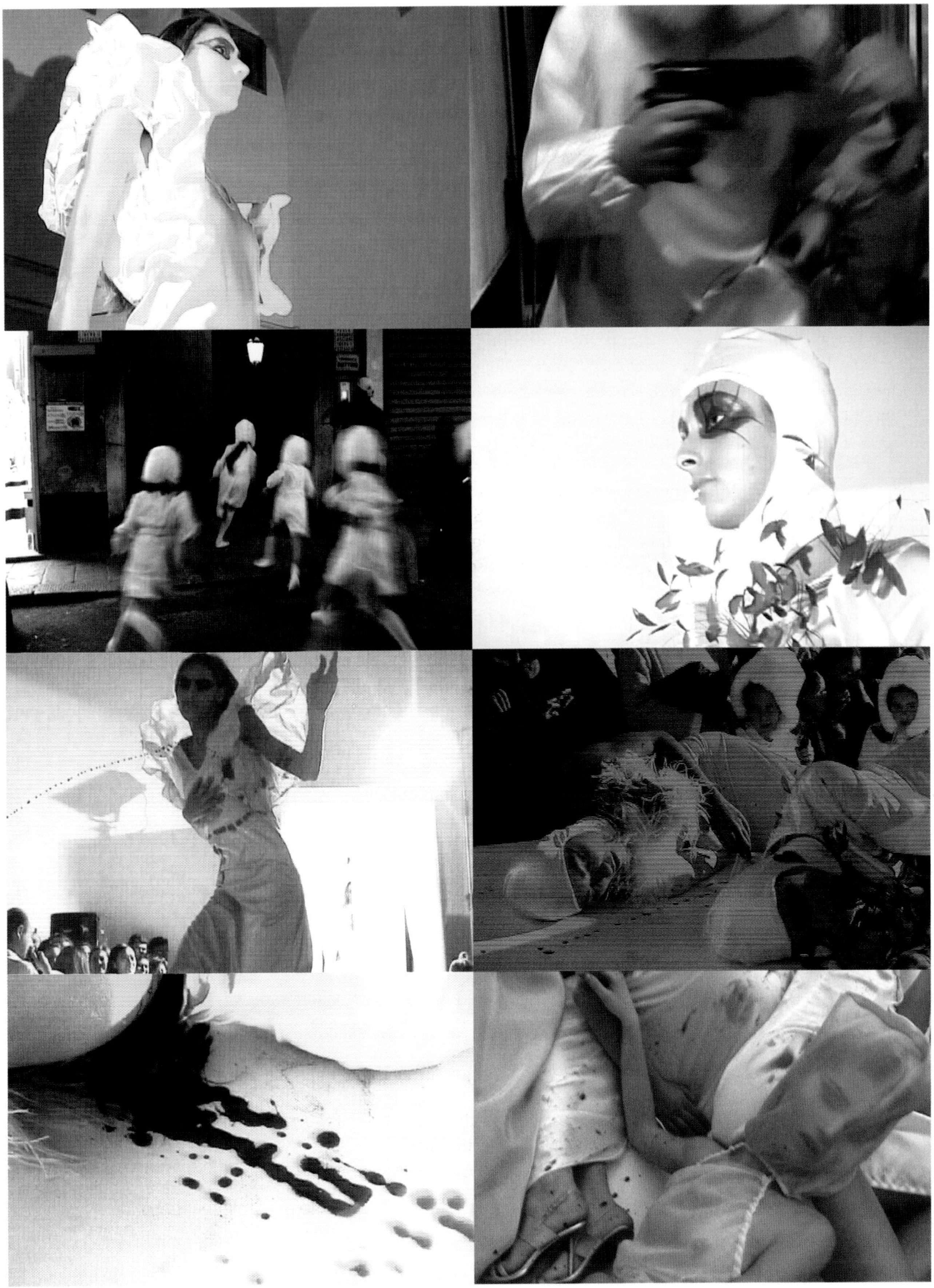

hon

What is possible? What is feasible if for a stitch in time, is to muffle the world and its affairs—only briefly, a mere wink—and in another moment we will set things back as they are. Not to worry. It is something that I do not often recommend, nor do often, but exceptions always exist. This is one.

This installation was always destined to stretch out in Venice as the intrepid, yawning metaphor it is. Its great reach into the world, free of the dreary cultural references droning on, was to be an instrument of contemplation that would be nearly theological. Do-Ho Suh's work can be attended to as a truly meaningful and truly rare example where international exhibitions are concerned, because it inspires by creating the proper atmosphere where art may grip universal themes and as a result provide a consequence of ideas with heart.

Last September in New York, every cultural allusion was thoroughly ambiguous as I strode *Floor 1997-2000*, supported, by each and every tiny upheld palm of thousands of women and men fashioned in a style reminiscent of social realism. Sheer numbers, compounded by a scrolling sense of scale allowed the subjugation of the individual to dissolve back into collective power. Scale became a way of organizing information and consciousness where cultural sociology was concerned. Do-Ho Suh possesses an uncanny gift for launching meaning from a sliding discrepancy between scale and perspective,

tasies where they lord over a ridiculous and funny world populated by miniature people who could even fight wars over the proper way to break an egg. At this blithe moment, his art disappears into the edge of entertainment and immediately gives rise to every stripe of imagination while still reaching deep into the real world. But there is another level, nearly theological where Do-Ho organizes this lesson in the balance between selfhood and the greatergood. In the way that *Powers of Ten*, the Charles and Ray Eames film, carried us through a cosmology otherwise unseen, vast and complex at any scale, or from any perspective, Do-Ho too is Unitarian. He envisions shifting scales to exemplify the balance between historical unconsciousness and cosmological realization, perhaps even something beyond this shift, something in the general direction of enlightenment. In such a secular age, all of this can be startling. He leans on stylistic ingenuousness and phenomenological utility to achieve a universalizing experience glimpsing what it means to be human *being*, not "being" as a noun, but as the theological form of that verb.

What is possible? Perhaps this work has made it possible to seriously consider, for the first time in a long while, a solitary moment walking across this glass floor where one glimpses their "hon", as Do-Ho translated for me; their "soul". It is worth considering even while Do-Ho's soulful morality tale waits to be told in some parts of this world I have shuttered out for the past few hundred words or so.

Ronald Jones

Floor
1997-2000
Plastic figures, glass plates, phenolic boards, polyurethane resin,
40 modules,
100 × 100 cm each

Do-Ho Suh 1962

and in such a way as to permit space to epitomize history. I think back to the way *High School Uni-Form*, 1997 was exhibited in a room custom made to boost the temperature of claustrophobia already congenital to military dress uniforms. At one level of course, *Who Am We?* is the swift demonization of humanity, where a homogeneous culture anesthetizes individuality *for some greater good*. Moral lessons and decisions are implied. In this way *High School Uni-Form* and *Who Am We?* are linked. But *Floor 1997-2000* presents something else, and something more subtle, even poignant.

It is important to acknowledge the lighthearted edge to *Floor 1997-2000* where adults can visit Lilliput, and watch children succumb to their fan-

Who am We?
1996-2000
Wallpaper, variable

What? *A-Portable, 2001.* A refurbished shipping container that functions as a mobile gynaecological clinic, transportable on ships and trucks. It includes a reception room, sanitary space and treatment room.

Who? A collaborative effort between Dr Rebecca Gomperts, founder of Women on Waves in Amsterdam, and Joep van Lieshout, founder of AVL (Atelier van Lieshout) in Rotterdam, where the container was designed and constructed. Dr Gomperts will make first-trimester abortions available to women in countries where the procedure is illegal by performing them in the A-Portable in international waters—19 km from shore and outside the jurisdiction of national laws. Van Lieshout just declared his collective atelier a free state; AVL-Ville, 2001- is a civic art work that challenges the Dutch state monopoly on community by producing its own food, education, arsenal, energy, sewage treatment and even currency.

When? In June 2001, Dr Gomperts set sail with a similar container and an all-women crew to an undisclosed location; she works only in collaboration with local women's groups and provides first trimester abortions as well as contraceptives, counselling, education and training for free. Van Lieshout has offered Dr Gomperts a place to operate A-Portable in AVL-Ville, which opened in April 2001, when she is not at sea.

year; abortion is the most-performed medical intervention, 20 times more common than an appendectomy; making abortion illegal increases the number of procedures since access to family planning is also curtailed; the Netherlands, where abortion and birth control are paid by the state, has the world's lowest abortion rate. For van Lieshout, the Women on Waves project reflects the philosophy and strategy of AVL-Ville, a place where existing rules are challenged and undecided ones are exploited. AVL does not approve projects but simply does them.

How? AVL has constructed shipping containers for making weapons, bombs, alcohol and medicine as well as the fully-operational AVL-Hospital, 1998. For Dr Gomperts, AVL was an obvious choice, not only for its experience, but also for its open designs. She and van Lieshout wanted to avoid the bunker aspect of most abortion clinics and create a comfortable and welcoming space. To make the small treatment room agreeable, sharp edges and straight angles have been eliminated.

Is this art? To ask reveals an outdated set of assumptions. To understand the work one must move from ontology (what is art?) to pragmatics (what can art do?). Herein lies a possible revival of avant-garde politics—no longer historically "ahead", nor operating through shock and estrangement, but rather producing works that make things possible

AVL / Joep Van Lieshout 1963

AVL / Joep

Why? For Dr Gomperts, A-Portable is a concrete solution to a world health problem and will provoke legislative change through media attention and activist pressure. The facts speak for themselves: The World Health Organisation estimates that 20 million illegal abortions cause the death of up to 100,000 women every

right now through their very materiality and use. In typical AVL style, A-Portable does not thematise, represent nor illustrate the problem of abortion; it imposes a new geo-political reality that challenges the status quo in ways that cannot be fathomed, let alone controlled.

Jennifer Allen

Atelier Van Lieshout was founded on 1966.

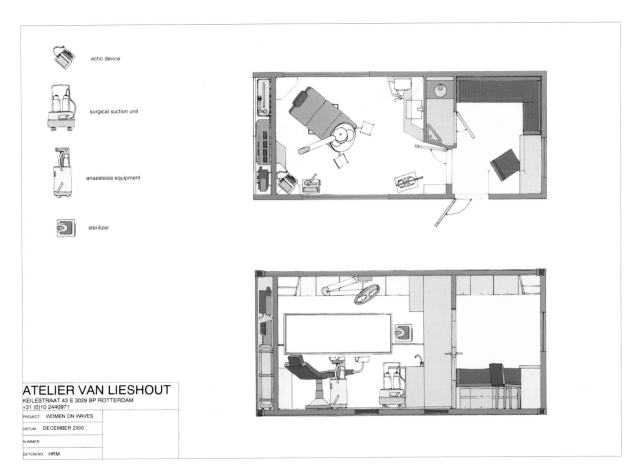

echo device

surgical suction unit

anaesthesia equipment

sterilizer

Women on waves
2000
Project

ATELIER VAN LIESHOUT
KEILESTRAAT 43 E 3029 BP ROTTERDAM
+31 (0)10 2440971
PROJECT: WOMEN ON WAVES
DATUM: DECEMBER 2000
NUMMER:
GETEKEND: HRM

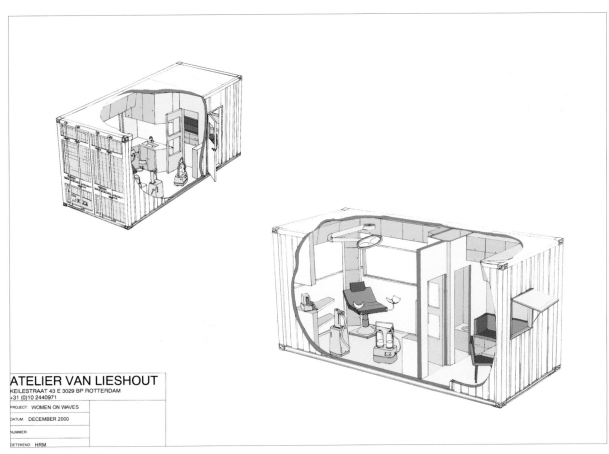

ATELIER VAN LIESHOUT
KEILESTRAAT 43 E 3029 BP ROTTERDAM
+31 (0)10 2440971
PROJECT: WOMEN ON WAVES
DATUM: DECEMBER 2000
NUMMER:
GETEKEND: HRM

A leaden, threatening sky, heavy with rank smog, looms over gagged buildings, empty hospitals, warehouses, factories, deserted schools, prefabs, derelict spaces. The asphalt is dank, like after a flood, and the puddles reflect bits of suburbia and patches of sky. Between the buildings silence-bound perspectives stretch out, glimpses, flights that depart and reach their destination far away. Over everything and everywhere, vacuum seems to prevail: yet a vacuum that is saturated, shapeless. Space seems a hemmed-in universe, time creeps along without a vanishing point.

To paraphrase a well-known philosopher, we might describe this suburb as a clearing, an opening in whose confines man is exposed to the risk of the vacuum. Beyond the boundary there does not seem to be any other possible civilization: what we see is a bounded world even if it can be trespassed. To say it in Hegel's terms, these metropolitan deserts are the image of a self-annihilating nothingness. They are, and at once are not, images of the end of history. They are, and are not, twilight glimpses, funereal scenarios, apocalyptic visions. The blow-ups by Botto and Bruno, a pair of Turinese artists, are a meditation on the question of art and architecture, that is, of the I and the We.

A meditation on existence as it unfolds on the extreme limit of the Western destiny "when the story of being is dissolving into pure nothingness, suspended in a sort of diaphanous limbo between no-longer-being and not-yet-being".

Botto and Bruno's suburb is that limbo, an existential dimension and a formal syntax, a senti-

tory, is running out; like after a flood water ebbs away, letting a desolate scene surface, the only possible landscape for millions of survivors. The master of Urbino's ideal city, picturesque views, metaphysical plazas, have dissolved. The center is a single great suburb, history is entirely now.

The only inhabitable world is the metropolis, the only livable dimension is computerized, technological globalization. In the vacuum of these suburbs a time confined within the limits of its own history draws near, a suspended, circular time, out of which you can break free only if you are willing to be subjected to drifting, nomads, internauts, citizens of a world and a net, that while it is true they are boundless, it is just as true that they are closed upon themselves, like inside a microcosmos. So this vacuum, suspended, formless, saturated with desolation, inside which things and people seem to exist is so because it is like the reversion of Nothingness into the Real world and the Virtual one.

Botto and Bruno's investigations, they claimed in an interview, have always approached borderline territories, "seeking therein a possible rebirth." The people who inhabit Botto and Bruno's Suburbias are melancholic youths, yet determined not to abandon the places of their childhood. Suburbia settlers, Suburbanites, that is, a social class capable of claiming its own political autonomy, its own ideological flight from ideologies, inhabit the post-modern condition but claim a politically edifying imagination, an expressivity capable of recreating a public art, iconographies that can be shared. Their blow-ups display the stuff

architectures. We are walking down a wet street. Under our feet the asphalt seems to utter a shapeless sentiment, a chaos of emotions and sensations, a magma of pulsions and visions; the smoggy sky and the eclectic architectures arouse in us exactly the same impression. The blow-up strives to be the picture of something, but also environment, stage, on which virtual people seem to float, figures placed like saints or dummies in the picture, the artists themselves, we the spectators, forced to be in the scene, to be put on the same level as virtual reality. Just try to leap in, into the beginning of the history of contemporary art. Just try to think about Frenhofer's painting, Balzac's unknown Masterpiece. The world represented by the artist is no longer that promise of happiness we could imagine a century ago. "My painting", Frenhofer tells Porbus and Poussin, "is not a painting, a sentiment, a passion... There is so much depth in this canvas, its art is so true, that you cannot distinguish it from the air around you. Where is the art? Gone, vanished!" The subject represented, the emotion are something like a shapeless mist. According to young Poussin on the canvas there is nothing; instead there is nothingness, and something that appearing on the threshold of the background of visibility seeks a dwelling in language. Reading ahead in the story you discover that a detail, a fragment, like a reef or a wreck appearing amidst the waters of the ocean, surfaces from the shapeless texture of the painting: it is the tip of a foot that stands out from the rest of the canvas "like a torso of a parian-marble Venus arising from the ruins of a fire-

Botto & Bruno

Botto & Bruno Botto

ment and a metaphysics, personal and collective, something that has to do with our own personal life, the social sphere. Beyond being a metropolitan landscape, suburbia is a way of life, is the inhabited world: that kind of cosmopolis that has sprung up at the end of modern civilization, of a notion of progress, of the proletariat, of the rationalistic design, when a new process of capitalist globalization began, something else, a new era, technologically and biologically different. That is, another beginning, a new dawning, that already conditions life in Suburbia. A new dimension of Western history that having gone beyond the shadowline of Humanism cast us into the era of post-technological globalization.

Modernism, that disastrous event in Western his-

Suburbanites' stories and dreams are made of, and the iconologies underlying this new metaphysical painting are those of the new iconauts that Botto and Bruno's striving is to recreate total works, connect fragments, tales, histories, the network of real and virtual, in a *telos* to be shared: theirs is a public art, democratic, made for the *agora* and not for drawing-rooms, produced for the telematics plaza and not for the media oligarchy. Like Klee's *Angelus Novus*, they live looking within themselves and inexorably must advance like nomads in an advancing desert. But unlike the angel of history they have the strength to gather up what has been shattered, to recompose the fragments, the ruins, to tell the odyssey of the Suburbanite.

The asphalt is surrounded by a forest of deserted

destroyed city". Giorgio Agamben has identified in that story the everlasting opposition between Terror and Rhetorics, that is, a crucial conflict in the unfolding of modern and contemporary art.

If Chatwin crossed deserts to leave behind metropolitan culture, so Botto and Bruno explore abandoned suburbs to experience that post-modern dimension which is suspended in a sort of diaphanous limbo between no-longer-being and not-yet-being.

This exploration gives rise to a sentiment that is somewhere between melancholy and present-ment; that tension is suggested by ruins of cities and crimson skies, toys discarded on the asphalt, figures with their backs turned, others sitting waiting, unexpected disclosing of spaces of blue

and mirages in the crystal puddles, bunches of familiar objects, traces of something that happened or may be about to happen.

Settlers in a drifting world, in an abandoned civilization, or else newborns in a coming world, Botto and Bruno experience twilight and dawn inside a closed world, even though henceforth virtually boundless. Is this perhaps the archipelago Cacciari spoke of, an image that eclectically reproduces the emblematic places of the modern era, the era of utopias, an era characterized by the myth of modernism, within which we can already discern the geopolitical outlines of a renovated subjectivity in myths and imagination.

The optimism, the vitality that permeated Boccioni's industrial suburbs is the remote origin of these images, the opposite shore of these cityscapes: in those days you entered the new century by standing on a terrace to depict the industrious city and yourself in the midst of the crowd of workers. At the end of the century that image has capsized. The gaze of the Angelus Novus conditions our way of seeing; this cohabits with our telematic, biotechnological and virtual optimism. Capable once again of a burst of hope, we are contaminated by an indissoluble melancholy, no longer the anguish, the nihilistic apathy of someone who at the end of modern progress could just see the end of history, but something mournful that characterizes the lightness of someone who has made up his mind to try out the possibility of rebirth.

Sergio Risaliti

Under my red sky
2000
Wall paper and pvc,
800 × 900 × 330 cm

Gianfranco Botto born on 1963;
Roberta Bruno on 1966.

Unassuming painting

1. Flaky aesthetics begin by ascribing therapeutic or redemptive abilities—religious, existential, socio-political—to artworks. Flaky aesthetics then proceed to fashion *truth*-driven artworks into illustrations of mystifying chimeras, and *goodness*-driven artworks into surrogates of well-intentioned activism.

2. Still, it shouldn't be denied that flaky aesthetics can be seedbeds for great artworks. Just think of Mondrian, whose esoteric convictions do not exactly add to his works aesthetic efficacy. Interestingly, we would find it difficult to accept the opposite— that great artworks can underscore flaky aesthetics. Great artworks may somehow outdo their authors and the aesthetics fuelling them. So perhaps a sensible aesthetic outlook should take the possibility of such dissociations into account.

3. My grammar-school teacher taught us in class, as required by the official curricula, that "Art is a form of expression" (*El arte es una forma de expresión*). Far from posing as a sufficient definition of Art (it is too vague for that) I believe this proposition can be a subdued and sobering directive as long as suggestions of therapeutic expressivism are avoided.

4. Late in life, Wittgenstein had left many lofty designs behind. He was no longer concerned with anchoring Truth (as the Positivists were) nor with

developed plastic syntax and by the ever-relevant constrains of its specific materiality. In painting, as in mature *forms of life*, presuppositions upheld by force of habit become stifling myths, clichés and articles of faith. A good painting may outdo its author's intentions and even his flaky aesthetics by contributing to the fluidity of painting's *form of life*—by oiling, tuning up, refurbishing its *forms of expression*. A lousy painting will simply contribute to the rusting of the gears (beware of the elegance of rust).

6. If Picasso reconfigured painting's engine, Mondrian streamlined its body, De Kooning and Pollock added turbo-drive, and Terry Winters recently refilled the anti-freeze, I would see my work as something of an injector cleaner that seeks to remove undesirable clogging particles. The obstruction here is a consequence of certain pseudo-categorical dichotomies that have become avant-garde commonplaces. I'm referring to dichotomies such as formalism/expressionism, form/content, figuration/abstraction, contemplative/critical, painterly/conceptual.
In order to disprove the mutual exclusivity of these terms, their repositioning must be carried out from within painting and through plastic articulation—that is, through staging a painterly dialectic that dissolves the exclusivity of the dichotomized categories, a dialectic resolved, if at all, in the work's pictorial efficacy.

7. Pictorial efficacy is not measured by what a

Yishai Jusidman 1963

dictating an ethical code (as, say, the Existentialists would be). Instead, he primarily devoted himself to analyzing the efficacy of human interchange. Following Wittgenstein liberally, a *form of expression* is eloquent (even conceivable) insofar as it conforms to a publicly acknowledged practice that bestows sense to individual behaviour. Such practices rely on shared dispositions and expectations which are shaped by natural and cultural circumstances. While natural law remains constant, culture's relative fluidity fosters the dynamics of such communal, meaning-bestowing practices, known in Ludwig's lingo as *forms of life*.

5. Painting's dynamics are circumscribed by the weight of its history, by its thoroughly

painting stands in for, but by what it does within the parameters defined by its elements (materials, colour, subject matter, public presentation). In my work, Sumo wrestlers are posited as triggers of plastic play; psychotics are cautiously assimilated as tools for reconditioning the appreciation of painterly expressiveness; painters are readily chosen as active operators in stagings of crisscrossing pictorial relations. But the efficacy of these paintings aspire to "notwithstanding my self-assertive justifications" must be carried through by virtue of the viewer's judgement—instigated, nourished and tempered by the firsthand experience of the works. I hereby rest my case.
Yishai Jusidman

F.A., Ciudad de México
2000-2001
Acrylic and oil on linen
mounted on wood
and synthetic carpet,
199,5 × 218 × 353,5 cm,
picture, 199,5 × 200,3 cm

Sumo X
1996
Oil on wood, 60 × 60 cm

Mutatis Mutandis: B.T.
1999
Installation,
248 × 276 × 215 cm

Stages of development in the works of Manfred Pernice cannot be ranked into the hierarchy of preparatory drawing, model and finished product. As the sculptures or installations can be read from the models, as if they were three-dimensional sketches, process and fragment are central for the sculptures themselves and become manifest in the repeated rebuilding and extension of his big installation-like works such as *Kü.mo* (begun in 1998 and to be viewed in extended version at the Hamburger Bahnhof Berlin in the year 2000) or *Fiat I-IV* (last exhibition at Kunsthalle Zürich 2000), a work that was first developed by Pernice in 1997 with manifold references to the Fiat plant at Lingotto in Turin. The extention of elements, the interchanging and addition of applied images and texts, that interact with the sculptures and explore the interchangeability of surface-classifications by presenting images or objects that are normally expected in interiors on exterior walls, again stress process and the transitory quality of the works, which also deny a final and universal statement and interpretation. Through multi-layered allusions—such as the often ironic titles of the works—a complex and at the same time playful system consisting in chains of references is created to confuse and amuse the viewer.

For the 49th Biennal in Venice Manfred Pernice will turn towards his concept of "containers", which he has developed since 1998 in parallel with his "cans" project. These "cans"—

open as possible. They represent, just like the "cans", mobile spaces and hollow bodies, that are able to store and transport some content and embody the global mobility of temporary places. On one hand the stacking of containers cites a logic implied by the time of transport and the place of destination of goods, which is not accidental. On the other hand, concrete but accidental neighbourhoods of contents, that remain invisible for the viewer, are created by piling up containers. These "nonsense-connections" (*Unsinnzusammenhänge*) are defined by the artist and partially made visible, so that the viewer can try to establish them. Pernice creates the paradox of this relative "nonsense-connection" through the coexistence of (intentional) coincidence and therefore the possible "imposition of neighbourhoods" of the most differing contents and the simultaneous denial of a logical system of these composed connections, that as such also reflect normality.

The provisional *non-finito* of the installation-like sculptures stands back in favour of a stronger focus on the constellation of the objects. The movable "containers" like the "cans" are parts of walk-through installations and do not only enclose a space within their outer walls, but also occupy and communicate with a specific space.

Sibilla Calzolari

Manfred Pernice 1963

to use the term Pernice himself has coined for this—are cylindrical sculptures of various sizes, consisting of wooden laths joined lenghtways and at first sight remind us of barrels or advertising pillars. According to Pernice, these reflect "a 'canned' world and existence" like those systems of regulation that structure everything into categories and patterns. The "can" works shift causalities, create fictional situations of encounter and finally develop "Unsinnzusammenhänge", which could be roughly translated as "nonsense-connections". The severe forms of the "containers" are, unlike the "cans", more like their "real" model, the goods and living container, in their outer appearance. Their initial function is, however, as

Untitled
2001
Mixed technique
and video, variable size

In her photographic work Heli Rekula gives a feeling of a matter of fact approach to reality. The photos are like statements of what has been seen and how it 'in fact' looked like. This straightforwardness in her visual gesture could be linked to a documentary tradition, but even more to a personal style often used in feature stories in magazines. Could the images be connected to a fictive story? Or are they evidences of events, traces of something real that in fact has been taking place?

image nearly simulates the surface of the human skin. This combination of two media, photography and video underlines the main role time plays in them both, technically as well as in the subject matter Heli Rekula circles around. You often find speed recognized in one way or another, as some kind of activity, as something that might happen, something you probably don't expect or want, or as a flash of the moment just afterward when it is already calm, something gone by.

women wind up wool into balls, the speed of the falling balls is slowed down into a dreamlike pace, the winding is repeated, turned backwards, eternally looped. The time surrounds the action, folds the symbolically charged rituals into unknown sections of our worldly dimension.

But in most cases the sharing atmosphere is left out and we are confronted with the question of a more general orientation of the

Rekula Heli Rekula Heli Rekula Heli Rekula Heli

Heli Rekula **1963**

Rekulas personage often introduces us to the contexts they have been placed in: sites that become signs of multilayered structures and discourses, ambiguous icons of contemporary reality.

Heli Rekula also works with moving image, both as monitor works and as video installations. She approaches both photography and video with an awareness of their ambiguous concrete, documentary quality and uses this quality intertwined into the worldview of her chosen contents. The worlds depicted in her pieces contain a vulnerability seldom seen, which gives them a certain kind of transparency and sensibility. The surface of the

Or maybe a scene a long time after the event, when time itself has been inscribed in the object, landscape or person depicted.

As Rekulas motives often involve women and girls, both in groups and as individuals, the narratives circulate around questions of gender. Many times it involves a discourse between women, as in her latest video installation *Skein* where Rekula opened up a strongly surreal, somehow comforting interpretative path. The work is based on Maya Derens experimental film *Ritual in Transfigured Time* (1946), the continuation of this duality of the narrative is build on a movement, shared between two women. The

abandoned individual within the wide world of the cold contemporary. In many of Rekulas images there is a sense of a loss of innocence, or even stronger, the feeling of "collective failure".

This concern for contemporary life includes an awareness of what Paul Virilio has called an exposure to the accidental. Virilio sees the accident as the inevitable backside of action and a result of the technologies of speed; in the development and invention of for example the ship it implicitly involves the invention of the shipwreck, in the caressing hand there is an inbuilt possibility of violence.

Maria Hirvi

Landscape n. 5
"American star"
1998
Colour print mounted
on aluminium and
laminated, 75 × 180 cm

Untitled (from theme
Pilgrimage)
1996
Colour print, mounted
on aluminium and
laminated, 120 × 90 cm

Provisional Home

ACCIDENT
The impossibility of maintaining any form of control.

CONTROL
An instinctive faculty which is often confused with conscience.

INCIDENT
An accident comes to form part of the history of our vital trajectory, when we incorporate it into our list of desires.

FURNITURE
The depository of our passing emotions (including the drawer we use for *bric-à-brac*).

HOUSE
A set of furniture.

MOBILITY
The ability to move between the stage and the flies, from the flies to the dressing-room, from the dressing-room to the box offices of multiple identities.

COINCIDENCES
Space and time are so elastic that they always manage to meet up occasionally (make a date).

MIGRATIONS
People, like birds, make nests with what they find wherever they happen to go.

GLOBALISATION
Everybody asks about the other person. Where are you from? Where do you live? But it gets harder and harder to give an answer. Soon, we'll stop asking.

MOVING
The motorways of destiny have different lanes; everything depends on the speed of the complex machinery of chance.

space which are subject to continuous alterations. We circulate between identities as if along the parallel lanes of a motorway. From our moving car it isn't easy to make out who is going the fastest.

PROVISIONAL HOME
The image after an accident, of a sudden run for it, of abandonment after a disaster.
Circumstances depend to a great extent on mere coincidences.
We are able to incorporate chance to the extent that we assume the intentional nature of accidents.
By penetrating the home and approaching things, we can see that in each piece of furniture there a hand mirror has been fixed. A small motor makes each one turn endlessly.
There is a slide projector pointing towards each mirror. Its projections are reflected on the walls. There are images of the same pieces of furniture and things scattered over the floor. They describe a complete circle around us, they move

Eulalia **Valldosera** 1963

HOME
A set of echos released by different subjectivities rooted in prenatal memory.

PROJECTION
Light is the only material which escapes the laws of gravity. It appears to act with complete freedom, but in reality corresponds to the mathematics (the compensatory law) of emotions.

MIRROR
I see in the other that which I am incapable of recognising in myself.

THEATRE
The stage of the subconscious.

plex machinery of chance.

FAMILY
Memory is not a deposit of objects, it is an activity that is highly useful when regenerating the present.

HAND MIRROR
An interface which works well with both solar and artificial light. At night we are all the same.

PROVISIONAL LIVING
The concepts of home and family, conventionally understood as universal, are to be found articulated around co-ordinates of time and

along the walls, hugging the floor, and some of them float, weightless, between the ceiling and the floor.
Every few seconds, all the projections come together and form a single image, the home, only to vanish at once and disperse themselves along the walls. They continuously speed up and vary in scale, as we come into contact with the fragility of our own instruments of perception.
Again and again we wait for the moment in which the objects, as if in an illusion, return to their natural place and size, and pause in order to tell us about who we are and where we come from, they appear in each brief encounter, held for a moment in a vast familiar landscape.

Provisional Home
(Provisional Living #1)
1999
Installation with slide
projection, installation
view, variable size

Provisional Home
(Provisional Living #1)
1999
Installation with slide
projection, installation
view, variable size

Provisional Home
(Provisional Living #1)
1999
Installation with slide
projection, installation
view, variable size

June 30 or the allegory in postmodern times

An army as part of an artistic problem? In Guatemala this question alone brings into mind the oxymoron that reads: military intelligence. It encloses in its contradiction the sentence that this human group governed by rules is not capable of the privilege of autonomous reason and only justifies its existence in terms of aggression and of the observation of the military codes. If we add to this that in Guatemala the image of the militia has an exact meaning in the history of this country's traumas, we will understand that breaking the stability of similar meanings can only be done from a daring perspective.

That is why in this action, titled *30 de Junio* (June 30), the Guatemalan artist A1-53167 generates a series of situations, the logical conditions of which cannot be considered exclusively as an exercise of criticism or denunciation of the actions that a specific authority group committed against civil society during the war years. For some time the Guatemalan artist Al-53167 has placed his work with in the possibility of seeing the words separately from their usual representations and original contexts, as well as engaging himself in destroying the status of the objects, of the ideas as they are, of "unique" meanings and questioning insistently the limits of the work of art itself.

At first it must be clarified that this series of images is the result of an action that the artist what had happened. The incident remained as an event of military domain.

Such a strategy is certainly romantic if it is trapped in the subversive anecdote. In this sense it is important to consider that charcoal is a material invested of a well-known code to the Guatemalans. It refers directly to the razed lands, the towns that, behind the battles and slaughters perpetrated by the army, were burnt to erase any trace of what had happened. However, A1-53167´s strategy is, from this collective notion, a change of rolls in an ambush of languages designed by the artist himself.

It is true that in Guatemala these figures will continue to conserve the enemy's equivalent, the hue of the established power and the memory's weight in historic events. But the artist, as an independent being, introduces himself into an analysis of what is kept as a traditional representation in the Guatemalans imagery, and enters a game where this monument is destroyed and drives into conflict every preconception of the allegory. Reasoning about the traditional notion of what an authority group is, A1-53167 invites as his unique audience precisely that group that, besides being an observer capable of understanding these codes, he makes transforms into an actor of his own deconstruction.

In this way this action of dematerializing something apparently inoffensive, confronts new paradoxes and leads to unexpected lessons. More than the documentation of

A1-53167 1964

performed in the date pointed out by the title, in which an annual parade celebrates the existence of the armed institution in Guatemala. The action consisted in introducing illicitly, over the road that the parade would go across, a charcoal path that was swept hours before the parade in an impressive display of subordinates sent to perform such task. The audience that attended the parade was not aware of images of an amazing aesthetics, A1-53167 enters the matter of the memory's abuses—as Tzvetan Todorov would say—without judgements or direct criticism. He transforms art into an entity capable of suggesting and dismounting the complicity with which we build the values and monuments that we establish in our culture and society.

Rosina Cazali

Never believe an artist
who says their work is about nothing
   The culture consumer's fear of the void

"Your paintings are like my films, they are about nothing... with precision".
(Michelangelo Antonioni to Mark Rothko, 1962)

"Polyphemus, what dire affliction has come upon you to make you profane the night with clamour and rob us of our slumbers? [...] Is someone threatening death to yourself by craft or by violence?"
[...]
"Friends, it is Noman's craft and not violence that is threatening death to me."
"[...] If you are alone, then this is a malady sent by almighty Zeus, from which there is no escape."
Homer, *The Odyssey* (trans. Walter Shewring)

One often has occasion to observe the remarkable degree to which the public simply accepts an artist's statement about a work of art, and in a way, maintains its trust in the faithful correspondence between the statement and the realisation. As if the statement was not a production in its own right with its own logic and motives but offered unmediated information about the way the work is to be perceived. And yet it must be allowed that a work may be motivated by circumstances that are alien to its definition. Quite dom... never is. We could even say that, for the observer who is not taken in or deluded by the statement, such works produce precisely the opposite effect. How can it be that nothing is always something, and what is it that makes an artist want to attain this dimension of absence if, ultimately, they already know that the undertaking is vain, the project impossible? I am not going to try to analyse the ways of formally expressing nothingness here, or the strategies of formally incorporating nothingness in the actual making of an artwork. I would simply like to show that the use of this concept of nothingness, as applied to the artist's statement about the work, constitutes a strategy designed to dash our hopes as viewers. But what are these hopes and on what are they based? More than ever, on the political and social context. Since art now speaks to an increasingly wide and, therefore, not necessarily educated audience, it cannot be presented on the basis of a shared artistic culture but must use values that are not specifically related to art and its history. These values are for the most part produced by an economic system based on production and consumption, on the belief in information and communication, on the need for events, tourism, distractions and signs of progress. Curiously, though, even the most disenchanted consumer may still harbour some credulity towards art. While he would be spontaneously sceptical towards the discourse surrounding consumer goods, he might well tend to believe an artist who egy that enables an artist to free his or her activity from any form of social pressure. This nothingness defines the absence of qualities from a sarcastic viewpoint, referring to the idea of an economic system based on the daily production of artificial values. The idea of making nothing both marks a refusal to take part in the blindness of all the hype, and anticipates the viewer's value judgements and possible disappointment. The artist who claims that his work is about nothing is doing nothing more than using the public language and judgemental values produced by this system. A work on nothingness, assuming it could exist, would in a sense be the essence of aesthetic production as it is habitually seen from a bourgeois perspective.

If viewers are not aware that this "nothing" is merely a trick of language embodying a critical attitude towards the social system and expectations of art, it is because they never think of assessing the discrepancy between the definition of the work and its physical reality—in other words, of analysing the way in which it is implemented and made and presented. If viewers do not undertake this task, that is because in most cases they position themselves as cultural consumers, outside the creative process, whereas in fact they should always consider themselves as the potential creator of the work. Each one of us creates at each moment of the day in the way we live and understand reality. The artist's sole quality is to be aware of this and to make it manifest in the context of art and in accordance with the artistic conven-

Pierre Bismuth 1964

simply because this definition corresponds either to what the artist wants to show (as opposed to what can be seen in the work) or to the position that the artist wants us to adopt with regard to the work. To call into question the meaning or value of the statement would not, however, imply calling into question the artist's good faith or intelligence. It is not a matter of knowing if the work is or is not what it is said to be but of understanding the motives behind a choice of definition and being aware of the possible gap separating it from what it designates. It's very simple. Art that claims to be about nothing, absence, silence, emptiness, vacuity, nothingness, ugliness, meaninglessness, uselessness, trivia, the negligible, the absurd, boredom vaunts the absence of aesthetic qualities in a blank canvas and to consider that there is indeed nothing here to be looked at. We are aware of the commercial impact of lies about quality when it comes to consumer goods, but we find it harder to understand why an artist might wish to devalue his or her own work. Why this publicity concerning the emptiness of the work if that was not really the case?

One of the answers put forward by maladroit upholders of an art based on negative values is to attempt to develop a discourse on the hidden qualities of nothingness. This presumptuous position makes the mistake of thinking that vacuity is a materially achievable quality and not just a concept. "Nothingness" constitutes a strattions to which he subscribes. Artists are artists only because they define themselves as such and, by using the strategy of nothingness, they confirm the old idea that the artwork is made by those who look at it. In art, "nothing" exists only for those who are ready to believe in it.

Pierre Bismuth

From Humanity
to Something Else
From Something Else
to Humanity
2001
Vinyl letters on wall
Project for installation
at the Italian Pavilion

Humanity	Art
Society	Craft
Civilisation	Skill
Culture	Technique
Edification	Process
Knowledge	Procedure
Erudition	Method
Refinement	Strategy
Manners	Plan
Behaviour	Plot
Adaptation	Machination
Acclimatisation	Manipulation
Conversion	Control
Transformation	Influence
Alteration	Authority
Shift	Power
Substitution	Strenght
Exchange	Energy
Transaction	Action
Commerce	Movement
Business	Traffic
Trade	Trade
Traffic	Business
Movement	Commerce
Action	Transaction
Energy	Exchange
Strenght	Substitution
Power	Shift
Authority	Alteration
Influence	Transformation
Control	Conversion
Manipulation	Acclimatisation
Machination	Adaptation
Plot	Behaviour
Plan	Manner
Strategy	Refinement
Method	Erudition
Procedure	Knowledge
Process	Edification
Technique	Culture
Skill	Civilisation
Craft	Society
Art	Humanity

A new face
2001
Collage on newspaper
(Guardian May 3th)

Thursday
May 3 2001
Britain's newspaper
for Europe

The Guardian

EUROPE

Published in France, Germany and Spain

What is Fay
Weldon up to?

Howard Jacobson in G2

David Lacey
on Leeds
vs Valencia

European Cup. In Sport

Albania US$ 2	Germany DM 4.00	Poland Z 8.00
Andorra FF 13	Greece D 550	Portugal E 330 CONT
Austria AS 30	Hungary F 380	Romania LEI 83,000
Belgium BF 85	Iceland IK 185	Russia US$ 2.75
Bulgaria BGL 4.20	Italy L 4,000	Slovakia SK 80
Croatia KN 16.00	Kenya KSH 150	Slovenia SIT 390
Cyprus C£ 1.10	Latvia US$ 2	Spain P 325
Czech Rep. KC65	Luxembourg LF 85	Sweden SK 19
Denmark DK 19	Madeira E 360	Switzerland SF 4.20
Estonia K 30	Malta ML 0.75	Thailand B 80
Finland FM 15	Netherlands G 5.75	Turkey TL 1000,000
France FF 13	Norway NK 20	Ukraine US$ 3.50

Former minister guilty of Maxwell deceit

Michael White
and David Hencke

The former paymaster general, Geoffrey Robinson, is guilty of misleading parliament over undeclared financial interests from his business dealings with the disgraced tycoon Robert Maxwell, a committee of MPs agreed last night.

The cross-party standards and privileges committee reached its verdict following two private sessions after hearing an unconvincing explanation from Mr Robinson earlier this week.

They did so on the basis of the fourth investigation into the Coventry North-West MP's tangled business affairs during the 1997 parliament — on what is virtually certain to be its last full working day before Tony Blair calls the expected general election.

The MPs had in front of them the latest report from the parliamentary commissioner for standards, Elizabeth Filkin, who is under attack from MPs for the rigour of her investigations into allegations that some MPs are not declaring all their private interests in the Commons register.

The inquiry centred on a £200,000 payment from Hollis Industries, an engineering company which Mr Robinson bought from Mr Maxwell and later resold. He has persistently denied claims, most recently in journalist Tom Bower's biography, that he received the payment.

Senior ministers and MPs, as well as the department of trade and industry, were told he had not received the money — though evidence of it existed in the Hollis accounts. Mr Robinson, who left Gordon Brown's treasury team in 1998, said the accounts were wrong.

Weekend reports suggested that Mrs Filkin had discovered that the MP had solicited such a payment from the then-owner of the Daily Mirror, who drowned in 1991 after robbing the paper's pension fund, and that the money may have been directed to an overseas trust, bank account or individual with which Mr Robinson could be linked.

There was no confirmation of such claims or any indication of how much of Mrs

Filkin's evidence the standards committee, chaired by the fastidious Labour veteran, Robert Sheldon, has accepted.

But the MPs have concluded that Mr Robinson did have a declarable financial interest because he worked for Hollis — whether he actually got the money or not.

Mr Robinson, 61, who is standing again at the election, has already been obliged to apologise to the Commons for non-declarations of interest, a 54-second apology in 1999. What punishment he may now face was unclear last night — though there will be no time for action before the election.

With evidence and annexes also likely to be published at the same time, so fellow MPs can judge what may be a controversial verdict, the report could appear this week — though next Tuesday or Wednesday may be more likely.

At question time yesterday, the Tory MP, Jacqui Lait, challenged Tony Blair to make sure the committee's findings are not kicked into the long grass before the election — or to publish the DTI inspector's report into Mr Robinson's affairs. Mr Blair said it was up to the committee.

The committee has been criticised in the past for not being tough enough on Labour ministers or backing Mrs Filkin firmly enough. They insist they have not been playing party politics — and that all the decisions have been unanimous, including those involving high profile MPs such as Peter Mandelson, Keith Vaz and the Northern Ireland secretary, John Reid.

One casualty of persistent controversy has been Mrs Filkin whose three year contract — after she succeeded Sir Gordon Downey — is due to end in January. "There are plenty of people on both sides who would love her to go, they feel she's overstepped the mark," one senior Labour MP said last night.

Mrs Filkin's fate lies in the hands of the House of Commons Commission, chaired the by Speaker Michael Martin, who is keen to maintain parliament's reputation in the post-Nolan era when rules on interests are being tightened.

Kim's Korea The North presents a new face - much like the old one

North Korean soldiers at a welcoming ceremony in Pyongyang for a high-level EU delegation designed to build on better relations between north and south Photograph: Stephen Shaver/Reuters

The People's Paradise crumbles

YES SUCCESS HAS A SMELL
THE KIND THAT NEEDS A PRE-SOAK
AND A 90° BOIL-WASH

The **Guardian**

Sport

A better breed of bagman
Exams for caddies are
a slur on golfing tradition **24**

Expanding contracts
Fletcher wants 12-month deals **27**

Premiership

Leeds aim to lead at quickstep

David Lacey on the Yorkshire club's prospects against Valencia

Pace can take Leeds United to their second European Cup final: speed of limb, quickness of thought, alacrity of movement and briskness of delivery. Valencia are unlikely to be beaten for technique in the opening leg of the semi-finals at Elland Road tonight but they can be harried and hustled to defeat by a superior tempo.

David O'Leary has tended to go into each Champions League match emphasising his team's lack of experience and only yesterday Ian Harte, the Leeds left-back, declared that "of the four teams in the semi-finals you would have to say that we are the weakest".

Yet, while Leeds are indeed relatively raw at this level, the fact that they have come so far rules out their still being considered novices. As Hector Cuper, the Valencia coach, said yesterday: "There are times to feign being the underdog but I don't think anyone will fall for that ploy now."

Of course not. Leeds, Valencia and Bayern Munich are evenly matched. Only Real Madrid, Bayern's opponents in the other semi-final, are a cut above, and central to the thoughts of O'Leary's players tonight should be the way Cuper's side were beaten by Real in last season's final.

Valencia might have lived with Real's quality in the Stade de France that night, and it is not as if the teams were complete strangers, but they could not combat the sheer speed at which the opposition set about winning the match 3–0.

O'Leary has the means to play tonight's game to a similar beat. In Alan Smith he has a keen, mean striker with the speed of reflex to challenge Cuper's ageing defence: Jocelyn Angloma (35), Mauricio Pellegrino (29), Roberto Ayala (28) and Amedeo Carboni (36).

When Manchester United shared a scoreless draw in the Mestalla stadium in the second phase, Angloma spent much of the time choking on the dust of Ryan Giggs. Harry Kewell is short of full match fitness but should still be able to stretch the Frenchman on the left.

The success Carboni had in laying up tight on David Beckham ought not to be repeated because of Lee Bowyer's penchant for moving inside to seek scoring opportunities. The timing of Bowyer's runs into the Valencia penalty area could be Leeds' best chance of taking a negotiable lead to Spain on Tuesday.

So much comes back to the way Olivier Dacourt and David Batty meet the challenge in midfield of Gaizka Mendieta

and Ruben Baraja. This is where the course, not only of this evening's match but of the semi-final as a whole, may be decided. Fundamental to Leeds' revival since the new year has been the strength of Dacourt and Batty in midfield and their understanding with the centre-backs, Rio Ferdinand and Dominic Matteo.

Given such a solid foundation, there is no reason why Leeds cannot achieve the sort of result tonight which will leave their chances of playing in the final in Milan on May 23 more than a little buoyant.

As O'Leary said yesterday: "We're two games away from playing in the biggest match anywhere after the World Cup final." It is now that the confidence bred by those gutsy performances against Milan and Lazio in the earlier rounds should serve Leeds well.

At the same time Valencia, defensively strong, remain the masters of the sudden counter-attack often followed by the sort of sucker punch which can upset the steepest odds in world heavyweight fights; Manchester United and Arsenal can vouch for that. And like many of the best creative players Mendieta is at his most dangerous when he appears to be drifting out of a game.

With Pablo Cesar Aimar, Valencia's talented young Argentine, Mendieta is capable of unlocking the tightest defence, while the long Norwegian legs of John Carew will doubtless command the attention of Ferdinand and Matteo.

In the 1975 semi-finals Jimmy Armfield's side beat the Barcelona of Johan Cruyff and Johan Neeskens 2–1 at Elland Road before drawing 1–1 at the Nou Camp after Gordon McQueen had been sent off. For Billy Bremner, Johnny Giles and Terry Yorath, read Dacourt, Batty and Bowyer tonight.

Leeds United (probable: 4–4–2): Martyn; Mills, Ferdinand, Matteo, Harte; Bowyer, Dacourt, Batty, Kewell; Smith, Viduka.
Valencia (probable: 4–4–2): Canizares; Angloma, Ayala, Pellegrino, Carboni; Mendieta, Baraja, Kily Gonzalez, Aimar; Carew, Sanchez.
Referee: P Collina (Italy).

Real v Bayern report, page 26

O'Leary: upping the tempo

Michael Owen touches the ball past the Bradford goalkeeper Gary Walsh to score Liverpool's first goal during last night's 2–0 victory at Valley Parade Photograph: Aubrey Washington

,198 Set by Quantum

27 The lender losing credit is the one to check (6)

Down
1 Genuine playing area raised in function (7)
2 Politician protected by first-class defence (5)
3 Refuse to steal a ship before first escaping (7)
5 Chicory is strangely veined (6)
6 An examination involving several questions (9)
7 A river in eg New Zealand — Tay, perhaps? (7)
8 In which a number of months are accounted for (9,4)
14 Could be applied to "The Twist" (9)
16 Bold footballer (7)
18 Engaged in fight against time on American vehicle (7)
19 Traffic light set up to indicate bend (7)
20 This attracts good artist around (6)
23 The sailor's a short distance nearer the stern (5)

Stuck? Then call our solutions line on 09068 338 238. Calls cost 60p per minute at all times. Service supplied by ATS

Solution No. 22,197

Across
1 Quiet church out East is run-down (6)
4 Excellent fruit year (6)
9 Opposing article backing Information Technology (4)
10 At work, hooter is kept to it (10)
11,12 One in opposition with advice saved lot in trouble (6,8)
13 The awareness of one sitting in judgement (9)
15 Light sack (4)
16 Company: one with branches at beginning of millennium (4)
17 I'm top name in performance at Christmas (3)
21,22 Common-or-garden salt (8,6)
24 It was shot as part of history (10)
25 Confidential assistant gives help with start of education (4)
26 Expand on obscure detail (6)

Solution tomorrow

In G2
Of all the violent crimes, those where the parent is the criminal are the most grimly baffling. How can parents turn on their children, hearing their cries, perhaps, and seeing their terrified faces, and murder them? **Angela Neustatter on what drives a loving father to murder page 10**

cross Chesterfield on next season's fixture list after a league disciplinary panel yesterday.

the league tomorrow. Chesterfield's manager Nicky Law said: "I'm glad. To be fair

ren Brown is also likely to be questioned. It is believed that the new owners have inherited

least 10 goals.

Brighton champions, page 26

The Guardian 119 Farringdon Road London EC1R 3ER, Telephone 020–7278 2332 Fax number: 020–7837 2114. In Manchester: 164 Deansgate, Manchester M3 3GG, Telephone 0161–832 7200; Fax 0161–832 5351 and 0161–834 9717. Telephone Sales: London 020–7611 9000; Manchester 0161–908 3900. Published by Guardian Newspapers Limited, 119 Farringdon Road, London EC1R 3ER, and at 164 Deansgate, Manchester M3 3GG. Printed at West Ferry Printers Ltd, 235 West Ferry Road, London, E14 8NX and at Trafford Park Printers, Longbridge Road, Manchester M17 1SL. Wednesday, May 2, 2001. Registered as a newspaper at the Post Office ISSN 0261–3077.

Upping the tempo
2001
Collage on newspaper
(Guardian May 2th)

ZZZZZZZZZZZZ

We have been on this planet for a long time, and it has been a long time since we started thinking, making questions, trying to understand who we are and what we are doing here, since we are surviving, we are making art.

Since that time, the beginning of history, we don't know what we are doing here, and since that time reality asks us what we are going to do today to keep life going on as a person, as a family, as a human being, as a society. Many things have changed from that time. But basically we are still the same lost human society. A long time ago we were just a simple community of "animals" completely part of nature, and we are animals still, even though it may sound strange. But today our responsibility is much bigger. Now we understand nature much greater. Now we can't let everything in the hands of God. We can't close our eyes and believe in a unique God as being responsible for everything—the master of divine laws. Now we know that, despite our power over nature, we are part of it and we depend on it. Despite belonging to different nations, different cultures, in the end we are all the same, and have the same fears. At least, we live on the same planet. The fact is that we can't escape our body. That's all we have—our body changing over our lifetime. And the beauty of our body and our living is our relationship to other people, to nature and to infinity. So here is the gap: how to connect organic life, necessity, hunger ...

in our actions. The planet is becoming too small for us.
Humanity where are you!!!?
I hope in this millennium art will become something more important than just a spectacle. I hope that art will get closer to the people in general, not just something for specialists. I hope art will become more spiritual. I hope it can fill the big emptiness of humanity today. I hope the old religions, that today are responsible for more war, more repression, more control than spiritual connection between people and the universe, get weaker, weaker and weaker due to the birth of a new religion, if we really need one; Amore spiritual, more abstract religion, that can hold the loneliness of humanity. I hope for an art less perverse and more sensual. I want an art that can connect us alone to a kind of spiritual place where we can breathe an idea of infinity, totality, where we can have a continuity between us and the universe. Also I want an art that will connect us to the other, that will help us interact with other people, that will show us the limit. But this limit between you and me is not a wall; it is a place of sensations, a place of exchange and continuity between people, a skin of existence and relationships.

Ernesto Neto

Ernesto Neto 1964

esto Neto Ernesto Neto Ernesto Ne

To the spiritual sensation of infinity. In the last few centuries we have approached the organic subject in a materialistic way, sociologically dividing, dividing, dividing; but the organic also means the spiritual.

We need gods from infinity, from nature, not a unique power, not an atomic idea in the Greek sense of one thing making everything, but an interaction of powers. The gods are here, we must celebrate them, but not as a father who protects us and gives orders, but at the most as brothers. They ask for our responsibility, we must know how to read them, we are in the same boat!

We must take care of our planet. We are so developed today, but we are still so primitive

**We fishing the time
(warm's holes
and densities)**
Lycra, tulle, poliamide
stockings, tumeric, black
pepper, clove and curry,
4,5 × 20 × 10 m
Installation view

We fishing the time (warm's holes and densities)
Lycra, tulle, poliamide stockings, tumeric, black pepper, clove and curry, 4,5 × 20 × 10 m
Installation view

We think of sport in terms of allegiance and competition. We witness it as a narrative performed and unfurled on an epic, heroic scale, even when it's compressed into the twenty-one inches of a TV set. As we watch, depending on the extent of our investment, we share our anxiety and elation with the rest of the crowd, or the rest of the bar, or our partners. Even if we are not physically in the stadium we can feel affiliated. It goes the other way too. We fantasise that we feel the emotions of the players themselves; they are, after all, doing it for us.

Roderick Buchanan makes art about sport as a means of exciting dialogue about our broader social behaviour. In the cultures of various sports, Buchanan shows us endlessly-varied microcosms: the team or the crowd, or the supporters thousands of miles away, as a social unit, and within that unit, the adhesion, affiliation, aggression and fragmentation of everyday life. Buchanan does not separate the sport from the context of its reproduction for the spectator or

Edited to produce a ceaseless, silent column of men, as one face leads to another face, so one team blends into another. It is an extended, multinational identity parade. As a viewer you find yourself somewhat uneasily, even guiltily, attempting to discern a "national type" to indicate which team you might be looking at. But by uniting the teams, Buchanan has taken away our bearings, uprooted the reference points of nationhood. Our allegiances have nowhere to go, our means of identification removed.

In *Deadweight* he turns his attention to the professional boxer. However, the spectacle of boxing is removed with the bodyweight of George Foreman or Mike Tyson now translated into bean-bags of low density vinyl which bear the boxer's name, weight and date of a lost bout. Up to 220 lbs in weight, the bean-bags are immovable, but the final round, described in text on the surrounding walls, tells a different story. "He rose on shaky legs and tried desperately to fend off the fighting machine—he moved straight onto a left and

Roderick Buchanan 1965

enthusiast, or the conditions governing that reproduction. He does not deal with sport as a self-contained abstraction but as a set of phenomena engaged in a mutual discourse with the regulations of society, both influential and influenced.

In the video work *Endless Column* (1999), Buchanan teases out our habitual and deeply subjective interpretation of appearances. A camera runs along teams of rugby players standing in line prior to kick off. It records the moment when national anthems are played, when players, evoke either a godhead or plain good luck to propel them to victory.

along right to the head which sent him to the floor beaten." Buchanan's translation of boxing into object and text reveals something shocking—a perverse poetry and vulnerability that lies in most of these games. How questions of cultural identity, including masculinity, intersect with the question of sport is what makes Buchanan's work so thought-provoking, even for those of us who think football is only a game.

Exercepts from Daniel Jewesbury's essay "Peloton"; Susanna Beaumont's essay "Friends vs Other friends"; and Nicky Bird's review "Roderick Buchanan at DCA", *Art Monthly*, Issue 243.

Deadweight + Peloton
(video)
2000
Installation view

Reflections within nature

What strikes us at first sight is the transparency, the fragility and lack of sophistication of the materials Christiane Löhr uses to erect her "micro-edifices". The forms cannot be immediately referred to functions, but all of them explicit a nexus with building, like in *Kleiner Turm – Small tower*, made of ivy seeds. You are instinctively reminded of the miracle of nature, its secret world, the variety of its expressions, but Löhr's figures are a far cry from poetic stereotypes. Instead there is the striving for a balance between inconceivable constructive forces. Who would ever imagine that ivy seeds could be used as elaborate brick-work assemblying walls, in a sort of jointing, that does not require any kind of "mortar" to hold? In *Kleiner Turm – Small tower* an elastic geometry becomes a bearing structure based on uncommon calculations. But all of Christiane Löhr's sculptures betoken an accurate calculation: conceived directly in

but actually the likeness is very vague: what leaps to the eye is the material they are made of and its unexpected expressive potential. So the association between form and object grows less important, becoming more than anything else a suggestive guide. However, her images are very different from Surrealist ones because, not presenting the slightest alteration of the natural materials, they do not suggest a severance from reality, but instead the opportunity to design and shape figures using biological elements.

We might say the images Löhr creates herald a dialogue between biologies and cultures, where the use of the plural is symptomatic of a less hierarchical research between materials and forms, since it displays a participation that has been performed, and not just the unfathomable mystery of nature.

An immediate emotional relationship arises. Christiane displays her works at a height that instinctively connects either with the eye or the heart or the belly of the viewer, precisely to

Christiane Löhr 1965

nature, heeding the variants it imposes. Thus seeds, flowers, horsehair, dog fur... serve as structural fibres that, in being assembled, confer cohesion onto fragility. This is neither an intellectual exercice nor a romantic-intimist approach, but an analytical investigation of expressive possibilities we are not used to separating from plant or animal forms.

When you use flowers or plants to represent an image, you usually do not use the individual parts of their body, whereas Löhr, by splitting up the components of ivy florescences, creates towers, edifices, and by analyzing those of burdock finds the rules to build a "Chalice" or a "Cushion" or a "Fan"... The titles recall objects,

recreate the type of emotion that led her to choose that particular seed, that flower. A connection appears between the images of art, of science, of nature through the idiom of primary handiwork, exactly that of picking fruit and arranging the objects of existence to observe them and understand their functions and truth. For milleniums that material knowledge was delegated to women as custodians of survival, whereas art and science had other, "loftier" tasks. It is not a coincidence if a woman is the one who revives the rules in keeping with which we do not have to separate mind from body, handicraft from science, art from the daily analysis of natural elements.

Francesca Pasini

It was the Italian Futurist musician and painter Luigi Russolo, who in 1913 published his manifesto *The Art of Noises*, that probably first proposed the incorporation of incidental noise in musical composition. Russolo, together with the painter Ugo Piatti, invented the *intonarumori*, an impressive new instrument that emitted different types of noises (gurgles, hisses, explosions, buzzes) with the capacity to regulate tone and pitch, which scandalized audiences at concerts in Modena, Milan and London just before the First World War. Naturally, instruments for making new sounds have been continually invented throughout history and each instrument, obviously, has a visual resonance. The violin has always been seen as well as heard as a beautiful woman. And, of course, many artists and composers of the last century have striven to make music and sounds visible—Scriabin, Schoenberg, Klee, Schwitters, Beuys, Stockhausen, Cage, to name just the obvious. Each of these artists have attempted in their own way to achieve the dream of holding the sounds of the everyday and of the universe, giving them a visual expression. John Cage in his famous Jiulliard Lecture of 1952 proclaimed in his inimitably gentle but authoritative manner that "one has to stop studying music. That is to say one has to stop all the thinking that separates music from living".

In the year 2001 things are the same and things are also different. The attempts go on to capture the sight of sound in terms that are adequate to the dreams and utopias and also

much as an alchemist's kitchen with primitive machines for making both objects and sounds. In the meantime, he has become ever more involved in the high-tech design of music machines, specifically turntables and the brilliant visual appearance of the shiny compact disc which have both become major signs and signals of our age. Music itself assumes the property of sculpture with a strong erotic charge. It becomes even more spatial and dreamlike—a hallucination, as it were, from outer space in which we can lose our identity, halfway between wakefulness and sleep. Nicolai has, with the help of scientific colleagues, picked up the rhythm signals from outer space so that we can literally dance to the sounds of stars—the classical music of the spheres brought to our own times.

But there is much more that we, through the mind and activity of this artist, can listen to and perhaps observe. We have here the sounds of the deep, the sounds of water through the medium of the instrument that is in the exhibition. It is the acoustic wave cannon, which through it s base tones is physically able to pull water into shape, to make waves that remain suspended whilst the tones are emitted. Huge echoing pipes on their metal tables hold in suspension the water in the smaller of the glass spheres or at any rate are suspended by virtue of the tonal frequency. The larger sphere, which is also full of water, is unaffected—the force is insufficient. It is a reminder of Venice, that most fragile Queen of the Seas, of the immense

Carsten Nicolai 1965

the realities of today. Even though we use them constantly, we can now harness astonishing, incredibly perplexing and ultimately mysterious new technologies that are continually and rapidly evolving. In discotheques, in studios, synthesisers of immense complexity transform sounds, manipulate pitch that act physically, and transform and hallucinate the brain as much as any artificial stimulant. Carsten Nicolai is an artist who grew up in the polluted and furtive world of the German Democratic Republic in Karl Marx Stadt (now Chemnitz) and whose studio, when I first saw it in the early nineties, resembled nothing as

forces that rule the tides and continually threaten to engulf so many of our shores and even our continents if we are not careful. Seeing is believing. Carsten Nicolai with his new musical canon/cannon presents us with what he describes as *Unantastbare Gedanken*—incontrovertible thoughts—thoughts and sounds made visible at a magic millennial moment in human history that is both full of hope and full of danger, that also speaks of the insignificance of man in the larger scheme of things. Art exhorts us to continue the fight —to be at one with nature, if not to overcome it.

Norman Rosenthal

Frozen water
2001
Installation, mixed media,
project

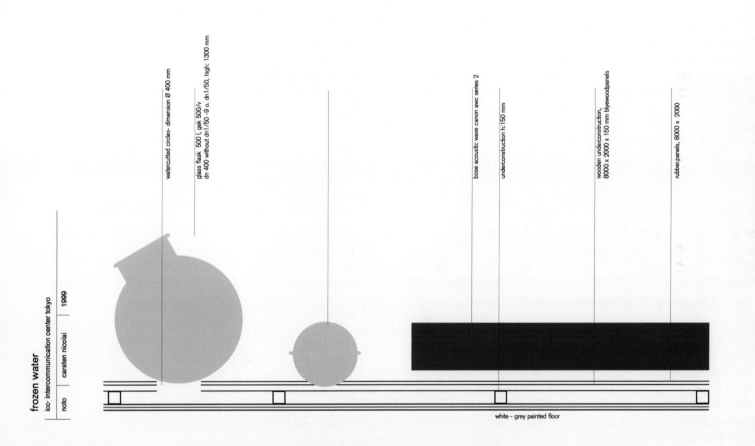

frozen water

icc- intercommunication center tokyo

| noto | carsten nicolai | 1999 |

watercutted circles- dimension Ø 400 mm

glass flask 500 l, gek 500/v
dn 400 without dn1/50 -9 o. dn1/50, high: 1300 mm

bose acoustic wave canon awc series 2

underconstruction h: 150 mm

wooden underconstruction,
8000 x 2000 x 150 mm b/yewoodpanels

rubber,panels, 8000 x 2000

white - grey painted floor

Painting on the Verge of a Nervous Breakdown

Manuel Ocampo is a painter who gives painting a hard time. Whether this is the result of Ocampo's playful questioning of contemporary painting or whether it is the case that painting itself is not up to answering any of Ocampo's questions—well this is difficult to say, but the paintings that emerge from Ocampo's studio seem on the verge of some kind of collapse.

Making sense of Ocampo's practice when an aesthetic appreciation of his paintings risks ridicule, when all attempts at piecing together narratives ends in frustration and when titles and imagery rarely match, means taking the senselessness of these paintings seriously. Hysteria was once thought to be a disease restricted to women, then male hysterics were

pure evil he does at least play the Devil's advocate. The once great tradition of oil painting , in Europe helped define the human in humankind walked hand in hand with the project of Enlightenment and became a banner for Modernist ideals, is on the verge of a nervous breakdown in Ocampo's hands...

There are other readings of Ocampo's work. Kevin Power, in his extended catalogue essay for *Heridas de la Lengua* (Wounds of the Tongue) held in Santa Monica, argues that Ocampo's practice should be viewed as a celebration of an expenditure that exposes the emptiness of representations of good and evil circulating within consumer culture: a reading that presents Ocampo's work as convergent with Baudrillard's concept of simulation and his notion that capitalist societies are consti-

Manuel Ocampo 1965

Manuel Ocampo Ma

written about by Charcot and Freud. Perhaps Ocampo has discovered the unthinkable—hysterical paintings! Hysteria has no physiological cause and appears as the symptoms of some repressed event or trauma. Hysteria is radically disconcerting as it upsets the order of things: speech is disturbed, bodies are paralysed and fears, anxieties and even hallucinations can erupt. Perhaps, then, Ocampo's paintings are hysterical allegories of painting's fragile state and also the fragile state of all that painting stands for. In an interview in *Flash Art*, May 1994, the artist rejected both multiculturalism and the role of the bad boy by claiming he would rather be Satan as "The Devil is God in exile". If Ocampo does not quite manage to be

tuted by an immense circulation and exchange of signs detached from history. While it is true that Ocampo consumes a mass of images and icons which are treated with equal violence and abandonment and that the artist also implies that the cross is equal to the swastika, it might not be true that the artist views all signs as empty or as "floating signifiers".

Ocampo spares nothing, then, when laying waste to culture. In this respect Kevin Power is not so far off the mark when he reads Ocampo's paintings through Baudrillard's writing—as the artist's practice is reminiscent of one of Baudrillard's lesser known slogans: "Even signs must burn".

David Burrows

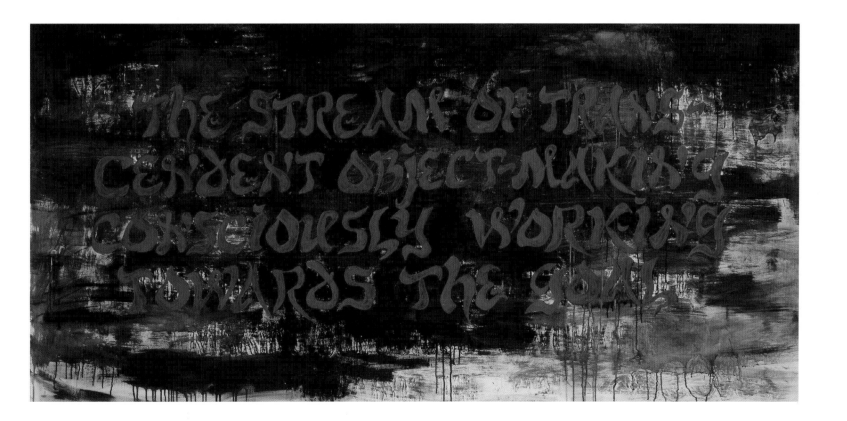

The Stream
of Trascendent Object –
Making Consciously
Working Towards
the Goal
2000
Acrylic on canvas,
122 × 244 cm

A raging fire blazes forth through a long corridor as several cripples hobble in panic in a futile attempt to escape the flames. Every time the fire consumes a cripple, a round of applause is heard. Athletic men, perched on trapezes, swing in succession into a vast emptiness. Their bodies are crushed against a high tower—the clock tower of the Berlin Olympic Stadium of 1936—and fall in pieces onto an examination table in an anatomical theatre. Magnus Wallin's computer animated video works, although possessing an aesthetics akin to that of computer games, are primarily stories about the human body. Or rather, stories concerning the manner in which the human body is portrayed and understood in contemporary western society. The short, animated sequences strike the viewer, with their intensity and subjective camera, and stage a series of events juxtaposing two body types. On the one hand: the perfect athletic bodies that submissively cast themselves into the void in *Skyline*, like cattle on their way to the slaughterhouse. The bodies that form perfect, symmetrical circles, like the decorative swimmers in *Limbo,* where each individual, as an exchangeable cog, constitutes a small part of a larger mechanism. It is the hero-ised body of the monumental aesthetics we see here, a symmetrical machine of pure muscle. We honour this body unconditionally in advertising and fashion, and enjoy watching it perform in our modern day equivalent to the gladiator games in sports arenas, or in game shows on television. On the other hand: the hobbling wretches desperately

key aspects of our culture. We tend to categorise bodies in terms of good and evil, beautiful and ugly, useful and useless. These notions are, in turn, based on the belief that symmetry, clean lines and surfaces, and perfect bodies reflect a divine harmony, as opposed to how bodies that violate these ideals instil horror. Wallin makes us aware of how the human body has, since the first dissections in the anatomical theatres of the Renaissance, steadily become more fragmentised, to the point where it is now presented as a machine—a system of information or codes, the parts of which can easily be improved or replaced. We have adopted an increasingly relentless attitude towards bodies that deviate, function poorly, or simply fail to fulfil the current criteria for beauty.

There is logic to the choice of working with three-dimensional animations in video, a medium normally associated with computer games and the entertainment industry. The world Magnus Wallin creates in his works makes no claims on realism or reality. Instead, his interest lies in how we create concepts and ideologies through the use of images. Hieronymus Bosch, pictorial quotations of Leni Riefenstahl's films, and psychedelic visions of paradise, reminiscent of new age imagery, appear side by side. Wallin does not categorise these various pictorial elements, nor does he grade them. They all play a part in our visual culture, and express how we view humanity. Through this cannibalistic borrowing of

strategy among artists working with new media. Instead, Wallin consciously takes advantage of the visual force inherent in the imagery of popular culture as a means of sending out a message, and readily makes use of a strong rhetoric to captivate his viewer.

Sara Arrhenius

Magnus Wallin 1965

trying to save themselves from the firestorm in *Exit.* These cripples represent the body that everyone chooses to turn a blind eye to, and that no one need be cursed with, as long as an effort is made to exercise, eat right, and undergo plastic surgery! A malformed exclamation mark, a grotesque deformity that reminds us of our pain and shortcomings; the body that we feel compelled to hide, correct, adjust and discipline.

Upon viewing Magnus Wallin's four video works, *Exit, Limbo, Physical Paradise* and *Skyline* together, the consistency of his work becomes apparent. A critical analysis is brought to bear, focusing on how these concepts of the human body are intimately intertwined with

imagery, Magnus Wallin demonstrates how certain age-old notions of man and the human body still prevail in contemporary iconography, and continue to convey a strong ideology. The use of video animation is not simply a choice of medium, but also a method of examining and commenting on the manner in which this medium is applied in our culture. When one chooses to work with video, as opposed to techniques exclusively identified with high culture, such as painting, one chooses a medium that is used in society at large, charged with aspects of the times and the fantasies therein. In Wallin's work, we find no trace of the media-critical distance and the visualisation of the conditions of the medium, a normal

Exit
1997
3D animation, stills
from video

Exit
1997
3D animation, stills
from video

Skyline
2000
3D animation, stills
from video

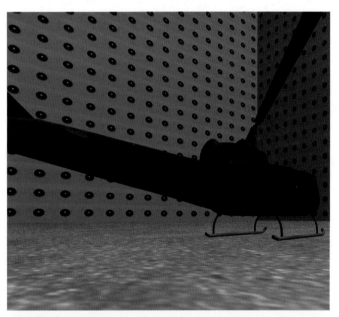

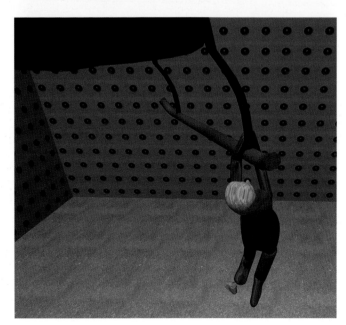

Welcome to a brave new world. It's an easy and accessible place. We know lots of people gladly living their lives there already. Foreign and familiar, it offers all the comforts and dis-ease of the culture whence it was conjured. Just jump right on in, the web waters are warm in this perverse, predatory and all too pervasive cyber-swamp. Here, full-time fools can spout half-baked ideas and semi-truths without any recourse to the skewered ratio of irrationality and ignorance. Think of it as a grand millennial costume ball, an endlessly unfolding shopping mall. You can come as anyone and leave with anything.

Yes it's a brave new world indeed, where everything is possible as long as you pay no attention to the cowards hiding behind streaming curtains. Just like the mighty all-powerful Oz, the substance is in the projection, not the weak and the geek riding on a mouse. And just as surely as that former fiction exploded the dimension of representation with the technology of Technicolor to birth a Pop planet, our new meta-fictions are here to collapse that space with an industry of icons that will just as surely give rise to an even more artificial Eden. Nick Waplington has been busy tending this garden of unearthly delights, cloning its illusory flowers of seduction into mutant hybrids of hucksterism, and mining the fecally fertilized soil for all its component contradictions and curious conformities.

These places.com don't really exist *per se*, but you will recognise them anyway as *a priori*

ibility and reality, you might just be surprised at how much stranger the truth is from fiction. There is no editorial here, just an index of our cultural idiocy. Of course whatever their spiel, Nick's got his tongue so firmly in cheek the logic gets tripped up in the lurid prose of its own visual and linguistic propaganda. The artist's position in all this is opaque, his politics as invisible as his hand in the slick spectacle of these hard-sell surfaces. But if the point is ambiguous, the perspective itself is far from ambivalent.

Waplington avoids the polemics of cultural critique in favor of a more sarcastically edged social satire. Portraits of the public discourse that are so outré they hardly need exaggeration, they are nonetheless unmistakable as piss-takes on the inherent stupidity of the medium and its message.

For the many who have come to regard Nick Waplington as one of the most honest and deeply humanist voices in contemporary art, the pleasure he now takes in perpetrating the same kinds of vulgar lies and cheap come-ons of the infotainment industry, and the brutally dark humour he bares here, constitutes an aesthetic shift so abrupt and outrageous that the very terms of continuity by which we measure creative evolution are all but obliterated.

Carlo McCormick

Nick Waplington 1965

projections of this domain's more probable terrain. In turn pathetic, provocative and prurient, Waplington's webscape may often be disturbing or just as likely appealing, but most of all it's just plain hilarious. No more a condescension than an endorsement, it's really a comic celebration of the chaos. The implicit content and barely-hidden agenda Waplington makes absurdly evident in these mock-sites are like generic caricatures of the various genres that populate and pollute the internet. Taken individually, these home pages can run the gamut from shocking to mundane, from the completely unbelievable to the all too likely. And just when you think something is so completely over the top that it defies all cred-

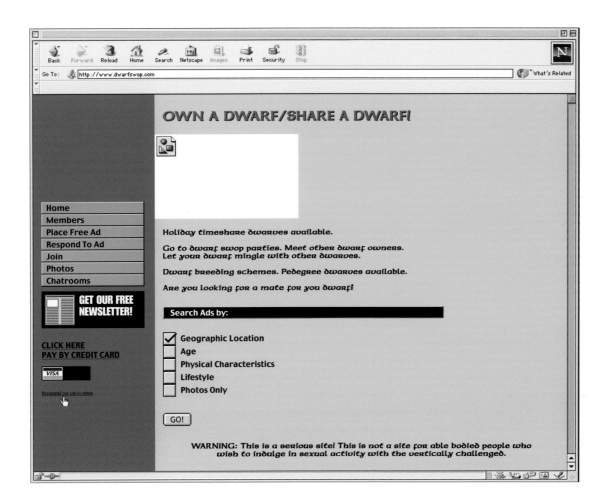

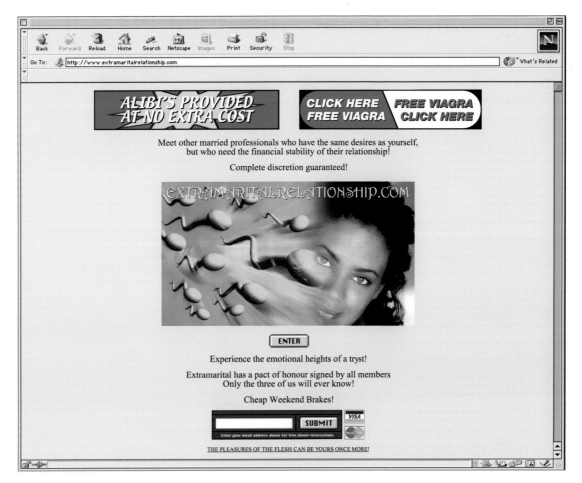

"We try to synthesize the world in keeping with our ideas, yet we are not willing to accept the consequences."

"Ruan" is the name of one of Xiao Yu's creatures, which he defines as "a predator animal with wings and mammae. Its physiological structure makes it impossible to date and classify it in terms of present-day biology. It is a crawling, amphibious animal, issued from a water creature equipped with just a spine. Its growth process is that of a mammal. It developed during the prehistorical period of dinosaurs, surviving after their extinction. In all probability it will keep on reproducing itself for a long time".

So Ruan bathes in a clear liquid, just like the many examples of animals conserved in natural science museums in Europe and China, and can be seen from all sides by the attentive observer. Comparable to the monsters—authentic or counterfeit—that were the curiosities of scholars' cabinets, and thronged

of the character Xiao Yu invented is composed of existing features, yet combined so as to have no phonetic or connotative matches. That is why, even in the Chinese text, Xiao Yu must write his transliteration next to the character, which is illegible. This is also the case for the "ideophonograms" invented for his other creatures, like Wu, an installation consisting of hybrid creatures formed by rabbits and ducks, and Jiu, where unlike the other instances, the laboratory rats used inside glass balls are still alive. The manipulation the artist performs on animals' or humans' bodies can undoubtedly be linked up with man's age-old longing—at least in the Western mind—to become a Creator, to invent new species no longer answering to environmental requisites, but instead to their inventor's imagination. In the past these attempts, performed for the most part on dead bodies, produced nothing but "laboratory fakes", exactly like Xiao Yu's creatures.

Xiao Yu 1965

Courts and *Wunderkammern* after the discovery of new worlds, Ruan is a disturbing, hybrid being, whose origin we wonder at. Among the "ingredients" of an exemplar of Ruan, we discover with horror the artist has used a premature foetus's head, a rabbit, a cat, a rat, and even condoms for eyes.

The Chinese character used to catalog the creature is not legible: Xiao Yu formed it *ex-novo* by using on the one hand the radical *zhi*, that also has the independent meaning of "footless and limbless insect (or reptile)" as mentioned in old books. The homophone *zhi* in classical Chinese refers to a legendary monster capable of distinguishing good men from evil, destroying the latter. The other half

But now that transgenic food has overwhelmed the market, and that the perspective of cloning human beings seems real, the game has grown more risky. Especially because in serious question is the human ability to understand—beyond the actual, physical difficulties—where our true good lies.

The appearance of Xiao Yu's monsters is both repulsive and true-to-life, precisely because the individual parts forming them—wings, head, body—are familiar to us. A combination that creates dismay and therefore warns us against the delusion of omnipotence that drives and at the same time blinds every creator of "monsters".

Monica Dematté

Ruan
1999
Holograph of installation,
70 × 50 cm

Eva Marisaldi's work consists of thirty-five post-card-size plaster bas-reliefs. Without end. Without end, as we all hope our relations with those we love will be. Thirty-five white images that focus our attention, in the same number of separate scenes, on the close-up where bodies draw near, where a head rests on a shoulder, arms meet, feet graze, the moment when the intimate dimension is displayed in one body's abandon to another, the moment when meeting becomes welcoming. Eva Marisaldi stages physical closeness, intimacy, contact.

The pictures, mainly touched up photographs from newspapers, in some cases shots from films, are bare, boiled down to the essentials, requiring neither further comment nor captions. In their simplicity, gestures, postures, say more than words. Keeping distances, holding at a distance, are not just manners of speech but expressions that describe in plain terms an emotional state, we also and mainly perceive the temperature of personal relationships in terms of space.

The images surface like ghosts from an unspecified time. The suspended narrative dimension is emphasized by the suggestion of a typical form of classicism, the explicit withdrawal from the noisy ambit of the news, conferring on the panels the character of *exempla*. Multiplication confirms that role; we are faced with a range of possibilities; there could be as many others: the individual story does not seem to matter much, a particular situation at a given moment, the central point

rows of ten and on each one she hand-embroidered the last ten frames of the same number of films and, alongside, four videos, respectively four possible ends to stories; if the introduction of a strictly handmade mark is a way to take over the swift motion of cinematic time, a way to enlarge individual perception within the collective imagination, on the other hand the videos relate a possible version of the facts, whose partiality, the fact of only knowing part of the story, is an extremely realistic rendering of the way our experience of the world is fashioned. The same partiality in rendering a comparison with reality, and the subjective terms of relationship with others, reiterates in an even more recent work (*Pallida Idea*, Tommaso Corvi Mora gallery, London 2001). Eva Marisaldi presented four portraits (three friends and a well-known racing-car constructor) where there were no photographs: on show there were only indications drawn from the interpretation of the artist's relationship with these people, plus an oral story regarding the friends. The result is anything but what we ordinarily call a portrait, but at the same time renders a far more intense degree of likelihood and intimacy than a picture.

In the stories Eva stages there is always something missing. Sometimes what is missing is only seemingly filled by the multiplication of possibilities (more finals, more sequences), but that is a temporary solution that actually extends the question rather than providing an answer. There are no shortcuts; the explo-

Eva Marisaldi 1966

being the detail present in all of them, becoming the actual guiding line.

Eva Marisaldi reduces details to a modicum. It is nearly impossible to recognize who the faces and bodies transformed into bas-reliefs belong to, so the image takes on a bare, essential character, background sound and context are pared to a strict minimum. Hence the artist adds another stage to her career, where the intentionally undisciplined use of the media and close confrontation with narrative rules create something akin to a reiterated theme. For instance, we again have both elements in the installation executed at the Museo d'Arte Moderna of Trento (*Lieto Fine*, 2000). There Eva Marisaldi arranged 120 cushions in twelve

ration of questions embodied in identity, never meant as an autonomous factor but always referring to the encounter with another, only offers temporary assumptions, the subjectivity played out in the relationship is the highest form of truth we are capable of experiencing. The awareness of this limit does not lead to a view of the world content with its relativity, but to the opportunity of real dialogue.

Absence, the point in which we feel a vacuum, is precisely the point that seems to interest the artist, the final point she means to lead us to, but beyond which the viewer can decide which road to take. It is up to us to choose what happened before, what will happen later.

Emanuela De Cecco

Senza fine # 1/5
2000
Series of 7 plaster
bas-reliefs,
10 × 15 cm each

Senza fine # 1/2
2000
Series of 7 plaster
bas-reliefs, 10 × 15 cm
each

In the early 1980s, graffiti was co-opted by the art world and graffiti writers were enticed to change the direction of their spray cans from walls to canvas, and from the street to the gallery, in a short-lived craze. Twenty years later, three graffiti writers—Barry McGee/TWIST, Stephen Powers/ESPO, and Todd James/REAS—have entered contemporary art on their own terms by bringing the street, both literally and figuratively, into the gallery. It is not just graffiti they practice, but graffiti in 3-D—a theme park of the streets. Their collaboration, which began at the Institute of Contemporary Art, Philadelphia, as "Indelible Market", last May, metamorphosed into "Street Market", shown at Deitch Projects, New York, where the installation took on the proportions of a miniature city block filtered through the ironic, witty, and at times, post-apocalyptic interpretations of the urban condition as perceived by McGee, Powers, and James.

texts resembling handpainted advertising signs. McGee likes to keep his gallery work separate from his outdoor work, yet there is traffic between these two worlds. For instance, the deep-red that has been so prevalent in his indoor art grows out of his love of tagging red doorways in San Francisco's Chinatown. As Eungie Joo, who curated *Regards, Barry McGee* at the Walker Art Center, has noted, McGee's indoor murals appear to be more *about* graffiti than graffiti itself, including its erasure, since the blotches of gray and liver-coloured paint we often see on the sides of buildings, on bridge pillars, and so on, remain its only record. Another component of McGee's art brings together drawings on found paper, fruit produce logos, photographs of favourite tags, graffiti writers in action, and photographs of both urban despair and quirkiness—all mounted in thrift-shop frames. As a graffiti writer, McGee is accustomed to tagging, drawing, and

visual noise of the cheap urban-retail experience. Mock businesses, including a *bodega* (urban corner store), a check-cashing store, liquor store, and limousine dispatching service, are animated by a cacophony of hand-painted and custom-fabricated signs featuring ESPO and REAS tags, invented store names, and gimmicky advertising slogans. Powers and James's collaboration is a variation on brand-building through logo and name identification, taking their cue from both capitalist consumer culture and graffiti. Ironically playing off the idea of transforming image into product, Powers and James designed consumer goods for the *bodega*, identified by their trademark tags and characters and/or invented product titles (which include cans of "Street Cred", "Dignity", "Sarcasm", "Guilt", and "Delusion", among others); they recall the Wacky Packages stickers that Art Spiegelman pioneered for Topps chewing gum thirty years

Barry McGee 1966 - Stephen Powers 1966 - Todd James 1969

McGee is known for his trademark down-and-out characters, use of red ground in his indoor installations, and his calligraphic tag TWIST, which often appears on "Hello my name is..." labels. McGee's gallery work emphasizes his impression of the sensory overload of the streets, where sad-sack figures, which recall anything from *Mad Magazine*'s Don Martin characters to Mexican mural art, to McGee's own mug, to the urban dispossessed, share space with drips, tags (some partly erased by imaginary, antigraffiti buff squads), amorphous honeycomb shapes, and miscellaneous

painting on any given surface. McGee's miniature paintings of characters on discarded liquor bottles, as well as his use of rusty, old letterpress type trays as a ground for painting—two other aspects of McGee's indoor art—demonstrate the agility acquired by the necessity of tagging and marking anything, anywhere, and is, perhaps, further evidence of the bridge between the worlds of his graffiti and "fine" art practice.

Powers and James counterbalance McGee's interpretation of the "cheerful hell of urban life" (as he has described it) by mimicking the

ago. The *bodega* is a site for the intersection of the illicit and the legitimate, where nickel bags of marijuana are sometimes sold alongside Lil' Hugs juices. In the constantly gentrifying neighbourhoods of New York and other cities, *bodegas* affront the sensibilities of the Dean and DeLuca crowd, maintaining their grittiness and authenticity. The *bodega* is a fitting metaphor for the graffiti writer: What is perceived as ugly, underground, and illegal—essentially an affront to the "quality of life"—continues to thrive alongside the gentrified.

Alex Baker

Street market
2000
Mixed media, variable
size, installation view
at Deitch Projects,
october-december 2000

Street market
2000
Mixed media, variable
size, installation view
at Deitch Projects,
october-december 2000

Street market
2000
Mixed media, variable
size, installation view
at Deitch Projects,
october–december 2000

"I know that, to the common apprehension,
this phenomenon of whiteness is
not confessed to be the prime agent
in exaggerating the terror of objects
otherwise terrible; nor to the unimaginative
mind is there aught of terror
in those appearances whose awfulness to
another mind almost solely consists
in this one phenomenon, especially when
exhibited under any form at all
approaching to muteness or universality.
What I mean by these two statements
may perhaps be respectively elucidated by
the following examples:"

Herman Melville, *Moby Dick*

Self-Portrait
as a fountain
2000
Mixed media installation,
183 × 549 cm

Paul Pfeiffer 1966

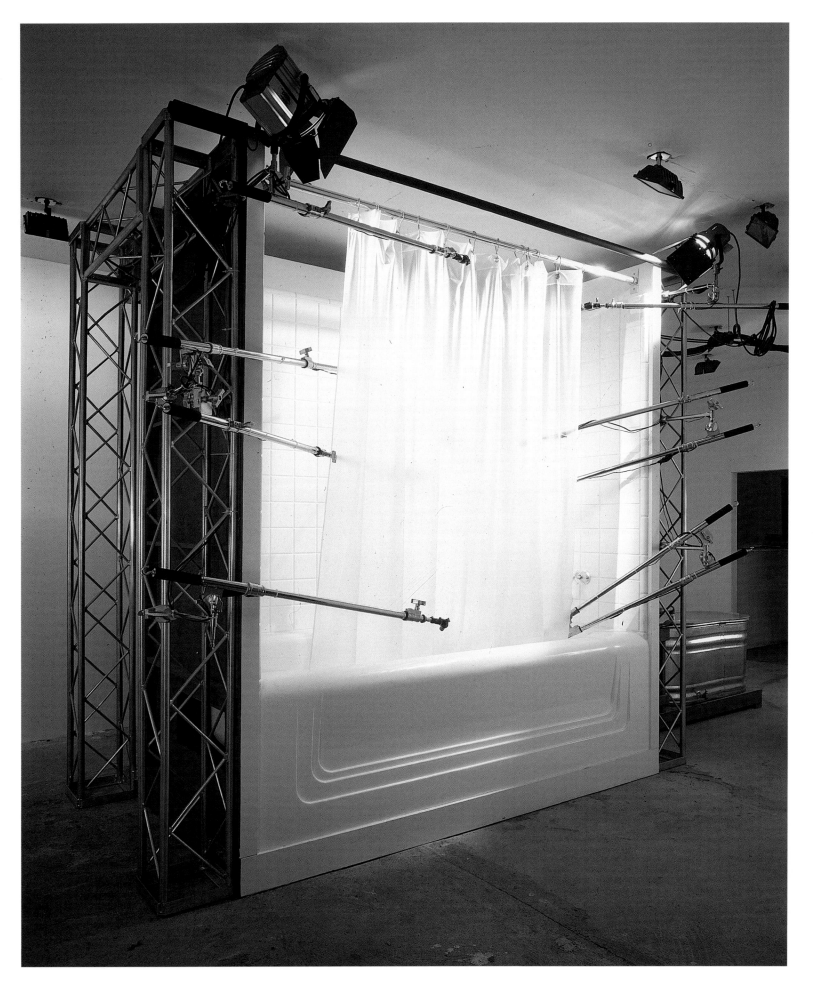

What Santiago Sierra proposes is a study of less "noble" ways of earning a wage. This is a work based on a stringent critique of the capitalist economic system as well as its racial and class scale. Sierra analyses the concept of "wage" in its crudest form: he creates activities in which idleness is the factor that determines the sum of money that is earned without recourse to the concept of productivity, and involving activities that simply correspond to the selling of time without allowing ideological or ethical readings to impinge on action.

Each of his performances is perversely designed: they take into consideration real wages in the geopolitical area in which the performance is undertaken as well as the social hierarchies in place among the inhabitants of the area and its racial characteristics. In Mexico, where Sierra lives, he used dark-skinned, medium-height males; in Europe and the United States he has concentrated on immigrant groups, whether they be Africans, Latin Americans, Asians or, as has recently happened, East Europeans.

On May 4 2000, in the small, alternative "Acceso A" in Mexico City, Sierra summoned five people to hold up an unfixed gallery wall which was inclined at a 60-degree angle. Each of them was contractually paid a total of 700 pesos (US$ 65) to make sure the wall, which they themselves had uprooted, did not veer from the acute 60-degree angle during the four-hour-a-day, five-day *Tarea Inocua* (*Innocuous Work*) performance. Zero produc-

rooms in the well-known P.S.1 Contemporary Art Center in New York into two perfectly-inhabitable spaces: one of these had only one small square opening for the delivery of food, and was used as a total confinement area for a worker who wanted to be paid for the equivalent of 360 continuous hours of work, without any further definition of whether his activity could be "economic" or leisure (what's more, the worker was the only person who could verify how he used his "working hours"); the other space was used by the general public, who would contemplate the concept of the selling of time, devoid of any productive sense or social retribution.

Perhaps the most oppressive and difficult of all proposed studies is the where the human body is forced to be the only interlocutor possible in obtaining remuneration in the form of wages. Sierra has come up with three distinct proposals by tattooing perfect lines on people who are then given about twice the minimum wage as defined in their respective countries. The first line was tattooed vertically along a worker's shoulders, and the tattoo was completed in Mexico City in 1998. Then, in 1999, Sierra, in collaboration with the Habana alternative Aghitinador space, summoned six men and offered them what was a rather hefty sum of money for Cuba and tattooed a horizontal line that ideally joined all six men. The most recent version of this tattooed line was undertaken with four salaried prostitutes in Salamanca who were also drug addicts. Sierra had already

pay anywhere between four and six times this amount for each shot of heroin: 12,000 pesetas. Photographs of this performance show, for the first time in Sierra's work, one of the participants grimacing in pain as she watches one of her friends being tattooed. Even for the artist himself, this social fact goes well beyond the abstractions of earning a wage.

When Sierra manages to find 200 immigrants in Italy who will be given a pre-established wage from the Venice Biennale staff, his conceptual proposal will undergo an all-important turning point in reference to what he has been after for a long time. Used to the problems inherent in evolving situations, the artist has managed to bring an absolute control to bear on the economic remuneration offered by his performances and to painstakingly negotiate the right amount of money for his workers (such an essential part of his artistic concept) with the institutions involved.

In these performances this group of immigrants can be clearly distinguished from the public by the colour of their hair. They will be given a wage that is not only the end result of the economic processes the artist has analysed; the institution itself has also accepted the process, thus demonstrating a contemporary "curatorial" opinion that is both shared and encouraging.

Taiyana Pimental

Santiago Sierra 1966

tivity, earning money as the only profitable use of time: unprofitability, yes, but a distinctly possible economic equation. The insistence on checking the 60-degree angle communicates two of the theoretical premises Sierra has developed. On the one hand the absurdity of the activity of symbolic economy; on the other, the successful corruption of neat, clean forms that, heirs to post-minimalism, and especially Robert Morris's and Richard Serra's post-minimalism, allowed him to understand the ability each object has to be transformed into a symbol for a process, into "action".

Following from this, in September 2000, the Madrid artist designed a diagonal wall of bricks he then used to subdivide one of the

dealt with the same theme in a performance held in conjunction with the Havana Biennale, where he offered the same amount of money a prostitute would earn for a night's work. But in the same performance, undertaken at the Reina Sofia in Madrid, the tattooed women simply privileged their payment over the activity for which they were paid. This was one of the most revelatory, eloquent and devastating responses the artist has ever received to his artistic proposals: there is an enormous difference between the wages prostitutes earn for this type of economic activity and the price they have to pay to satisfy their "sick" pleasures. Each blow job earns them between 2,000 and 3,000 pesetas, but these women have to

Linea de 160 cm
tatuada sobre cuatro
personas
Performance at El Gallo
Arte Contemporanea,
Salamanca,
December 2000
Cibachrome b/w

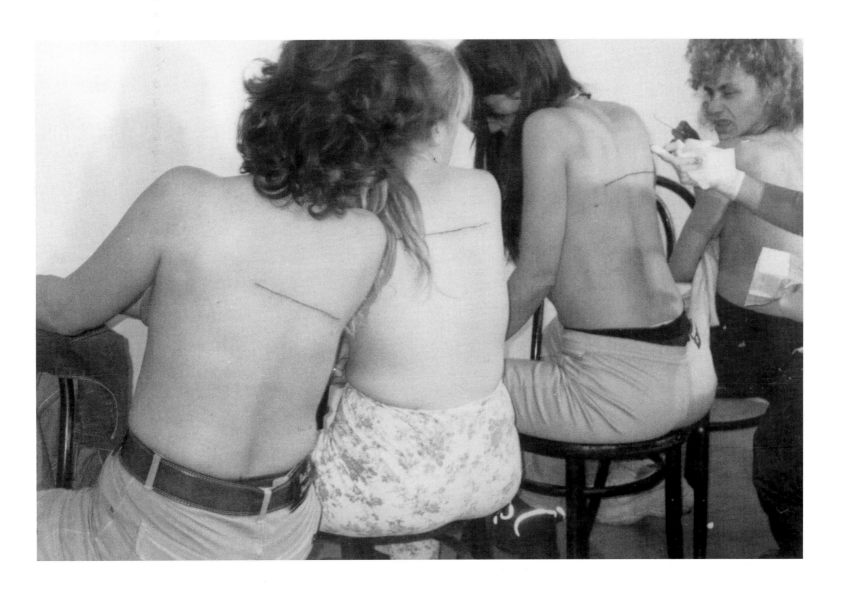

Facing Forward (1999) opens with a slow pan across rows of men, posed as if for a group photograph. The leaders are Europeans, the lower ranks "natives", the moment some time in the past when the still camera was the more familiar tool for recording. Most stare fixed towards the lens, holding a pose, deferential to the strictures of documentary witness. A second fragment is structurally similar but thematically and typologically quite other. In this archival extract, a single line of naked tribesmen is again revealed by the slow pan of the camera. This time the framing conventions resemble those of early ethnographic representation. The paralleling of these—the historicised social record contrasting with the 'timeless' anthropological data—conjure up two separate documentary traditions, and through that two distinct discourses.

The question of the relation of the past to the present offers an entry to Fiona Tan's primary preoccupation. For it introduces the structure, mechanisms and discourses through which she probes her thematic, the means by which self-awareness and, perforce, self-understanding may be construed.

In *Facing Forward* the principal vehicles for this enquiry are the dual figures of the traveller and the anthropologist, both represented by the anonymous white cameraman. He cranks his camera which points directly to the screen and hence to the viewer, indicating that the spectator is equally the subject of this work. Short segments of representative ethnographic

Smoke Screen (1997), which again uses archival ethnographic footage, raises the question of responsibility towards one's source material.

Prompted by the subtle insertion of multiple voices in text panels, doubts are raised both as to the authenticity of this brief episode, in which young Asian children are filmed smoking, and to the ethics of not only its original makers but subsequent appropriators. The shift in tone and idiom in this laconic commentary—"With my own eyes"; "Boys will be men"; "These infants take advantage of the opportunity that mother is shopping", "Indonesia, maybe 1930"—together with the uncertainty of the subject positions undermines the belief in a single source of authority. Intercutting an image of a contemporary filmmaker (herself) into the original footage, Tan proposes without actually instantiating a subjective ethnography. Additional postulates emerge. The truth of a statement proves to be merely a function of the particular discourse in which it is embedded and fiction occupies a central place within the documentary genre.

In *Facing Forward*, as in *Smoke Screen*, the faith of a former era in the evidentiary value of cinema as document is rewritten in order to explore ways in which knowledge of a different order may be conveyed, ways where neither medium nor genre are regarded as transparent or direct. Both photographic and filmic images are revealed to be synthetic and hybridised, infused with mis-readings and

Fiona Tan 1966

footage follow. The juxtaposition of diverse extracts emphasises the heterogeneity of this material which, given its wide-ranging geographical origins, becomes a prism for the world at large.

Overlaying the discourses of the traveller and the ethnographer Tan privileges poetics over politics. A site of multiple displacements and rearticulations of what is allegedly either documentary record or subjective witness, *Facing Forward* definately and incisively highlights a fundamental question; what James Clifford refers to as the absence of "a unified, inclusive historical consciousness" propels this young artist to search into issues of identity as a prerequisite to a larger understanding.

counter-assumptions as much as with shared beliefs, contractual agreements, and mutual convenience. A new, perhaps deeper understanding of these representational languages emerges from Tan's succinct and modest installations, one that is imbued with a disarming potency, a tense yet haunting charge.

Lynne Cooke

Abbreviated excerpt from 'Fiona Tan: Re-Take', essay written by Lynne Cooke, published in *Scenario - Fiona Tan*, vandenberg & wallroth, Amsterdam 2000.

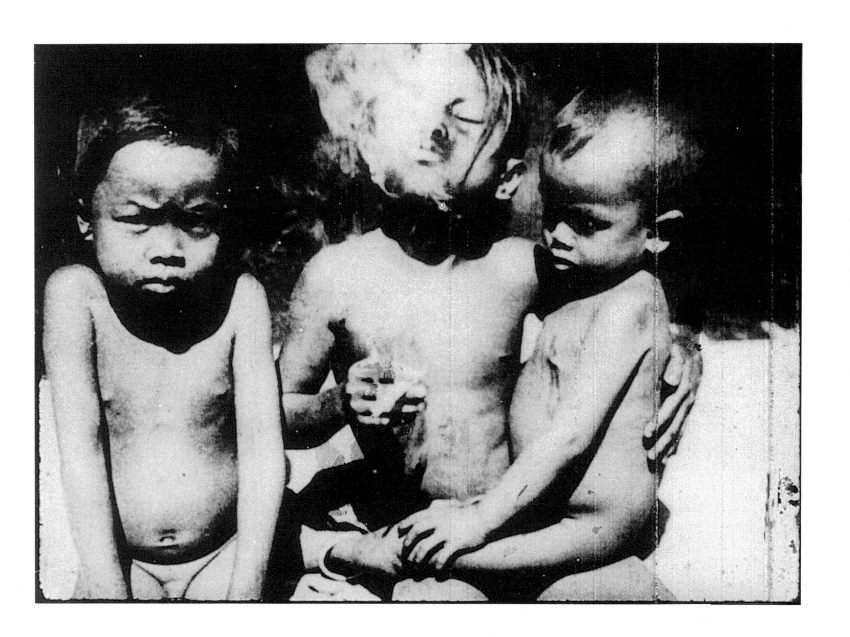

Facing Forward
1999
Video projection transfert
from 35 mm, 11',
still from video

Room with a view

Everybody is familiar with it: the door opens, you go in—wardrobe, bed, television, washing facilities—and the story begins. The hotel room as a middle room, as an intermezzo between here and there where this pleasant anonymity opens all doors and notions. It is attractive because of its location in no-man's land, the area between the place one is dreaming of and the one one is trying to escape from.

Alexandra Ranner's sculptural room is surrounded by nothing that would place it in a contextual meaning. It is a corpus cut off from the world and its exterior form and nature only repeats what is suggested—a semi-provisional construction with simple materials that reproduce the scenario of an exact room arrangement inside, and creates the strange atmosphere of a state of emergency. Although the room reminds one of the already mentioned hotel room, it still appears artificial, isolated, almost a model.

A pane of glass on the front divides the artificial atmosphere of the sculpure and thus preserves it. The objects seem slightly alien, a little exaggerated: the washbasin is slightly odd, the wardrobe a little hermetic, the shadows particularly sharp and the light like the twilight lighting of ambiguity. Nothing in the room stems from our presence and vice versa. The room remains alone in its perfect sterile isolation, while someone puts their suitcase down this side of the glass.

tion, of an empty space, of a person who might be there. Due to its form, the window next to the television suggests an exit that seems to promise a trap rather than a liberating view.

However, the situation changes dramatically while looking at the invisible mirror surface: neither the effect of the *trompe-l'oeil* that makes us think the mirror is real, nor the vampire-like fading of our own reflection is decisive, but rather the presence of a real room behind the fake mirror, on the other side of the reflection.

In that very moment in which the mirror asserts its own absence, one inevitably disappears in the wake and turbulence of this other room and re-finds oneself as a stranger on the very spot the television seems to point to. This place, protected from anything visible appears to be the secret centre that asserts its profound difference to the other rooms behind the false mirror and its inhabitant who leaves the room through the doors behind me is invisible to me at that moment.

It would be naive to believe that this piece can build its tension through the effect of the mirror alone. If it wants to push us away from an egocentric perspective through its twistings and turnings and we lose ourselves in this other room that lies beyond reflection then the absence of the Romantic notion of the empty space becomes a presence of progressively private area the other side of the individual.

Markus Ambach

Alexandra Ranner 1967

The immobility of the situation includes everything, from nothing happening to a murder ballad: everything is ready, the stage is ready but nobody begins. The ambivalence of the situation causes a sensation of ill-ease that increases the restlessness in the room, oscillating between paralysis and expectation. In its autonomy it remains in an incredible state of absence and whoever tries to locate and search the room has already become the absent leading actor.

After peering anxiously into the shower room to the right of the wardrobe, one finds oneself in front of the mirror hanging over the washbasin. It narrates what is hidden in the room: a television makes one aware of a hidden posi-

Après lude
2001
Plexiglass, styropor,
glass, artificial leather,
installation,
218 × 360 × 460 cm

Date: September 18, 2002. **Time**: 9 PM. **Place**: Brooklyn, New York; the home and studio of artist X. **Objective**: A weekly game of cards between six friends. **Socio-economic background**: 30ish, single, at the height of their professional life, working 24/7.

The friends:

"The Banker": Owner of a booming Internet services company that survived the great NAS-DAQ crashes of 2001; recently started buying real estate in Manhattan.

"The Snake": Owner of one of the hippest clubs in New York; dubiously associated with the New York mob.

"Euphoria": The only one in the group who picked out his own nickname. Poet and intellectual by nature, makes a living as a video editor for MTV.

"The Judge": Currently producing a series of documentaries about young artists in New York for the BBC; an acclaimed independent writer for *Art in America*; was nicknamed "Judge" several years ago, when two of his friends convinced him that an exhibition he criticized mercilessly in his column was actually an excellent production... The two were labeled "X" and "Y".

"Y" was among the most successful of the Cooper Union School of Art graduates. Already in his first year in the academy everybody knew that if Y didn't develop a mental illness and drop out of the academy, chances were he would become a prominent and influential

Jerry. X too was pigeonholed as a future Cooper Union *wunderkind*, however he developed a mental illness and dropped out of the academy. X tried to pass it on to Y. But even back then they fought about whether you should say "art world" or "art establishment".

X did quite well in the art establishment even without the Cooper Union's golden stamp of approval, and got almost as far as where he is now, just past the big money machine, which is where he has not yet gotten to... namely, at the top. At the same place where Y is.

The time machine:

Every weekend for the past seven years they have been meeting at X's home, which doubles as his studio. The pretext is to play a game of cards. The real reason is that they simply like hanging out together. X's home-studio is just as messy and dirty as it was ten years ago. It's like a time machine that takes them all back to when they were 20, when they had no inhibitions or masks, nothing to lose and nothing to gain, not even one day of standard work and certainly no concept of what was politically correct.

Rules of the Game:

1. No playing for money.
2. Cheating is allowed, but if you get caught the penalty is a $100 fine to each of the friends.
3. Ace of Hearts always wins.

both superb artists." But it was too late. The Snake had already come to life. "What do you mean there is no absolute way to measure who is the better artist," said the Snake, repeating the Judge's words. "Sure there are! Money! The better artist is the one whose art is worth more money!" The Banker concurred. At this point Euphoria joined in: "It's time you put yourselves on a scale. We all know there's always been a competition between you two. So why not put the cards on the table. Set a date, say a month from now, divide a space into two, and whoever sells his artworks for the most amount of money is the winner. Needles to say, the Snake liked the idea. The Judge was swept away in the excitement, in a manner more characteristic of Euphoria. It sounded delightfully dangerous. "Two artists of your calibre competing... competing about who's worth more of all things. I can't recall anyone who ever had the guts to do that before." The Banker immediately suggested that the competition be held in the lobby of the new building he recently purchased for his monstrous Internet services company (it surely couldn't hurt his company's dull image). X agreed at once. Y heard himself agreeing too. The whole thing got way out of proportion. The Banker's publicist also recognized the great business potential and got busy setting a huge PR and advertising campaign in motion. But what made the whole thing such hot news was a report that New York's black market gamblers hopped on the bandwagon with unprecedented enthusiasm. An aging mobster who was called in

Eliezer Sonnenschein **1967**

artist. Y did not develop any mental illness. Not only did he receive a diploma from the Cooper Union, he graduated with honours. Now, five and a half years later, Y has been described as a meteor in the contemporary art world, real close to becoming a prominent and influential artist. Y added: "It's scary. I got too far too fast. This dream could shatter in a split second, just before I reach the top." X agreed with Y for a change. Euphoria suggested that they just say they're already at the top now. The Snake added that instead of saying "the top" they should say "the big money machine". The Banker concurred. The Judge said nothing.

Y and X met during their first year at Cooper Union. Their classmates called them Tom and

In between the third and fourth games, the Banker went over to the pile of crates by the small sink (the kitchen) to make coffee. "Isn't it time you had a normal kitchen?" he asked. "Why should he have a normal kitchen!" Y interjected, "It would ruin his anti-establishment image." X flashed a half-smile at Y. Y knew he was right on the money and felt pretty smug. He knew that half-smile of X. Knowing that half-smile just as well, the Banker dropped the bomb: "Tell me, which one of you is the better artist?" With a leering gesture, the Judge immediately diffused the Banker's question. "There is no absolute way to measure which one is the better artist." And like a protective mother he added: "They are

as a commentator said on the news that this was a new crowd the majority of which had never before taken to gambling. X and Y found themselves in the eye of the storm. They could not back out now. The lobby of the Internet services company was divided into two closed spaces. X set out to work immediately. Y took a little longer. The competition posters were everywhere. Dozens of phone calls from reporters kept coming in. X and Y's faces were plastered all over the media. The Banker's publicist made sure there were news leaks. And to make matters worse, X had already begun working full speed ahead: wooden boards went in and out; the sound of hammering and smell of fresh paint emanated from his space. All this made Y feel he was los-

Come to kill
1998
Mixed media installation,
variable size

ing it. And then suddenly it dawned on him. When X went out, Y broke into his space and installed two hidden cameras. One quick glance around gave Y the impression that X was building cabinets and cubicles. Y knew that with his cameras, he had the ace up his sleeve. The public interest on the day of the competition was immense. Scores of big shot art collectors came from all over the world to participate in the auction. Y asked to present his work first. He talked about art as a current social factor, about a competitive, intrusive society that had lost all moral codes, about how copying and reproducing stolen ideas is no longer something to be ashamed of... etc. Members of the audience gazed at one another. And then he told them about the TV cameras he had planted in X's space, and that he, Y, had in fact copied detail-for-detail what X constructed in the adjacent space. The audience voiced their admiration. The doors of Y's space opened. At the center stood four red cabinets on wheels. The audience applauded at length. The Banker was the only one who could not figure out why everyone was so excited about some kitchen cabinets that X made for his apartment. His timing perfectly premeditated, Y added: "Why don't we let X describe the work I reproduced?" It was a knockout. The Judge calmed down the audience and gave X the floor. X looked in Y's direction and with that half-smile of his said to the Judge that according to the rules of the game Y owed him $100 for cheating. The audience, most of whom knew the rules of the game, burst into liberating laughter. Without another word, X quickly opened the doors of his space. It was totally empty! All eyes—the audience's and mainly Y's—looked for the cabinets-on-wheels that were supposed to be there. The room was empty! Well, not entirely empty. Sprawled out smack in the middle of the wall was the killer. Y closed his eyes. The audience gave him a standing ovation. Ace of Hearts always wins.

Eliezer Sonnenschein

A filled black refuse sack sits casually in the gallery space. Though familiar, its siting in this context arouses curiosity. On further inspection, it is apparent that things are not as they seem. Turk has cast the bag in bronze and has then painted it to further resemble the original subject.

With its strong presence and its shining black surface, it possesses a strange kind of beauty. Bronze, the material of gravity, permanence, status and values is used to represent the most transient and valueless symbol of contemporary life.

The enduring and the superflous combine in a provocative comment on monumental art and the preservation of value over time.

Much of Turk's previous work has been characterised by a playful subversion of the cult of the personality. *Cave*, a heritage plaque commemorating the artist's place of work, the artist's signature in eggshells, a paint roller cast in bronze and *Pop*, a full size wax figure of the artist as Sid Vicious in the pose of Elvis as seen in the pop prints of Andy Warhol... these are just some of Turk's works which draw on popular cultural icons and the history of art to subvert accepted values and traditions. In an age where for some modern artists, art and autobiography are virtually inseperable and Posh and Beck command front page news above war, famine and death, the priorities of our modern society are certainly questionable. It could be argued that the objects we choose to discard are the ones that define us the

Gavin Turk 1967

n Turk Gavin Turk Gavin Turk Ga

most. The paparazzi have commonly rooted around in celebrities' bins to try to discover not only their secrets but evidence of their more mundane daily routine. Objects can be used to define and detrmine our identities.

Local history and ethnographic museums commonly attempt to represent individuals, communities and cultures through a selection of objects.

D. Robinson,
In memoriam, The New Art Gallery,
Walsall, 2000

Bin Bag 3
2000–2001
Painted bronze,
55 × 56 × 58 cm

The enemy

I

Tania Bruguera has decided on silence.
On one occasion, I saw her transformed into a Caryatid; the ceiling and walls of the gallery forced her into a discomfiting reverence. One of the straps that held her also covered her mouth, impeding the free flow of her verbalization. When Homer described Ulysses' eloquence, he said Words sprung from his chest, not his mouth. But Tania is not exactly a hero, and from her breast come only humility and obedience. While silence served her as a precarious brace, she held in her hands the still warm heart of a lamb.

Tania's is a silence of profound intensity, even when her vulnerability is akin to a blank sheet of paper about to be squandered on inkblots and smudges. It's not an accident that cotton crops up often in her work—to cover the body or any surface that imposes limits on infinite space: an absorbent material, snow white and clinically pure.

Still, sometimes it's not clear if Tania "keeps silence" or sheathes herself with it. Indeed, to be silent is to keep the verb captive. Homer himself affirmed that teeth serve as a barrier against the tongue's natural impetuosity. But Tania isn't satisfied with what nature has prescribed; since the enclosure is not enough, she creates all sorts of ruses.

where the Words came from, we could say with certainty that these "in vitro cultures" are nothing less than self-portraits. Tania calls them The Body of Silence.

II

The story of art in Cuba—and in this sense it's no different than anywhere else—is surrounded by an anecdotal history that survives in the form of urban legend and rumor. One of these stories concerns the writer Virgilio Piñera at a meeting of intellectuals and politicos in the early 60s. To be true to this particularly persistent legend, it should be noted that the politicos were doing the talking and the intellectuals the listening.

Virgilio then respectfully asked to say a few Words. It was assumed that his Words would relate to what had been discussed that afternoon. But Virgilio was as laconic as he was intense: "I want to make a confession. I am afraid."

Fear is never in the past. We're overcome by a foreseeable turn of events that can put our security in doubt; a mistake that can alter routines which govern our existence; or the consequences of our inability to auto-suppress our disagreements. This kind of anguish always has a hint of premonition or instinct.

But it is not impossible to imagine Word and Fear meeting at some point, maybe even

III

There was a time when Tania felt beaten by arithmetic. As she tallied, she realized the nation could be a matter of numbers: add deaths over here, subtract lives over there, multiply bread and fish... divide and conquer—that's the perfect equation.

To be precise in her "statistics", all Tania had to do was refuse to separate the just from the unjust. Epic deeds intertwined with remorse, inequity and Fear. Heroes and traitors enveloped in the same shroud. In the kingdom of guilt, just as in that of the dead, everyone is guaranteed a place. Tania has woven funereal flags, in which she winds the intensely intricate workings of the nation. In these, guilt is spread all around.

Estadística began as a succession of marks on a wall. Obsessed with the limitations, Tania painted the wall black, as a silent requiem. Drawn with thread and strips of fabric, a tangle of hair was lined up on the wall with rigorous geometry. But a few details betrayed it. The flag had a beginning, but lacked an end. Ulysses' wife unravelled her work each night only to begin again at dawn. Tania drags out the wait with incomplete stitching. To compose the nation should not be an easy task. It's always the midway point, neither here nor there, exactly between two shores.

IV

If reversal can be made into victory, then many reversals would make for a great triumphant

Tania Bruguera 1968

Before her own verbiage could be contaminated by others, Tania has preferred to chew entire pages of alien Words. With her teeth, she repeats the same ponderous mechanism as the printing press, but her actions result in eroding all content from whole books. With her own spit she depopulates them of writing, until they are stamped only with silence and each of their pages has been turned to a sterile pulp. So much ink reduced to an overflowing mass of opinions in her mouth, she spits into glass vials, being careful not to spill a single letter.

Later, she seals each vial with the masticated paper, so white, so empty. If we didn't know

trading places. When this happens, Word and Fear enter into a calculated dance. Sometimes surreptitiously challenging, evasive at others, Word and Fear construct behaviors, claim territory and conceal realities. What remains is the need for masks, metaphors and a latent ambivalence which elude the weight of that which has now become unspeakable.

Virgilio's confession seems prophetic. Perhaps that's why his Words took flight from official history to find refuge in its margins. Words and guilt roll around behind Tania Bruguera's silence. Her Fear doesn't belong to her; it's just an echo that has finally caught up.

march for all eternity. By erecting a monument, no one can be sure the enemy doesn't exist. The most fitting pedestal will be a book of selected pages with all the weight of the monument on top; some loose pages might make a difference. There will be no strays. And those that do not fit into the canon of the nation will be torn out at once.

Victory should be cautious; whatever Word escapes means another book is written. It seems reversal and victory are complicated theorems. To resolve them, Tania respectfully keeps a minute of silence, then dedicates herself to spinning the intimate thoughts of the nation.

Eugenio Valdes Figueroa

LA ISLA EN PESO

La maldita circunstancia del agua por todas partes
me obliga a sentarme en la mesa del café.
Si no pensara que el agua me rodea como un cáncer
hubiera podido dormir a pierna suelta.
Mientras los muchachos se depojaban de sus ropas para nadar
doce personas morían en un cuarto por compresión.
Cuando a la madrugada la pordiosera resbala en el agua
en el preciso momento en que se lava uno de sus pezones,
me acostumbro al hedor del puerto,
me acostumbro a la misma mujer que invariablemente masturba,
noche a noche, al soldado de guardia en medio del sueño de los peces.
Una taza de café no puede alejar mi idea fija,
en otro tiempo yo vivía adánicamente.
¿Qué trajo la metamorfosis?

La eterna miseria que es el acto de recordar.
Si tú pudieras formar de nuevo aquéllas combinaciones,
devolviéndome el país sin el agua,
me la bebería toda para escupir al cielo,
Pero he visto la música detenida en las caderas,
he visto a las negras bailando con vasos de ron en sus cabezas.
Hay que saltar del lecho con la firme convicción
de que tus dientes han crecido,
de que tu corazón te saldrá por la boca.
Aún flota en los arrecifes el uniforme del marinero ahogado.
Hay que saltar del lecho y buscar la vena mayor del mar para desangrarlo.
Me he puesto a pescar esponjas frenéticamente,
esos seres milagrosos que pueden desalojar hasta la última gota de agua
y vivir secamente.
Esta noche he llorado al conocer a una anciana
que ha vivido ciento ocho años rodeada de agua por todas partes.
Hay que morder, hay que gritar, hay que arañar.
he dado las últimas instrucciones.
El perfume de la piña puede detener un pájaro.
Los once mulatos se disputaban el fruto,
los once mulatos fálicos murieron en la orilla de la playa.
He dado las últimas instrucciones.
Todos nos hemos desnudado.

Llegué cuando daban un vaso de aguardiente a la virgen bárbara,
cuando regaban ron por el suelo y los pies parecían lanzas,
justamente cuando un cuerpo en el lecho podría parecer impúdico,
justamente en el momento en que nadie cree en Dios.
Los primeros acordes y la antigüedad de este mundo:
hieráticamente una negra y una blanca y el líquido al saltar.
Para ponerme triste me huelo debajo de los brazos.
Es en este país donde no hay animales salvajes.
Pienso en los caballos de los conquistadores cubriendo a las yeguas,
pienso en el desconocido son del areíto
desaparecido para toda la eternidad,
ciertamente debo esforzarme a fin de poner en claro
el primer contacto carnal en este país, y el primer muerto.
Todos se ponen serios cuando el timbal abre la danza.
Solamente el europeo leía las meditaciones cartesianas.
El baile y la isla rodeada de agua por todas partes:
plumas de flamencos, espinas de pargo, ramos de albahaca, semillas de aguacate.
La nueva solemnidad de esta isla.
¡País mío, tan joven, no sabes definir!

¿Quién puede reír sobre esta roca fúnebre de los sacrificios de gallos?
Los dulces ñañigos bajan sus puñales acompasadamente.
Como una guanábana un corazón puede ser traspasado sin cometer crimen.
sin embargo el bello aire se aleja de los palmares.

Una mano en el tres puede traer todo el siniestro color de los caimitos
más lustrosos que un espejo en el relente,
sin embargo el bello aire se aleja de los palmares,
si hundieras los dedos en su pulpa creerías en la música.
Mi madre fue picada por un alacrán cuando estaba embarazada.
¿Quién puede reír sobre esta roca de los sacrificios de gallos?
¿Quién se tiene a sí mismo cuando las claves chocan?
¿Quién desdeña ahogarse en la indefinible llamarada del flamboyán?
La sangre adolescente bebemos en las pulidas jícaras.
Ahora no pasa un tigre sino su descripción.

Las blancas dentaduras perforando la noche,
y también los famélicos dientes de los chinos esperando el desayuno
después de la doctrina cristiana.
Todavía puede esta gente salvarse del cielo,
pues al compás de los himnos las doncellas agitan diestramente
los falos de los hombre.
La impetuosa ola invade el extenso salón de las genuflexiones.
Nadie piensa en implorar, en dar gracias, en agradecer, en testimoniar.
La santidad se desinfla en una carcajada.
Sean los caóticos símbolos del amor los primeros objetos que palpe,
afortunadamente desconocemos la voluptuosidad y la caricia francesa,
desconocemos el perfecto gozador y la mujer pulpo,
desconocemos los espejos estratégicos,
no sabemos llevar la sífilis con la reposada elegancia de un cisne,
desconocemos que muy pronto vamos a practicar estas mortales elegancias.

Los cuerpos en la misteriosa llovizna tropical,
en la llovizna diurna, en la llovizna nocturna, siempre en la llovizna,
los cuerpos abriendo sus millones de ojos,
los cuerpos, dominados por la luz, se repliegan
ante el asesinato de la piel,
los cuerpos, devorando oleadas de luz, revientan como girasoles de fuego
encima de las aguas estáticas,
los cuerpos, en las aguas, como carbones apagados derivan hacia el mar.

Es la confusión, es el terror, es la abundancia,
es la virginidad que comienza a perderse.
Los mangos podridos en el lecho del río ofuscan mi razón,
y escalo el árbol más alto para caer como un fruto.
Nada podría detener este cuerpo destinado a los cascos de los caballos,
turbadoramente cogido entre la poesía y el sol.

Escolto bravamente el corazón traspasado,
clavo el estilete más agudo en la nuca de los durmientes.
El trópico salta y su chorro invade mi cabeza
pegada duramente contra la costra de la noche.
La piedad original de las auríferas arenas
ahoga sonoramente las yeguas españolas,
la tromba desordena las crines más oblicuas.

No puedo mirar con estos ojos dilatados.
Nadie sabe mirar, contemplar, desnudar un cuerpo.
Es la espantosa confusión de una mano en lo verde,
los estranguladores viajando en la franja del iris.
No sabría poblar de miradas el solitario curso del amor.
Me detengo en ciertas palabras tradicionales:
el aguacero, la siesta, el cañaveral, el tabaco,
con simple ademán, apenas si onomatopéyicamente,
titánicamente paso por encima de su música,
y digo: el agua, el mediodía, el azúcar, el humo.

Yo combino:
el aguacero pega en el lomo de los caballos,
la siesta atada a la cola de un caballo,

el cañaveral devorando a los caballos,
los caballos perdiéndose sigilosamente
en la tenebrosa emanación del tabaco,
el último gesto de los siboneyes mientras el humo pasa por la horquilla
como la carreta de la muerte,
el último ademán de los siboneyes,
y cavo esta tierra para encontrar los ídolos y hacerme una historia.

Los pueblos y sus historias en boca de todo el pueblo.

De pronto, el galeón cargado de oro se mete en la boca
de uno de los narradores,
y Cadmo, desdentado, se pone a tocar bongó.
La vieja tristeza de Cadmo y su perdido prestigio:
en una isla tropical los últimos glóbulos rojos de un dragón
tiñen con imperial dignidad el manto de una decadencia.

Las historias eternas frente a la historia de una vez del sol,
las eternas historias de estas tierras paridoras de bufones y cotorras,
las eternas historias de los negros que fueron,
y de los blancos que no fueron,
o al revés o como os parezca mejor,
las eternas historias blancas, negras, amarillas, rojas, azules,
-toda la gama cromática reventando encima de mi cabeza en llamas-,
la eterna historia de la cínica sonrisa del europeo
llegado para apretar las tetas de mi madre.

El horroroso paseo circular,
el tenebroso juego de los pies sobre la arena circular,
el envenado movimiento del talón que rehúye el abanico del erizo,
los siniestros manglares, como un cinturón canceroso,
dan la vuelta a la isla,
los manglares y la fétida arena
aprietan los riñones de los moradores de la isla.

Sólo se eleva un flamenco absolutamente.

¡Nadie puede salir, nadie puede salir!
la vida del embudo y encima la nata de la rabia.
Nadie puede salir:
el tiburón más diminuto rehusaría transportar un cuerpo intacto.
Nadie puede salir:
una uva caleta cae en la frente de la criolla
que se abanica lánguidamente en la mecedora,
y «nadie puede salir» termina espantosamente en el choque de las claves.

Cada hombre comiendo fragmentos de la isla,
cada hombre devorando los frutos, las piedras y el excremento nutridor,
cada hombre mordiendo el sitio dejado por su sombra,
cada hombre lanzando dentelladas en el vacío donde el sol de acostumbra,
cada hombre, abriendo su boca como una cisterna, embalsa el agua
del mar, pero como el caballo del barón de Munchausen,
la arroja patéticamente por su cuarto trasero,
cada hombre en el rencoroso trabajo de recortar
los bordes de la isla más bella del mundo,
cada hombre tratando de echar a andar a la bestia cruzada de cocuyos.

Pero la bestia es perezosa como un bello macho
y terca como una hembra primitiva.
Verdad es que la bestia atraviesa diariamente los cuatro momentos caóticos,
los cuatro momentos en que se la puede contemplar
-con la cabeza metida entre sus patas - escrutando el horizonte con ojo atroz,
los cuatro momentos en que se abre el cáncer:
madrugada, mediodía, crepúsculo y noche.

Las primeras gotas de una lluvia áspera golpean su espalda
hasta que la piel toma la resonancia de dos maracas pulsadas diestramente.
En este momento, como una sábana o como un pabellón de tregua, podría
desplegarse un agradable misterio,
pero la avalancha de verdes lujuriosos ahoga los mojados sones,
y la monotonía invade el envolvente túnel de las hojas.

El rastro luminoso de un sueño mal parido,
un carnaval que empieza con el canto del gallo,
la neblina cubriendo con su helado disfraz el escándalo de la sabana,
cada palma derramándose insolentemente en un verde juego de aguas,
perforan, con un triángulo incandescente, el pecho de los primeros aguadores,
y la columna de agua lanza sus vapores a la cara del sol cosida por un gallo.
Es la hora terrible.
Los devoradores de neblina se evaporan
hacia la parte más baja de la ciénaga,
y un caimán los pasa dulcemente a ojo.
Es la hora terrible.
La última salida de la luz de Yara
empuja a los caballos contra el fango.
Es la hora terrible.
como un bólido la espantosa gallina cae,
y todo el mundo toma su café.

¿pero qué puede el sol en un pueblo tan triste?
Las faenas del día se enroscan al cuello de los hombres
mientras la leche cae desesperadamente.
¿Qué puede el sol en un pueblo tan triste?

Con un lujo mortal los macheteros abren grandes claros en el monte,
la tristísima iguana salta barrocamente en un caño de sangre,
los macheteros, introduciendo cargas de claridad, se van ensombreciendo
hasta adquirir el tinte de un subterráneo egipcio.
¿Quién puede esperar clemencia en esta hora?

Confusamente un pueblo escapa de su propia piel
adormeciéndose con la claridad,
la fulminante droga que puede iniciar un sueño mortal
en los bellos ojos de hombres y mujeres,
en los inmensos y tenebrosos ojos de estas gentes
por los cuales la piel entra a no sé qué extraños ritos.

La piel, en esta hora, se extiende como un arrecife
y muerde su propia limitación,
la piel se pone a gritar como una loca, como una puerca cebada,
la piel trata de tapar su claridad con pencas de palma,
con yaguas traídas distraídamente por el viento,
la piel se tapa furiosamente con cotorras y pitahayas,
absurdamente se tapa con sombrías hojas de tabaco
y con restos de leyendas tenebrosas,
y cuando la piel no es sino una bola oscura,
la espantosa gallina pone un huevo blanquísimo.

¡Hay que tapar¡ ¡Hay que tapar¡
Pero la claridad avanzada, invade
perversamente, oblicuamente, perpendicularmente,
la claridad es una enorme ventosa que chupa la sombra,
y las manos van lentamente hacia los ojos.

Los secretos más inconfesables son dichos:
la claridad mueve las lenguas,
la claridad mueve los brazos,
la claridad se precipita sobre un frutero de guayabas,
la claridad se precipita sobre los negros y lo blancos,
la claridad se golpea a sí misma,

va de uno a otro lado convulsivamente,
empieza a estallar, a reventar, a rajarse,
la claridad empieza el alumbramiento más horroroso,
la claridad empieza a parir claridad.
Son las doce del día.

Todo un pueblo puede morir de luz como morir de peste.
Al mediodía el monte se puebla de hamacas invisibles,
y, echados, los hombres semejan hojas a la deriva sobre aguas metálicas.
En esta hora nadie sabría pronunciar el nombre más querido,
ni levantar una mano para acariciar un seno;
en esta hora del cáncer un extranjero llegado de playas remotas
preguntaría inútilmente qué proyectos tenemos
o cuántos hombres mueren de enfermedades tropicales en esta isla.
Nadie lo escucharía: las palmas de las manos vueltas hacia arriba,
los oídos obturados por el tapón de la somnoliencia,
los poros tapiados con la cera de un fastidio elegante
y la mortal deglusión de las glorias pasadas.

¿Dónde encontrar en este cielo sin nubes el trueno
cuyo estampido raje, de arriba a abajo, el tímpano de los durmientes?
¿Qué concha paleolítica reventaría con su bronco cuerno
el tímpano de los durmientes?
Los hombres-conchas, los hombre-macaos, los hombres-túneles.
¡Pueblo mío, tan joven, no sabes ordenar!
¡Pueblo mío, divinamente retórico, no sabes relatar!
Como la luz o la infancia aún no tienes un rostro.

De pronto el mediodía se pone en marcha,
se pone en marcha dentro de sí mismo,
el mediodía estático se mueve, se balancea,
el mediodía empieza a elevarse flatulentamente,
sus costuras amenazan reventar,
el mediodía sin cultura, sin gravedad, sin tragedia,
el mediodía orinando hacia arriba,
orinando en sentido inverso a la gran orinada
de Gargantúa en las torres de Notre Dame,
y todas esas historias, leídas por un isleño que no sabe
lo que es un cosmos resuelto.

Pero el mediodía se resuelve en crepúsculo y el mundo se perfile.
A la luz del crepúsculo una hoja de yagruma ordena su terciopelo,
su color plateado del envés es el primer espejo.
La bestia lo mira con su ojo atroz.
En este trance la pupila se dilata, se extiende como mundo se perfila.
hasta aprehender la hoja.
Entonces la bestia recorre con su ojo las formas sembradas en su lomo
y los hombres tirados contra su pecho.
Es la hora única para mirar la realidad en esta tierra.

No una mujer y un hombre frente a frente,
sino el contorno de una mujer y un hombre frente a frente,
entran ingrávidos en el amor,
de tal modo que Newton huye avergonzado.

Una guinea chilla para indicar el angelus:
abrus precatorious, anona myristica, anona palustris.

Una letanía vegetal sin trasmundo se eleva
frente a los arcos floridos del amor:
Eugenia aromática, eugenia fragrans, eugenia plicatula.
El paraíso y el infierno estallan y sólo queda la tierra:
Ficus religiosa, ficus nítida, ficus suffocans.
La tierra produciendo por los siglos de los siglos:
Panicum colonum, panicum sanguinale, panicum maximum.

El recuerdo de una poesía natural, no codificada, me viene a los labios:
Arbol de poeta, árbol del amor, árbol del seso.

Una poesía exclusivamente de la boca como la saliva:
Flor de calentura, flor de cera, flor de la Y.

Una poesía microscópica:
Lágrimas de Job, lágrimas de Júpiter, lágrimas de amor.
Pero la noche se cierra sobre la poesía y las formas se esfuman.
En esta isla lo primero que la noche hace es despertar el olfato:
Todas las aletas de todas las narices azotan el aire
buscando una flor invisible;
la noche se pone a moler millares de pétalos,
la noche se cruza de paralelos y meridianos de olor,
los cuerpos se encuentran en el olor,
se reconocen en este olor único que nuestra noche sabe provocar;
el olor lleva la batuta de las cosas que pasan por la noche,
el olor entra en el baile, se aprieta contra el güiro,
el olor sale por la boca de los instrumentos musicales,
se posa en el pie de los bailadores,
el corro de los presentes devora cantidades de olor,
abre la puerta y las parejas se suman a la noche.

La noche es un mango, es una piña, es un jazmín,
la noche es un árbol frente a otro árbol sin mover sus ramas,
la noche es un insulto perfumado en la mejilla de la bestia;
una noche esterilizada, una noche sin almas en pena,
sin memoria, sin historia, una noche antillana;
una noche interrumpida por el europeo,
el inevitable personaje de paso que deja su cagada ilustre,
a lo sumo, quinientos años, un suspiro en el rodar de la noche antillana,
una excrecencia vencida por el olor de la noche antillana.

No importa que sea una procesión, una conga,
una comparsa, un desfile.
La noche invade con su olor y todos quieren copular.
El olor sabe arrancar las máscaras de la civilización,
sabe que el hombre y la mujer se encontrarán sin falta en el platanal.
¡Musa paradisiaca, ampara a los amantes!

No hay que ganar el cielo para gozarlo,
dos cuerpos en el platanal valen tanto como la primera pareja,
la odiosa pareja que servió para marcar la separación.
¡Musa paradisiaca, ampara a los amantes!

No queremos potencial celestiales sino presencias terrestres,
que la tierra nos ampare, que nos ampare el deseo,
felizmente no llevamos el cielo en la masa de la sangre,
sólo sentimos su realidad física
por la comunicación de la lluvia al golpear nuestras cabezas

Bajo la lluvia, bajo el olor, bajo todo lo que es una realidad,
un pueblo se hace y deshace dejando los testimonios:
un velorio, un guateque, una mano, un crimen,
revueltos, confundidos, fundidos en la resaca perpetua,
haciendo leves saludos, enseñando los dientes, golpeando sus riñones,
un pueblo desciende resuelto en enormes postas de abono,
sintiendo cómo el agua lo rodea por todas partes,
más abajo, más abajo, y el mar picando en sus espaldas;
un pueblo permanece junto a su bestia en la hora de partir,
aullando en el nar, devorando frutas, sacrificando animales,
siempre más abajo, **hasta saber el peso de su isla**,
el peso de una isla en el amor de un pueblo.

Virgilio Piñera, 1943

Chair (Fragment
from Selfportrait
as a Building)
1997-1998
This work was destroyed
and later reconstructed
on 88%,
220 × 322 × 625 cm

Fragment of an interview with Mark Manders

MM: Yes, in the sculpture *Reduced Night-scene with one beautiful Stone (reduced to 88%)*, for example. This is a glass display-case containing a miniature landscape, actually a small part of a cross-section of a garden. I made a small arrangement of various things. I then laid a rope over these things like a drawing prone to the force of gravity. Then I copied this whole scene, reducing it to 88% and covering it with a thin, black nocturnal layer.

ML: So the night really does cover the things like a thin membrane...

MM: Yes, and I have the feeling that all the light that falls on this night-scene is mine.

ML: You mean the light that hangs in between this thin layer of night and our eyes. It is unusual that it is a nocturnal scene that is illuminated, yet it remains night. Can you tell us anything more about the title?

MM: The title implies that I found one of the two stones unattractive. It is a strange, fascinating phenomenon that you can find a certain stone that is not beautiful, or one more beautiful than another.
Because I reduced everything to 88%, the garden scene has not been lost. The origional garden scene is gradually washed out by rain and windswept.

Mark Manders 1968

This work is a cross between a drawing and an actual photograph, but it is in fact about something more instinctive, about melancholy, the loss of youth, the *Titanic*.

The work *Reduced Night-scene with one beautiful Stone* will be shown in the exhibition *Plateau of Mankind*.

Marije Langelaar

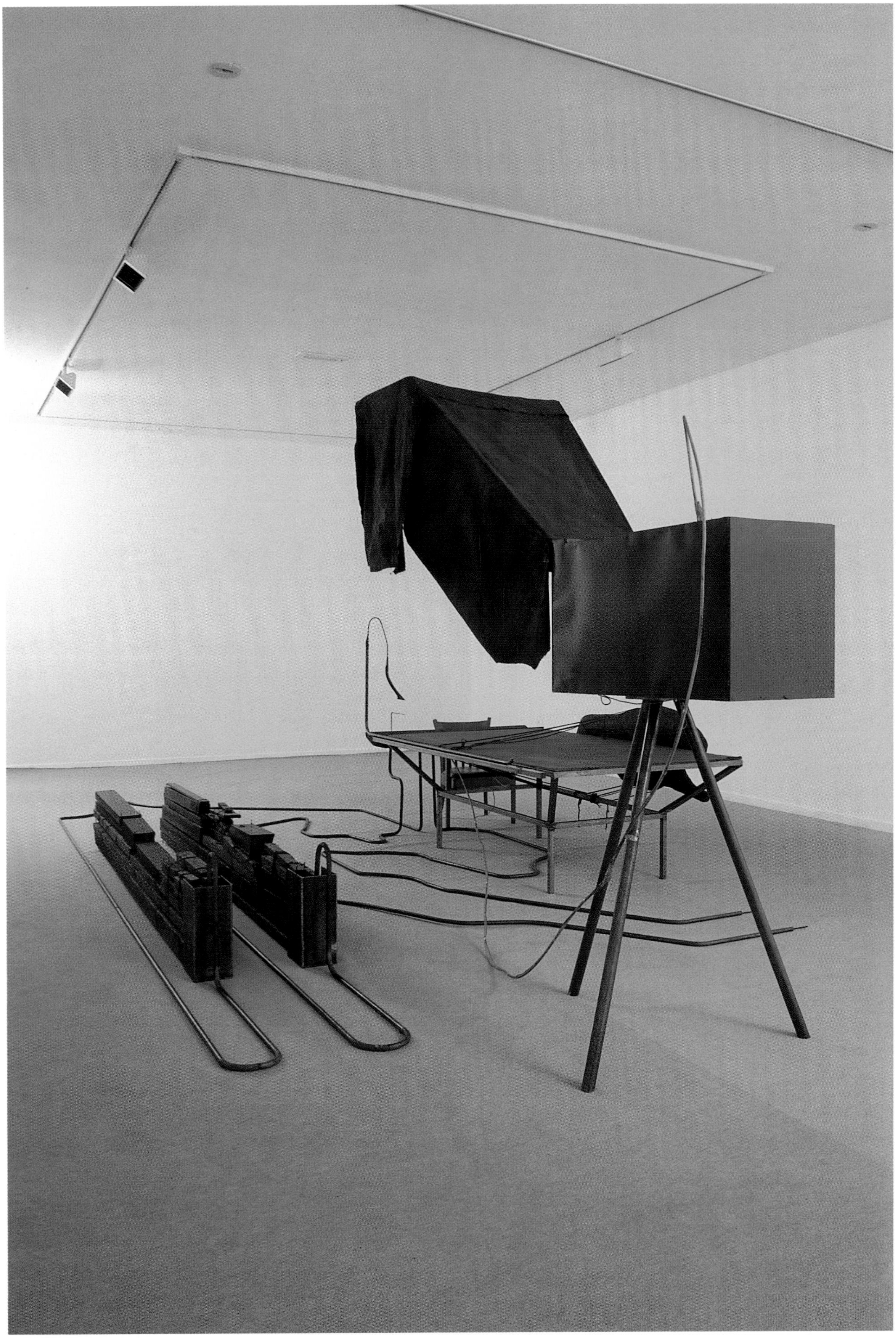

"A portrait must not just be the fac-simile of the face; there has to be, beyond the material likeness, a moral likeness. What must appear first of all, in a natural way, is expression, the model has to have a natural, easy pose, has to forget he is in front of the lens..."

André-Adolphe-Eugène Disdéri

Chantal Michel belongs to that young generation of artists who have an unfailing confidence in images: she practices video art, photography and performances. She also, brillantly, knows how to play with her own image, since she is the only figure in her scenarios. Staging her own woman's condition, but also her human condition nesting inside society and its possible oppressions, she seems to act in a decorative fashion, the choice of her dresses and her wigs perhaps emphasizing that notion, whereas her perception of reality is highly critical for anyone able to construe her. She might even be nudging Andy Warhol, who believed man defined himself, also and above all, by his make-up, his artifices, his appearance?

Her images are like self-portraits rendering not just the subject's physical likeness but its moral one, too. The image, exceptionally, would then coincide with her ego. What surfaces is not a model, but the very person as she is morally, as she sees her relationship with herself and the world. As for the universe she so poetically describes, it is as if suspended, so close to the one in fairy tales,

seize the human "becoming object" or "becoming animal", a human on the verge of animality, nearly alien to itself, its outward signs appearing at once so improvised and so reflected as to remind us of a cat wandering about in a street *à la* De Chirico.

Last of all, she sends us back to our own image, to our childhood, or even our origins. There is truly a kind of latent collective memory in Chantal Michel's images, a sort of wonderment tinged with a slight apprehension, a feeling we might have in front of a doll house (the *Puppenhaus* series) or the wardrobe full of mother's dresses, all those garments composing the artist's palette. Her impressive collection of dresses contributes to the work; she plays with their colours, their shapes, makes them spin, swirl, as a couple of decades earlier, with far less imagination, a famous actress had over an underground vent.

In her videos, unlike her photographs, the décor is always plain, even absent when space is just defined by a room. That is the case of *Weisses Rauschen*. A perfect *in camera* where the artist, entirely dressed in white, asserts her presence, a space that apparently does not distress Chantal Michel; instead, she assimilates its components, merges with them. Easy-going, she makes light of gravity, she rolls about, to one side and the other, effortlessly?, pleasurably?, just one more gesture and now she's up, she's rising, like a curl of smoke, she sways, making us nearly dizzy at the sight of that body with all its facets;

Chantal Michel 1968

a universe undoubtedly belonging to her dreams of yesterday, and why not, of today.

With Chantal Michel nothing is excluded, perhaps just slightly removed, a role that seems secondary yet allows her to shift her point of view, to certainly obtain an even more accurate observation.

The "fetichist" artist gives objects consistency. With her, objects come to life and humans become a bit less important. As a captivated artist, she pursues her stories, stages her fantasies and makes our heads swim. She tries to

again, she's whirling about like her well-oiled automats, but her gestures are so much more graceful that sensuality springs up from all sides. Her endless back-and-forths, that seemingly perpetual to-and-fro motion, sweeps the spectator into a waltz that forces him to take a position.

The point of view remains unique, but not the subject, composed of a thousand fragments, as any self-portrait striving to a bit more authenticity should be.

Vincent Juillerat

Weisses Rauschen
1997
Videoprojection,
123 × 171 cm, stills
from video

Priscilla Monge has repeatedly explored from different angles the crevices in the uses of language and of social expressions, both in their meanings and in their symbolic references. Her work is about what is known but not said, or about what is done but not shown, bringing out in these reinterpreted meanings the most uncomfortable aspects of everyday life, fractioned between the intimate and the social, under apparently innocent formulations, within a poetics of contradiction. Through subtle details she generates a context of confusion, acting inside the psyche, in the mechanisms that cause sensitivity to convulse.

Her narrative is experiential. The starting point may be a banal anecdote, but it ends up in a reflection that subverts and perverts the habits of innocent appearances, making use of the suspense of the unexpected, the surprise of grotesque or the acidity of black humour and irony as resources. The rendition is direct, flowing like a flash of lucidity and from there tending to produce a short-circuit in conventions, unsettles with new senses the understanding of reality, in an interpretative rewriting, like a vivid introspection, shared and critical. The lucidity of her gaze is somewhat perverse. It compels to a confrontation with the contexts, intensifying them, "normalising" the nightmares located in the intimacy of the unspeakable, insisting in vexation.

Violence is always present in her work but never appears expressed with crudeness. It is something latent and in ambush, it develops in con-

several languages and the different degrees that articulate the intention of humiliating and annoying the other, the boomerangs are now fabricated in marble, converting the insult in an epitaph of a language of the most daily violence. The trilogy of videos *Lessons* (*Make-up lesson*, *How to (un)dress oneself* and *How to die of love*, 1998-2000) outlines even more this meaning of violence as a tautology of behaviour, as a cultural formula and strategy or as the masking of innocence.

Room for Isolation and Protection, the work presented at this edition of the Venice Biennale, seems to deepen in that reflection about the ways in which violence develops. On this occasion a subtle and complex violence is approached, one that arises from within, in a metaphorical context of self-aggression, as a conflict of the feminine. It is a square space, entirely lined with sanitary napkins. The piece has been conceived as an imitation of the upholstered quarters used in psychiatric institutions to protect the patients from hurting themselves by striking their bodies against the walls. Inside this enclosure, voices like vague whispers and unrecognisable muttered words inhabit the room as the deadened echo of an internal discourse. The space also refers to soundproof rooms, meant to create the conditions of silence, and where that same silence makes audible the physiological sounds of the body, breath and vascular circulation. Metaphor of an (impossible) representation of silence, this work becomes a space to experience the void, in which the internal emerges.

The use of sanitary napkins as material or as tools

On the one hand the white colour isolates from interference in order to refer directly to the blood-red as its complementary, containing violence as a derivated symbol, "normalizing" the blood as an indicator of femininity, transforming the blood-red into a virtual content and stripping it of vindicating feminist connotations. The feminine as gender becomes an affirmation of a sensibility built from a bodily interior. That same affirmation confirms values expressed in the contradictions that cultural contexts represent to the feminine. Corporality and culture: the silenced word and the discourse, the body's voice and the rules of culture. On the other hand, the sanitary napkins establish a close formal analogy with the bricks in a wall of immaculate purity: protection and repression, isolation as muzzle, the inner voice as an echo of silence... The lightness of purity and the condensation of the obscure concentrate in the sanitary napkin. Contradictions of meanings, polar and complementary at the same time, generate associations that illuminate the symbolic levels of behaviours and discourses. The colour white and the neutral and aseptic texture of cotton place us in an extreme narrative minimalism and in an intense conceptual density.

This work condensates very clearly Priscilla Monge's working process, showing how the mingling of conceptual strategies with appropriating processes tend to generate a critical and reflexive context, of a visual character, linked to the experience of a daily life illuminated by symbolic and significant undertones.

Priscilla Monge 1968

texts of supposed tenderness, as in *Death sentences* (1993), texts and images embroidered on bare linen canvases as an innocent petit-point; or as in *Shut up and sing* (1997 IV Havana Biennial), in which wrestling helmets hold children's music boxes in their mouthpieces; or even more in the series of *Letters / Chains* (love letters, popular recipes to catch a man by bewitchment or a spell, and internet chains embroidered on crude linen, 1994-1998) in which the delirium of a language "fetishised" from the social hides the imposition of anxiety, fraud and deceit also conveyed as negative models of the feminine.

The series *Boomerangs* (1997-2001) place the verbal violence in a vicious circle of return: initially made out of wood and inscribed with insults in

is not new in her work. She has adopted different but always perturbing formulations. The *Football* (1997) was made by a manufacturer by hooking pieces of black leather to the sanitary napkins, reproducing the details of a real ball. Previously, in 1996, she had designed and made pants of different cuts and models, sewing sanitary napkins together. They were always exhibited as objects, but in 1997 in San José, Costa Rica, the artist presented a performance in which she walked the most crowded downtown streets wearing one of these pants, that progressively absorbed her own menstrual blood in the padded crotch.

The sanitary napkins used to build the space of *Room for Isolation and Protection* allow for the sliding of significance towards multiple readings.

In a way it is about free re-readings and reinterpretations of strategies and techniques; one could speak of a perverse pop hybridised with a conceptual minimalism.

Simplicity hides complexity, just the same as lucidity hides confusion or innocence hides perversity.

Santiago B. Olmo

Room
2001
Sanitary napkins,
installation, detail

Every flag says something about the country it belongs to. Just as the stars and stripes of the United States flag express their claim to be at once united and many, so a strip of embroidered cloth suggests for Bielorussia, maybe more than anywhere else, how intense the desire is to not lose touch with its traditions; just as it is natural for African flags to be composed of warm, solar colours, so it is for the flags of the northern countries of the world to be made in cold colours, and so on.

An amazingly accurate formal synthesis, flags codify the essential traits of the place they represent, render its prevailing landscape, and are a short story condensing, in a single sentence, climate, character, history, power relationships. The chromatic balances seem as perfect as the organization of the surface areas: with a simplicity verging on the commonplace, each flag expresses a collective identity with the few forms invented up to now.

Neri starts from existing signs and, copying them, he allows the brushstroke's inaccuracy to appear and avoids copyright issues—the pictures of the flags printed in a sort of handbook containing them all cannot be reproduced otherwise—, chooses to not delegate his task to a machine... this way he defends the force of a gesture and the time required to perform it, the cognitive possibility arising in that experience... He thus marks a further stage in his investigation focused on making the representation essential, and on rendering a live view of the world. Before, in the spare landscapes of *Skyline* (1998), but especially in *Sostenere lo sguardo* (1999)—a group of portraits where the title of each picture is the name of the subject portrayed, evidencing its personal relationship with the artist—and the series *Windows* (1999)—small paintings of windows shown side by side, a comment on a wide-spread condition of city life today—Marco Neri initiates a dialogue with the key moments of the tradition of

Marco Neri 1968

Marco Neri decided to paint all these flags, to face the present state of the world via a synthesis of forms and colours, build a political map of the world in the year 2000, review the differences but at the same time let the evidence reveal recurrent features, colonial and post-colonial relations, the world after '89, after the war in Yugoslavia, after the collapse of the Soviet empire, the growing autonomy of African countries... The artist faces a shifting political scene, the advent of new states, structuring of entire areas of the world, determination to break free from imposed rules, for which many are struggling. In this work Marco

Western painting, suggesting a contemporary layman's version. Human centrality, and a window as a symbolic reference to a painting, yield to a reflection, affective in the instance of the portraits, and attentive to the alterations of the landscape in the instance of the windows.

So with his series of flags the artist condenses the previous cycles of his work on landscapes and portraits—the flag being the portrait of the landscape—and communicates the freedom to travel with colours, to imagine landscapes, horizons, oceans, all the stories of the world those pieces of cloth have to tell...

Emanuela De Cecco

Quadro mondiale
2000
Tempera on linen,
192 canvas,
35 × 50 cm each

Two years after leaving Yale's photography programme, beginning a stretch of employment in Manhattan, John Pilson found himself gradually letting his "grad school" photography peter out under the influence of corporate "training". Taking advantage of the dead time available during weekend and night shifts, he began filming himself and his co-workers with a digital video camera; as he describes it, "Not so much 'subverting' the office space as 'ABUSING' it."

The fruits of this period are demonstrated in Pilson's 1999 work *Interregna* (the plural of "interregnum" = "between the kings", a period where authority is suspended). The work combines shots of Pilson himself—spinning on a swivel chair, hiding under a bank of printers, banging a plastic water container against the back of his head—with shots of his co-workers as they jump over cubicle dividers, look up when the lights are switched on and off, and sing Puccini. Towards the end of the piece, however, another element begins to dominate; the images become increasingly empty and eventually devolve into darkness, silence, and murk. This is an arch that comes to be repeated throughout Pilson's work: an initial period

doo-wop. This initial playfulness culminates in the appearance of dozens of multicolored rubber balls that bounce down a stairwell and roll into a waiting elevator, as if transported by the businessmen's serenades. But again, as the work continues it moves us away from this initial mood and towards stasis: Two figures seal off the hallway with tape, and the imagery darkens, giving us scenes of empty lobbies, views of the city at night, and elevators that open on nothing.

This dynamic is altered in *Mr Pickup* (2001). Here an unmoving camera observes a lawyer in his office as he spends a half hour trying (and failing) to put documents in a briefcase so he can leave for an important meeting. The piece is silent except for the sound of books, files, phones and office supplies crashing to the floor and the lawyer's occasional comments, including *Can't somebody help me, Jesus*, and (when singing birds become audible on the soundtrack) *Oh, the birds*. Even though this piece is more lighthearted than earlier work, with its echoes of vaudeville and an unmoving camera that suggests pre-Griffith slapstick, its stasis becomes even more obtru-

ed by a rubber-ball-wielding crowd of office workers in a scene that opens up any number of interpretations—is this the middle class turning on the underclass? Alienated workers trying to exorcise the monstrous spectre of International Capital? Or does it stage the exclusion of unacceptable feelings—weakness, fear, doubt—from the place of work? If the little girl and the monstrous figure are to be driven out, the question remains: where are they (and by extension, the viewer) supposed to go? A place without capital, without society, without labour? That would mean a place without bodies; and perhaps this is the greatest wish.

These problems bring to the fore another of Pilson's most significant influences—Stanley Kubrick. Like *The Shining* or *2001: A Space Odyssey*, echoes of which emerge in all of Pilson's works, the site that the camera traverses is in each case a frozen setting for the destruction of the individual. In contrast with Kubrick, however, the documentary aspect of Pilson's images—the fact that what he films is determined by where his employer puts him—gives overtones and complexity to this work that is unique. However it is described, as por-

John Pilson 1968

of release and dementia followed by silence and paralysis, as if the work were faltering before something unspeakable.

Pilson attributes much of the tension of this work—or of this aesthetic—to his reading Thomas Pynchon's *Gravity's Rainbow* during this time. Pilson speaks of this novel with reverence, and we find the novel's mixing of registers (of high and low, slapstick with apocalypse) taken up and repeated in his own work. The next major piece, *Above the Grid* (2000), gives us the adventures of two businessmen as they wander down corporate hallways singing

sive. The meanings that it circulates have to do with collapse, being trapped in a role, and punishment, even as this collapse is parodied and turned into comedy.

Pilson's most recent work is *À La Claire Fontaine*, which currently exists in two versions. The title comes from a traditional French tune sung by a little girl, who is seen in the first version breathing on a window and wrestling with a potted plant. In the second version of the piece, the girl's sequences alternate with footage of a figure wearing a heavy coat that obscures his face. This second figure is assault-

traying a return of the repressed (where the parts of a person that are pruned to create a "work persona" return), or delivering a social critique (our inability to comprehend and therefore control the influence of work and technology on our lives), or an exercise in desperate wage-slave Dada (an elaborate and deeply pleasurable thumbing of one's nose at the Employer/Father), Pilson's body of work has a way of defamiliarizing the issues involved and bringing them before us with a renewed force.

Jeffery Anderson

Lars Siltberg's video triptych *Man with Balls on Hands and Feet* (1998-2001) is a series of works where the artist has filmed a man whose hands and feet have been furnished with balls of polycarbonate. The man, clad in a bodysuit, can be found in three situations arranged by the artist, where, placed on such treacherous—not to say impossible—underlays as ice and water, and in the strong air flow of a wind tunnel, he is urged to get up, then later to try to remain in an upright position.

The pathos of this laborious activity recalls the situations in old newsreels where people dramatically crash-landed their ingeniously constructed and visually imaginative aircraft after a brief instant of technological triumph. Together, these two phenomena seem to describe a subject getting into a state he has little or no potential to control; a fundamental effort in mankind to explore his physical and mental limitations through action. Constantly lured by the same hard-to-explain lust to know more, control more, he tries to overstep his limits only to carry on towards new challenges.

Man with Balls on Hands and Feet reminds one of the performance art of the late sixties with the human body as an acting element in a space. However, the difference is that the spaces in which Lars Siltberg's explorations are methodically carried out are defined by their physical conditions, not by their physical extension. What we witness consists rather of aspects of performativity than performance, since *Man with Balls on Hands and Feet*, instead of referring to an individual act, turns towards the sets of representations that allow us to read and interpret the individual act. In fact one should not make too much of the art-historical perspective, since the artist, in his oeuvre as a whole, above all expresses an interest in phenomenological investigations of the most reduced, the most elementary, although in extremely contrived circumstances.

Action and duration are here elements to be controlled and directed by a human will. The man with the balls on his hands and feet is exposed to yet another related task—with his actions, with his reduced scope of action, he must create himself anew every time he stands up. The fact that the action in *Man with Balls on Hands and Feet* visually recalls the child's effort to learn to stand upright gives Lars Siltberg's project the impression of wanting to engage in a fundamental activity that exists immediately prior to language. The actor's megalomaniac obsession with what for the spectator seems to be an unknown undertaking, a kind of incessant climbing around his own secret, is underscored here by the actor's determination, a silence which also effectively excludes the viewer from the centre of the event. When the man then finally transcends, is able to overcome himself and find his balance, the film sequence breaks off and loops back to the initial situation; his labour of Sisyphus thus begins all over again, in an eternal, never-consummated learning process.

Mats Stjernstedt

Lars Siltberg 1968

Siltberg Lars Siltberg Lars Siltber

Man with balls
on hands and feet
1998-2001
Man on ice, 1998
Three channel video
installation, DVD
projection, 7'54"

Man with balls
on hands and feet
1998-2001
Man on water, 2000
Three channel video
installation, DVD
projection, 7'54"

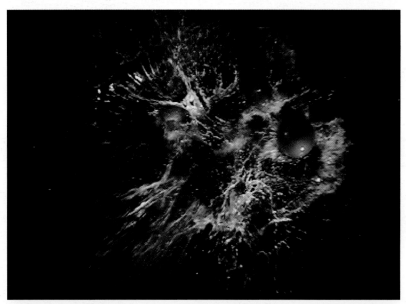

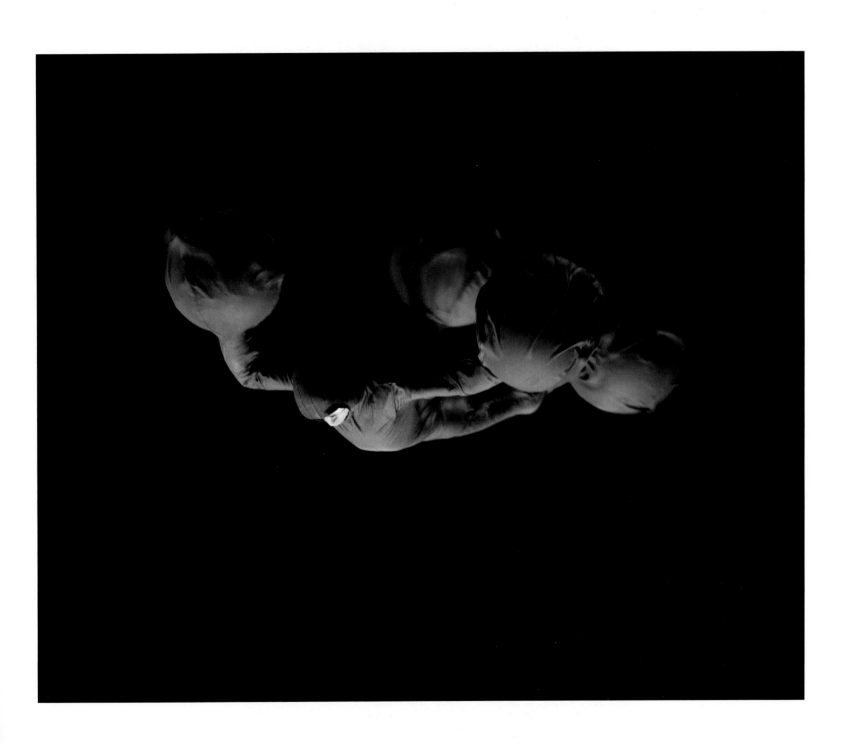

Man with balls
on hands and feet
1998-2001
Man on air, 2001
Three channel video
installation, DVD
projection, 7'54"

When used as an instrument against the forgetfulness of time, the strategies of art become volatile and impatient. Through my work I tear at the fabric of different realities, severing images from their origin and cleaving apart the logic of their familiarity. The links I make in this process can be chilling and brutal, but often the things we can't bear to face are the most telling witnesses of our times. Being both witness and participant, I provoke tension between the peculiarities of a mutating subjectivity and the specificities of my historical context.

Minnette Vári's video works explore the unfolding of historical events in South Africa and interrogate the way these events are recorded and rewritten through mass media. Imaged as autobiography, the artist performs naked in various digitally created scenarios. Vári's work speaks of the discomfit of a thousand ill-fitting interpretations. The artist has used television images of the transformative events between 1994 through until the present as an attempt to locate a sense of self within the larger overarching paradigm of global communication. The

Saturn, the god of Time, devoured his children in an attempt to evade his fate. The figure in *Oracle* desperately wants to bite into, over and beyond time. The artist, in researching the identities of the children of Saturn, selected footage from the media that resulted in a contemporary portrait of Southern Africa. The figure in *Oracle* is a powerful metaphor for the postcolonial condition—a craving to assimilate every fragment of information into one hybrid body.

In a work entitled *REM*, the projected figure of a woman suspended in hallucinatory slow motion appears in a dark landscape of apprehensive expectation. The image resembles a Bushman rock painting with tableaux of human and animal figures and various objects engaging in a flow of relationships. The figure is that of the artist asleep; the phases where she was the most restless were edited together into a trancelike choreography. Sleep is a state of transformation for the body and mind, and in this work the artist locates our experience of history and time somewhere between ritual, allegory and omen. Some scientists refer to REM (rapid eye movement) sleep as a third level of

find the best possible future. The official emblem of any ideology—a coat of arms—symbolically engenders images of family heritage, state, nation and regality. In *Mirage*, the mutating heraldic imagery of a coat of arms evokes the crises of changing times. Although historical events are commemorated on specific dates, the real transitions in politics and society occur in every aspect of daily life. *Mirage* mimics the illusion of imagined or erroneously represented facts, presenting a seemingly static coat of arms with a motto that reads, HISTORIAE ARDORE IN SPIRITU NOSTRO (the heat of history is in our breath). The illusion of stasis collapses when body parts of the heraldic figures are abruptly substituted with similar yet different fragments taken from local newspapers, and the coat of arms begins a transformation that resembles a meltdown. After a period of chaotic metamorphosis, the elements settle into a new coat of arms, bearing the inscription MEMORIAE FEBRE IN VENIS NOSTRIS (the fever of memory is in our veins). The first motto suggests that we, however fleeting our existence may be, contribute to the course of history. The second reflects how memory can be the

Minnette Vári 1968

works indicate a shift from the earliest video (*Alien*, 1998), a media based work, toward intrinsically surreal interpretations of public and private events.

In *Oracle*, Vári becomes a bald ogre who compulsively crams writhing handfulls of flesh into her mouth. This fit of hunger sees the artist gorging herself on media sequences from all the conflicting histories of present-day Africa and the world, as she relentlessly tries to incorporate disparate truths into one body in an attempt to make it whole again. Overcome by the excess of information, the figure in *Oracle* reaches saturation point and must reject mouthfuls of it, gagging, despite the forceful urgency to devour these socio-political realities.

consciousness, a 'dream state' that allows us to relive life's experiences through vivid dreams, filled with physical and emotional energy. As the subconscious processes the information, memories and neuroses gathered during wakefulness, so the artist's unconscious gestures seem to invite us to re-evaluate our relationship with this continent and its histories.

The images that float serenely past the orbital nude figure reflect a hundred years of great change. Selected from publications on Southern Africa and the continent, scenes of wild animals, urban clutter, modern day warfare and late twentieth century activities engage the hopes and fears of those who have lived through the turmoil of an infamous history and now have to

impetus of history, gathering our past, present and future into one gesture.

How do we begin to talk about South Africa after the euphoria of 1994? Ideologies collapsed and a nation has emerged that exists out of the urgency that was experienced in creating a democracy. Out of this arena, a fresh form of cultural hybrid has been born, compounded by images of the "new" and "immediate" South Africa that aims to give representation to a model multicultural society. The complexities of this society are efficiently demarcated in the video works of Minnette Vári, where the tension between a seemingly ordered fabric and the theatre of violence are so well conveyed.

Clive Kellner

Mirage
1999
Video animation, 40',
looped indefinitely, 100',
variable size, stills
from video

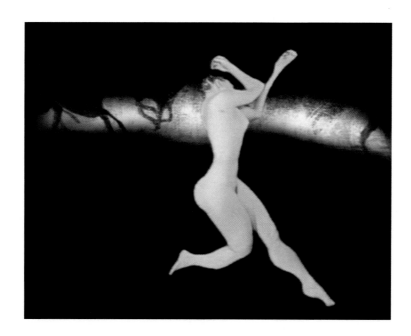

REM
2001
Video animation,
18' looped indefinitely,
variable size, stills
from video

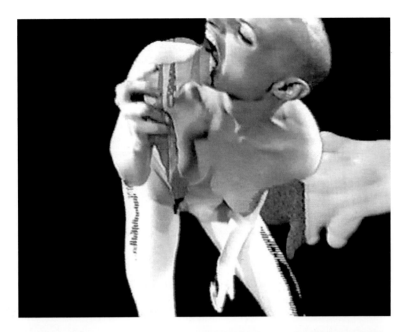

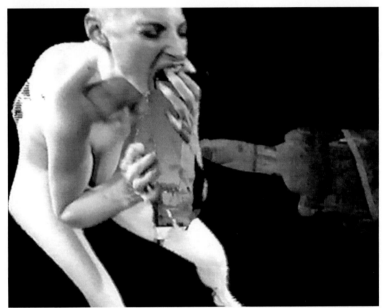

Oracle
1999
Video animation,
video 2', audio 6', looped
indefinitely, variable size,
stills from video

Sister melancholy
The colours of time

"Et haec melancholia nigra est"

Saint Hildegard of Bingen

The pose is a classic: it reminds us of David's Madame Récamier, later ironically revisited by Magritte, it reminds us of Paolina Borghese portrayed as Venus Victorious by Canova, it reminds us of Etruscan sarcophagi, but generally speaking of all art history, classical statuary, of that reclining figure, at length mistaken for Cleopatra, the Ariadne Chirico appropriated to drag into the centre of metaphysical squares. It reminds us of pictorial tradition and Douanier Rousseau surprising us by putting the image of a half-reclining woman on a couch in the midst of a jungle. So here we have, in the drawings turned the colour of the food. In this sequence of photographs there is also the idea of a psychological mutation in which the various seasons and the different colours are in correspondence with different moods. But after all this is nothing but the Renaissance theory of *temperaments*, a system of analogies between humours, elements, qualities, characters, seasons, ages and even colours. Among these temperaments there is *melancholy*, linked up with time, with the change of seasons, the diverse moments of the day and the phases of light, the dialectical alternation of light and night (what, with an imprecise word, we call depression and that it would be more accurate, as well as more suggestive, to call melancholy, is after all nothing but an alteration of the sleeping-waking rhythm). If two thirds of the people affected by melancholy are women, this also occurs because melancholy is shows was titled *Mädchen in uniform* and was dedicated to Carl Froelich's film, a film the artist had not seen but of which—a highly significant fact—she had felt the suggestiveness in the title. But we also think of her later performances and the attire of groups of girls, practically in uniforms, and last, of the sailors' military apparel in the works dedicated to the U.S. Navy. In certain cases military apparel or fabrics were worn by female figures (camouflage stockings in *VB28*, Venice 1997; or caps in *VB36*, Leipzig 1998). On the other hand, even in the artist's performances and the photographic works drawn from them the primacy of colour is essential (the drawings, from which the whole work springs, were recently shown arranged in series of twelve according to the same criterion). The variables are always pertinent to the portions of time represented, so in the spring Jennifer's hair was softer, in August she looked nearly

Vanessa Beecroft 1969

Vanessa Beecroft's latest work, her very young sister on the modern couch Mies van der Rohe designed. And she held that formal, natural pose, twelve times, for twelve photographs that form a motley calendar where colour variations rhythm the course of the year. Each season, in fact, the colour of the girl's hair is altered, while the intensity of the light changes from one month to another. The key notion is that outer atmospheric agents are reflected in the colours of the body. An idea not so removed from the one on which one of Vanessa Beecroft's first works was grounded, that food diary (*Despair*, 1985-93) where the artist repeatedly noted down every food intake in the female body, that body that, at the same time, cyclothymia, a disturbance of the cyclicity the female gender is bound to. The notion that with the succession of the seasons each of the four humors prevails in turn (blood, phlegm, yellow bile, black bile, the latter responsible for the melancholic temperament) belongs to Empedocles. A number of authors, mainly Aristotle in *Problema XXX*, mention wine as a food that can produce melancholy and in certain cases the term "melancholic foods" is used.

The result of every "picture" of the series of photographs Vanessa Beecroft has made is always monochrome in the tone of the many elements that repeatedly compose it: hair, skin, bikini, shoes, fingernails, nearly like a *uniform*. Here we should mention that one of her first destroyed... If Jennifer seems to have the profile of a Pollaiolo portrait, she also reminds us of movie stars, especially the series of blondes, from Jean Harlow to Marilyn Monroe... But above all she is a Lolita: when Humbert Humbert sees her for the first time in Stanley Kubrick's film, she is sitting on a lawn in the same position. Since she is the artist's sister, this work is permeated with a family air that Beecroft had already sought in her performance *Prima Linea* (Trevi, 1994), choosing as protagonists a mother and her two daughters. Jennifer looks like Vanessa, but also like her previous performers: the face the artist, beginning with a family album, has always pursued.

Laura Cherubini

The Sister Project
(November)
2000
C-print, 182,9 × 315 cm

BBBreathless

BBBreathless: stuttering. Or gasping for breath in an attempt to repeat a consonant that "blooms" laboriously and—as happens to infants, that is to those who are deprived of speech—it seems to form little bubbles between lips that are almost closed through lack of air. The breathing rhythm is such that it almost suggests agony. The rubber cell dilates, inflates threateningly and then gives in to its own force, as if it were passing away. We are faced not with an object, but a silent, claustrophobic mystery for those who have not been introduced to it. A grey room that must be avoided. An anguishing *mise en abîme* for anyone looking for an opening, an escape route through those fake walls. And yet these walls are real, because they are alive and animated by a mechanical flatus and by a cold engine that seems to feed shrewdly on the very breath it has taken from the spectator who is able to perceive its tragedy. The mechanics of it all actually breathes. We, dev-

of calques and recompositions, of negative games that seem to measure, comprehend and then alienate the objects from their original materials. Things are duplicated in a grey world of rubber, an invertebrate, compliant and destructured landscape that has been reduced to pure, uniform surface. They seem to be soft fossils—works that contain within themselves the sense of impotency, transience and yielding of our daily lives. They introduce a sense of surprise within the sudden, a lack of "thickness", the unchallenged being dragged to the ground, crushed by an invisible gravitational secret. We are alone before these impracticable sculptures, as if we were one of those characters that Cecchini immerses in photomontages devoid of narrative content. Subjects who are lost amongst detritus and dust; surroundings that leave no clue to action and time. People who are incapable of dialogue, who are often slumbering, lost in the depths of sleep. There is no greater solitude than in dreaming, closing your eyes and gaze to all extraneousness. In dreams you are

Loris Cecchini 1969

astated, do not. Our silence abandons the condemned and confirms the triumph of glacial rational folly. The distributive injustice of meting out death turns us into impotent witnesses to the cold engineering. The work is as simple as it is refined, just like the ritual of capital punishment: a room; then a chair covered in laces and electrical components; or gas; or an injection; and a macabre panoply of cynical accoutrements put together so that everything will "run smoothly" during the final moment.

Loris Cecchini, however, concedes nothing to this voyeuristic spectacle. Here there is no exhibited atrocity, nor are there any of the morbid and minute details offered by countless web sites. It gives us the cadenced rhythm of

the movement towards death via a mechanism that minimises slowness and, at the same time, the inexorable instantaneousness of a violence that displays the aggravating circumstance of arbitrariness and pretence of justice. A decision that can still be overturned, open to possible second thoughts or clemency but that, at the last moment, is allowed to proceed.

Hence: a decision without grace and, ineluctably, guilty; even if it is removed by the mask of the aesthetic space of these new, sophisticated stocks.

It is this perverse neutrality of space that Cecchini makes dramatic and at the same time accessible. The apparently simple forms of his works are the end result of a laborious system

dreamed, you are always autistically the actors of your own oneiric life. Armoured within ourselves, our solitude is reflected in that of the condemned within his own cell. Reclusion and pain within that scenic space offered up to the audience of humanity: further material for the human comedy or, perhaps, for its tragedy.

Gianfranco Maraniello

This work came about following a discussion with Sergio Risaliti about the problem of capital punishment when the Tuscan Regional government invited the artist to participate in a series of events commemorating the anniversary of the abolishing of capital punishment by the Grand Duke Leopold of Lorraine, who was the first in Europe to abolish capital punishment in 1786.

BBBreathless
2001
Model (urethanic rubber)

Stage evidence (untitled)
2000
Urethanic rubber,
installation

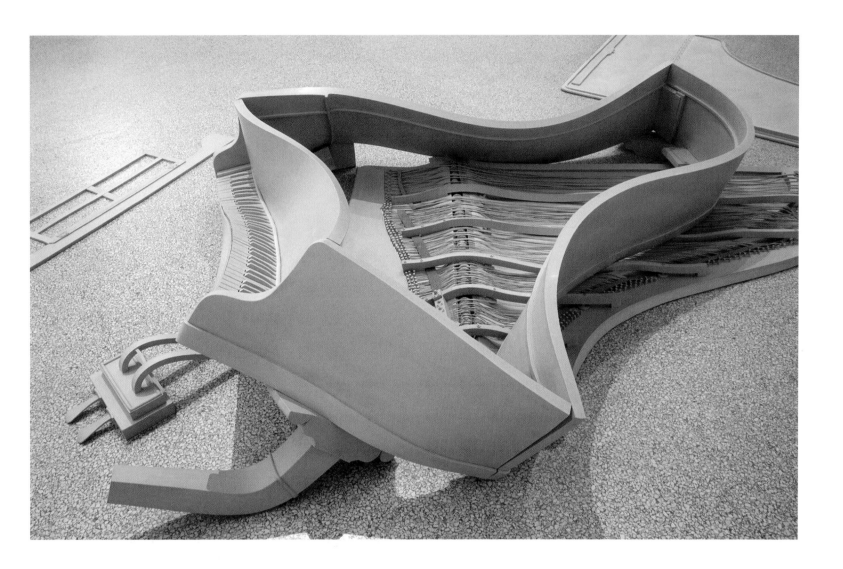

To see from within
on Charles Sandison's installation "Living Rooms"

Living Rooms is a computer generated artwork based on text. It is site specifically installed to embrace and surround the viewer in the exhibition space. The visitor sees projected words moving around a darkened space. The words indicate a very basic level of existence: Male, Female, Food, Father, Mother, Child, Old and Dead. After spending enough time in the space you notice that the words are acting and reacting, living their own lives, telling us their stories: "Males" compete for "Food". "Females" avoid "Males" until they have eaten "Food". Mature "Males" chase "Females" to reproduce. "Fathers" replace used "Food". A deadly virus starts to spread when population levels get too high. Everything is ageing and eventually becomes "Old" and "Dead".

In the tradition of art history *Living Rooms* follows the beaten tracks of conceptual art. It walks on the border of image and word, appearing in a sculptural format. It is also an ultimately reduced version of virtual reality.

Simulation

In the experimental field of virtual reality, models of worlds are constructed in order to make possible an examination and understanding of the basic functions of life and reality from a perspective not possible to take in real life. The field of endophysics operates with imagined viewpoints, treating our rela-

opens up for instant variability, machine generated variables. *Living Rooms* consists of 8000 lines of computer codes. It is a result of an advanced programming developed out of the idea of computer games.

The closed circuit of the work, its inner mental rhythm, brings it close to the system of a biological organism. The ultimate outcome of the work is something like a book that writes itself. A self-generating open narrative, a system of concepts, possible to be eternally reprogrammed, changed, altered and varied.

The work of Charles Sandison gives us a hint of what Peter Weibel has called post-ontological art. That means an existence of a kind of immaterial creation possessing human properties such as intelligence, life and conscience— all artificial—yet without any material existence. We would not be able to register their presence, they would represent a subject lacking ontological status

Re/Presentation

Living Rooms is designed to adapt to different architectural spaces and environments. By climbing stairs and moving between rooms it plays games with the tradition of site-specificity. The game of hide and seek includes us as viewers.

Through its immaterial characteristic *Living Rooms* is emphasising our position and our only possibility: to see a system from within. It forces us to be physically involved and become incorporated as the projections fall upon us,

Charles Sandison 1969

tion to the world as one to an interface. The aim is to transcend that interface relation, to go beyond the limits of body, time and space. *Living Rooms* is not a model of a world, it is an image of a suggestion of a basic structure. The method used is a simulation of a reduced structure of almost any kind of living system we know about. But what we see is only a sequence of an ongoing *perpetuum mobile*, a section made for presentation in the context of the art world.

Electronic art long ago introduced the image as a dynamic system. The digital technique

using our bodies as part of the screen. We are not able to interact or interfere, only invited to identify with the simulated system. Although it is impossible to predict the outcome of the simulation we can still recognise the struggle that happens around us.

The metaphorical levels rising from the work involves us in representations of biological rhythms, encounters with the interfaces of reality, interpretations produced in the juxtaposition of media discourse and the theory of psychoanalysis.

Maria Hirvi

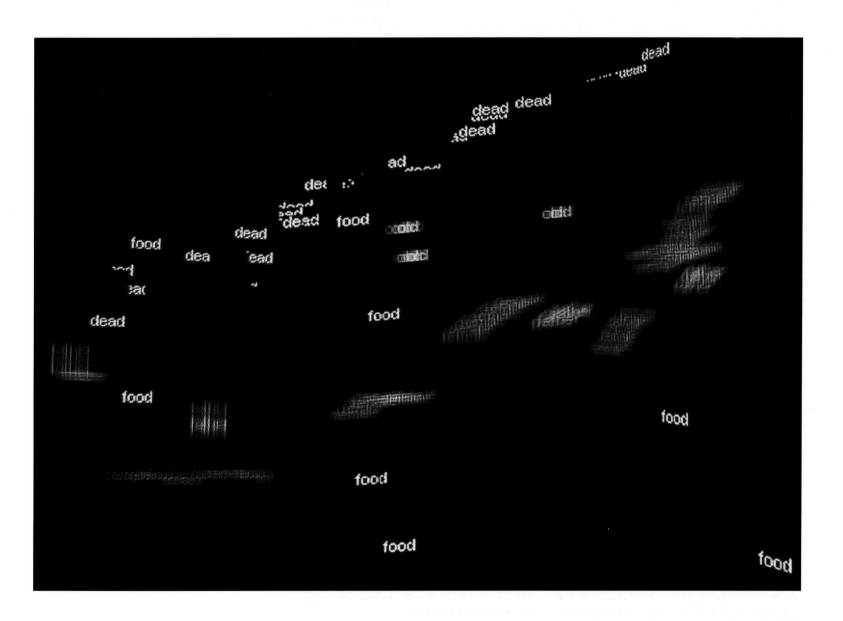

The work of Ene-Liis Semper with its body-focused rhetoric, both irritatingly provocative and intimately personal, seems to point at one central topic—"harassment in culture". It is difficult to find another name for it. Semper digs into her own world, penetrates deep under the layers of consciousness and the body. The artist apparently wants to say that a human subject can be treated as nothing else but a "'filthy stain' in the mirror of the world as a whole".[1] Ene-Liis Semper came to art in the early 1990s as an enigmatic heroine and a mysterious *femme fatale* of the ritual performances of "Group T." When the group almost ceased their activity in mid-1990s, Semper got rid of the cult woman aura promoted by "Group T", and her work may be understood as a radical inversion of that role.[2]

The transgressive gestures of Semper, whom the critics have called a cultural refugee, seem to allude to the artist's burning desire to cast off the strangling chains of culture and the burden of the body, and return to the pre-language and role state. Her work bears the eternal stamp of the tragedy of being here, where the ego is consequently precipitated as an imaginary misconstruction, alienating the subject in her own image. "The oscillation inherent in this situation (the self is always the other, the other is always the self), snares the subject in a constant search for the anterior state of asubjectivity."[3]

Her work, originating in the intermediate

Semper has a unique skill to freely manipulate the medium, and completely spellbind the viewers by perfectly controlling their reception. Using the features of the medium itself, she can make the means almost transparent, invisible. Paradoxically, the most vivid example of this is a work where she turns the characteristics of the video, itself into a fetish— *FF/REW* (1998). In a short film-like and rather self-ironical video that the critics were eager to interpret as a perfect metaphor of a cultural refugee's attempts to find a way out, the artist behaves in an emphatically theatrical manner. As a morbid heroine in the style of Dostoevsky, she is oscillating in the endless chain of suicides, accompanied by the absurdly pathetic music of Beethoven (hanging or shooting herself). Semper moves backwards and forwards with overwhelming indifference. The artist's wish to express the video's capability to manipulate time, to break down the linear and narrative structure of events, to continously change them around, to move both backwards and forwards from the starting point of events[4], and through that to point at the purely symbolic nature of her works, is actually amplifying the effect of reality. Precisely because there are no cuts (which an observant viewer certainly notices), and Semper's suicidal character ends up hanging in the gallows, in a total cultural vacuum.

Be that as it may, Semper's works nevertheless carry the viewers along, and by no means only in the "bewitching charm of horrors", but

-Liis Semper Ene-Liis Semper Ene-

Ene-Liis Semper 1969

Ene-Liis Semper Ene-

landscapes and peripheries of her Body and Self, Being and Word, finds a symbolic solution mostly in traumatic, tragic or almost suicidally brutal self-portraits/self-images. Be it as a softly sounding "morose embryo" (*Nameless I*, 1996); reading, slowly and in autistic incomprehension, the fundamental texts of cultural history (*Fundamental*, 1997); blending with nature in a forceful sacrifice (*Oasis*, 1999), or as a 'bodily bored' snake in its sinuous course upstairs (*Staircase*, 2000). All these videos seem to repeat the motif of mute pain, retreated into itself, although the works mentioned above actually form a fraction of Semper's relatively extensive video art production that started in 1994.

because the viewers have a chance to experience everything directly, recognise themselves, vacillate together with the author, identify with Semper's transgressive heroines.

Anders Härm

[1] Hanno Soans, "Vägivaldne autistlik Subjekt Eesti kunstis 1987-1998", *BA paper at the Academy of Arts*, Tallinn, 1998.
[2] *ibid.*
[3] Stuart Marshall, "Video Art, the imaginary and the parole wide", *Studio International*, 5-6, 1976.
[4] Ene-Liis Semper, "Borderline Syndrome. Energies of Defence", *Manifesta III Catalogue*, Ljubljana 2000, p.157.

FF / REW
1998
7', still from video

Learning from Spiders

An installation, in the hands of Javier Téllez, might be described as a "machine for seeing", and a "machine for thinking": for making an experimental cross-connection of ideas which can illuminate some of the great dualisms human beings labour or suffer under. Téllez's accumulations are often provocative, but they take a revitalising wit from their constant attempt to gain a liberty for worn-out signs. *Choreutics (A Motion Study)*, Javier Téllez's video installation for the 2001 Venice Biennale, has, for its main matter, film sequences shot by Téllez between December 2000 and March 2001 in his native country, Venezuela. They concern a community of fishermen who live

Javier Téllez's installation is a hexagonal structure made up of cells and a central area. Videos are projected from the centre radially towards the far wall of each cell. Téllez has compared the hexagon to a cobweb—by analogy the spider's threads are the trajectories of the looks, gazes, glances, linking the videos with the spectator. In one pair of projections, video-portraits of people affected by HD, the movements of their faces, hands or feet, are with children from the same villages playing with a top, which they pass, spinning, from hand to hand. In the other pair there is a 16mm black-and-white film made in 1972 by Dr Ramon Avila Giron, a Venezuelan doctor who was one of the first to study Huntington's Chorea in Lake Maracaibo; and speeded-up

obscure historical connection. In the late middle ages, in southern Italy, it was thought that the bite of the Tarantula produced the condition of chorea, those seizures of uncontrollable movement, which seems to have become a Europe-wide epidemic at the time, and which in English was known at St Vitus's Dance, and in French as La Danse de St Guy. In Italy it was believed that the only possible cure was the mimetic dance which became the tarantella, described by the historian of dance, Curt Sachs, as "wild, jumping and demoniacal [...] born perhaps out of the dances to avert the plague".[1] The medieval epidemic of "uncontrollable dance madness" (Sachs) was probably a psychological rather than a physiological phenomenon (if the two

Javier Téllez 1969

around or on Lake Maracaibo, many of whom suffer from Huntington's Chorea, or Huntington's Disease. The people of Barranquitas and Lagunetas represent the largest concentration in the world of the disease, an inherited neurodegenerative disorder that results in progressive motor, emotional and cognitive impairments, marked by "chorea" (uncontrollable movements), which eventually becomes fatal. Ironically, Lake Maracaibo is also the area where Venezuela extracts oil, the chief source of its national income. The fact that the profits obtained benefit only a small portion of Venezuelans is made dramatically evident by the extreme poverty in which the fishing communities live.

sequences of a spider spinning its orb-web. Finally, from the centre of the hexagon, extremely noisy tennis-practice machines fire balls at each of the projection screens, a perpetual and violent intervention which can only be taken as a metaphor for the gaze we cast as spectators.

From the present moment, and the "epicentre of the genetic tragedy" (in the artist's words), a web of connections spreads out. Clues are given by the work's title, and by the presence of the spider. "Choreutics" was the name given by Rudolph Laban, one of the pioneers of the theory and practice of modern dance, to his systemisation of expressive movement. The spider's presence unearths a more

can be definitively separated; certainly, it was not hereditary Chorea).

It is in the making of such connections that Téllez becomes provocative. How can he compare the movements of an HD sufferer—involuntary, "meaningless", indicative of a tragic disease and hellish experience—with the gestures of dancers, conscious and aimed at aesthetic pleasure? Isn't this to muddle up all our categories, ethical as well as aesthetic? To examine them, certainly, but in my view to refine them rather than confuse them. There are two things that can be said here which may derive from the age-old links between the disease and dance in the popular imagination. The introduction of Laban's dance theories in

the work's title is not gratuitous since modern dance was born from a challenge to classical ideas of beauty, just as modern art was. The German school of Laban especially, and his great pupil Mary Wigman, shattered the high-art codes of motion of classical ballet with a spasmodic, expressionist, contorted style. One contemporary writer described her dances as "petrified madness".[2]

In an even more remarkable example of the "psychogeographical leaps" which Téllez says articulate the structure of his work, Valeska Gert, the outlandish cabaret artist, dancer and contemporary of Mary Wigman, in describing the movements of her dance *Canaille* (1920s), wrote that, at a certain moment, "in a sudden spasm, as if bit by a Tarantula, I twitch upwards".[3]

The presence of Dr Avila Giron's film reminds us of the great process by which science bypasses the myths surrounding an affliction like Huntington's Chorea, searches for the fatal gene, finds it and neutralises it, thus holding up the possibility of the eradication of the disease. An essential part of the doctor's approach is his disclaimer that his "exhibition" of the Chorea of the fishermen, by filming it, has any other than a scientific purpose. Yet it is perhaps a feature of Téllez's conjunctions, weavings and reversals of ideas to suggest that "scientific truth" does not obliterate the wisdom of the popular conception of dance as

Bedlam
1999
Mixed media, video
installation, variable size

Hospital São Pedro
1997
Mixed media video
installation, variable size

an exorciser of demons. There is room, in other words, for a change of metaphor to underline the mutuality of science and art.

Operating as a visual artist rather than a scientist or historian, Téllez's recourse is to have the people in the grip of the Chorea stare back at the camera, meeting the observing gaze of the art-public emanating from the panopticon-like centre of the web-maze. The act of observing, which always carries with it an ethical ambiguity—does it signify authority over, engagement in, or indifference towards the lives of others? —is structured into a web by Téllez in an attempt to overcome polarisations and dualisms. Javier Téllez made this work, he says, "learning from spiders". In a letter he wrote to me while he was constructing the work, he goes on: "My labyrinth is composed of multiple lines that run from the periphery to the centre and vice-versa. It is the lines that our eyes draw when we see, it is the thread that makes tops spin and the lines traced in the hand of the child that supports it. It is also the long thread that ties all human beings, the umbilical cord: Aria-DNA."

Guy Brett

[1] Curt Sachs, *World History of the Dance*, London, George Allen and Unwin,1938, pp. 251-256.
[2] See Sally Banes, *Dancing Women: Female Bodies on Stage*, London, Routledge, 1998, pp. 125-136.
[3] Quoted, *ibid.*, p. 134.

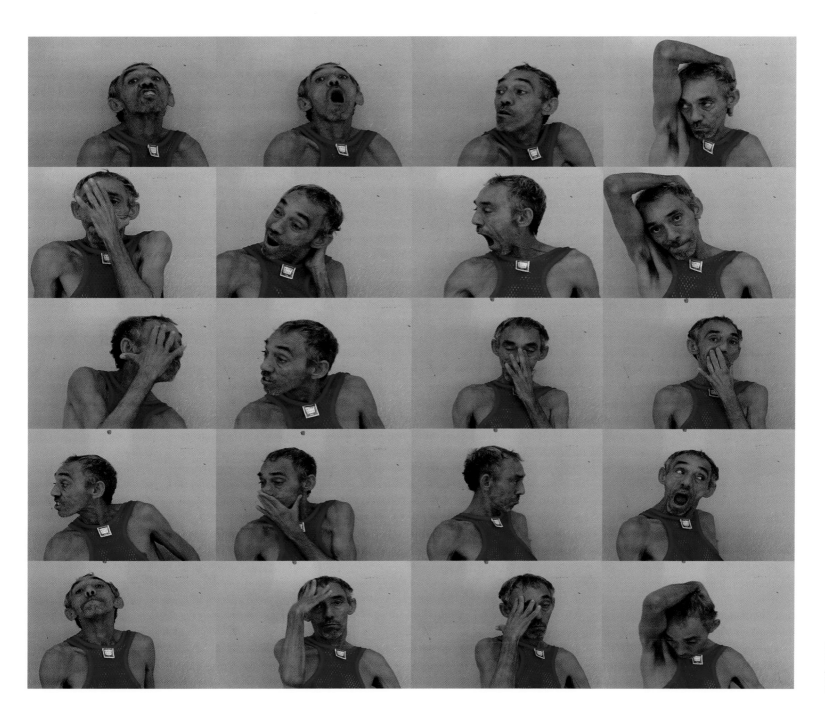

The Desire for Light

An animated image, in order to be fully perceived, requires a darkened environment; this is why, at this year's Biennale, the black boxes have been lined up alongside each other like monks' or nuns' cells in a convent. The price that must be paid in order to render a phenomenon in its temporal extension is a high one, from an architectural point of view—it is monotony.

A film is projected light; why, then, shouldn't it also be projected in a well-lit environment? Alessandra Tesi asked this question after having created many structures in the dark; and she has come up with a surprising solution. Thanks to the combination of a larger number of Ansilumen on a screen she devised herself, Alessandra Tesi manages to project a film in the light of day, locating within space an image in movement as if it were a painting. An obvious solution. The invention is as simple as it is ingenious, and the best way to describe it is to provide an extract from the "invention patent" that Alessandra Tesi presented to the patent office on April 9 2001 (patent application number MI 200/A 000687).

The image projection technique used thus far has a few limits. In fact, traditional screens are not suitable for projections in the presence of pervasive light, in that the intrinsic luminosity of the images projected is not sufficient to provide adequate contrast for the viewer; should one wish to project images in surroundings infused with pervasive light (such as in an outdoor cinema or in a naturally lit room), one would have to use very powerful projectors and this is unconvenient with regards to the oper-

same way, should one wish to use slightly concave projection screens, controlling and maintaining the correct curvature in the appropriate central areas of the screen becomes particularly difficult, due to the weight of the screen itself. What's more, traditional screens are not particularly suitable for outdoor projections, where they are subject to atmospheric phenomena such as wind and rain (which make them heavy or even flap violently, but in any case would compromise the quality of the screening).

In this context, the underlying technical aim of the present invention is to devise a projection screen able to offer a clear, neat vision of the image projected onto the screen itself, all of which will enhance the viewer's enjoyment of the screening.

Another important aim of the invention is to devise a projection screen that is able to confer pleasant aesthetic effects of brilliance, luminosity and three-dimensional consistency to the projected images, regardless of the type of projector used. The present invention also aims to provide a screen for even very large screening areas while at the same time avoiding distortions to the projected image even when enormous screens are used and/or when the projector is at quite some distance from the screen itself. For this latter technical aim, the present invention substantially aims to devise a projection screen with a structure sturdy enough to efficiently maintain the screen's original form even when used for outdoor screenings and/or for particularly large (flat or concave) screens.

A projection screen comprises an optically passive support for flat, concave or convex configurations and an optically active level, overhanging the optically passive support and designed to receive a light beam projected onto it in order to provide a refraction and/or an (at least partial) reflection: the optically active layer contains a multiplicity of reflecting and refracting polyhedral bodies arranged along the optically passive support.

This invention would thus obtain important advantages. Above all, it must be said that the structure of the present screen makes optimal use of the phenomena of light reflection and refraction, thus providing a substantial enhancement of the luminosity of the image perceived by the viewers watching the screen; in the final analysis, this provides greater visibility of the projected images, thus allowing them to be efficiently screened even in well-lit locations.

It must also be said that, thanks to its high degree of structural homogeneousness, the screen, according to the present invention, makes it possible to avoid potential image distortion, even with particularly large projection

structure, also provides intrinsic advantages in terms of structural resistance and maintenance of the original form: in fact, thanks to the fact that the bodies are adjacent to and along the same side as the support, they essentially lean against one another and thus contribute to maintaining the planarity of the screen itself.

It must also be noted that the bodies lean against each other in a largely homogeneous manner, even in those areas that are distant from the sides of the screen, and it is therefore possible to efficiently maintain the same form of the screen even in its central zone – substantially regardless of the size of the screen itself.

What's more, by exploiting the positioning and reciprocal adjacency of the bodies, it is possible, through a suitable distribution of the sizes of the bodies themselves, to enhance and maintain a given concavity/convexity of the screen; for example, by using larger spheres in the outer areas of the screen and gradually smaller ones towards the centre of the screen itself, it is possible to form a concave screen, while by using a substantially diametrically opposed choice of sizes it is possible to form a convex screen.

I personally followed the experimental phase and was surprised by the chromatic richness as well as by the dialogue between physical presence and pictorial effect. In Paris, Alessandra Tesi got the fire brigade to come to the Seine with all their equipment and fire helmets and direct jets of water from fire hydrants, with the pressure turned up full tilt, either up into the air or into the river. A powerful ejaculation *ad absurdum* of men in uniform, almost like a chapter from the cemetery of liveries and uniforms, adapted from Marcel Duchamp's famous mixed media on glass work, *La mariée mise a nu par ses célibataires, même | The Bride Stripped Bare by Her Bachelors, Even (Large Glass)*, who, in this seminal work, was already warning us against the perils of overpopulation: more eroticism, no procreation.

Alessandra Tesi 1969

ating expenses and the power input (these would also be potentially dangerous as they would overheat the projection mechanism itself and/or the film).

What's more, because of the fact that the only light source is constituted by the projector, the projecting of images onto traditional screens would result in a not insignificant loss of luminosity and brilliance in that the screen (which by its nature is opaque) absorbs part of the luminous energy; obviously, this part of luminous energy is not given back to reflected light (which is perceived by the viewer), and, in the final analysis, the images that can in effect be seen would not possess the overall luminosity that they might theoretically have were the illuminating potential of the projector to be fully exploited.

There is another, structural problem pertaining to traditional screens that should also not be overlooked. In fact, should one wish to use particularly large screens, there are problems inherent in maintaining the correct planarity of the screen in those areas which are furthest from the perimetrical frame (or from the supporting eyelets). In the

screens and/or when the projector is at some distance from the screen itself. What's more, it must also be noted that thanks to the characteristics of the present invention it is nonetheless possible to devise particularly large projection screens without incurring loss of planarity and/or without risking image distortion.

Furthermore, the present invention allows for exquisite three-dimensional effects to be conferred onto the projected images thanks, to the fact that the light projected onto the screen is "manipulated" via optically active elements (such as the glass spheres utilized) which redirect the projected light in directions that propel beyond the plane of projection; in this way it is possible to obtain an extremely convincing three-dimensional effect.

Another advantage of the present invention is that it is possible to increase both the resolution and quality of the image as perceived by viewers, without having to use sophisticated and expensive projecting devices.

Finally, it should be observed that the screen manifactured according to the present invention, and thanks to its

To go back to the projection: the screen devised by Alessandra Tesi with applied little glass spheres not only doubles the quality of color, but also gets the firemen's helmets to stand out clearly against the rest and the jet of water to dissolve in a chromatic flux—the same flux Monet sought and painted on his Waterlilies.

From the solid dimension to a liquid dimension in a new constellation, on the basis of an invention fed by the desire for light: this is the significant, enormously important contribution in that it offers us a new path to follow.

Harald Szeemann

252

Opale 00
1999-2001
Videoprojection
on canvas with glass
microspheres, installation
in daylight,
232 × 310 cm, stills
from video

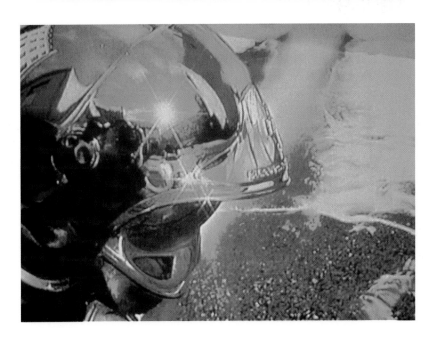

The Thinker (After Rodin) presented as part of the installation *Drawing and Thinking* is one of the series *The Seven Wonders of the World*. Tyson's Wonders are much more conceptual than Antipater's list of man-made architectural marvels, but they do, like those of the 2nd century writer, reside ultimately in simple, monumental forms.

Keith Tyson describes his practice as "traditional"—as traditional perhaps as cave painting or religious art—because it addresses itself to his sense of the ineffable, to a sense of awe at certain mysteries within the experiential world. Not the ancient mysteries of God or Natural divinity, but a contemporary sense of the ineffable framed through science as the new, secular "faith" with which we seek to understand the universe around us and our place within it.

The Thinker (After Rodin) has the form of a hexagonal tower wrought from aluminium—yet it embodies a complex idea, or rather, not so much an idea as the phenomenon of *thought* itself. The imposing, apparently mute monolith, emits an electronic hum and high up, two tiny LEDS signal the existence of hidden electrical activity. For inside is housed a bank of powerful computers running an Artificial Life programme, an evolutionary algorithmic system which defines and drives its own artificial universe, practically *ad infinitum*. Forms within this mathematically defined world are breeding, mutating, evolving, dying, being born again, and so on, all invisible to us. The system

In this way it is clearly related to its namesake, for Rodin's *Thinker* is similarly inarticulate, unable to share with us the nature of the question which caused his ponderous pose and his furrowed brow. Tyson's Thinker however is not a representation of thought. While Rodin formed a sculptural illustration of a human engaged in the process, with a rendering of what it *looks* like to think, Tyson's Thinker actively embodies the dynamic of thought within itself. For Tyson, the wondrous thing about this particular Wonder, is the fact that something as impossibly complex as thought—or cognition, or consciousness, or self-awareness—originates, and is contained within the inchoate carbon matter that is the human brain. And yet there's an irony in the fact that, although we are on the threshold of inventing silicon-based machines which can replicate human cognitive processes, we still can't entirely fathom what someone else is thinking, nor communicate particularly effectively what we, ourselves, think.

The second element in Tyson's *Drawing and Thinking* installation is an assembled mass of working drawings taken from the walls of his studio. Collectively, they represent a journal of Tyson's prodigious mental activity over a period of around 18 months. Some record interruptions from the outside world, a telephone conversation, something heard on the radio or read in the paper; some are preparatory sketches for pieces imagined but as yet unrealised; some are drawings for works generated

The thinker (After Rodin)
Technicals notes
2001
Mixed media on paper,
157 × 127 cm framed

Keith Tyson 1969

will keep doing what it is doing (at present memory capacity) for 33,000 years. Containing its own huge database, and its own systems of logic, the machine is entirely self-sufficient and entirely self-organising. It is impervious to any external influences that might interrupt its function, which is pure processing, or the pure operation of "thought". Tyson dubs it a "comatose God": "Godlike" because it is the master of its own self-contained Universe; "comatose" because it is a dynamic, functioning thing with absolutely no capacity to communicate with the outside world. We know it is thinking but we don't know *what* it is thinking.

by Tyson's *Artmachine*; some are more intimate and expressive tracings of his state of mind and his physical state of being. *En masse*, they add up to a drawn repository of the myriad things—ideas, experiences, feelings—flowing in and out of one individual brain: a kind of hard disk of the Self. *Drawing and Thinking*, as a bi-partite work, draws human consciousness, represented by the drawings, and mechanical cognition, embodied in the sculpture, into an artistic dialectic about the nature of Thought. As such it might be described as a piece which itself "thinks", about thought.

Kate Bush

2001: THE THINKER (AFTER RODIN) - TECHNICALS/NOTES

Note This work will be the 1st in the Series "The Seven Wonders of the World". Like all the Sculptures in the Series it combines a simple geometry with some philosophical, mathematical or Scientific concept That I find wondrous. It is not enough for these sculptures to illustrate the wonder, they must somehow embody it......

▶ Q What should the thinker be thinking about?

INITIALLY I JUST WANTED TO HAVE A SINGLE MATHEMATICAL ENTITY 'THINKING' BUT WHEN I BEGAN TO DESIGN SUCH A CALCULATION I CHANGED MY MIND. A BRAIN DOES NOT EXIST IN ISOLATION. A BRAIN OUTSIDE OF LANGUAGE ENVIROMENT OR EMBODIED IN SOME BIOLOGICAL SYSTEM CANNOT BE SAID TO THINK. BRAINS UNLIKE COMPUTERS ARE CONSTANTLY BEING FED INFORMATION FROM 5 SENSES AND WE HAVE INSTINCTIVE, SOCIAL, BIOLOGICAL AIMS TO FULFIL (OUR MOTIVATIONS). IT IS THE ATTEMPT TO FULFIL THESE + PROCESSING AND INPUT FROM OUR CONSTANTLY CHANGING AND UNPREDICTABLE ENVIROMENT THAT, for me, represents 'Thought'. There is also a possibility of Each brain being a single ... wired into the Global totality of knowledge and language. Thus I need to create a separa... ...rnal universe for this thinker to be Inhabiting - Complete with an enviromental evolver, breeding and life forms which will Their own motivations.)

BASE

A COMATOSE GOD RUNNING ITS OWN UNIVERSE

NOR

FIRST 12 UNITS OF THE SOCIAL GROUP OF A'S.

(A1) (A2) (A3) (A4)
(A5) (A6) (A7) (A8)
(A9) (A10) (A11) (A12)

B1
LOOPS IN 1 'INHABITANT' IN PROGRAMME

INTERNAL CHEMICAL + PHYSICAL STATES

IMAGINATION AND PREDICTION

OBJECTIVES

BRAIN I   BEHAVIOURS + ACTIONS

PROCESSING

THO

IF   ENVIROMENT ⟶ REACTION

MEMORY   IN

TURING TEST

NEURAL CONNECTIONS

FIRST 12 UNITS OF THE SOCIAL GROUP OF 'B's

(B6) (B1) (B2) (P) (B3) (B4) (B5)

(B7) (B8) (B9) (B10) (B11) (B12)

LIKE A COMPUTER WITH ITS VDU, KEYBOARD AND PERIPHERALS

(3 METRES)

DIAGRAM SHOWING EVERY POSSIBLE 2-WAY CONNECTION IN A MATRIX OF 12 UNITS - THERE ARE IN FACT 66 WAYS OF CONNECTING 2 UNITS, 220 3 WAY COMBINATIONS, 495 WAYS OF CONNECTING 4 UNITS, 792 WAYS OF CONNECTING 5 FROM A GROUP OF 12. 924 WAYS OF CONNECTING 6, 792 (again!) if connecting 7, 495 of 8, 220 of 9, 66 of 10. Thus they must be palindromic!

L   60   R   6

6

UNIVERSE
ENVIROMENT
SOC... OF THE...
THINKER

JAN 2001

39   39
1 2 3 4 5 6 7 8 9 10 11 12 13

Section of an Infinitive
Dam holding Back
the Terrible Weight
of the Abyss
Mixed media on paper,
157 × 126 m framed

Nov. 2000 - SECTION OF AN INFINITE DAM HOLDING BACK THE TERRIBLE WEIGHT OF THE ABYSS.

Lecture about current
problems with
Beatrix Ruf
Mixed media on paper,
157 × 126 m framed

Chasing a ball in the political field (fragment)

Theorem A. Two plus two makes a lot.
One country, two systems. One playing ground, two games. This fake post–Deng Xiao Ping slogan crawled into my mind when Gustavo Artigas, a young artist from Mexico City, showed me his work for the Insite 2000 Tijuana/San Diego exhibition: a double political metaphor he devised under the apparently innocent title of *The Rules of the Game (Las reglas del juego)*. The two part work is, at first glance, a transmogrification of sports. Instead of organising a clash, say, between a Tijuana and San Diego Baseball team, which would have exacerbated feelings of national hatred developed through the conflicting vicinity of two cities linked by their absolute opposition, Artigas fused a basketball match between two San Diego high schools and an indoor soccer match game between two preparatory school teams

hybridisation that would have tried to tame cultural and social differences through a creation of a mixed (albeit strident) common cultural repertoire. The proposition ought to become clearer after examining the first part of Artigas's project. In *The Rules of the Game I* Artigas had a handball court built against the border fence in one of the most paradigmatic shanty towns of Tijuana, Colonia Libertad, a neighborhood that grew in the desert-like slopes of the borderline on terraces erected with worn out car wheels filled up with cement, a practical solution that in itself describes a compensatory assimilation of the leftovers of capitalist affluence. This has also historically been one of the main crossing spots in the way of the illegal immigrants trying to get into the United States. So if the work seemed at first glance a slightly satirical attempt at urban improvement (a clean, perfectly designed piece of street furniture which instituted a proper

Gustavo Artigas 1970

from Tijuana, being played on the same field simultaneously. Soon, to the audience's exhilaration (similarly composed by the superimposition of impassioned American and Mexican sport audiences and overexcited Mexican and American art conscenti) the double match developed in the guise of an almost perfect lesson of cohabitation of differences without interference. Save for minor accidents, the players learned immediately to accept the interwined battle as one more contingency which would not distract them from the seriousness of their own ordeal. The situation pointed to critical operations far beyond the spirit of amateur fraternity or even the postulation of a form of

playground in the midst of an apocalyptic social scenery) it involved a cunning reading of the current situation of the Mexican/American Border. The mechanics of handball, throwing the ball to bounce it back and hitting it again to hit the wall, suggested the increasingly more frequent and dangerous attempts an immigrant makes today to cross to the north. Playing on Artigas's court is a melancholic reflection on the character of the wall between Mexico and the United States, incidentally made of recycled prefab roads used during the Desert Storm campaign, that is not solely a boundary, but is in fact a bouncer.

Cuauhtémoc Medina

The rules of the game
2000-2001
Video and photo
documentation, files and
sport props, variable size,
still from video

Richard Billingham's photographs and videos record everyday life with his family, at home in their council flat on the outskirts of Birmingham. His images, in which there is no condescension and no implied critique, have all the candour and remorselessness that only an insider can bring to their subject. In every sense, Billingham's is an interior view. The pensive video of Liz, smoking, with the condensation on the window behind her, the rain falling on the city beyond the glass, is in direct contrast to *Playstation*, a video which focuses entirely on Richard's brother Jason, manically playing at a Playstation game console. We never see the television heard in *Liz Smoking*, nor the screen on which Jason plays his computer game.

Ray in bed, the blanket right up to his neck, eyeing the intrusive camera and unable to escape; Ray, toothless, caught in a laughing grimace in a dusty bedroom mirror—laughing because he is being photographed, laughing at himself, or at whatever it is that is going on in his head. This last image has a terrible sincerity. At this moment, Ray seems altogether oblivious to the camera. Then Ray again, three times, in black and white portraits which have an almost monumental dignity.

The family's only escape seemed to be entirely inward—in drink, in smoking, in the family pets, in pastimes, in the constant round of arguments and reconciliations. It is an endless daily cycle. In recent photographs, Richard Billingham has been showing us the locality:

Richard Billingham 1970

Richard Billingham

the hinterlands of the city, the last scrappy remnants of nature, the promise of elsewhere. A path leads across a field to a near horizon, but you feel it leads no further.

Billingham records a circumscribed world, but one in which he discovers an inordinate richness and complexity. It is the details, of course, which count, the perceived moment, the opportunity taken, as much as what we imagine as the longer narrative or the explosive moments in the family drama. Billingham's, it turns out, is an art of patience and stoicism, and a surprising formality.

Adrian Searle

Untitled
1990
Black and white print on
aluminium, 98 × 147 cm,
editions of 5 plus 1 AP

"I'm freaked out by the body," says Chris Cunningham. "I used to pretend that I was hollow, because I couldn't stand the idea of having all those organs inside; it made me feel sick". Yet the body is a source of enormous fascination. His latest video, *flex* (2000), was partly inspired by a love of anatomy books. Caught in a beam of bright light, two naked figures curl round one another like embryos floating in deep space. A series of rapid edits shows a man and woman fighting and fucking. A mouth spews blood—a foretaste of things to come. Flashing lights, swirling mists and cosmic sounds suggest that we are witnessing the Creation. It could be pretentious; but the stark, monochrome beauty of the images saves it. Then we come down to earth. The man walks towards us, glancing nervously over his shoulder. The attack still catches him unaware, though.

Launching a violent assault, the woman downs him with a right hand to the solar plexus.

through a combination of visceral earthiness and haunting otherworldiness enhanced by the music of Richard James from Aphex Twin. Some sequences were shot underwater, others on a stage against a black background. "There's no gravity, no geography, no geometry," says Cunningham. "The sections are intercut so that the bodies have different weights from one shot to the next. The piece is totally organic; I asked the performers to improvise. Some sections were filmed very slowly so that when they're played back they become very fast and faces are distorted; others are violent, so it gets quite intense and starts to be suggestive on a psychological level. I wanted to do something like an abstract painting using figures, but in the edit room I started to create a sequence that feels like a narrative. One of my main objectives is to get a physical reaction, so I've made it as visceral as possible." Cunningham is a newcomer to the artworld, but he is well known to pop music fans for award-

much as the differences. Both explore the Creation myth (with God as a ray of light or a team of robots) and feature beings who, like Venus, are born sexually mature. One is filled with tenderness, the other is pervaded by violence but both are unashamedly erotic. One video is playful, the other is serious but an element of theatre turns them primarily into spectacle; the violence in *flex* is no more an article of faith than the lesbian caresses of *All is Full of Love*. This emotional distance is a source of strength—it prevents *All is Full of Love* from being too whimiscal and *flex* from being too expressionistic—but it is also a hazard. Technical eloquence enables one to be slick. Fortunately though, as a perfectionist, Cunningham is unlikely to be seduced by his own skill.

"My aim is to make images that are style-less but beautiful," he says. "If the image is too highly polished it detracts from the content. I wanted to be a sculptor; instead I got a job at

Chris Cunningham 1970

Retaliation comes quickly; an explosion of punches knocks her unconscious. As her body convulses painfully back to life, the man unsheaths his penis like a weapon, and rapid-fire edits suggesting premonition show violent coupling. She crawls away only to discover him lying prone. Caressing his cheek, she rolls onto him seductively. As they embrace in deep space, mist hangs suspended in a beam of light, like sperm in water—a cosmic ejaculation.

It's as though the Fall had been recast with sexually aware participants (Cunningham's Adam and Eve are mature adults)—a metaphor for the love/hate that binds men and women, with sex seen as a means of assault and a salve. This absurdly ambitious project succeeds

winning videos that are memorable both for their startling originality and stunning special effects. A pure white robot is being created on an assembly-line. She opens her eyes and begins to sing *All is Full of Love* (1999). Her face and voice resemble those of the pop star, Björk, who also appears as the robot's clone. As the pair kiss and caress, the assembly-line robots continue their work—driving rivets home and squirting lubricants into crevices—adding a witty, heterosexual frisson to the eroticism of lesbian love.

Two videos—one a sombre meditation on male /female relationships, the other a witty pop video featuring robots; seeing them together, though, what strikes one are the similarities as

Pinewood studios working as a make-up artist on a horror film". He later made models for *Alien 3* and special effects for Stanley Kubrick's *Artificial Intelligence*, a production that was eventually shelved. "I have a healthy disregard for special effects", he continues. "If they are convincing, you don't stop to think about what you've seen; but if they look fraudulent they become distracting."

Understandably, Cunningham is nervous about being judged as an artist; the beauty and professionalism of his imagery, on the other hand, is bound to make video artists sit up, take stock and realise how primitive many of their productions are.

Sarah Kent

Flex
2000
Shot on 35 mm film
transfered onto DVD Disc,
12', videoprojection,
still from video

By turning the laws of marketing and the mass media to his advantage, Matthieu Laurette incorporates his work within a strategy of infiltration and redistribution. In 1993, he established his artistic birth certificate by taking part in a TV game called *Tournez manège* where, when questioned by the presenter he said he was "A multimedia artist". Since then he has been using TV as both a work-place and a work-tool, by instrumentalising the ability of this medium to bring together not only means of production and broadcasting, but an audience to boot. In an initial phase, by assuming the status of passive viewer, which is offered to all citizens by the spectacle system, he took his place among the audience in a whole host of TV shows, putting together a series of *Apparitions/Appearances*—ready-made images which owed as much to Duchamp's idea of *rendez-vous* as they did to Warhol's fifteen minutes of fame. When the cable TV channel aptly named Spectacle offered him air time, he elected to make the video *Le Spectacle n'est pas terminé/The Spectacle isn't Over* (1998), where he got passers-by on the Champs-Elysées to read excerpts from Guy Debord's book, thus showing the extent to which the society of the spectacle had cynically encompassed his own criticism.

Being on TV can of course create a precarious form of fame, when it happens repeatedly, but not enough to earn a decent living. Based on a pragmatic line of thought about his

The same system of turning rules and laws inside out in favour of the individual informs the *Citizenship Project* (1998-∞), which involves him in investigating the conditions for obtaining several different nationalities by making this precious information available on a website. His goal is to obtain as many nationalities as he can, by going beyond the restrictions set by the idea of citizenship, in a world that is then truly globalised. This critical power of the artistic proposal also lies at the root of the *Laurette Bank Unlimited* project (1999-∞), which will help him to keep control of an offshore capital.

Matthieu Laurette systematically introduces a trading system, which invites the spectator to play an active part in his operations. *El Gran Trueque* (2000), the TV game he has created, with its copyrighted concept, thus offers TV viewers in Bilbao a chance to buy consumer goods at knockdown prices. A Fiat Seicento is bartered and bought in exchange for a computer, which is in turn swapped for a TV set, and so on, right down a pack of six blue glasses. This paradoxical system scales objects down using a principle of devaluation and equivalence. The negotiations required for this loose, informal economy set up a contract between the artist and the onlooker, which certainly informs Matthieu Laurette's transgressive economy, intentionally placed under the aegis of recycling in a world in the grip of commodification.

Pascal Beausse

Matthieu Laurette 1970

means of subsistence, Matthieu Laurette introduced, with his *Produits remboursés/ Money-back Products*, a system enabling him to meet his main needs. His method of consuming without spending anything is founded on the basic marketing system of the major food corporations. He feeds himself for nothing by only ever buying products with the rider: "Satisfied or your money back" or "Money back on first purchase". He makes the most of invitations from the media to broadcast the instructions for using his free consumer system. By merely systematically operating an advertising gimmick, Matthieu Laurette symbolically challenges the capitalist mercantile system.

Help Me to Become
a U.S. Citizen!
Financing contract for
citizenship
1998
Work in progress

J'y crois, j'y crois pas
TF1 TV, June 20, 1996
(excerpt)

C-Files: Tell Saga

The work *C-Files: Tell Saga* unfolds on the set of the eponymous feature film project by COM&COM. In this film, the two artists insert themselves into Schiller's drama as time-travelling secret agents. The classic, heroic drama is reflected through the genre of the quasi-supernatural detective series (*The X-Files*). On the set, the movie's trailer can be viewed together with records of its making: a documentary on *The Making Of*, props, stills and so on. The making of the fiction thus becomes the work of art, and the film—possibly fictional, never completed—is not an end in itself but hardly more than a condition of its making.

Passive melting into an undifferentiated context is not so very far removed from active camouflage; and this was the path that Marcel Duchamp traversed between his first *Objets à inscription* (procured from the Bazar de l'Hôtel de Ville in 1914) and his *Disques Optiques* (presented as optical inventions at the 33ème Concours Lépine in 1935). The "disintegration of the arts and their dissolution into the extra-artistic" (Sedlmayr) is not at all the same thing as the end of the arts. On the contrary: after the bankruptcy of the aesthetic programme of "Total art", running the world by means of *Gesamtkunstwerke*, this was the very process that kept artistic evolution going in the twentieth century. Every statement to the effect that "I hereby resign from art" (Beuys), every refusal to be art, tests and extends the boundaries of being art. Thus, an artist may perform an act of self-excommunication, demonstrating his or her freedom by renouncing freedom, or of self-commercialisation and submission to the dictates of economic rationality.

This has nothing to do with cynicism. A film is a product that is hard to distinguish from its own promotion. Together with that promotion, the film serves in its turn as a promotional tool for the merchandise that is derived from itself. This phenomenon has its exact counterpart in the world of art. The difference is that, in this case, the core product commonly has a different name: "The Artist". What goes for COM & COM, and also for Hedinger and Gossolt, also goes for *C-Files: Tell Saga*. The creator as *objet à inscription*: a verdict that, in a melancholy way, may not be so very remote from the sentiments that it would seem to threaten.

Tobia Bezzola

COM & COM

Johannes M. Hedinger (1971) and Markus Gossolt (1969) found Com & COM in 1997.

C-Files: Tell Saga, Poster
2000
Digi-Print, 128 × 90 cm

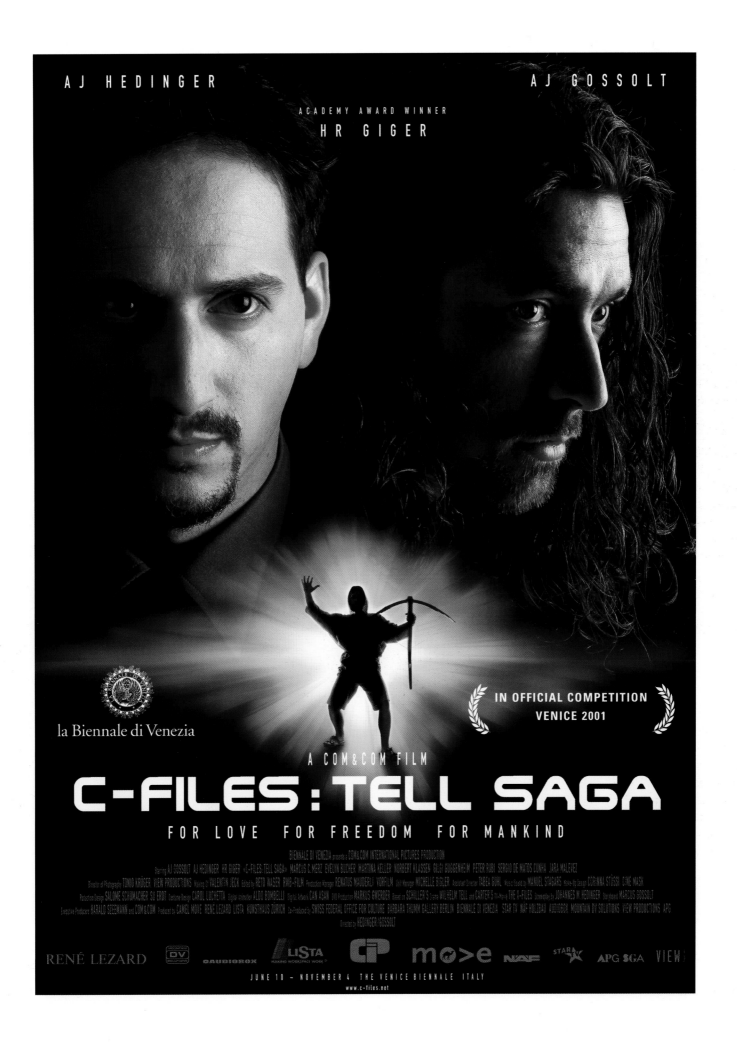

C-Files: Tell Saga,
Set Photography, Nr. 43
2000
Ilfochrome, 122 × 180 cm

A stitch in time...

Masterpieces in cross stitch and not. Special, wonderful drawings brilliantly created by golden hands from another time. Colours faded through time and stitches worn out by age. Examples of a special art which the German Museum of Embroidery in Celle, preserves as gems.
Elda Filippini, from *Rakam,* March 2001

Evviva il Ricamo! Long live embroidery!
From a private letter by Harald Szeemann, 2001

In a recent interview[1], Francesco Vezzoli says: "I hated being at college (Central St. Martins) and embroidery seemed to be a practice that allowed me to be on my own. At the beginning, it was neither a language or a stylistic choice. It was a way to be in peace and do what I liked best." This statement gives an indication of the value Vezzoli had already attributed to embroidery while he studied in London, firstly as a "practice", a word that nowadays defines "making" in art, and secondly as an autonomous and intimate space of expressive freedom.

"At the beginning, it was neither a language nor a stylistic choice": these words indicate how embroidery was at first a pretext to negotiate those moments of creativity which are not controlled by the academic institution, and then became a tool to build a detached

the Professor's revenge (the needle breaks at the end of "OK the Praz is Right!"), then in the wrath of Valentina Cortese when she continues to vent her anger on his bruised cheeks. Impassive at the centre of the scene full of silent disapproval, *Whistler's Mother* style, Vezzoli is the embroiderer and confirms his status as insider/outsider. And also that of the artist, and through this manual practice which is the domain of the "invisible" servant or the house-wife, it allows him to be both an actor and spectator of the *mise en scène*.

I believe there is a profoundly psychological reason for this bond between video and embroidery. It is a metaphor of a conflict grown by the obligations of public life and the requests of private life. The structure of Vezzoli's work is determined by precisely this unresolved conflict, dissolving the difference between reality and fiction.

The embroideries executed by the artist during the videos correspond to the narrative imagery of the videos, in obviously much longer fractions. This means that the filmic activity of Francesco Vezzoli's work does not describe real time reality but rather generates the embroidery as tangible reality. (The impossibility of interaction with the existing world is a lapse that produces alienation and hence solitude—widely demonstrated in '60s Italian films). The '60s sitcom *George Burns and Gracie Allen* (CBS)—to remain in the circuit of the television culture so dear to the artist—shows a 'positive' and very similar hybrid structure of reality and fiction. The everyday life of the protago-

dote to it and the social impropriety of its public expression[3]. Vezzoli's parody indicates with lightness all that is socially scornful[4] (in his work, "comedy of manners" is queen)[5]. The woven teardrops become skilfull and theatrical corrections of the images of the divas printed on canvas, just as in the work presented in Venice, where Vezzoli has embroidered make-up and maskara using color, golden and silver threads. The images in *Young at Any Age* (2000) are taken from a volume by Ira Von Fürstemberg by the same title, in which the author celebrates the beauty of 33 women: among these are Marisa Berenson, Isabelle Adjani and Diana Vreeland. The embroideries are of extraordinary perfection and great resolution and executed with "Rondine Cucirini Alba di Gallarate"[6] threads in half and diagonal stitches. Always attentive to the traps hiding in most commonplaces, Francesco Vezzoli has opted not to use the Venice embroidery stitch for the works in the Biennale, despite its fashionability in the 1960s.

Paolo Colombo

Francesco Vezzoli 1971

Francesco Vezzoli Francesco Vezzoli

and privileged "vantage point".

As in a '60s cinematographic fade-in, his words are in tune with those of Mariagrazia Lenti, director of *Giardino dei Punti*—The Garden of Stitches, School of Embroidery and the Lace Pillow in Milan—who in a recent conversation answered my question to define embroidery: "It is an area of creativity (unfortunately predominantly feminine), an exercise of ability, a technical expression and above all a solitary activity."

"The solitary activity" of the embroiderer, as in *An Embroidered Trilogy* (1997-99) takes shape in his role as an anti-character who operates outside the narrative while at the same having a strong stage presence[2]. Here he endures with

nists becomes a weekly television program. Here the device is that, when the protagonist George wants to know what his antagonist Gracie is doing in another wing of the house, he turns the tv in his studio on to the live channel to observe his wife in those moments of her role playing. Naturally, in the Irish tradition, and like postwar american housewives, Gracie Allen did not scorn "work" (labour) either.

Vezzoli often reminds us of how many characters other than Gracie have meticulously embroidered in their lifetime; from actors to directors to divas (from Cary Grant to Vincente Minnelli to Silvana Mangano). Often this activity started with a tragedy, as if embroidering was itself both the admittance of grief and an anti-

[1] Francesco Vezzoli in conversation with Helena Kontova and Massimiliano Gioni, *Flash Art,* 224, November 2000.
[2] A little thought to "the man with th McIntosh" whom Leopold Bloom meets twice in the streets of Dublin on th 16th of June.
[3] Public smiles, private tears.
[4] "... I just want to be the parody of the snob." Francesco Vezzoli in conversation with Helena Kontova and Massimiliano Gioni, *Flash Art,* 224, November 2000.
[5] In the context of social conventions and the use of embrodery as rethoric figure is associated a short paragraph from War and Peace: which denotes a peremptory use of embroidery as exclamation mark.
[6] "Special threads with high tenacity for embrodering and sewing."
[7] "First you do a drawing on paper which you lay onto two or three layers of canvas (sustain), the, you pinch holes around the silhouettes of the drawings. Proced with a machine sewn seam wich brings close drawing and canvas, along the contours of the drawing. Or procede with tacking going through the holes. Among the opposite contours of the drawing proced with "guipur" stiches, meaning those diverse stiches decorating flowers and leaves. Among a flower and another procede with streeps and pippiolini."

Embroidery of a Book:
Young at Any Age
2000
33 parts, 33 × 43,2 cm
each, detail

Francesco Vezzoli

Embroidery of a Book:
Young at Any Age
2000
33 parts, 33 × 43,2 cm,
detail

Provocation is a speciality of mine. My experience tells me that while art cannot quickly change social or political reality, it is important for art *not* be apolitical.

My need for direct communication led me to using my body and personality as a medium for art works. Sometimes I radically "sacrifice" my intimacy to confront certain existential, social or political subjects. *Looking for a husband with EU passport*, an interactive web project addressing gender and capital, criticises the ex-politics of Yugoslavia, and describes the collision of isolation, poverty and the elitism of European Union politics (www.cac.org.mk/capital/ostojic).

The personal contemporary space of individuals and human relationships, in and out of art circles, is in crisis. How can one revitalise essential human values through art? The Venice Biennale attracts the world press, art lovers and professionals; it seemed a natural opportunity to pose these questions here.

Black Square on White, made of pubic hair on my Mount of Venus, allows me to reconstruct a previous artwork (*Personal Space Photo Series*, 1995-96) in a very different context. Only the Biennale director, Mr Harald Szeemann, will have the right to see this "hidden Malevich" in order to declare it an official part of the 49th Venice Biennale. Walking around Venice during opening days, elegantly dressed, my work of art will be hidden. This intervention might provoke a reinterpretation of Eastern European spirituality, and non-material

Tanja Ostojić 1972

ideas; it is essentially about trust and power.

I'll Be Your Angel consists of my accompanying Mr Szeemann during the opening days around Venice (including cocktails, dinners, press conferences). I will be naturally performing as his escort—his Angel. This piece, integrated into everyday life, poses potentially ambiguous narratives concerning the scandalous artist (and the curator). It provokes an invitation/invasion, and questions the power structure in the art world. Speculations of morality, and artworld strategy will spin out; while the press will possibly construct a media support for this, it is not necessary. The structure of the piece is the process of mystery, both personal and public, encased in the glossy gossip of artworld whispers.

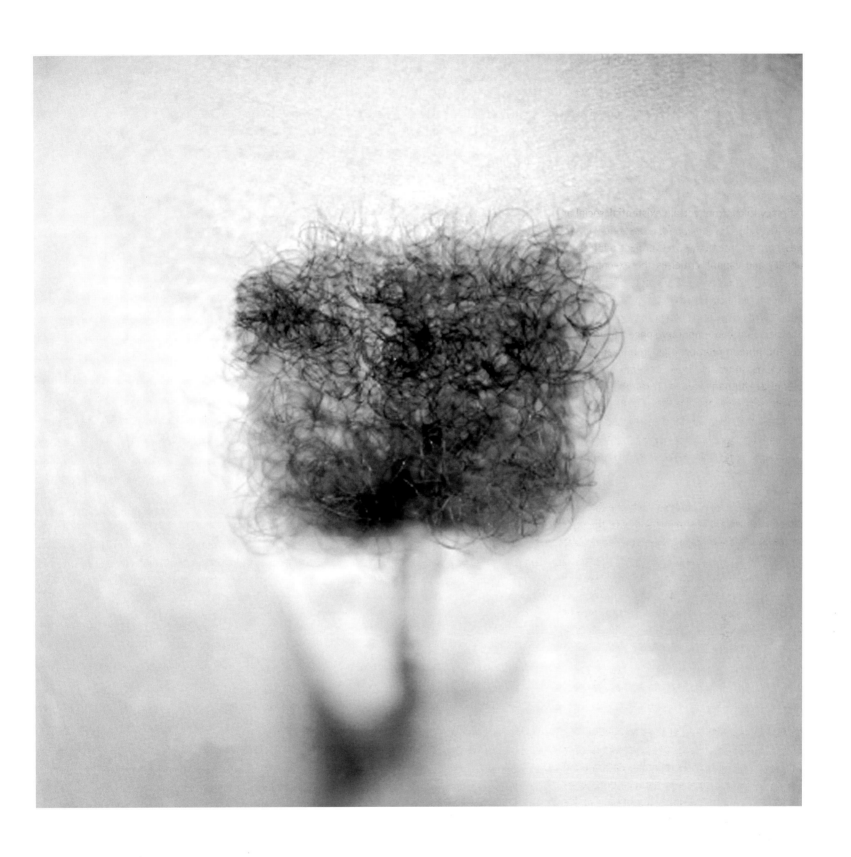

Black square on white
(on my Venus Hill)
1996–2001
Body art performance

Vertical Loops and Propassion in Salla Tykkä's Lasso

"Another of these small loops can be controlled vertically and brought up and over into a wedding ring around the roper's arm and then lifted off into a flat loop. This is the way you will find all the next loops acting. They are variations of the great Texas skip and in this trick the roper spins the loop clockwise on one side and counterclockwise on the other as he jumps through the loop."
("Will Rogers Rope Tricks" by Frank Dean, *The Western Horseman*, 1969.)

Salla Tykkä's video installation *Lasso* (2000) seizes on the sensation of wonder. It is like a spiral movement or emotion lasting for a few minutes; it starts from a relaxed concentration, lifts off at the centre point and moves towards a conclusion which is open to interpretation. The events of *Lasso* are, in brief: a girl who is out jogging takes a detour into the yard of a house and rings the doorbell, but nobody answers the door. She goes round the back of the house and peeps in a window. She can see a boy who is practising an amazing lasso trick. The girl looks on and a tear rolls down her cheek. She then turns away to look out across a calm sea.

Lasso airs the eternal question about the connection between art and emotion. It confronts us with the religious ecstasy we know so well from art history, for instance the Annunciation of the Virgin Mary or the sacred rapture of St Teresa. After all, one of the key arguments of

same in any culture, even if linguistic background and creed may influence the finer nuances. In *Lasso*, attention focuses on a clearly recognisable emotional response.

The music selected for *Lasso* was originally composed by Ennio Morricone for Sergio Leone's western *Once Upon a Time in the West*. The music directs the viewer's attention and heightens the work's intensity. In her childhood, Tykkä used to watch westerns on TV while her parents went about their daily chores around her. In that secure and drowsy milieu, gender roles were unobtrusively perpetuated, roles that were as clear-cut as those of the western.

The background or theme of Tykkä's work is often the role of emotional values as a background or determining factor for individual views of the world. Tykkä has also pursued a critical exploration of contemporary women's expectations of gender roles. To begin with, she played the main part in her work herself. The work became structured as a redefinition of self-image, female identity and physical presence. For instance, in her video *Bitch—Portrait of the Happy One* (1997), Tykkä deconstructs and reworks the methods for promoting a 'star cult' inherent in music videos.

In *Lasso*, the role of the work's inner narrator becomes a parallel for the situation where the work is viewed. What do I feel as a viewer in front of this work, and do other viewers feel the same? What if the work is not about the sensation of beauty, but about feelings of exclusion or about a sense of finality? Ought

work generates a sense of expectation, a "first movement". After that, *Lasso* goes through the entire gamut of emotions: the experience of pleasure, desire and its denial—the quelling of pre-passion, and suffering.

Does *Lasso* in fact show the wound between "the being in the world" of man and woman, the cut which prevents them from revolving as a mutually entwined totality, a cyclical creation of the universe? Does the boy and the lasso reveal to the girl the dynamic of human relationships (specifically theirs), the beauty and terror of their ins and outs, their wheeling and dealing, accompanied by music which evokes westerns and the to and fro motion of the "Texas skip"?

The sense of wonder presents the girl with the opportunity not just of approaching the boy, but also herself. His performance returns the formation of meaning to the articulation of gender differences. Un-awares, the man and his lasso represents what the woman is not capable of expressing, the feminine principle and the origin. In the reaching, expanding and contracting movement of the lasso, the girl discovers herself as a site for reoccurrence, a place of reproduction—a symmetrical, vertical loop, constantly seeking a shape, an opportunity for the boy to come and go.

Tykkä later said about her script that the girl in the main role is at the intersection of the role models she has acquired through her upbringing and the articulation of her own identity. The story is about siblings. The brother is an auxiliary character. The northern dimension of the narra-

Salla Tykkä 1973

the emotionalists has always been that the purpose of a work of art is to inspire emotion in the viewer.

"Admiration is a sudden surprise of the soul, which causes in her an inclination to consider with attention the objects which seem rare and extraordinary to her." (René Descartes, *The Passions of the Soul*, 70th Article.)

Emotion, a sensation of beauty, aesthetic pleasure. In *Lasso*, Tykkä builds up emotional impulses very skilfully using a variety of means: plot, music, careful direction of the camera work and the reactions of the work's inner narrator. On the level of definitions, emotion is seen as a spontaneous, non-calculated reaction to a concrete situation. The fundamental emotions are the

we as viewers to know more about the relationship of the film's characters to each other or to their surroundings?

Another essential feature of *Lasso* is movement. The work expresses the traditional concept of the significance of motion for emotion—motion can generate an emotion, while emotion may activate motion. The being of the main characters is tied to the way in which they are physically present. The work also draws attention to the gaze of the characters and the relationship between men and women. The gender roles follow the traditional roles of the western: the man is shown as a strong and independent loner, while the woman is an emotional onlooker on the sidelines. The introduction to the

tive is revealed in *Lasso* by the solid narrative structure combined with a straightforward perspective and the ability to tell a visual story with densely structured elements. *Lasso* poses the question of the boundary between personal feelings and a reaction pattern typical of any community. This applies more generally to Tykkä's work, too, where an individual perspective tends to expand in the work towards a more general observation. In the final scene of *Lasso*, the viewer appears almost to adopt the perspective of the camera. This requires the viewer to pause and reflect upon himself. A slightly melancholic sense of wonder swirls through the air like a lasso.

Leevi Haapala

Lasso
2000
Video, stills from video

Following pages
**From the series Pain,
Pleasure, Guilt**
2000
C-print, 100 × 120 cm

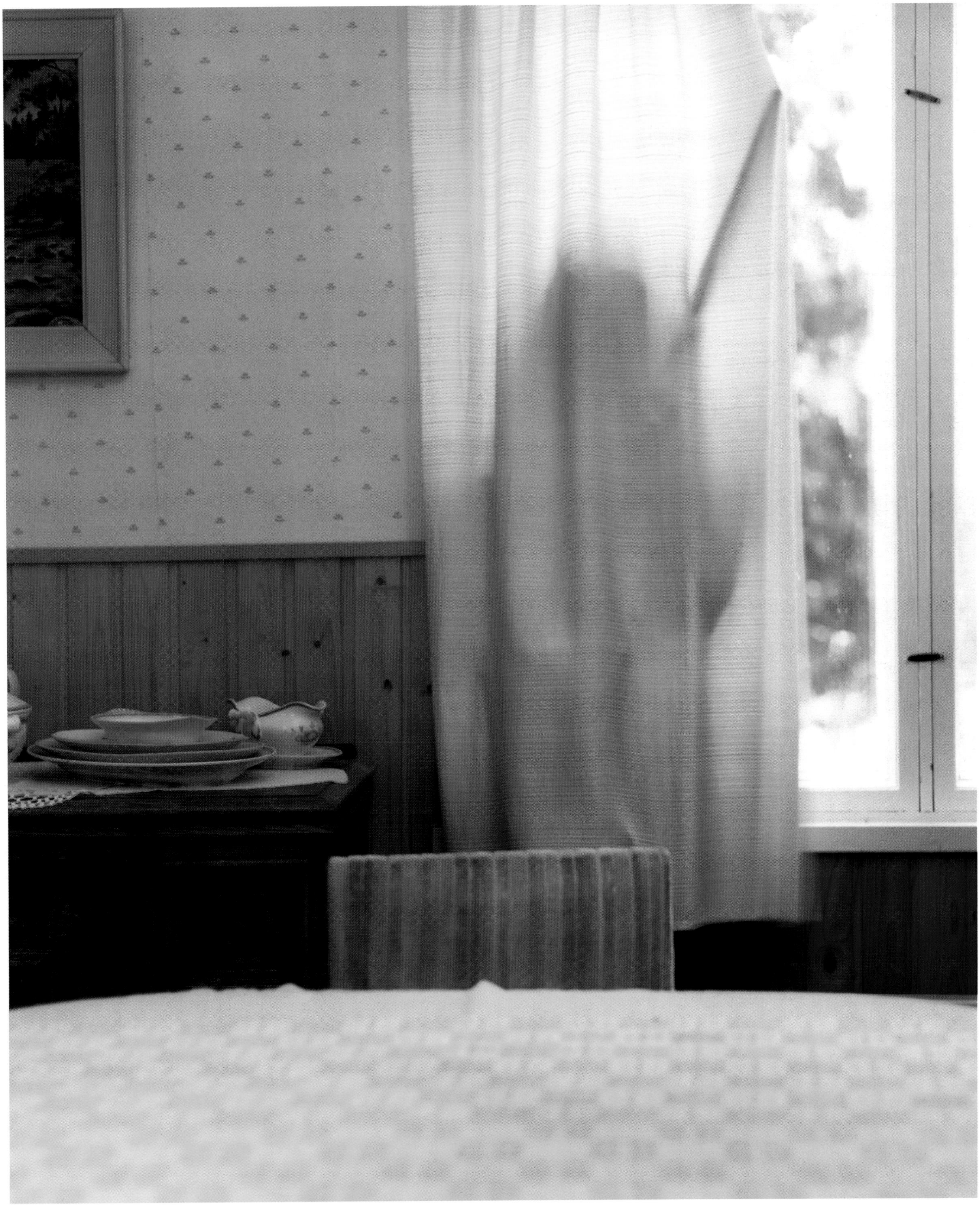

The Skin in Front of Space

Regina Galindo's introduction to the world of Guatemalan art was anything but straightforward. She herself finds it hard to recall the episode when, as a complete unknown, she put on a performance that consisted of her reciting poetry while hanging ten feet above a stunned crowd. She made more than one front page, where for most she was treated like just another news item even though for a select few she was seen as one of the most eccentric figures in the Guatemalan art community. However, it was only after her urban space performance that we were able to fully comprehend these encounters with the artist's performances, where each single step inaugurates its own cycle based on the highlighting of each instant and the reconfiguration of those spaces from which we have observed her not only as witnesses but also as participants.

To begin with, it is impossible not to note that in each single performance we are faced with a body which seems to emanate a potential it is impossible to avoid. Her body, which is fragile only in appearance, is such that it detonates reflections and discussions; it is willing to mesh in with the different spaces she has used for her works and with the ensuing sociological, psychological, aesthetic, economic and cultural implications.

This is perhaps why the artist, if she chooses materials for her performances, generally opts

is our starting point, we give shape to our belief systems.

It is therefore not strange that Galindo sometimes makes use of a quote from the Italian writer Curzio Malaparte, according to whom our skin is our own homeland. Human skin, genetically identical, is repeated in all bodies. It varies in colour and size. In any case, it necessarily implies a direct relationship with what lies around us and, in order to communicate with the outside world, personal codes are established which have to be adapted to the movements of bodies—like gestures.

Considering what we have just said, Galindo admits that divesting herself of all bodily covering and walking like an ambiguous being through the Venetian *calli*, immersing herself in and floating along the canals are two of the images that are possible within the context of the Venice Biennale. As a generic and political situation of *presence* in this incommensurable urban form, the artist will appear like an Epiphany, before which spectators are free to follow their own steps and recreate their own rituals.

Rosina Cazali

Regina Galindo 1974

for economical objects which, united to her gestures, provoke a symbolic and emotional relationship.

In truth, it is virtually impossible to escape emotion, or to decline the invitation to ceremony implied by Galindo's performances. Each action entails a series of elements and systems that are immediately translated into the suggestion of an intimate *vivencia* and a possible ritual practice. But her actions are not limited to a strategy that aims to move each individual. Silent forms and gestures suggest a comparison with or a reflection of our fears and the existential uncertainties we all have despite the immense variety of our cultural and social backgrounds. And almost as if this

El dolor en un pañuelo
1999, February
Video, still from video

Ciao Bella

Try to be a telescope
A plateau is a landmass. It is level. A stage. A table. A platform. Its fluctuations are mostly unapparent. It is stable. As an entity and as a concept. Being a plateau it is constant and enduring. It shrugs off any possible modulations to itself.

Staging a Plateau: "All the world's a stage"
By mildly laboured Shakespearean extension, then, those who find themselves strutting their hours upon respective stages do so largely within the confines of the roles allotted them. The case of how one learns to strut and who's authorised it: who's cast one in the role to begin with; the wrath of the casting agent and that of the audience one's playing for. The issue exists for artists clustered onto group exhibitions as much as it does for actors being typecast or for any individual trying to find placement in their world.

Staging the Players
Tracey Rose presents to the Venice stage what seems a familiar environment: a table of twelve characters and the suggestion of a godly presence—a Last Supper scenario. It intuits the standard iconic setting, the classic patriarchal supper club with, what one imagines, will be the standard clan of diners—if not the prescribed characters themselves, then individuals that at least personify the roles one expects to encounter. The site intuits the social

They taunt one another's historical time zones and scoff one another's histories and politics. Marie Antoinette/Queen E is arbitrarily involved in the frivolous operations of Empire. An *Afro'd* mermaid languishes with her plate of hot chips and "Katch-Up" singing a siren song of Panis Angelicus. An intersexual Lolita, fluttering big blue eyes and seemingly possessed by an ominously darker presence, interacts with coy hysteria over a bowl of cherries, while Mami oversees all goings on. There is a severity amongst the characters in their limited interaction. They act and communicate mostly obliviously within their own small zones of consciousness. And yet, there is a common humanity that binds these players. An unspoken empathy that underlies their combined existence. They exist within a circuit that is highly politicised in terms of what each character references and embodies: socially, iconically; of the roles that they play as women and who they are able to explore themselves to be as players.

"His own frontal bone blocks his way (he bloodies his brow by beating against his own brow)."
Franz Kafka, *Aphorisms from the 1920 Diary*
"Love me. Fuck me. Love me. Fuck me" is the uneasy, visually enacted mantra of a character wearing boxing gloves, who sits catatonically, beating herself up. It is an ambivalent tension of lust and self-loathing that pervades the ethos of the entire group of characters, though: the recognition and desire to relinquish that which pins them into submission, coupled with

fractured domain. And the dimensionality of these characters is not dependent on the squared parameters of the stage set—their presence fluctuates at whim. Their existence exudes upon and through the stage. They appear to move in and out of the spaces, porously beyond; above, beneath and before the stage in a type of battle against stasis. Each one motioning in search of purpose and meaning. Their acts are self-conscious assertions beyond victim status. It is almost a quantum space, existing in simultaneous time zones and geographical references and renderings. Its stability and this sense of space, not ironically, like Venice as its larger backdrop, are fluid and in continuous flux.

Ciao Bella, the title of Rose's work, speaks plainly of that ambivalence. *Ciao* is at once an allowance and welcoming, but also a dismissal or denial of beauty. An attempt to embrace that which is restorative and nurturing, to opt for a conscious joy rather than a deliberate laceration, claiming agency rather than victimhood.

One might view these characters as being potential facets of one another, playing themselves out individually in acknowledgement of a particular state of being and searching for a gap to move into new self-defined territory. And beyond their individual existences, they come together to comprise a collective godhead: congregating, in turns and in passing, under the coloured spotlight presence—the thirteenth character revealed in infinite exchange and transformation.

Tracey Rose 1974

dynamics of the anticipated group and its familiar subtle undercurrents: a central leading figure, closely committed followers and at least one inevitable dubious quisling other... within the rules and parameters that remain predictable to the storyline. The stage in memory at first encounter is still a plateau intact. Likely modulation to plot minimal.

But Rose's *Ciao Bella* is a notably altered scenario. For one, they're all girls. But that is this modified tableau's most obvious element. The revised guest list that reveals itself is not a straight substitution. The characters that unexpectedly inhabit this environment are, at first glance, an infinitely disparate congregation.

an internalised instinct to self-destruct. Each character speaks/acts/features as a symbolic moment of herself. As a group, though, they are not set up in opposition to one another—they do not reveal themselves as binary solutions of one another. They also lay no distinct claim to any nationality or collective grouping: even those that feel familiar by look or by apparent nature are not assumably predictable within the progression of their actions.

Rose's characters engage with the parameters of the stage not as a clearly defined territory, that is they do not confine themselves to playing *on* the stage, but rather explore the stage as a launching pad of sorts. The stage itself is a

Each of *Ciao Bella*'s characters die—some enacting a type of sacrificial crucifixion, having reached a climax of spiritual and existential journeying. Saartjie Baartman's transformation in this regard is both profound and idyllic. Crassly preserved and labelled in recorded history; identified only by her genitalia, and hanged by her necktie in Rose's enactment, Saartjie re-enters the stage, having sprouted a pair of extraordinary crystalline wings, flying off into exhilarated limitlessness and a resurrection of breathless supremacy.

Rose has commented that theatre has always been an integral socially, accepted domain—a place where questions can be posed and new

Ciao Bella
2001
Film performance
installation – DVD
Ms Cast: MAQUE II

roles adopted, especially when those possibilities do not readily exist in the immediacy of one's lived environment. It is of significance that Tracey Rose plays all the characters on the stage that she has constructed, and it is significant that she creates her characters by transforming simple materials into wondrously fantastical physical constructions. Rose's trademark and tendency are a discreet balance of a veering towards iconoclasm immersed with searing wit and a profound aesthetic. Choosing to bypass the aesthetics of Rose's works to give priority only to the strong socio-political insights that she draws, would amount to missing a critical element of what she does. These entities, conceptually, are not mutually exclusive. They reveal and refer to one another in the most intimate and intrinsic ways.

Where a plateau's overarching feature is its appearance of consistency and stasis, Tracey Rose's project makes a point of bringing out the small modulations of what might have been unexpected, vividly under the spotlight.

Tracy Murinik

UOMODUOMO

AS
It's very important to Uomoduomo that there is no sound, because it makes you wonder if even the image will crash in a minute.

HUO
No image no cry

AS
(laughs)

HUO
It's also interesting in terms of the electronic billboards in Seoul to which you recently consented, and them having no sound, due to the car culture there (whereas in Tokyo the billboards have sound). Seoul has a kind of Blade Runner or apocalyptic technological futuristic ambiance that has become the present with all of these electronic billboards or video screens in the streets, but at the same time it's very interesting that their silence brings them back to low-tech or Charlie Chaplin.
How did you meet Uomoduomo?

AS
I was in Milan, where I actually went to work on another project that would take more time, and would go every day to the Duomo. I saw this man there twice, but I always had the camera with me, a small camera like yours. I had to be discreet. It's very difficult because

AS
I saw him twice, two days out of the five days I was there.

HUO
There are strange people that inhabit public spaces. Since I live near Stalingrad, whenever I take a train or a plane (I catch the RER) I always pass by the Gare du Nord, and there is one woman who is permanently standing at the corner there by the pharmacy, every day from 6:30-7:00 am to midnight, every day, even if it is snowing or raining. It's really scary.

AS
And there is also a woman in Les Halles, a black woman; you see her when you go in through the main entrance where you buy tickets. She spends her entire day cleaning the glass there.

HUO
She's not employed to do the work?

AS
No, and it's an open place, public glass, it's not her property, but still she has a strong relationship of belonging with it. She is like your character. I remember seeing her there four years ago when I came to Paris and she is still there now.

HUO
There is also this person who used to be at

Anri Sala 1974

Sala Anri Sala Anri Sala Anri Sal

everybody is like this [makes a gesture] and because in the cathedral there is a part where everyone can enter and sit but you must be careful because people may be praying. Everybody is facing the front of the church, like the Uomoduomo, so it's very difficult because I had to be facing the people to film him.

HUO
Did he realise you were shooting him?

AS
No.

HUO
Was he there every day?

Café Carette at Trocadero who was waiting for this person who never arrived. She would sit at the table all day long, occasionally walking out and asking if the person had arrived. The first time you didn't notice anything unusual, you would just think she was waiting for an appointment, and then you realised it was a loop kind of thing. That's why I thought Uomoduomo was Beckett-like.

AS
And you know Beckett was one of the most fashionable and popular playwrights in Albania in the 1990s. The first plays you had right after the Communist and socialist plays were Beckett's and Ionesco's.

Uomoduomo
2000
Video – DVD, variable
size, stills from video

Current Female Presidents

Laura Horelli's work presents the six current women presidents. She also includes a map showing the countries where these women hold power. The work was inspired by the fact that Finland got its first woman president in March 2000. Horelli started doing research and found that, at that time, there were five, and later, with the change of president in the Philippines, six women presidents in the world. She discovered that the women presidents were in small countries that are on the periphery if our gaze is situated in one of the so-called centres. She also found that the European women presidents had long political or other official careers, while their Asian counterparts usually came from well-to-do families who had been active in national politics. The father of the current president of the Philippines was also president, while the mother of the Sri Lankan president was the world's first woman prime minister. In this

Horelli excluded all other groups of women in power—prime ministers, chancellors etc., as she wanted to look at the picture through this specific lens. This lens is an interesting one as it also contains the aspect of symbolic or representational power, with the president being the head of state in a democratic society.

Reflecting upon the information that she was collecting, she became acutely aware of the strange normalisation of the situation. It is normal that presidents are not women, and when they are it also seems normal for people to start wondering why and how they got this position. Typically, they look for masculine character traits.

In the exhibition space, the results of Horelli's visual investigation are collected together in cascade-like collages of pictures hung side by side. This accurately conveys the ways we receive visual information and create our own image of the person in question.

It is interesting to see, that there is a uniformity in their dress and self-presentation, even

The suite of images is completed by shifting the perspective from that of an individual president pictured in different modes of presentation and representation to that of a world map with countries with women presidents marked in grey. The shift of distance is from close-up to that of an overview, and from the microworld to the macroworld, or more specifically to the global scale. On the scale of the map, these small geographical/national areas look like pebbles or small islands in a vast ocean.

Questions of representation and presentation abound here. The president represents the nation. In doing so, she presents herself in a certain way. This presentation is in turn presented in the media in deliberately chosen ways, so as to create a focus that achieves certain purposes. The images chosen for the exhibition are a combination of these two modes of presentation. From these the artist has further selected the ones that serve her own purposes, and at the same time function as her

Laura Horelli 1976

way, these women are carrying on and in a way guaranteezing the work started by their families. All the women presidents have academic backgrounds. The president of Sri Lanka studied in France, while the new president of the Philippines studied in the US.

Horelli continued her investigations on the internet to see how these women are presented, both on their own PR pages and more generally in various media. This, she says, led to an almost obsessive collecting of images. The internet proved to be the most democratic source of images, as the world press rarely pays attention to the women presidents of these small countries. The world press usually reacts to their election to office, as this still has news value.

though national costumes are also worn as marks of their cultural and ethnic backgrounds. The uniformity of their habitus—well-groomed, middle-aged women wearing business-like blazers, shows that there is already a dress culture for women in power.

The uniformity of their appearances covers up differences in their political backgrounds and social situations. They look more alike than they actually are, or than their situations are. When looking at their pictures, I also became aware of my own thoughts. When alone they seemed to look more alone than men do in similar situations. Undoubtedly, this is also one of the conventions surrounding women in new situations in life.

own artistic representation in an exhibition situation.

Beyond these positions, we can talk about the presentation and representation of power, and in this case power held by women, which also includes gender representation. Its dominant presence in the viewing of these pictures is yet more testimony to the situation in which seeing women in high positions is something abnormal, something extraordinary. The grey spots on the map draw our attention to unusual and, on a global scale, highly exceptional situations. In our normal perception, a man in power is a grey spot that we no longer see or think about.

Maaretta Jaukkuri

Current Female
Presides (3/2001)
Chandrika Kumaratunga,
Sri Lanka 1994;
Mary McAleese, Ireland
1997;
Vaira Vike-Freiberga,
Latvia 1999;
Mireya Moscoso,
Panama 1999;
Tarja Halonen, Finland
2000;
Gloria Macapagal-
Arroyo, Philippines
2001-2001
DDI - 6 photoportraits
prints on aluminium,
84 × 120 cm each

Casting, 2000, is a determining work in the course of João Onofre's production. The artist brought together a group of advertising models for the holding of a casting session. Each participant was asked to say the final words from the movie *Stromboli*, by Rossellini, uttered by Ingrid Bergman on the edge of despair, "che io abbia la convinzione, la forza e il coraggio."

The film is a landmark of neo-realism and this statement is the belief in man as a product of man, being for this reason declaredly humanist, and João Onofre, after showing the models a screening, asked each of them to interpret the phrase on camera.

This is what the video continuously shows us. Each model steps out of the lined-up group and faces the camera to state their name and to say the phrase, after which they have to stare at the camera in silence, step back and join the other participants awaiting their turn. The impossibility of an adequate representation does not lie only in the lack of quality shown by the models-promoted-to-actors (a situation which is more and more common in Hollywood circles) but above all in the absolute and irreducible difference in the universe which separate this group of young people from a time of historical protagonisms to which individual *conviction, strength and courage* were united in a narrative legitimising an historic achievement of mankind.

In their being out of step with this time, of which our time is the heir, these young people

in a volte-face of history, but rather that of understanding, or filming, the microstructures that make up the forms of signification throughout contemporary western societies. The comical nature of the situation lies not only in the ludicrous deliveries of the phrase, but also in the determined wilfulness suggested by the phrase. When we laugh on seeing this video we are laughing in a no man's land, between a monstrous demand and the monstrous nature of our contemporary tics.

The fixed camera shot rejects editing as a configuration of time and with a unequivocal sense. The image may thus reveal time as its substance or strategy. The gestures and words are played within a repetition that moves them away from the intentional and strips away any declarative meaning. Thus, the out-of-step aspects of the deep ambiguity that runs through the image forms the possibility of a mediating space, with is counterpoised to the performing and immediate understanding that carries out the construction of reality in contemporary societies. Between the humanist sense of the declaration and the meaning aroused by the indexical field of the image—like the narcissism drawn out by the relationship between the models and their appearance, with the respective panoply of codified tics—there is a relationship not of continuity but of superimposing. Above all, this video is a questioning, in the superimpositions it deals with, of the respective confinements of the different conceptions of the medium itself.

João Onofre 1976

attempt at a possible attitude on camera. The rhetoric of the poses assumed, clearly evident and assimilated in the advertising style, functions as the sole place of possible enunciation, which is no longer any place at all. The more or less ridiculous resources used allow one to see the great homogenisation that the culture industries have reached in the post-spectacle society. Everything is likened to the sale of a product and the respective comical strategies that stand out in the way that each model faces the viewer.

This is not a question of counterpoising this context with the realising of the idea of a message releasing a wondrous meaning, as if

That wider place of the relationships and pressures of power in which a determined conception exists. It is thus a critical project on the various configurations that have provided the base for the image itself in modern and contemporary culture.

The fact that João Onofre has chosen a casting session as the motif thus becomes somewhat significant. Here nothing is definitive, and the possibilities are continuously brought into play. The scene is repeated in its possibilities, not as a premeditated whole, but as the unforeseen event that shudders the unthought fact of an enunciation.

Pedro Lapa

Casting
2000
"Che io abbia la forza,
la convinzione e il
coraggio", based upon
Roberto Rossellini's
screenplay of Stromboli
(1949)
DVD, colour, sound,
12' 59", stills from video

Rainbow (*caihong*) is the title of a short video by Xu Zhen, four minutes of tension in which an anonymous back, of undefined sex, naked, gradually changes color, a pale flesh-colour with a few moles scattered about turning into a diffused red becoming bright fuchsia. The rhythm of the shots is uneven, with caesuras that coincide with the sound of a slap, unexpected and unseen, striking the skin, whereas the mark on the flesh and the intense sense of pathos preceding the next smack are clearly defined. As the blows hail, the single handprints merge in a more diffused flush.

Xu Zhen's world, here as in other works, is circumscribed to what has to do with the body, his own and that of others': general categories such as life-death, male-female... are real only when experienced by the individual, insofar as they belong to what the five senses can perceive. Thus in the long video *I am not asking for anything*, a dead cat is repeatedly struck against the paving, in a mysterious ritual where gratuitousness blends with a disquieting, sinister cruelty.

of the body are printed on yellow post-its that, arranged in a disorderly, random manner on a surface, remind us of a boundless proliferation of bodily fragments that will never, despite their number, be able to reconstruct a body in its wholeness.

In the artist's works we always find the viewer's dual relationship of detachment and involvement. Detachment is produced by the unquestionable difference there is between "being seen" and a "seeing" that here often has voyeuristic features. On the other hand involvement is sought and obtained by simple but efficient modes, devices that challenge the viewer's secure intimacy. In a video-installation presented at the show *Art for Sale* in Shanghai in 1999, titled *From inside the Body*, the viewer, seated on a brown imitation-leather couch, witnessed a video showing a boy and a girl, part naked, intent on smelling their own body and the other's, meticulously and with a seeming nonchalance, seated on the same couch. In another exhibition,

Xu Zhen 1977

Or else, in an unfinished work, Xu Zhen massages at length the body of a dead man to verify the different consistencies of flesh.

In *Sewer*, parts of the male and the female body are photographed and then "sewn" together so as to merge in a series of smooth surfaces surrounded by corporeal creases arranged like a frame. In *A Problem of Colourfulness*, a nude body, unmistakably male, photographed in its entirety and its parts, but always from the back, exposes between his legs trickles of menstrual blood, producing an effect—that Grace Fan deems a constant in the young artist's work—of "beauty and violence". The work titled *Actually, I Am Also Dim* (2000) is utterly simple and "poor" in materials. Here photographs of parts

Developing Time, again in Shanghai (2001), the action designed by the artist is set up so that when the spectator goes in, some people hidden behind a fake partition raise their arms and point at him, following him as he moves. Obviously embarassed, the visitor is given the final surprise of being confronted with his own image on the mirror-wall in front of him when, turning around, he goes toward the exit. Xu Zhen ironically questions the widely accepted borderlines between one's own space and that of others, passive and active roles, male and female connotations, volumes and surfaces, the use of our five senses, challenging prejudices and commonplaces.

Monica Dematté

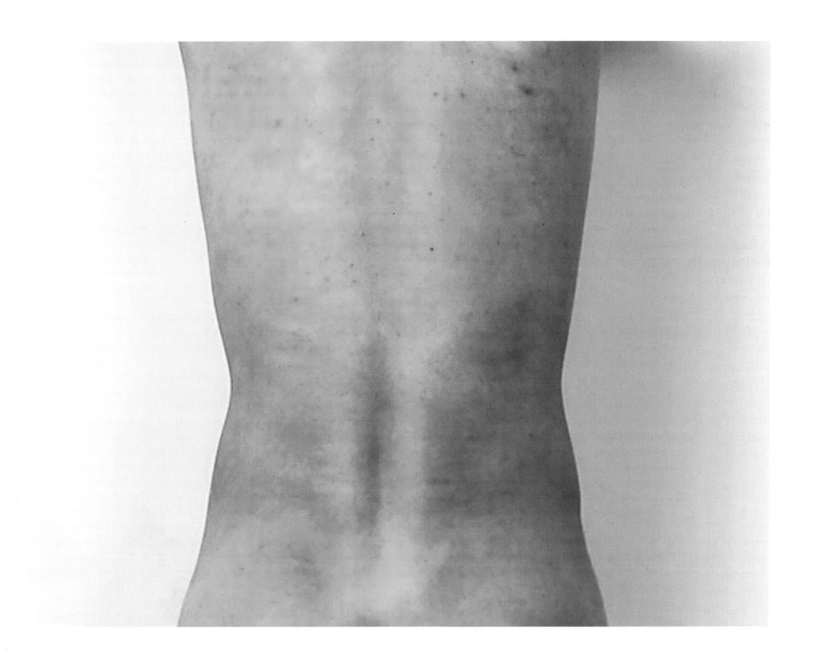

Rainbow
Body part being slapped
– graduately turning red
Video, 4', still from video

Differently from former times, present-day artists face a contradictory scene just as the century starts. The strong diversification of cultural and artistic practices drives the attention of a rising generation of creators to focus on the transformation of a complex political awareness and on the social space as observed from everyday life and from an autobiographical perspective.

The metropolis as a failed nature, the fall of the myths about modernity and the vertigo of technology all lie as isolated pieces altered and converted into resources of a personal experience. The act of scanning existence, image manipulation, deconstruction of information, artificial nature, memory and utopia of happiness in the days of globalisation—among other references—translate, alter and oppose the external break-ups and transformations from a subjective reality.

Now, in the sphere of artistic production, and in front of the superposition of manifold and antagonistic categories of time and space, we are witnessing the apparent exhaustion of the pictorial experience. In the coexistence and the encounter between material or digitally-elaborated universes, in the travelling of the experience displaced between fiction and reality, artists are subjected to negotiating a creative response within a heterogeneous space that may seem familiar and updated to them.

Federico Herrero, a rising young artist from the generation of peripheral artists in Costa Rica, paradoxically belongs in an odd occurrence of

universe based on brilliant colour grounds, the whimsical spots, organic secretions of sorts, coexist with the discrete drawing of detailed writings, done on ball-point pen, markers and industrial spray, inserting a fantastic imagining of monstrous figments in an automatic and crammed act: an inventory of images later edited by the artist as the pieces of electronic and fragmented building blocks having their composing equivalent in the culture of videogames and the syncopated sound of today's music.

These paintings, some sort of contemporary bricolage, loaded with referents and influences, reveal their origin in modernistic practice. Miro, Matta or Gorky are reinterpreted with ease on these canvases in which the hybrid and the bizarre highlight their interest. A pictorial genealogy, rooted in the languages inherited from recent tradition, is emptied from its contents in order to incorporate polluting elements and thus violate the rational order, based on the deconstruction and reconfiguration of formal patterns.

Being distant from the implicit rhetoric and away from all scholarly narrative, even when their titles have been randomly appropriated from the literary world, these canvases—fresh and spontaneous, allow—through a gaming act—to interact with and communicate a heterogeneous sign system adapted to the present-day dimension. In these nonjudgemental "paintings from the unconscious" everything is play, pleasure, humor, emotionality, libido.

Federico Herrero 1978

legitimation of painting—as a medium—at a time when the excesses of mediatiing trends prevail in art. On his wide canvases, the explicit attraction for the art of painting, the paint's resistance and the vigorous enjoyment of practising it, create a flexible structural space in which the forms are joined together with personal sensitiveness and intuitive impulses.

What at first sight would seem to be abstractions of a chromatic—verging on decorative—landscape hides something "dirty" underneath, which apparently brings to mind just beauty and happiness. In that pictorial constructed

Among them, however, formal strategies and technical operations alternate with each other restlessly in a process of constant construction and edition of patterns in order to put together a pictorial space laid out between reality and fictionalised thought. Between the strategic coexistence of a lyric poetics of the pictorial and an urban expression of graffiti, within the realm of the psychological and the individual, Herrero delves into and frees in the search for new relations allowing him at least to reinvent the ability to gaze.

Ruth Auerbach

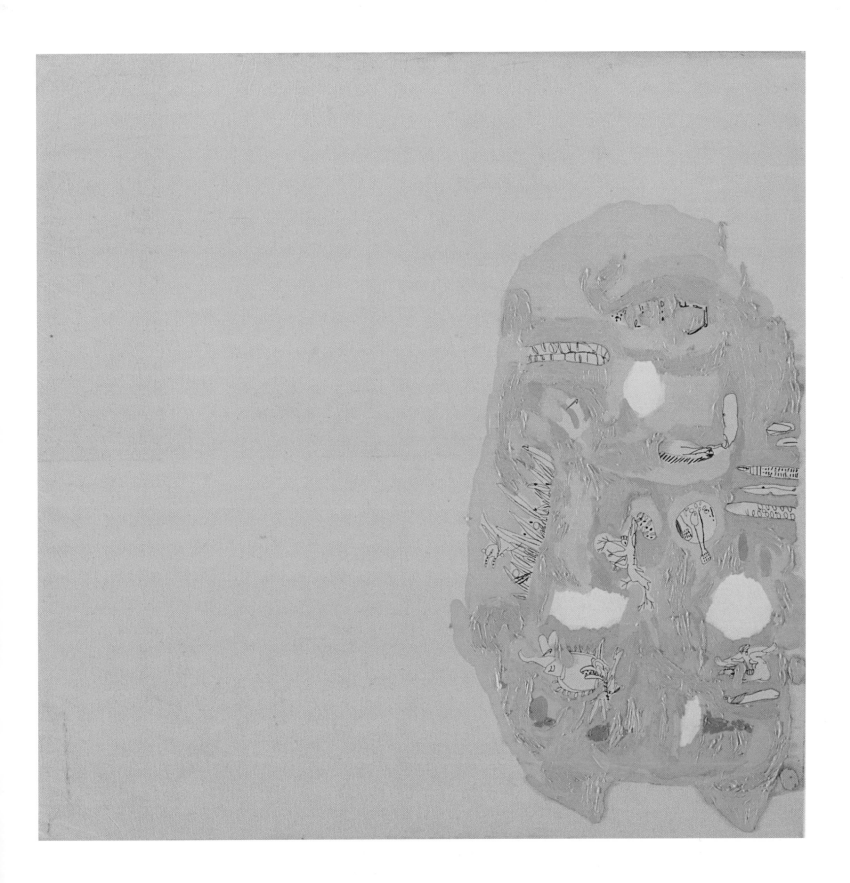

Head
2000
Oil, pen, pilot on canvas,
50 × 50 cm

Bunker poetico

Chen Zhen: hommage

Heli Global Art Tour

Human condition

museum in progress

Refreshing_

Secession

Adonis
Sua Santità Dalai Lama
Adrian Arias
Ahmad Abdul Mu'ti Hijazi
Alba Donati
Huber Bertand
Fernanda Pivano
Yves Bonnefoy
Younis Tawfik
Wolfgang Ziemer
Paul Mccartney
City Lights Italia
Antonio Bertoli
Vitaldo Conte
Viviana Penkhues
Vincenzo Consolo
Caterina Davinio
Casa Del Tibet
Vera Lucia De Oliveira
Valentino Zaichen
Alan Shapiro
Gail Mazur
Ellen Bryant Voigt
Heather Mchugh
Rita Dove
Valentine Verhaeghe
Umberto Piersanti
Adam Vaccaro
Ubaldo Giacomucci
Guy Bennet
Tomaso Binga
Tom Bell
Edward Estlin Cummings
Tiziano Salari
Tiziano Broggiato
Thanasis Chondros
Catherine Wagner
Delfina Provenzali
Enrica Salvaneschi
Tamas St. Auby

Tom Sleigh
Louise Gluck
Sandra Cisneros
June Jordan
Garrett Hongo
Lloyd Schwartz
Marc Mcmorris
Michael Collier
Gary Snyder
Willis Barnstone
David Gewanter
Sallie Vanderhoof
Carlos German Belli
Egla Morales Blouin
Rosario Ferrè
Enrique Fierro
Marjorie Agostin
José Kozer
Kofi Awoonor
Bei Dao
Nissim Ezechiel
Kedar Nath Singh
Kirti Chandhary
Naresh Metha
Kunwar Narayan
Vishnuchandra Sharma
Prayag Shukla
Shaligram Shukla
Anna Santoliquido
Silvia Accorà
Cheryl Clarke
Pat Parker
Sergio Zuccaro
Sergio Beltramo
Raffaella Bonetti
Giovanna Bemporad
Senadin Musabegovic
Scott Rettberg
Ryu Yotsuya
Rossana Brambilla
Rosa Pierno
Rosa Foschi
Rosita Copioli
Roland Baladi
Roger Mayer
Rocco Giudice
Roberto Severino

Reid Wood
Ray De Palma
Raul Ferrera - Balanquet
Ramadan Abdelmoneem
Raffaella Di Ambra
Pino Guzzonato
Pierre Yves Freund
Pierre Balpe
Piero Cademartori
Piero Bigongiari
Pierfrancesco Paolini
Pedro Lopez Casuso
Metta Gislon
Standard Schaefer
Jacques Brault
Gwendalyn Mac Ewen
Patrick Lane
Pawel Kawasniewski
Paul Vangelisti
Paul Parcellin
Patrizia Molinari
Patrizia Cavalli
Paolo Ruffili
Paolo Iacuzzi
Daniel David Moses
Paolo Donadello
Paola Campanile
Osvaldo Coluccino
Oretta Dalle Ore
Olu Oguibe
Oliver Gomez Valenti
Nizla Amaral
Nina Zivancevic
Nina Reis
Niji Fuyuno
Nathan Zach
Nanni Balestrini
Nadia Cavalera
Nada Savkovic
Muzio Clementi
Mohammad Afifi Matar
Mirko De Angelis
Mirella Bentivoglio
Mimoza Ahmeti
Milo De Angelis
Michel Orel
Michel Collet

Mariano Baino
Maria Tsantsanoglou
Maria Teresa
Ciammaruconi
Maria Sebregondi
Alfredo De Palchi
Milli Graffi
Meeten Nasr
Maria Pia Quintavalla
Maria Modesti
Maria Luisa Spaziani
Marga Clark
Marco Tornar
Marco Palladini
Marco Guzzi
Marco Giovenale
Marco Furia
Marco Flo Meneguzzo
Marco Cardini
Marco Cagnolati
Marco Berisso
Marchetti Lamera
Marcello Mercado
Marc Mercier
Marc Delouze
Manorah Shetty
Alberto Curi
Madison Morrison
M. Consuelo C. Campos
M. Celia Bombana
Luigi Di Ruscio
Luigi Cannillo
Luigi Briselli
Luca Patella
Luca Menegaldo
Luca Guerneri
Loretto Rafanelli
Loredana Magazzeni
Lina Angioletti
Lelio Scanavini
Lavinia Greenlaw
Laura Marchig
Laura Cantelmo
Lamberto Pignotti
Lamberto Garzia
Klaus Peter Dencker
Karl Young

James Koller
Ivano Mugnaini
Iulita Iliopoulu
Irene Pavlova
Ines Scarparolo
Indiani Lakote
Ilian Berk
Igor Ulanovsky
Ida Travi
Hoda Hussein
Helen Clare
Guido Oldani
Guido Caserza
Gryzko Mascioni
Gregory Ford
Gregorio Scalise
Grace Wychowanska
Stefano Zecchi
Giuseppina Rando
Giuseppe Tomacelli
Giuseppe Conte
Giuseppe Caracausi
Giulio Giorello
Nino Mustica
Fernando Bandini
Giuliano Mesa
Giuliano Gramigna
Giovanni Zaniello
Giovanni Strada
Giovanni Raboni
Giovanna Sicari
Giorgio Luzzi
Giorgio Guglielmino
Giorgio Bonacini
Giorgio Barberi
Squarotti
Gio Ferri
Gilberto Finzi
Gianni Pozzi
Franco Jonda
Gianni Godi
Gianni D'Elia
Gianni Cappi
Gianni Caccia
Gianluca Seimandi
Gianfrancesco
Chinellato

Francesco Forlani
Florinda Fusco
Flavio Ermini
Filippo Senatore
Filip Marinovic
Fernando Bandini
Federica Beltrame
Fausta Squatriti
Fabrizio Venerandi
Fabio Zanzotto
Fabio Doplicher
Eyrem Basha
Eugenio De Signoribus
Eugenie Umansky
Ettore Bonessio Di Terzet
Enis Batur
Endre Szkarosi
Elisa Biagini
Elio Pecora
Elena Cologni
El Fakith Salem
Eftim Ketn
Edoardo Zuccato
Edoardo Sanguineti
Donatella Bisutti
Donald Datti
Domenico Cipriani
Domenico Cara
Dimitry Bulatov
Diane Caney
Diadji Iba Ndiaye
Dennis Philips
Demosthenes Agrafiotis
Deena Larsen
Davide Rondoni
Davide Campi
Davide Argnani
Daniela Matronola
Daniel Donahoo
Daniel Daligand
Daniel Acosta
Cristina Pianta
Costantino Badalotti
Constanca Lucas
Comunità Pakistana
Comunità Gahanese
Coco Gordon

Bunker poetico

Susana Aragon
Stefano Pasquini
Wendy Barnes
Robert Pinsky
Frank Bidart
Jorie Graham
Stavros Pandgiotakis
Robert Hass
Skipsilver
Simon Armitage
Silvio Ramat
Silvia Tessitore
Allyssa Wolf
Brenda Hillman
Charles Simic
Sandra Gilbert
Anthony Hecht
Ishmael Reed
John Ashbery
Carol Muske
Leslie Marmon Silko
Charles Wright

Roberto Roversi
Roberto Rossi Precerutti
Roberto Mussapi
Roberto Cogo
Eugenio Miccini
Laurence Ferlinghetti
Massimo Mandolini
Pesaresi
Luigi Manzi
Leslie Scalapino
Roberto Carifi
Roberto Bianchi
Roberto Bartoli
Roberta Castoldi
Robert Kendall
Rita Degli Esposti
Rinaldo Caddeo
Rifaa't Sallam
Richard Piegza
Riccardo Giove
Alberto Caramella
Reiner Strasser

Nico Orengo
Max Rooy
Max Hordre
Mauro Ferrari
Mauro Arrighetti
Maurizio Cucchi
Tomaso Franco
Maurice Pozor
Matvei Yankelevich
Massimo Sannelli
Massimo Mori
Mary De Rachewiltz
Priscilla Uppal
David Wevill
Margaret Avison
Marosia Castaldi
Mario Santagostino
Mario Luzi
Mario Lunetta
Joe Rosenblatt
Shannon Bramer
Marica Larocchi

Julien Poirier
Julien D'Abrigeon
Julien Blaine
Juan Diaz Infante
Ju Gosling
Jorge Luiz Antonio
Jonathan Silverman
Jonathan Asser
Jon Uaristi
John M. Bennett
John Gian
Joe Oppedisano
Joachim Montessuis
Jo Shapcott
Jj Runnion
Jill A. Samuels
Jenni Mastoraki
Jean Flaminien
Jean Baptiste Para
Janine Gordon
Janet Wondra
Jamie Mckenrick

Giancarlo Majorino
Gian Marco Chiavari
Giampiero Neri
Giacomo Martini
Giacomo Guidetti
Giacomo Bergamini
Georges
George Albon
Garcia Movero
Gabriella Girelli
Gabriella Galzio
Gabriele Pipia
Frank Smith
Mimma Pisani
Franco Romanò
Franco Rella
Franco Falasca
Franco Buffoni
Francesco Romano
Francesco Muzzioli
Francesco Mandrino
Francesco Leonetti

Clemente Padin
Claus Groh
Claudio Recalcati
Claudio Pezzin
Claudio Damiani
Claudia Zannoni
Claudia Azzola
Christian Tarting
Christian Popp
Charles Flores
Charlemagne Palestine
Ribka Sibhatu
Pap Khouma
Gezim Hajdari
Nasos Vaghenas
Hans Raimund
Alfred Temba Qabula
Ugo Entità
Cesare Viviani
Cesare Ruffato
Cecil Touchon
Catherine Hewitt

Carol Starr
Carmelo Causale
Carla Paolini
Caishlan Herd
Alberto Mari
Antonio Mori
Bruno Ceccobelli
Brice Bowman
Mahmud Darwish
Fawzi Al Delmi
Thea Laitef
Unsi Al Hajj
Fadwa Tuqan
Amal Dunqol
Amira El Zein
Victor Sosnora
Vladimir Gandelsman
Ivan Zhdanov
Timur Kibirov
Elena Shvarts
Vitaly Kalpidy
Alexander Eremenko
Olga Sedakova
Lev Losev
Olesia Nikolaeva
Bahyt Kenzheev
Oleg Ohapkin
Velery Petrochenkov
Yuri Kublanovsky
Ilya Kaminsky
Bianca Frabotta
Biagio Cepollaro
Bernard Simeone
Bernard Mazo
Benedicta Marzinotto
Beatrice Comte
Barbara Gabotto
Athos Agapitos
Athanase Vantchey De Thracy
Arturas Bumsteinas
Arias And Aragon
Antonio Santori
Antonio Rossi
Antonio Riccardi
Antonio Radaelli
Antonio Marchetti
Antonio Curcetti
Antonio Arevalo
Antonietta Dell'Arte
Antonella Doria
Annie Abrahams
Annarita Chierici
Annamaria De Pietro
Antonio Porta
Annalisa Manstretta
Anna Maria Ercilli
Angelo Tonelli
Angelo Ricciardi
Angelo Gaccione
Andy Bejtja
Andrea Zanzotto
Andrea Raos
Andrea Inglese
Andrea Gibellini
Alvaro Andrade Garcia
Aline Schreck
Ali Verban
Alfonso Lentini
Alexandre Pazmandy
Alexandra Katsiani
Alex V. Cook
Alex Sus
Alessandro La Motta
Alessandro Fo
Alessandro Ceni
Alda Merini

Alckmar Luiz Dos Santos
Indiani Sioux
Bettsimar Diaz
Soledad Farina
Peter Waterhouse
Ingrid Fichtner
Tuvia Rubner
Linda Paula Gunn Allen
Elisabeth Cook Lynn
Charlotte De Clue
Joy Harjo
Linda Hogan
Wendy Rose
Roberta Hill Whiteman
Elisabeth Woody
Massimo Giannotta
Andrea Balzola
Lucio Zinna
Fabio Dainotti
Ottavio Rossani
Fulvio Sgambati
Mariella De Santis
Salvatore Carbone
Luciano Parinetto
Tiziano Rossi
Ida Boni
Antonio De Marchi Gherini
Ignazio Apolloni
Barry Callaghan
Miguel James
Rose Anne Mcgreevy
Antonio Di Mauro
Carmelo Panebianco
Elio Tavilla
Angelo Maugeri
Andrea Visioli
Fulvio Fontana
Valerio Magrelli
Mark Strand
Derek Walcott
Norma Cole
Ruggero Maggi
Avery E.D. Burns
Massimo Gezzi
Ermanno Krumm
Arnaldo Ederle
Marco Marangoni
Olimpio Cari
Vittorio Mayer Pasquale
Silvio Tanoni
Santino Spinelli
Bruno Morelli
Rasim Sejdic'
Karoly Bari
Eguiluz Luisa
Adele Milo
Giorgio Tentolini
Alberto Federici
Maura Rinaldini
Tania Belletti
Cristina Magni
Manuela Barozzi
Irene Scioti
Arianna Bonato
Laura Caruso
Vasatko
Antonietta Casini
Daniela Bellotti
Marco Molinelli
Giorgio Farbetta
Emanuela Fiorani
Emiliano Gori
Ada Tentolini
Giovanni Zanichelli
Elisa Montanari
Giorgio Pognani

Marco Nereo Rotelli, poetry section
artist-curator, born in Venice in 1955.

Marco Nereo Rotelli
Bunker poetico
General project
2001
Photomontage

Being a Chinese artist—what does it really mean to be Chinese? It is in the spirit that one is Chinese (of Buddhist inspiration), but with a rather universal message. This is the reason for I am very interested in the relationship between East and West, even though I am now more interested in working, as an artist, on the problems of being human in general, beyond artistic or cultural questions.

As reference point in Western-global art, the history of art is only one part, but at the end of the century plastic language became a sort of digestion. By this I don't mean that it has become secondary, but at the end of the century the primary source of creation was the experience of life.

I am aware of all currents—from Duchamp etc. I find some artists interesting, but now I am putting together a sort of trans-experience that derives from my own personal experience with other people in different countries—in Israel, for example. Last year I worked with

n Zhen: hommage

Chen Zhen: hommage

nage Chen Zhen: ho

some Quakers, and this year I will be working with Brazilian *meninos da rua*. It's clear that my creative method is different in each context, since I take in influences from each situation. For me, globalisation is not homologation but the celebration of differences. It's not a question of loving or not loving; the problem is whether you respect others or not. Art is an evacuation that follows digestion and goes beyond personal taste. Since I started working here I've found an enormous contrast between different works—otherwise I would have gone back to schools and trends.

From the interview with Monica Dematté, during the setting of the 40. Esposizione Internazionale d'Arte La Biennale di Venezia in 1999.

Chen Zhen was born in Shanghai in 1955, dead in Paris in 2000.

*Chen Zhen and his wife
during the setting
of his last exhibition*

Those who wish to realise a Utopia have first to set out on a Grand Tour. Many artificial paradises born of the history of literature lie in remote and distant parts of the world—from Shangri-La to Eldorado. However, since global economic networking increasingly wipes the map of unknown regions, artistic fiction focuses more and more on travelling itself. Some artists of the 20th century chose a kind of cultivated restlessness as an aesthetic life plan. A figure like James Bond—chasing across continents in a helicopter, always dressed impeccably, Martini in one hand—is unthinkable without the concept of an aesthetic existence riding piggy-back on the hand luggage carted along.

For a long time open, process-invested artistic work has been devoted to the aesthetic of the journey as well as to the overcoming of cultural and religious borders. The modular and also process-invested concept of "Global Heli Art Tour" which the Rome-based cosmetic dentist and implantologist Michael Schmitz has outlined, takes its place within the tradition of such art projects but pursues other goals beyond them. Thus there is a continua-

and to other cultural institutions. The distance is approximately 50,000 miles long and should be covered in 100 to 150 flight days. The route, however, can be totally modified—suggestions are welcome. The aim is to integrate in the project the largest number of people as possible. Sponsors and the artist himself will bear the finances of the undertaking. The pilot is the artist himself, appearing as a kind of Phileas Fogg of the 21st century. Celebrities such as famous Hollywood actors will be taking part in the "Global Heli Art Tour". Indeed it is still possible to fly with the pilot if you are willing to sponsor one of the project's route sections. Sponsoring proceeds are to be donated to a Swiss foundation for orphans in South Africa or Latin America. The helicopter doesn't simply transport passengers but also functions like a communication channel between nations, religions and cultures, carrying information further and finally spreading it via media worldwide.

Michael Schmitz

Michael Schmitz
I-SEEL R22 beta
The Helicopter
of Heli Global Art Tour
project

Heli Global Art Tour

tion of the Venice Biennale beyond the time of the exhibition itself and the idea of a collective art work created by all of the Biennale's participants, as well as a fundraising for a children's home in South Africa.

During the Biennale a travel-ready helicopter, around ten metres long and three metres high, will be exhibited. Bit by bit various Biennale artists will decorate it with greetings. At the same time the project of circling the globe will be presented. When the Biennale closes its gates the helicopter will set off on an 18-month journey where it will fly and be shipped over five continents, flying to museums and places where artists work

May 4, 2000

Dear Dr Schmitz,
It was indeed a great pleasure to meet you yesterday and be briefed of your proposed project "Global Heli Art Tour" that will have a fund-raising aspect for the setting up of a children's home in South Africa.
I would like to assure you my support for this project.
The idea of a children's home that will also provide education for future employment is definitely welcomed.
I wish you all the possible success in this project.
Your sincerely, Anthony Mongalo,
Ambassador
South African Embassy in Rome

Michael Schmitz, born in Burscheid in 1963.

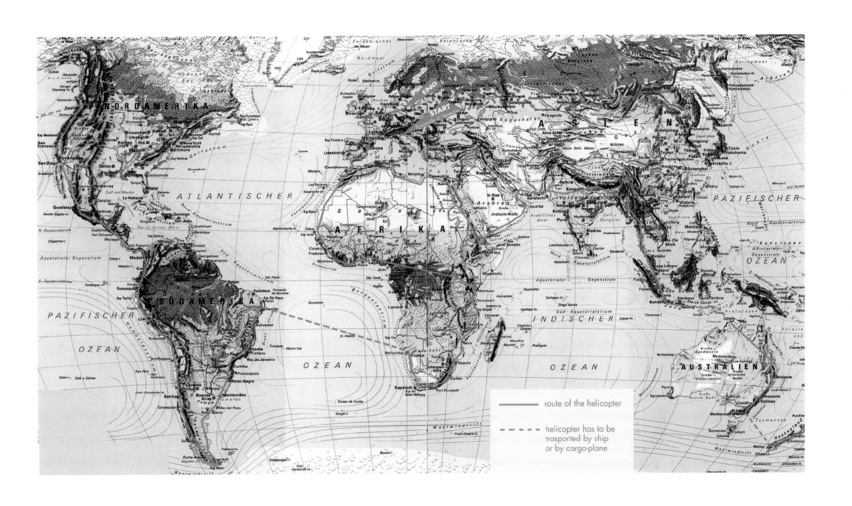

	route of the helicopter
	helicopter has to be trasported by ship or by cargo-plane

Michael Schmitz
Heli Global Art Tour
2001
Helicopter flying plan

Anur: a bridge between visual arts, other languages and the human condition

Anur, whose genetic code has already been programmed for the multimedial, has artistic and cultural interests that are strictly linked to the human condition. This characteristic of his work could be seen as early as his first solo show at the Centro Arte Contemporanea Spazio Umano (Milan, October 1998). In this exhibition, entitled *Human Condition*, he presented a series of works utilising a different languages, including visual art, graphic and design art, striking an essential balance in the conceptual manipulation of photographic technique and linguistic communication. Post-war Sarajevo is a painful place, where most people have lost virtually everything; but even though the city is exhausted, it has not succumbed—the wounds still hurt, yes, but people are already looking to the future. Young people above all want to get their city and Bosnia-Herzegovina back on their feet as soon as possible. And there is just as much urgency about their desire to reconnect the torn tissue of their own culture and civilisation. There is an enormous energy potential, as well as favourable conditions for group work in the realisation of projects of common interest. Anur perceives the importance of working together in specific socio-political-cultural situations. Perhaps he feels, like many others, the need to group together, discuss, confront and collaborate with a view in order to realise an experience able to insert the creative energies of Bosnia-Herzegovina and of the

Anur
Buy five, get one free
From the project
Human Condition
1999
C-print, 130 × 180 cm

Human condition

European Union into an open circuit. It is perhaps the pregnancy of this humus that has helped him take the decisive step and put together his Creative Centre Cardea as a place for meetings, the free exchange of ideas between visual artists, designers, photographers, fashion designers models, actors, musicians, video makers and others. A place where, under his direction, individual and collaborative works can be devised and brought to fruition—projects capable of bridging the gap between visual art, the graphic arts used in advertising, and other languages besides.

Enrico R. Comi

Human Condition

Human Condition is made of insights and fragments from my life.
It is a journal in which instead of words, which I do not manage as well, I use a visual vocabulary. *Human Condition* is the title of a series of posters which began to emerge from adversity, during at the time of the war Bosnia, in the context of my refugee life in Milan. They were created out of necessity, out of a personal need to expel built up dissatisfaction, and in this way materialise and ease my inner pain. Instead of hitting my head against the wall in situations with I had no control of. I made collages from photocopies that synthesised my

thoughts and presented the consequent conclusions about social phenomena of the time. *Human Condition* is a series of subjective notes about a period of time that begun in 1993 and continues to this day.
I believe that it is possible to speak in simple terms about all things, even those that are considered as philosophical or "deep" and "complex." I find confirmation for this in the simple language of our elderly people who, using just one or two words, are able to explain an issue more successfully then volumes of text.
Human Conditions is not afraid of banal expression. If someone were to characterise these messages as banal or literal, I would take it as a compliment. *Human Condition*

With God On Our Side

wants to communicate with people using the language of posters, because it is readable and accessible to everyone. I would like for it to step out of the gallery and address those who do not define themselves as gallery clientele. *Human Condition* does not require any previous knowledge about art or the biography of its author or a familiarity with the entire opus... nor does it require a manual to clarify, it or the aid of a dictionary in order to read its message. *Human Condition* does not address art, because in that case the work of art would become a purpose in itself.

Art for the sake of art. I have always seen this as a problem of contemporary art. *Human Condition* deals with this problem using banal poetics and literal synthesis.

This is not a symphony, it only has three chords.

Anur   Anur was born in 1971.

I'm never made to feel
at home here
I don't feel at home here

Wow, I really like it here
I don't think I ever want
to go home!

I'm sick of your views
about immigrants
This is our home too!

museum in progress

There is no Place like Home

The fact that my work is placed in public spaces means that my concept is founded on a culture of people within this context. By this I mean the accumulation of signs and symbols that "seize" public space and therefore the public's attention. People are very knowledgeable about the different forms of advertising, such as posters and hoardings, even if they react differently to the adver-

tisement itself. And my project was based precisely on the recognition of this type of culture in people. A type of culture that concerns public space, which is strongly defined by commercial and private interests through advertising itself.

Billboards therefore allow for direct participation and a broader dissemination of the work.

Another problem was how I could artistically present myself within the cacophonic context

of our contemporary cities. As Foucault puts it, when will we have full control over all systems of production and communication, and full control over speech? This became clear to me, and so my project had to attempt to throw open the space of advertising to such a degree that it would negatively underline the domination exerted by the system. By this I mean that my work had to create contradiction by using established communicative means (structures, codes, messages); but,

Ken Lum was born in Vancouver in 1956.

304

Ken Lum
*There is no place
like home*
Museum in progress
2000
Installation, variable size

ou call this a home?
his ain't no goddamn
ome

Go back to where you
come from!
Why don't you go home?

I don't want to go home
Mommy
I don't want to go home

despite this, my work presupposed a collective culture that was potentially articulated in a different way. In other words: my idea had to be registered as art, despite the fact that it looked like the "non art" used in advertising.

A third problem is linked to globalisation: globalisation, in fact, obliges artists to give a common meaning to a series of signs that have up to now been perceived differently according to one's race, sex and class dynam-

ics, such as the meaning of "home", "identity" and "belonging" themselves. This problem is not peculiar to Austria, despite the FPO (a virulently xenophobic party led by Haider). I didn't want my work to be translated into German.

I therefore use the English word "home" because of its multifarious meanings. It is a key to the meaning of many things—as opposed to Heimat or maison. We might say that "home" has more meaning for

Americans, because of their mythical roaming from one city to another. "Home" is the concept that expresses nostalgia ("home-sickness") when it flows freely within you; it is where you live. If the basis for identity is the stylistic repetition of action within time, then "home" is the locus for the repetition of these acts. In our cybernetic age these repetitions might seem to be mere mental exercises.

In other words: "home" is also a mood.

Ken Lum

A new generation of artists began to make their presence felt on the art scene in the first half of the 1990s. And their occupation, which is light, partial and progressive—but for how long, and until when?—tones down the sense of the podium for the winner, just as the "other", who seemed connaturalised with the Being itself of Western art, tones down the sense of the solitary, melancholic pedestal for the individual who was cut off from the social context s/he belonged to. What the scene continues to manifest is therefore its being a privileged site thanks to a long tradition of affirmation, more than its being a scene of representation or self-representation, of an individual liberty freed from conditionings imposed by society and the culture of roles. It appears to be the privileged site, both real and symbolic, of this freeing. A neutral space conceded by the general system of production and power to those a-systematic, dis-organic and substantially non-productive practices that the West celebrates as art, handing it over to the unresolved aspects of its own destiny.

By privileging the possibility of concrete experi-

us a vision of the collapse of the most recent myth of participation and interactivity: what counts is the skopic and bodily traversing of the work. In the same way, in Olafur Eliasson's work light is not relegated to the point where it fixes the gaze, but permeates the entire space, which also includes the *locus* and body of the observer. The work is not *in front* of the viewer, but expands in all directions. The perspectival distance that once assured the viewer's immunity and solicited his/her abstract will to domination is reduced to a zero degree, producing an area of uninterrupted continuity in which the viewer is immersed in and melted into the work itself.

For Massimo Bartolini, and equally so for Cai Guo Qiang, the relative terms are again different: on the one hand we have a proposition which is constantly being renewed according to the relativity of space; while on the other we have a series of crases and non-linear breaks within time. Hence, perhaps, that sense of exile implied by both artists.

Bartolini's environments are devoid of sharp edges; Cai offers a rapid self-consuming of forms within an opus containing fireworks, the

Refreshing_

ence what is lessened is their symbolic value, and it further opens out as a space which is made accessible for direct and immediate practicability. Symbols, metaphors, association and linguistic puns and games do not lose their *significance* because of this transformation of the area in which they have been inscribed. But they no longer constitute the ultimate and unique goal of artistic production; they are, rather, components which have exactly the same weight as technological tools, physical materials, aesthetic forms, individual and collective memory, historical consciousness and the sense of belonging to a cultural tradition.

If Rirkrit Tiravanija's work goes beyond the *voyeur* vs *performer* dichotomy, Tobias Rehberger's offers

remains of which testify to an original combustion: in both there is a fluidity which is neither Edenic nor salvific, a flexibility of experience beyond the concept of canons. And this does not imply that the field has been enlarged according to older criteria of positive and progressive evolution, but rather an immersing within its own texture, within its own weave.

All of this implies a slowing down, a reduction of speed, a pause, a withdrawal, an a-specific specific detour.

Hence *Refreshing_*: a cafeteria, a restaurant, vendors' carts, on the scene of art, on the "stage of humanity."

Pier Luigi Tazzi
Fabio Cavallucci

Massimo Bartolini, Cai Guo Qiang, Olafur Eliasson, Tobias Rehberger, Rirkrit Tiravaanija

Massimo Bartolini
Rot Bostane
2001
Project for *Refreshing_*

Secession: facade project

In addition to disgust and anger, there was also a high degree of disconcerted perplexity in the reactions of many people in Austria one year ago, when the coalition of a moderate conservative party with the FPÖ—the "Freedom Party"—, generally regarded as being too far to the right, as racist, sexist, xenophobic—and which has also always behaved antagonistically toward contemporary art in particular—, became a reality. There was perplexity in the face of a situation that might have been vaguely foreseen or at least conjectured, but which was disregarded as being too abstruse or unrealistic. Of course, this indicates a certain short-sightedness particularly with respect to the politicians and parties, which neither hindered nor prevented the rise of the FPÖ into government power, but rather even actively enabled this rise to power and certainly failed to provide for the appropriately irreversible legal and political structures of a modern democracy to preclude a relapse into mental patterns that were thought to be long since overcome.

Perplexity in the sphere of art was often coupled with a desire for action, for finding possi-

themselves here in their own field, art. The range of contributions that the artists presented for discussion is naturally as extensive as the oeuvre of each participating artist, yet one thing remains consistently clear: the contempt for politics that marginalizes those who are weaker, attempts to pit groups of people against one another, wants to establish rusticity as being superior to urbanity, and generally prefers to view art merely as a market-compatible, compliant economic factor. Mediocrity so forcefully promoted denies and hinders everything that interests art at all and makes it significant: what is new to us, complex and something we did not know before.

Matthias Herrmann

Secession

bilities to somehow actively counter this situation, to intervene (better late than never) in a self-determined way in the political discourse, and—ultimately—to dismiss the FPÖ from the government.

Both as an exhibition house and as an artists' association, the Secession has repeatedly made efforts to take part in shaping sociopolitical processes (the Secession's ignominious (vanguard) role during the Nazi era can unfortunately not be left unmentioned in this context). For this reason, it seemed entirely logical to make room for expressing the objections of the house to this government coalition on the facade as the most public of all available space, and to invite artists to express

Franz West, John Baldessari, Dorit Margreiter, Günter Brus, Jochen Gerz, Peter Land, Richard Prince, Markus Geiger, Joseph Kosuth, Werner Reiterer, Louise Bourgeois, Renée Green, David Shrigley, Paul McCarthy, Extra Territoria, Heimo Zobernig, Monica Bonvicini

Secession
Ballad for Midgest, # 1
2000
Project for the facade

Secession
*Smile (with Hair
and Moustache)*
2000
Project for the facade

Index Index Index Index Index Index Index Index Index

A-1 53167

1964, born in Guatemala.
Lives and works in Guatemala City.

Solo Exhibitions

2000
El Préstamo, Action, Contexto, Guatemala.
Oficio de Salida, BF15, Contexto, Guatemala México, México Guatemala.
Línea de 12,000 Puntos de Largo, Monterrey, México.
Día Internacional de la Paz, Intervention in urban site, Contexto, Guatemala.
30 de Junio, Intervention, Contexto, Guatemala.
Foto Reportaje, Museo Ixel, Vivir Aquí, Guatemala.
Mancha de 55,000 puntos, Intervention on the review: *Siglo XXI,* Contexto, Guatemala.
Punto en movimiento, Action in urban site, Contexto, Guatemala.

1999
Acción No. ––– 507 D.O., vídeo projection: (Making coffee action), Quidam Soleil, Guatemala.
Significado, Intervention in urban site, Guatemala.
Colectiva, Sol Del Río, Arte Contemporáneo, Guatemala.
Percepción, Colloquia, Museo de Arte Moderno de Guatemala.

1997
100% 50/50, Sol Del Río, Arte Contemporáneo, Guatemala.

Group Exhibitions

2000
La Cena, Octubre Azul, Guatemala.
VII Bienal de la Habana, La Habana.
Contexto Arte Contemporáneo en Guatemala, Sala Municipal de las Francesas, Valladolid.

1999
Boceto, Coloquia, Museo de Arte Moderno de Guatemala.

1998
1265 Km, Centro Wifredo Lam, La Habana.
Sin Título, PAI (Proyecto de Arte Independiente), Guatemala.
Jaula, Intervention in urban site, Guatemala.

1997
VII Gathering of contemporary Latin American Writers & Visual Artist, Providence.
ARCO 97, Madrid.

Seleccionado *ES97,* Salón Internacional de Estandartes Museo Rufino Tamayo, México D.F.
ES97, Salón Internacional de Estandartes, Tijuana, México.

1996
HACIA ARCO 1997. Sol Del Río, Arte Contemporáneo, Guatemala.
Visión del Arte Contemporáneo de Guatemala III (1975-1995), Museo de Arte Moderno de Guatemala.

Bibliography

2001
Contexto, Arte Contemporáneo en Guatemala, exhibition catalogue, Sala municipal de Exposiciones De la Iglesia de la Francesas.

2000
VII Bienal de la Habana, exhibition catalogue.

1998
1265km, exhibition catalogue, Centro Wifredo Lam.

1997
Arco 1997, exhibition catalogue.

1996
Visión de Arte contemporáneo en Guatemala III, exhibition catalogue, Museo Nacional de Arte moderno.

Chantal Akerman

1950, born in Brussels.
Lives and works in Paris.

Solo exhibitions

1998
Selfportrait/Autobiography – a work in progress, Sean Kelly Gallery, New York; Frith Street Gallery, London; Paris; Bruxelles; Clermont-Ferrand.

1995
D'est: au bord de la fiction, Galerie Nationale du Jeu de Paume, Paris; Walker Art Center, Minneapolis; San Francisco Museum of Modern Art, San Francisco; Société des Expositions du Palais des Beaux Arts de Bruxelles, Bruxelles; Kunstmuseum Wolfsburg, Germany; IVAM Centre del Carme, Valencia; The Jewish Museum, New York.

Filmography

1999
La Capitve, 35 mm. Production: Gemini Films.

1998-99
Sud, vidéo, 70 min. Production: Amip, Chemah I S, Arte.

1997
If jour ou, 35 mm, colour, 7 min. Production: WAKA Films, Switzerland.

1996
Chantal Akerman par Chantal Akerman, vidéo, 63 min. Production: Amip, Chemah I S, Arte.
Un divan a New York, 35 mm, colour, 105 min. Production: Les Films Balenciaga, Parsi; Babelsberg Films, Germany; Paradise Films, Bruxelles; RIBF. Screenplay: Chantal Akerman, with the collaboration by Jean-Louis Benoit. Cast: Juliette Binoche, William Hurt.

1993
Portrait d'une jeune fille de la fin des années 60, a Bruxelles, 35 mm, colour, 60min. Production: IMA, Paris. Screenplay: Chantal Akerman. Cast: Circé, Julien Rassam, Joëlle Marilor.
D'Est, 35 mm, coulour, 107 min. Production: Paradise Films, Bruxelles; Lleurac Production, Paris. Screenplay: Chantal Akerman.

1992
Le Déménagement, 35 mm, colour, 42 min. Production: Le Poisson Volant, Paris. Screenplay: Chantal Akerman. Cast: Sami Frey.

1991
Nuit et jour, 35 mm, colour, 90 min. Production: Pierre Grise Production, Paris; Paradise Film, Bruxelles; George Reinhart Production, Zurich; C.N.C.; Canal Plus; RTBF. Screenplay: Chantal Akerman in collaboration with Pascal Bonitzer. Cast: Guillame Londez, Thomas Langmann, Françoise Négret.

1989
Trois strophes sur le nom de sacher, Henri Dutilleux, vidéo, colour, 30 min. Production: Mallia Films, La Sept, Arcanal, CGP. Cast: Sonia Wieder-Atherton.
Les tres derniers sonates de Franz Schubert, video, colour, 49 min. Production: La Sept, INA. Actor: Alfred Brendel.

1988
Histoires d'Amerique, 35 mm, colour, 92 min. Production: Mallia Films, Paris; Paradise Films, Bruxelles; La Sept; La Bibliothèque Publique d'Information; Le Centre Georges Pompidou; RTBF. Screenplay: Chantal Akerman. Cast: Judith Malina, Roy Nathanson.

1986
Mallet-Stevens, vidéo, colour, 7 min. Production: BRT. Cast: Sonia Wieder-Atherton, Coralie Seyrig, Chantal Akerman.
Letters Home, vidéo, colour, 104 min. Production: Centre Simone de Beauvoir, Paris. Cast: Delphine Seyrig, Coralie Seyrig.
Le marteau, vidéo, colour, 4 min.
La paresse, 35 mm, colour, 14 min. Cast: Chantal Akerman, Sonia Wieder-Atherton.

1985
Golden Eighties, 35 mm, colour, 96 min. Production: La Cécilla, Paris; Paradise Films, Bruxelles; Limbo Film, Zurich. Screenplay: Chantal Akerman, Léora Barish, Henry Bean, Pascal Bonitzer, Jean Cruault. Cast: Delphine Seyrig, John Berry, Jean François Balmer, Myriam Boyer, Fanny Cottençon, Charles Denner, Lio, Pascale Salkin, Nicholas Tronc.

1984
Lettre d'une cinéaste, 16 mm, colour, 8 min. Production: Paradise Films, Bruxelles.
New York, New York bis, 35 mm, black and white, 8 min.
Family Business, 16 mm, colour, 18 min. Production: Large Door LTD, Londre. Rôle principaux: Chantal Akermon, Marilyn Watelet, Leslie Vandermeuler, Cleen Camp, Aurore Clément.
Paris vu par 20 ans apres... J'ai froid, 35 mm, black and white, 12 min. Production: JM Production, Films A2. Screenplay: Chantal Akerman. Cast: Maria de Medeiros.

1983
L'homme a la valise, 16 mm, colour, 60 min. Production: INA, Paris. Screenplay: Chantal Akerman. Cast: Chantal Akerman, Jeffrey Kime.
Un jour Pina m'a demandé, 16 mm, colour, 57 min. Production: INA, A2, R.M., Arts, RTBF, SSR. Screenplay: Chantal Akerman.
Les années 80, vidéo/35 mm, colour, 82 min. Production: Paradise Films, Bruxelles; Abliene Productions, Paris. Screenplay: Chantal Akerman, Jean Gruault. Cast: Aurore Clément, Magall Noël, Lio.

1982
Toute une nuit, 35 mm, colour, 89 min. Production: Avidla Films, Paris; Paradise Films, Bruxelles. Screenplay: Chantal Akerman. Cast: Aurore Clément, Samy Szlingerbaum, Natalia Akerman, Simon Zalewski.

1980
Dis-moi, 16 mm, colour, 45 min. Production: I.N.A.

1978
Les rendez-vous d'Anna, 35 mm, colour, 127 min. Production: Hélène Films, Paris; Unité Trois, Paris; Paradise Films, Bruxelles; ZDF, Mainz, Germany. Screenplay: Chantal Akerman. Cast: Aurore Clément, Jean Pierre Cassel, Helmut Griem, Magali Noël, Léa Massari, Hans Zleschler.

1976
News from Home, 16 mm, colour, 85 min. Production: Unité Trois, Paris; INA, Paris; Paradise Films, Bruxelles. Screenplay: Chantal Akerman. Rôle du narrateur: Chantal Akerman.

1975
Jeanne Dieiman, 23 Quai du commerce, 1080 Bruxelles, 35 mm, colour, 200 min. Production: Paradise Films, Bruxelles; Unité Trois, Paris. Screenplay: Chantal Akerman. Cast: Delphine Seyrig, Jan Decorte, Henri Storch, Jacques Doniol-Valcroze, Yves Bical.
Je tu il elle, 35 mm, black and white, 90 min. Production: Paradise Films, Bruxelles. Screenplay: Chantal Akerman. Cast: Chantal Akerman, Niels Arestrup, Claire Wauthion.

1973
Hanging out yonkers, Inachevé, 16 mm, colour, 90 min. Production: Paradise Films, Bruxelles. Screenplay: Chantal Akerman.
Le 15/8, 16 mm, black and white, 42 min. Production: Paradise Films, Bruxelles. Screenplay: Chantal Akerman, Samy Szlingerbaum.

1972
La Chambre 2, 16 mm, colour, 11 min. Production: Paradise Films, Bruxelles. Screenplay: Chantal Akerman.
Hotel Monterey, 16 mm, colour, 65 min. Production: Paradise Films, Bruxelles. Screenplay: Chantal Akerman.

1971
L'enfant aimé ou jouf à etre une femme mariée, 16 mm, black and white, 35 min. Cast: Chantal Akerman, Claire Wauthlon, Daphna Merzer.

1968
Saute ma ville, 35 mm, black and white, 13 min. Rôle principal: Chantal Akerman.

Bibliography
1998
Une famille a Bruxelles, Récit, Editions de l'Arche.

1996
Un divan a New York, Editions de l'Arche.

1992
Hall de nuit, théâtre, Editions de l'Arche.
Le demenagement, théâtre, Editions de l'Arche.

Sunday Jack Akpan
1940, born in Ikot Ide Etukudo.
Lives and works in Ibesikpo-Uyo, Akwa Ibom State.

Solo Exhibitions

2001
Oh my way to Venice, Centre Culturel Français, Lagos.
Contemporanea, Arti e Culture, Milan.

1996
Haus der Kulturen der Welt, Berlin.

1994
Art Front Gallery, Tokyo.

1988
Institut für Austandsbezeichung, Stuttgart.

1987
Goethe Institut, Lagos.

1985
Association Française d'Action Artistique, Paris.

1977
Festac 77, Lagos.

Group Exhibitions

1989
Les Magiciens de la Terre, Centre Georges Pompidou e La Villette, Paris.

1986
Festival d'Avignone.

Francis Alÿs
1959, Born in Antwerp, Belgium.
Lives and works in Mexico D.F.

Solo Exhibitions

2001
Peter Kilchmann, Zurich.
The Last Clown, Lisson Gallery, London.
Musée Picasso, Antibes.

2000
The Last Clown, Galerie d'art de l'Université du Québec, Montreal.

Residue, edited by Pip Day, Vienna.
Plug In, Winnipeg.
The Last Clown, Sala Moncada, La Caixa Foundation, Catalonia.
ACME., Los Angeles.

1999
Stand-by, Lisson Gallery, London.
Peter Kilchmann Galerie, Zurich.
Mario Flecha Galería, Girona.

1998
Le temps du sommeil, Contemporary Art Gallery, Vancouver.
PICA, Portland.
Web Site Project, Dia Center For the Arts, New York.

1997
Jack Tilton Gallery, New York.
The Liar, The Copy of the Liar, Museo de Arte Moderno, Mexico D.F.

1996
ACME, Santa Monica, California.
Museo de Arte Contemporaneo de Oaxaca, Oaxaca.

1995
Galeria Camargo Vilaça, São Paulo.
Jack Tilton Gallery, New York.
Opus Operandi, Ghent.
Galería Arte Contemporàneo, Mexico City.

1991
Salón des Aztecas, Mexico City.

Group Exhibitions

2001
Da Adversidade Vivemos, ARC/Musée d'Art Moderne de la Ville de Paris, Paris.
The Whitechapel Centenary, Whitechapel Gallery, London.
Subject Plural: Crowds in Contemporary Art, Contemporary Arts Museum, Houston.
Nothing, NGCA, Sunderland, touring to Contemporary Arts Centre, Vilnius, Lithuania and Rooseum, Malmö.
Painting at the Edge of the World, Walker Art Center, Minneapolis.
Making Time, UCLA Hammer Museum, Los Angeles.

2000
Cinema without walls, Rotterdam 2000, Rotterdam.
Un siecle d'arpenteurs, les figures de la marche, Musée Picasso, Antibes, exhibition touring to Koldo Mitxelena Kulturunea, San Sebastian.
Film/Video Works - Lisson Gallery at 9 Keane Street, Lisson Gallery, London.

Making Time, Palm Beach ICA, Florida.
Age of influence: reflections in the mirror of American Culture, MCA, Chicago.
Dream Machines, edited by S. Hiller, Dundee Contemporary Arts, Scotland, touring to Mappin Art Gallery, Sheffield and Camden Arts Centre.
Stimuli, Witte de With, Rotterdam.

1999
The Passion and the Wave, 6th Istanbul Biennial, Istanbul.
Reality and Desire, Fundacion Joan Miro, Barcelona.
La Biennale di Venezia, 48. Esposizione Internazionale d'Arte, Venice.
Mirror's Edge, Bild Museet, Umeå, Sweden, edited by O. Enzewor, touring: Vancouver Art Gallery, Canada; Castello di Rivoli, Turin; Tramway, Glasgow.
Signs of Life, 1st International Melbourne Biennial, Australia.
Thinking Aloud, touring exhibition edited by R. Wentworth and organized by the Hayward Gallery, U.K.

1998
Loose Threads, Serpentine Gallery, London.
Roteiros, XXIV San Paulo Biennale, San Paulo.
Insertions, Arkipelag, Stockholm.

1997
Antechamber, Whitechapel Art Gallery, London.

1996
NowHere, Louisiana Museum, Copenhagen.
Pittura Figurativa, Castello di Rivoli, Turin.

1994
V Biennial de la Habana, Havana.

1993
Lesa Natura, Museo de Arte Moderno, Mexico City.

Bibliography
2001
Francis Alÿs, Musée Picasso, Antibes, France, texts by C. Basualdo, C. Medina, T. Davila.
Nothing, edited by G. Gussin, E. Carpenter, August .

2000
Un siecle d'arpenteurs, les figures de la marche, Musée Picasso, Antibes, France.
Torres, D., "Francis Alÿs, simple passant", *Art Press International*, cover, December 2000, pp. 18-23.
Romano, G., "Francis Alÿs - Streets and Gallery Walls", *Flash Art*, March-April

2000, pp. 70-73.
The Last Clown, Galerie d'art de l'Université du Québec, Montreal, Canada.
Francis Alÿs - The Last Clown, Fundacio "la Caixa", text by D.G. Torres, C. Medina, M. Flecha.
Mirror's Edge, Bild Museet, Umeå, Sweden, text by O. Enwezor, J. Fisher, M. Alexander, C. Basualdo, M. De Bord, J.E. Lundström, J.P. Nilsson.
Europa - Different Perspectives in Paintings - 51° Premio Michetti, Museo Michetti, Palazzo San Domenico, Francavilla al Mare, Chieti, Italy, texts by G. Romano, M. Dumas, M. Maloney, L. Relyea, W. Peters, B. Casavechia, Giancarlo Politi Editore.
Withers, R., "Francis Alÿs, Lisson Gallery", *Artforum*, March, pp. 140-141.
Medina, C., "Mexican Strategies", *Flash Art*, January-February, p. 77.

1999
Signs of Life, Melbourne International Biennial Catalogue, text by J. Engberg
Basualo, C., "Head to Toes - Francis Alÿs' paths of resistence", *Artforum*, March-April, pp. 104-107.

1998
Le Temps du Sommeil, Contemporary Art Gallery, Vancouver, Canada, text by K. Scott.
Gallo, R., "Francis Alÿs at Jack Tilton", *Flash Art*, January-February.

1997
Walks/Paseos, Museo de Arte Moderno, Mexico, texts by F. Alÿs, I. Mequita, B. Ferguson.
Medina, C., *Francis Alÿs: Tu Subrealismo*, third text, Summer.
Darling, M., "Francis Alÿs and the Return to Normality", *Frieze*, March-April.
Guilbaut, S., "Rodney Fraham and Francis Alÿs", *Parachute 87 Poiliester*, Spring.
Ferguson, B., "Francis Alÿs", *Flash Art*, May-June, 96.
Hollander, K., "Francis Alÿs", *Poliester*, Summer, pp. 16-21.
Iannaccone, C., "Francis Alÿs", *art & text*, May-July, pp. 89-90.
Pagel, D., "Francis Alÿs", *Art Issues*, March-April, p. 36.

1995
Alÿs, F., *Other Peoples, Cities, Other Peoples, Work*, Galeria Camargo,Vilaça, San Paulo, Brazil, text by K. Hollander.
Rubinstein, R., "Francis Alÿs", *Art in America*, November.

1994
Francis Alÿs: The Liar, The Copy of the Liar, text by T. McEvilley, Arena Mexico Arte Contemporaneo, Guadalajara, Mexico and Galeria Ramis Barquet, Mexico.
Fabiola, Curare, Mexico City, text by C. Medina.

Tiong Ang
1961, born in Surabaya.
Lives and works in Amsterdam.

Solo Exhibitions

2001
Timeline Underworld, Kolenmuur, Europapark, Groningen.

2000
Ray of Light, Lumen Travo, Amsterdam.

1999
Like a Zombie, Het Torentje, Almelo.

1998
Not Dark Yet, Art Book, Amsterdam.

1997
REHEARSALS / incestuous, Proton ICA, Amsterdam.
Insomniacs, Lumen Travo, Amsterdam.

1996
The Making of Painted Strokes / INCES-TUOUS, with Carter Kustera, Thread Waxing Space, New York.

1995
Insist to Exist, Lumen Travo, Amsterdam.
The Making of Painted Strokes, with Carter Kustera, Proton ICA, Amsterdam.

1993
Bring Your Own Light, Van Rooy Galerie, Amsterdam.
Insides, Stedelijk Van Abbemuseum, Eindhoven.

1992
Initiation, Van Rooy Galerie, KunstRAI, Amsterdam.

1991
Tiong Ang, Van Rooy Galerie, Amsterdam.

1990
Tiong Ang, Galerie Basket, Middelburg.

1988
In.Aan-Uit, Galerie Goem, Nijmegen.

1987
MaleMalerMalevich, Foundation Roest, Amsterdam.

1986
Bijziend-Verziend, Foundation De Bank, Enschede.

Group Exhibitions

2000
Flaming Youth, Galerie Nouvelles Images, Den Haag.
Reflective Figurations, Galerie Ferd van Dieten/D'Eendt, Amsterdam.
Neues Leben, Galerie für Zeitgenössische Kunst, Leipzig.
Holland-South Africa Line, AKKA Foundation, De Bagagehal, Amsterdam.
Holland-South Africa Line, The Castle of Good Hope, Capetown.

1999
Not a Chinese Show, with Roy Villevoye, Gate Foundation, Amsterdam.
Spiral TV-The 3rd Art Life, with Carter Kustera, Spiral/Wacoal Art Center, Tokyo.
De Verzameling, Deel I, Acquisitions from the directorship Jan Debbaut (1988-present), Stedelijk Van Abbemuseum, Eindhoven.
Trouble Spot: Painting, with Roy Villevoye, MUHKA, Antwerpen.
Come In and Find Out, Vol. 1, Art Club Berlin, Podewil, Berlin.
Serendipity, The Borders of Europe, Poëziezomer Watou.
Kind, Stadsmuseum Woerden.
'...' Free Space, NICC, Antwerpen.
1. School 2. Ray 3. Race, Tankhalle, Künstlerhaus Schloss Wiepersdorf.

1998
NL, Stedelijk Van Abbemuseum, Eindhoven.
Meeting Point, Lumen Travo, Amsterdam.
After the Orgy, Smart Project Space, Amsterdam.
Onbegrensd en ingekaderd, Harmoniege-bouw, Rijks Universiteit, Groningen.
It takes two to tango, De Lakenhal, Leiden.
Copy Culture, Arti & Amicitiae, Amsterdam.
Length, Width, Depth, with Roy Villevoye, De Gele Rijder, Arnhem.
De Droom van een Fontein, De Kabinetten van de Vleeshal, Middelburg.

1997
Festival aan de Werf, Annie M.G. Schmidt-huis, Utrecht (School Pictures, with Roy Villevoye).
Aanwezig / Afwezig, People in The Collection Almere, De Paviljoens, Almere.
Triple X Festival, Westergasfabriek, Amsterdam (*Silent Movies*, with Roy Villevoye).
Reushering in Sacrality, Galerie Ferd van Dieten / D'Eendt, Amsterdam.
(No) Vacancies II, Vantaa City Museum/ Myyrmäki Shopping Center, Vantaa-Helsinki.

1996
Goodbye Be Welcome, Proton ICA, Amsterdam.
Recent Acquisitions, Stedelijk Van Abbemuseum Entre'Acte, Eindhoven.

1995
Niet Bien/Très Goed, Espace Brasseurs, Liège.
Acquisitions, Stedelijk Van Abbemuseum Entre'Acte, Eindhoven.
The Conimex Cinema, Galerie Witzen-hausen + Partners, Amsterdam (curatorship).
Het land dat in mij woont, Museum voor Volkenkunde, Rotterdam.
4th International Biennial of Istanbul 1995, Antrepo, Istanbul Foundation for Culture and Arts, Istanbul.

1994
The Spine, (Tiong Ang, Janine Antoni, Christine Borland, Willy Doherty, Pépé Espaliú, Doris Salcedo), De Appel Foundation, Amsterdam.
Quinta Bienal de La Habana, Centro Wilfredo Lam, Havana.
Ik + De Ander: Dignity for All, Reflections on Humanity, Beurs Van Berlage, Amsterdam.

1993
Prospect '93, Frankfurter Kunstverein/ Schirn Kunsthalle, Frankfurt.
Prothesen, Galerie Nouvelles Images, The Hague (curatorship).
1992
The Comfort Zone, The Living Room, Amsterdam.
Frontiera 1'92, Forum Junger Kunst, Messehalle Bozen, Bolzano.

1991
Koninklijke Subsidie voor Vrije Schilder-kunst, Royal Palace, Amsterdam.
L'Invitation Au Voyage, Rijksdienst Beeldende Kunst, Centre Borschette, Brussels.
Peiling '91,10 Young Dutch Artists, Haags Gemeentemuseum, The Hague.

Bibliography

2000
Altmann, S., *Neues Leben*, Galerie für Zeitgenössische Kunst, Leipzig.
Lütticken, S., "Framed and Frozen", *Flash Art*, XXXIII, 211, March, pp. 96-98.
Koplos, J., "Tiong Ang at Lumen Travo", *Art in America*, 12, December 2000, p. 130.
Slager, H., & Balkema, A., *Reflective Figurations*, Global Vernunft, Amsterdam.

314

Ang, T., "Der Geschichtenerzähler", *Neues Leben #2*, Galerie für Zeitgenössiosche Kunst, Leipzig.

1999
Nijmeijer, P., "Gedichten als nagedachten", *Vrij Nederland*, July 17, pp. 54-56.
Barragan, P., "Fragmentos de Cotidaneidad", *Lapiz 155*, July, pp. 18-31.
Wallner, K., *Come In and Find Out, Vol. 1*, Podewil, Berlin.
Di Pietrantonio, G., "De vleugels van de vlinder", *Serendipiteit*, Poëziezomer Watou.
Ang, T., "Rethinking Calaf", *Transversal*, 10, p. 105.
Ang, T., "Over luie beelden", *The dummy speaks*, 2, pp. 36-39.

1998
Horne, S., "Painting in the shadows", *Parachute 91*, July, pp. 25-28.
Steevensz, B., *NL*, Van Abbemuseum, Eindhoven.
Slager, H., Balkema, A., "Artistieke transities", *Reushering in Sacrality*, Global Vernunft, Amsterdam.
Kraijer, Z., "Tiong Ang; tussen video en schilderkunst", *Onbegrensd en Ingekaderd*, Rijks Universiteit, Groningen.
Kremer, M., "Becoming a Gook", *Not Dark Yet*, Artimo Foundation, Breda.

1997
Steevensz, B., "Tiong Ang: STUDIO INT. DAY", *Metropolis M*, 18, 1, February, pp. 32-35.
Hettig, F.-A., "Tiong Ang", *Artforum*, 36, 1, September, p. 135.
Kremer, M., "Geef me een lichaam met vleugels van papier", *Metropolis M*, 19, 6, November, pp. 22-33.
Ang, T., "The Making of Painted Strokes", *HTV De IJsberg*, 13, pp. 4, 5.

1996
Pelsers, L., "Het land dat in mij woont", *Kunst en Museum Journaal*, 7, 1/2/3, pp. 8-11.

1995
Pingen, R., "Tiong Ang", *Kunst van Nu*, Encyclopedisch overzicht vanaf 1970, Primavera Pers, Leiden.
López, S., "Landschappen van herinnering", *Het land dat in mij woont*, Museum voor Volkenkunde, Rotterdam.
Ang, T., "Suppose There would be Something like a new Image", cat. *Biennial 4*, Istanbul Foundation for Culture and Arts, Istanbul.

1994
Gibbs, M., "The Spine", *Art Monthly*, 174, March, pp. 26, 27.
van Giersbergen, Marieke, "De marge

schuift op naar het centrum", *Archis*, 3, March, pp. 10, 11.
Morgan, Stuart, "The Spine", *Frieze*, 16, May, pp. 52, 53.
Perrée, Rob, "De versluierde identiteit van Tiong Ang", *Kunstbeeld*, 7/8, July-August, pp. 23-25.
Bos, S., Van Duyn, E., *The Spine*, De Appel, Amsterdam.
Ang, T., "Insides", cat. *6 Projects*, Van Abbemuseum, Eindhoven.
Ang, T., "A diferencia del pensamiento", cat. *Quinta Bienal de La Habana*, Centro Wilfredo Lam, Havanna.

1993
Beer, E., "Tiong Ang", *Rijksaankopen 1992*, Rijksdienst Beeldende Kunst, Den Haag.
Guldemond, J., "Tiong Ang", *6 Projecten*, Van Abbemuseum, Eindhoven.
Ruyters, Domeniek, "Tiong Ang", *Metropolis M*, 14, 4, August, p. 50.
Ang, T., "Schöne Gemälde zeugen: Malerei ist schamlos", cat. *Prospect '93*, Frankfurter Kunstverein/Schirn Kunsthalle, Frankfurt.

1992
Ang, T., "Prothese(n)", Stichting De Bank, Enschede.

1991
Beer, E., "Tiong Ang", *Rijksaankopen 1991*, Rijksdienst Beeldende Kunst, Den Haag.
Janssen, H., *Peiling' 91*, Haags Gemeentemuseum, Den Haag.
Ang, T., "Hollands Dagboek", *NRC Handelsblad*, January 12.

1989
Ruyters, Domeniek, "Tiong Ang", *Metropolis M*, 10, 4, September-October, pp. 36, 37.
Ang, T., "Meester van het heelal", *De Rijksakademie*, 10, Amsterdam, pp. 10-13.

Gustavo Artigas
1970, Born in Mexico City.
Lives and works in Mexico D.C.

Solo Exhibitions

2001
vs., BagFactory, Johannesburg, South Africa; Iturralde Gallery, Los Angeles.

2000
Tell her that she is making a mistake, Iturralde Galley, (Video room) Los Angeles.
Porqué no me has llamado?, Intervención, Arte in situ - La Torre de los vientos, México.
Cuarto 6001, Laboratorio México-Cuba; Marina Hemingway, La Habana.

1998
A clock. The shape of time, Basel.

1997
Ritual and rhythm, Instalaciones, The Other Gallery, Banff Centre for the Arts, Alberta, Canada.

1996
Desalojo/Muro de sonido, Instalación/Acción radiofónica, Jesús María 42, Centro Histórico, México.

Group Exhibitions

2001
Armory Show, Art Fair, New York.
Miami Art Fair, Miami, Florida.

2000
7ma Bienal de la Habana, Plaza Vieja, Havana, Cuba.
inSITE 2000, San Diego, CA, USA y Tijuana, B.C. México, Proyecto Binacional.
Action videos, Artists space, New York, New York.
La amistad, Holguín, Cuba.
3SafMc, Arizona State University West, Phoenix, Arizona.

1999
Ruido. Primer Festival de Arte sonoro, ExTeresa Arte Actual. México, D.F.

1998
Non-Lieux. Poesie des Nich-ortes, Exposición internacional de arte en espacios públicos, Kaskadenkondensator espacio alternativo, Basel, Switzerland.
caMac Site specific projects, caMac, Centre des Arts, Marnay sur-Seine, France.
Glubos Window projects, Brokenbrude Glubos, Basel, Switzerland.
In the 90's. Mexican contemporary art, Instituto Mexicano de Cultura, Washigton D.C./ New York, NY.
Everyday life objects, PAC, Post d'Art, Fribourg, Basel.

Bibliography

2001
Bousteau, F., "Cuba: La Belle Américaine", *Beaux Arts*, 200, Janvier, pp. 68-81.
Weiss, R., "The orbit of the 7th Havana Biennial, Planet Buenavista", *Art Nexus*, 39, February-April, pp. 48-55.
Chattopadhyay, C., "inSite 2000", *Art Nexus*, 39, February-April, pp. 82-85.

2000
Seventh Havana Biennial, exhibition catalogue, Centro de Arte Wifredo Lam - Art for the World, Havana, Cuba, pp. 54, 55.

1999
Lozano, L.M., *In the nineties. Contemporary Mexican Art*, exhibition catalogue, Mexican Cultural Institute, Washington D.C. and Buffalo, USA, pp. 85, 96-97.
Noise. first sound art festival, exhibition catalogue, Ex Teresa Arte Actual, Mexico City, p. 24.

1996
Morales, S., *Coordenadas*, exhibition catalogue, Unodosiete Gallery, Mexico City, pp. 7-10.
Granados, M., *Exchange. Installation Festival*, Monterrey, Nuevo León, Mexico, pp. 5-24.
Tibol, R., *Third Monterrey Biennial*, exhibition catalogue, Monterrey, Nuevo León, Mexico, pp. 48.
Volkow, V., *Creation in motion*, exhibition catalogue, Young Artists Grant Program Exhibition, Mexico City.
Martínez, V., *Second Installation Contest*, exhibition catalogue, Ex Teresa Arte Alternativo, Mexico City.
<sum> Aranda, Carlos, Enviromex, *Poliéster Magazine*, 5 # 17, Mexico City, pp. 58-59.

Atelier Van Lieshout
Established in 1995.
Joep Van Lieshout, born in 1963 in Ravenstein. Lives and works in Rotterdam since 1987.

Solo Exhibitions

2001
PS1, New York.
Jack Tilton Gallery, New York.
Galeria Gio Marconi, Milan.
BAWAG foundation, Vienna.
AVL-Ville, Rotterdam.

2000
Galerie Fons Welters, Amsterdam.

1999
USF Contemporary Art Museum, Tampa, Florida.
Museum für Gegenwartskunst, Zürich.
The Contemporary Arts Center, Cincinnati.
AVL Equipment, Transmission Gallery, Glasgow.
Museum of Contemporary Art, Miami.

1998
Galeria Gio Marconi, Milan.
The Good, the Bad and the Ugly, Rabastens.
The Good, the Bad and the Ugly, Le Parvis, Ibos/Tarbes.
Modulare Multi-Frauen-Betten, Sprengel Museum, Hannover.

1997
Saucisson, Galerie Roger Pailhas, Paris.
Hausfreund I, Kölnischer Kunstverein, Cologne.
Museum Boijmans Van Beuningen, Rotterdam.

1996
Jack Tilton Gallery, New York.
Plug In Inc., Winnipeg.

1995
Galerie Bob van Orsouw, Zürich.

1993
Castello Di Rivara, Turin.

1992
Galerie Roger Pailhas, Marseille.
Galerie Blancpain/Stepczynski, Génève.

1991
Galerie Roger Pailhas, Paris.
Gallery 1 og 1, Reykjavik.

1990
Galerie de Bruxelles, Brussels.
Museum Boijmans Van Beuningen, Rotterdam.

1988
Galerie Fons Welters, Amsterdam.

Group Exhibitions

2001
Milano Europa 2000, Milan.
Sonsbeek 9, Arnhem.
La Biennale di Venezia, Venice.

2000
Against design, Philadelphia.
Over the Edges, SMAK, Gent.
Wonderland, St. Louis.
Exorcism, esthetic terrorism, Museum Boijmans van Beuningen, Rotterdam.
LKW, Kunsthaus, Bregenz.
House show - the House in Art, Deichtorhallen, Hamburg.

1999
In the Midst of Things, Bourneville/ Birmingham.
Arte all'Arte, San Gimignano.
Le Fou dédoublé, Moscow.

1998
NL, Van Abbe Museum, Eindhoven.
The Good, the Bad and the Ugly, Walker Art Center, Minneapolis.
artranspennine98, The Henry Moore Institute, Leeds.

1997
De kunst van het verzamelen, Palais des Beaux-Arts, Brussels.
Sculpture Projects 97, Münster.
The 2nd Kwangju Biennale, Joongwoe Park, Kwangju City, Korea.

1996
Bars, Kunstverein Recklinghausen, Recklinghausen.
Museum für Gegenwartskunst, Zürich.
De Muze als Motor, De Pont Foundation, Tilburg.

1995
Dutch Design Café, MOMA, New York.

1994
Het Grote Gedicht, The Hague.
Biannual, San Paulo.
Ateliers '63, Palais des Beaux Arts, Brussels.

1993
Gallery Jack Tilton, New York.
Wiener Sécession, Vienna.

1991
Negen, Witte de With, Rotterdam.

1990
Stedelijk Museum, Amsterdam.

1989
Museum Boijmans Van Beuningen, Rotterdam.

Bibliography

2000
Borg, L. ter, "Vrijstaat bij Zestienhoven", *Volkskrant*, 19 January.
Lootsma, B., "The Good, the Bad and the Ugly, or: Sympathy for the Devil", *Daidalos*, 75, May.
Floor, M., "Kunst op vuil", *Rotterdams Dagblad* , 12 Mei.
Milgrom, M., "Target: AVL", *Metropolis*, May.
Depondt, P., "Pionieren op de vuilnisbelt", *Volkskrant Magazine*, 35, 16 September.
Ibelings, H., *Het kunstmatig landschap. Hedendaagse architectuur, stedenbouw en landschapsarchitectuur in Nederland*, Nai uitgevers, Rotterdam.
Lootsma, B., *Superdutch. New Architecture in the Netherlands*, Thames and Hudson.
Reijnders, T., "Portrait de l'artiste en Mobile Home: L'Atelier van Lieshout", *Septentrion. Arts, Lettres et Culture de Flandres et des Pays Bas*, revue trimestrielle, 29e annee, 2.
Allen, J., "Up the organization", *Artforum*, April, pp. 104-111.
van Ulzen, P., "Atelier van Lieshout", *Parachute*, 102, pp. 44-57.

1999
Maurer, S., "Das Modulaire Multi-Frauen-

Bett im Museum", *Tagesanzeiger*, April 5.
A Supplement, M.A. Miller, D. Hickey, J. Dellinger, Contemporary Arts Museum, Tampa, tent.cat.
Hickey, D., "Joep van Lieshout's Rebel Housing. Architecture as Rock and Roll", *Issues*, December.
Ankerman, K., "Kunstenaar-aannemer. De wondere wereld van Joep van Lieshout cs", *Het Financieel Dagblad*, 27 November.

1998
Lütticken, S., "Markteconomie en libido-economie", *De Witte Raaf*, July-August, pp. 5-7.
Atelier van Lieshout – The Good, The Bad & The Ugly (English edition) / *Le Bon, La Brute & Le Truand* (French edition) / *The Good, The Bad & The Ugly* (German edition), Hoefnagels, P.J., Noordervliet, M.J., Lootsma, B.O., Les Abattoirs/Toulouse, Migros Museum für Gegenwartskunst/Zürich, Atelier van Lieshout/NAi Publishers/Rotterdam, tent.cat.

1997
Atelier van Lieshout - A Manual / Ein Handbuch, Lieshout, J. van, Lootsma, B., Jonge, P. de, Kölnischer Kunstverein/Cologne, Museum Boijmans Van Beuningen/Rotterdam, Cantz Verlag/Ostfildern, tent.cat.
Winkelmann, J., "Joep van Lieshout", *Artist Kunstmagazin*, 3/97, pp. 18-21.
Wesseling, J., "Een echte man slacht zijn eigen varken", *NRC Handelsblad-CS*, August 29, p. 4.
Ulzen, P. van, "Ik en mezelf", *Metropolis M*, 5/97, pp. 50-55.
Vanstiphout, W., "Dirty, delicious and direct, Joep van Lieshout's manual of architecture", *Archis*, 11/1997, pp. 38-41.

1996
Sütö, W., "Atelier Van Lieshout", *De Muze als Motor II: Beeldende kunst in Brabant 1945- 1996*, Tilburg, De Pont Stichting/ Breda, De Beyerd/ Eindhoven, Van Abbe Museum, pp. 118-121, tent. cat.

1995
"Klaar van der Lippe interviewt Joep van Lieshout" (kunstenaarspagina), *Jong Holland* , 2, pp. 32-33.

1994
Pontzen, R., "De kunst van het klussen: Joep van Lieshout helpt Rem Koolhaas in Lille", *Vrij Nederland*, June 11, pp. 56-58.
Bierens, C., "Joep van Lieshout", *Het Grote Gedicht, Nederlandse Beeldhouwkunst 1945-1994*, Gent, Snoeck-Ducaju & Zoon, pp. 66-67.

1993
Linders, D., "Amorphophallus en de schemering: een nieuwe sculptuur van Joep van Lieshout", *Vormgeven aan Veelzijdigheid: opstellen aangeboden aan Wim Crouwel ter gelegenheid van zijn afscheid als directeur van Museum Boymans-van Beuningen*, Rotterdam, Museum Boijmans Van Beuningen, pp. 196-205.

1991
9 artisti olandesi contemporanei, Prato, Museo d'Arte Contemporanea Luigi Pecci, tent. cat. (vertaling van cat. '9 (negen)' Witte de With, Rottterdam).
Collection 1991, Rotterdam, cat. Joep van Lieshout in eigen beheer.
Coelewij, L., "The art of exhibiting: the exhibition as art: Joep van Lieshout", *Metropolis M*, 1, pp. 30-31.

1990
Joep van Lieshout: beelden/sculpture, Rotterdam, Museum Boijmans Van Beuningen, tent. cat.

Samuel Beckett
1906, born in Foxrock (Dublin).
1989, died in Paris.

Samuel Beckett studied and taught in Paris before settling there permanently in 1937. He wrote primarily in French, frequently translating his works into English himself. His first published novel, *Murphy* (1938), typifies his later works by eliminating the traditional elements of plot, character, and setting. Instead, he presents the experience of waiting and struggling with a pervading sense of futility. The anguish of persisting in a meaningless world is intensified in Beckett's subsequent novels including *Watt* (1942-44); the trilogy *Molloy* (1951), *Malone Dies* (1951), and *The Unnamable* (1953); *How It Is* (1961); and *The Lost Ones* (1972). In his theater of the absurd, Beckett combined poignant humor with an overwhelming sense of anguish and loss. Best known and most controversial of his dramas are *Waiting for Godot* (1952) and *Endgame* (1957), which have been performed throughout the world. Beckett was awarded the 1969 Nobel Prize for Literature.
Beckett's other works include a major study of Proust (1931); the plays *Krapp's Last Tape* (1959) and *Happy Days* (1961); a screenplay, *Film* (1969); short stories, *Breath* (1966) and *Lessness* (1970); collected shorter prose in *Stories and Texts for Nothing* (tr. 1967), *No's Knife* (1967), and *The Complete Short Prose: 1929-1989* (1996, ed. by S. E. Gontarski); volumes of

collected writings, *More Pricks than Kicks* (1970) and *First Love and Other Shorts* (1974); and *Poems* (1963). His *Collected Works* (16 vol.) was published in 1970, and his first works of fiction and drama were both published posthumously, the novel *Dream of Fair to Middling Women* (1932) in 1992 and the play *Eleuthéria* (1947) in 1995.

Vanessa Beecroft

1969, born in Genoa, Italy.
Lives and works in New York.

Solo Exhibitions & Perfomances

2001
Gagosian Gallery, Beverly Hills.
Kunsthalle Wien, Vienna.
Museum of Contemporany Art, Oslo.

2000
The Intrepid Sea, Air, Space Museum / Whitney Museum of American Art Biennial, New York.
Gagosian Gallery, London.
Sydney Biennial, VB 40, Sidney.

1999
Galleria Massimo Minini, Brescia.
Museum of Contemporary Art, (MCA), San Diego.
Museum of Contemporary Art, (MCA), Sydney.
Wacoal Art Center, Tokyo.

1998
Galleria d'Arte Moderna, Bologna.
Galerie fur Zeitgenossische Kunst, Leipzig.
Solomon R. Guggenheim Museum, New York.
Fondation Cartier pour l'Art Contemporain Paris.
Moderna Museet Sockholm.

1997
Institute of Contemporary Art (ICA), Boston.
Institute of Contemporary Art (ICA), London.
FRAC, Le Nouveau Musee, Lyon.
Galleria Lia Rumma, Naples.
Site Santa Fe, IIBiennial, Santa Fe.
La Biennale di Venezia, XLVII Esposizione Internazionale d'Arte, Venice.

1996
The Dakis Joannou Collection, The Factory, Athens.
Musee d'Art Contemporain, Bordeaux.
The Renaissance Society at the University of Chicago, Chicago.
Ludwig Museum, Cologne.
Stedelijk Van Abbemuseum, Eindhoven.

Netherland Fri Art, Centre d'Art Contemporain, Kunsthalle, Fribourg.
Deithc Projects, New York.
Institute of Contemporary Art, ICA, Philadelphia.

1995
Galerie Analix, Geneva.
Fondation Cartier pour l'Art Contemporain, Paris.
Fuori Uso 95, Pescara.

1994
P.S. 1 Museum, Long Island City.
Courtesy Fac-Simile, Milan.
Castello di Rivoli, Museo d'Arte Contemporanea, Rivoli.

Group Exhibitions

2001
Metamorphosis and Clones, Musee d'Art Contemporain de Montreal, Montreal.
Recent Acquisitions The Doron Sebbag Art Collection, ORS, Tel-Aviv Museum.
Subject Plural, Contemporary Arts Museum, Houston.
La Biennale di Venezia, 49. Esposizione Internazionale d'Arte, Venice.

2000
Perfoming Bodies, Tate Modern, London.
The Sydeny Biennial, Sydney.

1999
Moving Images, Film-Reflexion in der Kunst, Galerie fur Zeitgenossische Kunst, Leipzig.
Examining Pictures, Whitechapel Art Gallery, London.
Get Together, Kunsthalle Wien, Karlsplatz, Vienna.
Unheimlich (Uncanny), Fotomuseum Winterthur, Winterthur.

1998
Kritische Elegantie (Critical Elegance), Museum Dhondt-Dhaenens Deurle, Deurle.
Photography as Concept, Photographie als Handlung, 4th Internationale Photo-Triennale, Galerie der Stadt Esslingen, Esslingen.
Veronica's Revenge, from Man Ray to Matthew Barney, Prague City Gallery, Lambert Art Collection, (LAC), Prague.
Wounds, Between Democracy and Redemption in Contemporary Art, Moderna Museet, Stockholm.

1997
Arte Italiana, Ultimi Quarant'anni Materiali Anomali, Galleria d'Arte Moderna, Bologna.
Enterprise, Venture and Process in

Contemporary Art, Institute of Contemporary Art (ICA), Boston.
Fatto in Italia, Institute of Contemporary Art, (ICA), London.
Some Kind of Heaven, South London Gallery, London.
Identity, FRAC, Le Nouveau Musee, Lyon.
Vanessa Beecroft, Diana Thater, Tracey Moffatt, Stadtisches Museum Abteiberg, Munchengladbach.
Young and Restless, Museum of Modern Art (MOMA), New York.
Ein Stuck vom Himmel, Kunsthalle Nurnberg, Nurnberg.
Partito Preso Internazionale, Galleria Nazionale d'Arte Moderna, Rome.
Persona X, Salzburger Kunstverein, Salzburg.
Truce, Echoes of Art in an Age of Endless Conclusions, Site Santa Fe, II Biennial, Santa Fe.
Future, Present, Past, La Biennale di Venezia, XLVII Esposizione Internazionale d'Arte, Venice.

1996
Everything that's Interesting is New, The Dakis Joannou Collection, Deste Foundation, The Factory Athens.
Persona (The Renaissance Society at the University of Chicago), Kunsthalle Base, Basel.
Traffic, CAPC Musee d'Art Contemporain, Bordeaux.
Museumsfest, Wallraf-Richartz-Museum and Museum Ludwig, Cologne.
ID; An International Survey on the Notion of Identity in Contemporary Art, Stedelijk Van Abbemuseum, Eindhoven.
Autoreverse 2, Le Magasin, Grenoble.
Campo 96, Konst Museet, Malmo.
You Talking to me? Conversation Piece II, Institute of Contemporary Art, Philadelphia.

1995
Videos et Films d'Artistes, Ateliers d'Artistes de la Ville de Marseilles, Marseilles.
Anni 90, Arte a Milano, Palazzo delle Stelline, Milan.
Show must go on, Les Soirees Nomades, Fondation Cartier Pour l'Art Contemporain, Paris.
Aperto Italia 95, Trevi Flash Art Museum, Trevi.
Campo 95, Corderie dell'Arsenale, Venice; Turin; Malmo.

1994
Winter of Love, P.S. 1 Museum, Long Island City.
Soggetto-Soggetto, Una Nuova Relazione Nell'Arte di Oggi, Castello di Rivoli, Museo d'Arte Contemporanea, Rivoli.

Bibliography

2001
Metamorphosis and Clones, exhibition catalog, Musee d'Art Contemporain de Montreal, Quebec, Canada.
I am a Camera, The Saatchi Gallery, Booth-Clibborn Editions, London.
"The Sister Project", *I.D. Magazine*, February.
Labro, C., "Artiste du Mois: Vanessa Beecroft", *Beaux Arts*, March.
Kazanjian, D., "The Body Artist", *Vogue*, April.

2000
Whitney Biennial 2000, M. Auping, V. Cassel, H. Davies, J. Farver, A. Miller-Keller, L. Rinder, The Whitney Museum of American Art, New York, NY.
Fresh Cream, Phaidon Press, London.
VB 08–86–Vanessa Beecroft Performances, text by D. Hickey, Cantz, Germany.
Biennale of Sydney 2000, edited by E. McDonald, Sydney, Australia.
Presumed Innocents: L'art Contemporain et l'enfance, CAPCMusee d'art contemporain de Bordeaux, France.
Manchester, C., "Fresch cream; Contemporary Art in Cutlure", *fresh cream*, Phaidon press, November, UK.
Sharp A., "Clip Joint", *Frieze*, March, NY.
Casadio, M., "Artists. On Location", *L'uomo Vogue*, May, Italy.
Shave, S., "Hello Sailor", *i-D Magazine*, 198, June, UK.
Kazanjian, D., "Art Talk: Vanessa Beecroft", *Vogue*, August, New York.
Leffingwell, E., "Vanessa Beecroft aboard the USS Intrepid", *Art in America*, October, NY.
Furlong, W., "Audio Arts Magazine", *Audio0 Arts magazine*, 19. October, UK.
Rosenblum, R., "Vanessa Beecroft", *Artforum*, December, NY.
Casadio, M., "VBGDW – An Artwork", *Vogue Italia*, December.

1999
Art at the Turn of the Millennium, Edited by U. Grosenick & B. Riemschneider, Taschen, Cologne, Germany.
Collection: Rhone-Alpes 1998-1999, Institut d'Art Contemporain Frac Rhone-Alpes / Nouveau Musée, France.
Contemporanea, text by E. De Cecco, G. Romano, Costa & Nolan, Milan.
Examining Pictures, Like Hands Stuck in a Mattress, Whitechapel Art Gallery, edited by J. Nespitt & Bonami, London.
Get Together, Kunst als Teamwork, Kunsthalle Wien, Vienna.
Moving Images: Film-Reflexion in der Kunst. Galerie fur Zeitgenossische Kunst Leipzig, text by J. Roberts, Leipzig.

Regarding Beauty: A View of the Late Twentieth Century, text by N. Benezra, O.M.Viso, AC.Danto, Smithsonian Hirshhorn Museum, Washington, D.C.
Smith, R., "The New York Artist Is Now From Everywhere", *The New York Times*, April 18, New York.
Kamiya, Y., "Vanessa Beecroft", *Esquire Japan* 13, May, Japan.
Gopnik, B., "Vanessa Beecroft", *Art News*, June, NY.
Vogel C., "Art in Summer Whites", *The New York Times*, June, CA.
A.A., "What They Were Thinking "Vanessa Beecroft U.S. Navy", *The New York Times Magazine*, July, NY.
Bryson, N., Luigi Tazzi, P., Seward, K., "Classic Cruelty, Parades, US Navy Seals", *Parkett*, September, Switzerland, New York, Germany.
Karcher E., "Armee der Schonheit", *German Vogue*, September, Germany.
Casadio, M., "U. Navy. A New Performance by Vanessa Beecroft", *Vogue Italia*, October, 590 Conde Naste, Milan.
Angus, D., "Fall of the Model", *Beaux Arts Magazine*, December, Paris, France.
Rimanelli, D., "Best of the 90s", *Artforum* XXXVIII 4, December, NY.

1998
Cream, edited by G. Williams, Phadion, New York.
Performance: Live Art Since 1960, text by R. Goldberg, Sean Kelly Gallery, New York.
Photography as Concept, Photographie als Handlung, 4. Internationale Photo-Triennale Esslingen, edited by R. Wiehager, Galerie der Stadt Esslingen am Neckar, Esslingen, Germany.
Wounds. Between Democracy and Redemption in Contemporary Art, Edited by D. Elliot, P.L. Tazzi, Moderna Museet, Stockholm, Sweden.
Davis, J., "The Girlie Show", *The Face* , 12, January, UK.
Tatley, R., "Vanessa Beecroft", *Dazed & Confused*, 38, January, UK.
Slyce, J., "Made in Italy", *Flash Art International*, January-Febrary, Italy.
Fleiss, E., Zahm, "235 Berry Street", *Purple Fashion* , 4, Winter, France.
"Bologna", *Il Manifesto*, Saturday, June 6, Italy.
Beecroft, V., "Flash Art XXXI Years", *Flash Art International*, XXXI, 201, Summer, Italy.
Koestenbaum, W., "Bikini Brief", *Artforum*, 10, Summer, NY.
Kontova, H., Politi, G., "Arte, Vanessa Beecroft", *Intervista* ,14, July/August, Italy.
Rimanelli, D., "Whirl Weary", *Artforum*, XXXVII, 3, November, NY.
Homes, A.M., "The best of 1998", *Artforum*, XXXVII, 4, December, NY.
Rosenblum, R., "The Best of 1998",

Artforum, XXXVII, 4, December, NY.

1997
Arte Italiana, Ultimi Quarant'anni Materiali Anomali, edited by D. Eccher, D. Auregli, Galleria d'Arte Moderna, Bologna, Italy.
BV 97 Future, Present, Past, La Biennale di Venezia, XLVII Esposizione Internazionale d'Arte, Venice, Italy. Edited by G. Celant.
Ein Stuck vom Himmel - Some Kind of Heaven, Kinsthalle Nurnberg, Germany. Soouth London Gallery, UK. Edited by S.Coles and E. Meyer-Hermann.
Enterprise, Venture and Process in Contemporary Art, The Institute of Contemporary Art, Boston. Edited by C. Grunenberg.
Fatto in Italia, edited by P. Colombo, Centre d'Art Contemporain, Geneva.
Truce, Echoes of Art in an Age of Endless Conclusions, Site Santa Fe, NM. edited by F. Bonami.
Zahm, O., Fleiss, E., "Vanessa Beecroft, 1996, Performance, Galleria Massimo De Carlo, Milan", *Purple Fashion*, 2, 1996-97, France.
Romano, G., "Vanessa Beecroft", *Zoom Vision*, January, Italy.
Schorr, C., "The Girlie Show", Art, *Harper's Bazaar*, September, NY.
C., L., "This is an Art", *The Face* , 11, December, UK.
Corrigan, S., "Artrageous", *I-D Magazine* ,171, December, UK.

1996
Collezionismo a Torino, Le opere di sei Collezionisti d'Arte Contemporanea, Castello di Rivoli, Italy.
Echoes, Contemporary Art at the Age of Endless Conclusions, edited by F. Bonami, New York.
Everything that's Interesting is New, text by J. Deitch, The Dakis Joannou Collection, Athens, Greece.
ID; An International Survey on the Notion of Identity in Contemporary Art, edited by M. Bloemheuvel, J. Guldemond, Stedelijk Van Abbemuseum, Eindhoven, Netherlands.
Persona, The Renaissance Society at The University of Chicago, Kunsthalle Basel, Switzerland, edited by S. Ghez.
Traffic, CAPC Musee d'Art Contemporain, Bordeaux, France, edited by N. Bourriaud.
Casadio, M., "Pelle d'Artista", *Italia Vogue* , 548, April, Italy.
Romano, G., "Todo lo que es interesante es nuevo", *Lapiz* , 122, June, Spain.
Angus, D., "Trop belles pour toi", *Technikart* , 7, November, France.
De Cecco, E., "Vanessa Beecroft", Review, *Flash Art*, October/November, Italy.

1995
Anni 90 Arte a Milano, Artisti e artisti designer nella città, Milan, Italy, edited by R. Bellini. Text by A. Vettese.
Ca,po 95. Fondazione Sandretto Re Rebaudengo per l'Arte, Turin, Italy, edited by F. Bonami.
Fuori USO '95, Caravanserraglio Arte Contemporanea, Pescara, Italy, edited by G. Di Pietrantonio.
XXISecolo, Arte e Architettura, Zerynthia, Contemporary Art Association No. 5, Italy, edited by J. Hoet and G. Di Pietrantonio.
Cherubini, L., "Strange Girls", *El Guia*, May, Spain.
Janus, E., "Vanessa Beecroft", *Artforum* , 9, May, NY.
Di Pietrantonio, G., "Vanessa Beecroft", Ouverture, *Flash Art International* , 183, Italy.
Furlong, W., "Cologne Art Fair 1994, Painting: a Symposium at the Camdem Arts Center", *Audio Arts Magazine* , 3, 14, UK.
Polla, B, "Vanessa Beecroft", Review, *Frieze* , 20, UK.

1994
Incertaine Identite, Galerie Analix B&L Polla, Geneva. edited by B. S. Polla, O. Zahm and L.L.Polla.
Prima Linea, The New Italian Art, Trevi Flash Art Museum No. 3, Trevi, Italy. edited by F. Bonami and G. Di Pietrantonio.
Soggetto-Soggetto, Una nuova Relazione nell'Arte di Oggi, Castello di Rivoli, Italy. edited by F. Pasini and G. Verzotti.
Papadopoulos, H., "Vanessa Beecroft", *Bob* , 1, May 1994, Greece.

Joseph Beuys
1921, born in Krefeld.
1986, died in Düsseldorf.

Joseph Beuys was born in Krefeld, Germany on May 12, 1921. His first one-person exhibition was held in 1953 in Kranenburg. In 1961 he was appointed Professor at the Düsseldorf Art Academy, where he had earlier been a student, and he continued teaching there until 1972 when he was dismissed amidst great controversy, a dismissal that finally, in 1978, was deemed unlawful. From the beginning of the 1970s he exhibited widely throughout Europe and the United States, representing Germany at the Venice Biennale in 1976. Beuys died January 23, 1986, in Düsseldorf, where he had lived for most of his career. Notable among the many retrospectives of his work are those held in New York in 1979, in Berlin in 1988, and in Zürich, Madrid, and Paris in 1993-94.

Bibliography

1995
Liveriero Lavelli, C., *Joseph Beuys e le radici romantiche della sua opera,* Bologna, Clueb.

1993-1994
Joseph Beuys, edited by H. Szeemann, T. Bezzola, Kunsthaus Zürich, 1993; Museo Reina Sofia, Madrid, 1994 e Centre Pompidou, 1994.

1993
Thinking Is Form: The Drawings of Joseph Beuys, Philadelphia and New York, Philadelphia Museum of Art and Museum of Modern Art, text by A. Temkin, B. Rose, D. Koepplin.

1991
Joseph Beuys: Natur, Materie, Form, edited by A. Zweite, Düsseldorf, Kunstsammlung Nordrhein Westfalen.
Stachelhaus, H., *Joseph Beuys,* translated into English by D. Britt, New York, Abbeville Press.

1988
Joseph Beuys: Retrospektive, edited by H. Bastian, Berlin, Martin Gropius Bau.

1987
Joseph Beuys, New York, Dia Art Foundation.

1979
Joseph Beuys, The Solomon R. Guggenheim Museum, New York, text by Caroline Tisdall.
Adriani, G., Winfried Konnertz, K.T., *Joseph Beuys: Life and Works,* New York, Barron's.

Richard Billingham
1970, born in Birmingham.
He lives and works in the Stourbridge, UK.

Solo Exhibitions

2001
Micro Museum, Palermo.

2000
Ikon Gallery, Birmingham touring to Douglas Hyde Gallery, Dublin; Nikolaj Contemporary Art Centre, Copehagen; Brno House of Arts, Czech Republic; Hasselblad Centre, Göteberg, Sweden; Kunsthalle Willhelmshaven, Germany. Contemporary Art Museum, Nuoro, Italy.

1999
British School at Rome, Rome.
Galerie Mot & Van den Boogaard, Brussels.
Galerie Monica Reitz, Frankfurt am Main.

1998
Anthony Reynolds Gallery, London.

1997
Galeria Massimo De Carlo, Milan.
Galerie Jennifer Flay, Paris.
Regen Projects, Los Angeles.
Luhring Augustine, New York.

1996
Portfolio Gallery, Edinburgh.
National Museum of Film and Photography, Bradford.
Anthony Reynolds Gallery, London.

Group Exhibitions

2001
Valencia Biennale, Valencia.
Milano Europa, Milan.
IMMA Award, IMMA, Dublin.
Emotional Ties, Tate Gallery, Liverpool.
New Acquisitions from the Dakis Joannou Collection, Deste Foundation, Athens.
I Am a Camera, Saatchi Gallery, London.
Give & Take, Serpentine Gallery, London.
2000
Cities/Faces, Centre régional de Cherbourg-Octeville Quotidiana, Castello di Rivoli, Turin.
Scene de la vie conjugale, Villa Arson, Nice.
Bleibe – ein Projekt von 'art in dialog' (Jorg & Karen van der Berg, Universitat Witten/Herdecke), Akademie der Kunste, Berlin.
Body Beautiful, Galerei Jennifer Flay, Paris.
WarningSHOTS, Royal Armouries, Leeds.
The Sleep of Reason, Norwich Gallery and tour.

1999
Close-Ups, Contemporary Art and Carl Th. Dreyer, Nikolaj, Copenhagen Contemporary Art Centre.
Interior Britannia, Richard Billingham/Anna Fox, Saidye Bronfman.
Centre for the Arts, Montreal (le mois de la photo a Montreal 1999).
Officina Europa, Villa delle Rose, Galleria d'Arte Moderna, Bologna and tour.
Endzeit, Galerie Six Friedrich Lisa Ungar, Munich.
Common People, Fondazione Sandretto Re Rebaudengo, Guarene.
La Casa, Il Corpo, Il Cuore, 20er Haus, Museum Moderner Kunst Stiftung. Ludwig, Vienna.
Anthony Reynolds Gallery, London.
International Neurotic Realism: Bern Now!, Galerie Francesca Pia, Bern.
Janviers en Bourgogne, Xn, L'Espace des Arts, Chalon-sur-Saône.
1998
Mois de la Photographie, Galerie Agnès b., Paris.

Family, Inverleith House, Edinburgh.
Remix, Musée des Beaux Arts, Nantes.
Malos Habitos, Galerie Soledad Lorenzo, Madrid.
Life is a Bitch, De Appel Foundation, Amsterdam.
Galerie Barbara Gross, Munich.
U.K.Maximum Diversity, Benger Areal, Bregenz.
Edinburgh Film and Television Festival, Edinburgh.
7de Zomer van de Fotografie, Museum voor Fotografie, Antwerp.
Not Strictly Private, Shed im Eisenwerk, Frauenfeld.
Le Printemps de Cahors, Cahors.
Women, Galerie Klemens Gasser und Tanja Grunert, Cologne.
Close Echoes, Public Body and Artificial Space, City Gallery, Prague, Kunsthalle, Krems.
Wounds: Between Democracy and Redemption in Contemporary Art, Moderna Museet, Stockholm.
Head First, City Art Gallery, Leicester and tour.

1997
Galerie Francesca Pia, Bern.
Private Face-Urban Space, Gasworks, Athens; L. Kanakakis Municipal Gallery of Rethymnon, Crete.
Strange Days, Claudia Gian Ferrari Arte Contemporanea, Milan.
Sensation: Young British Artists from the Saatchi Collection, The Royal Academy, London; Hamburger Banhof, Berlin; Brooklyn Museum of Art, New York.
Pictura Britannica, Museum of Contemporary Art, Sydney; Art Gallery of South Australia, Adelaide; Te Papa, New Zealand.
Home Sweet Home, Deichtorhallen, Hamburg.
:Engel :Engel, Kunsthalle, Vienna; Galerie Rudolfinum, Prague.
Observaties/Observations, Recent acquisitions, PTT Museum, The Hague.
Vis-à-vi(e)s, Galerie Art et Essai, Université Rennes 2, Rennes.
The Citibank Private Bank Photography Prize, Royal College of Art, London.
Anthony Reynolds Gallery, London
SIAFO, Seoul.

1996
Full House, Kunstmuseum Wolfsburg.
Blick von innen, Galerie Monika Reitz, Frankfurt-am-Main.
Photos Leurres, Mois de la Photo, Galerie de Jour Agnès B, Paris.
New Photography 12, Museum of Modern Art, New York.
Life/Live, ARC, Musée d'Art Moderne de la Ville de Paris, Fundação das Descobertas,

Centro Cultural de Belem, Lisboa.
Radical Images, Museum of Contemporary Art, Szombathely, Hungary.
Galerie du Jour Agnès B, Paris.
'Radical Images', Second Austrian Triennal on Photography, Graz.
Herkunft?, Fotomuseum, Winterthur.
Passage à l'acte, Galerie Jennifer Flay, Paris.
Anthony Reynolds Gallery, London.

1995
Night and Day, Anthony Reynolds Gallery, London.

1994
Who's Looking at the Family?, Barbican Art Gallery, London.

Bibliography

2001
I Am a Camera, Saatchi Gallery, London.

2000
Richard Billingham, exhibition catalogue, Ikon Gallery, text by M. Tarantino, A. Capasso, *Tema Celeste*, January-February.
Marziani, G., *Flash Art*, February-March, p. 112.
WarningSHOTS, exhibition catalogue, Royal Armouries, Leeds.
The Sleep of Reason, exhibition catalogue, Norwich Gallery.

1999
Close-ups, Contemporary Art and Carl Th. Dreyer, Nikolaj Copenhagen Contemporary Art Centre, text by H. Meyric Hughes
La Casa, Il Corpo, Il Cuore, exhibition catalogue, 20er Haus, Museum Moderner Kunst Stiftung Ludwig, Vienna.
Interior Britannia, Richard Billingham/Anna Fox, exhibition catalogue, Saidye Bronfman Centre for the Arts, Montreal (le mois de la photo a Montreal 1999).
Officina Europa, exhibition catalogue, Galleria d'Arte Moderna, Bologna.
Common People, exhibition catalogue, Fondazione Sandretto Re Rebaudengo, Guarene.
Searle, A., "Family Fortunes", *Frieze*, no 34, January-February.

1998
Wounds: Between Democracy and Redemption in Contemporary Art, exhibition catalogue, Moderna Museet, Stockholm.
Life is a Bitch, exhibition catalogue, De Appel Foundation, Amsterdam.
Close Echoes, Public Body and Artificial Space, exhibition catalogue, City Gallery, Prague.

Malos Habitos, exhibition catalogue, Galerie Soledad Lorenzo, Madrid.
Le Printemps de Cahors, exhibition catalogue, Cahors.
Lingwood, J., "Inside the fishtank", *Tate*, Winter.
Lingwood, J., "Family Values", *Tate*, Summer.

1997
Lewis, J., "No Place Like Home", *Artforum*, January, pp. 62-67, cover.
Sensation: Young British Artists from the Saatchi Collection, exhibition catalogue, The Royal Academy, London.
Private Face-Urban Space, exhibition catalogue, Gasworks, Athens.
Pictura Britannica, exhibition catalogue, Museum of Contemporary Art, Sydney.
:Engel :Engel, exhibition catalogue, Kunsthalle, Vienna.
Vis-à-vi(e)s, exhibition catalogue, Galerie Art et Essai, Université Rennes 2, Rennes.

1996
Ray's a Laugh, Scalo, Zurich (second edition published 2000).
Williams, G., "Richard Billingham", *Art Monthly*, September, pp. 31-32.
Life/Live, ARC, exhibition catalogue, Musée d'Art Moderne de la Ville de Paris.
The Citibank Private Bank Photography Prize, exhibition catalogue, Royal College of Art, London.
Photos Leurres, exhibition catalogue, Mois de la Photo, Galerie de Jour Agnès B, Paris.
Herkunft?, exhibition catalogue, Fotomuseum Winterthur.
Sladen, M., "A Family Affair", *Frieze*, May.

1994
Who's Looking at the Family?, exhibition catalogue, Barbican Art Gallery, London.

Pierre Bismuth
1964, born in Paris.
Lives and works in London.

Solo Exhibitions

2001
CAC, collaboration with Jonathan Monk, Vilnius, Lithuania.
Centre d'art contemporaine, Bretigny, France.
Dvir Gallery, Tel Aviv, Israel.

2000
Galerie Mot & Van Den Bogaard, Brussels.

1999
Galerie Yvon Lambert, Paris (exhibition catalogue.).

1998
The Showroom, London.
Galerie Mot & Van den Boogaard, Brussels.

1997
Box, Palais des Beaux Arts, Brussels.
Plus Min, Renesse, Netherlands.
Witte de with, Rotterdam.
Kunsthalle Vienna.
Arborétum, public project for la DRAC d'Orleans, France.

1996
Galerie Mot & Van den Boogard, Brussels.
Le bruit de son, Lisson Gallery, London.
The blind film, Tramway, Glasgow.

1995
Centre de Création Contemporain, Tours.
FRAC Langedoc Rousillon, Montpelier.

1992
Galerie M Duchamp, Chateauroux.
Galerie One Five, Anvers.

Group Exhibitions

2001
Nothing, NGCA, Sunderland, Touring to Contemporary Arts Centre, Vilnius, Lithuania and Rooseum-Malmö.

2000
Film/Video Works - Lisson Gallery at 9 Keane Street, Lisson Gallery, London.
Korean Biennale, Seoul, edited by J. Millar and B. London.
Collection Yvon Lambert, Avignon.
Be seeing you, Centre d'art Contemporain de Brétigny, Brétigny.
Cinema without walls, Museum Boymans Van Beuningen, Rotterdam.

1999
Cinema, Cinema / Contemporary Art and the Cinematic Experience, Stedelijk Van Abbemuseum, Eindhoven.
8e Biennale de L'Image en Mouvement, Geneva.
Patch work in progress / expositions monographiques, Mamco, Musée d'art moderne et contemporain, Geneva.

1998
Yokohama Museum, Japan.
Speed, Whitechapel Gallery, London.

1997
Junction, Palais des Beaux Arts, Brussels.
Instants données, Musée d'Art Moderne de la ville de Paris/ARC.
At one remove, Henry Moore Sculpture Trust, Leeds, exhibition catalogue.

1996
Il futuro dello sguardo, Museo Civico, Prato.

1995
Stoppage, Nice, Villa Arson and C.C.C. Tours.

1994
Watt, Witte de With, Rotterdam.
Beyond Belief, Lisson Gallery, London.

Bibliography

2001
Our Trip Out West, exhibition catalogue, with J. Monk, Contemporary Art Centre, Vilnius.
Nothing, exhibition catalogue, edited by G. Gussin, E. Carpenter.
Moisdon, S., "Never believe an artist", Marcel Duchamp Prize, exhibition catalogue, la DIAF, Paris.

2000
Sausset, D., "Pierre Bismuth", L'œil, May, 2000.
Lequeux, E., "Bismuth traverse les apparences", Le Monde / Aden, 16- 22 June.

1999
Barak, A., "Silence according to Pierre Bismuth", Art Press, September - October, p. 30.
Newman, M., "Pierre Bismuth", essay, Lisson Gallery, exhibition catalogue.
Augé, M., "Pierre Bismuth", essay, Galerie Yvon Lambert, exhibition catalogue.

1996
Bismuth, P., "Introduction to Blind Film", Paletten, 1, January.
Doove, E., "P.S. De vertalingen van Pierre Bismuth", Metropolis M, 5, Utrecht, October, pp. 38-41.

1994
Dannatt, A., Exposé, 1.

1993
Brayer, M.A., Forum International, 17.
Migayrou, F., "Revers de l'identique", Fonds régional d'art contemporain du centre, 93, exhibition catalogue.

Botto & Bruno

Gianfranco Botto, 1963, born in Turin.
Roberta Bruno, 1966, born in Turin.
Both live and work in Turin.

Solo Exhibitions

2000
Under my red sky, Sottozero, Palazzo delle Esposizioni.
My song goes down into the water, Galleria Alfonso Artiaco, Pozzuoli, Naples.
Suburb's Day, Fondazione Teseco per l'Arte, Pisa.

1999
My beautiful box, Galleria Alberto Peola, Turin.
Le Case d'Arte, Milan.

1998
Il posto dove vivo, Juliet Room, Trieste.
Studio Pino Casagrande, Rome.

1997
Gli stessi sogni, Le Case d'Arte, Milan.
Studio Barbieri, Venice.
Wall Paper, Bullet Space, New York.

1996
Galleria Alberto Peola, Turin.

Group Exhibitions

2000
Paysages urbains, Le Quartier, Centre d'Art Contemporain de Quimper, Bretagne.
Futurama-arte in Italia 2000, Museo Pecci, Prato.
Atlantide, installazioni permanenti, Palazzo delle Papesse, Siena.
Videoplace, Fabbrica Europa, Florence.
Dire Aids, Promotrice delle Belle Arti, Turin.
Insights, Fondazione Adriano Olivetti, Rome.
Big Torino 2000, sezione Arti Visive, Cavallerizza Reale, Turin.
Nursery Crime, Williamsburg Art & Historical Center, New York.
L'Assurdo quotidiano, Galleria comunale d'Arte Contemporanea di Ciampino, Rome.

1999
Passaggi Invisibili, Palazzo delle Papesse, Siena.
Artbeat, Arte Narrativa Videoclip, Salara, Bologna-La Posteria, Milan.
XIII Quadriennale, Proiezioni 2000, Palazzo delle Esposizioni, Rome.
Turin à Nice, une nouvelle génération, Galerie des Ponchettes et Galerie de la Marine, Nice.
Atlante, Geografia e Storia della Giovane Arte Italiana, MACS, Sassari.
Ateliers d'Artistes, Marsiglia.

1998
Tracce significanti. Arte italiana oggi, Gazi, Athens.
Nuovo paesaggio italiano, multimedial exhibition.
A Noir, Palazzo della Triennale, Milan.
Senza Titolo, International Festival, Trento and Rovereto.

1997
Duos Duels, 5° Biennale Internationale d'Art de Groupe, Centre Cargo, Marseilles.
Arcate Art Fabrica, Murazzi del Po, Turin.
Aperto '97, Trevi Flash Art Museum, Trevi, Perugia.
Festival Internacional de Arte Ciudad, Medellin, Colombia.
1996-4x2, Galleria Caterina Fossati, Turin.
Modernità, Progetto 2000, Palazzo Bricherasio, Turin.
Reportage, Galleria Giancarla Zanutti, Lanciano, Chieti.
June Trailers, L'Atlantique cafè, Milan.

1995
Konrad Lorenz's Duck, Ex Lanificio Bona, Carignano, Turin.
Nuovi Arrivi, Galleria di San Filippo, Turin.

Bibliography

2001
Verzotti, G., la ville idéale, Le Quartier, Quimper.
Chiodi, S., "Botto & Bruno", Tema Celeste, 84, March.
Romeo, F., "Botto & Bruno", Artforum, January.
Romeo, F., "Botto & Bruno", Flash Art, 226, February.

2000
Macri, T., Tolomeo, M.G., Pratesi, L., exhibition catalogue, Palazzo delle Esposizioni, Rome.
Fiz, A., Paesaggi fluttuanti, Oropa, Biella, Charta.
Chiodi, S., Maraniello, G., Cerizza, L., Espresso, arte oggi in Italia, Electa, Milan.
Lacagnina, S., "Botto & Bruno", Tema Celeste, 82, October.
Bigi, D., "Botto & Bruno", Arte Critica, 24, October.
"Botto&Bruno", Futurama, exhibition catalogue, Museo Pecci, Prato.
Verzotti, G., L'arte nell'epoca dell'AIDS, mostra Promotrice delle Belle Arti, Turin, Charta.
"Botto & Bruno", Suburb's Head, Lindau, Big Torino 2000, Turin.
"Botto & Bruno", Un giorno a Suburbia, Fondazione Teseco per l'Arte, Pisa.
Cochrane, G., Botto & Bruno, Fondazione Teseco per l'Arte, Pisa.
Bigi, D., "Vivere il nostro presente. Oltre il vuoto", Arte e Critica, 21, January.
Vescovo, M., L'assurdo quotidiano, exhibition catalogue, Galleria comunale d'Arte Contemporanea di Ciampino, Rome.
Mulatero, I., Nursery Crime, cat. mostra, Williamsburg Art&Historical Center, New York.
Pieroni, A., Fototensioni, Castelvecchi editore.

1999
"Botto&Bruno, Storie di ordinaria soprav-
vivenza", *Artel*, 1.
Beccaria , M., "Botto & Bruno", *FWD Italia*,
Passaggi invisibili, exhibition catalogue,
Palazzo delle Papesse, Siena.
Tolosano, E., "Botto & Bruno", *Flash Art*,
219, December.
Comisso, F., "Botto & Bruno", *Segno*, 171,
December.
Beatrice , L., "Il porto di Torino", *Atlante*,
MACS, Politi editore, Sassari.
Fabbri, F., Bartorelli, G., Altavilla, M., Frillici,
P.F., Lotta, D., *Artbeat*, Mazzotta.
mostra spazio Salara, Bologna e La
Posteria, Milan.
Conti, T., "Botto&Bruno", *Tema Celeste*, 76,
October.

1998
Curto, G., "Botto&Bruno", 2° edizione del
premio Torino incontra l'Arte, Associazione
Arte Giovane, Centro Congressi, Turin.
Torri, M.G., "Piccola storia del paesaggio(a
360°)", *Nuovo paesaggio italiano*, Lupetti.
Verzotti, G., "It's academic", *Artforum*, 10.
Fanelli, F., "Lettera dall'Italia", *Tracce sig-
nificanti. Arte italiana oggi*, Athens.
Colasanti, C., "Botto & Bruno", *Flash Art* ,
210, June.
Bertola, C., "Botto&Bruno", *Flash Art*, 207.
Pieroni, A., *Botto & Bruno*, catalogo
mostra, Studio Pino Casagrande, Rome.
Papa, D., "Botto&Bruno", *Juliet* , 89,
October.

1997
Romano, G., *Botto & Bruno*,catalogo
mostra, Studio Barbieri, Venice.
Mulatero, I., "Botto & Bruno", *Juliet*, 83
June.
Curto, G., "Un'ipotesi oltre il 2000", *Aperto
Italia '97*, Trevi Flash art Museum, exhibi-
tion catalogue, Politi editore, Trevi.
Curto, G., "Botto & Bruno", *Flash Art*, 204,
June-July.
Romano, G., "Botto & Bruno", *Juliet*, 80,
December.

1996
Curto, G., "Botto & Bruno", *Flash Art*, 198,
Giugno-Luglio.
Conti, T., *Modernità – progetto 2000*,
Palazzo Bricherasio, Turin, Milan, Electa.

1995
Piccato, P., Mulatero, I., Papa, D., *Konrad
Lorenz's Duck*, exhibition catalogue, Ex
Lanificio Bona, Carignano, Turin.
Conti, T., "Botto & Bruno", exhibition cat-
alogue, *Nuovi Arrivi*, Galleria San Filippo,
Turin.

Martin Bruch

1961, born in Hall in Tirol.
Lives and works in Vienna.

Solo Exhibitions

2000
Bruchlandungen, Kulturlabor Stromboli,
November, Hall in Tirol.

2001
Bruchlandungen, Museumquartier, März,
Hall A 1, Vienna.
Verzogene Haller, Beteiligung, Mai,
Stromboli, Hall in Tirol.

Bibliography

Bruchladungen, erschienen im November
2000 im Haymon Verlag, Innsbruck.

Tania Bruguera

1968, born in Havana.
Lives and works in Havana and Chicago.

Solo Exhibitions

2001
Liebman Magnan Gallery, New York.
Casa de las Americas, La Habana, Cuba.
Project Room, Algunas Islas ARCO:
Feria de Arte Contemporáneo, Recinto
Ferial Juan Carlos I, Madrid,Spain,
cdited by R. Martinez, O. Zayas, Y.
Hasegawa.

1999
Recent work, Vera van Laer Gallery,
Antwerp.
*Lo que me corresponde, Colloquia-proyec-
to para el arte contemporáneo*, Ciudad
Guatemala.

1997
El peso de la culpa, Tejadillo 214, Havana.
Anima, The Base Space, The School of the
Art Institute of Chicago.

1996
Cabeza abajo, Espacio Aglutinador,
Havana.
Lágrimas de tránsito, Centro de Arte
Contemporáneo Wifredo Lam, Havana.

1995
Lo que me corresponde, artist's home,
Havana.
Soñando, Gasworks Studios Gallery,
London, with Fernando Rodriguez, .

1993
Memoria de la postguerra, Galería Plaza
Vieja, Fondo Cubano de Bienes Culturales,
Havana.

1992
Ana Mendieta, Sala Polivalente, Centro de
Desarrollo de las Artes Visuales, Havana.

1986
Marilyn is alive, Galeria Leopoldo
Romañach, Academia de san Alejandro,
Havana.

Group Exhibitions

2001
Do you have time?, LiebmanMagnan
Gallery, New York, cdited by P. Liebman
and K. Magnan.

2000
Uno mas cerca del otro, VII Bienal de la
Habana, Fortaleza de San Carlos de la
Cabaña, Galería de Contraminas de San
Ambrosio, La Habana, edited by Centro de
Arte Contemporáneo Wifredo Lam.
Arte all 'Arte, 5th edition, Fortezza di
Poggio Imperiale, Arte Continua,
Poggibonsi, cdited by R. Pinto and G.
Williams.
Exotica Incognita, 3rd. Kwangju Bienale,
Kwangju, cdited by Yu Yeon Kim.

1999
Videodrome, The New Museum of
Contemporary Art, New York, cdited by D.
Cameron.
Looking for a Place, III International
Biennial, SITE Santa Fe, cdited by R.
Martinez.
Happening, Stedelijk Museum voor
Actuele Kunst, Gent, cdited by J. Hoet.
Cuba – Maps of desire, Kunsthalle Wien,
Austria, cdited by E. Valdes, G. Matt.

1998
Art in Freedom, Boymans van Beuningen
Museum, Rotterdam, cdited by E. van der
Plas, C. Dercon.
The Garden of Forking Paths, traveling
exhibition, 1998-1999, Helsinski City Art
Museum, Helsinski; Kunstforeningen,
Copenhagen; EdsuikKunst & Kultur,
Stockholm; cdited by O. Zayas.
Obsesiones, Centro de Arte
Contemporáneo Wifredo Lam, Havana,.
cdited by M. Ileana González.

1997
Trade routes, 2nd Johannesburg Biennale,
The Electric Workshop, Johannesburg,
cdited by O. Enwezor, exhibition catalogue.
1990's Art from Cuba, a national residency
and exhibition program, traveling exhibi-
tion 1997-1999, Betty Rymer Gallery, The
School of the Art Institute, Chicago; Art in
General, New York; Hallwalls Center for
Contemporary Art, Buffalo, New York,
cdited by H. Block, B.-S. Hertz.
New Art from Cuba: Utopic Territories,
Morris and Helen Belkin Art Gallery,
Vancouver, cdited by S. Watson, E. Valdés.

1996
23rd Sao Paolo International Biennial,
Parque do Ibirapuera, Sao Paolo, cdited by
L. Yanes .
*The visible and the invisible – representing
the body in contemporary art and society*,
St. Pancras Church, Institute of
International Visual Art, London.
La carne, Espacio Aglutinador, Havana,
cdited by S. Ceballos, E. Suárez

1995
La Isla Posible, Centro di Cultura
Contemporania, Barcelona, Spain, cdited
by I. de la Nuez, J. P. Ballester.
New Art from Cuba, Whitechapel Art
Gallery, London.
Tullie House Museum and Art Gallery,
Carlisle, Cumbria, England, cdited by J.
Peto.

1994
La otra orilla, V Havana Biennial,
Castillo de los Tres Reyes del Morro,
Centro Wifredo Lam, Havana, cdited by
E. Valdés, M.I. González.

1993
La nube en pantalones, Museo Nacional
de Bellas Artes, Havana, cdited by C.
Matamoros.

1989
Es sólo lo que ves (arte abstracto),
Havana, cdited by G. Novoa.

1988
*No por mucho madrugar amanece más
temprano*, Fototeca de Cuba, Havana,
cdited by R. Torres Llorca.

Performances

2000
Untitled, Uno mas cerca del otro, VII
Bienal de la Habana, Fortaleza de San
Carlos de la Cabaña, Galería de
Contraminas de San Ambrosio, La
Habana, November 18.

From the series *El peso de la culpa*:
No. IV, *Exotica Incognita*, 3rd Kwangju
Bienale, Kwangju, South Korea, March
29, 2000.
Utopía/Distopía, 8va. Muestra
Internacional de Performance, Mexico
City, Mexico, October 15, 1999.
No. III Hapenning, Stedelijk Museum
voor Actuele Kunst, Gent, May 8, 1999.
No. II, *Looking for a Place*, III International

Biennial, SITE Santa Fe, New Mexico, United States, July 10, 1999.
Vera van Laer Gallery, Antwerp, March 26, 1999.
No. I, *Cuba - Maps of desire*, Kunsthalle Wien, Vienna, Austria. March 19, 1999.
Desde el cuerpo: Alegorías de lo femenino, Museo de Bellas Artes, Caracas, February 15, 1998.
Tejadillo 214, La Habana, Cuba, May 8, 1997.

From the series *El cuerpo del silencio*:
Silencio Lo que me corresponde, Museo de Arte Contemporáneo, Fundación Colloquia, Ciudad Guatemala, Guatemala, April 24, 1999.
No. II, *Tejadillo 214*, Havana.
No. I, *Fragmentos a su imán*, Galería Latinoamericana, Casa de las Américas, Havana. June 17, 1998.
The Garden of Forking Paths, Kunstforeningen, Copenhagen, April 25, 1998.

Destierro Obsesiones, Centro de Arte Contemporáneo Wifredo Lam, Havana. August 13, 1998.
II Bienal Barro de América, Museo de Bellas Artes, Caracas, Venezuela, July 9, 1998.

From the series *Dédalo o el imperio de salvación*:
No. II, *De discretas autorías, Cuba y Venezuela: Nuevas poéticas*, Museo de Arte Contemporáneo Mario Abrey, Maracay, March 8, 1998.
No. I, Museo de Bellas Artes, Havana. November 25, 1995.

Cabeza abajo Cabeza abajo, Espacio Aglutinador, Havana. December 20, 1996.
Trabajo por cuenta propia, Facultad de Artes y Letras, University of Havana, Havana. May 6, 1997.
New Art from Cuba: Utopian Territories, The Western Front, Vancouver. April 1997.

From the series *Lo que me corresponde*:
Estudio de Taller, 23rd Sao Paolo Biennale, Parque de Ibirapuera, Sao Paolo, October 5, 1996.
Centro Wifredo Lam, Havana, July 18, 1996.
Lo que me corresponde artist 's home, Havana.

From the series *Memoria de la Postguerra*:
Miedo La otra orilla, V Havana Biennial, Castillo de los Tres Reyes del Morro, Havana. May 8, 1994.

Bibliography

2000
Fresh Cream – Contemporary Art in Culture, text by I. Blazwick, A. Cruz, B. Curiger, V. Kortun, M. Lind, V. Misiano, G. Mosquera, O. Oguibe, A. Poshyananda, O. Zaya, Ed. Phaidon Press Inc., London, England; New York, pp. 160-165.
Espacios Híbridos, text by J. Fernández, Ed. La Casona, Havana, p. 5.

1999
Corpus Delecti -Performance Art of the Americas, text by C. Fusco, T. Bruguera among others. Edited by Coco Fusco. Ed. Routledge, London, England; New York, pp. 152-153.
Cuba -Los mapas del deseo, interview with O. Zayas, text by E. Valdes Figueroa, among others, Ed. Folio, Kunsthalle Wien, Vienna, pp. 113, 136-140, 144, 155-157, 235-254.
Bruguera, T., *Lo que me corresponde*, interview with V. Garzón, Ed. Colloquia proyecto para el arte contemporáneo, Guatemala.
Arte cubano: Mas allá del papel, text by L. Yanes, Ed. Caja Madrid, Madrid, pp. 56-59.
La dirección de la mirada, texts by G. Mosquera, A. Mena, E. Valdes. Ed. Voldemeer, Springer Wien, New York, pp. 29, 32-33.

1998
Performance Live Art since 1960, text by R. Golberg, Ed. Thames and Hudson Ltd, London, England; Harry N. Abrams Inc., New York, p. 142.
Contemporary Art from Cuba, "The infinite island: introduction to new Cuban art" by G. Mosquera, p. 37; "Tree of many beaches: Cuban art in motion" by Tonel (Antonio Eligio Fernandez), p. 61, Ed. Delano Greenidge Editions, New York.
Caribe insular, Ed. Casa de América, Madrid; Museo Extremeño e Iberoamericano de Arte Contemporáneo, Extremadura, Spain, pp. 96-99, 1998.
The Garden of Forking Paths, Ed. Tabapress, S.A., pp. 30-35.
De discretas autorías. Cuba y Venezuela: nuevas poéticas Evanescencia de la imagen (The evanescence of image), texts by N. Gutiérrez. Ed. Fundación Museo de Arte Contemporáneo de Maracay Mario Abreu, pp. 38-41, 86-87, 102.
II Salón de Arte Cubano Contemporáneo, Ed. Centro de Desarrollo de las Artes Viduales, La Habana, Cuba, p. 37.

1997
Trade Routes – 2nd Johannesburg Biennale, text by O. Enwezor, among others. Ed. Johannesburg Metropolitan Council, The Prince Claus Fund, New York, pp. 84-85.
1990's Art from Cuba: A National Residency and Exhibition Program, interview by B.S. Hertz, T. Bruguera, V. Cassel, *Cronology: selected events in cuban art and history since 1959*, Ed. Art in General, New York, p. 29-31.

1996
Valdés Figueroa, E., *El arte de la negociación y el espacio del juego. El coito interrupto del arte cubano contemporáneo*, Ed. Centro Atlántico de Arte Moderno (CAAM), Las Palmas de Gran Canaria, p. 108.
Cuba siglo XX, Modernidad y Sincretismo, introduction M.L. Borrás, A. Zayas. Texts by A. Zayas, I. de la Nuez, G. Mosquera, N. Herrera Ysla, J.A. Molina, among others; "El arte de la negociación y el espacio del juego. El coito interrupto del arte cubano contemporáneo", by E. Valdés Figueroa, Ed. Centro Atlántico de Arte Moderno (CAAM), Las Palmas de Gran Canaria, Spain, 1996.
23rd Bienal Internacional de Sao Paolo *Nothing to see, everything to feel*, by Nelson Herrera Ysla, Ed. Fundação Bienla de Sao Paolo, Brazil, pp. 116-119.
23rd Bienal Internacional de Sao Paolo *Entre la ida y el regreso. La experiencia del otro en la memoria* by J.A. Molina, Ed. Centro de Arte Contemporáneo Wifredo Lam, Havana, brochure.

1995
Cuba: La Isla Posible, texts by I. de la Nuez, G. Mosquera, R. Rojas, A. Benítez Rojo, O. Sánchez, M.M. Fraginals, N. Bolívar, G. Pérez Firmat, among others, Ed. Centro di Cultura Contemporania de Barcelona, p. 183.
New Art from Cuba, text by A. Eligio (Tonel) Fernández, Ed. Whitechapel Art Gallery, London, brochure.

1994
New Art of Cuba, text by L. Camnitzer, Ed. University of Texas Press, Austin, pp. 194, 326.
Fragmentos a su imán, text by T. Diaz Bringas. Ed. Casa de las Américas, La Habana, Cuba, p. 10.

Looking for a place, text by R. Martinez and the artists, pp. 44-45, s.d.

Roderick Buchanan
1965, born in Glasgow, Scotland.
Lives and works in Glasgow, Scotland.

Solo Exhibitions

2001
Uppsala Kunstmuseum.
Lisson Gallery, London.

2000
Dundee Contemporary Arts.
Galerie Praz-Delavallade, Paris.

1999
FRAC Languedoc-Roussilon.

1998
Turnaround, Hayward Gallery, London.
Galerie Praz Delavallade, Paris.
Play & Record, Catalyst Arts, Belfast, with Fanni Niemi-Junkola.

1997
Lotta Hammer Gallery, London.
YYZ Gallery, Toronto.

1996
Jack Tilton Gallery, New York, with Jaqueline Donachie.
Mai de la Photo, Reims.

1995
City Racing, London, with David Allen.
Glasgow Print Studios.
Work in Progress, the Project Room, Tramway, Glasgow.

1994
Knoll Galeria, Budapest, with Ross Sinclair.
Knoll Galerie, Vienna, with Ross Sinclair.

Group Exhibitions

2001
Circles, ZKM, Karlsruhe.
Lost & Found: Critical voices in New British Design, Kulturhuset, Stockholm.
Open Country, Musee Cantonal des Beaux arts, Lausanne.

2000
Au-dela du spectacle, Pompidou Center, Paris.
Sporting Life, MCA, Sydney.
Printemps de Cahors.
Becks Futures, touring to ICA, London, Cornerhouse, Manchester and CCA Glasgow.
Lets Entertain, Walker Arts Center, Minneapolis.

1999
Printemps de Cahors.

dAPERTutto, La Biennale di Venezia, 48. Esposizione Internazionale d'Arte.
Rue Louise Weiss, Centre d'art Contemporain, Meymac.
Mayday, Photographers Gallery, London.

1998
In Visible Light, Moderna Museet, Stockholm.
Host, Tramway, Glasgow.
Nettverk, Museet for Samtidskunst, Oslo.

1997
Johannesburg Biennial, Johannesburg.
Material Culture, Hayward Gallery, London.

1996
Girls High, Fruitmarket Gallery, Glasgow.
Life/Live, Musee d'Art modern de la ville de Paris, Paris and Centro Cultural de Belem, Lisbon.

1995
Instant, Camden Art Centre, London.
Ideal Standard Summertime, Lisson Gallery, London.
Karaoke, South London Gallery.

1994
Institute of Cultural Anxiety, ICA, London.
The Curators Egg, Anthony Reynolds Gallery, London.
Modern Art, Transmission Gallery, Glasgow.

1993
Wonderful Life, Lisson Gallery, London.

1992
Guilt by Association, Irish Museum of Modern Art, Dublin.

1991
Speed, Transmission Gallery, Belfast.

1990
Self Conscious State, Third Eye Center, Glasgow.

1989
Information, Paisley Museum & Art Gallery.
The Festival of Plagerism, Transmission Gallery, Glasgow.

Video Programmes

2001
Swiss Institute, New York.

2000

Moderna Museet, Stockholm.
Black Box Recorder, British Council International Touring Exhibition.
Shoot, Kunsthall, Malmo.

1999
This other world of ours, Art Media Centre, Moscow.
Magnetic North, National Film Theatre, London.
Screenings, Iconoscope, Montpelier.
Fourth Wall, PADT at the Royal National Theatre, London.
Les nuits de la pleine lune, SWITCH 1, TV Channel Arte, France.
This is now, Travelling Gallery, London.
What is love, Five Year Gallery, London.

1998
Artcrash, Kulturhus, Arhus.
Muu Media Festivali, Kiasma, Nykytaiteen Museum, Helsinki.

1997
New Video from Great Britain, Musem of Modern Art, New York.
Take 2, Institute of Contemporary Art, London.
Nerve, Glasgow Projects, Sydney.

1996
Wish you were here, De Appel, Amsterdam.
Looking Awry, Brazilian Embassy, Paris.

1995
Sixth International Video Week, Saint-Gervais, Geneva.

1994
Scottish Video, Museum of Installation, London.

Bibliography

2001
www.planey-britain.org, *Foreign Office What's On*, January.
Buck, L., "Beautiful Games", *Esquire*, p. 37, February.
Mottram, J., "He shoots he scores", *The Face*, pp. 30-31, February.
Brd, N., "Roderick Buchanan Dundee Contemporary Arts", *Art Monthly*, 243, pp. 37-38, February.
www.beme.com, *Culture & Trends*, Innovate, April.

2000
Bradley, W., *Nu*, 2000.
Paini, D., "Le retour du flaneur", *Art Press*, 225, pp. 33-41, March.
Huitorel, J.-M., "L'effet traveling. Another Country", *Art Press*, 253, pp. 42-45, January.

1999
Beausse, P., "Nouveaux scenarios sportifs", *Le Journal*, (Centre national de la photographie), p. 11, September 1999.
Ellis, P., "Smells Like Teen Spirit", *Flash Art*, pp. 85-86, October.
Marguerin, M., "Global Game", *Blocnotes*, 17, pp. 164-173, Autumn.
Loubet, C., "Le regard des videastes sur l'an 2000", *Le Dauphine Libere*, p. 8, 9, December

1998
Jouanno, E., "Roderick Buchanan", *Flash Art*, 203, p. 114, November/December.
Ellis, M., "This Island Earth", *Art Monthly*, 219, pp. 30-32, September.
Jewesbury, D., *Circa Magazine*, 40, pp. 86-87, May.
Huitorel, J.M., "Le Terrain des Sports", *Art Press*, 237, Front Cover & pp. 30-35, July/August.
Timoney, P., "Play/Record", *Frieze*, 40, pp. 86-87, May
Boyesen, P., *K.I.T. magasin*, 17, pp. 46-47, December.

1997
Esche, C., "Collision Discourse", *Coil Magazine*, 5, October.
Beaumont, S., "Club Land", *The List*, 316, p. 84, September.
Williams, G., "A League of His Own", *Art Monthly*, 209, pp. 24-25, September.
Herbert, M., "Roderick Buchanan", *Time Out*, p. 48, June 4-11.
Beagles, J., "Tales from the city", *The List*, 316, p. 83, October.
Yankees, publication with Art Metropole, Toronto.

1996
Garnett, R., "A frame of two halfs", *Tate Magazine*, p. 43, 47, Summer.
Perreau, D., "Roderick Buchanan", *Documents Sur L'Art*, 10, pp.6-8, Winter.

1995
Tamas, K., "A Kocsma az en Muzemom", *Magyar Narancs*, pp. 30-31, November.
Findlay, J., "Roderick Buchanan, Work in Progress", *Flash Art*, pp. 131-132, January.

1994
Janos, S., "Csac R & R, De Nekem Tetszik", *Balkon Magazine*, p. 26, July.
Sinclair, R., "Global Village Idiots", *Frieze Magazine*, 16, pp. 22-23, May.

Chris Burden
1946, born in Boston, Massachusetts.
Lives and works in Topanga (CA).

Solo Exhibitions

2000
Crown Point Press, San Francisco.
Gagosian Gallery, New York, Beverly Hills and London.

1999
Tate Gallery, London, England.
Magasin 3 Stockholm Konsthall, Sweden.
Austrian Museum of Applied Arts, Vienna.
Galerie Krinzinger, Vienna.
Centre d'Art Santa Monica, Barcelona.
Galerie Anne de Villepoix, Paris.
Le Consortium, Dijon.
FRAC Champagne-Ardenne, Reims.

1996
Gagosian Gallery, New York, Beverly Hills and London.

1994
Gagosian Gallery, New York, Beverly Hills and London.

1993
Gagosian Gallery, New York, Beverly Hills and London.

1992
The Lannan Foundation, Los Angeles.
Josh Baer Gallery, New York.

1991
The Brooklyn Museum.
Josh Baer Gallery, New York.
Kent Fine Arts, New York.

1989
Carnegie Mellon Art Gallery, Pittsburgh.
Institute of Contemporary Art, Boston.
Josh Baer Gallery, New York.
Kent Fine Arts, New York.
Christine Burgin Gallery, New York.

1988
Newport Harbor Art Museum, Newport Beach.

1987
Hoffman-Borman Gallery, Santa Monica.
Christine Burgin Gallery, New York.

1985
Lowe Art Museum, Miami.
Wadsworth Atheneum, Hartford.

1983
Ronald Feldman Fine Arts, New York.

1980
Ronald Feldman Fine Arts, New York.

1977
Ronald Feldman Fine Arts, New York.

1976
Ronald Feldman Fine Arts, New York.

1975
Ronald Feldman Fine Arts, New York.
Galerie Stadler, Paris.
Ronald Feldman Fine Arts, New York.
Riko Mizuno Gallery, Los Angeles.

1974
Ronald Feldman Fine Arts, New York.

Group Exhibitions

2000
Orbis Terrarum, Antwerp.
Made in California 1900-2000, Los Angeles County Museum of Art, Los Angeles.
La Biennale di Venezia, XLVIII Esposizione Internazionale d'Arte, Venice.
Le monde reel, Cartier Foundation, Paris.

1998
Out of Actions: Between Performance and Object, 1949-1979, Museum of Contemporary Art, Los Angeles.
Biennale de Lyon, Lyon.
Sunshine & Noir, Louisana Museum of Modem Art, Humelbaek, Denmark.

1997
Whitney Biennial, Whitney Museum of Modem Art, New York. .

1996
Blurring the Boundaries, San Diego Museum of Art, San Diego.

1995
Endurance, Exit Art, New York.
After Hiroshima, Hiroshima City Museum of Contemporary Art, Hiroshima, Japan.

1994
Virtual Reality, National Gallery of Australia, Canberra.
Hors Limites, Centre Georges Pompidou, Paris.

1993
Action/Performance and the Photograph, Turner/Krull Gallery, Los Angeles.
Whitney Biennial, Whitney Museum of Modem Art, New York.

1992
LAX, Galerie Krinzinger, Vienna.
Helter Skelter: L.A. Art of the 1990s, Museum of Contemporary Art, Los Angeles.

1991
Dislocations, Museum of Modem Art, New York.

Places With A Past: Site Specific Art in Charleston, Spoleto Festival, Charleston.

1990
New Works for New Spaces: Into the Nineties, Wexner Center for the Visual Arts, Columbus.
TSWA: Four Cities Project, Newcastle.
Seven Obsessions, Whitechapel Gallery, London.

1986
Individuals: A Selected History of Contemporary Art 1945-1986, Museum of Contemporary Art, Los Angeles.

1985
NO! Contemporary American DADA, Henry Art Gallery, University of Washington, Seattle.

1983
Deeds and Feats, Contemporary Art Center, New Orleans.

1982
War Games, Ronald Feldman Fine Arts, New York.
Eight Artists: The Anxious Edge, Walker Art Center, Minneapolis.

1981
The Museum as Site: Sixteen Projects, Los Angeles County Museum of Art, Los Angeles.

1977
Documenta 6, Kassel.
Whitney Biennial, Whitney Museum of Modem Art, New York.

1971
Body Movements, La Jolla Museum of Contemporary Art, La Jolla.

Bibliography

2000
Montano, L., *Performance Artists Talking in the Eighties*, University of California Press, pp. 343-347, 496.
Ward, F., "The technology We Deserve", *Parkett*, 60, pp. 190-193.
Millar, A., "Chris Burden at Crown Point Press", *Artweek*, July-August.
Neumaier, O. von, "Pizza City", *Frame*, March-April, pp. 90-91.

1999
When Robots Rule: The Two Minute Airplane Factory, Tate Gallery Publishing, London.
Chris Burden, Magasin 3 Stockholm Konsthall, Stockholm.
The American Century: Art and Culture

1900-2000, Whitney Museum of American Art, New York.
Johnstone, M., *Contemporary Art in Southern California*, Craftsman House, pp. 40-43.
Singerman, H., *Art Subjects Making Artists in the American University*, UC Press.
Ward, F., "Chris Burden Transfixed: Between Public and Private", *Collapse*, May, pp. 10-19.
Sanders, M., "Chris Burden", *Dazed and Confused*, April, pp. 110-117.
Hipperson, D., "The Two Minute Airplane Factory", *International Flying Model Designer and Constructor*, Spring, 6, 3, pp. 116-118.

1998
Out of Actions: Between Performance and the Object, 1949-1979, Museum of Contemporary Art, Los Angeles.
Millar, J., "Speed", *Dazed and Confused*, November, pp. 132-137 (English publication).
Knight, C., "Chris Burden and the Potential for Catastrophe", *Art Issues*, March-April, pp. 14-18.

1997
4e Biennale d'Art Contemporain de Lyon, Reunion des Musées Nationaux, Lyon.
Sunshine & Noir Art in L.A. 1960-1997, Louisiana Museum of Modern Art, Humelbaek, Denmark.
Phillips, L. and Neri, L., *1997 Biennial Exhibition*, Whitney Museum of American Art, New York.
Gallo, R., "Chris Burden", *Poliester*, Winter, pp. 2-7 (Mexican publication).

1996
Chris Burden France 1994-1995, Le Consortium, Dijon.
Chris Burden: Beyond the Limits, Museum of Applied Arts, Vienna.
L'art au Corps, Musees de Marseilles, Marseilles.
"...usurpar la volubilidad del destino. Chris Burden", *Sin Titulo*, Facultad de Bellas Artes de Cuenca, Fall, 3, p. 4, 51-86 (Spain).
Neumaier, O. von, "Chris Burden der Diskrete Charme der Technologie", *Noema*, 41, pp. 44-49.
"Chris Burden: America's Darker Moment", Grand Street, Spring, 13, 4, pp. 121-128.
Umeni, V., "Chris Burden", *Art in America*, January-February, pp. 74-89 (Czech publication).

1995
Chris Burden, Centre d'Art Santa Monica, Barcelona.
Chris Burden, Frank Perrin. Blocnotes, Paris.

Albertini, R., *Chris Burden/Bill Viola*, Museo d'Arte Moderna, Bolzano.
Knight, C., *Last Chance for Eden*, edited by M. Wilson, Art Issues-Press, Los Angeles, pp. 31-34.
Perrin, F., *Chris Burden*, Blocnotes, Paris.

1994
Noever, P. editor, *Positions in Art MAK Round Table*, Austrian Museum of Applied Arts, Vienna, p. 64-89.
Schimmel, P., "Chris Burden Another World", *Art Press*, December, p. 24-32.

1993
1993 Biennial Exhibition, Whitney Museum of American Art, New York.

1992
Action/Performance and the Photograph, Turner/Krull Gallery, Los Angeles.
Helter Skelter: L.A. Art in the 1990's, essays by Klein, N. and Relyea, L., The Museum of Contemporary Art, Los Angeles.
Dislocations, edited by R. Storr, The Museum of Modern Art, New York, Harry N. Abrams, New York.

1988
Chris Burden: A Twenty Year Survey, Newport Harbor Art Museum, Newport Beach.

1984
Butterfield, J., The Art of Performance. A Critical Anthology, *edited by G. Battock and R.Nickas, E.P. Dutton, New York, p. 222-239.*

Maurizio Cattelan

1960, Padova.
Lives and works in Milan and New York.

Solo Exhibitions

2001
Maurizio Cattelan, Fargfabriken, Stockholm.

2000
Project Gallery, CCA Kitakyushu, Kitakyushu.
Migros Museum für Gegenwartskunst, Zurich.
Kunsthalle Basel, Basel.
Project #65, Museum of Modern Art, New York. Castello di Rivoli, Turin; Le Consortium, Dijon; Wiener Secession, Vienna.

Group Exhibitions

2001-2000
Home is where the heArt is, Museum van

Loon, Amsterdam. *Let's Entertain*, Walker Art Center, Minneapolis, Minnesota; Musée National d'Art Moderne-Centre Georges Pompidou, Paris, France; Museo Rufino Tamayo, Mexico City, Mexico; Miami Art Museum, Miami, Florida.

2000
Apocalypse: Beauty and Horror in Contemporary Art, Royal Academy, London.
Presumed Innocent, Musée d'Art Contemporain de Bordeaux, Bordeaux. *Age of Influence: Reflections in the Mirror of American Culture*, Museum of Contemporary Art, Chicago.
Over the Edge, Ghent. Expo 2000, Hannover.
La Ville, le Jardin, la Memoire, Villa Medici, Rome. *Abracadabra*, Tate Gallery, London.
Wiener Festwoken, Vienna. *dAPERTutto*, La Biennale di Venezia, Esposizione Internazionale d'Arte, Venice.

Actions

1999
6th Caribbean Biennial, co-curated with Jens Hoffmann, St. Kitts, British West Indies.

Bibliography

2001
Gioni, M., "Maurizio Cattelan, Giù la maschera", *Flash Art*, April, 227.
Jouannais, J.-Y., Kihm, C., "Les Witz de Maurizio Cattelan", *Art Press*, 265, February
Kazanjian, D., "The Lying Game", *Vogue*, February 2001.
Belcove, J.L., "To Market", *W Magazine*, May.

2000
Bourriaud, N., "A Grammar of visual delinquency", *Parkett*, 59.
Gingeras, A.M., "A Sociology without truth", *Parkett*, 59.
Bonami, F., "Every Artist can be a Man, The silence of Beuys is understandable", *Parkett*, 59.
Vogel, M., "Maurizio Cattelan im Migros-Museum", *Neue Burder Beitung*, July 16.
Aaronovitch, D., "Brash, innovative, my kind of show", *The Independent*, September 20.
Wakfield, N., "Where the human condition and the animal kingdom merge", *Interview Magazine*, June.
Smith, R., *The New York Times*, Friday, March 17.
Shave, S., "Dodger", *I.D.*, March.
The Hugo Boss Prize 2000 Guggenheim Museum, contributor Jan Avgikos.

Maurizio Cattlean, Phaidon, contributors F. Bonami, N. Spector, B. Vanderlinden.
Art at the Turn of the Millenium, edited by F. Bonami, H.U. Obrist, Taschen.
In Between, Art Expo 2000, Hannover.

1999
Nickas, B., "Maurizio Cattelan", *Index Magazine*, September/October.
Maurizio Cattelan, Museo d'Arte Contemporanea, Castello di Rivoli, Carta.
Abracadabra, edited by C. Grenier, C. Kinley, Tate Gallery, July 15 - September 26.

1998
Maurizio Cattelan, Museum of Modern Art, New York. *Projects 65*, November 6 - December 4.

1997
Maurizio Cattelan, Museo d'Arte Contemporanea, Castello di Rivoli, Carta.
Maurizio Cattelan, Wiener Secession, January 31 - March 9.
Perreau. D., "Maurizio Cattelan l'idiot du village", *Art Press*, 1997

1996
Rian, J., "Maurizio Cattelan Went Home", *Flash Art*, October.

Loris Cecchini
1969, born in Milan.
Lives and works in Milan.

Solo Exhibitions

2001
Loris Cecchini, Heidelberger Kunstverein, Heidelberg.
h( )me, Armani Store, Milan.

2000
Stage evidences (around&taround), Galleria Continua, FIAC, Paris.
Loris Cecchini, Fondazione Bandera, Busto Arsizio, Milan.
Cargo, Maschio Angioino, Napoli.
Waste, galleria Max Estrella, Madrid.
Loris Cecchini, Centro Galego de Arte Contemporanea, Santiago de Compostela.
Stage evidences, Galleria Hyperion, Turin.
Project room, ARCO 99, Galleria Continua, Madrid.

1999
Loris Cecchini, Istituto Italiano di Cultura, Colonia.
Loris Cecchini, Galleria Claudia Gian Ferrari Arte Contemporanea, Milan.

1998
FWD>>: Loris Cecchini, cdited by A.

Pieroni, Palazzo delle Papesse, Centro Arte Contemporanea, Siena.
No casting, Galleria Continua, San Gimignano.

1997
Pause in background, Galleria Studio Legale, Caserta.

1996
Farfalle e propano, Galleria Bordone, Milan.

Group Exhibitions

2001
Body & Sin, cdited by A. Bonito Oliva, Biennale di Valencia, Valencia.
Lombard-Fried Fine arts gallery, New York.
Le Odissee dell'Arte, cdited by A. Bonito Oliva, Museo Revoltella, Trieste.
Poetiche del Quotidiano, edited by L. Ragaglia, Galleria Civica, Bolzano.

2000
The sky is the limit, edited by J. Sans, M. Hzu, Biennale di Taiwan, Taipei.
Futurama, Arte in Italia 2000, cdited by B. Corà, M. Meneguzzo, Centro per l'Arte Contemporanea Luigi Pecci, Prato.
Simili, galleria De Chiara / Stuart, New York.
No Confines, Mandarina Duck / Medicins sans Frontieres, London, Paris, Madrid, Milan, Berlin.
3nds Milano, Bologna, Salara, edited by A. Galasso, G. Maraniello.
Fantapop, cdited by V. Baradel, Fondazione Bevilaqua La Masa, Venice.

1999
Il sentimento del 2000. Arte e foto 1960-2000, Photomedia Europe, galleria Continua, S. Gimignano.
In Uso, cdited by L. Pratesi, P. Magni, Fondazione Michetti, Pescara.
MIR. Art in Space, cdited by E. Francalanci, Arte nello Spazio, Kunst in Raum, galleria Civica, Bolzano.
Porta d'Oriente, cdited by G. Romano, Bisceglie (Bari).
Nuovo nomadismo individuale, Casa Rigoletto, Mantova.
Video virtuale - Foto Fictionale, Ludwig Museum, Colonia.
Fantasimilia - dalla fotochimica alla fotoelettronica, cdited by I. Zannier, S. Zannier, CRAF centro di ricerca e archiviazione della fotografia, Lestans.
Arbeat, Salara, Bologna, Posteria, Milan, cdited by G. Bartorelli, F. Fabbri.
XIII Quadriennale, Palazzo delle Esposizioni, Rome.
MoltepliCittà, cdited by B. Pietromarchi,

Fondazione Adriano Olivetti, Rome.
Arte in Giro, cdited by A. Fiz, Oropa, Biella.
Effetto Notte, cdited by L. Pratesi, P. Magni, Napoli Sotterranea, Napoli.
Alta definizione, cdited by P. Magni, Rome.
Digitalia, cdited by P. Campiglio, Studioventicinque, Milan.

1998
Oraperora, progetto per www.Undo.net.
Eccentrica, cdited by M. Manara, G. Gianuizzi, Rocca Sforzesca, Imola.
Rock around the Clock, cdited by A. Galasso, Galleria Ciocca, Milan.
Standby, cdited by A. Pieroni, Galleria Romberg Arte Contemporanea, Latina.
Attraversamenti, cdited by C. Corbetta, D. Grandi, CRT Teatro dell'arte, Milan.
Pre-millennium tension, cdited by L. Beatrice, Galleria Eos, Milan.

1997
Crash, cdited by G. Del Vecchio, Ex officina meccanica, Caserta.
Arena, cdited by C. Perrella, C/O Mel Bookstore, Rome.
Generazione media, Palazzo della Triennale, Milan.
Periscopio, cdited by P. Campiglio, F. Tedeschi, A. Madesani, Cascina grande di Rozzano, Milan.
Città aperta 1997, cdited by R. Bianchini, Città S. Angelo, Pesaro.
Aperto '97), cdited by C. Perrella, Trevi Flash Art Museum, Trevi, Perugia.
Il punto, cdited by E. Grazioli, Galleria Continua, San Gimignano, Siena.

1996
Invita, Galleria Continua, San Gimignano, Siena
Mutoidi, cdited by M. Sgroi, Maschio Angioino, Napoli.
0" video 1', cdited by D. Esposito, AA. BB. AA., Milan.

1995
Storm, Plastic & Juboxhero, Milan.
Anni '90 arte a Milano-Profanazioni, cdited by L. Saccà, Openspace, Milan.
The meridian crossings - Ent/artic shelf - Hermit IV - interdisciplinary symposium, Plasy, Czech Republic.

Bibliography

2001
Gerke, H., "Mind the gap", Cerizza, L., "L'ultimo spettacolo", *Loris Cecchini*, Heidelberger Kunstverein, Heidelberg.
Ragaglia, L., Zannier, S., *Poetiche del quotidiano 2*, Galleria civica/Stadt-Galerie, Bolzano.

Bonito Oliva, A., *Odissee dell'arte*, Prearo editore, Milan.

2000
Cicelyn, E., "Al limite dell'insignificanza", Maraniello, G., "Essere giocati dall'artista", Perosino, M., "Il senso del nonsenso", *Loris Cecchini - Cargo*, Associazione Percorsi, Museo di Castel Nuovo, Naples.
Fernandez-Cid, M., *Centro Galego Arte Contemporanea*, Aprile, Santiago de Compostela.
Lodi, S., "Chi ha paura della tecnologia?", Pioselli , A., "Palcoscenici per giocare", Pieroni , A. "21st century schyzoid man", *Loris Cecchini*, Galleria Continua, San Gimignano.
Bonito Oliva, A., *Arte e sistema dell'arte*, Prearo Editore, Milan.
Pieroni, A., *Fototensioni*, Castelvecchi, Rome.
Maraniello, G., "Con la debita distanza", *3nds - Milano*, Bologna, Salara.
Pietromarchi, B., *Molteplicittà*, Fondazione Adriano Olivetti, Rome.
Futurama, Museo Pecci per l'arte Contemporanea, Prato.
Bonito Oliva, A., *Gratis - A bordo dell'arte*, Skira, Milan.
Sans, J., Hzu, M., *The sky is the limit - Taipei Biennal 2000*, Taipei Fine Arts Museum, Taiwan.
Espresso - Arte oggi in Italia, Electa, Milan.
DISERTORI - Sud: racconti della frontiera, immagine di copertina, "Tascabili Stile libero", Einaudi, Turin.

1999
Pieroni, A., "Stereoreale", Pratesi, L, "Note e appunti sul lavoro di Loris Cecchini", *Loris Cecchini*, Istituto Italiano di Cultura, Cologne.
Magni, P., Mino, E.N., "Effetto notte", Castelvecchi Arte, Rome.
Pontiggia, E., "Nuove tecnologie: l'imma-terialità del quadro", XIII Quadriennale, *Lo spazio delle arti visive nella civiltà multi-mediale*, De Luca, Rome.
Zannier, S., *Fantasimilia. Dalla fotochimica alla fotoelettronica*, Milan, Motta / CRAF editore.
Bonazzi, F., "Senza fissa dimora", *Nuovo nomadismo individuale*, Mantova.
Romano, G., *Porta d'Oriente*, Bisceglie.
Francalanci, E., Masieno, R., Polese, V., *MIR. Art in Space, Arte nello Spazio, Kunst in Raum*, Skira, Milan.

1998
Beatrice, L., Perrella, C.,*Nuova arte italiana*, Rome, Castelvecchi.

1997
Tanzi Mira, F., "The impossible Man", *Loris Cecchini - Pause in Background*, Galleria Studio Legale, Caserta.

Perrella, C., *Aperto Italia '97*.
Campiglio, P., *Periscopio*, Mazzotta.
Generazione Media, Triennale di Milano, Milan.

COM & COM

Johannes M. Hedinger, 1971, born in St. Gallen.
Marcus Gossolt, 1969, born in St. Gallen.
Both live and work in Zurich, Switzerland.

Solo Exhibitions

2002
Galerie Barbara Thumm, Berlin.

2001
Shed im Eisenwerk, Frauenfeld.

2000
Kunsthaus, Zurich.

1999
Raum für aktuelle Kunst, Lucerne.
Gallery Scott Thatcher, New York.

1998
Galerie Sima, Nuremberg.

Group Exhibitions

2001
SCCA Gallery, Soros Center of Contemporary Art, Kyiv, Ukraine.
Firemouth God, Galerie Barbara Thumm, Berlin.
Pandaemonium, Biennal of Moving Images, LUX-Center, London.
Zurich-Urban Diary, Galerie Bob van Orsouw, Zurich.

2000
Ostschweizer Kunstschaffen, Kunstmuseum St. Gallen.
Kunstszene Zürich, Hürlimann Areal, Zurich.
Viper, Internationales Filmfestival, Basel.
No Vacancies, Galerie Barbara Thumm, Berlin.
Z 2000, Akademie der Künste, Berlin.
International Videoprogramm, touring exhibition, Galerie Barbara Thumm, Berlin; Badischer Kunstverein, Karlsruhe; TRAFO, Budapest; Galerie Bunkier Sztuki, Krakau.

1999
Sozialmaschine Geld, O.K. Zentrum für Gegenwartskunst, Linz.
Xposition, Swiss Institute, New York.
art pleasure, Linienstrasse 155, Berlin.

1998
Albrecht Dürer Gesellschaft, Kunstverein, Nuremberg.

commercé, Galerie Gaxotte, Porrentruy.
anstadt.98, GSMBA, St. Gallen.

1997
Ostschweizer Kunstschaffen, Kunstmuseum, St. Gallen.

Bibliography

2001
In Hoc Signo Vinces, artist book with texts by T. Bezzola, P. Bianchi, D. Binswanger, C. Blase, E. Bronfen, B. Groys, V. Hediger, G. Jetzer, T. Macho, H.-U. Obrist, H. U. Reck, D. Signer, R. Wolfs and F. Zelger, edition fink, Zurich.
The Odyssey (English version, reprint), artist book, edition fink, Zürich.
Meier, P., "We are # 1", *NZZ*, March 8, p. 44, ill.
Renggli, H., "Wo Kleinbürger und Starkünstler sich treffen", *Tages-Anzeiger*, March 16, p. 58.

2000
C-Files: Tell Saga - Das Buch zum Film, artist book, text by J.M. Hedinger, Kunsthaus Zürich and edition fink, Zurich.
The Book of COM & COM (extended version, reprint), artist book with texts by von D. Baumann, D. Binswanger, K. Bitterli, T. Feuerstein, A. Göldi, G. Mack and R. Walch, edition fink, Zürich.
Bitterli, K., "Kunst zwischen Kommerz und Kommunikation", *Kunstforum International*, 152, pp. 220, ill.
Blase, C., "Der ultimative Schweiz-Schweiz Film-Film", *Blitz Review*, 639, www.blitzreview.de, ill.
Signer, D., "Trashkunst gegen die Einsamkeit", *Magazin*, Tages-Anzeiger, September, 23, pp. 40, ill.
Vachtova, L., "Optische Attacken auf die Klassiker", *Weltwoche*, September, 14, p. 55, ill.
Hess, E., "Nichts als Kunst", *Sonntags-Zeitung*, September, 10, pp. 61, ill.
Herzog, S., "Die Welt im Magnumformat", *NZZ*, September 9, p. 66, ill.
Krebs, E., "Perfekter Act", *Züritipp*, Tages-Anzeiger, September, 8, p. 59, ill.
Berg, S., "Leichenfund im Tiergarten", *Zitty*, 17, p. 51.
Lange, R., "Satellit", *Z 2000*, exhibition catalogue, Akademie der Künste, Berlin, p.161, ill.
Nolte, M., "Kohle als Kunst", *Der Tagesspiegel*, February, 17, p. 34.

1999
The Book of COM & COM, artist book with texts by D. Baumann, D. Binswanger, K. Bitterli, T. Feuerstein, A. Göldi, G. Mack and R.r Walch, edition fink, Zurich.
Hattinger, G., Baumann, D., "Interview mit COM & COM", *Sozialmaschine Geld*, exhi-bition catalogue, O.K Zentrum für Gegenwartskunst Linz, Berlin, pp. 152, ill.
Feuerstein, T., "COMmix & COMmunity", *K-Bulletin*, 1, exhibition catalogue, Helmhaus Zurich und Exner Allee Wien, p. 58, ill.

1998
Die Odyssee, artist book, edition fink, Zürich.
Mack G., "COM & COM in der Galerie Sima", *Das Kunst-Bulletin*, Zürich, 11, p. 42, ill.
Rigendinger, B., "Label-art oder wie Luxusautos und Plastikstühle zu Kunst werden", *Sonntags-Zeitung*, May, 3, p. 23, ill.

Cracking art Group

Omar Ronda, Renzo Nucara, Marco Veronese, Alex Angi, Carlo Rizzetti, Kikko, Alessandro Pianca. Cracking art work in Biella.

Solo Exhibitions

2001
Premio Villa Caruso, Villa Caruso, Florence.
Green Frozen Dollar, Caltex Gallery, Biella.
Nel segno della solidarietà, Fabriano.
Nuovi codici rosa, Villa Vidua, Conzano.
Irene, monumento alla pace, Comune di quattro castella, Reggio Emilia.

2000
Cracking Art/Naturale Artificiale, Caltex Gallery, Biella.
Celebration of Creativity, Denim Art, Los Angeles.
Etna, Palazzo Duchi di S. Stefano, Taormina.
Naturel/artificiel, Artiscope Kanal 20, Bruxelles.
Musicarte, Chiari,Cracking, Gilardi, Galleria Santo Ficara, Florence.

1999
Giungle, Scultura 99, Sondrio.
Andy Warhol/Carcking Art, Galleria Pananti, Florence.
Salon des art mediterraèes, Cannes.
La Casa di Lucrezia, Bolognano.
Scultura contemporanea, Caltex Gallery, Biella.
Omaggio all'Arno, Villa Bellosguardo Caruso, Lastra a Signa.
Progetti di Sacro, Fallani Best, Florence.
Paesaggi notturni, Palazzina Piacenza, Biella.

1998
Pop/Graffiti/Cracking, Galleria Pananti, Florence.
Art Jonction, Nizza.

Verso il Sole, Galleria Melesi, Lecco.
Istituto superiore di comunicazione, Milan.
Golden Stars, La Posteria, Milan.
Banca popolare di Milano, Monza.
Epocale, Pop/Graffiti/Cracking, La Posteria, Milan.
Antico castello della Pretuara, Castell'Arquato.

1997
Galleria d'Arte Moderna Aroldo Bonzagni, Cento.
Palazzo della Triennale, Milan.
Studio B&D Cracking Art, Milan.
Cappella del Buon Gesù, S. Michele, Mondovì.
Kanal, Galleria Zaira Miss, Brussels.

1996
Arte fiera, La natura per la natura, Bologna.
Palasport, Ecologica 96, Casalecchio di Reno.
Made in Bo, Bologna.
Cracking Art, Comune di Filottrano, Ancona.
Corteo contro l'inceneritore Fenice, Biella.
Amordimare, Piazza del Popolo, Rome.
Replastic Factory, Melzo.
1000 delfini a Milano, Arengario di Palazzo Reale/Piazza del Duomo, Milan.

1995
XII Premio Alfons Roig, Casa della Cultura, Bellreguard.
Death Life, Ponte alle Grazie/Ponte Vecchio, Florence.
Ecologica 95, Fortezza da Basso, Florence.
Art Jonction 95, Palais des Festival, Cannes.
Fondo imperatrice nuda per LAV, Palazzina Liberty, Milan.

1994
Ministere des affaire Culturelles, Lussemburgo.
Musei Civici, Sala delle colonne, Rimini.
Progetto Firenze per l'arte contemporanea, Florence.
Galleria EOS, Milan.
Cracking Girls, Galleria Il Ponte, Rome.
Crackingfoodfest, Palazzina Reale, Florence.
Corteo per la Natura, Ponte Vecchio, Florence.
Animal Amnesty, Galleria Made 21, Florence.
I love You, Galleria Il Ponte, Rome.
Chicago Art Fair, Chicago.
Chandelle verte, Gallerie Vinciana, Eos, Milenium, Milan.
Pro Natura, Lotta per gli indicatori ambientali, Biella.
Palazzo Lanfranchi, Pisa.
Museo De Pero, Rovereto.

Palazzo Ducale, Massa Carrara.
Palazzo Pretorio, Certaldo.
White Plastic Flight, Santa Maria degli Angeli/ Chiostro del Brunelleschi, Florence.
Crackingmaremuore, Mole Vanvitelliana, Ancona.
40x40, Galleria Eva Menzio, Turin.
Galleria Continua, San Gimignano.
Arroccamenti, Rocca stellata, Bondeno.
Centro polifunzionale Giovanni Arpino, Bra.
Ritorno al mare, Omaggio a Pino Pascali, Polignano.
Art Energie, Paris.

1993
L'arca, Galleria Melesi, Lecco.
Fortezza da Basso, Florence.
Accademia di Belle Arti Carrara, Bergamo.
Biennale internazionale, Fine Art Museum, Taipei.
La ragione trasparente, Galleria EOS, Milan.
Palazzo La Marmora, Biella.
Indian Stories, Galleria Cavellini, Brescia.
Scuderie di palazzo Ruspoli, Rome.

1992
Arte fiera 92, Studio Cavalieri, Bologna.
Studio Soligo, Rome.
Alle origini della materia, Galleria La Polena, Genova.
Fortezza da Basso, Florence.
Art Basel 92, Galleria La Polena, Genova.
Paraxo 92, Castello di Andora, Savona.
Green Pyramid, Raffineria SARAS, Cagliari.
SOS, Galleria Gian Enzo Sperone, Rome.
Internazionale di Bergamo, Galleria Melesi e Rino Costa, Bergamo.

1991
La piramide d'oro, Galleria la Polena, Genova.
Museo civico, Palazzo Lomellini, Carmagnola.
Galleria Piero Cavellini, Brescia.
Galleria Massimo Minini, Brescia.
Art 91, Galleria La Polena, Basilea.
Agravitazionale, Palazzo dei Diamanti, Ferrara.
Casa della Cultura, Bellreguard.

1990
Studio Cavalieri, Bologna.
La piramide d'oro, ghiacciai del Monte Bianco, Aosta.
Sala chierici e Bastioni ex Forte Spagnolo, L'Aquila.
Agravitazionale, Palazzo Farnese, Ortona.

1989
Mutazioni genetiche, Reggia di Caserta, Caserta.
Galleria Murnik, Milan.
La notte dei poeti, Teatro Romano di Nora, Cagliari.

Chris Cunningham

1970, born in Reading.
Lives and works in London.

Solo Exhibitions

2001
Chris Cunningham: flex, De Vleeshal Kunsthalle, Middelburg.

2000
Chris Cunningham, Anthony d'Offay Gallery, London.

Group Exhibitions

2001
Sur Face, edited by P. Kyander, Lunds Kunsthalle, Sweden.

2000
Apocalypse, edited by N. Rosenthal and M. Wigram, Royal Academy, London.
Exit, edited by S. Morgan, Chisenhale Gallery, East London.

1999
Video Vibe: Art, Music and Video in the UK, edited by C. Perrella, The British School in Rome.

Music videos

1999
All is Full of Love (*Bjork*) - created and directed by Chris Cunningham. For this extraordinary video, Chris received four "Silver Awards" and the first 'Gold Award' ever given to a music video at the 2000 D&AD Awards. This video features Bjork as a stunning white robot making love to a replica of herself. This was also Chris Cunningham's last music video.

1998
Windowlicker (*Aphex Twin*) - created and directed by Chris Cunningham. Filmed in LA, this video is the sequel to *Come to Daddy*. Awarded 'The Best Alternative Video of the Year' at the 2000 CAD Awards. Chris also received two 'Silver Awards' at the D&AD Awards.
Frozen (*Madonna*) - created and directed by Chris Cunningham.
The first video from Ray of Light album, set in the Mojave desert.

1997
Only You (*Portishead*) - created and directed by Chris Cunningham.
This striking video features a little boy rolling and swimming under water trying to reach the surface. Chris received the Best Dance Video of 1998 at the CADS Awards and a Silver Award at the 1999 D&AD Awards.

Come to Daddy (*Aphex Twin*) - created and directed by Chris Cunningham. For his work on *Come to Daddy*, Chris received the MCM Grand Prix du Jury 1997, three separate awards, Best Video, Best Cinematography and Best Editing at the 1997 Creative and Design Awards, held by Music Week. He also received two Silver Pencils Awards at the 1998 D&AD Awards.

Josef Dabernig

1956, born in Kötschach-Mauthen, Austria.
Lives and works in Vienna.

Solo Exhibitions

1997
Berlinführer, Künstlerhaus Bethanien, Berlin.

1996
Neue Galerie am Landesmuseum Joanneum, Graz.

1994
Galeria Potocka, Cracow.

1993
Atelier beim Ambrosi-Museum, Österreichische Galerie Belvedere, Vienna.
Kärntner Landesgalerie, Klagenfurt.

1992
Wiener Secession, Vienna.

Group Exhibitions and Film screenings

2001
False Start, spring thesis exhibition, Center for Curatorial Studies, Bard College, New York.
14. Stuttgarter Filmwinter.
Avanguardia nel presente, Museo Laboratorio di Arte Contemporanea, Università degli Studi di Rome, Rome.

2000
the big screen, Stadtkino, Vienna.
34th New York EXPOsition of Short Film and Video.
10a Semana de Cine Experimental, Madrid.
Les rumeurs urbaines/Urban Rumors, Fri-Art, Fribourg.
Manifesta 3, Ljubljana.
Delay, Forum Stadtpark, Graz.
29th International Film Festival Rotterdam.
living inside – subjektive räume/private dimensionen, Technische Universität Wien, edited by Matthias Michalka/Josef Dabernig).
viatico di arte e critica # 1, Galleria Change, Rome.

1999
translocation (new) media/art, Generali Foundation, Vienna.

1998
interim, Mecklenburgisches Künstlerhaus Schloß Plüschow.

1997
Presently, Galerie Menotti, Baden.

1996
Jenseits von Kunst, Ludwig Museum, Budapest / Neue Galerie am Landesmuseum Joanneum, Graz.

1994
Lokalzeit - Wiener Material im Spiegel des Unbehagens, Raum.
Strohal, Vienna / Moderna Galerija-Museum of Modern Art, Ljubljana / Fondazione Querini Stampalia, Venice.

1993
making art, Kunstverein für Kärnten, Klagenfurt.

1992
Drei scultori viennesi, Sala 1, Rome.

Films

2001
WARS, 16 mm, black and white, 11 min.

2000
JOGGING, 35mm, color, 11 min, music: Olga Neuwirth.

1998
TIMAU, 16 mm, black and white, 20 min, with Markus Scherer.

1996
WISLA, 16 mm, black and white, 8 min.

1994
GEHFILMEN 6, 16 mm, black and white, 17 min, with Thomas Baumann/Martin Kaltner.
Films distributed by sixpackfilm, Vienna

Bibliography

2000
Les rumeurs urbaines/Urban Rumors, edited by Hans Ulrich Obrist for Fri-Art, Fribourg and ACTAR/arc en rêve centre d'architecture, Bordeaux.
Manifesta 3 - European Biennal of Contemporary Art, text by F. Bonami, O. Bouman, M. Hlavajová, K. Rhomberg a.o., Ljubljana.
Avanguardia nel presente, text by Domenico Scudero, Lithos editrice, Rome, p. 141.

1998
interim, text by P. Funken a.o., Künstlerhaus Schloß Plüschow, pp. 28-31.
Be Magazin, Künstlerhaus Bethanien, Berlin, pp. 94-95.
Transparent 1988 11/12, edited by G. Feuerstein, text by G. Held, E. Köb, Manuskripte für Architektur, Theorie, Umraum, Kunst, Wien, pp. 37-46.

1997
Jenseits von Kunst, edited by P. Weibel/Neue Galerie Graz, Passagen-Verlag, Vienna, S 325.
Opening - Periodico di Arte Contemporanea, text by C. Kravagna, XI, 30, Progetto Città, Rome, pp. 29-33.

1996
Co wlasciwie sprawia, ze dzisiejsze miasta sa tak odmienne, tak seksy? - Just what is it, that makes today's cities so different, so sexy?, text by G. Gawlik, J. Ladnowska, Panstwowa Galeria Sztuki, Lodz.
Dabernig, J., *Montage-System*, Neue Galerie am Landesmuseum Joanneum, Graz, text: Günther Holler-Schuster.
TUMULT 12, edited by Maria Anna Potocka, Cracow, pp. 36-41.

1995
Dabernig, J., Salle de Bal - Institut Francais de Vienne, Vienna, text by A. Spiegl.
Dabernig, J., *2x2x6 3x12+3x10 11+2x12+3x10*, text by C. Kravagna, Atelier beim Ambrosi-Museum, Österreichische Galerie Belvedere, Vienna.
making art, text by C. Kravagna, G. Schöllhammer, Kunstverein für Kärnten, Klagenfurt.
Dabernig, J., *4x6+3x3+2x2+1=38*, text by A. Rohsmann, L. Safred, Kärntner Landesgalerie, Klagenfurt.

1992
Dabernig, J., *Wiener Secession, Wien*, text by C. Kravagna, A. Krischanitz.
"Drei" scultori viennesi, text by B. Schmidt, Sala 1, Rome.

1990
2x2x6, text by J. Dabernig, Projektraum Wien, WUK, Vienna.

Raffaello D'Andrea

Raffaello D'Andrea is a professor at Cornell University specializing in Control of Complex Systems. He is a leading scholar in this area, with many honors and awards to his name, including several best paper awards at national and international conferences. In the last five years, he has given over forty invited talks at national and international universities, companies, research labs and research agencies, and published over forty research papers. He is also the manager and supervisor of the Cornell RoboCup team, the two time international Robot Soccer champions (1999 Sweden and 2000). He has appeared with the Cornell RoboCup team on Scientific American Frontiers (1999), the Lemelson Center at the Smithsonian in Washington, D.C. (1999), the Tech Museum of Innovation in San Jose, California (2001), and will be featured on an upcoming episode of Scientific American Frontiers on games and competitions (2001). His current research projects include control of autonomous airplane formations, high performance control of autonomous flying vehicles, adaptive optics control for high performance telescopes, and cooperative control of autonomous vehicles in uncertain environments.

Max Dean
1949, born in Leeds.
Lives and works in Toronto.

Solo Exhibitions

2000
Any Moment, Susan Hobbs Gallery, Toronto.

1996
As Yet Untitled, Art Gallery of Ontario, Toronto.

1992
Skins, Georgian College, Barrie, Ontario.

Group Exhibition

2001
Quality Control, Site Gallery, Sheffield.

2000
Canadian Stories, Ydessa Hendeles Art Foundation, Toronto October 28, 2000 - June 2002.
The Fifth Element, Kunsthalle, Düsseldorf.
Umedalen Skulptur 2000, Umea.
Voici, 100 ans d'art contemporain, Palais des Beaux-Arts de Bruxelles.

1999
Still Life, York Quay Gallery, Toronto.
dAPERTutto, La Biennale di Venezia, 48. Esposizione Internazionale d'Arte, Venice.

1996
Prospect 96, Frankfurter Kunstverein, Frankfurt.

1994
Three Small Rooms, The MacLaren Art Centre, Barrie.

1992
Masks and Metaphor, The MacLaren Art Centre, Barrie, Ontario.

Localmotive, Toronto.

1991
Storefront Installation, 31 Maple Avenue, Barrie, Ontario.

1989
Luminous Sites, Or Gallery, Vancouver.
Gardens, Artscourt, Ottawa.

1987
Memory/Souvenir, The Festival of Arts, Ottawa.

1986
Artist-in Residence (1985-86 Program), The National Museum of Science and Technology, Ottawa.

1983
O'Kanada, Academie der Kunste, Berlin.
The Berlin Project, The Montreal Museum of Fine Arts.

1980
Pluralities, The National Gallery of Canada, Ottawa.
Compass Winnipeg: Artists as Printmakers, Harbourfront Art Gallery, Toronto.

1979
Form and Performance, The Winnipeg Art Gallery.

1978
Obsessions, Rituals, Controls, The Norman Mackenzie Art Gallery, Regina.

1977
Sculpture on the Prairies, The Winnipeg Art Gallery.
Artists' Prints and Multiples, The Winnipeg Art Gallery.
True Confections, The Burnaby Art Gallery.

1976
The Mid-Western 1976, The Winnipeg Art Gallery.
Mosaicart, Cultural Olympics, Montreal.

1975
Royal Horse's Mouth Piece, The Dandelion Gallery, Calgary.

1974
SCAN (Survey of Canadian Art Now), The Vancouver Art Gallery.

1973
Pacific Vibrations, The Vancouver Art Gallery.

Events

1982
The National Gallery of Canada, Ottawa.
1981
Pass It On. An installation of Performance organized by *Parachute*, revue d'art contemporaion Inc., Montreal. Drummond Medical Building, Montreal.

1980
A, B, ou C, The Montreal Museum of Fine Arts.
11e Biennale de Paris, Musée d'art moderne de la ville de Paris.

1979
Untitled, The Living Art Performance Festival, Vancouver.
Thirty Minute Sketch, The Norman Mackenzie Art Gallery.

1978
Room 321, A Collective Work with the Students of the University of Ottawa.
Performance Festival, The Montreal Museum of Fine Arts.

1977
Two Hands for CAR, CAR Miniature Show, Fleet Gallery, Winnipeg.
Drawing Event, The Winniopeg Art Gallery.
Max Dean: A Work, The Winnipeg Art Gallery.

1976
ART (A Snow Sculpture), The Ottawa River Parkway, Ottawa.

1975
To Be Read As It Is (Billboard), Near the intersection of Georgia and Denman Streets, Vancouver.

1973
Large Yellow Duck, Lost Lagoon, Stanley Park, Vancouver.

Bibliography

2001
Gabrielle Mark, L.G., "Button Pusher", *Canadian Art*, 18, 1, Spring/March, p. 54-59.

2000
Harten, J., *Das fünfte Element - Geld oder Kunst*, Kunsthalle Düsseldorf, Düsseldorf.
de Duve, T., *Voici 100 ans d'art contemporain*, Palais des Beaux-Arts, Brussels.

1999
Szeemann, H., *dAPERTutto*, La Biennale di Venezia 48ª Esposizione Internazionale d'Arte, Venice.

1997
Kirby, W., *Sculpture on the Prairies*, The Winnipeg Art Gallery, Winnipeg.
Miller, E., "Max Dean", *Parachute*, 86, Spring.
Nemeczek, A., "Und Noch Immer Erwweitert Sich Der Kunstbegriff", *Art Das Kunstmagazin*, 6, p. 48-50.

1996
Weiermair, P., *Prospect 96*, Franfurter Kunstvereins, Frankfurt.
Mason, J., "Selection Necessary", *C International Contemporary Art*, 51, October-December, p. 20-25.
Dault, G.M., "Mixed Media", *Canadian Art*, 13, 2, Summer, p. 77.
Spring, J., "Photo Finish", *Art+Text*, 54, p. 74-75.
Herholzier, M., "Fotographie Als Hohe Kunst Der Inszenierung", *Frankfurter Allgemeine*, March 10.
Gopnik, B., "Sacrificial Icons Led To The Shredder", *The Globe and Mail*, Toronto, July 27.

1994
Bradley, J., Johnstone, L. (editors), *Sightlines. Reading Contemporary Canadian Art*, Artexte Editions, Montreal.

1986
Augaitis, D., Henry, K., *Luminous Sites*, , Video Inn/The Western Front, Vancouver.

1982
Théberge, P., *Okanada*, Akademie der Kunste, Berlin.

1981
Pontbriand, C. (editor), *Performance Text(e)s & Documents*, Parachute, Montreal.
"Max Dean: Made to Measure", *Impressions*, 27.

1980
Holmes, W., *Pluralities*, The National Gallery of Canada, Ottawa.

1979
McKibbon, M., *Form and Performance*, The Winnipeg Art Gallery, Winnipeg.
Fry, P., "Max Dean", *Parachute*, 14, Spring.
Payant, R., "Notes sur la Performance", *Parachute*, 14, Spring.

1978
Froelich, P., "Blurbs: Performance Festival - The Montreal Musueum of Fine Arts",

Parachute, 12, Autumn.
Racine, R., "Festival de Performances du M.B.A.M.", *Parachute*, 13, Winter.

1975
Grayson, J., *Sound Sculpture*, A.R.C. Press, Vancouver.

Lucinda Devlin
1947, born in Ann Harbor, Michigan.
Lives and works in Hattiesburg, MS.

Solo Exhibitions

2001
The Omega Suites, Ludwig Museum im Deutscherrenhaus, Koblenz.
Lucinda Devlin, Other Series: Corporal Arenas, Habitats and Water Rites, Fotografie Bochum.

2000
The Omegas Suites und *Water Rites*, daadgalerie, Berliner Künstlerprogramm.
The Omega Suites, Paul Rodgers/9W, New York.

1999
The Omega Suites, in der Austellung *Räume*, mit Candida Höfer und Andreas Gursky, Kunsthaus Bregenz, Austria (catalogue).
Erpis Gallery, Tokyo.
Photo Gallery of Naniwa, Osaka.

1998
Un-Räume, The Omega Suites und weitere Photographien aus den Serien Pleasure Ground und Corporal Arenas, m Fotografie Bochum.

1995
The Omega Suites, Fotofe '95, Aberdeen Art Gallery and Museum, Schotland Invited Artist.
Stills Gallery, Edinburgh.

1993
The Omega Suites, Tartt Gallery, Washington D.C.; Gallery TPW, Toronto; The Photographer's Gallery, Saskatoon, Kanada; Blue Sky Gallery, Portland.

1992
The Omega Suites, Menschel Gallery, Syracuse.

1990
Fotografias, Centro Colombo Americano, Medellin, Kolumbien, Ausst.-Tournee.

1987
Pleasure Ground, Northlight Gallery, Arizona State University, Tempe.

1985
Pleasure Ground, with John Orentlicher, Lightwork Gallery, Syracuse.

1982
Chicago Center for Contemporary Photography, Chicago.

Group Exhibitions

2001
SHELTER, Bochum Kunstvermittlung.
In a Lonely Place, National Museum of Photography, Film & Television, GB-Bradford.

2000
Katastrophen und Desaster. Das Jahrhundert am Ende, Museum Folkwang Essen.
Landschaft in der zeitgenössischen Fotografie. Aus der Sammlung der DG Bank.
Landesmuseum Oldenburg, Schloss und Augusteum.

1998-99
Under/Exposed, Stockholm Underground, Stockholm.

1996
Discipline and Photography, The Peace Museum, Chicago, Il.
Photography In the 1990's, Wright State University Art Galleries, Dayton.
Macht/OnMacht, Internationaal Cultureel Centrum, Antwerpen.

1995
Meta/Physics: Crossing Boundaries in Contemporary Photography, DePree Art Center and Gallery, Hope College, Holland, MI.
Crimes and Punishments, Philadelphia Art Alliance, in conjunction with "Prison Sentences", PA.

1994
Evidence of Death: Andres Serrano, Sophie Calle, Lucinda Devlin, James VanderZee, The Light Factory, Charlotte.

1992
Medicine Body, University Galleries, Illinois State University, Bloomington.
Murder As Phenomena, SF Camerawork, San Francisco.

1991
Myth, Spirituality and Culture, College Art Gallery, SUNY New Paltz.

1989
Photograph As Document, Downey Museum of Art, Downey.

1987
Photo Environments: Real and Imagined, University of Northern Iowa Gallery of Art, Cedar Falls.
American Color, New Mexico State University Art Gallery, Las Cruces. Ausst.-Tournee.

1986
New Developments, Contemporary American Photography, Louis K. Meisel Gallery, New York.
Personification of Space: Lucinda Devlin and Michelle Van Parys, Light Factory, Charlotte.

1985
Lightwork, Photography Over the 70's and 80's, Everson Museum, Syracuse, Featured Artist (Catalogue).

1982
CAPS Photography Award Show, Nikon House Gallery, New York.
Everson Biennial, Everson Museum of Art, Syracuse.

1976
How America Lives, Midtown Y Gallery, New York.
Americana, Creative Eye Photo Gallery, Los Angeles.
Photography and Language, Camerawork Gallery, San Francisco.

Bibliography

2001
In a Lonely Place, exhibition catalogue, National Museum of Photography, Film & Television, Bradford.

2000
Katastrophen und Desaster - Das Jahrhundert am Ende, text by M. Vignold, *Künstliche Höllen*, Catalogue-beitrag zu *Lucinda Devlin, The Omega Suites*, Museum Folkwang Essen.
Lucinda Devlin, The Omega Suites, edited by Susanne Breidenbach, text by B. Rose, *Clean Death/ Der Saubere Tod*, daad Galerie, Berliner Künstler-programm und Museum Ludwig im Deutschherrenhaus, Koblenz, exhibition catalogue.

1999
European Photography, 64/65, Göttingen, März.
Räume. Lucinda Devlin, Andreas Gursky, Candida Höfer, text by U. Erdmann Ziegler, *The Omega Suite: Mit dem Töten zu leben*, exhibition catalogue, Kunsthaus Bregenz, Bregenz.
auch in: *Ulf Erdmann Ziegler, Foto-*

grafische Werke, DuMont, Koln.

1998
Hitchens, C., "Scenes From An Execution", *Vanity Fair*, Januar.
Contact Sheet 25th Anniversary Edition Book, Lightwork, Syracuse.

1997
"Death's Doors", *Time Magazine*, 16, june.
"Amerika", *Arbeiter Fotografie*, Köln, Sommer.

1996
Photography In The 1990's, exhibition catalogue, Wright State, CD Rom Catalogue, Dayton.
Macht/OnMacht, exhibition catalogue, Internationaal Cultureel Centrum, Antwerpen, Belgien.
Discipline And Photography, exhibition catalogue, The Peace Museum, Chicago.

1995
META/PHYSICS: Crossing Boundaries in Contemporary Photography, exhibition catalogue, DePree Art Center and Gallery, Holland, MI.
fotofeis, InternationalFestival of Photography in Scotland, Aberdeen, October.
Portfolio, Feature and review, The Catalogue of Contemporary Photography in Britain, 22.

1994
"Lucinda Devlin: The Omega Suites", *Creative Camera Magazine*, February.

1993
Hlynsky, D., "The Authority Of Silence-Lucinda Devlin's Omega Suites", *Black Flash*, 11, 3.

1992
The Omega Suites, #29, exhibition catalogue, Menschel Gallery, Syracuse.
"Murder As Phenomena", *Camerawork*, San Francisco, 19, 2, Herbst.

1990
"Nature vs Human Nature", *Views*, TPW, 7, 1, February.

1987
American Color, exhibition catalogue, New Mexico State University, Las Cruces.

1985
Lightwork, Photography Over The 70's And 80's, exhibition catalogue, Lightwork, Syracuse.

1979
CAPS Visual Artists Catalog, exhibition catalogue, New York State Council on the Arts.

Rineke Dijkstra
1959, born in Sittard, the Netherlands. Lives and works in Amsterdam.

Solo Exhibitions

2001
Israel Portraits, Herzliya Museum of Art, Herzliya, Israel.
Focus: Rineke Dijkstra, The Art Institute, Chicago.

2000
Anthony d'Offay Gallery, London.
Marian Goodman Gallery, New York.

1999
Portraits, DAAD Gallerie, Berlin.
The Herzliya Museum of Art, Herzliya, Israel.
The Buzzclub, Liverpool/Mysteryworld, Zaandam, MACBA, Barcelona.
Anthony d'Offay Gallery, London.
Anne Frank Museum, Amsterdam.

1998
Menschenbilder, Folkwang Museum, Essen and Galerie der Hochschule fur Grafik und Buchkunst, Leipzig.
Museum Boymans van Beuningen, Rotterdam.
About the World, Sprengel Museum, Hannover.

1997
Location, The Photographer's Gallery, London.
Galerie Mot & Van den Boogaard, Brussels.

1996
Le Consortium, Dijon.
Galerie Sabine Schmidt, Cologne.
Galerie Bob van Orsouw, Zurich.
Galerie Paul Andriesse, Amsterdam.

1995
Stedelijk Museum Bureau Amsterdam, with Tom Claassen.
Time Festival, Rineke Dijkstra, with Hugo Debaere, Museum of Contemporary Art, Gent.

1994
Amstelveen Art Encouragement Award, Aemstelle, Amstelveen.

1988
The Creation of Form, de Moor, Amsterdam.

1984
Paradiso Portraits, de Moor, Amsterdam.

Group Exhibitions

2001
At Sea, Tate Liverpool.
Uniform - ordine e disordine, Pitti Immagine, Florence.

2000
Eurovision, The Saatchi Gallery, London.
Interventions. New Art in Unconventional Spaces, Milwaukee Art Museum, Milwaukee.
Let's Entertain, Walker Arts Center, Minneapolis; Portland Art Museum, Portland; Centre Georges Pompidou, Paris; Museo Rufino Tamayo, Mexico City; Miami Art Museum, Miami.
Breathless! Photography and Time, V & A, London.
How to look at it. Fotografien des 20. Jahrhunderts, Sprengel Museum, Hannover.
Presumed Innocent, Capc, Mus,e d'Art Contemporain de Bordeaux.
Museum Boymans van Beuningen, Rotterdam.
CLOSE UP, Kunstverein Freiburg im Marienbad and Kunsthaus Baselland, touring to Kunstverein Hannover 2001.
Photocollection Elton John, The High Museum of Art, Atlanta.
Performing Bodies, Tate Modern, London.
World without End - photography and the twentieth century, Art Gallery of New South Wales, Sydney.

1999
The Citibank Private Bank Photography Prize, The Photographer's Gallery, London.
Modern Starts: People, Places, Things, The Museum of modern Art, New York.
Macht und Fürsorge: Das Bild der Mutter in der zeitgenössischen Kunst, Trinitatiskirche, Cologne.
L'Occidente Imperfetto, VIII Biennale Internationale di Fotografia, Palazzo Bricherasio, Turin.
Regarding Beauty in Performance and The Media Arts, Hirshhorn Museum and Sculpture Garden.

1998
Sightings, New Photography Art, ICA, London.
Wounds, Between democracy and redemption in contemporary art, Moderna Museet, Stockholm.
Rineke Dijkstra, Tracy Moffat, Fiona Tan, Museum van HedendaagseKunst, Gent.

XXIv Bienal Internacional de San Paulo, San Paulo, Brasil.
Berlin, Berlin, Berlin Bienale.
Global Vision, New Art from the 90's, Part III, Deste Foundation, Athens.

1997
Future, Present, Past, Corderie, La Biennale di Venezia, 42. Esposizione Internazionale d'Arte, Venice.
Work in Progress/Constructing Identity: Rineke Dijkstra, Wendy Ewald, Paul Seawright, Nederlands Foto Instituut, Rotterdam.
Rotterdam 97 Festival: Rineke Dijkstra, Nan Goldin, Mike Kelly, Sharon Lockhart, Museum Boymans van Beuningen, Rotterdam.
New Photography 13, The Museum of Modern Art, New York.

1996
Prospect 96, Schirn Kunsthalle, Frankfurt am Main.
Fotofiction, exhibition catalogue, Kasseler Kunstverein, Kassel.
100 foto's uit de collectie, exhibition catalogue, Stedelijk Museum, Amsterdam.
Zeitgenossische Fotokunst aus den Niederlanden, exhibition catalogue, NBK, Berlin and Badischer, Kunstverein Karlsruhe.

1995
The European Face, Talbot Rice Gallery, Edinburgh.

1994
De ander, der Andere, l'autre, Het Domein, Sittard and Ludwig Forum fur Internationale Kunst, Aachen.

1993
The Power of Present, Loods 6, Amsterdam.

Bibliography

2000
Darwent, C., "Eurovision", *The Independent on Sunday*, January 9.
Dorment, R., "Modern-day monuments", *The Daily Telegraph*, January 19.
Grant, S., "A vision with no focus, Eurovision", *Evening Standard*, January 20.
Lutyens, D., "Snap ruling", *The Times*, February 5.
Andrews, M., "Eurovision", *Contemporary Visual Arts*, 28.
Belcove, J.L., "Lens Crafters", *W*, May.
Sumpter, H., "miss frisbee", *i-D*, June.
Darwent, C., "Eurovision", *The Independent on Sunday*, January 9.
Dorment, R., "Modern-day monuments", *The Daily Telegraph*, January 19.

Grant, S., "A vision with no focus, Eurovision", *Evening Standard*, January 20.
Lutyens, D., "Snap ruling", *The Times*, February 5.
Andrews, M., "Eurovision", *Contemporary Visual Arts*, 28. Belcove, J.L., "Lens Crafters", *W*, May.
Sumpter, H., "miss frisbee", *i-D*, June.

1999
Searle, A., "Every picture tells a porkie", *The Guardian*, March 2.
Wieder, A.J., "Fleeding Portraits", *Frieze*, May.
Schmitz, E., "The Citibank Private Bank Photography Prize 1999", *Contemporary Visual Arts*, 23.

1998
Lyle, P., "One night in 1994, a Dutch artist called Rineke Dijkstra...", *The Face*, March.
Wahjudi, C., "Sightings. New Photographic Art", *Kunstforum*, July-September.

1997
Lamoree, J., "De jeugd van tegenwoordig, een avondje uit met Rineke Dijkstra", *Het Parool*, August 29.
Dik, I., "Chaos en toeval bepalen het lot", *Vrij Nederland*, August 30.
Van Dijck, R., "Resultaten van Photowork(s) in Progress", *Foto*, September.
Marsman, E., "Carrousel aan identiteiten gevangen door de camera", *NRC Handelsblad*, September 6.
Haytema, A., "De onzekerheid belicht van pubers in de disco", *De Volkskrant*, September 24.
Thijssen, M., "Photowork(s) in Progress", *Het Financieele Dagblad*, September 27.
Neefjes, A., "Betrapte onhandigheid", *Vrij Nederland*, October 4.
Bracewell, M., "Costume Dramas", *The Independent Saturday Magazine*, November 22.
Schube, I., "Photowork(s) in Progress", *Photonews*, December/January.
Geerling, J., "Children of Chaos", *Metropolis M*, 6.
Catalogue, The Photographer's Gallery, London.
Januszczak, W., "Baring witness to a truth made flesh", *The Sunday Times*, December 14.
Haase, J., "If you're now looking at a picture of your son, you might like to know he's an icon of Modern Art", *Daily Liverpool Post*, December 19.
Haase, J., "Boy from gallery tracked down, thanks to the Post", *Daily Liverpool Post*, December 22.

1996
Prospect 96. Photographie in der Gegenwartskunst, catalogue, Frankfurter

Kunstverein, Frankfurt am Main.
Gynaika, catalogue, Cultureel Centrum Knokke, Belgium.
Fotofiktion, catalogue, Kasseler Kunstverein, Kassel.
Zeitgenossische Fotokunst aus den Niederlanden, catalogue, Neuer Berliner Kunstverein.
Thijssen, M., "Prospect 96 blijft overeind dankzij thematische ordening", Het Financleete Dagblad.
Thijsen, M., *Le printemps de Cahors, Photographie & Arts Visuels*, catalogue, June.
Wauters, C., "Prospect 96", *Art Press*, 214, June.
Ollier, B., "6eme Printemps de Cahors, Photographie & Arts Visuels", *Liberation*, June 26.
Vogele, C., "Rineke Dijkstra in der Galerie Bob van Orsouw", *Das Kunst-Bulletin*, 9, September.
Maurer, S., "Zwischen Magie und Sachlichkeit", *Tages-Anzeiger*, Zurich, September 9.
Volkart, Y., "Nackte Identitat", *Annabelle*, 16/96.
Lindo, M.A., "Ik zie meteen een Botticelli voor me, de fotocollectie van het Stedelijk", *Het Parool*, September 14.
Steiner, J., "Suche nach Wurde - Fotografie von Rineke Dijkstra in Zurich", *Neue Bildende Kunst*, May.
Schwartz, I., "Lolita's uit Liverpoolse disco", De Volkskrant, Coleur Locale, October 30.
Catalogue, *Habitus*, Galerie Fotohof Salzburg, September.
Haak, B.van der, "Fotografe Rineke Dijkstra 'Iedereen is alleen'", *Elle*, November.
Singels, H., "Fotograferen op het strand", *Kunstschrift*, 4.
100 foto's uit de collectie van het Stedelijk Museum, catalogue, Stedelijk Museum, Amsterdam.
Lutticken, S., "Lichaamstaal in de Engelse disco", *Het Parool*, November 1.
Stigter, B., "Rineke Dijkstra", *NRC Handelsblad*, November 1.
Catalogue, *Rineke Dijkstra, Beaches*, Codax Publisher, Zurich.
Blindspot Photography, 8.

1995
Schwartz, I., "Meedogenloze camera van Rineke Dijkstra", *De Volkskrant*, January.
Seelig, T., "Rineke Dijkstra", *Pakt*, 5, January/February.
"Rineke Dijkstra's Wall Street", *Vrij Nederland*, 6, February 11.
Berg, M.v.d., Wallroth, T., *Wim Janssen, Rineke Dijkstra, Jan Koster*, ultgave Galerie Paul Andriesse, May.
Wilson, M., "Rineke Dijkstra", Stedelijk Museum Bureau, *Flash Art*, March/April.
"Rineke Dijkstra", *5 Fotos*, 3, 2.

Groot, P, "De geboorte van een nieuwe muze. Bij de foto's van Rineke Dijkstra", *Metropolis M*, 2, April.
Leenheer, I., "De naakte man", *Elle*, April.
Lamoree, J., "De manipulators", *Het Parool*, April 15.
Hemmerechts, K., "Het taboe van het hoogstpersoonlijke", *Vrij Nederland*, 21, May 27.
Vlinderslag, *Het Parool*, August 16.
Boecker, S., "Art Cologne, Angebot grosser denn je", *Kolner Stadt Anzeiger*, 267, November 17.
Scherphulus, A., "Verkracht voor Volk en Vaterland", *Vrij Nederland*, 48, December 2.
Zoetendaal, W.v., "Rineke Dijkstra/Jacob Molenhuis", *Het Parool*, December 21.
Catalogue, Vlinderslag, Beeldende Kunst in het Zuiderbad.
Catalogue, *The European Face, Portrait Photography from the Fifteen Member States of the European Union*.
Catalogue, *A Europa e o Mar, Encontros da Imagen*, Braga, Portugal.
Gkf 50 jaar, exhibition catalogue, fotografie 1994-1995.
Catalogue, *Stofgoud*, Jacob Molenhuis/Rineke Dijkstra.

1994
Steenbergen, R., "Eenzaamheid vastgelegd in een moment voor de camera", *NRC Handelsblad*, July 18.
Catalogue, Visser, H., "De ander, der Andere, l'autre", *Werner Mantz Award*, October.
Visser, H., "Rineke Dijkstra", *Nieuwsbrief Stedelijk Museum Bureau Amsterdam*, 10, December.
Koemans, M., "Lachen is niet Interessant", *Het Parool*, December 17.
Haveman, M., "Het bijzondere van het gewone", *Vrij Nederland*, 51-52, December 24.
Berg, M.v.d., Wallroth, T., "Rineke Dijkstra", *Rulmte*, 3/4.
Vos, J.D., "Rineke Dijkstra", *Nogal onfatsoenlijk maar zeker verleidelijk*, December.
Coelewij, L., "Rineke Dijkstra/Tom Claassen", *Stedelijk Museum Bulletin*, December.

1993
"Fotofestival Naarden", *Trouw*, May 13.
Morrien, A., Aarsman, H., "Bij de Vloedlijn, Strandportretten van Rineke Dijkstra", *Vrij Nederland*, 19, May 15.
"De kracht van Heden", *The Netherlands Foundation of Fine Arts, Design and Architecture*, May.
Catalogue, *Fotofestival Naarden*, May.

Stan Douglas

1960, born in Vancouver.
Lives and works in Vancouver.

Solo Exhibitions

2001
Stan Douglas, Kunsthalle Basel, Basel.
Stan Douglas, Winnipeg Art Gallery, Winnipeg, Canada.
La Biennale di Venezia. 48. Esposizione Internazionale d'Arte, Venice.
Stan Douglas: Le Detroit, Neue Gesellschaft für bildende Kunst, Berlin, Germany, Summer.

2000
Stan Douglas: Le Detroit, Art Gallery of Windsor, Ontario.
Stan Douglas: Le Detroit, Art Institute of Chicago.

Filmography

1999/2000,
Le Detroit, 35 mm film installation for two 35 mm film projectors, looping device, anamorphic lens, one screen, Dimensions vary with installation, Edition 1/3.

Bibliography

2000
Enwezor, O., *Stan Douglas, Le Detroit*, exhibition brochure, The Art Insitute of Chicago, 20 September (text and illustrations).

Atom Egoyan

1960, born in Cairo.
Lives and works in Toronto.

Filmography

2001
Ararat, in production with Serendipity Point Films.

2000
Krapp's last tape, 65 min., 35 mm, colour, Dolby Digital.
The line, 4 min, 35 mm, colour, made for the 25th Anniversary of the Toronto International Film Festival.

1998
Felicia's journey, 120 min., 35 mm, colour, Dolby Digital, Cinemascope.

1996
The sweet Hereafter, 100 min., 35mm, colour, Dolby Digital, Cinemascope.
Sarabande, 60 min, 16 mm, colour.

1995
Portrait of arshile, 4 min., 35 mm, colour.

1994
Exotica, 104 min., 35 mm, colour, Dolby Stereo.

1993
Gross misconduct, 120 min., 16 mm, colour, CBC.
Calendar, 75 min., 16 mm, colour.

1992
Montreal vu par, episode 4; *En Passant*, 20 min., 35 mm, colour, Dolby Stereo.

1991
The Adjuster, 102 min., 35 mm, colour, dolby stereo, Cinemascope.

1989
Speaking parts, 92 min., 35 mm, colour.

1988
Looking for nothing, 30 min., 16 mm, colour.

1987
The Final Twist, 30 min., 16 mm, colour.
Family Viewing, 86 min., 16 mm, colour.

1985
In this corner, 60 min., 16 mm, colour.
Next of kin, 72 min., 16 mm, colour.

1982
Open House, 25 min., 16 mm, colour.

1981
Peep Show, 7 min., 16 mm, black and white and colour.

1980
After Grad with Dad, 25 min. 16 mm, colour.

1979
Howard in particular, 14 min., 16 mm, black and white.

Theatre/opera/music

2001
Coke Machine Glow
Gord Downie solo album.
Collaboration and classical guitar on two songs.
Diaspora
Phillip on film.
Short film with music composed by Philip Glass.
To premiere at Lincoln Center in July.

1998
Elsewhereless
Premiere production of the opera by Rodney Sharman, libretto by Egoyan. Tapestry Music. World premiere, Buddies in Bad Times Theatre, Toronto, Spring. Remounted at the National Arts Centre, Ottawa, and the Vancouver Playhouse.
Dr. Ox's experiment
World premiere of the opera By Gavin Bryars, libretto by Blake Morrison. English National Opera, Summer.

1997
Bolex/Sextet
Collaboration with Nexus / Steve Reich, commissioned by Autumn Leaf Performance.
Live music/film projection piece. Walter Hall, Toronto.

1996-1997
Salome
Canadian Opera Company, Fall 1996.
Houston Grand Opera, Winter 1997.
Vancouver Opera, Fall 1997.
Canadian Opera Company remount, Winter 2002.

Installations

2002
Hors D'usage, Le Musée D'Art Contemporain de Montréal, Montreal.

2001
The origin of the non-descript, with G. James, The Power Plant, Toronto.
In Passing, White Box, New York.
Close, with J. Sarmento, La Biennale di Venezia, Venice.

1999
Evidence, Notorious: Alfred Hitchcock and Contemporary Art, Museum of Modern Art, Oxford.

1997
Early Development, Le Fresnoy, Tourcoing.
America, America, La Biennale di Venezia, Armenian Pavilion, Venice.

1996
Return To The Flock, Museum of Modern Art, Dublin.

Helmut Federle

1944, born in Solothurn.
Lives and works in Düsseldorf and Vienna.

Solo Exhibitions

2001
Jensen Gallery, Auckland.

1999

Kunsthaus Bregenz, Bregenz.
Galerie Max Hetzler, with Peter Zumthor, Berlin.

1998
Aargauer Kunsthaus Aarau, Aarau.
Staatliche Kunsthalle Karlsruhe, Karlsruhe.
IVAM Centre Julio González, Valencia.

1997
La Biennale di Venezia, Venice.

1995
Galerie nationale du Jeu de Paume, Paris.
Kunstmuseum Bonn, Bonn.

1994
Peter Blum, New York.

1993
Museum Fridericianum, Kassel.
Museum Folkwang, Essen.
Galerie nächst St. Stephan Rosemarie Schwarzwälder, Vienna.

1992
Kunsthalle Zürich, Zürich.
Moderna Museet Stockholm, Stockholm.
Galerie Durand-Dessert, Paris.

1991
Wiener Secession, Vienna.

1990
Barbara Gladstone Gallery, New York.

1989
Museum Haus Lange, Krefeld.
Kunsthalle Bielefeld, Bielefeld.
Kunstverein Hamburg, Hamburg.
Musée de Grenoble, Grenoble.

1985
Museum für Gegenwartskunst, Basel.
Haags Gemeentemuseum, Den Haag.

1984
The Living Art Museum, Reykjavik.

1983
Musée Cantonal des Beaux-Arts, Lausanne.
Musée d'Art et d'Histoire, Fribourg.

1979
Kunsthalle Basel, Basel.

Group Exhibitions

2001
Pleasures of Sight and States of Painting – Radical Abstract Painting since 1990, Museum of Fine Arts, Florida State University, Tallahassee.

Ornament und Abstraktion, Fondation Beyeler, Basel.
Abstraction: The Amerindian Paradigm, Palais des Beaux-Arts, Brussels; IVAM, Valencia.

2000
Body of Painting – Günter Umberg mit Bildern aus Kölner Sammlungen, Museum Ludwig, Cologne.
Das Gedächtnis der Malerei, Aargauer Kunsthaus Aarau, Aarau.

1999
'99 respektive '59 – Rücksicht auf 40 Jahre Kunst in der Schweiz, Aargauer Kunsthaus Aarau, Aarau.

1998
Im Reich der Zeichnung, Aargauer Kunsthaus Aarau, Aarau.
Das Jahrhundert der künstlerischen Freiheit, Wiener Secession, Wien.

1997
Abstraction/Abstractions, Musée d'Art Moderne, St. Etienne.
Voglio vedere le mie montagne - Die Schwerkraft der Berge 1774 -1997, Aargauer Kunsthaus Aarau, Aarau; KunstHalle Krems, Krems.
KünstlerInnen - 50 Positionen zeitgenössischer internationaler Kunst - Videoporträts und Werke, Kunsthaus Bregenz, Bregenz.

1996
Monochromie Geometrie, Sammlung Goetz, Munich.
Colour and Paint, Kunstmuseum St. Gallen, St. Gallen.
Chaos & Wahnsinn, Kunst Halle Krems, Krems.

1995
Meisterwerke aus dem Kupferstichkabinett Basel, Westfälisches Landesmuseum, Münster.

1994
Aura, Wiener Secession, Vienna.

1993
Der zerbrochene Spiegel, Messepalast and Kunsthalle Wien, Deichtorhallen Hamburg.
Equilibre, Aargauer Kunsthaus Aarau, Aarau.

1992
Geteilte Bilder - Das Diptychon in der neuen Kunst, Museum Folkwang, Essen.

1991
Extra Muros - Art Suisse Contemporain, Musée des Beaux-Arts, La Chaux-de-

Fonds; Musée d'Art Moderne, Saint-Etienne.

1990
Gegenwart Ewigkeit, Martin-Gropius-Bau, Berlin.

1989
Prospect 89, Frankfurter Kunstverein, Frankfurt am Main.
Bilderstreit, Museum Ludwig, Cologne.
256 Farben & Basics on Form. Werkdialoge zwischen Analogie und Widerspruch, Stiftung für konkrete und konstruktive Kunst, Zurich.

1988
The Biennial of Sydney, Sydney.
The Image of Abstraction, MOCA, Los Angeles.
Arbeit in Geschichte - Geschichte in Arbeit, Hamburger Kunstverein, Hamburg.

1986
Geometria Nova: Helmut Federle, John Armleder, Matt Mullican, Gerwald Rockenschaub, Kunstverein München, Munich.
The Spiritual in Art: Abstract Painting 1890–1985, Los Angeles County Museum of Art, Los Angeles; Museum of Contemporary Art, Chicago; Haags Gemeentemuseum, Den Haag.

1984
Zeichen, Fluten, Signale, Galerie nächst St. Stephan, Vienna.

Bibliography

2000
Ermen, R., "Helmut Federle: Personale", Kunsthaus Bregenz, *Kunstforum*, 150, April-Juni, p. 429.
Pühringer, A., "Helmut Federle, Kunsthaus Bregen", *frame*, 01, January-February, p. 129.

1999
Helmut Federle, texts by J. Yau, F. Schmatz, E. Samsonow, Kunsthaus Bregenz, Bregenz.

1998
Helmut Federle, texts by J.M. Bonet, D. Abadie, G. Boehm, IVAM Centre Julio González, Valencia, 1998.
Helmut Federle, Black Series I + II und Nachbarschaft der Farben, Aargauer, texts by B. Wismer, J. Jonas-Edel, J. Gachnang, Kunsthaus Aarau, Aarau.
Kuspit, D., "Helmut Federle", *Artforum International*, 3, p. 112.

1997

Gerold Wiederin, Helmut Federle, texts by J. Gachnang, Herzog & de Meuron, Nachtwallfahrtskapelle Locherboden (Tirol), edited by Kunsthaus Bregenz, Gerd Hatje Verlag, Stuttgart.
Helmut Federle, La Biennale di Venezia, Venice, texts by E. Franz, G. Boehm, G. Franck, chronology by J. Jonas-Edel, Lars Müller Verlag, Baden/Schweiz.
Wechsler, M., "Genauigkeit und Sehnsucht - Zur Malerei von Helmut Federle", *Noëma Artjournal*, 44, pp. 30-35.

1996
Ermen, R., "Helmut Federle – Kunstmuseum Bonn, 12.10.1995 – 21.1.1996", *Kunstforum International*, 133, Ruppichteroth, pp. 342-343.

1995
Helmut Federle, texts by K. Schrenk, E. Franz, M. Bockemühl, J. Jonas-Edel, Kunstmuseum Bonn, Bonn.
Helmut Federle, text by B. Ceysson, chronology by A. de Andrès, Galerie nationale du Jeu de Paume, Paris.
Königer, M., "Helmut Federle im Kunstmuseum Bonn und im Jeu de Paume, Paris", *Kunstbulletin*, 12, p. 29.

1994
Adolf Krischanitz, Helmut Federle, text by O. Kapfinger, Neue Welt Schule (Vienna/Leopoldstadt), edited by Kunsthaus Bregenz, Gerd Hatje, Stuttgart.

1993
Helmut Federle, texts by J. Jonas-Edel, F. Meschede, J. Yau, Galerie Franck + Schulte, Berlin.
Symbol Sinn Struktur - Helmut Federle - Zwei Räume und eine Intervention in der Sammlung des Museum Folkwang, text by G. Finckh, Museum Folkwang, Essen.
face à face, Espace de l'Art Concret, Mouans-Sartoux.
Fleck, R., "Eminenz in Schwarz und Gelbgrün", *Art*, 11, pp. 76-86.

1992
Helmut Federle, texts by Bernhard Bürgi, V. Loers and J. Yau, Kunsthalle Zürich, Zurich.
Fleck, R., "Helmut Federle. Kunsthalle Zürich", *Flash Art*, 167, pp. 108-109.
Wechsler, M., "Die Ordnung der Abweichung - Zur Malerei von Helmut Federle", *Artis*, June, pp. 30-35.

1991
Helmut Federle, texts by E. Badura-Triska, F. Meschede, V. Loers, H. Federle, G. Boehm, B. Strauss, H. Küng, E.

Stegentritt, Wiener Secession, Vienna.
Badura-Triska, E., "Helmut Federle", *Noëma Artjournal*, 36, pp. 77-79.

1990
Helmut Federle 5 + 1, texts by E. Badura-Triska, E. Franz, D. Koepplin, D. Kuspit, F. Meschede, T. Vischer, Peter Blum Edition, New York.

1989
Helmut Federle, Bilder und Zeichnungen 1975-1988, texts by D. Kuspit, B. Buhlmann, E. Franz, M. Hentschel, E. Stegentritt, H. Federle, edited by Wilfried Dickhoff, Karl Kerber Verlag, Bielefeld.
Helmut Federle, Peintures, Dessins, texts by S. Lemoine, D. Kuspit, X. Douroux/F. Gautherot, H. Federle, Musée de la Peinture et de la Sculpture, Grenoble.
Puvogel, R., "Helmut Federle – Nächst St. Stephan, Vienna, Haus Lange, Krefeld, Kunsthalle Bielefeld, Kunstverein Hamburg", *Noema Artjournal*, 24/25, p. 99.
Blase, C., "Von Streifen und Flächen nach 1960", *Artis*, Juni, pp. 54-58.
Bochynek, M., "Unentschiedenheit als Wahrheit", *Wolkenkratzer Art Journal*, 2, p. 84.

1988
Selwyn, M., "The Image of Abstraction", *Galleries Magazine*, 26, p. 69.
Westfall, S., "Helmut Federle. Mary Boone/Barbara Gladstone", *Flash Art International*, 138, p. 123.
Kuspit, D., "Helmut Federle. Mary Boone Gallery/Barbara Gladstone Gallery", *Artforum International*, January, p. 111.

1987
Helmut Federle, texts by C. Ratcliff, K. Kertess, Mary Boone Gallery/Barbara Gladstone Gallery, New York.
Schmidt-Wulffen, S., "Helmut Federle", *Flash Art International*, 133, p. 80.

1986
Helmut Federle, Zeichnungen 1978-1986, Galerie Borgmann-Capitain, Cologne.
Jedes Zeichen ein Zeichen für andere Zeichen - Zur Ästhetik von Helmut Federle, texts by V. Loers, W. Reiss, J. Herzog, M. Brüderlin, E. Stegentritt, C. Schenker, H. Federle, B. Bürgi, J. Zutter, edited by Galerie nächst St. Stephan, Vienna, Ritter Verlag, Klagenfurt.
Helmut Federle, John M. Armleder, Matt Mullican, Gerwald Rockenschaub - Geometria nova, text by V. Loers, Kunstverein München, Munich.
Nemeczek, A., "Neo Geo weder Trend

noch Stil", *Art*, 12, p. 96.
Brüderlin, M., "Postmoderne Seele und Geometrie. Perspektive eines neuen Kunst-phänomens", *Kunstforum International*, 86, Ruppichteroth, p. 80.
Kuspit, D., "New Geo and Neo Geo", *Artscribe International*, 59, p. 52.
Rein, I., "Helmut Federle, Galerie nächst St. Stephan, Wien", *Artforum International*, September.
Wechsler, M., "H.F., Die Anmassung der Bescheidenheit", *Wolkenkratzer Art Journal*, 13/3.
Schenker, C., "H.F. Haags Gemeentemuseum", *Flash Art International*, 125.

1985

Helmut Federle, Bilder, Zeichnungen, Museum für Gegenwartskunst, Basel, texts: J. Zutter, F. Bool and D. Koepplin.
Brüderlin, M., "Geometrie der Einfühlung. Zum Werk von Helmut Federle", *Kunstforum International*, 81, Ruppichteroth, p. 156.

1984

Helmut Federle, Zeichnungen/Drawings 1975–1984, text by P. Suter, The Living Art Museum, Reykjavik, and Galerie Elisabeth Kaufmann, Zurich.

1983

Arbeit der neuen Ordnung (NSG II) – Helmut Federle, AQ-Verlag, Dudweiler.

1981

New Suicide Graphic, Faces and other Pieces - Helmut Federle, Nachbar der Welt Verlag, Zurich.

1979

Helmut M. Federle, Bilder 1977–1978, texts by J.-C. Ammann, B. Curiger, E. Stegentritt, Kunsthalle Basel, Basel.

Regina José Galindo
1974, born in Ciudad de Guatemala.
Lives and works in Ciudad de Guatemala.

Solo Exhibitions

2000

Todos estamos muriendo, performance, Simposio Centroamericano Temas Centrales, TEOR/ética, Museo del Niño, San José.

1999

El cielo llora tanto que debería ser mujer, performance, Contexto, Guatemala.
Sobremesa, instalación y performance, Proyecto Jóvenes Creadores Bancafé, Guatemala.

Group Exhibitions

2001

Diez Piedras de crak, Intervención en el espacio, Escultura Actual Guatemalteca, Gran Teatro Miguel Angel Asturias.
Nostalgia del lodo, Performance, Zonas Adyacente, Galería Sol Río.

2000

No perdemos nada con nacer, performance, Basurera Municipal, Festival Octubre Azul, Guatemala.
No perdemos nada con nacer, performance, Zócalo, Novena Muestra Int. de Performance, Ex. Teresa Arte Actual, México, D.F.
Esperando al príncipe azul, performance, Colectivo Tripiarte, Guatemala.
Valium 10, Performance, Vivir Aquí, La Curandería, Museo Ixchel, Guatemala.
Encierros, performance, Colectiva Paréntesis, Proyecto de Arte Independiente PAI, Parque Nacional Zoológico La Aurora, Guatemala.

1999

Lo voy a gritar al viento, Arco de Correos, II Festival del Centro Histórico de la Ciudad de Guatemala.
El dolor en un pañuelo, Colectiva sin pelos en la lengua, Proyecto de Arte Independiente PAI, Plaza G&T, Guatemala.

Bibliography

2001

Mujeres que Cuentan, Antología de Narradoras Guatemaltecas, Guatemala.

2000

Personal e Intransmisible, Editorial Colloquia, Guatemala.
Catálogo Novena Muestra Int. de Performance, ExTeresa Arte Actual, México.
Latin American Literature and Arts, 62, Americas Society, New York.

1999

Tanta imagen tras la puerta, Antología de Poetas Jóvenes Guatemaltecos, Guatemala.

1998

Para conjurar el sueño, Antología de Mujeres Poetas Guatemaltecas, Guatemala.

Cristina García Rodero
1949, born in Puertollano (Ciudad Real).
Lives and works in Madrid.

Solo Exhibitions

2001

Lo Festivo y lo Sagrado, Red de Exposiciones Itinerantes de la Comunidad de Madrid.

2000

Cristina García Rodero. Historia de una pasión, PhotoGalería, Madrid.
Eye of Spain, Meadows Museum, Dallas.
Grabarka. El Monte de las 6.000 cruces, Una peregrinación ortodoxa en Polonia, Museo de las Peregrinaciones, Santiago de Compostela.
¿Angeles?, FotoFórum (Web).

1999

España oculta, Aspekte Gallerie, Munich.

1998

Cristina García Rodero. 1974-1992, Facultad de Bellas Artes de la Universidad Complutense de Madrid, Madrid.
España oculta, Museo Álvarez Bravo, Oaxaca, México.
España oculta, Museo de Bellas Artes, Caracas.

1997

España oculta, Encontros de Fotografía de Coimbra.

1995

España oculta, Centro Mediterranée de la Photographie, Bastia, Córcega.

1994

España oculta, Mitaka Gallery of Art, Tokio.

1993

España oculta, The Gallery of Contemporary Photography, Santa Mónica.
España. Fiestas y Ritos, Museo Nacional de Antropología, Madrid.

1992

Europa: El Sur, Arco'92, IFEMA, Madrid.

1991

Old World, New World, Seattle Art Museum, Washington.

1990

España oculta, FotoFest '90, George R. Brown Convention Center, Houston.
España oculta, La Méditerranee, La Lumiere Eblouie, V Recontres Photographiques, Carcassonne.
España oculta, Photographers'Gallery. Londres.

España oculta, Diaframma, Milán.
España oculta, Galería Reckerman, Photokina, Colonia.
España oculta, Landesbildstelle Wuttemberg. Zentrum fur Audiovuelle Medien. Stuttgart
España oculta, Münchner Stadtmuseum, Munich.

1989

España oculta, Museo de Arte Contemporáneo, Madrid.
España oculta, XX Recontres Internationales de la Photographie, Palais Lärchevech, Arlès.

1988

Four Spanish Photographers, Center for Creative Photography, University of Tucson.

1985

Practiques Religueuses en Pays Méditerraneens, Journées Internationales de la Photographie. Montpellier.
Foco 85, Círculo de Bellas Artes, Madrid.

1984

Fiestas Tradicionales en España, Consejo Mexicano de Fotografía, México D.F.

Group Exhibitions

2000

Pasión por el mundo, Sala de Exposiciones del Deutsche Bank, Madrid.
Arco 2000, Stand del diario El País, Recinto ferial Juan Carlos I, Madrid.
Roma 2000. Uno sguardo spagnolo, Sala dell'Istituto Cervantes, Rome.
España Ayer y Hoy. Escenarios, costumbres y protagonistas de un siglo, Museo Nacional Centro de Arte Reina Sofía, Madrid.
Faire le Point, Recontres Photographies à Niort. L'Espace d'Art Contemporain Ecreuil, Niort.
Parallel Journeys, Photographs Do Not Bend Gallery, Dallas.
Memoria y Modernidad. *Fotografía y Fotógrafos del siglo XX en Castilla La Mancha*, Centro Cultural Conde Duque, Madrid.

1999

Emotion, Galeria Photo Fnac Étoile, París.
Visión mediterránea. 12 fotógrafos y el Mediterráneo español, Sala de Exposiciones CAM, Murcia.
Portraits de femmes – Portraits de fermes, Espace Commines, Paris.
La Bretagne dans la collection de l'imagerie, Lannion.
La image de l'altre, Forum Universal de las Cultures, Barcelona.

150 años de fotografía en España, Círculo de Bellas Artes, Madrid.

1998
Femmes photographes. Du temoignage à l'engagè. Maison Robert Doisneau, Gentilly, París.
El Largo Viaje. Fotografía Española del Siglo XX, PHotoEspaña 98, Madrid.

1997
Linha de Frontera. 700 anos de tratado de Alcañizes, Museo de Guarda, Portugal.
Zürich - Ein Fotoportrait, Kunsthaus, Zúrich
FotoPres.97, Centro Cultural Fundación "La Caixa", Barcelona.

1996
Retratos (Fotografía Española, 1948 – 1995), Sala de Exposiciones de la Fundación "Caixa de Catalunya", La Pedrera, Barcelona.
Fotografía y Sociedad en la España de Franco (Las Fuentes de la Memoria III), Centro Cultural de la Fundación "la Caixa", Barcelona.
Testigos, Canal de Isabel II, Madrid.
Sul, Museo Antropológico, Encontros de Fotografía de Coimbra.

1995
De la Rebelión a la Utopía (Fotografía de los años 60 – 70), Centro Cultural de la Fundación "la Caixa", Barcelona.

1994
Chefs d'Oeuvre de la Photographie, les Années 70 (Collection de la Fondation Select), Musée de L'Elysée, Lausana.
Géneros y tendencias en los albores del siglo XXI, Casa Municipal de la Cultura, Alcobendas, Madrid.

1992
Open Spain, The Museum of Contemporary Photography, Chicago.
Astilleros. Del Ayer al Hoy, Museo Español de Arte Contemporáneo, Madrid.
Imagina (Un proyecto en torno a la Fotografía), Mediterránea'92, Pabellón Español Expo.92, Palacio de la Maestranza, Sevilla.

1991
Artistas Españolas en Europa, Museo de Arte Moderno de la Villa de París.
Vanishing Spain, International Center of Photography, New York.
The Legacy of Eugene Smith (Twelve Photographers in the Humanistic Tradition), Centre Georges Pompidou, París; International Center of Photography, New York.
Cuatro Direcciones de la Fotografía

Contemporánea Española, Museo Nacional Centro de Arte Reina Sofía, Madrid.

1990
Alhambra, últimas miradas, Palacio de Carlos V, Granada.

1989
Artistas Españolas en Europa, Waino Aalronem Museum, Finlandia.

1988
Sefarad, Jewish Roots in Spain, Bernard Hilken, Los Angeles.
III FotoBienal, Vigo.

1987
After Franco, Marcuse Pfeiffer Gallery, New York.

1985
Contemporany Spanish Photography, University Art Museum, University of New Mexico, Alburquerque.
Photographen Aus Spanien, Fotografische Sammlun in Museum Folkwang, Essen.

Bibliography

2001
Lo Festivo y lo Sagrado, Consejería de Cultura de la Comunidad de Madrid, Madrid.

2000
Grabarca. O Monte das 6000 cruces, Museo de las Peregrinaciones, Santiago de Compostela.
Cristina García Rodero, prólogo de J. Llamazares. La Fábrica, Madrid

1995
España Oculta, Prólogo de M.M. Crain, Public Celebrations in Spain, 1974 – 1989, Smithsonian Institution Press, Washington.

1994
Spagne: Feste e Riti, prólogo de W.A. Christian Jr., text by C. Bonald, Jaca Book, Milan.
España Oculta, prólogo de Christian Caujolle, Mitaka City Gallery of Art, Tokio.
1992
Europa: El Sur, introducción de P.L. de Osaba, prólogo de C. Caujolle, Madrid. Consorcio para la Organización de Madrid Capital Europea de la Cultura.
Spanien: Festes und Riten, prólogo de W.A. Christian Jr., text by C. Bonald. Stemmle, Schaffiausen.

1990
Espagne occulte, prólogo de C. Nori y C.

Caujolle, Contrejour, Paris.
España Oculta, prólogo de J.C. Baroja, Bucher, Munich.
España: Fiestas y Ritos, prólogo de W.A. Christian Jr., text by C. Bonald. Lunweg, Barcelona.

1989
España Oculta, Prólogo de J.C. Baroja. Lunwerg, Barcelona.

Yervant Gianikian
Angela Ricci Lucchi
1942, Yervant Gianikian born in Merano.
1942, Angela Ricci Lucchi born in Lugo di Romagna.
Both live and work in Milan.

Solo Exhibitions

2001
Visioni del deserto, Fundacio "la Caixa", Barcelona.
Visioni del deserto, Centro Andaluz de Arte Contemporaneo, Sevilla.

2000
Festival du Reel, Nyon.
Festival Vila do Conde e Oporto, Portugal.
Cineteca Italiana Spazio Oberdan, Milan.
Cinemathéque Francaise, Paris.
The Museum of Modern Art, New York.
Fondacio Antoni Tapies, Barcelona.
Proiezioni: "Dal Polo all'Equatore", "Su tutte le vette è pace", "Prigionieri della guerra".
Visioni del deserto, Commande Fondation Cartier Pour l'Art Contemporain, Paris, per la mostra *Desert*.

1999
Coté Court, Pantin, Paris.

1995
Galerie Nationale du Jeu de Paume, Paris.

1992
Museo Nazionale del Cinema di Torino.

1989
De Unie, Rotterdam.
Group Exhibitions

2000
Inventario balcanico/*Balkan Inventory*, 16 mm, colour, 62 min. Production: Biennale Cinema di Venezia. Music by D. Gasparyan.
Visioni del Deserto/*Visions of the Desert*, video, colour, 16 min. Production: Fondation Cartier pour l'Art Contemporain, Paris.

1998
Trasparenze/*Trasparences*, colour, 6 min.
Su tutte le vette è pace/*Peace on Every Peak*, 16 mm e 35 mm, colour, 72 min. Music by G. Marini. Production: Musei Storici di Trento e Rovereto.

1997
Nocturne, video, colour, 18 min.
Io ricordo/*I Remember*, video, colour, 11 min.

1996
Lo Specchio di Diana/*Diana's Mirror*, video, colour, 31 min.

1995
Prigionieri della guerra/*Prisoners of the War*, 16 mm e 35 mm, colour, 67 min. Music by G. Marini. Production: Musei Storici di Trento e Rovereto.

1994
Animali Criminali/*Criminal Animals*, 16 mm, colour, 7 min.
Diario Africano/*African Diary*, 16 mm, colour, 16 min.
Aria/*Air*, 16 mm, colour, 16 min.

1993
Mario Giacomelli, Serie "Contact"/ *"Contact" series*. 35 mm, black and white, 13 min. Production: Arte.

1991
Archivi italiani n. 1. Il fiore della razza/ *Italian Archives n. 1. The Flower of Race*, 16 mm, colour, 25 min.
Archivi italiani n. 2 /*Italian Archives n. 2*, 16 mm, colour, 20 min.

1990
Uomini anni vita/*People Years Life*, 16 mm, colour, 70 min. Production: ZDF.
Interni a Leningrado/*Interiors in Leningrad*, 16 mm, black and white and colour, Materiali non montati/*Unedited material*.

1988
La più amata dagli italiani/*The One the Italians Love Best*, 20 giugno 1988, video, col.
Passion, 16 mm, colori originali a tampone/*original pad tinting*, 7 min.

1987
Frammenti/*Fragments*, 16 mm, colour, 60' (*Coproduction with RAI for Folco Quilici's television program* Geo).

1986
Dal Polo all'Equatore/*From the Pole to the Equator*, 16 mm, colour, 101 min. Produzione: ZDF. Music by K. Ulrich, C. Anderson.

Ritorno a Khodorciur. Diario armeno/*Return to Khodorciur. An Armenian Diary.* Video, colour, 80 min.

1982
Das Lied von der Erde – Gustav Mahler, 16 mm, colour, muto/*silent*, 17 min.

1981
Essence d'absinthe/*The Essence of Absinthe*, 16 mm, colour, muto/*silent*, 15 min.

1979-1981
Catalogo 9,5 – Karagöez/*Catalogue 9,5 – Karagöez*, 16 mm, colour, muto/*silent*, 56 min.

1980
Catalogo n. 4 – Un due tre: immagini. Un due tre: profumi/*Catalogue n. 4 – One Two Three: Images. One Two Three: Perfumes*, 16 mm, Eastmancolor, muto/*silent*, 18 min.

1979
Milleunanotte/*One Thousand and One Night*, 16 mm, black and white, incompiuto/unfinished.
Karagöez et les Brûler d'herbes parfumés/*Karagöez and the Burners of Scented Herbs*, 8 mm, colour, muto/*silent*, 16 min. Odore di damascena e mandorle amare/*Scent of damask-rose and bitter almonds.*

1978
Un prestigiatore, una miniaturista/*A Conjurer, a Miniaturist*, 8 mm, colour, muto/*silent*, 10 min.

1977-1979
Catalogo n. 3 – Odore di tiglio intorno alla casa/*Catalogue n. 3 – Lime Scent Around the House*, 8 mm, colour, muto/*silent*, 12 min.

1977
Profumo/*Perfume*, 8 mm, colour, muto/*silent*, 27 min. Odori e profumi diversi/*Different scents and odors.*

1976
Cesare Lombroso – Sull'odore del garofano/*Cesare Lombroso –On the Smell of Cloves*, 16 mm, Ektachrome, muto/*silent.*
Di alcuni fiori non facilmente catalogabili/*Of Some Not Easily Classifiable Flowers*, 8 mm, colour, muto/*silent.*
Cataloghi – non è altro che gli odori che sente/*Catalogues – It's Nothing But the Scents She Smell*, 16 mm, Ektachrome, muto/*silent*, 20 min.
Catalogo n. 2/*Catalogue n. 2*, 8 mm, colour, muto/*silent*, 20 min.
1975-76

Dal 2 novembre al giorno di Pasqua/*From 2nd November to Easter Sunday*, 8 mm, colour, muto/*silent*, 10 min.

1975
Erat-Sora/*Erat-Sora*, 8 mm, colour, muto/*silent*, 10 min.
Wladimir Propp – Profumo di Lupo/*Wladimir Propp – Wolf Smell*, 8 mm, colour, muto/*silent*, 10 min.
Del sonno e dei sogni di rosa limitata al senso dell'odorato/*Of sleep and Rose dreams limited to the sense of smell*, 8 mm, colour, muto/*silent*, 10 min.
Alice profumata di rosa/*Rose-scented Alice*, 8 mm, colour, muto/*silent*, 10 min.
Klinger e il guanto/*Klinger and the Glove*, Super 8, colour, muto/*silent*, 5 min.
Catalogo della scomposizione/*Catalogue of Decomposition*, 8 mm, colour, muto/*silent*, 10 min.
Non cercare il profumo/*Don't Look for the BNL Perfume*, 8 mm, colour, muto/*silent*, 10 min.
Catalogo comparativo/*Comparative catalogue*, 8 mm, colour, muto/*silent*, 10 min.
Stone-Book/*Stone-Book*, 8 mm, colour, muto/*silent*, 10 min.

Bibliography

2001
Parsons, M., "From the Pole to the Equator", *Pix*, 3, London.

2000
Benoliel, B., "Archéologues de la pellicule", *Cahier du Cinéma.*
Bonnaud, F., "À la rencontres des fantomes", *Les Inrockuptibles.*
Gianikian & Ricci Lucchi, "Voyages en Russie", *Trafic.*
Gianikian & Ricci Lucchi, "Aquarelles", *Cinémathèque.*
Signorelli, A., "Scrivere la storia", *Cineforum*, 394.
Retour à Khodorciur, Galerie Nationale du Jeu de Paume, Paris.
Cinema Anni Vita, Yervant Gianikian e Angela Ricci Lucchi, Quaderni Fondazione Cineteca Italiana, Provincia di Milano Settore Cultura, Editrice Il Castoro.

1999
Bellour, R., "L'arrière monde", *Entre-Image.*
Bonnaud, F., "Le temps retrouvé", *Les Inrockuptibles.*
Kermabon, J., Vatrican, V., "Propos de YG & ARL", *Bref*, 42.

1996
Bluminger, C., "Ins innere des einzelbildes", *Meteor 3.*
Bluminger, C., "Film makers in the archives", *Fondation Tapies.*

1995
Gianikian & Ricci Lucchi, "Notre caméra analytique", *Trafic.*
Sipe, D., "From Pole to Equator, a vision of a wordles past", *Revisioning History. Film and Construction of a New Past*, Princeton University Press, Princeton.

1993
Mac Donald, S., "From Pole to Equator" *Avant-Garde Film*, Cambridge press).
Mac Donald, Scott: "Gianikian & Ricci Lucchi" (A Critical Cinema 3, University California press, 1998).
Macnab, G., "From Pole to Equator", *Sight and Sound*, June.

1992
Yervant Gianikian, Angela Ricci Lucchi, Edizione Hopefulmonster editore, Florence; Museo Nazionale del Cinema di Torino e Cinemazero, Pordenone.
Hoberman, J., "Pre-industrial light and magic", *Premiere.*

1989
Mac Donald, S., "From Pole to Equator", *Film Quarterly*, Spring.

1987
Gianikian & Ricci Lucchi, "Dal polo all'equatore", *Griffithiana.*
Hoberman, J., "Explorers", *Village Voice.*

1981
Lipzin, J.C., "Engaging the olfactory", *Cinemanews* S.Fr.

1980
Farassino, A., "Cataloghi e profumi", *Patalogo Due*, Ubu libri.
Koch, G., "Karagoez", *Jahrabuch Film 1983-1984.*
Rosenbaum, J., "Sight and Smell", *The Soho News*, July, New York.
Morandini, M., *Dizionario dei film*, Zanichelli.
Mereghetti, P., *Dizionario dei film*, Baldini & Castoldi.

Luis Gonzalez Palma

1957, born in Ciudad de Guatemala. Lives and works in Ciudad de Guatemala.

Solo Exhibitions

2000
Palazzo Ducale, Genoa.
Mes de la fotografía de Mérida, Mérida.
Pinacoteca Diego Rivera, Veracruz.
Schneider Gallery, Chicago.
Denton University, Texas.

1999
Steve Cohen Gallery, Los Angeles.
Martin Weinstein Galery, Minneapolis.
Museo Ken Damy, Brescia.
Foto España, Centro cultural la Villa, (Mes de la fotografía en Madrid).
Festival de Invierno, Ouro Preto, Brasil.
Sicardi-Sanders Gallery, Houston.
Photo & Co. Gallery, Milan.
David Perez-MacCollum, Guayaquil, Ecuador.
El Ojo ajeno, Lima, Perú.
Art and Humanities Council, Lake Charles.
Lissa Sette Gallery, Scotsdale, Arizona.
Galería Nina Menocal, México D.F., México.

1998
Lissa Sette Gallery, Scottsdale.
Photo & Co. Turin.
Galeria Pelliti, Rome.
Museo de Arte y diseño contemporáneo, San José.
James Danziger Gallery, New York.
ArtexArte, Buenos Aires.
Festival de Iverno, Ouro Preto, Minas Gerais, Brasil.
Centro Cultural UFMG, Bello Horizonte, Brasil.
Galería Observatorio, Recife, Brasil.
Jane Jackson Fine Arts, Atlanta.
Galería Visor, Valencia.

1997
Mes de la Fotografía, San Paulo.
Casa de las Américas, Havana.
MIT List Visual Art Center, Cambridge.
Centro de Artes Visuales, Museo del Barro; Asunción, Paraguay.
Steve Cohen Gallery, Los Angeles.
Weinstein Gallery, Minneapolis.
Fondo Nacional para el Arte Contemporáneo, Río de Janeiro.
Schneider Gallery, Chicago.
James Danzinger Gallery, New York.

1996
Museo Palacio de Bellas Artes, México D.F.
Museo de Guadalajara, México.
Biblioteca Luis Angel Arango, Santafé de Bogotá.
Museo de Arte Moderno de Medellín.
Robert Mc Clain Gallery, Houston.
Lisa Sette Gallery, Scottsdale.
Schneider Gallery, Chicago.
Biuro-Wystaw-Artystycznych, Jelenia Gora, Osrodek Kultury, Wroclaw/Lodzki Dom Kultury, Lodz/Centrum Kultury, Katowice, Polonia.
V Bienal de Cuenca, Cuenca, Ecuador.
Galería Tomás Andreu, Santiago de Chile.

1995
Galleria Il Diaframma, Milan.

The Photographers Gallery, Saskatoon SK, Canada.
Southeast Museum of Photography, Daytona Beach.
Galería Spectrum, Zaragoza.
Mes de la Fotografía, Quito, Ecuador.
Galería Antonio de Barnola, Barcelona.

1994
Royal Festival Hall, London.
Museo de Bellas Artes, Caracas.
25 Recontres de la Photographie, Arles.
Cleveland Center for Contemporary Art, Cleveland.
Month of Photography, Bratislava, Slovaquia.
Steve Cohen Gallery, Los Angeles.
Galería Visor, Valencia.

1993
Moderna Museet, Fotografiska Musset, Stochkolm.
Musee de la Photographie de Charleroi.
Lowinsky Gallery, New York.
A.B. Galeries, Paris.
Fotofeis, Scottish International Festival of Photography, Scotland.
Schneider-Bluhm-Loeb Gallery, Chicago.
Steve Cohen Gallery, Los Angeles.
Jane Jackson Gallery, Atlanta.

1992
Art Institute of Chicago, Chicago.
V Fotobienal de Vigo.
Lowinsky Gallery, New York.
Galleri Image, Arhus, Denmark.
Schneider-Bluhm-Loeb Gallery, Chicago.
Fotofest International Month of Photography, Houston.
Galería Sol del Río, Guatemala.

1991
Galería Arte Contemporáneo, México D.F.
Galería El Cadejo, Antigua Guatemala.

1990
Fotogalería Teatro San Martín, Buenos Aires.

1989
Museum of Contemporary Hispanic Art, New York.

Group Exhibitions

2000
Bienal internacional de Fotografía, Venezuela y República de China.

1999
10 Años de Centro Cultural UFMG, Belo Horizonte, Brasil.

Lisieres LatinoAmericaines, Strasburg, Francia.
Contemporay art from Guatemala, El Salvador, Nicaruagua and Costa Rica, Taipei Fine Art Museum, Taipei.
Tracing Times, photogravures by eight latin american photographers, Trinity college, Hartfort.
I Bienal Internacional de Fotografía, Centro de la Imagen, México D.F.
Viejas Técnicas, Nuevas Tendencias, Museo de Bellas Artes de Salta, Argentina.
Peintures et Sculptures d'Amerique Latine. Chef-d'oeuvre de Xxeme siécle, Colección del Museo de Bellas Artes de Caracas, Festival de Biarritz, Francia.

1998
Center for Latino Art, San José.
Galería Nina Menocal, Mexico D.F.
1,254KM, Centro Wifredo Lam, Havana.
Lumo triennal, Jyvaskyla Art Museum, Finlandia.

1997
VI Bienal de la Habana, Havana.
Festivales de Arte de Lima, Lima.
Festival Internacional de Arte de Medellín, Medellín.
New Realities, Hand Colored Photographs – 1839 to the present, Wyoming Art Museum, Boise Art Museum.
Así está la cosa: Instalación y Arte Objeto de América Latina, Centro Cultural de Arte Contemporáneo, México D.F.
Arqueología del Silencio, Museo de Arte Moderno, Guatemala.
Real Maravilloso, Piazza dei Macelli, Prato.

1996
Bienal de San Paulo, Brasil.
Relaciones, Museo de Arte y Diseño Contemporáneo, San José, Costa Rica.
Visión del Arte Contemporáneo en Guatemala, Museo de Arte Moderno, Guatemala.
Image & Memory, Museo del Barrio, New York.
Common Bonds, Photogravure, Spectrum Gallery, New York.
Photogravure, A Survey 1903-1996, Marlborough Gallery, New York.
Pushing Image Paradigsm: Conceptual Maneuvers in Recent Photography, Portland Institute of Contemporary Art, Portland.
Arqueología del Silencio, Museo del Chopo, México D.F.
Figuratively Speaking 20th Century, Paintings, Sculptures and works on Paper, Santa Barbara Museum of Art, Santa Barbara.

Cuerpo, Galería de Nina Menocal, México D.F.
Mesótica II, Museo de Arte y Diseño Contemporáneo, San José, Costa Rica. Casa de América, Madrid.

1995
Triangular, Antigua Guatemala, México D.F., Stockholm.
Arte Contemporáneo Latinoamericano, Haus der Kulturen der Welt, Berlín.
Image & Memory, Latin American Photography 1880-1992, Crocker Art Museum, Sacramento.
Traces: The Body in Contemporary Photography, Bronx Museum, New York.
Cruzando Caminos: 6 fotógrafos latinoamericanos, Museo de Arte de Lima, Lima.
Quest for the Moon, Museum of Fine Arts, Houston.

1994
V Bienal de la Habana.
Ludwig Forum fur International Kunst, Aachen.
Image & Memory, Latin American Photography 1880-1992, Akron Art Museum, Meadous.
Museum of Art, Southern Methodist University, Dallas.
Schneider Gallery, Chicago.
Le Courage, Chateux Beychevelle, Bordeux.
Indagaciones, Galería Sol del Río, Guatemala.
Encuentro Interamericano de Artistas Plásticos, Museos de las Artes, Guadalajara, México.
Tierra de Tempestades, Nuevo Arte de Guatemala, El Salvador y Nicaragua, Harris Museum, England (travelling).

1993
Encuentro Latinoamericano de Fotografía, Caracas.
Canto a la Realidad, Fotografía Latinoamericana 1860-1990, Casa de América, Madrid (travelling).

1992
Salón Latinoamericano del Desnudo, *Bienal de San Paulo*, Brasil; Alianza Francesa, Lima, Perú.

1991
Recontres Internationales de la Photographie, Arles.
Fotografía Contemporánea de Latinoamérica, Museo de Huelva, Spain.

1990
Cents Ans de Photographie au Guatemala, Maison de L'Amerique Latine, Paris.

1989
Presencia Imaginaria, Museo de Arte Moderno de México, Museo de Arte Moderno de Guatemala.

1988
Angelogía, Galería Imaginaria, Antigua Guatemala.
Refigura, Arte Moderno Gallery, San Antonio.

Paul Graham
1956, born in Stafford, England.
Lives and works in London.

Solo Exhibitions

2001
Karen Lovegrove Gallery, California.

2000
Paintings, Anthony Reynolds Gallery, London.
Galerie Bob Van Orsouw, Zurich.
Lawrence Rubin Greenberg Van Doren Fine Art, New York.
End of an Age, Scalo, New York.

1998
Hippolyte Gallery, Helsinki.
Portfolio Gallery, Edinburgh.
Galerie Bob van Orsouw, Zurich.

1997
Anthony Reynolds Gallery, London.

1996
Empty Heaven, Galleri Tommy Lund, Odense.
Hypermetropia, Tate Gallery, London.

1995
Empty Heaven, Kunstmuseum, Wolfsburg.
Le Case d'Arte, Milan.

1994
Television Portraits, Galerie Paul Andriesse, Amsterdam.
Television Portraits, Raum Aktueller Kunst, Vienna.
Television Portraits, Galleri Tommy Lund, Odense.
Anthony Reynolds Gallery, London.
Television Portraits, Claire Burrus, Paris.

1993
Television Portraits, Esther Schipper, Cologne.
Bob van Orsouw, Zurich.
Television Portraits, Anthony Reynolds Gallery, London.
New Europe, Ikon Gallery, Birmingham.
New Europe, Fotomuseum Winterthur.

1992
Anthony Reynolds Gallery.
Galerie Claire Burrus, Paris.

1991
PPOW Gallery, New York.
Germany / November 1990, Aschenbach, Amsterdam.

1990
XPO, Hamburg.
Esther Schipper, Cologne.
National Museum of Film and Photography, Bradford.
Anthony Reynolds Gallery, London.

1989
Fotobiennale Enschede 1989, Enschede.
Centre Regional de la Photographie, Douchy.
Galerie Claire Burrus, Paris.

1988
Museum Het Princessehof, Leeuwarden.
PPOW Gallery, New York.

1987
Chapter Arts Centre, Cardiff.
Cornerhouse Arts Centre, Manchester.
Stills Gallery, Edinburgh.
FNAC Les Halles, Paris.
Kodak Gallery, Tokyo.
Arles Rencontres, Arles, France.
Jones Troyer Gallery, Washington.

1986
Watershed Gallery, Bristol.
Photographers' Gallery, London.
National Museum of Photography, Bradford, touring to Birmingham, Kendal, Cheltenham, Cardiff.

Group Exhibitions

2001
Heads and Hands – loans from the nvisible museum, Decatur House Museum, Washington.

2000
Protest and Survive, Whitechapel Art Gallery, London.
Ghosts, Memphis.
Invitation to the City, Centre Bruxelles 2000, Brussels.
The British Art Show, national touring exhibition organised by the Hayward Gallery, Edinburgh and tour to Southampton, Cardiff and Birmingham.
Some Parts of This World: Helsinki Photography Festival, The Finnish Museum of Photography, Helsinki.

1999
Endzeit, Galerie Six Friedrich Lisa Ungar, Munich.

Common People, Fondazione Sandretto Re Rebaudengo, Guarene.
Ursula Rogg vs Paul Graham, Galerie Andreas Binder, Munich.
Art Life 21, Spiral/Wacoal Art Center, Tokyo.

1998
Das Grosse Rasenstueck, Galerie der Stadt Schwaz, Austria.
Yesterday Begins Tomorrow, Bard College for Curatorial Studies, New York.
Laurent Delaye Gallery, London.
Rencontres Internationales de la Photographie, Arles.
Women, Galerie Klemens Gasser und Tanja Grunert, Cologne.
The Citibank Private Bank Photography Prize, Photographers' Gallery, London.
Homo Zappiens Zappiens, Université Rennes 2, Rennes.
Tuning Up #5, Kunstmuseum, Wolfsburg.

1997
Pittura Britannica, Museum of Contemporary Art, Sydney, Art Gallery of South Australia, Adelaide, Te Papa, New Zealand.
Strange Days, Claudia Gian Ferrari Arte Contemporanea, Milan.
Zurich, Kunstlerhaus, Zurich.
Photography in Europe, Green on Red Gallery, Dublin.
Galerie du Jour Agnès b., Paris.
Threats and Containments, Byam Shaw School of Art, London.
Kunstverein, Hamburg.

1996
Die Klasse, Museum für Gestaltung, Zurich.
Prospect, Schirn Kunsthalle Frankfurt and Kunstverein Frankfurt.
EV+A, Limerick City Gallery of Art, Eire.
Colorealismo, Galleria Photology, Milan.

1995
Esslingen Triennale, Esslingen.
Witness, Photoworks from the Collection, Tate Gallery, Liverpool.
Printemps de Cahors, Cahors, France.
Mai de la photo, Reims, France.

1994
Project for Europe, Copenhagen and tour.
Seeing the Unseen, Thirty Shepherdess Walk, London.
Europa 94, Munich.
Anthony Reynolds Gallery, London.

1993
Photographs from the Real World, Lillehammer Bys Malerisamling, Lillehammer and tour.
European Exercises, Galerie D-BS, Antwerp.

The Legacy of W.Eugene Smith, San Jose Museum of Art, San Jose.
PPOW, New York.
New World Images, Louisiana Museum, Humlebaek.

1992
Vers Une Attitude, Groupe Caisse des Depots, Paris.
Une seconde pensee du paysage, Domaine de Kerguehennec, Britanny.
Whitechapel Open, Whitechapel Art Gallery, London.
The Billboard Project, commissioned by BBC TV, London.
More than One Photography, MOMA, New York.

1990
The Human Spirit, The International Center of Photography, New York and Centre Pompidou, Paris.
British Photography from the Thatcher Years, Museum of Modern Art, New York.
Conflict Resolution Through the Arts: Focus on Ireland, Ward Nasse Gallery, New York.
XPO Galerie, Hamburg.

1989
PPOW, New York.
Anthony Reynolds Gallery, London.
Framed, Artspace, San Francisco.
Corporate Identities, Cornerhouse Gallery, Manchester.
Towards A Bigger Picture, Victoria & Albert Museum, London; Tate Gallery, Liverpool.
Hot Spots, Bronx Museum of the Arts, New York.
Through the Looking Glass-Independant Photography in Britain 1946-1989, Barbican Art Gallery, London – touring to USA.
The Art of Photography 1839-1989, Museum of Fine Arts, Houston – touring to Royal Academy, London; Australian National Gallery, Canberra.

1988
Towards A Bigger Picture, V & A Museum, London.
Recent British Photography, XYZ Gallery, Belgium.
Selected Images, Riverside Studios, London.
Camouflage, Curt Marcus Gallery, New York.
Third Fotobienal, Vigo, Spain.
A British View, Museum fur Gestaltung, Zurich.

1987
Open Exhibition, Whitechapel Gallery, London.

Troisieme Triennale, Musee de la Photographie, Belgium.
Attitudes to Ireland, Orchard Gallery, Londonderry.
Konigreich, Forum Stadtpark, Austria.
Recent Acquisitions, Museum of Modern Art, New York.
Mysterious Co-incidences, Photographers' Gallery, London.
Future of Photography, Corcoran Gallery, Washington.
Recent Histories, Hayward Gallery, London.
New British Photography, Modern Arts Museum, Tampere, Finland.
New Photography 3, Museum of Modern Art, New York.

1986
Recent Acquisitions, V & A Museum, London.
Modern Colour Photography, Photokina, Frankfurt.
British Photography, Houston Foto Fest, Houston.
The New British Document, Museum of Photography, Chicago.
Force of Circumstance, PPOW Gallery, New York.

Bibliography

2000
Paintings, Anthony Reynolds Gallery, London; Galerie Bob van Orsouw, Zurich; Lawrence Rubin Greenberg Van Doren Fine Art, New York.
The British Art Show, exhibition catalogue, UK.

1999
End of an Age, Scalo Books, Zurich.
Townsend, C., "Poetical Journeys in a Political Landscape", *Parachute*, April/May/June.

1998
The Citibank Private Bank Photography Prize, exhibition catalogue, Photographers' Gallery, London.
Homo Zappiens Zappiens, exhibition catalogue, Université Rennes 2, Rennes.

1997
Pittura Britannica, Museum of Contemporary Art, Sydney, Art Gallery of South Australia, Adelaide, Te Papa, New Zealand.
Strange Days, Claudia Gian Ferrari Arte Contemporanea, Milan.

1996
Paul Graham, Phaidon Press, London.
Die Klasse, exhibition catalogue, Museum für Gestaltung, Zurich.

Prospect, Schirn Kunsthalle Frankfurt and Kunstverein Frankfurt.

1995
Empty Heaven, Kunstmuseum Wolfsburg/Scalo Books, Zurich.
Paul Graham, exhibition catalogue, Le Case d'Arte, Milan.
Esslingen Triennale, exhibition catalogue, Esslingen.
Printemps de Cahors, exhibition catalogue, Cahors, France.
Mai de la photo, exhibition catalogue, Reims, France.
Baqué, D., "Hybridations", *Art Press*, Summer.

1994
Europa 94, exhibition catalogue, Munich.
Durden, M., "Paul Graham", *Frieze*, January-February, 20.
Uccia, B., "Paul Graham", *Artis*, December /January.
Bonaventura, P., "The Man with the Moving Camera", *Artefactum*, XI/51.

1993
God in Hell, artists books, Grey Editions, London.
New Europe, Fotomuseum Winterthur/Cornerhouse Publications, Manchester.
New World Images, exhibition catalogue, Louisiana Museum, Humlebaek.
Mack, G., *Das Kunst-Bulletin*, 12, December.

1991
Paul Graham 'Germany November 1990', exhibition catalogue, Aschenbach, Amsterdam.

1990
In Umbra Res, National Museum of Photography, Film and Television, Bradford / Cornerhouse Publications, Manchester.
Paul Graham, exhibition catalogue, Anthony Reynolds Gallery, London and Esther Schipper, Cologne.
Roberts, J., *Frieze*, April.
Reindl, U.M., "Paul Graham at Esther Schipper", *Kunstforum*, 109, August/October
Renton, A., *Blitz Magazine*, May.
Bush, K., *Artscribe*, September-October, 83.

1989
Fotobiennale Enschede 1989, exhibition catalogue, Enschede.
Framed, exhibition catalogue, Artspace, San Francisco.
Corporate Identities, exhibition catalogue, Cornerhouse Gallery, Manchester.

Hot Spots, exhibition catalogue, Bronx Museum of the Arts, New York.
Through the Looking Glass-Independent Photography in Britain 1946-1989, exhibition catalogue, Barbican Art Gallery, London – touring to USA.
The Art of Photography 1839-1989, exhibition catalogue, Museum of Fine Arts, Houston.
Saltz, J., "Notes on a Photograph", *Arts Magazine*.

1987
Selected Images, exhibition catalogue, Riverside Studios, London.
Third Fotobienal, exhibition catalogue, Vigo, Spain.
Troubled Land, Grey Editions, London.
Bishop, W., "Troubled Land", *British Journal of Photography*.

1986
Beyond Caring, Grey Editions, London.

1983
A1-The Great North Road, Grey Editions, London.

Veli Granö
1960, born in Kajaani.
Lives and works in Helsinki.

Solo Exhibitions

2000
The Star dweller / Tähteläinen, Hippolyte gallery, Helsinki.

1999
The Tangible Cosmologies, Imatra Museum of Art, Imatra, Finland.
The Tangible Cosmologies, Oulu Art Museum, Oulu, Finland.
The Tangible Cosmologies, Museum of Contemporary Art, Helsinki.
The Lost Expedition, TM Gallery, Helsinki.

1994
The Illuminated Room, several galleries in Finland.

1992
The Solar Eclipse, several galleries and museums in Finland.

1991
Septembre de la photo, Nice.
Union, installation, several galleries in Finland.

1989
The Son of Moses, several galleries in Finland.

1986
Onnela / A Trip to Paradice, several galleries in Finland.

Group Exhibitions

2001
Surface and Whirlpools, Artmuseum Borå, Sweden.
Cooper Gallery, Dundee.
Real of Photography.- photo- and video installation, invitation project for City Douro, Portugal.
Empathy, Pori Art Museum, Pori, Finland.
ITE, Helsinki Art museum, Helsinki.

2000
Identiteté Fictive, Institut Finlandais, Paris.
Kylä/Byn, Tensta Arthall, Stocholm, Sweden.
Manifesta 3, Lublijana.
Utopias, Warwick Arts Centre/Mead Gallery, Coventry.
ITE, Art Museum Kajaani, Finland.

1999
What is Real, Haus am Waldsee, Berlin.
What is Real, Art Hall Helsinki, Helsinki.
Identiteté Fictive, Gallery Contretype, Brussels.

1998
Unknown Adventures, Stadtgalerie im Kulturviertel, Kiel.
Unknown Adventures, Rostock.
Granny pine, Gallery Annika Sunvik, New York.

1997
Unknown Adventures, Badisher Kunstverein, Karlsruhe.
North-West, Moscow.
Northern Realities, Museum of Contemporary Art, Thessaloniki.

1992
Decennium, International touring exhibition in 8 countries.

1989
The Bridge, Moscow.

Documentaries and Videos

1998
A Strange Message from Another Star, a documentary, 16 mm, 30 min.

1993
Attempt to Raise Hell - Dennis Oppenheim, a documentary, 16 mm, 20 min.

1992
The Imaginary Life of Matias Keskinen, a documentary, 16 mm, 55 min.

1986
Onnela / A Trip to Paradice, several galleries in Finland.

Group Exhibitions

2001
Surface and Whirlpools, Artmuseum Borå, Sweden.

Bibliography

2001
Surface and Whirlpools, Artmuseum Borå, Sweden.
Manifesta 3, Lublijana.

2000
ITE/Diy-lives, cooperation with E. Pirtola, a documentary book.
Utopias, Warwick Arts Centre/Mead Gallery, Coventry.

1999
What Is Real, Art Hall Helsinki, Haus am Waldsee, Berlin.

1997
Tangible Cosmologies, a documentary book.
Tangible Cosmologies, cooperation with H. Haaslahti, CD-Rom.
Unknown Adventures, Badisher Kunstverein, Karlsruhe.

1993
Northern Realities, Museum of Contemporary Art, Thessaloni.

1989
Onnela/A Trip to Paradice/, a documentary book.

Screenings

2000
Double Take, Filmfestival, Durham.

1999
Kiasma, Museum of Contemporary Art, Helsinki.
31st Auckland International Film Festival, New Zealand.
Edinburgh International Film Festival.
28sh Wellington Film Festival, New Zealand.
23rd International Film Festival, Dundine, New Zealand.
23st Houston International Film Festival, USA.
Nordisk panorama,Rejkjavik.
5th International Short Film Festival of Drama, Greece.
Uppsala Int Short Film Festival, Sweden.
Pori Art Museum, Finland.
Int Documentary Filmfestival, Amsterdam.

1998
The Kitchen, New York.
Digital Days, Copenhagen.

1994
Pori Art Museum, Finland.

1993
The Kitchen, New York.

1992
Berlin video festival, Berlin.

Hai Bo
1962, born in Changchun, province of Jilin. Lives and works in Beijin.

Solo Exhibitions

2000
Shanghai Biennale, Shanghai.
CCAA, Chinese Contemporary Art Award.
Home, Contemporary Art Proposals, Shanghai.
Exhibition of Chinese Internet and Photographic Works.

1999
Back and Forth, Left and Right. Exhibition of Photography and Installations, Beijing.

1996
First Annual Exhibition of Chinese Oil Painting Institute, Beijing.

1995
7th International Biennial of Sketch and Print, Taiwan.

1994
12th Chinese Print Work Exhibition, Shenzhen.

1992
Tibet: Photographic Work Exhibition, Jilin Museum.

Federico Herrero
1978, born in San José, Costa Rica. Lives and works in San José.

Solo Exhibitions

2000
Recuadros (with Carlos Garaicoa), Jacobo Karpio Gallery, San José.

Group Exhibitions

2001
Ex 3, Museo de Arte y Diseño Contemporàneo, San José.

2000
Puertos y Costas Ricas, TEOR/éTica, San José (Five artists from Costa Rica and Puerto Rico).
Costas y Puertos Ricos, Michelle Marxuach arte contemporàneo, San Juan, Puerto Rico (Second part of the project).
Of a generation, at the New School of Art, San José
Carlos Quintana and invited artists, Jacobo

Karpio Gallery, San José.
The artist through the objects, National Gallery, Costarican Center for Science and Culture, San José.
Mapping, Schafter Gallery, Pratt Institute, New York.
Ventana hacia Venus, curada por el artista cubano Carlos Garaicoa en coordinación con el proyecto Zerynthia (Italy), coincidiendo con la VII Bienal Internacional de la Habana, Ciudad de la Habana, Cuba (*Window onto Venus*, edited by Carlos Garaicoa in coordination with Zerynthia Project, coinciding with Havana Biennale).

1998
Bienarte, Galería Nacional, del Centro Costarricense para la Ciencia y la Cultura, San José.
(painting biennale)

Gary Hill
1951, born in California. Lives and works in Seattle and Rome.

Solo Exhibitions

2001
Gary Hill: Remembering Paralinguay, SITU Fabienne Leclerc, Paris.
Kunstmuseum Wolfsburg, Wolfsburg.

2000
Donald Young Gallery, Chicago.
Centro Cultural Recoleta, Buenos Aires; Museo Caraffa, Córdoba.
Gary Hill: The Performative Image, WATARI-UM, The Watari Museum of Contemporary Art, Tokyo; Towers Plaza Hall, Nagoya.

1999
Aarhus Kunstmuseum, Aarhus.

1998
Musée d'art contemporain de Montréal, Montreal.
Fundação de Serralves, Porto.
Capp Street Project, San Francisco.
Museu d'Art Contemporani, Barcelona.
Center for Contemporary Images, Saint-Gervais Genève, Geneva.

1997
Westfälischer Kunstverein, Münster.
Gary Hill: o lugar do outro/where the other takes place, Centro Cultural Banco do Brasil, Rio de Janeiro, Brazil; Museu de Arte Moderna de São Paulo, Brazil.

1996
Galleria Lia Rumma, Naples.
Barbara Gladstone Gallery, New York.

1995
Gary Hill, traveling exhibition organized by Riksutställningar, Stockholm, Sweden, Moderna Museet, Spårvagnshallarna, Stockholm; Museet for samtidskunst, Oslo; Helsingin Taidehalli, Helsinki; Bildmuseet, Umeå, Sweden; Jönköpings läns museum, Jönköping; Göteborgs Konstmuseum, Göteborg.

1994
Gary Hill, traveling exhibition organized by Henry Art Gallery, Seattle; Hirshhorn Museum and Sculpture Garden, Washington; Henry Art Gallery, Seattle; Museum of Contemporary Art, Chicago; Museum of Contemporary Art, Los Angeles; Guggenheim Museum Soho, New York; Kemper Museum of Contemporary Art and Design, Kansas City.
Musée d'art contemporain, Lyon.
Imagining the Brain Closer than the Eyes, Museum für Gegenwartskunst, Öffentliche Kunstsammlung, Basel.

1993
Gary Hill: In Light of the Other, Museum of Modern Art, Oxford, England; Tate Gallery, Liverpool.
Gary Hill: Sites Recited, Long Beach Museum of Art, Long Beach.

1992
Gary Hill: I Believe It Is an Image, WATARI-UM – The Watari Museum of Contemporary Art, Tokyo.
Gary Hill, traveling exhibition organized by the Centre Georges Pompidou, Musée national d'art moderne, Centre Georges Pompidou, Paris; Instituto Valenciano de Arte Moderno (IVAM), Centre del Carme, Valencia, Spain; Stedelijk Museum, Amsterdam, The Netherlands; Kunsthalle Wien, Vienna. Stedelijk Van Abbemuseum, Eindhoven.

1990
Galerie des Archives, Paris.
Museum of Modern Art, New York.

1986
Whitney Museum of American Art, New York.

1982
"Gary Hill: Equal Time, Long Beach Museum of Art, Long Beach.

1981
Museum of Modern Art, New York.

Group Exhibitions

2000

Between Cinema and a Hard Place, Tate Modern, London.
Vision Ruhr, 235 Media, Dortmund.
12th Biennale of Sydney, Sydney.
Voici, 100 ans d'art contemporain, Palais des Beaux-Arts, Brussels.

1999
The American Century: Art & Culture, Part II 1950 – 2000, Whitney Museum of American Art, New York.
Seeing Time: Selections from the Richard and Pamela Kramlich Collection of Media Art, San Francisco Museum of Modern Art, San Francisco; Zentrum für Kunst und Medientechnologie (ZKM), Karlsruhe.

1998
Tuning up #5, Kunstmuseum Wolfsburg, Wolfsburg, Germany, March 7 – August 9.
Voices, Witte de With, Center for Contemporary Art, Rotterdam, The Netherlands; Fundació Joan Miro, Barcelona, Spain; Le Fresnoy, Studio national des arts contemporains, Tourcoing, France.

1997
The Twentieth Century: The Age of Modern Art, Martin-Gropius-Bau, Berlin, Germany; Royal Academy of Art, London.
Angel, Angel, Kunsthalle Wien, Vienna; Galerie Rudolfinum, Prague.

1996
NowHere, Louisiana Museum of Modern Art, Humlebaek, Denmark, May 15 – September 8.
Foreign Bodies, Museum für Gegenwartskunst Basel, Öffentliche Kunstsammlung, Basel.
Being & Time: The Emergence of Video Projection, traveling exhibition organized by the Albright-Knox Art Gallery, Buffalo; Cranbrook Art Museum, Bloomfield Hills; Portland Art Museum, Portland; Contemporary Arts Museum, Houston; Site Santa Fe, Santa Fe.

1995
MultiMediale 4, Zentrum für Kunst und Medientechnologie, Karlsruhe.
Identità e Alterità, Venice Biennale.
Video Spaces: Eight Installations, Museum of Modern Art, New York.
Carnegie International, Carnegie Museum of Art, Pittsburgh.
3e Biennale d'art contemporain de Lyon, Musée d'art contemporain, Lyon.

1994
Múltiplas Dimensões, Centro Cultural de Belém, Lisbon.

Cocido y Crudo, Museo Nacionale Centro de Arte Reina Sofia, Madrid.

1993
Passageworks, Rooseum, Malmö.
American Art in the 20th Century: Painting and Sculpture 1913-1993, Martin-Gropius-Bau, Berlin, Germany; Royal Academy of Arts and the Saatchi Gallery, London.

1992
Doubletake: Collective Memory and Current Art, Hayward Gallery, London; Kunsthalle Wien, Vienna.
Documenta IX, Museum Fridericianum, Kassel.

1990
Passages de l'image, Musée national d'art moderne, Centre Georges Pompidou, Paris; Centre Cultural de la Fundació, Caixa de Pensions, Barcelona; The Power Plant, Toronto; Wexner Center for the Arts, Columbus; San Francisco Museum of Modern Art, San Francisco.

1989
Video and Language, Museum of Modern Art, New York.

1987
Documenta VIII, Museum Fridericianum, Kassel.

1984
Arte, Ambiente, Scena, La Biennale di Venezia, Venice.

1983
Whitney Biennial, Whitney Museum of American Art, New York, New York (also included in Whitney Biennials of 1985, 1987, 1989, 1991, and 1993).

1981
Projects Video XXXV, Museum of Modern Art, New York.

Bibliography

2001
Gary Hill: Around & About: A Performative View, Paris, Éditions du Regard, 2001. Boxed edition containing a DVD compilation by G. Hill (entitled *Performative Images* and containing video excerpts from videotapes, installations and performances) and three books: G. Hill, *Withershins 1995*; J. Lageira, *Des premiers mots aux derniers silences* (in French); and G. Quasha and C. Stein, *La performance elle-même*, including "Liminal Performance: Gary

Hill in Conversation with George Quasha and Charles Stein" and "How Great It's Going to Be: Liminal Performance 2: Gary Hill, George Quasha and Charles Stein in Conversation" (in French with English translations).
Gary Hill: Around & About: A Performative View, Limited Edition, Paris, Éditions du Regard, 2001 (Edition of 100, plus 20 artist' proofs; signed and numbered). Boxed edition containing *Performative Images* DVD by Gary Hill; texts by Gary Hill, Jacinto Lageira, George Quasha and Charles Stein, plus an additional DVD by Gary Hill entitled *Goats and Sheep* and poster designed by Gary Hill.
Gary Hill: The Performative Image, Tokyo, Gary Hill Exhibition Committee, 2001, unpaginated (Japanese and English).

2000
Gary Hill, edited by R.C. Morgan, introductory text by R.C. Morgan; reprinted texts by G. Hill and R. Bellour, L. Cooke, R. Cornwell, J. Derrida, C. Diserens, L. Furlong, J.C. Hanhardt, J. Lageira, L.-J. Lestocart, H. Liesbrock, B. London, A. Machado, R. Mittenthal, G. Quasha, S. Sarrazin, C. Stein, C. van Assche, W. van Weelden, PAJ Books / The Johns Hopkins University Press, Baltimore.
Gary Hill en Argentina: textos, ensayos, dialogos, texts by G. Hill, A. Machado, G. Quasha, C. Stein and R. Alonso, Buenos Aires, Centro Cultural Recoleta, in Spanish.
Gary Hill: Instalaciones, texts by D. Capardi, R. Alonso, A. Machado, G. Quasha, C. Stein, Córdoba, Ediciones Museo Caraffa, in Spanish.

1999
Gary Hill, edited by A. Kold, texts by J.E. Sørensen, J. Harboe, A. Kold, G. Ørskou Madsen, G. Quasha and C. Stein, J. San, Aarhus Kunstmuseums, Aarhus.
Gary Hill: Video Works, NTT InterCommunication Center, Tokyo.

1998
"Liminal Performance: Gary Hill in Conversation with George Quasha and Charles Stein", *PAJ (Performing Arts Journal)*, 58, XX, 1, January, pp. 1-25.
Bélisle, J., *Gary Hill*, essay by G. Quasha and C. Stein (french and english), Musée d'art contemporain de Montréal, Montreal.
Gary Hill: HanD HearD – Withershins – Midnight Crossing, texts by H. Liesbrock, G. Quasha and C. Stein, J. Lebrero Stals, Museu d'Art Contemporani de Barcelona, Barcelona.

1997
Quasha, G., Stein, C., *Tall Ships*, Gary Hill's

Projective Installations 2 Station Hill Arts, Barrytown, New York.
Quasha, G., Stein, C., *Viewer*, Gary Hill's Projective Installations 3, Station Hill Arts, Barrytown, New York.
Dantas, M., *Gary Hill: O lugar do outro/where the other takes place*, texts by A. Machado, G. Quasha and C. Stein (portuguese and english), Magnetoscópio, Rio de Janeiro.
Liesbrock, H., *Gary Hill: Midnight Crossing*, text by R. Mittenthal (german and english), Westfälischer Kunstverein, Münster.

1996
Quasha, G., Stein, C., *Gary Hill: HanD HearD/liminal objects*, Galerie des Archives, Paris; Station Hill Arts, Barrytown, New York.

1995
Gary Hill: Tall Ships, Clover, texts by T. Sandqvist, G. Quasha, M. Och Pål Wrange,, Riksutställningar, Stockholm.
Vischer, T., *Gary Hill: Imagining the Brain Closer than the Eyes*, texts by H. Belting, G. Boehm, G. Hill, B. Kempker, K. Lüdeking, F. Malsch, Museum für Gegenwartskunst, Basel; Ostfildern, Cantz, (In German: *Gary Hill: Arbeit am Video*, Basel, Museum für Gegenwartskunst; Ostfildern, Cantz).

1994
Bruce, C., *Gary Hill*, texts by L. Cooke, B.W. Ferguson, J.G. Hanhardt, R. Mittentha, Henry Art Gallery, Seattle; University of Washington, Washington.
Thériault, M., *Gary Hill. Selected videotapes 1978-1990*, Art Gallery of Ontario, Toronto, unpaginated (in French with English translation by D. McGrath)

1993
Gary Hill: Sites Recited, Long Beach, California, Long Beach Museum of Art, 1993, texts by H.B. Nelson, C.A. Klonarides, S. Kolpan, G. Quasha, and R. Bellour.
Mignot, D., *Gary Hill*, texts by R. Fuchs, T. Stooss, G. Hill, W. Van Weelden, L. Cooke, and G. Quasha, Stedelijk Museum, Amsterdam; and Vienna Kunsthalle, Vienna, pp. 8-9. English with Dutch and German translations.
Van Assche, C., Diserens, C., *Gary Hill*, texts by G. Hill, J. Lageira, L. Cooke, and H. Massardier, Instituto Valenciano de Arte Moderno (IVAM), Centre del Carme, Valencia.
Gary Hill: In Light of the Other, texts by L. Nittve, R. Mittenthal, C. Diserens, B.W. Ferguson, S. Morgan, The Museum of Modern Art Oxford, Oxford; Tate Gallery Liverpool, Liverpool.

1992
Sarrazin, S., *Chimaera Monographe No. 10*

(Gary Hill), Montbéliard, Centre International de Création Vidéo Montbéliard, Belfort.
Shizuko Watari, *Gary Hill – I Believe It Is an Image*, Watari Museum of Contemporary Art, Tokyo.
Van Assche, C., *Gary Hill* texts by L. Cooke, J. Lageira, H. Massardier, translations by A. Walker, Editions du Centre Georges Pompidou, Paris.

1991
Lageira, J., *Gary Hill: Between Cinema and a Hard Place*, OCO, Espace d'art contemporain, Paris.

1990
OTHERWORDSANDIMAGES, Video by Gary Hill, texts by A. Dorph Christoffersen, R. Bellour, G. Hill (Danish and English), Video Gallerie/Ny Carlsberg Glyptotek, Copenhagen.
Mittenthal, R., *Gary Hill: And Sat Down Beside Her*, Galerie des Archives, Paris.

1988
Quasha, G., Fargier, J.-P., *Gary Hill: DISTURBANCE (among the jars)*, Villeneuve d'Ascq, France, Musée d'Art Moderne, 1988 (French and English).

1980
Quasha, G., "Notes on the Feedback Horizon", *Glass Onion*, Program notes, Station Hill Press, Barrytown, New York. Reprinted in *Gary Hill*, edited by R.C. MorganPAJ Books / The Johns Hopkins University Press, Baltimore, pp. 109-113.

Laura Horelli

1976, born in Helsinki.
Lives and works in Frankfurt.

Solo Exhibitions

2001
Galerie Barbara Weiss, Berlin.

2000
Artists-in-Residence, AIAV-Gallery, Yamaguchi.

1999
Installaatio, Kuvataideakatemian Galleria, Helsinki.

Group Exhibitions

2001
Arbeit Essen Angst, Kokerei Zollverein, Essen.

1999
Cities on the Move, Kiasma, Helsinki.

1998
Stuttgart 17.7.1956 - Salem (Wis) | USA 3.3.1977, Portikus, Frankfurt.

Bibliography

2000
Kopomaa, T., *Kännykkä-Yhteiskunnan Synty ("The Birth of the Mobile Phone Society")*, Helsinki.

1999
Metronome or Backwards Translation: (No. 4-5-6), edited by C. Deliss.

Todd James
1969, born in New Haven, Connecticut.
Lives and works in New York.

Group Exhibitions

2001
Untitled 2001 Art Event, The Keith Haring Foudation, Tokyo.

2000
Point of Purchase, Parco Gallery, Tokyo.
Indelible Market, Institute of Contemporary Art, Philadelphia.

1998
Crash and Daze, Enrico Coveri Gallery, Florence.

Bibliography

2001
Cohen, M., "Street Market", *Flash Art*, January-February.

2000
Street Market, Little More Publishers, Tokyo.
Indelible Market, essay by Alex Baker, Institute of Contemporary Art, Philadelphia.
Attitude Dancer, Privately published, New York.
"Juicy Fruits", October.
Siegal, N. "Exhibit Becomes Opportunity for Arrest". *The New York Times*, October 10.
Oliver, S., "Bombs Away", *The Face*, November.
Yablonsky, L., "Street Market", *Time Out*, November 2-9.
Flannigan, E., "Soho Exhibit Sparks Mental Flames", *New York Amsterdam News*, October 26-November 1.
Valdez, S., "Street Market at Deitch Projects", *Art in America*, December.
Avgikos, J., "Street Market", *Artforum*, December.

1999

The Art of Getting Over, St. Martin's Press, New York.
1996
New York Graffiti 1970-1995, Edition Aragon, Germany.

1987
Spraycan Art, Thames and Hudson, England.

Yishai Jusidman
1963, born in Mexico D.F.
Lives and works in Mexico D.F.

Solo Exhibitions

2001
Stedelijk Museum voor Actuele Kunst, S.M.A.K., Gante.
Centro Fotográfico Manuel Alvarez Bravo, Oaxaca.

2000
mutatis mutandis, Centro de la Imagen, México, D.F., Galería Camargo Vilaça, São Paulo.

1999
en-treat-ment, Ramis Barquet Gallery, New York
Sumo (1995-98) / Bajo tratamiento (1997-99), Museo de Arte Carrillo-Gil, México, D.F.

1998-1996
Investigaciones Pictoricas / Pictorial Investigations 1989-1996, University Gallery, San Diego State University; Otis Gallery, Otis College of Art and Design; Wolfson Galleries, Miami-Dade Community College; Nevada Institute for Contemporary Art, Blaffer Gallery, University of Houston, EUA.

1997
Sumo/Geishas, Instituto Cultural Cabañas, Guadalajara, Jal, México.

1996
Sumos, Galería OMR, México, D.F.

1995
Investigaciones Pictoricas / Pictorial Investigations 1989-1994, Galería OMR, México, D.F.
Jardín Borda, Cueravaca, Morelos, México.

1994
Los Payasos, CURARE. México, D.F.

1990
Galería Sloane-Racotta, México, D.F.
Jack Shainman Gallery, New York.

1989
Elizabeth McDonald Gallery, New York.

Elizabeth McDonald Gallery, (Projects Room), New York.
1988
Ollantay Center for the Arts, New York.

1985
Attack Gallery, Los Angeles.

1984
Cal Arts Main Gallery, Los Angeles.

Group Exhibitions

2001
La Biennale di Venezia, 49. Esposizione Internazionale d'Arte, Sección Aperto, selección de Harald Szeemann, Venice.
ARS '01, Museo de Arte Contemporáneo Kiasma, Helsinki, Finland.
Ultrabaroque, Aspects of Post-Latin American Art, Modern Art Museum of Fort-Worth, Texas, EUA.
Self-made men, DC Moore Gallery, New York.

2000
Mexican Contemporary Art, travelling exhibition, Ludwig Museum, Budapest; Art Gallery of the Mexican Embassy, Berlin.
Visiones, Di-versiones, Lourdes Sosa Galería, México, D.F.
Ultrabaroque, Aspects of Post-Latin American Art, San Diego Museum of Contemporary Art, CA, EUA (travelling).
La Beauté du Geste, Centre dArt Contemporain, Vassiviére.
The Figure: another side of modernism, Newhouse Center for Contemporary Art, New York.
Caleidoscopio: Lenguajes contemporáneos, Banco Nacional de Comercio Exterior (BANCOMEXT), México, D.F.

1999
México eterno, Arte y permanencia, Palacio de Bellas Artes, México, D.F.
Vistas y conceptos, Museo de Arte Moderno, México, D.F.
Cinco Continentes y Una Ciudad, Museo de la Ciudad de México, México, D.F.
Zonas, Naturalezas y Suburbios en México, Museo de Arte Moderno, México, D.F.
A vueltas con los sentidos, Casa de América, Madrid, España. Curada por Estrella de Diego.
México Nuevo, Centre d'Arts de Villefranche-sur-Saône, Museé de la Valleé de Barcelonnette.
Tierra, Identidades dispersas, Museo Universitario de Artes y Ciencias, México, D.F.
Talleres, Track 16 Gallery, Los Angeles.
Viviendo la metáfora, Kunsthaus, San

Miguel de Allende, Guanajuato, México.
Artistas promotores, Out Gallery, México, D.F.
25 x 25, Galería El Espacio, México, D.F.
Creación en movimiento, Becarios del FONCA en el Centro Nacional de las Artes, México, D.F.
V Salón Bancomer, México, D.F.
FIAC, Stand Galería OMR, París.

1998
El cuerpo aludido; representaciones, anatomías y construcciones, México Siglos XVI-XX, Museo Nacional de Arte, México D.F.
Mexico: Reconfigured, Associated American Artists, New York.
In the 90's, Mexican Contemporary Art, Instituto Cultural Mexicano, Washington y Nueva York.
No soy chino, Art & Idea, México D.F.
ARCO, Stand Galería OMR, Madrid.
IV Salón Bancomer, México D.F.

1997
Mexico Now. Point of Departure (México Ahora. Punto de Partida), The Ohio Arts Council's Riffe Gallery, Columbus; El Arsenal de la Buntilla, San Juan; The Mint Museum of Art, Charlotte; Woodstreet Gallery, Pittsburgh; The Mexican Fine Arts Center Museum, Chicago; Delaware Art Museum, Wilmington; The Contemporary Arts Museum, Houston; The Mexican Cultural Institute, Washington.
The Conceptual Trend, cdited by R. Gallo, T. Gower, Museo del Barrio, New York.
ARCO, Stand Galería OMR, Madrid.

1996
Corona Roja, Sobre el Volcán. Centro Atlántico de Arte Moderno, Islas Canarias, Spain.
The Counterfit Subject; Francis Alÿs and Yishai Jusidman. Boulder Museum of Contemporary Art, CO, EUA.
Trip Wire, cdited by C. Ianaconne, LACE, Los Angeles.
Obras Recientes, Galería OMR, México, D.F.
ARCO, Stand Galería OMR, Madrid.

1995
Clown Oasis, edited by J. Vallance, Ron Lee's World of Clowns Museum, Las Vegas.
Fifteen Paintings, Richard Telles Fine Art, Los Angeles.
Tendencies: New art from Mexico City, San Francisco Art Institute, San Francisco.
Vancouver Gallery of Contemporary Art, Canadá, cdited by R. Gallo.
Pieza del Mes: E.K., Museo de Arte Contemporáneo de Oaxaca.
XI Muestra de Gráfica, Fundación Cultural Curitiba, Brazil.
Continental Discourse, cdited by D. Bacigalupi, San Antonio Museum of Art, San Antonio.

Quimeras, edited by M. Guerra, Museo Casa Diego Rivera, Guanajuato, Gto, Mexico.
Juntos y Revueltos, edited by O. Sánchez, Hospicio Cabañas, Guadalajara, Jal, Mexico.
ARCO, Stand Galería OMR, Madrid.

1994
XIV Muestra de Arte Joven. Casa de la Cultura, Aguascalientes; Pinacoteca de Nuevo León, Monterrey; Museo de Arte Carrillo Gil, Mexico, D.F.
Arte en Movimiento. Becarios del Consejo Nacional para la Cultura y las Artes. Museo de Arte Carrillo Gil, Mexico D.F.

1993
Summer Invitational, Patricia Shea Gallery, Los Angeles.
El Nopal Press, SPARC, Los Angeles.

1991
Waxworks, Tibor de Nagy Gallery, New York.
Window to L.A., ART L.A., Los Angeles.

1990
Summer Invitational, Pence Gallery, Los Angeles.
Greenberg Wilson Gallery, New York.
Landscape, Griffin McGinn Gallery, New York.

1989
Rugged Terrain, Shea & Becker Gallery, New York.
Landscape, Tibor de Nagy Gallery, New York.
New Landscape, Frank Bernarducci Gallery, New York.
La Agencia, New York.
1985
Attack LA, Piezo Electric Gallery, New York.
New Attitudes, Bank of Los Angeles, Los Angeles.

Bibliography

2000
Ultrabaroque. Aspects of Post-Latin American Art, exhibition catalogue, texts (spanish and english) by E. Armstrong, M. García, V. Zamudio-Taylor, *et alii*, San Diego Museum of Contemporary Art (travelling).
1900-2000. Un siglo de Arte Mexicano, texts by J. Coronel Rivera, L.-M. Lozano, T. del Conde, A. Arteaga, CONACULTA/INBA, Landucci Editores.
Gonzales-Day, K., "Sourires distants: les peintures de Yishai Jusidman Distant Smiles: Painting of Yishai Jusidman", *Art Press*, 260, Septembre, pp. 38-42.

1999

Cinco Continentes y Una Ciudad / Five Continents and One City, exhibition catalogue, texts (spanish and english) by K. Kellner, B. Ferguson, G. Minglu, M. Seppälä, C. Medina, D. Joseph Martínez, Museo de la Ciudad de México, Mexico.
Yishai Jusidman. bajo tratamiento / en treat ment, exhibition catalogue (individual), texts (spanish and english) by D. Pagel y Y. Jusidman, México, Museo de Arte Carrillo Gil, INBA, February-April.
A vueltas con los sentidos, exhibition catalogue, text by E. de Diego, Casa de América, Madrid.
McDonough, T., "Yishai Jusidman at Galeria Ramis Barquet", *Art in America*, December.
Mallet, A.E., "Yishai Jusidman. Museo Carrillo Gil", *Art Nexus*, 33, Julio-Septiembre, p. 150.
García Ponce de León, U., "Yishai Jusidman / Visión e Ideología", *ArtVance*, 1, June-July, pp. 54-57.
Cruzvillegas, A., "Sumo. Bajo Tratamiento", *Curare*, 14, Enero-June, pp. 33-38.
Nahas, D., "Yishai Jusidman en-treatment", *Review*, June 1, pp. 11-12.

1998-1999
El Cuerpo Aludido. Anatomías y Construcciones México, Siglos XVI – XX, exhibition catalogue, texts by K. Cordero, I. Vivanco, I. Benítez, P. Mues, J. Luis Barrios, *et alii*, Museo Nacional de Arte, Mexico.

1998
Nahas, D., "Yishai Jusidman at Blaffer Gallery", *New Art Examiner*, July-August, p. 15.

1997-1998
México Now: Point of Departure, México, , text (spanish and english) by O. Sánchez, Ohio Arts Council (travelling).

1997
Yishai Jusidman. Sumo, exhibition catalogue (individual), text (spanish and english) by O. Sánchez, Instituto Cultural Cabañas, Guadalajara, Jalisco, Mexico, September-October.
Birbragher, F., "Yishai Jusidman / Miami-Dade Community College", *Art Nexus*, October-December, pp. 146-147.
Iannaccone, C., "Yishai Jusidman at Otis Gallery", *Art Issues*, Summer.
Turner, E., "Worlds Collide in spheres, portraits", *Miami Herald*, July 25, p. 30G.
Knight, C., "'Jusidman': Going Beyond the Face Value of Clowns", *Los Angeles Times*, Tuesday February 18.

1996-1997
Gallo, R., "Yishai Jusidman, La serie Sumo", *Poliester*, 5, 17, Winter, pp. 26-31 (portada).

1995
Yishai Jusidman. Investigaciones Pictóricas, exhibition catalogue (individual), texts by C. Medina y D.A. Greene, Cuernavaca, Morelos, México, Instituto de Cultura de Morelos, México.
Continental Discourse, exhibition catalogue, text by Don Bacigalupi, San Antonio Museum of Art.
González Mello, R., "Yishai Jusidman. Investigaciones Pictóricas", *Poliester*, 13 Otoño, pp. 54-55.
Schneider Enriquez, M., "Yishai Jusidman / OMR", *Art News*, Summer, p. 138.
Hollander, K., "Yishai Jusidman at Galeria OMR", *Art in America*, June.
Bautista, S., "Yishai Jusidman" (Jardín Borda, Cuernavaca, Morelos, April 27-June 4, 1995). ARTI. U.S.A., 1995, p. 219.

1990
O'Rourke, M., "Yishai Jusidman", *Arts Magazine*, November, p. 102.
Kornblau, G., "New York Fax", *Art Issues*, December - January.

1989
Johnson, K., "Yishai Jusidman at Elizabeth McDonald", *Art in America*, December.
Lewis, J., "Yishai Jusidman, Elizabeth McDonald Gallery", *Art Forum*, November.

Ilya and Emilia Kabakov

1933 & 1945, born in Dniepropetrousk (Ukraina). Both live and work in New York.

Solo Exhibitions

2001
20 ways to get an apple. Listening to Mozarts Music, Museum of Fine Arts, Columbus.
50 installations + 2 big paintings from Charles Rosenthal, State Museum of fine Arts, Chemnitz.
The Palace of Projects, Kokerei Foundation, Essen.

2000
The Palace of Projects, Public Art Fund, The Armory on 26st and 1st Av, New York.
The Sick child, Ilya and Emilia Kabakov, Galerie Lia Romma, Naples.
Ilya Kabakov 50 installations, Wiesbaden Museum, Germany.
The life and Creativity of Charles Rosenthal, Städel Institute Frankfurt.

1999
Gallerie Thaddaeus Ropac.
Ilya Kabakov. Zeichnungen, Spregel-museum, Hannover.
Ilya and Emilia Kabakov, The Monument of a Lost Civilization, Cantieri della Zisa, Palermo.

The Boat of my Life, Duke University Museum.The Old Library, University of Amsterdam.
The Life and Creativity of Charles Rosenthal, Museum of Contemporary Art, Mito.

1998
Art Angel Project, The Roundhouse, London.
The Palace of Projects by Ilya and Emilia Kabakov, travelling to Upper Campfield Market, Manchester; Reina Sofia, Crystal Palace, Madrid.
The Children's Hospital by Ilya and Emilia Kabakov, The Irish Museum of Modern Art, Dublin, with biography published by Phaidon Press.

1997
The Artist's Library, Satani Galery, Tokyo.
The Life of Flies, Barbara Gladstone Gallery, New York.

1996
The Healing with Paintings, Kunsthalle Hamburg, permanent installation.
Op het Dak (On the Roof), Palais des Beaux-Arts, Brussels.

1995
Ilya Kabakov-Ein Meer von Stimmen (A Sea of Voices), Museum für Gegen-wartskunst, Basel.
C'est ici que nous vivons (We are living here), Centre G. Pompidou, Paris.
The Man Who Never Threw Anything Away, Museet for Samtidskunst, Oslo, permanent installation.

1994
Album of My Mother, The Golden Underground River, The Boat of My Life, Le Magasin, Grenoble.
Operation Room, Nykytaiteen Museo, Helsinki, traveling to Museet for Samtidskunst, Oslo, book *5 Albums*.

1993
NOMA oder der Kreis der Moskauer Konzeptualisten (NOMA or Moscow Conceptual Circle), Kunsthalle Hamburg.
Deserted School or School N.6, perma-nent installation, Chinati Foundation, Marfa.
Communal Kitchen, permanent installa-tion, Musée Maillol, Paris.
Het Grote Archief (The Big Archive), Stedelijk Museum, Amsterdam.

1992
Unaufgehängtes Bild (Unhung Painting), permanent installation, Ludwig Museum, Cologne.

Illustration as a Way to Survive, Kanaal Art Foundation, Kortrijk, traveling to Ikon Gallery, Birmingham; Hessisches Landes-museum, Darmstadt, "Zwischenfall im Museum".
Das Leben der Fliegen (The Life of Flies), Kunstverein, Cologne.

1991
Ilya Kabakov, Sezon Museum of Modern Art, Nagano.

1989
Sieben Ausstellungen eines Bildes (Seven Exhibitions of a Painting), Kasseler Kunstverein, Kassel.
Ten Characters, Hirshorn museum and Sculpture Garden, Washington.
He Lost his Mind, Undressed, Ran Away Naked, RFFA, New York.
Ausstellung eines, Buches (Exhibition of a Book), DAAD-Galerie, West-Berlin, installation De Appel, Amsterdam *Witte Schilderijen en witte Mensjes*, installation.
Ilya Kabakov: the Untalented Artist and OtherCharacters, Institute of Contemporary Art, London.

1988
10 Albums, Portikus, Frankfurt.
Ten Characters, RFFA, New York.

1987
Gegenwartskunst aus der Sowjetunion: Ilya Kabakov und Iwan Tchuikow, Museum für Gegenwartskunst, Basel.

1985
Ilya Kabakov, Galerie Dina Vierny, Paris.
Ilya Kabakov: Am Rande (along the Marginis), Kunsthalle Bern, travelling to Galerie de la Vieille Charité, Marseille, *Ilya Kabakov: En Marge*.

Group Exhibitions

2000
Vision du Future, Incident at the Museum or Water Music, Le Grand Palais, Paris.
Art gallery of New South Wales, Museum of Contemporary Art, The 12th Biennale of Sydney 2000, The Milan Italy, Rotonda della Besana, Stanze e Secreti, Ilya and Emilia Kabakov.

1999
Global Conceptualism, Queens Museum of fine Arts, New York.

1998
Wounds Between Democracy and Redemption in Stadel Institute, Moderna Museet, Stockholm.
The History of Interior: from Vermeer to Kabakov, Frankfurt.

1997
Sculpture of XX Century, Münster, permanent installation *Looking at the Sky, Reading the Words. Monde Future*, La Biennale di Venezia, 47. Esposizione Internazionale d'Arte, Corderie dell'Arsenale, Venice, installation *We Were in Kyoto*, by Ilya and Emilia Kabakov.
The Age of Modernism - Art in the 20th Century Martin-Gropius Bau, Berlin, installation *Three Nights*.
Whitney Biennial, New York, installation *Treatment with Memories*.

1996
G7 Summit, Musée d'Art Contemporain, Lyon, installation *Monument to the Lost Glove*.

1994
The Man who Never Threw Anything Away, installation, Kunst und Ausstellungshalle der Bundesrepublik Deutschland, Bonn.
Tyrannei des Schönen, Österreichisches Museum für Angewandte Kunst, Vienna.

1993
Russische Avantgarde im 20. Jahrhundert: von Malevitch bis Kabakov, Kunsthalle, Cologne, installations *Before Supper, Red Pavilion*.
Et tous ils changent le monde, Biennale d'Art Contemporain, Lyon, installation *Emergency Exit*, La Biennale di Venezia, 45. Esposizione Internazionale d'Arte, Venice, installation *Red Pavilion*, musical arrangement by V. Tarasov.
Rendez(-)Vous, Museum van Hedendaagse Kunst, Ghent, April 28 - June 27, installation *Unfinished Installations*.

1991
Wanderlieder, Stedelijk Museum, Amsterdam, installation *Before Supper*.
Carnegie International 1991, Carnegie Museum of Art, Pittsburgh, installation *We Are Leaving Here Forever*.
Dislocations, Museum of Modern Art, New York, installation *The Bridge*.

1990
Die Endlichkeit der Freiheit Berlin 1990: ein Ausstellungsprojekt, DAAD-Galerie, Berlin.
The Readymade Boomerang: Certain Relations in the 20th Century Art, 8 Biennale, Sydney, installation *Three Russian Paintings*.
Artisti Russi Contemporanei, Museo d'Arte Contemporanea Luigi Pecci, Prato, installation *The Underground Golden River*.

1989
Documenta IX, Kassel, installation *The Toilet*.

1988
Aperto, La Biennale di Venezia, Venice, installation *Before Supper*.

1987
Magiciens de la Terre, MNAM, Paris, installation *The Man Who Flew Into Space*.

1977
La nuova arte sovietica, una prospectiva non ufficiale (New Soviet Art, an Unofficial Perspective), La Biennale di Venezia, Venice.

Bibliography

2000
Der Text als Grundlage des Visuellen / The Text as the Basis of Visual Expression, edited by F. Zdenek, Oktagon, Cologne.
"Ilya Kabakov Flies into His Picture", *Art in America*, November, pp. 145-53.

1999
Kabakov, I., Kabakov, E., *Monument to a Lost Civilization/ Monument alla Civiltà Perduta*, Charta, Milan.
Vettese, A., "Storie d'un paese che sembra il nostro", *Sole*, 18 May, p. 41.

1998
Ilya Kabakov, dialogues with D. Ross and R. Storr, texts by B. Groys, I. Blazwick, I. Kabakov, Phaidon Press, London.
Haden-Guest, A., "Ilya Kabakov", interview, *Paris Review*, 149, pp. 104-121.
Hunt, I., "The People's Palace", *Art Monthly*, May, pp. 9-12.
Morgan, S., "Ilya Kabakov The Round House, London", *Frieze*, June-August, pp. 94-95.

1997
Siebold-Bultmann, U., "Unangetastete Räume: Natur und Geschichte als Themen neuer Kunst", *Neue Züricher Zeitung*, 28 June.

1996
Wallach, A., *Ilya Kabakov: The Man Who Never Threw Anything Away*, texts by I. Kabakov, R. Storr, Harry N. Abrams, New York.
"Ilya Kabakov: The Secret Antropologist", *Tate*, Winter, pp. 52-58.

1995
Kabakov, I., *Installations 1983 - 1995*, edited by N. Pouillon, texts by J.-H. Martin, R. Storr, B. Groys, I. Kabakov, Centre Georges Pompidou, Paris.

1994
Bonami, F., "Ilya Kabakov: Tales from the Dark Side", dialogue, *Flash Art*, 177, Summer, pp. 91 e sgg.

1993
Beaucamp, E., "Ästhetisches trotzdem", *Frankfurter Allgemeine Zeitung*, 29 October.

1992
Storr, R., "The Architect of Emptiness", *Parkett*, 34, pp. 42-51.
Becher, J., "Ilya Kabakov - Das Leben der Fliegen", *Kunstforum International*, 118.

1991
Kabakov, I., Groys, B., *Die Kunst des Fliehens: Dialogue über Angst, das heilege Weiß und den sowjetischen Müll*, Carl Hanser, Munich-Vienna.

Marin Karmitz
1938, born in Romania.
Lives and works in Paris.

After graduating from the l'IDHEC, he was the assistant to such film makers as Jean-Luc Godard, Agnès Varda, Jean Charles Tacchella and Pierre Kast.
In 1964 Karmitz produced his first short film, *Nuit Noire Calcutta*, according to the text written by Marguerite Duras, then his first full length film in 1968, *Sept Jours Ailleurs*, with Jacques Higelin. The events in May of 1968 inspired him for the next two films: *Camarades* (1970) and *Coup pour Coup* (1972).
In 1971 Marin Karmitz created his own production company, MK2, and he added a distribution structure and developed a chain of movie theatres of which the first is called '14 Juillet Bastille' and inaugurated May 1, 1974.
The Palm d'Or Award for *Padre Padrone* from the Taviani brothers at the Cannes Festival in 1977 and the award for best interpretation given to Michel Piccoli and Anouk Aimee for *Le Saut dans le vide* by Marcellocchio in 1980 in Cannes, confirm the quality of cinema concept defended by MK2. In 1982 the company achieves an exceptional success in Cannes: five films produced and distributed by MK2 are awarded a prize including the Palme d'Or for *Yol* by the Turkish Director Ylmaz G_ney.
Amongst the main films produced by Marin Karmitz, the trilogy by Krzystof Kieslowski (*Three Colors: Blue, Three Colors: White, Three Colors: Red*), the last eleven films by Claude Chabrol (*Poulet au Vinaigre, Inspecteur Lavardin, Masques, Madame Bovary, Berry, Une Affaire de Femmes, The Torment, A Judgement in Stone, Rien ne va Plus, The Colour of Lies*, and *Merci Pour Le Chocolat*), *Melo* and *I Want to Go Home* by Alain Resnais, *Little Felins* by Jacques Doillon, *Gabbeh, A Moment of*

Innocence and *The Silence* by Moshen Makhmalbaf, *The Apple* by Samira Makhmalbaf, *The Wind Will Carry Us* by Abbas Kiarostami, *Signs and Wonders* by Jonathan Nossiter and the co-production of some other films by Taviani brothers (*La Notte di San Lorenzo, Kaos, Good Morning Babylon*), to *Au Revoir Les Enfants* by Louis Malle and *The Beekeeper* by Theo Angelopoulos.

Marin Karmitz presented *Code Inconnu* by Michel Haueke with Juliette Binoche at the Official Competition at the Cannes Festival last year and *Un Temps Pour L'Ivresse des Cheveaux* by Bahman Ghobadi at the Director's Fortnight. This last film obtained a Camera d'Or.

Many official events have paid tribute to Marin Karmitz's work: the French Film Archives in 1985, the Georges Pompidou Center in 1987, the MOMA in New York in 1989, the Tel Aviv Film Archives in 1992, the Madrid Film Archives in 1998, the Munich Film Archives and the European Cinema Forum in Strasbourg in 1999.

In 1995 he published a book of memoirs entitled *Bande à part*.

In 1985 he was elevated to the rank of Knight of the Legion of Honour and to the rank of Officer of the Legion of Honour in 1999.

Abbas Kiarostami
1940, born in Teheran.
Lives and works in New York.

Filmography

1999
The wind will carry us.

1997
Taste of charry, Palma d'oro al festival di Cannes nel 1997.

1996
Viaggio verso l'alba.

1994
Through the olive trees.

1992
And life goes on..., Premio Rossellini al festival di Cannes nel 1992.

1990
Close-up.

1989
Homework.

1987
Where is the friend's home?, Golden Pardo d'oro at Locarno festival in 1987.

1984
First Graders.

1977
The report.

1974
The traveller.

Susan Kleinberg
1949, born in Phoenix (Arizona).
Lives and works in New York.

Solo Exhibitions

1999
Madresfield Court Fountain Design, Worcestershire.
Cal-a-Vie, Vista.

1998
Wilshire Blvd, Temple, Los Angeles.

1996
Studio D'Arte Barnabo, Venice.
AmeriCares Kobe Airlift Project.
AmeriCares, New Canaan.

1995
La Biennale di Venezia, Venice.
ArteLaguna, Casini Stal Vitale, Varese.

1994
International Headquarters, Human Rights Watch, New York.

1993
Zand Projects, New York.

1986
Cite des Artes, Paris.

1983
Castelli Uptown, New York.

1982
The American Center, Paris.

1985
New York Shakespeare Festival Public Theater, New York.
Thomas Babeor Gallery, La Jolla.

1981
University of Southern California, Los Angeles.
Gallerie Alain Oudin, Paris, France.
William Patterson College, Wayne.

Group Exhibitions

1996
Lingotto, Turin.

1995
Vietri Sul Mar.

1994
Fashion Moda, Bronx Museum, South Bronx, New York.

1993
Los Angeles Design Center, Los Angeles.

1992
Zand Projects, New York.

1991
University of California, San Diego Shiley Eye Center.

1989
BlumHelman, Green St., New York.
P.S. 1, Long Island.

1986
Cincinnati Museum, Orton Collection.
Thomas Babeor Gallery, La Jolla.

1985
Museum of Modern Art, Traveling Exhibition.

1984
Sarah Lawrence College, Bronxville.

1981
Monumental Sculpture '81, Brooklyn.

Matthieu Laurette
1970, born in Villeneuve St Georges, France.
Lives and works in Paris.

Solo Exhibitions

2001
Deitch Projects, New York.
Jousse entreprise, Paris.

2000
The Secret of Free Shopping, in collaboration with the Proto Academy, ECA research, Edinburgh College of Art, as part of *Vivre sa vie*, Edinburgh, Scotland, edited by T. Leighton & A. Patrizio in collaboration with The Proto Academy.
Social Hackers (Part 2), with Gunilla Klingberg, Muu galleria, Helsinki, Finland, edited by C. Ricupero & P. Topila.
Applaus (teil 2), project in public space as part of C/O Berlin, Berlin, Germany, edited by C/o Berlin /N. Boutin & M.-B. Carlier.
El Gran Trueque, Consonni, Bilbao, Basque Country, Spain, edited by F. Larcade.

1999
Applaus (teil 1), Institut Français, as part of

C/O Berlin, Berlin, edited by N. Boutin, M.-B. Carlier.
Patchwork in Progress, exposition monographique, edited by C. Bernard, Mamco – Musée d'Art Contemporain de Genève, Geneva.
Quand ça ne sert plus, ça sert encore, Le Pavé dans la Mare, Besançon.
Efficace et Commode, Propositions 99 pour la Collection, joint project with A. Pérez González, F. Larcade, Capc Musée d'Art Contemporain, Bordeaux, France.

1998
Free Sample 2, Slide Demix, Live Remix featuring Bosco, Mr Learn, S. Comte, Soirée Nomade, Fondation Cartier pour l'Art Contemporain, Paris.
Free Sample, Galerie Jousse Seguin, Paris.
Comment faire ses achats remboursés, invited by Le Confort Moderne, Médiathèque François Mitterrand, Poitiers.
Applaus, edited by L. Smits, M. Dölle. CASCO, Utrecht.

1997
Vivons remboursés, Le Camion-vitrine des produits remboursés, invited by Entre 2, project in public space, Nantes.
Mangez remboursé, showroom et visites guidées de supermarché, edited by L. Hazout, Réserve de Jean@ Chatelus, 28 rue Rousselet, Paris.
Matthieu Laurette, edited by A. Barak, with Pierre Joseph, FRAC Languedoc-Roussillon, Montpellier.
Nourrissez un artiste à partir de 100 Francs, c/o Ghislain Mollet-Viéville, Art Agent, Paris.

Group Exhibitions and Projects

2001
Il dono, edited by G. Maraniello, A. Somaini, Palazzo delle Papesse, Centro Arte Contemporanea, Siena.
Camo Show, edited by A. Vaillant, Wiesbaden Museum, Germany.
Really, edited by B. Hunt, Artists Space, New York.

2000
Au-delà du Spectacle, edited by P. Vergne, B. Blistène, Centre Georges Pompidou, Paris.
All you can eat!, edited by S. Sembill, Galerie für Zeitgenössische Kunst, Leipzig,
I love Paris, edited by A. Vaillant, as part of the exhibition *Duchamp's Suitcase*, Arnolfini, Bristol.
Négociations, edited by N. Bourriaud, B. Marcadé, Centre Régional d'Art contemporain, Sète.
Fuori uso 2000 (The Bridges), edited by H. Kontova, Pescara.

Voilà, le monde dans la tête, edited by S. Pagé, B. Parent, H.-U. Obrist, A. Schaerf, L. Bossé *et alii*, Musée d'Art Moderne de la Ville de Paris, Paris.
What, How & for Whom, edited by A. Devic, N. Ilic, S. Sabolovic, Zagreb.
Plan B, edited by M. Badia, S. de Jong, J. Bhoyroo, B. Kremer, F. Derieux, S. O'Brien, De Appel, Amsterdam.
Hairstyling, The Haircut of the Month, edited by Toasting Agency, Salon Coiffure Complice, Paris.

1999
Crash!, Corporatism and Complicity, edited by E. Dexter, CRASH!, V. Gaskin, ICA, London.
Equinox Now, edited by C.A. Klonarides, L.A. Edge Festival, The Geffen Contemporary at MoCA, Los Angeles.
French Video Art, edited by C. Van Assche, Santa Monica Museum of Art, Santa Monica.
Rebecca Bournigault, Matthieu Laurette, Marie Sester, 3 french artists explore the unseen, edited by S. Miller, New Langton Arts, San Francisco.
Direct Translation, edited by E. King Torrey, San Francisco Art Institute, San Francisco.
Le capital (tableaux, diagrammes et bureaux d'études), edited by N. Bourriaud, Centre Régional d'Art contemporain, Sète.
Soft Résistance, Galerie Gebauer, Berlin.
Le temps libre: son imaginaire, son aménagement, ses trucs pour s'en sortir, edited by Jean-Charles Masséra, Deauville.

1998
Propos Mobiles, edited by D. Gaudel, Projet 10, 10th arrondissement, Paris.
Premises: invested spaces in visual arts, architecture and design from France, 1958-1998, edited by C. Van Assche, M.-A. Lanavère, Guggenheim Museum Soho, New York.
In vitro et altro, Hors scène #3, edited by C. Cherix, G. Motti, Cabinet des estampes, Musée d'Art et d'Histoire, Geneva.
Bruitsecrets, edited by C. Saraiva, O. Reneau et A. Julien-Laferrière, CCC, Tours.

1997
Ici et maintenant, edited by Y. Jammet, Parc de la Villette, Paris.
Version originale, edited by G. Rey internet show http://www.lyon-city.org/mac-vo, Musée d'Art Contemporain, Lyon.
Nouvelles acquisitions vidéos, Musée National d'Art Moderne, Centre Georges Pompidou, Paris.

1995
Un monde chez soi / World at home, edited by S. Lamunière, St Gervais-Geneva.
Cosmos, des fragments futurs, edited by F. Perrin, MAGASIN-CNAC, Grenoble, France.

Bibliography

2000-2001
Balice, D., "Matthieu Laurette. Interview", *InterVista*, IV, 24, Fall-Winter, pp. 50-53.

2000
Vivre Sa Vie, exhibition catalogue, essay by A. Barak, Vivre Sa Vie, Glasgow. Artist project.
All You Can Eat!, exhibition catalogue, Galerie für zeitgenössische Kunst, , Leipzig.
Fuori Uso 2000, The Bridges, exhibition catalogue, Giancarlo Politi , Milan.
Plan B, exhibition catalogue, De Appel, Amsterdam.
Jeffries, S., "Young, gifted and French", *The Guardian - G2*, Thursday November 16, pp. 12-13.
Allen, J., "Reviews. Matthieu Laurette, C/O Berlin", *Artforum*, 39, 2, October, pp. 153-154.
Ellis, P., "The Great Exchange", *Flash Art*, 211, March - April, pp. 43.
Gonzalez Carrera, J.A., " Arte en agitación", *El Correo*, March 6.
Vaillant, A., "¿No nos hemos vistos antes en algun sitio?", *Zehar*, 41, Winter, pp. 8-17.

1999
Masséra, J.-C., *Amour, gloire et CAC 40*, Essay, Paris, POL, 1999, pp. 297-302.
Bourriaud, N., *Le Capital, tableaux, diagrammes & bureaux d'études*, exhibition catalogue, Centre Régional d'Art Contemporain, Sète.
Vaillant, A., "Questions for a champion. An interview with Matthieu Laurette", *Casco Issues*, 5, May, pp. 84-93.
Kellmachter, H., "Hervé Chandès présente Matthieu Laurette", *Connaissance des Arts*, 557, January, pp. 72-73.

1998
Laurette, M., *Free Sample Demix*, Artist publication, , essay by A. Vaillant, Galerie Jousse Seguin, Paris; documentation of works 1993-1998; biography; exhibition chronology; bibliography.
Masséra, J.-C., *A quoi rêvent les années 90?*, exhibition catalogue, Montreuil, Centre d'Art Moderne.
Beausse, P., "Matthieu Laurette", *Flash Art*, 211, November-December, p. 115.
Colard, J.-M., "Superdiscount", *Les Inrockuptibles*, 172, November 4-9, p. 75.
Hahn, C., "Économies parallèles, interview with Matthieu Laurette", *Blocnotes*, 15, Summer, pp. 48-51.
1997-1998
Demir, A., "Matthieu Laurette", *Documents sur l'art*, 14, Fall-Winter, pp. 16-17.

1997
Vaillant, A., "Matthieu Laurette: La folie des Produits remboursés", *Ici et maintenant*, exhibition catalogue, Le Méjean, éditions Actes Sud.
Cosmos des fragments futurs, exhibition catalogue, MAGASIN, Grenoble.
Mollet-Viéville, G., "Les bons plans de Matthieu Laurette", *Sans Titre*, 38, February, p. 3.

Marko Lehanka
1961, born in Herborn.
Lives and works in Frankfurt.

Group Exhibitions

2000
Szenenwechsel XVII, Museum für Moderne Kunst, Frankfurt am Main.
Mixing memory & desire, Neues Kunstmuseum, Luzern.
Forwart – a choice, Banque Bruxelles Lambert, Brussels.
Spicesbreadcompetitioneating, Leo Koenig Inc., New York.
Schipperme, Schaltern, wie vom Sinnen, Galerie Art Attitudes, Hervé Bize, Nancy.
Der Waas–Komplex, Neuer Kunstverein, Gießen.

1999
Pizzeria Sehnsucht, Quinzièmes Atelier du Frac des Pays de Loire, Nantes.

1998
Wer die Heimat liebt: 12 Jahre Offenbach, Galerie Martina Detterer, Frankfurt am Main.

1996
Semikolo, Portikus, Frankfurt am Main.

1993
Szenenwechsel IV, Museum für Moderne Kunst, Frankfurt am Main.
Salone, Villa Romana, Florence.

Jouko Lehtola
1963, born in Helsinki.

Solo Exhibitions

2001
Institut Finlandais, Paris.

2000
Young Heroes, 1% Gallery, Copenhagen, Denmark.

1998
Young Heroes, Gallery Zebra, Karjaa.

1997
Young Heroes, Peri Photo Centre, Turku.

Young Heroes, Viktor Barsokevich Centre, Kuopio.

1996
Young Heroes, Old Student House Gallery, Helsinki.

1994
Potrait of Finnish Rock, Kuopio City Art Museum, Kuopio.
Lionheart, Peri Photo Centre, Turku.

1993
Lionheart, Gallery Vapauden Aukio, Helsinki.

1992
Potrait of Finnish Rock, Alvar Aalto Museum, Jyväskylä.

1991
Potriait of Finnish Rock, Old Student House Restaurant, Helsinki.

Group Exhibitions

2001
fotoFINLANDIA!, Fotografisk Center, Copenhagen.
Encontros da Imagem/Festival of Light, Antigo Tribunal, Braga.
ITE, DIY Lives, Helsinki City Art Museum.
ITE, DIY Lives, Lönnström Art Museum, Rauma.

2000
Les Boreales, Caen.
Le(s) Nord(s), Batofar, Paris.
Urban Youth, Helsinki City Art Museum, Helsinki.
Organising Freedom, Charlottenburg, Copenhagen.
ITE, DIY Lives, Kajaani Art Museum.
ITE, DIY Lives, Kaustinen.
Viva Scanland, Art Tank, Belfast.
Centro de Arte la Estancia, Caracas.
Encontros da Imagem/Festival of Light, Antigo Tribunal, Braga.
BIG Torino 2000, Biennial of Emerging Artists, Cavalerizza, Turin.
Organising Freedom, Moderna Museet, Stockholm.

1999
Finnish Line: Starting Point, Musée d'art Moderne et Conteporain, Strasbourg.

1998
PhotoEspana98, Museo Arguelogico Nacion, Madrid.
Photo/Realities, Sörlandets Art Museum, Kristiansand.
Granny Pine, Annika Sundvik Gallery, New York.

1997

Heartbreak Hotel, Hotel Otava, Pori.
Contact, Finnish Museum of Photography, Helsinki.
The Art of Growing Up, Palazzo de Renzzo, Bologna.
The Young in the North, Peri Photo Centre, Turku.
The Young in the North, Finnish Cultural Centre, Antwerpen.

1996
Finland 80-years, Peri Photo Centre, Turku.
The Young in the North, Rådhuset, Copenhagen.

1994
Suvipinx, Sysmä.
Fotofinlandia-The Competition Final, Old Cable Factory, Helsinki.

1992
The Printed Photograph, Gallery Zebra, Karjaa.
Stop, The Dreams and Rusty everyday, Finnish Museum of Photography, Helsinki.

1991
The Colliding Interpretations, Art Hall, Helsinki.

1989
Focus - An Invitational Exhibition for Young Finnish Photographers, Finnish Museum of Photography, Helsinki.
The Young Photographers Exhibition, Old Student House, Helsinki.

1986
The Young Photographers Exhibition, Von Fersen-Sveaborg, Helsinki.

Bibliography

2000
Stadin Nuoret/Urban Youth, Tammi, Works included.
Itse tehty elämä ITE/DIY Lives, Maahenki, Works included.

1996
Vile Bodies: Photography and the Crises of Looking, Prestel, Works included.

1991
The Dreams and Rusty Everyday, Tammi, Participant photographer in the book project.

Tv programs

1996
Vile Bodies-Three Films about Photography and Our Taboos, Channel Four, U.K

Christiane Löhr

1965, born in Wiesbaden.
Lives and works in Cologne.

Solo Exhibitions

2000
Artothek, Cologne.
Camera Oscura, San Casciano dei Bagni.

1998
Galleria Salvatore + Caroline Ala, Milan.
Galerie Hafemann, Wiesbaden.
Objects, Forum Kunst, Rottweil.
Objects, Studentisches Kulturzentrum, Belgrade.
Objects and Drawings, Galerie im Kelterhaus, Winningen/Mosel.

1997
Objects and Drawings, Associazione artistica, Trier.
Preponderance of the small thing, Mittelrhein Museum, Coblenza.

1995
Objects and natural materials, Umweltberatung Österreich, Vienna.
Objects and installations, Galleria Brückenturm, Magonza.

Group Exhibitions

2000
Zeitsprung, Museo Mittelrhein, Coblenza.

1999
Galerie S., Aachen.
Fondazione Il Giardino di Daniel Spoerri, Seggiano.
Ville international des Arts, Paris.
The Secret Life of Plants, Galerie Conrads, Düsseldorf.

1998
Art and Artists in Rheinland-Pfalz, Jockrim.
Untitled, Museo Mittelrhein, Coblenza.
Eingemacht, Museo delle Donne, Bonn.

1997-1998
Claus Brunsmann, Brigitte Dams, Ursula Habermacher, Bärbel Schulte Kellinghaus, Christiane Löhr, Sandra Voets, Galleria Salvatore + Caroline Ala, Milan.

1997
Galleria S, with Sandra Voets and Felix Ersig, Aachen.
15 + 15, Capitale della Cultura Europea 1997, Salonika.
BASE, work by 28 artists, Hombroich Museum.
Klasse Kounellis, Modern Art Museum, Belgrade.

1996
Costructive drawing, Haus zum Stein, Mainz.
4a biennale Kleinplastik, Hilden.
FIELD, Künstlerforum, Bonn.
Klasse Kounellis, Royal Gallery of The Haag.
Young Artist of Rheinland-Pfalz, Artistic Association "Ludwigshafen", European Academy of Trier and Gallery Mennonitenkirche, Neuwied.
Animated dimension, Mittelrhein Museum, Coblenza.

1995
Albert Haueisen Preis, Jockrim.
Art and Music of Rheinland-Pfalz, Landesvertretung Bonn.
Photography and Graphic, Künstlerhaus Metternich, Coblenza.

1994
Art and Artists Rheinland-Pfalz, Germersheim.
Trofei, Galleria ARTicle, Cologne.
Doppelgänger, exchange project exhibition between 10 artists from Magonza and 10 artists from Glasgow, Old Fruit Market Hall, Glasgow.

1993
Paper, Galleria Brückenturm, Mainz.

1991
10x10x10, Kunsthaus, Wiesbaden.

Bibliography

2000
Verzotti, G., "Christiane Löhr", *Artforum*, January.
Menegoi, S., "Un'armonia possibile", *Activa*, January.
Castello, S., "Cardi, girasoli e metamorfosi della Löhr", *Arte*, February.
Horáková, D., "Nichts als Wachstum und Zerfall", *Welt und Sonntag*, 19, May 7.
Szeemann, H., "Die Expertise", *Welt und Sonntag*, May 7.

1999
"La Löhr espone a Milano", *La provincia di Cremona*, September 25.
"Bacche, crine di cavallo, cardi, semi questi i materiali di Christiane Löhr", *Il Giorno*, September 29.
"Christiane Löhr", *Il Giornale*, September 29.
"Christiane Löhr", *Arte e Critica*, October.
Tabozzi, R., "Christiane Löhr", *Corriere della Sera*, October 6.
Silvestri, C., "Christiane Löhr", *ebcnews*, October 7.
"Christiane Löhr", *Herald Tribune - Italy Daily*, October 13.

"Mostre in Italia: Christiane Löhr", *i Viaggi di Repubblica*, October 14.
Barile, S., "Christiane Löhr", *Lombardia Oggi*, October 17.
Bonalumi, F., "Triangolo d'arte tra Milano e Bergamo", *Avvenire*, October 21.
"Christiane Löhr", *Herald Tribune - Italy Daily*, October 25.
Bonazzoli, F., "Christiane Löhr", *ViviMilano - Corriere della Sera*, October 27.
"Christiane Löhr", *Interni*, November.
"Gallerie d'arte", *Milano Mese*, November.
Ceresoli, J., "Allucinanti cartoline dal terzo millennio", *Stile*, November.
"Natura astratta", *L'Unità*, November 1.
"Christiane Löhr", *Ottopiù*, supplemento del *Giornale di Brescia*, November 3-9.
Ridolfi, R., "Christiane Löhr", *Segno*, December-January.
Gravagnulo, E., "Christiane Löhr", *Titolo*, Winter.

Ingeborg Lüscher

1936, born in Freiberg.
Lives and works in Ticino.

Solo Exhibitions

2001
Fondazione Trussardi, Milan.
Kunstmuseum, Chemnitz.

2000
Ausstelungshalle Kraft, Basel.
53° Festival Internazionale del Film, Locarno.

1999
Plenty/Vaste, Gallery the Box, Turin.
Sette porte e una parete, Centro Culturale Svizzero, Milano.

1998
OceanPodpecPlecnikIngeborgLüscher (Catalogue), Museum of Modern Art, Mala galerija, Lubljana.

1997
Galerie Heinz Holtmann, Cologne.
Galerie Hans Mayer, Düsseldorf.
Städtische Galerie, Göppingen.

1996
Aargauer Kunsthaus Aarau, Aarau.
Omikuji – japanische Glückszettel, Völkerkundermuseum, Zurich.

1995
Brightness/Stillness, Moore College of Art and Design, Goldie Paley Gallery, Philadelphia.

1994
Galerie Marianne Grob, Luzern.

1993
Retrospektive Ingeborg Lüscher, Museum, Wiesbaden.

1991
Ingeborg Lüscher, Haags Gemeentemuseum, Den Haag.

1988
Lichtmasse, Galerie Farideh Cadot, Paris.

1987
Soirée bi-socque – Hôtel Touring Balance, Musée d'art et d'Histoire, Genf.

1986
Die Augen der Solfatara – gelb und rot, Galerie Elisabeth Kaufmann, Zurich (1988; Basel, 1990).
Ingeborg Lüscher – La Alquimia del Ser (Catalogue), Museum Diputacion Provincial, Madrid.

1985
Dei molteplici approcci al liocorno, Galleria Marilena Bonomo, Bari.
Pinturas 1981-1985, Galeria Juana de Aizpuru, Madrid (1986, Catalogue; 1994, Sevilla; 1998).

1982
Kunstmuseum, Solothurn.

1980
Galerie Dany Keller, München.
Steirischer Herbst, Kulturhaus, Graz.

1979
We all are magiciens, C Space, New York.

1977
Arbeiten von 1972-1977, Galerie nächst St. Stephan, Vienna (1982, Catalogue; 1985, Catalogue).
Arbeiten von 1972-1977, Galerie Krinzinger, Innsbruck (1980, Catalogue; 1982, Catalogue; 1985, Catalogue; 1988, Catalogue; 1989, Vienna, Catalogue; 2000, Vienna).
Centre d'Art Contemporain, Genf.

1976
Rester disponible (Faltblatt), Musée d'Art Moderne de la Ville de Paris, ARC 2, Paris.

Group Exhibitions

1997
Engel, Engel, Kunsthalle, Vienna.
Voglio vedere le miei montagne, Aargauer Kunsthaus, Aarau.
L'autre, 4e biennale d'art contemporain, Lyon.
Unmapping the Earth, 2nd Biennale, Kwangju.

Odeurs; ...une odyssée, Passage de Retz, Paris.
Die Schärfe der Unschärfe – Aspekte zeitgenössicherSchweizer Kunst, Kunstmuseum, Solothurn.
La Biennale di Venezia, XLVIII Esposizione Internazionale d'Arte, Arti Visive, Venice.
999, Centro d'Arte Contemporanea, Palazzo ex Troesch, Bellinzona.
Progetti di sacro: Arte e Architettura per il Giubileo, *Fallani Best, Chiesa di San Nicolò, Florence.*

1996
I love Yellow, Galerie Beyeler, Basel.

1993
Abstrakt, Deutscher Künstlerbund, Dresden.

1992
Documenta IX, Kassel.
Geteilte Bilder – Das Diptychon in der neuen Kunst (Catalogue), Museum Folkwang, Essen.
Weltausstellung Sevilla, Schweizer Pavillon, Sevilla.
Sonderfall? – Die Schweiz zwischen Réduit und Europa, Schweizerisches Landesmuseum, Zurich.

1991
Bildlicht, Wiener Festwochen, Museum des 20. Jahrhunderts, Vienna.
Visionäre Schweiz, Kunsthaus, Zurich; Museo Nacional Reina Sofia, Madrid; Kunsthalle, Düsseldorf.

1989
4. Triennale der Kleinplastik, Fellbach.
Unikat und Edition, Helmhaus, Zurich.
Einleuchten, Deichtorhallen, Hamburg.

1988
Aspects of Abstraction, Holly Solomon Gallery, New York.
Australian Biennale, Sydney.
Zeitlos, Hamburger Bahnhof, Berlin.

1987
Die Gleichzeitigkeit des Anderen, Kunstmuseum, Bern.

1981
Erweiterte Fotografie, Biennale, Vienna.

1980
Zorn un Zärtlichkeit, Galerie Maeght, Zurich.
Aperto, La Biennale di Venezia, XXVII Esposizione Internazionale d'Arte, Venice.

1978
Monte Verità, Museo Casa Anatta, Ascona; Akademie der Künste, Berlin; Museum des 20. Jahrhuderts, Vienna.

1972
Documenta 5, Kassel.
Welt aus Sprache, Akademie der Künste, Berlin.

Bibliography

1999
Manuale, Ingeborg Lüscher, text by S. Herzog, edited by.: A.T. Schmid, Verlag Niggli.

1996
Japanische Glückszettel, Schrkamp, ... Verlag, Frankfurt am Main und Liepzig, mit A. Muschg und O. Minako.

1985
Der unerhörte Tourist – Laurence Pfautz, Verlag Sauerländer, Aarau, Frankfurt am Main und Salzburg.

1982
Die Angst des Ikarus oder Hülsenfrüchte sind Schmetterlingsblütler, Verlag Sauerländer, Aarau, Frankfurt am Main and Salzburg.
Avant-apres/Sheer Prophecy – True Dreams, edited by A. von Fürstenberg, Centre d'Art Contemporain.

1975
Erlebtes und Erdäumeltes einander zugeordnet, Publikation des Prix Concours Oumansky, 1974, Société des Arts, Palais de l'Athénée, Genève.

1972
Dokumentation über A.S. – Der grösste Vogel kann nicht fliegen, Du Mont, Cologne.

Mark Manders
1968, born in Volkel.
Lives and works in Arnheim, Holland.

Solo Exhibitions

2000
The drawing center, New York.
Stedelijk Museum / Museum overholland, Amsterdam.
Greene Naftaly Gallery, New York.

1999
Galerie Erika + Otto Friedrich, Bern.

1998
Staatliche Kunsthalle, Baden Baden.

1997
De Appel, Amsterdam.
The Douglas Hyde Gallery, Dublin.
Zeno X Gallery, Antwerpen.

1995
Galerie Erika + Otto Friedrich, Bern.

1994
Zeno X Gallery, Antwerpen.
Van Abbemuseum, Eindhoven.
MUHKA, Museum voor Hedendaagse Kunst, Antwerpen.

Group Exhibitions

2001
Stedelijk Museum, Amsterdam / Museum overholland.
Sonsbeek 9.
La Biennale di Venezia, 49. Esposizione Internazionale d'Arte, Venice.
Museum de Servalles, Porto.

2000
Museum voor moderne kunst, Oostende.
Barbara Gladstone Gallery, New York.
Tokyo City Opera Art Gallery, Tokyo.

1999
S.M.A.K. in Watou, Watou.
XXIV Biennale Sao Paolo, San Paolo.
3 Raume 3 Flusse, Hann Munden.
S.M.A.K., Gent.
Fondazione Sandretto Re Rebaudengo per l'Arte, Turin.
Bonner Kunstverein, Bonn.
Zeeuws museum, Middeburg.

1998
Barbara Gladstone Gallery, New York.
Stedelijk Van Abbemuseum, Eindhoven.

1997
ICA, London.
Fondazione Sandretto Re Rebaudengo per l'Arte, Turin.

1996
Stedelijk Museum De Lakenhal, Leiden.
Centraal Museum, Utrecht.
Van AbbeMUSEUM, Eindhoven.

1995
De Vleeshal, Middelburg (films),
Van Abbemuseum, Eindhoven.
National Museum of Modern Art, Jakarta.

1994
Musée d'Art Moderne de la Ville de Paris, Paris.
Museum van Hedendaagse Kunst, Gent.
Vereniging voor het museum van hedendaagse kunst, Gent.

1993
Sonsbeek 93, Arnhem.
La Biennale di Venezia, Scuola, Venice.
1992
Prix de Rome, Museum Fodor, Amsterdam.

Bibliography

2001

"Mark Manders / Marije Langelaar", *Angus*, Rome / Internationale Beelden Colectie Rotterdam.
Mark Manders / Marije langelaar - Waiting for the laundry, Rome.
"Mark Manders", *Newspaper with fives*, Rome / Sonsbeek 9.
Mark Manders – China, Rome.
Mark Manders - Pressure points, Rome / Sonsbeek 9.

2000

Mark Manders - Ornament met brandpunten, Rome.
"Mark Manders / Marije Langelaar",*Tokyo newspaper*, Rome / Tokyo City Opera Art Gallery.
"Mark Manders", *Newspaper with drawings*, Rome / Greene Naftaly Gallery.

1999

"Mark Manders", *Newspaper with fives*, ROMA, S.M.A.K., Gent.
Mark Manders, Coloured room with black and white scene, ROMA, Galerie Friedrich Bern.
Mark Manders / Roger Willems, Assoziative Wortkörper, ROMA, S.M.A.K., Gent.

1998

Mark Manders, Self-portrait in a surrounding area, XXIV Biennale Sao Paolo, Mondriaan Foundation.

1997

Mark Manders, Fragments from Self-portrait as a building, De Appel, Amsterdam , The Douglas Hyde Gallery, Dublin.

1994

Mark Manders - De afwezigheid van Mark Manders, Museum voor Hedendaagse Kunst, Antwerpen.

Tuomo Manninen
1962, born in Jyväskylä.
Lives and works in Helsinki.

Solo Exhibitions

2000

Me-We, Norden I fokus, Stockholm.
Me-We, VR:n makasiinit, Helsinki.

1999

Me-We, Fredrikinkatu, Helsinki.

1998

Flora & Fauna, Galleria Zone, Helsinki.

1997

Average, Main exhibition of Nordic Autumn of Arts, Helsinki.
Galleria Harmonia, Jyväskylä.
Rantagalleria, Oulu.

1996

Galleria Zone, Helsinki.
Galleria Nykyaika, Tampere.
Galleria Zebra, Karjaa.

Group Exhibitions

1999

Exhibition of Finnish Photography, Brussels.

1998

Flight of thought, Jyväskylä.

1997

Window-Mirror: Finnish-Latvian exhibition of modern art, Kunsthalle, Helsinki.
Contact: Finnish documentarism, Museum of Photography, Helsinki.
Window-Mirror: Finnish-Latvian exhibition of modern art, Arsenals, Riga.

1996

ENTER, Kunsthalle, Helsinki.

Bibliography

1998

Me/We, Graal/Anfortas, Helsinki.

1997

"Anthology of Finnish Photography", *Musta Taide magazine*.

1996

Helsingin Sanomat Magazine, April.

1995

"Anthology of Finnish Photography", *Musta Taide magazine*.

Eva Marisaldi
1966, born in Bologna.
Lives and works in Bologna.

Solo Exhibitions

2001

Pale idea, Corvi Mora, London.

2000

Lieto fine, Palazzo delle Albere, Trento.
Tristan, Massimo De Carlo, Milan.
Eva Marisaldi, Sales, Rome.

1999

Accampamenti, Massimo Minini, Brescia.
Jet lag, Robert Prime, London.
A4 extra, Galleria d'arte moderna di Bologna, Bologna.

1998

Indifferentemente, Massimo De Carlo, Milan.
Omissioni, Sales, Rome.

1997

Avanti e indietro sul linoleum fino all'alba, Robert Prime, London.
Molte domande non hanno una risposta, Neon, Bologna.

1996

X e il Disegno della Cancellazione, Massimo De Carlo, Milan.
Maestri, Massimo De Carlo, Milan.

1995

Il corso tace, Iconoscope/Frac Languedoc-Roussillon, Montpellier.
Minima arteria, Massimo Minini, Brescia.
5 Giornate, Kunsthaus, Essen.

1994

Film, Analix, Geneva.
A un'ora, Studio Guenzani, Milan.

1993

Ragazza Materiale, Raucci/Santamaria, Naples.
Prét, ARC Musèe de la Ville de Paris, Paris.
La portata umana è nulla, Neon, Bologna.

1992

Studio Guenzani, Milan.

1991

Risoluzione d'immagine orizzontale, Antonella Melari, Rome.

1990

'ee', Neon, Bologna.

Group Exhibitions

2001

Sonsbeek 9, Arnhem

2000

Talent\um Tolerare, Fondazione Querini, Venice
Migrazioni, Centro per l'Arte Contemporanea, Rome

1999

Biennale di Istanbul 6, Istanbul

1998

Subway, Metropolitana, Milan.
La ville, le jardin, la memoire, Villa Medici, Rome.

1997

Fatto in Italia, Centre d'art contemporain, Geneva.

Pittura italiana da collezioni italiane, Castello di Rivoli, Turin.

1996

Uccelli/Birds, Rome.
Manifesta, Witte de With, Rotterdam.
Exchanging Interiors, Museum Van Loon, Amsterdam.
Presente/Gegenwart, Kunstlerwerkstatt Lothringer Strasse, Munich.

1994

Soggetto/soggetto, Museo d'Arte Contemporanea Castello di Rivoli, Rivoli, Turin.
L'Hiver de l'Amour, ARC Musèe de la Ville de Paris, Paris.
Rien à signaler, Analyx, Geneva.
L'Hiver de l'Amour, P.S.1, New York.
Incertaine Identité, Analyx, Geneva.

1993

Documentario/Privacy, Spazio Opus, Milan.
Aperto. Emergenze, La Biennale di Venezia, XLV Esposizione Internazionale d'Arta, Venice.
Hotel Carlton Palace chambre 763, Hotel Carlton, Paris.

1992

Una domenica a Rivara, Castello di Rivara, Rivara.
Venti pezzi fragili, Analyx, Geneva.

1991

Provoc'arte, Galleria ferroviaria Montale, Repubblica di San Marino.
Nuova Officina Bolognese, Galleria Comunale d'Arte Moderna, Bologna.

1990

Italia '90, Ipotesi Arte Giovane, Fabbrica del vapore, Milan.

Bibliography

2001

Il premio del centro 2000, Rome.

2000

Belli, G., *Eva Marisaldi*, Skira.
Daolio, R., *Eva Marisaldi*, Skira.

1999-2000

Bertola, C., *Eva Marisaldi*, P.S.1 Bureau Italia, ed. Castelvecchi.
Vettese, A., *Eva Marisaldi*, Spazio Aperto, 19, Bologna.

1999

Amadasi, G., *Eva Marisaldi*, 6 Istanbul Biennial.

1998

Beatrice, L., Perrella, C., *Nuova arte italiana*, Castelvecchi.

1997
Verzotti, G., "Viatico per quarant'anni di pittura italiana", *Pittura italiana*, exhibition catalogue, Charta.
Colombo, P., *Fatto in Italia*, exhibition catalogue, Electa, Milan.
Barilli, R., "Una marcia progressiva verso gli 'immateriali'", *Officina Italia*, Mazzotta.
Barilli, R., *Eva Marisaldi*, il Patalogo, Ubulibri.
Marisaldi, E., *Molte domande non hanno una risposta*, exhibition catalogue.

1996
Daolio, R., *Presenze/Gegenwarten*, exhibition catalogue.
Vergine, L., *Arte in trincea*.
Tazzi, P.L., "Or of lightness", *Exchanging Interiors*, exhibition catalogue, Amsterdam.

1994
Di Pietrantonio, G., *Prima Linea*, exhibition catalogue, Politi, Milan.
Romano, G., *Rien à signaler*, exhibition catalogue, Analyx, Geneva.
Pasini, F., Verzotti, G., *Soggetto/soggetto; Una nuova relazione nell'arte di oggi*, exhibition catalogue, Charta, Milan.
Incertaine identitè, exhibition catalogue, Analyx, Geneva.

1993
Daolio, R., "Postscriptum", *Aperto*, Politi.

1992
Romano, G., *Twenty fragile pieces*, exhibition catalogue.

Viktor Marushchenko
1946, born in Novosibirsk.
Lives and works in Kyiv.

Solo Exhibitions

1998
Ukraine, Werkstattgalerie J. Gloor + E. Vogel, Aarau.
Galéria Profil, Bratislava.

1997
Ausstellung in der Kornschütte, Luzern.
Ausstellung im Verwaltungsgebäude Hostett, Sarnen.

1996
Leben mit Tschernobyl, Seidlvilla, Munich.
Leben mit Tschernobyl, Stadtmuseum Weilheim.

Retrospektive 1976-1996, Ukrainische Künstlerunion, Kyiv.

1994
Theaterfotografien, Schauspielerhaus, Moskow.
Ein Fenster zur Ukraine, Stadthaus Zurich.
Die Ukraine, Galerie Goldenes Kalb, Aarau.

1993
Folio Gallery, Calgery (CAN).
Theaterfotografien, Theaterfestival, Sevastopol.

1992
Photoforum Pasquart, Biel (CH).
Die Ukraine nach Tschernobyl, Soroptimist International, Glückstadt.

1987
Theaterfotografien, Chisinau.

Group Exhibitions

2000
Meine Welt, mit Künstlerin Marija Pryjmachenko, Kommunale Galerie, Berlin.

1999
Unsere ukrainische Welt, in Zusammenarbeit mit W. Miloserdov, Ukrainisches Haus, Kyiv.
Wir, in Zusammenarbeit mit W. Miloserdov, Ukrainisches Kulturzentrum in Moskow.

1996
Filmregisseur S. Paradzhanov, Fotocollage zur Ausstellung in Zusammenarbeit mit R. Balajan, Nationale Universität "Kyjevo-Mohyljanska Akademija", Kyiv.
"Ein Fenster zur Schweiz", Ukrainische Künstlerunion, Kyiv.

1995
Multiple Exposures: Ukrainian Photography Today, Rudgers Art Center, New Brunswick.
Nach 5 Jahren, Kulturhaus, Bratislava.

1993
Galerie Municipale du Château d'Eau, Toulouse.

1992
Galerie Basta, Lausanne.

1990
100 Fotografen aus Osteuropa, Musée de l'Elysée, Lausanne.

1987

Ein Jahr nach Tschernobyl, Kyiv.

1984-1986
Journalistenunion, Moskow.

1983
Fotogalerien Vilnius, Kaunas.

Bibliography

1997
Viktor Marushchenko. Ukraine. Fotografien, Fotobuch, Benteli, Verlag Bern.

Barry McGee
1966, born in San Francisco.
Lives and works in San Francisco.

Stephen Powers
1968, born in Philadelphia.
Lives and works in New York.

Todd James
1969, born in New Haven.
Lives and works in New York.

Solo Exhibitions

2000
UCLA hammer Museum, Los Angeles.

1999
Hoss, Rice University Art Gallery, Houston.
The Buddy System, Deitch Projects, New York.

1998
Regards, Walker Art Center, Minneapolis.

1995
Installation, Art & Design Studio/ K&T Lionheart LTD, Boston.

1994
Installation, Center for the Arts Yerba Buena Gardens, San Francisco.

1993
Installation, Museum Laser Segall, San Paulo.

Group Exhibitions

2000
Street Market, Parco Gallery, Tokyo.
Street Market, Deitch Projects, New York.
Indelible Market, Institute of Contemporary Art, Philadelphia.

1998
Art From Around the Bay, Museum of Modern Art, San Francisco.

1997
Drawing Installation, Galerie Tanya Rumpff, Harlem.
Drawing Today, San Francisco.

1996
1997-SECA Art Award, Installation, Museum of Modern Art, San Francisco.
WAVEFORMS, Installation, Santa Cruz.
Figureheads & Red Herrings, Koplin Gallery, Los Angles.
Acme Custom, Acme Gallery, San Francisco.
Wall Drawings, The Drawing Center, New York.
City Folk, Group Exhibition, Holly Solomon Gallery, New York.
Degenerate Art, Group Exhibition, The Lab, San Francisco.
Post No Bills, Acme Gallery, Wall Installation, San Francisco.
Group Installation, Pro Arts Gallery, Oakland.
Missed Connections, Market Street Installation, Luggage Store/509.
Cultural Center Annex, San Francisco.
Installation, Street Art Exhibition, Los Angeles.
The Library, New Langton Arts, San Francisco.
Big Jesus Trash Can, Victoria Room, San Francisco.

1993
Twelve Bay Area Painters: The Eureka Fellowship Winners, San Jose Museum of Art, San Jose.
Texture of Nature, Berkeley Art Center, Berkeley.
Folklore, Luggage Store, 509 Cultural Center, San Francisco.
Installation, La Raza Graphics Center, San Francisco.

1992
U.C. Santa Cruz, Mary Porter Sesnon Gallery, Santa Cruz.

1991
Wet Paint, Southern Exposure, San Francisco.
3/Play, Southern Exposure, San Francisco.
Installation, Diego Rivera Galley, San Francisco.
Wall of Resistance, Wall of Shame, UC Berkeley, Berkeley.
Art Aginst the War. A.T.A. Gallery, San Francisco.
Multicultural Show, Diego Rivera Gallery, San Francisco.

Bibliography

2001
Cohen, M., "Street Market", *Flash Art*,

January – February.
Strenght, March.

2000
Street Market, Tokyo, Japan, Little More Publishers.
Indelible Market, essay by A. Baker, Institute of Contemporary Art, Philadelphia.
Venus, R., "The Artists in Their Studios", *Flaunt Magazine*, March.
Tokyo Jammin', October.
Siegal, N., "Exhibit Becomes Opportunity for Arrest", *The New York Times*, October 10.
Flannigan, E., "SoHO Exhibit Sparks Mental Flames", *New York Amsterdam News*, October 26-November 1.
Oliver, S., "Bombs Away", *The Face*, November.
Yablonsky, L.,"Street Market", *Time Out New York*, November 2-9.
"Juicy Fruits", *Tokion*, November-December.
Valdez, S., "Street Market at Deitch Projects", *Art in America*, December.
Avgikos, J., "Street Market", *Artforum*, December.
Stecyk, C.R., "Some Other Small Planet" *Super X Media*, 4.1.2.

1999
Buddy System, New York, Deitch Projects.
Mccormich, C., "Barry McGee's Twist of Faith", *Paper*.
Leffingwell, E., "Barry McGee at Deitch Projects", *Art in America*.
Blake, N., "Barry McGee", *Interview Magazine*, February.
Smith, R., *The New York Times*, April.
Scherr, A., "Stealing Beaty", *San Francisco*, November.
Kalm, J., "Old School, New School", *NY Arts*.

1998
Caniglia, J., *ArtForum*.

1996
Bonetti, D., *San Francisco Examiner*, September.

1994
Baker, K., *San Francisco Chronicle*, June.

Marisa Merz
1925.
Lives and works in Turin.

Solo Exhibitions

1998
Galleria Christian Stein, with D. Bianchi, Milan.

1996
Stedelijk Museum, Amsterdam.

1995
Kunstmuseum, Winterthur.

1994
Centre Georges Pompidou, Paris.
Barbara Gladstone Gallery, New York.

1993
Galleria Christian Stein, Milan.

1990
Galleria Christian Stein, with Mario Merz, Turin.

1984
Galerie Jean & Karen Bernier, Athens.

1983
Galerie Konrad Fischer, Düsseldorf.

1980
Citta irreale, with Mario Merz, Galleria Lucio Amelio, Naples.

1980
Galleria Antonio Tucci Russo, Turin.

1979
Galerie Jean & Karen Bernier, Athens.

1978
Galleria Franco Toselli, with N. de Maria e Mario Merz, Milan.

1977
L'eta del Rame, Galleria Salvatore Ala, Milan.

1975
Galleria L'Attico, Rome.

1974
Galleria Franco Toselli, Milan.

1970
Galleria L'Attico, Rome.

1969
Aeroporto di Ciampino, Rome.

1967
Galleria Luna 2, Turin.
Galleria Sperone, Turin.
Piper Club, Turin.

Group Exhibitions

1997
Arte Italiana Ultimi Ouarant'anni. I Materiali, Galleria d'arte moderna, Bologna.

1996

Città Natura, Palazzo delle Esposizioni, Rome.

1995
Die Italienische Metamorphose 1943-1968, Kunstmuseum, Wolfsburg.

1994
Italiana. From Arte Povera to Transavanguardia, Nicaf, Yokohama.
The Italian Metamorphosis 1943- 1968, Guggenheim Museum, New York.

1993
Viaggio verso Citera, Casinò d'Inverno, Venice.

1992
La Collection M.me Christian Stein: Un regard sur l'art italien, Le Nouveau Musée, Villeurbanne, Lyon.
Documenta IX, Kassel.
Avanguardie in Piemonte 1960- 1990, Palazzo Cuttica, Alessandria.
Arte povera, Kodama Gallery, Osaka.

1991
Ottanta Novanta, Monastero dei Benedettini, Monreale.
Visionäre Schweiz, Kunsthaus, Zurich.

1990
Ponton Temse, Museum van Hedendaagse Kunst, Ghent.

1989
Verso l'Arte Povera, PAC, Milan; ELAC, Lyon.
Bilderstreit: Widerspruch Einheit und Fragment in der Kunst seit 1960, Museum Ludwig e Rheinhallen, Cologne.
Einleuchten, Deichtorhallen, Hamburg.

1987
Disegni italiani, Galleria Civica d'Arte Moderna, Modena.
Italienische Zeichnungen, Frankfurter Kunstverein, Frankfurt.
Turin 1965-1987: de l'Arte Povera dans les collections publiques françaises, Musée Savoisien, Chambéry.
Zeitlos, Hamburger Bahnhof, Berlin.
Sculptures de chambre, Centre d'Art Contemporain, Geneva.
La Biennale di Venezia, XLIII Esposizione Internazionale d'Arte, Venice.

1986
Sculture da camera, Gipsoteca del Castello Svevo, Bari.
Chambres d'amis, Museum van Hedendaagse Kunst, Ghent.
Fideliter 1966-1986, Galleria Christian Stein, Turin.

De sculptura , Messepalast, Vienna.
Sonsbeek, Arnhem.
La Biennale di Venezia, XLII Esposizione Internazionale d'Arte, Venice.
Skulptursein, Stadtische Kunsthalle, Düsseldorf.

1985
Del Arte Povera a 1985, Palacio de Cristal e Palacio de Velàzquez, Madrid.
Promenades, Parc Lullin, Genthod Geneva.
Il museo sperimentale di Torino. Arte italiana degli anni sessanta nelle collezioni della Galleria Civica d'Arte Moderna, Museo d'arte contemporanea Castello di Rivoli, Turin.
The Knot: Arte Povera at P.S.1, P.S.1, New York.
De sculptura, Messepalast, Vienna.
Spuren Skulpturen und Monumente ihrer präzisen Reise, Kunsthaus, Zurich.

1984
Il modo italiano, Laica Los Angeles Institute of Contemporary Art, Los Angeles; University of California, Irvine; Newport Harbor Art Museum, Newport Harbor.
Coerenza in coerenza: dall'Arte Povera al 1984, Mole Antonelliana, Turin.
Ouverture: Arte Contemporanea, Museo d'Arte Contemporanea Castello di Rivoli, Turin.
Il disegno in dialogo con la terra, Galerie Albert Baronian, Bruxelles; Musée d'art moderne de la ville de Liege, Liege.

1983
Eine Kunst-Geschichte in Turin 1965-1983 Kölnischer Kunstverein, Cologne.
Tema Celeste, Museo Civico d'Arte Contemporanea, Gibellina.
Il cielo, come il fuoco e la terra, Centro d'Arte Contemporanea, Siracusa.

1982
Avanguardia Transavanguardia, Mura Aureliane, Rome.
Documenta 7, Kassel.
Spelt from Sibyl's leaves: Explorations in Italian Art, University Art Museum, University of Sidney; Power Gallery, Brisbane.
Galleria Christian Stein, Turin.

1981
Linee della ricerca artistica in Italia 1960-1980, Palazzo delle Esposizioni, Rome.

1980
La Biennale di Venezia, XXXIX Esposizione Internazionale d'Arte, Venice.
Arte e critica 1980, Galleria Nazionale

d'Arte Moderna, Rome.

In autunno, disegni di A. De Maria, Gastini Mainolfi, Mario Merz, Marisa Merz, Zorio, OOLP Libreria Internazionale, Turin.

1979

Magma, Museo di Castel Vecchio, Verona.

Le stanze, Castello Colonna, Genazzano, Rome.

1978

Scatola d'amore, Galeter Centro Arte, Adro, Brescia.

XII Rassegna Internazionale d'Arte, Acireale.

1977

Arte in Italia 1960-1977, Galleria Civica d'Arte Moderna, Turin.

Incontri internazionali d'arte, Palazzo Taverna, Rome.

Festival of Celtic People, Wrexham.

1976

Autori vari per "Europa-America", Galleria Franz Paludetto, Turin.

La Biennale di Venezia, XXXVII Esposizione Internazionale d'Arte, Venice.

Identité italienne: l'art en Italie depuis 1959, Musée National d'Art Moderne Centre Georges Pompidou, Paris.

1975

Mostra per le fabbriche occupate, Galleria Multipli, Turin.

1973

X Quadriennale nazionale d'arte La ricerca estetica dal 1960 al 1970, Palazzo delle Esposizioni, Rome.

1972

La Biennale di Venezia, XXXVI Esposizione Internazionale d'Arte, Venice.

1970

III Biennale Internazionale della giovane pittura: Gennaio 70, Museo Civico, Bologna.

1969

Op losse schroeven: Situaties en cryptostructuren, Stedelijk Museum, Amsterdam.

Verborgene strukturen, Museum Folkwang, Essen.

1968

Arte povera + azioni povere, Arsenali dell'Antica Repubblica, Amalfi.

1967

*Museo sperimentale d'arte contempo-

---

ranea, Galleria Civica d'Arte Moderna, Turin.

Deposito d'arte presente, Turin.

Bibliography

1995

Marisa Merz, edited by D. Schwarz, Kunstmuseum, Winterthur.

1994

Corgnati, M., Poli, F., *Dizionario d'Arte Contemporanea*, Feltrinelli, Milan.

Marisa Merz, Editions du Centre Pompidou, Paris.

1993

Austellungen bei Konrad Fischer, Düsseldorf Oktober 1967-Oktober 1992, Edition Marzona, Bielefeld, p. 208.

1992.

Celant, G., " Marisa's Swing", *Artforum*, XXX, 10, Summer, pp. 97-101.

Semin, D., *L'Arte Povera*, Edition du Centre Pompidou, Paris.

1991

Kurzmeyer, R., "Marisa Merz", *Visionare Schweiz*, edited by H. Szeemann, Aarau, Frankfurt, Salzburg, Sauerländer, pp. 178-180.

1989

Soutif, D., "La famille pauvre", *Artstudio*, 13 (été), pp. 6-19.

Meyer-Thoss, C., "Heaven can wait... Konstruktionen für den freien Fall: Gedanken zu Werk und Person der Amerikanischen Bildhauerin Louise Bourgeois und den Künstlerinnen Eva Hesse, Marisa Merz und Meret Oppenheim", *Bilderstreit Widerspruch, Einheit und Fragment in der Kunst seit 1960*, J. Gachnang; S. Gohr, DuMont Buchverlag, Cologne, pp. 195-208.

1986

Celant, G., "Art Pauvre", *Libération*, September 26.

1985

Calabrese, O., *L'Italie aujourd'hui/Italia oggi: Aspects de la création contemporaine de 1970 à 1985*, Villa Arson, Nice.

Cora, B., "Figure", *AEIUO*, 12, January, pp. 70-73.

Merz, M., "Senza titolo. 1982", *ibid.*, pp. 68-69.

Il museo sperimentale di Torino: Arte italiana degli anni Sessanta nelle collezioni della Galleria Civica d'Arte Moderna, edited by M. Bandini, R. Maggio Serra, Fabbri, Milan, pp. 17, 276- 277,426.

Celant, G., *Arte Povera. Storie e protagonisti/Arte Povera. Histories and Protagonists*, Electa, Milan.

Celant, G., *The Knot: Arte Povera at P.S.1*, Umberto Allemandi, Turin, pp. 134-147.

Merz, M., "Perme", *Spuren, Skulpturen und Monumente ihrer präzisen Reise*, Kunsthaus Zurich, Zurich, p. 52.

1984

Zacharopoulos, D., "Arte Povera Today", *Flash Art International*, Milan, March, pp. 52-57.

La Palma. M., "Paradoxes of Association and Object", *Art Week*, March 3.

Rogozinski. L., "La position crépusculaire", *Parachute*, mars-avril-mai, pp. 5-17.

Tazzi, P.L., "Marisa Merz", *Il modo italiano*, Laica, Los Angeles, p. 94.

1983

Grüterich, M., "Was Du mir nicht sagst. frage ich mich trotzdem", *Eine Kunst-Geschichte in Turin 1965-1983*, edited by W. Herzogenrath Kölnischer Kunstverein, Cologne, Daniela Piazza Editore, Turin, pp. 71-77.

1982

Bonito Oliva, A., *Mostra d'arte. XV Rassegna Internazionale d'Arte*. Acireale Turistico-Termale.

1981

Merz, B., Merz, M., "Interview, décembre 1972", Asor Rosa, A. [et alii], *Identité Italienne: L'art en Italie depuis 1959*, Centro Di, Florence.

Paris, Musée National d'Art Moderne Centre Georges Pompidou, Centro Di, Florence, p. 406.

1980

Celant, G., "20 ans d'art en Italie", *Art Press*, 37, May, pp. 8-9.

Celant. G., "L'interno di Marisa", *Arte e critica*, Galleria Nazionale d'Arte Moderna, De Luca, Rome.

Bandini, M., "Immagini della natura e invenzioni neoclassiche", *Avanti!*, Rome, September 7.

Rogozinski, L., " Marisa Merz" , *Flash Art*, 98-99, Milan.

1979

Merz, M., "Fiore", *Le stanze*, edited by A. Bonito Oliva, Centro Di, Florence.

Barilli, R., *Informale, oggetto, comportamento*, 2, Feltrinelli, Milan.

Mussat Sartor, P., *Fotografo 1968-1978. Arte e artisti in Italia*, Stampatori, Turin, pp. 147-161.

1978

Licitra Ponti, L., "Marisa Merz", *Domus*, 579, February, pp. 48-49,

Merz, M., "Da dove viene il rame? Una mostra di Marisa Merz", *ibid.*, p. 49.

Merz, Marisa. "Legni abbandonati sui campo", *ibid.*, p. 50.

Toselli, F., "L'arte fuori luogo", *ibid.*, p. 51.

Ferrari, C., "L'età del rame", *Data*, 31, March-May.

Loda. R. "Scatola d'amore", *Galeter Centro Arte*, June-July.

1977

Celant, G. "Una scarpetta di nylon con tanti chiodi", *La Repubblica*, 4-5 dicembre, Rome.

1976

Brizio, G.S., "Torino da Persano. Concettuali per le lotte operaie", *Avanti!*, January 22, Rome.

Bonito Oliva, A., *Europa-America. The Different Avantgardes*, Deco Press, Milan.

Bonito Oliva, A., "Process. Concept And Behaviour In Italian Art", *Studio International*, 191, 979, January-February, pp. 3-10.

Merz, M., "L'apprendimento dell'artigianato calzolaio per il poeta Lenz", *La Città di Riga*, 1, p. 42.

Sauzeau Boetti, A.-M., "Negative Capability as Practice in Women's Art", *ibid.*

Vergine, L., "Italian Art Now", *ibid.*

1975

Trini, T., "Arte e storia dell'arte", *Data*, 16-17, July-August, pp. 49-53,

Boetti. A.-M., "Lo specchio ardente", *Data*, 18, settembre-ottobre, p. 50-55, Milan.

1974

Celant, G., "Piccole cose, fatti personali", *Domus*, 534, May.

1970

Volpi Orlandini, M., "L'art pauvre", *Opus International*, 16, March, pp. 39-43.

1969

Trini, T., "Nuovo alfabeto per corpo e materia", *Domus*, 470, January, pp. 45-51, Milan.

Millet, C., "Petit lexique de l'Art Pauvre", *Les Lettres françaises*, June 4.

1968

Trini, T., "Marisa Merz", *ibid.*

Apollonio. U., "Deposito d'Arte Presente a Torino", *Flash Art*, 7, March-April.

Calvesi, M., "Lo spazio, la vita e l'azione", *L'Espresso*, September 15.

van Elk, G., "Amalfi: Arte povera in azioni povere", *Museum Journal,* 1, Stedelijk Museum Amsterdam.

1967
Trini, T., "Marisa Merz: una mostra alla Galleria Sperone", *Domus,* 454. p 52.
Celant, G., "Arte povera. Appunti per una guerriglia", *Flash Art,* 5, November-December.
Barilli, R., *Dall'oggetto al comportamento,* Ellegi, Rome.

Chantal Michel
1968, born in Bern.
Lives and works in Thun.

Solo Exhibitions

2001
Galerie Kabinett, Zürich.
Galerie Haus Schneider, Ettlingan.
Galerie Hubert Winter, Vienna.
Galerie Klara Sais, Düsseldorf.
Büchsenhausen Kunstraum, Innsbruck.

2000
Kunsträume Zermatt.
Galerie Kabinett, Bern.
Maison de la Culture d'Amlens.
Kunstverein Freiburg I.Br.
Espace d'Art Yvonamor Palix, Paris.

1999
Galerie Naumann, Stuttgart.
Büro für Fotografie, Stuttgart.
Next Stop, Kunstmuseum Thun.
Galerie Karin Sachs, München.

Group Exhibitions

2001
Ghost, Galerie Clocca, Milan.

2000
Au centre l'artiste, Centre Pasquart, Biel.
Puisions, Centre Culturel Switzerland, Paris.
Berneraustellung, Kunsthalle Bern.
Artistes Indépendantes, Galerie Hubert Winter, Vienna.
recycle, Kunstraum Kreuzlingen.
Galerie Clara Sels, Düsseldorf.
Girls, art plessures 3, Zürich.
Les trahisons du modèle, Café Creme, Luxemburg.
Mare Nostrum, Palazzo Ferretto, Genua.

1999
24h deluxe, Hôtel Scribe, Paris.
Young – Junge Schweler Fotografie, Fotomuseum Winterthur.
I never promised you a rosegarden, Kunsthalie Bern.

...imagine, Galerie Haus Schneider, Ettingen.
Heartbreakhotel, Hotel Beau-Rivage Thun.
Come in and find out, Podewll, Berlin.

1998
Larmes artificielles, Galerie Montenay-Giroux, Paris.
In the summertime..., Galerie Haus Schneider, Ettlingen.

Priscilla Monge
1968, born in San José.
Lives and works in San José.

Solo Exhibitions

2000
Relaciones, Galeria Jacobo Karpio, San José.

1999
Priscilla Monge, Galería Jacobo Karpio, San José.
Priscilla Monge, (MUA Instala), Galeria del Museo de Bellas Artes, Tegucigalpa, Honduras.
Cuatro Artistas, Museo de Arte y Diseño Contemporaneo, San José.

1997
Priscilla Monge, The Soap Factory, Athens.

1996
Vereniging voor het Museum van Hededaagse Kunst Gent, Gent.
A Radical Complicity, Gandy Gallery, Prague.
Thomas Cohn Arte Contemporanea, Rio de Janeiro.

1995
Priscilla no Pinta, Galería Jacobo Karpio, San José.

Group Exhibitions

2000
Mega Fino, Miami Beach Convention Center, Miami.
X, Museo de Arte y Diseño Contemporaneo, San José.
Visiones de Hombres, Museos del Banco Central, San José.
No solo lo que ves. Pervitiendo el minimalismo, Museo Nacional Centro de Arte Reina Sofía, Madrid.
Puerto Rico 2000, San Juan, Puerto Rico.
El enigma de lo cotidiano, Casa de America Latina, Madrid.
El Poder de Narrar, IVAM, Valencia, España.
Territorios Ausentes, Casa de America Latina, Madrid.
Central American Art, Fine Art Museum, Taipei, ROC.

1998
Galería Jacobo Karpio, San José, Costa Rica.
Thomas Cohn Arte Contemporanea, San Paulo.
XXIV Bienal de San Paulo.
Adquisiciones Recientes Arte Latinoamericano, Museo Centro Nacional de Arte Contemporaneo Reina Sofía, Madrid.
Mesótica, Van Reekum Museum, Apeldoorn, Holanda.
Instituto Italo – Latino, Rome.

1997
Sexta Bienal de la Habana , Cuba.
Bienal de Medellin, Colombia.
Mesótica, Casa América Latina, Madrid.
Maison de l'Amerique Latine, Paris.
Asi esta la cosa | Instalacion y arte objeto en America Latina, Centro cultural Arte Contemporaneo, A.C., Mexico, D.F.

1996
Tijuana 96, Centro Cultural Tijuana, Mexico.
Colección de Museo Iberoamericano de Badajoz, Spain.
Relaciones, Museo de Arte y Diseño Contemporaneo, San José.

1995
Juguetes, Museo de Arte y Diseño Contemporaneo, San José.
Costa Rica en las Bienales, Museo de Arte y Diseño Contemporaneo, San José.

1994
XXII Bienal de Valparaiso, Valparaiso, Chile.
Bienal de Pintura de Santo Domingo, Republica Domenicana.
Arte Contemporaneo Costarricense, Museo Sofia Imber, Caracas.
Arte Contemporaneo Costarricense, Museo Mario Abreu, Maracay.
Salones Nacionales de Arte, Museo de Arte Costarricense, San José.
VI Bienal de Pintura Lachner y Saénz, Museo del Banco Central, Plaza de la Cultura, San José.

1991
V Bienal Lachner y Saénz, Museo del Niño, San José, Costa Rica.

Bibliography

1998
Loria, V., "Las argucias seductoras de la (in) significancia", *Revista Lápiz,* 146, October, pp. 44-49.
Borras, M.L., "De vuelta con el cliché y el Tabù", *Art Nexus,* October, pp. 44-48.
Mosquera, G., *Fresh Cream,* Phaidon Press, London.

1997
Hanappe, E., "Priscilla Monge", *Catálogo de La Sexta Bienal de La Habana,* May, p. 158.
Scott–Fox, L., "Priscilla Monge", *Revista Poliester (On Sport),* 17, Winter.
Perez–Ratton, V., "Victima–Victimario", *Catálogo Bienal de Medellin.*
"Bordados violentos", *Catálogo Paises XXIV Bienal de San Paulo,* Brazil.

1996
Martens, H., *Kunst Nu,* January, Gent.
Ruyters, M., "Melktandjes", *Weekend Knack,* February 25, p. 121.
Perez–León, D., "A Bridge Between Two Cultures", *Art Nexus,* 22, October-December, p. 121.

1995
Pérez, D., "Priscilla Monge en la Jacobo Karpio", *Art Nexus,* 17, July- September, pp. 120-121.
Casanova, S., "Pintura, pintura, pintura", *Revista Estilo,* June, pp. 64-65.
Rubinstein, R., "Priscilla Monge at Jacob Karpio", *Art in America,* Summer, p. 117.

Ron Mueck
1958, born in Melbourne.
Lives and works in London.

Solo Exhibitions

2000
Anthony d'Offay Gallery, London.

1998
Anthony d'Offay Gallery, London.

Group Exhibitions

2000
Ant Noises, Saatchi Gallery, London.

1999
Unsichere Grenzen, Kunsthalle zu Kiel, Kiel.
The Mind Zone, Millennium Dome, London.

1997
Sensation: Works of Art from the Saatchi Collection, Royal Academy of Arts, London; Hamburger Bahnhof, Berlin.

1996
Spellbound, Hayward Gallery, London (exhibited as part of Paula Rego installation).

Marco Neri

1968, born in Forlì.
Lives and works in Torriana (RN).

Solo Exhibitions

2001
Tilt, Galleria Fabjbasaglia, Rimini.

2000
Scorrere, Gianni Giacobbi Arte Contemporanea, Palma de Mallorca.
A grandi linee, Juliet, Trieste.
Come into my room, Galerie Hilger/Artlab, Vienna.
Travel, Galerie Haus Schneider, Ettlingen/Karlsruhe.

1999
Windows 99, Galleria dell'Immagine, Musei Comunali, Rimini.
Windows 99, Galerie Hübner, Francoforte.

1998
Familiarizzare, Galerie Hübner, Francoforte.
Skyline, Galerie Haus Schneider, Karlsruhe.
Sostenere lo sguardo, Galleria Fabjbasaglia, Rimini.

1997
Progetto Museo d'Arte Italiana 1985-1997, Castello di Rivara, Turin.
Dinamiche interne, Wassermann Galerie, Munich.

1996
Gravity, Galleria Ponte Pietra, Verona.
Rinverdire il classico, Galleria Fabjbasaglia, Rimini.

1995
Galleria Rasponi Arte Contemporanea, Ravenna.
Ex Chiesa di Sant'Anna, Galleria Nazionale d'Arte Moderna, Repubblica di San Marino.

1993
L'età del ferro, Pinacoteca Cleofilo e Centro Culturale Una Arte, Fano.

1991
Galleria Rasponi Arte Contemporanea, Ravenna.

Group Exhibitions

2000
Futurama, Museo Pecci, Prato.
Sui Generis, PAC, Milan.
Premio Michetti, Museo Michetti, Francavilla a Mare, Pescara.
1999
Mitomoto, Chiostri di San Domenico, Reggio Emilia.

Nuovo nomadismo individuale, Casa del Rigoletto, Mantova.
Porta d'oriente, Palazzo Tupputi, Bisceglie, Bari.
Figuration, Fondazione Blickle, Rupertinum Museum, Saltzburg.

1998
Mitovelocità, Galleria d'Arte Moderna, Repubblica di San Marino.
Nuovo Paesaggio Italiano, Spazio Consolo, Milan.
Il nuovo ritratto in Italia, Spazio Consolo, Milan.

1997
Exelisis, Fondazione M. Merkouri, Pneumatiko Kentro, Athens.
La bella addormentata, Palazzo Basile, Città Sant'Angelo, Pescara.
Collezione permanente, Galleria Civica d'Arte Moderna, Siracusa.
Vodka Orange, Galleria Dirarte, Caserta.
Malerei, Galerie Linding in Paludetto, Norimberga.

1996
Figurazione Fantastica, Studio d'Arte Cannaviello, Arte Fiera Bologna.
Romantico Contemporaneo, Castello di Bentivoglio, Bologna.
Fade Out, La sparizione del paesaggio, Conc. Vicentini, Verona.
Martiri e Santi, Galleria L'Attico, Rome.
Adicere Animos, Palazzo del Ridotto, Cesena.
Il nibbio di Leonardo, Cortile del Castello, Carpi.
Nuovo luogo per l'arte, Ex manifattura tabacchi, Città Sant'Angelo, Pescara.
Ultime Generazioni 1950, 1990, Quadriennale Nazionale d'Arte.
Palazzo delle Esposizioni, Rome.
Pittura, Castello di Rivara, Turin.

1995
Museo d'Arte Paolo Pini, ex O.P., Milan.
Gallerie Elisabeth Krief, Paris.
Cambio di Guardia, Studio d'Arte Cannaviello, Milan.

1994
Stanze del Paesaggio, Palazzo Albertini, Forlì.
Ora, Pinacoteca di Pavullo, Modena.

1993
Pittura Italiana dopo la Transavanguardia, Galleria Rasponi, Ravenna.

1990
Intercity Uno, Fondazione Bevilacqua La Masa, Venice.
Premio Marche, Ancona.
XXXIV Edizione Premio Campigna, Santa Sofia di Romagna, Forlì.

1988
XL Edizione Premio F.P. Michetti, premiato, Francavilla al Mare, Chieti.

1987
Indagine '87, Palazzo del Podestà, Bologna.

Bibliography

2000
De Cecco, E., "Marco Neri", *Premio Michetti 2000*, exhibition catalogue, G. Politi Ed. Milan.
Romano, G., "Siempre clandestinos", *Lapiz*, 160, Spain.
Riva, A., "Marco Neri", *Sui generis*, exhibition catalogue, PAC, Milan.

1999
Marziani, G., "Windows 99", *Windows 99*, catalogo, Galerie Hübner, Frankfurt.
Romano, G., "Sostenere lo sguardo", *Flash Art Italia*, 219, G. Politi.

1998
Romano, G., "Ceci n'est pas un paysage", *Skyline*, exhibition catalogue, Galerie Haus Schneider, Karlsruhe.
Romano, G., "Ceci n'est pas un portrait", *Sostenere lo sguardo*, Galleria Fabjbasaglia, Rimini.
Sciaccaluga, M., "Marco Neri", *Tema Celeste*, 68.

1997
Bellasi, P., "Marco Neri, intervista", *Tema Celeste*, 59\60.

1996
Meneghelli, L., *Fade out, la sparizione del paesaggio*, exhibition catalogue, Vicentini, Verona.
Spadoni, C., "Rinverdire il classico", *Martiri e santi*, exhibition catalogue, L'Attico, Rome.

1993
Spadoni, C., "Dipingere le cose", *L'età del ferro*, exhibition catalogue, Ass. Cult. Una Arte, Fano.
Mingotti, A., "Per Marco Neri", *L'età del ferro*, exhibition catalogue, Ass. Cult. Una Arte, Fano.

1990
Spadoni, C., "Gilardi, Sartelli, Neri", *Premio Marche 1990*, exhibition catalogue, Ed. De Luca, Rome.

Ernesto Neto

1964, born in Rio de Janeiro. Lives and works in Rio de Janeiro.

Solo Exhibitions
2001
Directions, The Smithsonian Hirshhorn Museum and Sculpture Garden, Washington.
Centro Galego de Arte Contemporaneo, Santiago de Compostela, Spain.

2000
Institute of Contemporary Art, London.
SITE Sante Fe, New Mexico.
Wexner Center for the Arts, Columbus.
Dundee Contemporary Art, Scotland.

1999
Contemporary Arts Museum, Houston.

1998
Museo de Arte Contemporano Carrilo Gil, Mexico D.F.
Bonakdar Jancou Gallery, New York.

1997
Tanya Bonakdar Gallery, New York.
Galeria Camargo Vilaca, San Paulo.
Fundação Cultural do Distrito Federal, Brasilia.

1996
Paço Imperial, Rio de Janeiro.
Espacio 204, Caracas.

1993
Desenhos, Espaço, Cultural Sergio Porto, Rio de Janeiro.

1992
Museu de Arte Moderna de São Paulo, São Paulo.
Centro Cultural São Paulo, São Paulo.

1990
Galeria Millan, São Paulo.

1989
FUNARTE, Rio de Janeiro.

1988
Petit Galerie, Rio de Janeiro.

Group Exhibitions

2000
La Repetition, La Tête dans les nuages, Villa Arson, Nice.
Sense and Sensuality, Body and Soul in Pictures, Neues Museum Weserburg, Bremen.
Carnegie International, Carnegie Museum of Art, Pittsburgh.
Wonderland, The St. Louis Art Museum.
Centro de Arte Reina Sofia, Madrid.

1999
Collectors Collect Contemporary: 1990-1999, ICA, Boston.
Liverpool Biennial.
Amnesia, Biblioteca Luis Arango, Bogota.
A Vuelta com los Sentidos, Casa de America, Madrid.
La Metamorfosis de las Manos, Irma Arestizabal, Mar Del Plata.

1998
XXIV Bienal Internacional de São Paulo, São Paulo.
Sidney Biennial, Sydney, Australia.
Poeticas de Cor, Centro Cultural Light, Rio de Janeiro.
Loose Threads, Serpentine Gallery, London.
Bienal Barro de América, Roberto Guevara, Memorial da America Latina, Museu Brasileiro da Escultura and Paço das Artes, São Paulo.

1997
Material Immaterial, The Art Gallery of New South Wales, Sydney.
Esto es: Arte Objeto e Instalacion de Piberoamerica, Centro Cultural Arte Contemporano, Mexico D.F.
As Outras Modernidades, Haus der Kulturen der Welt, Berlin.
A Arte Contemporânea da Gravura Brasil-Reflexão 97, MUMA, Museu Metropolitano de Arte de Curitiba, Curitiba.

1996
Transformal, Wiener Secession, Vienna.
Defining The Nineties, Consesus-making in New York, Miami and Los Angeles, Museum of Contemporary Art, Miami.
Suenos Concretos, Biblioteca Luis Angel Arango, Bogota.
Sin Fronteras/Arte Latinoamericano Actual, Museo Alejandro Otero, Caracas.
Internationales Projekt Für Bildende Kunst, 1996 Kunstbrau, Next, Verein für Bildende Kunst, Graz.
Pequenas Mãos, Paço Imperial, Rio de Janeiro; Centro Cutrural Alumni, São Paulo.
Transparencias, Museu de Arte Moderna, Rio de Janeiro.

1995
The Drawing Center, New York.
The Five Senses, White Columns, New York.
Anos Oitenta: O Palco de Diversidade, Museu de Arte Moderna, Rio de Janeiro.
Entre o Desenho e a Escultura, Museu de Arte Moderna de São Paulo, São Paulo.
Kwangju International Biennale, Kwangju, Korea.
1994
Escultura Carioca, Paco Imperial, Rio de Janeiro.
Esapço Namour, São Paulo

A Espessura do Signo, Carmeliter Kloster, Frankfurt.

1993
Brasil Hoy, Galeria Vanezuela & Klenner, Bogota.

1992
Museu de Arte Moderna de São Paulo, São Paulo.

1991
Brasil, la Nueva Generacion, Fundação Museu Bella Artes de Caracas, Caracas.
Panorama de Arte Brasileira Atual, Museu de Arte Moderna de São Paulo, São Paulo.

1990
Premio Brasilia de Artes Plásticas, Rio de Janeiro.

1989
XI Salão Nacional de Artes Plasticas, Rio de Janeiro.
O pequeno Infinito e o Grande Circunscrito, Galeria Arco, São Paulo.

1988
X Salão Nacional de Artes Plasticas, Rio de Janeiro.

Bibliography

2000
Ward, F., "Carnegie International", *Frieze*, March-April.
Arning, B., "Ernesto Neto", *Bomb*, Winter, pp. 78-84.
Siegel, K., "1999 Carnegie International", *Artforum*, January, pp. 105-106.

1999
"Carnegie International 1999/2000", essay by M. Grynsztejn, *Curator*, pp. 61, 103, 184.
Arning, B., "Ernesto Neto", *Bomb Magazine*, Winter 2000, pp. 78-84.
Fulchéri, F., "Ernesto Neto, feinte de coprs", *FIAC le quotidien*, 6, 19-20 September.
Frehner, M., "Trace - sinnliche Kunst mit Sinn, The Liverpool Biennale of Contemporary Art", *Neue Zürcher Zeitung*, October 12, p. 65 (image).
Brenson, M., Grynsztejn, "Fact and Fiction", *Artforum*, September, pp. 67-70.
Fortin, S., "Ernesto Neto", *Parachute*, 94, April/May/June, pp. 58-59.
Ebony, D., "Review of Exhibitions: Ernesto Neto at Bonakdar Jancou", *Art In America*, June, p. 118.
Liebmann, L., Brooks, A., "A Summer Place", *Art In America*, June, pp. 100-107, 130.
Leffingwell, E., "Reports From San Paulo: Cannivals All", *Art in America*, May, pp. 48-55.

Haye, C., "Plays well with others... (part four)", *Dutch, #20*, Spring, p. 46.

1998
XXIV Bienal de São Paulo: arte conemporânea brasiliera, Pavilhão Ciccillo Matarazzo, Parque Ibirapuera, October 3 - December 13, p. 110, ill. 65.
Arning, B., "Ernesto Neto", *Time Out New York*, November 19-26, 165, p. 64.
Basualdo, C., "Ernesto Neto", *Cream: Contemporary Art in Culture*, London, Phaidon, pp. 296-299.
Johnson, K., "Ernesto Neto at Bonakdar Jancou", *The New York Times*, November 13, p. 40.
Perderoas, A., "Ernesto Neto/Galerie Camargo Vilaça", *Frieze*, 39, March-April, p. 91.

1997
Pedrosa, A., "Ernesto Neto - Tanya Bonakdar Gallery", *Art/Text*, November, pp. 87-88.
Israel, N., "Ernesto Neto - Tanya Bonakdar Gallery", *Artforum*, October, p. 101.
Angeline, J., "Ernesto Neto at Tanya Bonakdar", *Art Nexus*, September, pp. 140-141.

1996
Olivares, R., *Lapiz*, June, pp. 70-71
Taylor, S., "Ernesto Neto at Zolla/Lieberman", *Art in America*, December, p. 108.
Artner, A.G., "Erneesto Neto's sometimes symbolic sculptures", *Chicago Tribune*, August 23.

1995
Basualdo, C., "Ernesto Neto - Galeris Camargo Vilaça", *Artforum*, January, p. 93.
Herkenhoff, P., "Ernesto Neto - Galeria Camargo Vilaça", *Poliester*, Winter, pp. 60-61.
Basualdo, C., "Studio Visit Ernesto Neto", *Trans*, November, pp. 137-42.

1994
Tager, A., "Report from Brasil: Paradoxes and Transfigurations", *Art in America*, July, pp. 44-5.
Pederosa, A., "El Arte de la Vida - Una Nueva Generacion", *Poliester*, Spring, pp. 16-23.

1993
Herkenhoff, P., "Ernesto Neto: Entre El Nadir y La Nada", *Arte Internacional*, pp. 15-16.

Carsten Nicolai

*1965, born in Karl-Marx-Stadt.
Lives in Berlin and Chemnitz.*

Solo Exhibitions

2001
Paolo Curti & Co, Milan.

2000
Galerie EIGEN + ART, Berlin.
Plug In, Winnipeg.
Ystad Kunsthalle, Ystad.
Polar, collaboration with M. Peljhan, Canon Artlab 10, Tokyo.

1999
1% Space, Copenhagen.

1998
Galerie für Zeitgenössische Kunst, Leipzig.

1997
Galerie EIGEN + ART, Berlin.

1996
The New York Kunsthalle, New York.

1994
Neue Nationalgalerie, Berlin.

1993
Galerie EIGEN + ART, Berlin.
Städtische Kunstsammlungen Chemnitz, Chemnitz.

1992
Galerie Springer, Berlin.

1991
Kunstwerke Berlin, Berlin.

1986
Galerie EIGEN + ART, Leipzig.

Group Exhibitions

2001
Wilde Zone, Witte de With, Rotterdam.
Let's Entertain, Kunstmuseum Wolfsburg.
Art/Music, Museum of Modern Art, Sydney.

2000
!HOP, Lund Konsthall, Lund.
Sound aka space, Hamburg.
Kabusa Konsthall, Kabusa.
Audible Light, Museum of Modern Art Oxford.
Sound Art, NTT InterCommunication Center, Gallery A, Tokyo.
Volume, P.S.1, New York.
Taktlos, Bern.

1999

cycle (collaboration Ryoji Ikeda), Watari-Um Museum, Tokyo.
Examining Pictures: exhibiting paintings, Whitechapel Art Gallery, London.
Museum of Contemporary Art, Chicago.
Liverpool Biennial, Liverpool.

1998
Last House on the Left, Archipelago-Newrooms, Stockholm.

1997
documenta X, Kassel.
P.S.1 reopening, New York.

1996
mikro makro, collaboration with M. Vainio, Industriemuseum, Chemnitz.

1995
Drawing Center, New York.

1994
Welt-Moral, Kunsthalle Basel, Basel.

1993
Cadavre Exquis, Drawing Center, New York.

Discography

2001
cyclo.(r.ikeda + noto), raster -noton

2000
alva noto.prototypes, mille plateaux
noto.telefunken, raster -noton
Ø+noto.wohltemperiert, raster -noton
opto .files (opiate + noto), raster -noton

1999
noto. time.dot, raster -noton, 20´ to 2000
noto.empty garden, watari-um, museum, on sundays

1998
noto.kerne, plate lunch
noto.polyfoto, noton-raster

1997
noto.∞, noton-rastermusic

1996
noto.spin, noton-rastermusic
Ø+noto.mikro makro, noton-rastermusic

Performances

2001
Museum of Modern Art, San Francisco.
Sydney Opera House, Sydney.
Dissonancia, Rome.

2000
Guggenheim Museum, New York.

Ars electronica, 20´ to 2000, Linz.
Raster-noton-oacis, taktlos, Bern.
Museum of Modern Art , Bombay.
Spiral - experimental express, Tokyo.
Paradiso, Amsterdam.

1999
ZKM, Karlsruhe.
Phonotaktik, Vienna.
Beta festival, Berlin.
Galerie für Zeitgenössische Kunst - new forms, Leipzig.
Rote Fabrik - electrip, Zürich.
Impakt, Utrecht.
Volksbuehne - 20´ to 2000, Berlin.

1998
Ars electronica, Linz.
Steim festival, Amsterdam.
v2_archiv, Rotterdam.
Spiral - experimental express, Tokyo.

1997
Documenta X, Kassel.
Sonar festival, Barcelona.
Bauhaus, Dessau.

Bibliography

2001
Weskott, H., "Wenn Kunst sich selbst-ständig macht", *Süddeutsche Zeitung*, 25 January, p. 20.

2000
Pesch, M., "Nachrichten aus der Produktion", *Kunstforum*, 7/9, p. 253.
Gutmair, U., "Carsten Nicolai - Charmante storingen", *Metropolis M*, 5.
Gutmair, U., "Was kommt, wenn der Club geht?", *DE:BUG*, 032|0200, S.18.
Sherburne, P., "Carsten Nicolai", *Surface*, 24, p.150.
The Wire, London, 3/2000.
"Welcome to the ear-splitting, eye-popping disco", *The Times*, April 26.
Prototypen, Heft 1. Carsten Nicolai, Erweiternder Beitrag zur Ausstellung "Produktionen 1999/2000", edited by G. Harry Lybke, Galerie EIGEN+ART, C. Tannert, Künstlerhaus Bethanien, Berlin.

1999
Nicolaus, F., "Carsten Nicolai - Ich bin ein Mauerspringer", *Art*, 12/99, pp. 78-83.
BT, Art Magazine, August, p.188.
"Ton / Nichtton", *Art*, 3/99, p. 21.
Ratliff, B., "Fluffs, Tremors and Skeletal Noises", *The New York Times*, January 29.
Hergeth, A., "Techno, Vogelstimmen und unbeschreibliche Töne", *Der Tagesspiegel*, December 16.
Koehler, S., "Watari-um cultivates creative spaces", *The Japan Times*, May 16, p. 13.

1998
Frieze, September/October, 42.
Guth, P., "Modelle für ein Leben im Zwischenraum", *FAZ*, July 30.
Polyfoto, exhibition catalogue, text by C. Doswald, F. Eckart, D. Grünbein, R. Rimbaud, S. Russ, R. Young, Carsten Nicolai in der Galerie für Zeitgenössische Kunst, Leipzig, edited: Institut für Moderne Kunst Nürnberg und Galerie für Zeitgenössische Kunst, Leipzig, Gestaltung: Olaf Bender, Benedict Press, Chemnitz.

1997
noto. archiv für ton und nichtton, Layout: O. Bender, C. Nicolai, Druck: Druck-werkstätten Stollberg.

1996
NERV + SPIN, Katalog zur Ausstellung, Städtische Kunstsammlungen Augsburg, 1996, Gestaltung: C. Nicolai, Druck: Druckwerkstätten Stollberg, Compactdisc: NOTO.SPIN Carsten Nicolai, Auflage: 2000 Exemplare

1995
SPIN & KÄFIG / Material, Kunstverein Konstanz Leonardi Museum Dresden, Re-Print eines Zeichenbuches.

1994
TwinTwin, edited by Staatliche Museen zu Berlin, Neue Nationalgalerie, Berlin.
Schwarz + Holz, edited by Städtisches Kunstmuseum Spendhaus Reutlingen, Altenburg.

1993
Corpus, edited by Susanne Anna, mit einem Beitrag von Heiner Stachelhaus, Darmstadt 1993.

1991
"...", zusammen mit Thomas Schliesser, edit by Edition Eigen+Art und "981", Leipzig 1991.

Olaf Nicolai
1962, born in Halle/Saale.
Lives and works in Berlin.

Solo Exhibitions

2001
Migros Museum für Gegenwartskunst, Zurich.
Galerie für Zeitgenössische Kunst, Leipzig.

2000
Bonner Kunstverein am August-Macke-Platz, Bonn.
Pantone wall, instrumented and *Odds and Ends (Edition 1994-2000)*, Kunstverein Bonn.

...fade in, fade out, fade away..., Westfälischer Kunstverein, Münster.

1999
Labyrinth, Galerie für Zeitgenössische Kunst, Leipzig.
Parfum für Bäume, International Artproject at the Bundesgartenschau, Magdeburg.

Group Exhibitions

2001
Squatters, Museum Serralves Porto/ Witte de With, Rotterdam.
Sous les Ponts, le long de la Riviere..., Casino Luxembourg.
Casino 2001, Stedelijk Museum Voor Actuele Kunst, Gent.

2000
What If – Art on the verge of Architecture and Design, Moderna Museet, Stockholm.
La Ville 1998, le Jardin 2000, la Mémoire 1999, Villa Medici, Rome.
4. werkleitz biennale real[work], Werkleitz.

1999
Konstruktionszeichnungen, Kunst-Werke, Berlin.
1999, P.S.1 Museum, New York.
Empty Garden, Watari-Um Museum, Tokyo.
Peace, Migros Museum für Gegenwartskunst, Zurich.

1998
Etre Nature, Foundation Cartier, Paris.
Grandeur Nature, Parc La Courneuve, Saint-Denis, France.
Berlin biennale, Berlin.

1997
documenta X, Kassel.

Bibliography

2001
Nicolai, O., *...fading in, fading out, fading away...*, Susanne Gaensheimer, for the Westfälischer Kunstverein, Münster.
Liebs, H., "Olaf Nicolai", *Frieze*, September.

2000
Stange, R., "Olaf Nicolai", *artist*, 43/ May.
Pohlen, A., "Language of Color", *30 Farben*, Salon Verlag.

1999
Nicolai, O., *show case*, Verlag für Moderne Kunst, Nürnberg.

1997
Irmer, T., "Natur Gestalten", Insert and Interview, *Neue Bildende Kunst*, 1/ 1997.

1994
Nicolai, O., *Sammlers Blick*, Verlag der Kunst, Amsterdam and Dresden.

Manuel Ocampo
1965, born in Quezon City, Philippines. Lives and works in Berkeley.

Solo Exhibitions

2000
Presenting the Undisclosed System of References in the Loophole of Misunderstanding, Galeria OMR, Mexico City.
Those Long Dormant Pimples of Inattention Counterattacking the Hyper-Convuluted Dramas of the Gaze, Galerie Philomene Magers, Munich; Galerie Baerbel Grasslin, Frankfurt.
Those Long Dormant Pimples of Inattention Meandering through the Cranium Arcade of Pitiless Logic Swastikating between Love and Hate, Jack Shainman Gallery, New York.
The Stream of Transcendent Object-Making Conciouly Working towards the Goal, Galerie Michael Neff, Frankfurt.

1999
The Nature of Culture – Manuel Ocampo/Gaston Damag, Centro Andaluz de Arte Contemporaneo, Seville.
The Inversion of the Ideal: Navigating the Landscape of Intestinal Muck, Swastikating between Love and Hate, Galeria Soledad Lorenzo, Madrid.

1998
To Infinity and Beyond: Presenting the Unpresentable – The Sublime or the Lack Thereof, Galerie Nathalie Obadia, Paris.
Yo Tambien Soy Pintura, El Museo Extremeno e Iberoamericano de Arte Contemporaneo, Badajoz, Spain.
Why Must I Care For a Girl Who Always Scratches Wherever She Itches: 1-1/2 Centuries of Modern Art Twelve Step Program, Delfina, London; Centre Cultural Tecla Sala, Barcelona.

1997
Heridas de la Lengua, Track 16 Gallery, Santa Monica, California.
Hacer Pintura Es Hacer Patria, Galeria OMR, Mexico City.

1996
Annina Nosei Gallery, New York.

1995
Galerie Nathalie Obadia, Paris.
Musee d'Art Contemporain de Montreal, Canada.

1994
Paraiso Abierto a Todos, The Mexican Museum, San Francisco.
Stations of the Cross, Annina Nosei Gallery, New York.

1993
New Paintings, Salander-O'Reilly Galleries/Fred Hoffman, Beverly Hills, California.
Manuel Ocampo, Galeria OMR, Mexico City.

1992
Matrix – Berkeley 150, University Art Museum, University of California, Berkeley.

1991
Manuel Ocampo, Fred Hoffman Gallery, Santa Monica, California.

Group Exhibitions

2001
Berlin Biennale II, Berlin.
Vom Eindruck zum Ausdruck: Graesslin Collection, (From Impression to Expression), Deichtorhallen, Hamburg.

2000
Partage d'Exotismes, 5th Biennale d'Art Contemporain de Lyon, Lyon.

1998
Double Trouble: The Patchett Collection, Museum of Contemporary Art, San Diego.

1996
Unmapping the Earth, '97 Kwangju Biennial, Korea.

1993
Jean-Michel Basquiat & Manuel Ocampo, Henry Art Gallery, University of Washington, Seattle.
43rd Biennial Exhibition of Contemporary American Painting, The Corcoran Gallery of Art, Washington.

1992
Documenta IX, Documentahallen, Kassel.
Helter Skelter: L.A. Art in the 1990s, The Museum of Contemporary Art, Los Angeles.

1990
Mike Bidlo, Manuel Ocampo, Andres Serrano, Saatchi Collection, London.

Bibliography

2001
Les Chiens Andalous, Smart Art Press, Santa Monica.
Asian Collection 50, From the Collection of the Fukuoka Asian Art Museum, Fukuoka.
Angeline, J., "Manuel Ocampo: Jack Shainman Gallery", *Art Nexus*, February-April.
Leffingwell, E., "Manuel Ocampo at Jack Shainman", *Art in America*, February.

1999
Why Must I Care For a Girl Who Always Scratches Wherever She Itches: 1-1/2 Centuries of Modern Art Twelve Step Program, Delfina, Londres; Centre Cultural Tecla Sala, L'Hospitalet, Barcelona.
La Naturaleza de la Cultura – Manuel Ocampo & Gaston Damag, Centro Andaluz de Arte Contemporaneo, Sevilla.
The Inversion of the Ideal: Navigating the Landscape of Intestinal Muck, Swastikating between Love and Hate, Galeria Soledad Lorenzo, Madrid.
Bright, S., "Manuel Ocampo", *Art Asia Pacific*, 22.

1998
At Home & Abroad: 20 Contemporary Filipino Artists, Asian Art Museum of San Francisco.
Double Trouble - The Patchett Collection, Smart Art Press, Santa Monica.
Yo Tambien Soy Pintura, Museo Extremeno e Iberoamericano de Arte Contemporaneo (MEIAC), Badajoz, Spain.
Burrows, D., "Manuel Ocampo", *Art Monthly*, July-August.
Chattopadhyay, C., "Manuel Ocampo at Track 16 Gallery", *Asian Art News*, January-February.
Maison, A., "Agony and Ecstasy: Manuel Ocampo's Artistic Vision of the Postcolony", *Amerasia Journal*.
Ocampo, M., "To Infinity and Beyond", *ARTI International*, 39, May-July.

1997-1998
Power, K., "Manuel Ocampo: Rough Gatherings at the Edges of the Mind", *Third Text*, Winter.

1997
American Stories: Amidst Displacement and Transformation, Setagaya Art Museum, Tokyo.
Hacer Pintura es Hacer Patria, Galeria OMR, Mexico City.
Heridas de la Lengua, Smart Art Press, Santa Monica.
Unmapping the Earth, Kwangju Biennial, Korea.
Hammond, A., "Manuel Ocampo at Annina Nosei, *Artnews*, March.
Joanou, A., "Furious Desire", *World Art*, 13.
Katz, V., "Manuel Ocampo at Annina Nosei", *Art in America*, May.
Lutfy, C., "Asian Artists in America: Manuel Ocampo", *Atelier*, March-April.

1995
Manuel Ocampo: Ciocca Raffaelli, Arte Contemporanea, Milan.
Alba, V., "Master of the Macabre", *Asian Art News*, March-April.
Dagbert, A., "Manuel Ocampo at Galerie Nathalie Obadia", *Art Press*, November.
Ferrario, R., "Manuel Ocampo – Ciocca Raffaelli", *Flash Art*, July.

1994
Virgin Destroyer: Manuel Ocampo, Hardy Marks Publications, Honolulu.
Asia/America: Identities in Asian American Art, The Asia Society Galleries, New York.
Apostol, S., "An Interview with Manuel Ocampo", *ARTI*, 21.
Edelman, R.G., "Springtime in New York – Manuel Ocampo at Annina Nosei", *Art Press*, July-August.
Jana, R., "Manuel Ocampo at the Mexican Museum", *Asian Art News*, July-August.
Mahoney, R., "Manuel Ocampo – Annina Nosei", *Flash Art*, Summer.
Santiago, C., "Manuel Ocampo at the Mexican Museum – San Francisco", *World Art*, November.
Scarborough, J., "Manuel Ocampo – One Man-National Movement", *Flash Art*, May-June.

1993
43rd Biennial, The Corcoran Gallery of Art, Washington D.C.
In Out of the Cold, Center for the Arts, Yerba Buena Gardens, San Francisco.
Duncan, M., "Manuel Ocampo at Salander-O'Reilly/Fred Hoffman", *Art in America*, November.

1992
"Young Old Master: Galaxy of Rising Stars", *Time*, November 18.

1991
Laurence, M., "Manuel Ocampo at Christopher John", *Art in America*, January.
Selwyn, M., "Manuel Ocampo at Fred Hoffman", *Flash Art*, May-June.
Weissman, B., "Manuel Ocampo at Fred Hoffman Gallery", *Artforum*, May.

1990
Documenta IX, Kassel.
Helter Skelter: LA Art in the 1990s, The Museum of Contemporary Art, Los Angeles.

Arnold Odermatt

1925, born in Oberdorf, Kanton Nidwalden.
Lives and works in Stans.

Solo Exhibitions

2000
Springer & Winckler Galerie, Berlin.

1998
Karambolage, Polizeipräsidium Frankfurt am Main (during the Bookfair, Frankfurt).

1996
Meine Welt, Viewpoint Gallery, Salford.

1993
Seeplatz 10, Buochs.

Group Exhibitions

1999
Automobility - Was uns bewegt, Vitra Design Museum, Lörrach.
Wohin das Auge reicht, Deichtorhallen, Hamburg.

1995
Heimat - Auf der Suche nach der verlorenen Identität, Jüdisches Museum, Vienna.
Ein deutscher Sammler - ein deutsches Auto: Peter Ludwig und der Volkswagen, Museum Ludwig, Aachen.

Bibliography

2000
Wolff, T., "Der Scharfschütze", *Frankfurter Rundschau*, 3, pp. 4-5.
Tröster, C., "Abgründiger Humor, Ein Schweizer Polizist fotografierte Zeit seines Lebens Unfälle und produzierte damit Unfälle", *Die Woche*, 23. Juni.
Steiger, C., *Klick im Unglück, auto, motor und sport*, 23, pp. 208-212.

1998
Euler, R., "Karambolagen werden zu Kunst, Fotos von Arnold Odermatt im Polizeipräsidium", *Frankfurter Allgemeine Zeitung*, October 4.

1994
Kleinschmidt, K., "Mein Revier - Das photographische Protokoll des Schweizer Polizisten Arnold Odermatt", *Süddeutsche Zeitung*, 1, pp. 24-33.

1993
Arnold Odermatt, Meine Welt, Photographien 1939-1993, edited by Urs Odermatt, Bern.

João Onofre

1976, born in Lisbon.
Lives and works in Lisbon.

Solo Exhibitions

2001
Cutting Edge, ARCO, Madrid.

Group Exhibitions

2001
Opponents, Paraplufabriek, edited by S. de Haan, Nijmegen, Holland.
Disseminations, Culturgest, edited by P. Lapa, Lisbon.
The Mnemosyne Project, edited by D. Sardo, CAPC, Coimbra.

2000
Performing Bodies, Tate Gallery of Modern Art – Millbank, edited by H. Blaker, I. Blazwick, S. Mckinlay, A. George, London.
Full Serve, edited by K. Schachter, Rove – West 27th Street, New York.
Piano XXI – Portuguese Contemporary Art, edited by P. Mendes and A. Rego, Intermedia Gallery, Glasgow.
XXVI Bienal de Pontevedra, edited by Ma. de Corral, Pontevedra.
Olhar da Contemporaneidade, edited by I. Nunes, Lisbon.
Arritimia, Mercado Ferreira Borges, edited by J. Sousa Cardoso, Porto.
I hate New York, edited by K. Schachter, Rove – Shoreditch High St., London.
Sweet & Low, edited by K. Schachter, Rove – Lispenard St., New York.

1999
António Cachola Colleciont – Portuguese Art, years 80-90, MEIAC – Museo Ibero-Americano de Arte Contemporânea, Badajoz.
7 Artistas ao 10° Mês, edited by J. Pinharanda, Fundação Calouste Gulbenkian, Lisbon.
MA Fine Art Show, Goldsmiths College, London.
Non-stop opening, Central Point Gallery, London.
Bienal da Maia, Maia.
Chainstore, edited by N. Fox, Trinity Buoy Wharf, London.

1998
Bienal A.I.P., Europarque, St. Maria da Feira, Portugal.
Acasos & Materiais, edited by P. Mendes, CAPC, Coimbra.

Tamsuti Orimoto

1946, born in Kawasaki-City.
Lives and works in Kawasaki-City.

Solo Exhibitions

2000
Hara Museum, Tokyo.
Foto Galerie Win, Austria.
Tallinn Kunsthoole Gallery, Tallinn.
Museum fur photographe, Braunschweig.

1999
Neurologisches, Theraplecentrum Hospital, Cologne.
Galerie Moriogai + Action Gallery, Berlin.
Lichtblick Downtown Gallery, Koln.
Art Space Niji, Kiyoto Japan.
Galerie Neue Anstandigkeit, Berlin.

1998
Galerie 7/8 Barmherzigkeit, Hamburg.

1997
Kunst Park Forum, Munchen.
Galerie 7/8 Barmherzigkeit, Hamburg.

1996
30 Underwood St, Gallery, London
Galerie 7/8 Barmherzigkeit, Hamburg

1995
House of culture Odorheiu, Romania.
New Galerie, Landshut.
Ladengalerie, Munich.

Group Exhibitions

1992
Museum City Tenjn, Fukuoka.

1991
The Biennale of Sâo Paulo.

1989
P.S.I. Museum – Clocktower, New York.

1988
The Biennale of Sydney.

Performance (Public Space)
Bread–Man (Communication)

2000
Wiener Naschmarkt, Vienna.
Insa Main St, Seoul Korea.
Shinagawa Station, Tokyo.
Bereich Damm – Bohlweg, Braunschweig.

1999
Tachikawa Station, Tokyo.
Hackeschen Market, Berlin.
Ehrenstr, Cologne.
Konigsstadtbrauerei, Berlin.
Augustus Brige, Dresden.

Hauptplatz, Linz.

1998
Cinema Bortfabrik, Berlin.
Kunst Werke Cafe, Berlin.

1997
Konigliche Garden, Hannover.
Dock II, Berlin.
Saitama Museum, Urawa.

1996
Museumdorf, Cloppenburg.
Kensington Garden, Brighton.
House of Parliament, London.

1995
River side St, Lewes England.

1994
Ordu caddes, Istanbul.
Edge space, Tokyo.
English Garden, Munich.
Piata Libertatii St, Sf. Gheorghe.
Gum Depertment Store, Moscow.
Swayambhunath Stupa, Kathmandu.

1993
Labirynt Gallery, Lublin.
Plish Army Museum Warszawa.
Kunsthalle Rathaus, Altonaer Museum, Hamburg.
Kunst & Nutzn, Stadtbadmitte, Bremerhaven.
Bowery Mission ministries, New York.
Wallraff Richartz Museum, Cologne.

1992
Trips, Koln-Bonn.
Kurihamm National Hospital, Japan.
Theater Teatro Municipal, Saô Paulo.
Gallery K,Tokyo.

Bibliography

2000
Nanjo, F., "Art: Tatsmumi Orimoto, Art Mama + Bread Man Exhibition", *Ryuko Tsushin*, 444, July, INFAS, p. 151.
Yasuda, A., "Tatsumi Orimoto", *Tatsumi Orimoto – Art Mama + Bread Man*, exhibition catalogue, Hara Museum of Contemporary Art, Tokyo.
Interview, "Artist interview 2: Orimoto Tatsumi, Bread Man Borne by Art Mama", *Bijutsu Techo*, 52, 791, August, Bijustu Shuppan sha, pp. 137-144.
"Tokyo Schockt Kölnä Deutsch – jaianische Künstlerprojekte im dritten Jahr erfolgreich", *Junge Kunst*, 41, January-March, pp. 35, 36.
Interview, "Photo Watching: Tatsumi Orimoto", *Asahi Camera*, 887, November, pp. 172-176.

1999
"Tatsumi Orimoto", *Tokyo Shock*, exhibi-

tion catalogue, ARTicle Galerie & Edition, Cologne.

1998
Earle, J., "Asian Avan Garde", *Christie's Magazine*, October, pp. 48-51.
Weiler, N., "Mutter im Reifen: Tatsumi Orimoto", *Szene Hamburg*, June, Szene Verlag Klaus Heidorn KG, Hamburg, p. 88.

1997
DiPietro, M., "Against the Grain", *Tokyo Journal*, April, Internet Access Center, pp. 17-19.
Schmidt, E., "Tatsumi Orimoto", *Alle Tage Kunst*, exhibition catalogue, Agora e V., Hannover.
Johannes Lothar Schröder, "Verständigung durch das Reifenrohr", *Silvia Schreiber, Tatsumi Orimoto*, exhibition catalogue, Kunstpark Forum, Munich.
"Tatsumi Orimoto", *Plantsüden*, Plantsüden, Munich, pp. 63-71.

1996
"Tatsumi Orimoto", *Pull to Ear: Tatsumi Orimoto*, exhibition catalogue, 30 Underwood Street Gallery, London.

1995
Orimoto, T., "Tatsumi Orimoto", *MILCH-wirtschaft*, KUBUS, Städtische Galerie, Hannover.

1992
"OrimotoTatsumi", *Museum city Tenjin '92*, exhibition catalogye, Museum City Project, Fukuoka, pp. 22, 23.

1991
Orimoto, T., "Event Pull to Ear (Communication Art)", *déjà-vu*, 3, November, Photo-Planet, pp. 111-113.

1988
Iizawa, K., "Tatsumi Orimoto", *Australian Biennale 1988*, exhibition catalogue, The Biennale of Sidney, Sidney, pp. 212, 213.
"Artrageous: Pull to Ear", *Good Weekend*, May 14, John Fairfax and Sons Ltd., Sidney, p. 31.

1985
Izawa, K., "Correspondence between Photography and Performance", *Art '85*, 111, May, Maria Shobo, p. 87.

Tanja Ostojić
1972, born in Užice.
Lives and works in Belgrade.

Solo Exhibitions, Performance and Art Actions

2000
There is no rest until the renovation is on, Solo Exhibitions, Remont Gallery, Belgrade and IZBA Novi Sad, Yugoslavia.
The interactive web project "Looking for a husband with EU passport" http://www.cac.org.mk/capital/ostojic/.
Social and political roll of Art: free political postcards project, SKUC Gallery Ljubljana, Slovenia. http://www.galerija.skuc-drustvo.si/ostojic.
Stutzen macht frei, performance action, Schloss Damtschach, Austria.
Illegal border crossing, art-action, Slovenia, Austria.

1999
Would You Digitalize Your Soul, performance, ICA, London.

1998
MA Show, FLU, Belgrade.

1997
Personal Space, Hollywood Leather Venue, London.

1996
Hopscotch, performance, Student Cultural Canter Gallery, Belgrad.
Personal Space, exhibition with S. Gajin, Gallery 12+, Belgrade.
(Re)action to the opening..., Happy Gallery, Belgrade.

1995
Honours Student Exhibition, Faculty of Fine Arts Gallery, Belgrade.
Exhibition of Sculptures, with Apostolovic and Glid, Lada Gallery, Belgrade.
Intervention from burnt materials, In the burnt Sculpture Department, Faculty of Fine Arts, Belgrade.

Group Exhibitions

2001
Call me Sarajevo, winter festival, Sarajevo.
Perfect Match, City Shopping Mall, Skopje.
Serbia File, Fine Art Academy, Berlin.
Body and the East, Gallery Exit Art, New York.

2000
Serbia File, Fine Art Academy, Vienna.
Utopia, Rogaland Kunstmuseum, Stavanger.

Digital media festival, Maribor.
Video and film festival, Oberhausen.
Salon, Gallery Schloss Damtschach.
Festival of short digital forms, REX, Belgrade.

1999
SKIN, DESTE Foundation, Athens.
Collaboration in André Stitt's performance *Witness*, PS1 Contemporary Art Centre, New York.
I Want You to Demand..., exhibited unofficially on the streets, La Biennale di Venezia, Venice.
Stirring, Streaming, Dreaming, Forum Stadtpark, Graz.
Glassbox Gallery, Paris.
Post-Diplôme Internationale 1998-99, Musée des Beaux-Arts de Nantes, Espace delrue and Zoo Galerie, Nantes.
Polysonneries, live arts festival, Lyon.
Lelabo, performance festival, Nantes, France.

1998
MANIFESTA 2, Musee d'Histoire de la Ville de Luxembourg, Luxembourg.
ARCO, Sala de Arte Joven, Madrid.
Utopia, Chateau de Beaumanoar, Quentin.
Body and the East, Moderna galerija, Ljubljana.
Critics Choice, Cultural Centre, Belgrade.

1997
Would You Digitalize Your Soul, exhibited unofficially, with Gajin, La Biennale di Venezia, Venice.
Lamparna '97, Abandoned coal mine, Labin, Croatia.
Du bon usage de l'emballage, Musee des Beaux-Arts, Verviers, Belgium.
Photographs, and my *Josephine Beuys performance*, Salon of the Museum of Modern Art, Belgrade.

1996-1997
In the Context of the Student and Civil Protest, street actions, performances and graffiti, Belgrade.

Bibliography

2001
Ostojic, T., "Nema odmora dok traje obnova", *Remont magazine #2*, Belgrade.
Rose, M., web art magazine, http://www.art-themagazine.com/paris3.htm.

2000
Slijepcevic, N., "Art in Yugoslavia", *Metro issue # 2*, March.
Ubrilo, J.,"Etre une artist", *Profemina*, Belgrade.
Grzinić, M., "Tanja Ostojić", *The body caught in the computer intestines and*

beyond, MKC, Maribor & MASKA, Ljubljana.

1999
Howell, A., *The Analysis of Performance Art*, by Harwood Academic Publishers, London.
Krivokapic, J., *ArtPresse*, January.

1998
Dimitrijevic, B., *MANIFESTA 2*, Luxembourg.
KUNSTFORUM, 142, October-December, pp. 319, 347, 360.
Sretenovic, D., *Body and the East*, Museum of Modern Art, Ljubljana.
Crabtree, A., *ART MONTHLY*, 219, September '98, pp. 22-24.
Ferre, S., *Inter*, 71, Quebec.
Cubrilo, J., "Belgrade Art Scene - the Nineties", *Radio B92*, pp. 105-107.

1997
Suica, N., "Personal Space", *ARTI*, 36/1997, Athens.

1996
Tanja Ostojić and Sasa Gajin, Personal Space, published by Gallery 12+, Belgrade.
Cubrilo, J., "Tanja in First Person", *A Look at the Wall 1994-1996*, published by Radio B92, Belgrade.

Manfred Pernice
1963, born in Hildesheim.
Lives and works in Berlin.

Solo Exhibitions

2001
Sprengel Museum, Hannover.
Sieg, Anton Kern Gallery, New York.
Galerie Neu, Berlin.

2000
Herbst 2000, Produzentengalerie Hamburg, Hamburg.
Der Wanderer, Stella Lohaus Galerie, Antwerpen.
Witte de With, Rotterdam.
Portikus, Frankfurt am Main.
Kunsthalle Zurich.
Galerie Neu, Berlin.

1999
Institute of visual arts, Wisconsin/ Milwaukee.
Galerie Nächst St. Stephan, Vienna.

1998
Galerie Konrad Fischer, Düsseldorf.
E-Welten (maritim), Kunstverein Bremer-haven.

A+J, London.
Bad, bath, Anton Kern Gallery, New York.
Pilmut, Stella Lohaus Galerie Antwerpen.
Migrateurs, Museé d'Art Moderne de la Ville de Paris, Paris, exhibition catalogue, Platz, Galerie NEU, Berlin.

1997
Verkranzlerung, Kabinett für aktuelle Kunst, Bremerhaven.
D & A -Punkt, Galerie Nächst St. Stephan, Vienna.

1996
Stralau 1, Kunsthalle Moabit, Berlin.
Galerie Klemens Gasser, Cologne.

1995
Zeichnungen + Modelle, Galerie NEU, Berlin.

Group Exhibitions

2000
Räumen, Kunsthalle Hamburg (exhibition catalogue)
escape-space, Blickle Stiftung, Kraichtal exhibition catalogue.
Projekt Außendienst, Kunstverein Hamburg.
Das Haus in der Kunst, Deichtorhallen Hamburg.
Manifesta, Lubjana.

1999
The space is everywhere, Villa Merkel, Esslingen.
Kraftwerke Berlin, Kunstmuseum Aarhus.
Children of Berlin, PS 1, New York.
Officina Europa, Galleria d'Árte Bologna, Rimini.

1998
Side Construction, South London Gallery.
Museum of Fine Arts, Warschau.
ars viva 98/99, Cottbus, Kunstverein Braunschweig, Portikus.
Berlin Biennale, Berlin.
Mai 98, Joseph Haubrich Halle, Cologne.
Made in Berlin, Städtische Galerie L. Kanakakis, Rethymnon.

1997
surprise II, Kunsthalle Nürnberg, Nürnberg.
Biennale de Lyon, Lyon.
Fiat, Künstlerhaus Stuttgart, Stuttgart; Städtisches Museum Zwickau.

Bibliography

2001
Herbstreuth, P., "Manfred Pernice-Hamburger Bahnhof", *Flash Art*, January/February.

2000

Manfred Pernice, Kunsthalle Zürich, Ausstellungskatalog.
escape_space, exhibition catalogue Ursula Blickle Stiftung.
Vogel, S., "Von Originalbehältern und Gedichten", *Kunst-Bulletin*, April.
Schneider, C., "Systematisch voorbehoud, Manfred Pernice", *Metropolis M*, April-May.
Sonna, B., "Das Prinzip Dose", *Art*, 4, April.

1999
Dziewior, Y., "Manfred Pernice", *German Open*, Wolfsburg.
Wiehager, R., *Manfred Pernice*, exhibition catalogue, Villa Merkel, Esslingen.
Pesch, M., "Installationen", *unstforum*, May/June.
<Ferien Utopie Alltag> in der Künstler-werkstatt..., *Kunst-Bulletin*, January/February.
Ritchie, M., "The new City", *art/text*, 3/1999.
Dziewior, Y., "Manfred Pernice", *Artforum*, April.
Smolik, N., "Manfred Pernice", *Kunst-forum*, January/February.
Titz, S., "Manfred Pernice", *Art*, Taschen.

1998
Archer, M., "Manfred Pernice", *Artforum*, November.
Müller, S., *Art*, 10/1998.
Graw, I.,*Texte zur Kunst*, September.
Williams, G., *Frieze*, 42, September/October.
Sonderdruck aus dem Katalog ars viva 98/99, Cologne.
Mai 98, Positionen zeitgenössischer Kunst seit den 60er Jahren, Katalog, Kunsthalle, Cologne.
Herbstreuth , P., "Manfred Pernice in der Galerie Neu", *Kunst-Bulletin*,3/1998.
Schmid, K.-H., "Cocktail...", *Kunstzeitung*, 2/98.
Brytniningstider, Katalog, Norrköingsmuseum, Norrköping.
Katalog 1998 Prix Whanki Exhibition, Whanki Museum Seoul.

1997
Clewing, U., "Modelle der Unwirtlichkeit", *Art* , 10.
Schmidt , E., *Fiat*, exhibition catalogue, Städtisches Museum Zwickau, Oktober.
Meyer Herrmann , E., exhibition catalogue, *suprise 2*, Kunsthalle Nürnberg.
Szeemann, H., *Biennale de Lyon*.
Flash Art, XXX, 195, Summer.
Obrist, Hans Ullrich: "Unbuilt roads", 107, unrealized projects.
Podeschwa, I., "I.P. über Manfred Pernice", *Artist*, 1.
Kreibohm, J., *Artist*, 2.

Paul Pfeiffer

1966, born in Honolulu.
Lives and works in New York.

Solo Exhibitions and Projects

2001
Whitney Museum of American Art, New York.
UCLA Hammer Museum, Los Angeles.
The Project, Los Angeles. Kunsthaus Glarus.
Orpheus Descending, The Public Art Fund, New York.
Barbican Centre, London.

2000
The Project, New York.
Kunst-Werke, Berlin.
Duke University Museum of Art, with Romuald Hazoumé, Durham.

1998
The Pure Products Go Crazy, The Project, New York.

1997
The Pure Products Go Crazy, Cendrillon, New York.

1994
Santo Niño Incarnate, Colonial House Inn, New York.

1993
Survival of the Innocents, Art In General, New York.

Group Exhibitions

2001
Gio Marconi, Milan.
Maze, Turin.
Salo Uno, Rome.
Zero Gravity, Fondazione Adriano Olivetti, Rome.
Race In Digital Space, List Visual Art Center, MIT, Cambridge.
Bitstreams, Whitney Museum of American Art, New York.
Subject Plural, Contemporary Arts Museum, Houston.
Refresh, Cantor Center for the Visual Arts, Stanford University.

2000
The Whitney Biennial, The Whitney Museum, New York.
Greater New York, PS1/MoMA, New York.
Hypermental, Kunsthaus, Zurich (travelling).
City Visions, media_city seoul 2000, Seoul.
Extraordinary Realities, Columbus Museum of Art, Columbus.

1999
Tête de Turkois, The Project, New York.

Hocus Focus, New Video, Rare Gallery, New York.
Surface Tension, Art In General, New York.
A Place Called Lovely, Greene Naftali, New York.

1998
Warming, The Project, New York.
At Home and Abroad, 21 Contemporary Filipino Artists, Asian Art Museum, San Francisco (travelling).

1996
Memories of Over-development, Philippine Diaspora in Contemporary Art, UC Irvine Art Gallery, California (travelling).

1995
In a Different Light, UC Berkeley Museum, Berkeley.
Pervert, UC Irvine Art Gallery, CA.
14 Artists, Sugod sa Katapusan, Dumaguete City, Philippines.

1994
Extreme Unction, Panchayat / Market Gallery, London, England.
Reframing a Heritage, University of Hawaii, Manoa.
Picturing Asian America, Communities, Cultures, Difference, Houston Center for Photography, Houston.

1993
The Curio Shop, Artists Space, New York.
Kayumanggi Presence, Academy of Art, Honolulu (travelling).

1992
Altars, Divinations and Icons, Painted Bride Art Center, Philadelphia, PA.
(en)Gendered Visions, Race, Gender and Sexuality in Asian American Art, Guada-lupe Cultural Center, San Antonio.
Made in America, Remembering Vincent Chin, Art In General, New York.

1991
DisMantling Invisibility, Asian Americans Respond to the AIDS Crisis, Art In General, New York (travelling).

Bibliography

2000
Whitney Biennial, exhibition catalogue, Whitney Museum of American Art, New York.
Greater New York, New Art In New York Now, exhibition catalogue, New York, PS1/MoMA.
Romuald Hazoume/Paul Pfeiffer (brochure), Duke University Museum of Art, Durham.
Hunt, D., "Man Trap", *Frieze*, 53, June/July/August.

Berwick, C., "Maybe Race Has Nothing To Do With It", *FEED Magazine*, April 24.
Siegel, K., "Openings, Paul Pfeiffer", *Artforum*, Summer.
Siegel, K., "The Max Factor, Whitney Biennial 2000", *Artforum*, March.
Rush, M., "New Media Rampant", *Art In America*, July.
Gopnik, B., "Window Shopping At The Whitney", *The Globe Online*, March 22.
Plagens, P., "Art in the Fast Lane", *Newsweek*, April 10.
Schjeldahl, P., "Pragmatic Hedonism", *The New Yorker*, April 3.
Halle, H., "State of the Art", *TimeOut New York*, 234, March 16-23.
Halle, H., "2000 and none", *TimeOut New York*, 237, April 6-13.
Saltz, J., "My Sixth Sense", *Village Voice*, April 4.
Saltz, J., "Greater Expectations", *Village Voice*, March 14.
Vogel, C., "Inside Art, Whitney Prize", *The New York Times*, April 14.
Solomon, D., "A Roll Call of Fresh Names and Faces", *The New York Times*, April 16.
Cotter, H., "Greater New York", review, *The New York Times*, March 1.
Kimmelman, M., "A New Whitney Team Makes Its Biennial Pitch", *The New York Times*, March 24.

1999
Adelman, S., "Paul Pfeiffer, The Project ", *Frieze*, NY, 45, March/April.
M., Rush, "Hocus Focus", review, *Review*, February 1.
Turner, G., "Abstracted Flesh", *Flash Art*, 32, 204, January-February.
Chattopadhyay, C., "At Home And Abroad", *Art Asia Pacific*, 22.
Johnson, P., review, *Houston Chronicle*, January 12.

1998
Cotter, H., "Paul Pfeiffer and Nadar", review, *New York Times* , November 13.
Sirmans, F., "Get A Little Closer", *ArtNet Magazine*, December 17.
Turner, G., "Paul Pfeiffer and Nadar", review, *Review*, November 1.
Jana, R., "Home and Away", review, *Asian Art News*, July/August.
Bliss, K., "Crazy", review, *Dutch Magazine*, #18.
Baker, K., "Modern Art Redefined", review, *San Francisco Chronicle*, July 11.
At Home And Abroad, 20 Contemporary Filipino Artists (exhibition catalogue), Asian Art Museum, San Francisco.

1997
Memories of Overdevelopment, exhibition catalogue, Plug In Gallery, Winnipeg.

1995
In A Different Light, exhibition catalogue, UC Museum/ City Lights, Berkeley.
Art In General Annual Catalogue, Art In General, New York.
Pervert, exhibitioncatalogue, UC Gallery, Irvine.

1994
Extreme Unction, exhibition catalogue, Panchayat, London.
Hirsh, D., "Christian Iconography", review, *New York Native*, April 4.
Village Voice, Scene & Heard, (reproduction), March 22.

1993
"1991 In Review, Alternative Spaces", (reproduction), *Art In America*, August.
Consul, W., "The Agony and Apostasy", *Filipinas Magazine*, June.
Ty-Tomkins, N., "Philippines International", *Honolulu Weekly*, October 13.

1992
Asian American Arts Dialogue, (cover reproduction), 11, 1, January/February.
Altars, Divinations and Icons, exhibition catalogue, Painted Bride Gallery, Philadelphia.
(en)Gendered Visions, Race, Gender and Sexuality in Asian American Art, exhibition catalogue, Guadalupe Cultural Center, San Antonio.
Nelson, N., "Artists Find Their Own Religions", *Philadelphia Daily News*, September 24.

1989
Bernstein, N., "Portrait of the Artists", *San Francisco Bay Guardian*, October 11.

John Pilson
1968, born in New York.
Lives and works in New York.

Solo Exhibitions

2001
Nicole Klagsbrun, New York.
Raucci/Santamaria, Naples.

Group Exhibitions

2001
Open Ends, Museum of Modern Art.

2000
Greater New York, PS1, New York.
Nancy Davenport / John Pilson, Nicole Klagsbrun Gallery, New York.
John Pilson / Torbjorn Vejvi, Raucci/Santamaria Gallery, Naples.
World Without Ground, Chase/Freedman Gallery, West Hartford.

Ghosty, 1000eventi Gallery, Milan.
Some New Minds, P.S.1-MoMA Contemporary Art Center, New York.
Moma2000: Open Ends "Video/Performance", Museum of Modern Art, New York.
Above The Grid, special project, P.S.1-MoMA Contemporary Art Center, New York.
Shoc@kwave, Raucci/Santamaria Gallery, Naples.
Work 312 Gallery, Chicago.
Foxey Mark Pasek Gallery, New York.
The City Nicole Klagsbrun Gallery, New York.
Hope Ginsberg, Justine Kurland, John Pilson Kunst-Werke, Berlin.
Greater New York, P.S.1-MoMA Contemporary Art Center, New York.

1998
Citizens, New York Public Library, New York.

1994
Building, Dwelling, Thinking, Lowinsky Gallery, New York.

Bibliography

2001
Stephanson, A., "Openings", *Artforum*, April.
Huberman, A., "Ouverture", *Flash Art International*, March/April.
Romeo, F., "Shockwave", *Flash Art*, Italian Edition, January.

2000
Caroli, E., "Raucci e Santamaria, Cartoline da Los Angeles", *Corriere del Mezzogiorno*, November.
Anderson, J., "Interregna", P.S. 1 Greater, New York Catalogue.
Gopinath, G., "2 Critical Comments: Greater New York at P.S.1" Review New York, May.

1998
"In Progress", *DoubleTake Magazine*, December.

1994
Aletti, V., "Building Dwelling Thinking", *Village Voice*, March.

Stephen Powers
1968, born in Philadelphia.
Lives and works in New York.

Group Exhibitions

2000
Indelible Market, Institute of Contemporary Art, Philadelphia, May.
Street Market, Deitch Projects, New York.
Point of Purchase, Parco Gallery,Tokyo, Japan.

1999
Coup d'Etat, Alleged Gallery, New York.

1998
407 Gallery, New York.

Bibliography

2001
Cohen, M., "Street Market", *Flash Art*, January-February.

2000
Street Market, Tokyo, Japan, Little More Publishers.
Indelible Market, essay by A. Baker, Philadelphia, Institute of Contemporary Art.
Siegal, N., "Exhibit Becomes Opportunity for Arrest", *The New York Times*, October 10.
Tokyo Jammin', October.
Flannigan, E., "SoHOExhibit Sparks Mental Flames", *Amsterdam News*, October 26 - November 1, New York.
Oliver, S., "Bombs Away", *The Face*, November.
Yablonsky, L., "Street Market", *Time Out New York*, November 2-9.
Valdez, S., "Street Market at Deitch Projects", *Art in America*, December.
Avgikos, J., "Street Market", *Artforum*, December.
"Juicy Fruits", *Tokion*, November-December.

1999
Powers, S., *The Art of Getting Over: Graffiti at the Millenium*, St. Martin's Press.

1993-1997
Powers, S., *On the Go*, a graffity and hip-hop lifestyle magazine, 1993-1997.

Alexandra Ranner
1967, born in Osterhofen .
Lives and works in Munich.

Solo Exhibitions

2001
Aprèlude, Six Friedrich Lisa Ungar Gallery, Munich.

2000
Statements, Art Basel 2000, Six Friedrich Lisa Ungar Gallery, Munich.

1999/2000
Bedroom, M+R Fricke Gallery, Berlin.

Group Exhibitions

2001
International Triennale of Contemporary Art, Yokohama.

2000
Kunsthalle Mannheim, Mannheim.
Mnemosyne, Encontros de Fotografia 2000, Coimbra.

1999
Der bevorzugte Ort, Kunstverein Ludwigsburg.
Untitled, M + R Fricke Gallery, Düsseldorf.
Künstlerhaus Palais Thurn und Taxis, Bregenz.
Künstlerwerkstatt Lothringerstraße, Munich.

1998
Bolseiros e Finalistas, Ar.Co, Lisbon.
Galeria Pedro Cera, Lisbon.

Bibliography

2000
H.W. & J. Hector-Kunstpreis, Kunsthalle Mannheim.
The Mnemosyne Project, Coimbra.

1997
Alexandra Ranner, Galerie der Künstler, Munich.

Neo Rauch

1960, born in Leipzig.
Lives and works in Leipzig, Germany.

Solo Exhibitions

2001
Haus der Kunst, Munich.
Deutsche Guggenheim, Berlin.
Kunsthalle Zurich.
Collection Deutsche Bank, Mannheimer Kunstverein, Neues Museum Weserburg Bremen.
The Douglas Hyde Gallery Dublin.
International Culture Centre Krakow.
Squatters, Museu Serralves, Porto Witte de With, Rotterdam.

2000
Galerie EIGEN + ART, Berlin / Leipzig.
Contemporary German Art / The Last thirty Years / Thirty Artists from Germany, Goethe Institut, Bombay, Bangalore, Calcutta, New Delhi.
After the Wall, Hamburger Bahnhof, Berlin.
Salon, The Delfina Studio Trust, London.
Galerie für Zeitgenössische Kunst Leipzig.
David Zwirner Gallery, New York.

1999
Galerie EIGEN + ART, Berlin.
The Golden Age, ICA, London.
Malerei, INIT Kunst-Halle-Berlin.
After the Wall, Moderna Museet Stockholm.
German Open, Kunstmuseum Wolfsburg.
Beitrag zur Gestaltung des Bundestagsgebäudes "Paul-LöbeHaus", Berlin.

1998
Transmission, Espace des Arts, Chalon-sur-Saône.
Die Macht des Alters - Strategien der Meisterschaft, Deutsches Historisches Museum Berlin, Kunstmuseum Bonn.
Galerie EIGEN + ART, Berlin.
Galerie der Stadt Backnang.

1997
Museum der Bildenden Künste Leipzig, Verleihung des Kunstpreises der Leipziger Volkszeitung.
Manöver, Galerie EIGEN + ART, Berlin.
Vitale Module, Plauen, Dresden, Prag, Ludwigshafen, Wrozlaw.
Need for Speed, Grazer Kunstverein, Austria.

1996
Der Blick ins 21ste, Kunstverein Düsseldorf.
Contemporary Art at Deutsche Bank, London.

1995
Goethe House, New York.
Marineschule, Overbeck-Gesellschaft Lübeck.
Galerie EIGEN + ART, Berlin.
Dresdner Bank, Leipzig.

1994
1. Sächsische Kunstausstellung, Dresden.
Projekt Galerie, Kunstverein Elsterpark e. V., Leipzig.

1993
Galerie EIGEN + ART, Leipzig.
Galerie Voxx, Chemnitz.
Dresdner Bank, Frankfurt am Main.

1992
Junge Künstler aus Leipzig, BASF, Ludwigshafen.

1989
Galerie am Thomaskirchhof, Leipzig.

1988
X. Kunstausstellung der DDR, Dresden.
Leipziger Sezession, Krochhochhaus.

1986
Junge Künstler im Bezirk Leipzig, Staatliches Lindenau-Museum, Altenburg.

Bibliography

2001
Mack, G., "Mit den Waffen des Malers", *art, Das Kunstmagazin*, 1, January, pp. 12-23.
Beaucamp, E., "Schattenboxen im Randgebiet", *Frankfurter Allgemeine Zeitung*, 5, January 6, Feuilleton, p. 41.
Birnbaum, D., "Neo Rauch", reviews, *ART-FORUM*, March, p. 137.

2000
Smith, R., "Neo Rauch", *New York Times*, March 10.
Halle, H., "Back to the Wall", *Time Out New York*, March 16, p. 81.
Volk, G., "Neo Rauch at David Zwirner", *Art in America*, May, pp. 161-162.
Neo Rauch, Sammlung Deutsche Bank, edited by Deutsche Bank AG, Leipzig.
Neo Rauch, "Randgebiet" exhibition catalogue at Galerie Zeitgenössische Kunst Leipzig, Haus der Kunst München, Kunsthalle Zürich, edited by K. Werner für die Galerie für Zeitgenössische Kunst, Leipzig.

1998
Neo Rauch, exhibition catalogue, texts by B. Brock, M. Schick, C. Tannert, Galerie der Stadt Backnang, exhibitions catalogue, Galerie der Stadt Backnang und Galerie EIGEN+ART, Leipzig.

1997
Guth, P., "Machtspiele gegen die terroristische Realität: Neue Bilder von Neo Rauch in Leipzig", *Frankfurter Allgemeine Zeitung*, May 16.
Manöver, exhibition catalogue, Galerie EIGEN+ART, Leipzig.
Exhibition catalogue, Museum der bildenden Künste Leipzig, edited by H. Guratzsch, Leipzig 1997.

1995
Neo Rauch. Marineschule, exhibition catalogue, edited by Overbeck-Gesellschaft Lübeck, Leipzig.

1993
Neo Rauch, Ausstellungskatalog, edited by Galerie Alvensleben, München, Munich.

Heli Rekula

1963, Born, Helsinki.
Lives and works in Helsinki and abroad.

Solo Exhibitions

2000
Here Today, Gone Tomorrow, Fotogalleriet, Oslo.
Gallery Kari Kenetti, Helsinki.
Artspace 1%, Copenhagen.

1999
Nordisk Videokunst, Uppsala Artmuseum, Uppsala.

1998
Paradise Lost, edited by S. Huits, Stedelijk Museum Het Domein, Sittard.

1997
Pyhiinvaellus – Pilgrimage, Helsinki City Art Museum, Gallery Kluuvi & Gallery Struts, Oslo.

1995
Luontotutkielmia - Nature Studies, Helsinki City Art Museum, Gallery Kluuvi.
Häpeä Ja Halu - Shame And Desire, MUU Gallery, Helsinki.

1993
Muotokuvia – Portraits, Gallery Hippolyte, Helsinki.

Group Exhibitions

2001
Milano - Europe 2001, Milan.
Anteprima Bovisa. Milano Europa 2000, edited by M. Hirvi, Settore Cultura Musei e Mostre, Milan.
Get that Balance, edited by U. Vorkoeper, Hamburg.
Gallery Christian Dam, Oslo.

2000
Momentum, Nordic Biennial of Contemporary Art, Moss.
The Future is now, videoprogram edited by Artspace 1%, Stockholm Art Fair & Louisiana Museum, Copenhagen.
Premate - Impakt Festival 2000, edited by A. Dunnevind, Utrecht.
Identité Fictive, Centré Culturelle des Institutions Europeens, Luxemburg.
Centré Cultural, Varegem.
Finnish Instutute, Paris.
Shoot - moving pictures by artists, Malmö Konsthall.

1999 -2001
Can You Hear Me - 2nd Ars Baltica, edited by K. Becker, Triennial of Photo graphic Art.

1999
666999 - six days, six events, six countries, Annecy.
Nuoret / Vanhukset (Young Ones/Old Ones), edited by M. Hannula, T. Vaden, Wäinö Aaltonen Museum of Art, Turku.
Identité Fictive, Galerie Contretype, Bryssel.
Come in and find out, 2, edited by K. Wallner, Podewill, Berlin.
Pink For Boys / Blue For Girls, edited by

K.Becker, Neue Gesellschaft für bildende Kunst, Berlin.
Mmm...but not for marabou, edited by Frame & AV-ARKKI, Stockholm Art Fair.

1998
Mikä on todellista - What is real, The Third Triennial of photographic Art, Helsinki Kunsthalle.
Mikkelin Taidemuseo, edited by U. Jokisalo.
Photo / Realities, Biennale Syd, Kristiansand Art Museum, Norway.
Alastomat ja naamioidut (Naked and Masked), Helsinki City Art Museum, Helsinki.

1997
Unknown Adventure - Positions of Contemporary Finnish Art, Sophienhof, Kiel & Kunsthalle, Rostoc.
Darkside, Gallery Kenetti, Helsinki.

1996
Likat - Sju Flickor, Galleri Otto Blonk, Bergen.
Women breaking the boundaries of Ar, The Lönnström Art Museum, Rauma.
When the shit hits the fan, Scandinavian Art in Recent Time, edited by T.O. Nielsen, Overgaden, Copenhagen.
Postmorality, edited by A. Elovirta, Sofia, Bulgaria.
Body as membrane, edited by Valie Export & Kirsten Justessen, Kunsthallen Brandts Klaedefabriken, Odense, The Nordic Arts Centre, Helsinki.

1995
Living Texture, Scandinavian Art Productions, Zurich.
Smart Show, Stockholm.
Art Attack, Scandinavian Art Happening, Oslo.

1994
Lady Shave, Gallerie Kluuvi, Helsinki.

Works on Film & Video

2000
Vyyhti – Skein, Videoinstallation for two videoprojectors, DVD, á 2,52 min production Lasse Saarinen / Kinotar Oy.

1998
pyhiinvaellus - pilgrimagre, 35 mm / digital betacam, 10 min.
Täällä tänään, huomenna mennyttä, Here today, gone tomorrow, 4 min, orig. S-16 mm, colour, digital betacam, production: Chrystal Eye / Ilppo Pohjola.
MUU Media Festival, Helsinki.
French-Baltic-Nordic Video and New Media Festival, Tallinn, Estonia.

1997
Women in Film and New Media, Nordic Glory, J:skylä.
Short Spring, Bio Illusion, Helsinki.

1996
MUU Media Festival, Helsinki.

1995
Luontotutkielmia - Nature Studies, S-VHS 13 min.
MUU Media Festival, Helsinki.

1993
No Budget Film Festival, Q-Theatre, Helsinki.

1992
Institute of Contemporary Arts, Brisbane, Australia.
Metro Arts, Brisbane, Australia.
Pleasure Dome, Toronto, Canada.
London Film Festival.
Cinema Jové '92, Valencia.
Off FestivaaLi, Espoo, Finland.
Espoo Ciné, Finland.
Iisalmen Kamera.
No Budget Film Festival, Hamburg.
Tampere Film Festival, National competition serie.

1991
Hotelli - Hotel, 16 mm/black and white/Com-mag.

Bibliography

2000
The Artists Body, Phaidon Press.
Park - Momentum, Nordic Festival of Contemporary Art, exhibition catalogue, text by S. Huits, Stedelijk Museum, Het Domein.

1999
The young ones, the old ones, exhibition catalogue, conversation with T. Vaden about Maya Derens works, Wäivö Aaltonen Art Museum.
Come in and find out, exhibition catalogue, 2, edited by K. Wallner.
Rosa für Jungs, Hellblau für Mädchen, Pink for Boys, Blue for Girls, exhibition catalogue.
FRAMES Viewing Finnish Contemporary Photography, FRAME Finnish Fund for Art Exhange.

1998
Paradise Lost, exhibition catalogue, Stedelijk Museum Het Domein.
Mikä on todellista -What is real, The Third Triennial of Photographic Art, exhibition catalogue, Helsinki Kunsthalle.
Alastomat Ja Naamioidut 1998, Helsinki City Art Museum.

Biennale Syd, Photo/Realities 1998, exhibition catalogue, Sorlandets Kunstmuseum.

1997
Taide, art magazine 3/97, cover + artists pp. 32-33.

1996
Nielsen, T.O., *When the shit hits the fan*, exhibition catalogue.
Elovirta, A., "Masking and Unmasking of the self in Heli Rekula's works", *Body as membrane*, exhibition catalogue.

1995
Lintonen, K., "Luontotutkielmia - Nature Studies", *Valokuvalehti*, 6/95.
Elovirta, A., "Finland: The Ideological Body. The Grotesque Moment: Corpo/Real Anxities", *Magazyn Sztuki*, Art Magazine Quarterly, 8, 4/95.

1994
Elovirta, A., "The Grotesque Moment", *Siksi*, Nordic Art Review, 1/1994.

Gerhard Richter
*1932, born in Dresden.
Lives and works in Cologne.*

Solo Exhibitions

1999
Gerhard Richter, Städtische Galerie im Lenbachhaus, Kunstbau, Prato, Fundacio Museo d'Arte Contemporaneo (MACBA), Munich/Barcelona; Centro per l'Arte Contemporanea Luigi Pecci, Museo d'Arte Contemporanea, Prato.
Gerhard Richter, Astrup Fearnely Museum of Modern Art, Oslo.
Gerhard Richter: Zeichnungen und Aquarelle 1964 – 1999, Kunstmuseum Winterthur, Winterthur.
Gerhard Richter: the Complete Editions, Anthony d'Offay Gallery, London.

1998
Gerhard Richter, Wexner Center for the Arts, Columbus.
Gerhard Richter: Ein Saal und ein Kabinett für die Sammlung, Kunstmuseum Winterthur, Winterthur.
Gerhard Richter, Druckgrafik, Neue Galerie, Munich/Dachau.
Gerhard Richter, Bilder 1972-1996, Galerie Bernd Lutze, Friedrichshafen.
Gerhard Richter, Printing, Neuer Aachener Kunstverein, Aachen.
Gerhard Richter, New Paintings, Anthony d'Offay Gallery, London.
Gerhard Richter, Landschaften, Sprengel Museum, Hannover.

1997
Gerhard Richter: Fuji, Städtische Galerie im Lenbachhaus, Munich.
Gerhard Richter: Halifax, Kaiser-Wilhelm-Museum Krefeld, Krefeld.
Gerhard Richter, Wako Works of Art, Tokyo.

1996
Gerhard Richter, Carré d'Art Contemporain de Nîmes, Nîmes.
Gerhard Richter, Museum für Koderne Kunst, Bozen.
Gerhard Richter, Wako Warks of Art, Tokyo.
Gerhard Richter, Marian Goodman Gallery, New York.
Two Sculpures for a Room by Palermo, Marian Goodman and Anthony d'Offay Gallery, New York/London.

1995
New Paintings, Anthony d'Offay Gallery, London.

1994
Grafik und Auflagenbilder, Galerie Bernd Lutze, Friedrichshafen.
Prints and Multiples 1966-1993, David Zwirner Gallery, New York.
Bilder 1962-1993, Moderna Museet, Stockholm.
Gerhard Richter und die Romantik, Kunstverein Essen, Essen.
Bilder 1962-1993, Centro Reina Sofia, Madrid.

1993
Gerhard Richter, "Ausschnitt", 20 Bilder von 1965-1991, Neuer Berliner Kunstverein, Berlin.
Gerhard Richter, Wako Works of Art, Tokyo.
Gerhard Richter, Marian Goodman Gallery, New York.
Gerhard Richter, Peinture, Museé d'Art Moderne de la Ville de Paris, Paris
Gerhard Richter, Editionen 1965-1993, Kunstverein/Kunsthalle Bremen, Bremen.
Editionen, Galerie Löhrl, Mönchengladbach.
Bilder 1962-1993, Kunst und Ausstellungshalle der Bundesrepublik Deutschland, Bonn.
Bilder 1992 und Arbeiten auf Papier, Galerie Fred Jahn, Munich.

1992
Gerhard Richter, Sils Maria/Engadin Sils, Nietzsche-Haus.
Gerhard Richter, Antony d'Offay Gallery, London.
Gerhard Richter, Galerie Bernd Slutzky (FrüheDruckgrafik), Frankfurt.
Gerhard Richter, Galerie Nächst St. Stephan, Vienna.

Associazione per l'Arte Contemporanea, Rome.
Gerhard Richter, Nolan/Ekman Gallery, New York.

1991

Gerhard Richter, Anthony d'Offay Gallery, London.
Gerhard Richter, Galerie Fred Jahn, Munich/Stuttgart.
Gerhard Richter, Galerie Durand-Desert, Paris.
Gerhard Richter, Douglas Hyde Gallery, Dublin.
Gerhard Richter, Tate Gallery, London.
Gerhard Richter, Galerie Achenbach, Frankfurt.
Gerhard Richter, Galerie Bernd Lutze, Friedrichshafen.

Group Exhibitions

1998

Zeichnungen deutscher und osterreichischer Künstler, Galerie Fred Jahn, Munich.
Artificial Figuracions contemporanies, Museu d'Art Contemporani, Barcelona.
Melancholie und Eros in der Kunst der Gegenwart, Sammlung Murken, Ludwig Forun für Internationale Kunst, Aachen.
Wounds between democracy and redemption in contemporary art, Moderna Museet Stockholm, Stockholm.
More Pieces for the Puzzle: Recent Additions to the Collection, Museum of Modern Art, New York.
Photoimage: Printmaking 60s to 90s, Museum of Fine Arts, Boston.
Puheenvuoroja Inlagg Dialogue, Museum of Contemporary Art, The Finnish National Gallery, Helsinki.
Artist's Proof, Kaiser Wilhelm Museum, Krefeld.
Breaking Gound, Marian Goodman Gallery, New York.
Museum Ludwig im Russichen Museum, St Petersburg.
Surrogate: The Figure in Contemporary Sculpture and Photography, Henry Art Gallery, University of Washington, Seattle.

1997

Documenta X, Fridericinaum, Kassel.
Objects of Desire: The Modern Still Life, Museum of Modern Art, New York.
De Re Metallica, Anthony d'Offay Gallery, London.
German Art: 30 Years of Contemporary Art from the Collections of the Kunstmusem Bonn, Singapore Art Museum, Singapore.
Passato Presente Futuro, La Biennale di Venezia, Venice.
Die Maler und Ihre Skulpturen - Von Edgar Degas bis Gerhard Richter, Museum Folkwang, Essen.

Le Collection du Centre Georges Pompidou, Museum of Contemporary Art, Tokyo.

1996-1997

Froehlich Collection, Tate Gallery, London.

1996

Abstraction in the 20th Century, Solomon R Guggenheim Museum, New York.
New Displays, Tate Gallery, London.
New Abstraction, Centro Reina Sofia, Madrid.
NowHere, Louisiana Museum of Modern Art, Humblebæk.
Munch and after Munch, Stedelijk Museuk and Munch Museet, Amsterdam/Oslo.
Recaptured Nature, Marian Goodman Gallery, New York.
Zeitstromungen - Kunst aus der Sammlung der Niedersachsischen Sparkassenstiftung, Sprengel Museum Hannover, Hannover.
Portrait of the Artist, Anthony d'Offay Gallery, London.
Face à l'histoire, 1993-1996, Paris.

1995

Desire, Disaster, Document, San Francisco Museum of Modern Art, San Francisco.
Still Life, National Museum, Stockholm.
The Romantic Spirit in German Art, Munich.
Ars Helsinki, Museum of Contemporary Art, Helsinki.
Singular Objects, National Museum of Modern Art, Tokyo/Kyoto.
Auf Papier - Kunst des 20 Jhd. aus der Deutschen Bank, Schirn Kunsthalle FFM, Berlinische Galerie, Museum der bildendon Künste Leipzig, Berlin/Leipzig.
Junge deutsche Kunst der 90er Jahre aus NRW: Die Generation nach Becker, Beuys, Polke, Richter, ruthenbeck, Sonje Museum of Contemporary Art, Kyongju, Korea.
Degrees of Abstraction: From Morris Louise to Mapplethorpe, Eunica and Julian Cohen Gallery, Boston.
Gerhard Richter, Sigmar Polke, Bruce Nauman, Yuji Takeoka Noritoshi Hirakawa, Wako Works of Art, Tokyo.
Kunstler - Raum, Sammlung Hans Goethe, Kunstmuseum, Bonn.
Kunst in Deutschland, KAH, Bonn
Blumenstillepen, Kunsthalle, Bielefeld.
Colour and Paint, Kunstmuseum, St Gallen.
Still Life, Stadtische Galerie Helmhaus, Zurich.
National Museum of Modern Art, Osaka.

Bibliography

1999

Schumacher, R., "Gerhard Richter: Atlas", *Flash Art*, 99, March-April.
Wilson, A., "The Same but Different", *Art Monthly*, October.

Schwarz, *Gerhard Richter: Zeichnungen 1964-1999*, Kunstmuseum Winterthur.

1998

Hierholzer, M., "Gerhard Richter", *Deutschland*, Magazine on Politics, Culture, Business and Science, Frankfurt, 1.
Rosenthal, M., "Gerhard Richter" (interview), *Mark Rothko*, National Gallery of Art, Washington.
Boller, G., "Gerhard Richter: Illusionen 1989", Dies: Kunst und Architektur, Universitat St Gallen, Bern.
Tosatto, G., "The feeling of having come closer to something of the reality of appearanches", *Ninety: Art in the 90s*, 29.
Hentschel, M., "On Shifting Terrain: Looking at Richter's Abstract Paintings", *Gerhard Richter: Paintings*, Anthony d'Offay Gallery.
Hemken, K.-U., *Gerhard Richter: 18 Oktober 1977*, Frankfurt am Main und Leipzig.
Morley, S., "The Friedrich Factor", *Contemporary Visual Arts*, 19.
Gayford, M., "Zen and the abstract use of the squeegee", *The Daily Telegraph*, September 16.
Pecker, W., "Paintings on the nature of abstraction", *The Financial Times*, October 3.
Elger, D., *Gerhard Richter: Landschaften*, Sprengel Museum, Hannover.
Hubbard, S., "Gerhard Richter", *Time Out*, October 14.

1997

Gerhard Richter Notes: 1964-1965, Indiferencia Y Singularidad, La fotografie en el pensamiento artistico contemporeneo, Musea d'Art Contemporani do Barcelona.
Ronte, D., "Gerhard Richter: Limited Possibilities", *German Art: 30 Years of German Contemporary Art*, Singapore Art Museum.
Ehrenfried, S., *Ohne Eigenschaften: Das Portrait bei Gerhard Richter*, Vienna, New York.
Jones, G. R., *Redstarts, Richter, Sparrows, Richter: Aphorisms on the Names of Birds and the Art of Gerhard Richter*, Edinburgh.
Alberro, A., Gerhard Richter, March.
Schwarz, D., "Leserbrief (zu S mit Kind Bildern)", *Texte zur Kunst*, 27, September.
Jacobi, F., "Gerhard Richter's Zyklus: 18 Oktober 1977", *Museumsjounal*, Museumspadagogischer Dienst Berlin, IV, October.
Butin, H., *Gerhard Richter, der kapitalistische Realismus und seine Malerei nach Fotografien von 1962-1966*, Deutschlandbilder, Kunst aus einem getailten Land, Berlin, Cologne.
uping, M., *Paintings from the Decades: Realism, Memory and Re-Figuration*, Modern Art Museum Fort Worth, Texas.
Gandy, M., *Contradictory Modernities:*

Conceptions of Nature in the Art of Joseph Beuys and Gerhard Richter, Annals of the Association of American Geographer, Oxford.

1996

Haxthausen, C., "Gerhard Richter", *Burlington Magazine*, January.
Hohmeyer, J., "Selbstenblossung in Schmelz und Wut", *Der Spiegel*, March 25.
Crow, T., *Living with Pop, The Rise of the Sixties.*
Koniger, M., "Vom Text zum Kontext-100 Bilder Gerhard Richter im Carre d'art Nimes", *Newue Bildende Kunst*, 4, August-September.
Dietrich, D., "Gerhard Richter's ATLAS: One man show in a shipping crate", *The Print Collector's Newsletter*, XXVI, 6 January-February.
Buchloh, B., "Divided Memory and Post-Traditional Identity: Gerhard Richter Work of Mourning", *October 75*, Winter.
Wallenstein, S.-O., "The Force of Necessity: History and Freedom in the work of Gerhard Richter", *Material: Journal of Contemporary Art*, 29, Summer.
Huser, "L'Incroyable Monsieur Richter", *LeNouvel Observateur*, August 15.
Jurgensen, G., "Entre abstraction et figuration: Gerhard Richter peint l'inquietude", *La Croix*, August 29.
Rosernthal, M., *Extreme Statements, Abstraction in the Twentieth Century: Total Risk, Freedom, Discipline*, Guggenheim Museum, New York.
Weiermair, P., "Der Maler als Sisyphus", *Gerhard Richter*, Museum für Moderne Kunst, Bonn, Vienna, Bozen.
Brehm, M., "Uber das Konstituieren visueller Wahrheit beim Malen", *Sammlung Frieder Burda: Gerhard Richter, Sigmar Polke, Arnulf Rainer*, Staatliche, Kunsthalle Baden-Baden, Ostfildern.
Williams, A., "Saying Nothing", *American Book Review*, December-January.

1995

Spies, W., *Emotional und eisig - In der Holle der Beruhrungsangste: Gerhard Richter, Schnitt durch die Welt*, Aufsatze zu Kunst und Literatur, Cantz Verlag.
Schuster, P.K., *Gerhard Richter*, Staatsgaleire moderner Kusnt Munchen.
Smith, R., "A German Master Takes an Epic Journey", *New York Times*, 4 June.
Butin, H., "Zwei Kerzen für Dresden", *Cameria Aurstira*, 50.
Obrist, H.U., "Interview with Gerhard Richter", *Flash Art*, 192.
Moch, G., "Zwei Kerzen Mahnen an der Kunstakacademie", *Sachsische Zeitung*, February 8.
Searle, A., "Visual Arts - Gerhard Richter", *The Independent*, June 10.

Vogel, C., "Inside Art - Gerhard Richter", *New York Times*, June 16.
Currah, M., "Richter Scale", *Time Out*, June 28.
Kramer, H., "MoMA Helps Martyrdom of German Terrorists", *New York Observer*, August 2.
Jefferey Kastner Art Monthly, 188, July/August.
Cork, R., "Testaments to the scars that never heal", *The Times*, July 25.
Forstbauer, N.A., "Abschied als marlische Mahnung", *Stuttgarter Nachrichten*, July 8.
Hecht Wohlfeile, A., "Klagen um das deutsche Gesamtbild", *Art*, July 7.
Richter, G., *The Daily Practice of Painting: Writing 1962-1993*, Anthony d'Offay Gallery, London.
Huck, B., "Bine Erregung, Springer, Bank 1", *Heft 4*, September.
Druger, K., *Der Blick ins innere des Bildes*, Pantheon, Munich.
Ruthe, I., "Unscharf ist das Bild der Realitaet", *Berliner Zeitung*, 13, 12.
Kimmelman, M., Serra, R., "One Provocateur Inspired by Another", *New York Times*, August 11.
Baker, K., "Richter's ATLAS at Dia", *San Francisco Chronicle*, July 17.
Chelsea Pearl Neville Wakefield, *Artforum*, December.
van Drathen, D., "Gerhard Richter-An die Macht der Bilder glauben", *Kunstforum*, August-October.
von Drathen, D., "Malen ist etwas ganz und gar Lebensnotwendiges, Gerhard Richter im Gesprach mit Doris von Drathen", *Kunstforum*, August-October.
Meinhardt, J., "Ende der Malerei und Malerei nach dem Ende der Malerei", *Kunstforum*, August-October.
Seymour, A., *Gerhard Richter*, Anthony d'Offay Gallery, London.
Gidal, P., *The Polemics of Paint in Gerhard Richter: Painting in the Nineties*, Anthony d'Offay Gallery, London.
Pelzer, B., "The Elision of the Gaze", *Gehard Richter*, The Israel Museum, Jerusalem.
Lewis, J., *A Two Part Invention, Gerhard Richter: Selected Works 1963-1987*, Luhring Augustine Gallery, New York.
Spies, W., "Lachende Leere", *FAZ*, 234, October 9.
Butin, H., "Mit der RAF in Museum of Modern Art - Gerhard Richter im Gesprach", Interview, *Neue Zurichter Zeitung*, 246, October 23.
Koldehoff, S., "Stammheim in New York", Interview, *Die Tageszeitung*, October 28/29.
Storr, R., "Des diverses manières d'echorcher un chat doté de sept vies", *Art Press Hors Serie*, 16.

1994
Perrin, F., "The Absolute Presence of Painting", *Flash Art*, 1/2, 1994.

Gerd Rohling
1946, born in Krefeld.
Lives and works in Berlin.

Solo Exhibitions

2001
The 66 CUP, Ghana, National Museum, Accra.

2000
Drei Affen erstochen, Galerie Borgemeister, Berlin.

1999
Made in India, Government Museum, Chennai, Madras.
First Biennale Liverpool, Art Forum, Berlin.

1998
All and nothing, Max Mueller Bhavan Bombay, Mumbai.
Blue Blood, David Sassoon Library Bombay, Mumbai.
Arena, Galerie Rainer Borgemeister, Berlin.

1997
3 x 3, Galerie Gutshof Langen, Langen.

1996
Form + Inhalt, Kunstwerke e.V. Berlin, Berlin.
Àgua e vinho, Museu de arte moderna do Rio de Janeiro.
Gerd Rohling, Chiesa di san Giovanni e Paolo, Spoleto.
A Porcelana da rainha, Museu de Arte moderna da Bahia, Salvador de Bahia.

1995-96
Plastische Metamorphosi, Museo Archeologico Nazionale di Napoli, Naples.

1995
Al re di Napoli, Casina Vanvitelliana, Fusaro.

1994
Der lange Weg zum guten Bild, Kunsthalle, Nürnberg.

1993
Back to Bombay, Christie's Berlin.

1992
Dirty Windows Gallery, Berlin.
Der Sprung, Flohmarkt Wedding, Berlin.

1989
Gerd Rohling. Poestenkill. Bilder aus Amerika, Kutscherhaus Berlin.
Die Ahnenreihe, Nationalgalerie im Kunstforum der Grundkreditbank, Berlin.

1986
Galerie Fahnemann, Berlin.

1984
Galerie Fahnemann, Berlin.

1983
Galleria Peccolo, Livorno.
Kunstverein Freiburg, Schwarzes Kloster.

1982
Cars and Bikes, P.S.1, New York.

1981
Gerd Rohling, Objekte, Environments 1979/80, Neuer Berliner Kunstverein.
Pink Panther Raum.
P.S.1, New York.

1980
Gerd Rohling, Bilder - Objekte, Galerie 1/61, Berlin.
Galleria Schema, Florence.

Group Exhibitions

2000
ter Hell, Mang, Metzel, Pods, Rohling, Kunstverein Offenburg.
Ein/räumen, Hamburger Kunsthalle.

1999
Sammlung Böckmann, Kunsthalle Lingen
Liverpool Biennal 1999 (Tracey).
Berlin 80er Jahre, Kunsthalle Göppingen.

1998
Brandenburgische Kunsttage, Drewen.
Von Rodin bis Trockel, Museum Kleve.
Missing Links, Kunsthalle Rostock.

1997
Eröffnungsausstellung, Hamburger Bahnhof, Berlin.

1996
Artedomani - Punta di vista, Spoleto.
Metropole e Peripheria, Museu de arte moderna, Rio de Janeiro.

1991
Interferenzen. Kunst aus Westberlin, Riga, St. Petersburg.
Das goldene Zeitalter, Württembergischer Kunstverein, Stuttgart.

1990
Animalia, Haus am Waldsee, Berlin.
Ambiente Berlin, XLIV Venice Biennale, Kunsthalle Budapest.

1989
Art in Berlin, The High Museum of Art, Atlanta.
D&S-Ausstellung, Kunstverein Hamburg.

1987
Auf der Spur, Sammlung Stober, Haus am Waldsee, Berlin.
Olaf Metzel, Gerd Rohling, Ina Barfuß, Thomas Wachweger, Institute of Contemporary Arts, London.
Berlin, Goethe House, New York.
Ten Painters: Berlin, Crescent Gallery, Dallas.
Desire for Life, Ausstellung des Goethe-Instituts für USA.

1986
Berlin Aujourd'hui, Musée de Tulon.
Vorsatz Eins, Galerie Vorsetzen, Hamburg.
Momente, Kunstverein Braunschweig.

1985
1945-1985. Kunst in der Bundesrepublik Deutschland, Nationalgalerie, Berlin.
Zeichnungen. 12 Künstler aus Berlin, Ausstellung des Goethe-Instituts für Kairo, Tel Aviv, Athen, Sarajevo.
Middelheim-Biennale, Antwerpen.

1984
Neue Malerei Berlin, Kestner Gesellschaft, Hannover.
Zwischen Plastik und Malerei, Haus am Waldsee, Berlin, Kunstverein Hannover.
Skulpture, Art Palace, New York.
Ein anderes Klima, Städtische Kunsthalle Düsseldorf.

1983
Skulpture 83, Kunststichting Rotterdam.
Montevideo Diagonale, Antwerpen.
Neue Malerei in Deutschland (dimension IV. Wettbewerb und Ausstellung der Phillip Morris GmbH), National galerie, Berlin, Städtische Kunsthalle Düsseldorf, Haus der Kunst, München.
Generics, Berlin.

1982
Old World, New Works, The Clocktower, New York.
Gefühl und Härte. Künstler in Berlin, Kulturhaus Stockholm.
Gefühl und Härte. Neue Kunst aus Berlin, Kunstverein München.
Kunst wird Material, Nationalgalerie, Berlin.
Kunst, Kutscherhaus, Berlin.
Dada. Montage, Konzept, Berlinische Galerie, Berlin.

1981
Situation Berlin, Galerie d'Art Contemporain des Musées de Nice, Nizza.
Szenen der Volkskunst, Württembergischer Kunstverein, Stuttgart.
Berlin, eine Stadt für Künstler, Kunsthalle Wilhelmshaven.
ars viva. Skulpturen und Installationen der Preisträger, Kunsthalle Bielefeld.

1980
1/61, Berlin.

1979
Kunstpreis Junger Westen, Kunsthalle Recklinghausen.
Kunstlandschaft Bundesrepublik, Württembergischer Kunstverein, Stuttgart.
Exotismen, Württembergischer Kunstverein, Stuttgart.

1977
Kunstpreis Junger Westen, Kunsthalle, Recklinghausen.
Ausblicke-Einblicke. 7 Künstler, Kurfürstendamm-Karree, Berlin.

1976
Schuhwerke, Kunsthalle, Nürnberg.

1975
Forum junger Kunst, Staatliche Kunsthalle, Baden-Baden.

Alexander Roitburd
1961, born in Odessa.
Lives and works in New York.

Solo exhibition

2000
The Benefit-night, State Cultural Center Ukraine, Odessa.

1999
Pompey's cycle, Liberty Gallery, Odessa.

1997
Ordinary Life in Pompey, Karas' Atelier Gallery, Kiev.

1995
Blank Art Gallery, Kyiv.

1993
The Lying Nude, Tirs Gallery, Odessa.
A Portrait. Of the Lady. In White, Galleries 1.0, Guelman Gallery and Shkola, Moscow.

1991
Classics and Contemporaries, Center for Contemporary Art, Moscow.

1990
Guelman Gallery, Moscow.

Group Exhibitions

2000
2000+, Lyublyana.
Crime, Odessa.
It could be Obsession, Graz.

1999
On the Margin, Saskatoon.
Regards sur l'Ukraine, Paris.
New Pinakotheka, Kyiv.
Future is Now, Zagreb; Maribor, Slovenia.

1998
Academy of Cold, Odessa.
Publik Interest, Kyiv.

1997
Unnatural Selection, Odessa.
Supermarket, Odessa.
Art & Fact, Odessa.
New File, Odessa.
Near the Beginning, Plasy, Czech Republic.

1995
Phantom-Opera, Odessa.
Doctor Frankenstein Studio.
Neochimerism, Odessa.
Kandinsky Syndrome, Odessa.
Configura 2, Erfurt.

1994
Free Zone, Odessa.
Space of Cultural Revolution, Kyiv.

1993
Steppes of Europe, Warsaw.
Kunst-Kammer, Moscow.
Angels over Ukraine, Edinburgh.

1992
Post-anaesthesia, Munich-Leipzig.

1990
Ukrainian malARTstvo of 1960-80, Odesse.
Babylon, Moscow.
Artists of Empty House, Bratislava.
Ukrainian Art of the XX Century, Kyiv.

1989
All-Union Painters' Competition, Moscow.

1988
Soviart, the first Soviet-American art exhibition, Kyiv.

Bibliography

1997
ARTnewsletter, New York, July.

1993
Art News, 7.
Khudozhesvenniy Zhurnal, art magazine, Moscow, 2.

1992
ARTnewsletter, September.

1990
Art News, 5.
Art review, yearbook.

1987
Tvorchestvo, art magazine, 8.

Tracey Rose
1974, born in Durban.
Lives and works in Jojannesburg.

Solo Exhibitions

2000
The Project, New York, USA.
ArtPace, San Antonio Texas.
Goodman Gallery, Jojannesburg, South Africa.

Group Exhibitions

2001
Cross+Over, CPC Path Studios, Johannesburg.
Fresh, South African National Gallery, South Africa.

2000
South Meets West, Kunsthalle, Bern.
Dakar Biennale, Dakar.
Johannesburg, Mostra d'arte contemporanea, Milan.
Mostra Africana de Arte Contemporanea, San Paolo.

1999
Dialog: Vice versa, OK Centrum, Linz.
Video cult/ures, Zentrum für Kunst und Medientechonologie/Museum fur neue Kunst, Kalsruhe.
Channel, South African National Gallery, Cape Town.
Vedeodrome, New Museum of Contemporary Art, New York.

1998
Dark Continent, Klein Karoo Nationale Kunstfees Oudshoorn, South Africa *Art of the World 1998*, Passage de Retz, Paris.
Democracy's Images, Bildmuseet, Umea, Sweden.
Gaurene: Fondazione Sandretto per l'arte, Turin.
Triennale of Small Sculptures, SudwestLB Forum, Stuttgart.

1997
Purity & Danger, Gertrude Posel Gallery, Johannesburg.
Cross/ings, Museum of Contemporary Art, Tampa.
FNB Vita Awards, Sandton Civic Gallery, Johannesburg.
Graft, 2nd Johannesburg Biennale, South African National Gallery, Cape Town.

1996
Scramble, Civic Theatre Gallery, Johannesburg.

Hitchhiker, Generator Art Space, Johannesburg.

Curated exhibitions

1997
50 Stories, Carlton Centre, Johannesburg.

Bibliography

2000
Smith, R., "The Project", *The New York Times*, March 24.
"Aus Afrika – und jenseits von Afrika" *Berner Zeitung BZ*, April 12.
Tobler, K., "Tracey Rose 00.1", *Judith Russi Kirshner Artpace* (The International Artist in residency Program), February – March.

1999
"Venus 2000: Baartman and Beyond, , edited by Deborah Willis and Carla Williams, Temple University.
Kellner, C., "A history of invention", *co@rtnews*, February.
Smith, G., "Coming up Rose", *Elle*, September.

1998
"Spin City" Christian Haye, *Frieze*, January.
van Bosch, C., "Lang arm gryp in toe die doilies begin krap", *Krit*, April 6.
Shantall, L., "Feathers Fly at Fest", *Mail and Guardian*, April 9-16.

1997
Geers, K., "Planet Art", *Elle*, South Africa, October.
Atkinson, B., "Vita(1) Signs", *Mail and Guardian*, October 24 - October 30.
Roper, C., "Hair and Now", *Mail and Guardian*, October 31 - November 6.
Jones, D., "The view from the top", *The Star*, November 11.

Mimmo Rotella
1918, born in Catanzaro.
Lives and works in Milan.

Solo Exhibitions

2001
Galleria Spaziotempo, Florence.
Galerie Fish Platz, Ulm.
Galerie Binz Kramer, Cologne.

2000
Charles Cowlws Galerie, New York.
Guy Pieters Galerie, Knokke-Zut.
Espace Ernest Hilger, Paris.

1999
Museo d'Arte Modema e Contemporanea, Nizza.

1998
Galleria-Museo Baviera, Zurich.
Galleria Cannaviello, Milan.
Kunstverein, Braunschweig.
Galleria Fabibasaglia, Rimini.
Wurttembergicher Kunstverein, Stuttgard.

1996
Galleria Dionne, Paris.
Galleria Marisa del Re, New York.

1993
Fondo Regionale d'Arte Contemporanea, Digione.
Museo Ludwig, Cologne.

1992
Museo Civico, Piacenza.

1991
Studio Marconi, Milan.

1990
Galleria Tomwall, Stockholm.
Galleria Sonia Zanettacci, Geneve.
Galleria Beaburg, Paris.

1989
Daad Gallery, Berlin.
Galleria Reckermann, Cologne.

1987
Galleria Keeser Bohbot, Hamburg.

1981
Galleria Denis Renè, Paris.

1975
Rotonda della Befana, Milan.

1974
Galleria Crafen, Paris.

1972
Studio Marconi, Milan.

1971
Galleria Mathias Fels, Paris.

1967
Galleria "20", Amsterdam.

1966
Galleria del Naviglio, Milan.
Teatro la Fenice, Venice.

1965
Galleria La Tartaruga, Rome.

1964
La Biennale di Venezia, XXXII Esposizione Internazionale d'Arte, Venice.

1963
Galleria Apollinaire, Milan.

1962
Galleria "J", Paris.
Galleria Seven Arts, London.
Galleria Bonino, Buenos Aires.
Galleria del Leone, Venice.

1959
Galleria La Salita, Rome.

1957
Galleria Beno, Zurigo.
Galleria Del Naviglio, Milan.
I.C.A., London.

1955
Galleria Del Naviglio, Milan.

1952
Galleria Rockjill Nelson, Kansas City.

1951
Galleria Chiaruzzi, Rome.

Group Exhibitions

2001
Les annèes pop, Centre G. Pompidou, Paris.

1999
Pop Art Europe/Usa, Moma, New York.

1996
Davant l'Histoire, Centre G. Pompidou, Paris.
Art and Film, Museum of Contemporary Art, Los Angeles.

1994
Italian Metamorphosis, Guggenhein Museum, New York.

1991
Pop Art, Royal Academy, London.

1990
Art and Pub, Centre George Pompidou, Paris.

1989
Arte italiana del XX secolo, Royal Academy of Art, London.

1986
Arte italiana oggi, Galleria Di Laurenti, New York.

1982
Contemporary Italian Art, Hayward Gallery, London .
Les nouveaux rèalistes, Musèe d'Art Moderne et Contemporain, Nice.

1981
Linea della ricerca artistica in Italia, 1960-1980, Palazzo delle Esposizioni, Rome.

1979
Sei artisti italiani di Paris, Galerie Denis Renè, Paris .

1977
Tre città, tre collezioni, Centre G. Pompidou, Paris.

1970
Festival del Nuovo Realismo, Milan.

1967
Omaggio a Marylin Monroe, Sidney Janes Hallery, New York.

1966
Movimento Dada, Galleria Schwarz, Milan.

1964
Pop art, Nouveau Realisme, Palais des Beaux-Arts, Bruxelles.

1963
Biennale internazionale d'Arte Moderna, Tokio.

1962
New Realism, Sidney Janes Gallery, New York.
Premio Apollinaire, Venice.

1961
The Art of Assemblage, MoMa, New York.
Aspect of collage, Brook Street Gallery, London.
Collages e costruzioni tridimensionali, Galleria la Salita, Rome.

1960
Six Techniques – Six Nationalities, Berta Schaefer Gallery, New York.

1958
Contemporary Italian drawing collages, Federazione Americana delle Arti del Museo Brooklyn Traveling Show, New York.

1954
Sei pittori sul Tevere, Rome.

Bibliography

1999
Fagiolo dell'Arco, M., "Un giovane pittore verso il duemila", exhibitions catalogue *L'Arte Oggi*, Skirà Editore, Milan.

1998
Fabbri, P., *A Federico Fellini*, exhibition catalogue, Galleria Fabibasaglia, Edizioni Tiperti, Rimini.

1990
Calvesi, M., "Cronache coordinate di un'avventura", *Roma Anni '60. Al di là della pittura*, exhibition catalogue, Edizioni Carte Segrete, Rome.

1989
Bonito Oliva, A., "Ruota dell'arte, Rotella", *Mimmo Rotella. Lamiere*, Studio Marconi, Milan.
Fagiolo Dell'Arco, M., Restany, P., "Mimmo Rotella. Uno sguardo sempre all'altezza della situazione", inserto monografico, *Prospettive d'Arte*, V, 29.

1988
Restany, P., "Le nuove lamiere di Mimmo Rotella", *Mimmo Rotella. Sovrapitture 1987*, Studio Marconi, Milan.
Schwabsky, B., "Rotellascopio", *Mimmo Rotella. Sovrapitture 1987*, Studio Marconi, Milan.

1986
Martucci, G., "Rotella: Risposte e considerazioni sull'arte", *Artecultura*, 1, Milan.

1984
Hunter S., *Dècollages 1954-1964*, Edizioni Electa – Studio Marconi, Milan.
Restany, P., " Cinecittà 2", exhibition catalogue, Milan.

1982
Ginesl, A., "Arte-Industria", *Le Arti*, 2, Milan.

1981
Tadini, E., "Mimmo Rotella", *D'Ars*, 96, Milan.

1974
Trini, T., "Rotella", presentazione alla monografia, Giampaolo Prearo Editore, Milan.
Argan, G.C., *L'Espresso*, July 19.

1972
Rotella, M., *Autorotella, Autobiografia di un artista*, Sugar Editore, Paris.

1971
Jaime, M., "Linha cultural. Rotella cartaz lacerado", *Corriero de Manha*, March.
Galy-Charles, H., "Rotella", *Les Lettres Française*, May.
Hahn, 0., "Profession: Lacerateur", *L'Expressi*, May.

1965
Hahn, 0., "Reportage surrèels", *L'Express*.
Vivaldi, C., "Intervista a Mimmo Rotelli", *Marcatrè*.

1963
Wescher, H., "Quoi de neuf chez les Nouveaux Rèalistes", *Cimaise*, March-June.

Rubiu, V., " Scheda n.1: Mimmo Rotella, *Collage*, II, 1, December.

1962
Aschbery, J., "Mimmo Rotella", *Art International*, Lugano.
Galy-Charles, H., "De Spoerri à Rotella", *Aujourd'hui*, April.
Nbuia, A., "Rotella", *Mizue*, Tokyo.
Restany, P., "Le Nouveau Rèalisme de Rotella", *Metro*, 6, Milan.
Ragon, M., *Arts*, 6, Paris.

1961
Alfieri, B., "Rotella nel paese delle meraviglie", *Metro*, Milan.
Menna, F., "Rotella", *Telesera*, Rome, April.

Anri Sala
1974, born in Tirana.
Lives and works in Paris.

Solo Exhibitions

2001
Galerie Chantal Crousel, Paris.
Galerie Rüdiger Schöttle, Munich (& Martin Creed).

2000
Anri Sala, Stichting De Appel, Amsterdam.
Intervista, Galerie Rüdiger Schöttle, Munich.
Nocturnes, MAMCO, Geneva.

Group Exhibitions

2001
Wiener Festwochen, Vienna.
BB2, Berlin Biennal, Berlin.
passwor(l)ds : Anri Sala - Hollis Frampton - Jonas Mekas, Künstlerhaus Stuttgart, Stuttgart.

2000
Géographies : Darren Almond - Graham Gussin - Anri Sala, Galerie Chantal Crousel Paris.
City Vision: Clip City, inter media_city seoul, Seoul.
Man muss ganz schön viel lernen um hier zu funktionieren, Frankfurter Kunstverein, Frankfurt.
Coast to Coast, Placentia Arte, Piacenza.
Martin Boyce & Anri Sala, Johnen et Schöttle, Cologne.
Voilà - Le Monde dans la Tête, Musée d'Art Moderne de la Ville de Paris, Paris.
Manifesta 3, Biennale Européenne de l'Art Contemporain, Ljubliana.
Wie Weg - Disappeared, Rotor Association for Contemporary Art, Graz.
Wider Bild Gegen Wart / Positions to a Political Discourse, Raum Aktueller Kunst, Vienna.

1999
After The Wall, Musée d'Art Moderne, Stockholm, Ludwig Museum, Budapest.
Albanian Pavillion, La Biennale di Venezia, 47. Esposizione Internazionale d'Arte, Venice.

1997
Ostrenanije-97, Video Festival, Bauhaus, Dessau.

1995
Tunnel 95, Galerie Nationale, Tirana.
Spring 95, 1er prix, Galerie Nationale, Tirana.
Symposium Kultur Kontakt, Kunsthaus Horn.

Bibliography

2001
Obrist, H.-U., "Anri Sala, First Take", *Artforum*, January.

2000
Higuinen, E., "A la rencontre de l'intime", *Cahiers du Cinéma*, 535.
Jones, R., "After the Wall: Art and Culture in Post- Communist Europe", *Artforum*, March.
Verwoert, J., "Mun muss ganz schön viel lernen um hier zu funktionieren", *Springerin*, April.
Verwoert, J., "Manifesta 3", *Frieze*, 55, November-December.
Anri Sala, DeAppel, Amsterdam.
Muka, E., "Anri Sala", *Manifesta 3*, European Biennal of Contemporary Art, Ljubljana.
Ostria, V., "Anri Sala/Vladimir Perisic", *Voilà - Le Monde dans la Tête*, Musée d'Art Moderne de la Ville de Paris, Paris.
"Anri Sala", *Media-City Seoul 2000*, Seoul Metropolitan Museum.
"Nocturnes", *La Ville, Le Jardin, La Memoire*, Villa Medicis.
"Beautiful rumours", *Mutations*, arc en rêve centre d'architecture.

1999
Muka, E., *After the Wall, Art and Culture in Post-Communist Europe*, Moderna Museet.

Sandison
1969, born in Great Britain.
Lives and works in Tampere, Finland.

Group Exhibitions
2001
Nuorten Näyttely, Kiasma Museum of Contemporary Art, Helsinki.

1994
Museum of Cultural Anxiety, Institute of Contemporary Art, London.

1993
Wonderful Life, Lisson Gallery, London Art, London.

1992
Invisible Cities, Fruitmarket Gallery, Edinburgh.

Sarenco
1945, born in Brescia.
Lives and works in Verona e Malindi.

He is: poet, performer, film maker, editor, art merchant, expert in historical and contemporary avantgarde, expert in African and Asian contemporary Art, writer, actor.

Exhibitions
1972
In the section "Il libro come luogo di ricerca". Documenta, Distel Schubladen Museum, Kassel.

Julião Sarmento
1948, born in Lisbon.
Lives and works in Estoril, Portugal.

Solo Exhibitions

2001
Julião Sarmento Obra Recent, Galería Joan Prats, Barcelona.

2000
Julião Sarmento: Flashback, Centro de Arte Moderna José de Azeredo Perdigão, Fundação Calouste Gulbenkian, Lisboa.
Julião Sarmento, Akira Ikeda Gallery, Nagoya.
Julião Sarmento Slow Motion, ESTGAD, Caldas da Rainha.

1999
Julião Sarmento: Fundamental Accuracy, Hirshhorn Museum and Sculpture Garden, Washington.
Segredos e Mentiras, Galeria Camargo Vilaça, São Paulo.
Maverick, Xavier Hufkens, Brussels.
Segredos e Mentiras, Paço Imperial, Rio de Janeiro.
The Wrong Person, Dan Bernier Gallery, Los Angeles.
Julião Sarmento: Flashback, Palacio de Velazquez, Museo Nacional Centro de Arte Reina Sofia, Madrid.
A Film Installation, Sean Kelly Gallery, New York.

1998
Julião Sarmento, Galleria d'Arte Moderna, Bologna.
Carpe Diem / Racial Makeup, Galeria Pedro Oliveira, Porto.

Veneno, Galerie Bernd Klüser, München.
Julião Sarmento, Sean Kelly Gallery, New York.

1997
Julião Sarmento, La Biennale di Venezia, XLVII Esposizione Internazionale d'Arte, Padiglione Portoghese, Palazzo Vendramin ai Carmini, Venice.
Urban Corpo, CCA Kitakyushu - Project Gallery, Kitakyushu.
Julião Sarmento - Werke 1981-1996, Haus der Kunst, Munich.
Suffering, Despair and Ascent, Sean Kelly Gallery, New York.

1996
Selfish, Proud, Cunning, and Regardless of Others, Sean Kelly, New York.
Two Rooms, Van Abbemuseum, Eindhoven.
The House with the Upstairs in it, London Projects, London.
Julião Sarmento, Galeria da Universidade do Minho, Museu Nogueira da Silva, Braga.

1995
Julião Sarmento, Galeria Pedro Oliveira, Porto.
Laura and Alice, Galerie Béla Jarzyk, Cologne.
Quatre Mouvements de la Peur, Edifício das Caldeiras, Universidade de Coimbra, Coimbra.
Julião Sarmento, Palácio Nacional de Sintra, Sintra.
Only a moment or two of brutal madness, Galerie Xavier Hufkens, Brussels.

1994
The White Paintings, Centre des Arts Saidye Bronfman, Montréal.
Julião Sarmento, IVAM, Centre del Carme, València.
Laura and Alice, Galerie Bernd Klüser, Munich.
Julião Sarmento, Ruth Bloom Gallery, Santa Monica.

1993
Julião Sarmento, Centro de Arte Moderna, Fundação Calouste Gulbenkian, Lisbon.

Group Exhibitions

2001
Re-Location:on moving, Sean Kelly Gallery, New York.
Wir sind die Ander(en), Herford.

2000
Lisson Gallery @ Covent Garden, Millennium Lofts, 9 Kean Street, London.
On Language, Sean Kelly Gallery, New York.

Um Oceano Inteiro para Nadar / Spanning An Entire Ocean, Culturgest, Lisbon.
Uma galeria é uma galeria é uma galeria, Galeria Pedro Oliveira, Porto.
Helena Almeida, Georg Baselitz, Francesco Clemente, Anselm Kiefer, Richard Long, Gerhard Richter, Julião Sarmento, Pedro Cabrita Reis, Rachel Whiteread, Galeria Mário Sequeira, Braga.
00 Drawings 2000, Barbara Gladstone Gallery, New York.
The Mnemosyne Project, Encontros de Fotografia de Coimbra, Coimbra.
Colecção Banco Privado para Serralves, Museu Serralves, Porto.
Het oorkussen van de Melancholie The Pillow of the Melancholy, Museum voor Schone Kunsten, Gent.

1999
Damenwhal - Rita McBride & To Be Announced, Kunstverein München.
Linhas de Sombra, Fundação Calouste Gulbenkian, Centro de Arte Moderna José de Azeredo Perdigão, Lisbon.
De Verzameling (deel 1), Stedelijk VanAbbemuseum, Eindhoven.
Tage der Dunkelheit und des Lichts - Zeitgenössische Kunst aus Portugal, Kunstmuseum Bonn, Bonn.
Circa 1968, Museu Serralves, Porto.
The Painted Canvas, John Berggruen Gallery, San Francisco.
Das Gedächtnis öffnet seine Tore - Die Kunst der Gegenwart im Lenbachhaus, Städtische Galerie im Lenbachhaus, Munich.

1998
En qué estás pensando?, Galeria Joan Prats, Barcelona.
Anos 80, Culturgest, Lisboa (catalogue).
A Conversation Piece John Murpy - Julião Sarmento, The Museum of Modern Art, Oxford.
Figuration/Abstraction, John Berggruen Gallery, San Francisco.
Corpus Virtu, Sean Kelly Gallery, New York.
Camargo Vilaça BIS 46, Galeria Camargo Vilaça, San Paulo.
Alternativa Zero. Tendenze polemiche dell'arte portoghese nelle democrazia, Galleria Bianca, Cantieri Culturali, Palermo.
Corpos em Trânsito, Galeria Pedro Oliveira, Porto.

1997
Form und Funktion der Zeichnung Heute, Art Frankfurt 1997, Messe Frankfurt, Frankfurt (catalogue).
En la piel de toro, Museo Nacional Centro de Arte Reina Sofia, Palacio de Velázquez, Madrid.
Von Kopf bis Fuss - Fragmente des Körpers,

Ursula Blickle Stiftung, Kraichtal; Kunstraum Innsbruck, Innsbruck; Burgenländische Landesgalerie, Eisenstadt.
A Arte, o Artista e o Outro, Fundação Cupertino de Miranda, Vila Nova de Famalicão.
Magnetic - Drawings in Dialogue, Sean Kelly, New York.
Absence/Presence - Christine Borland, Kristján Gudmundsson, Julião Sarmento, Kópavogur Art Museum, Kópavogur.
Perspectiva: Alternativa Zero, Fundação de Serralves, Porto.
Colección de Arte Contemporáneo, Fundació "La Caixa", Barcelona.
Anatomias Contemporâneas, Fundição de Oeiras, Oeiras.

Bibliography (dal 1997)

2001
Power, K., "Talking about what makes a writer great: Writing about what makes a talker great", exhibition catalogue, *Julião Sarmento*, Galería Joan Prats, Barcelona.

2000
Melo, A., "Julião Sarmento, Palacio de Velázquez/Museo Nacional Centro de Arte Reina Sofía", *Artforum*, XXXVIII, 8, April, pp. 145-146.
Staple, P., "Video Show House", *Art Monthly*, 238, July-August, pp. 11-14.
Pinharanda, J., Costa Pinto, A., (Coordinator), *Portugal Contemporâneo*, Sequitur, Madrid.
Pinto de Almeida, B., *Duplo constrangimento*, Edições Radar, Porto.
Catálogo de la Colección de Arte Contemporáneo, Fundación "la Caixa", Barcelona.
Pinto de Almeida, B., "Una dramaturgia blanca", *Lapiz*, 161, March, pp. 55-63.
Gardner, B.G., "Der begehrliche Blick der Bilder", *Verführung des Blics. Das Haus der Kunst, München*, Hamburg, Helmut Metz, pp. 150-159.

1999
Avgikos, J., "Julião Sarmento: Flashback", *Artforum*, XXXVIII, 1, September, p. 50.
Chaimovich, F., "Julião Sarmento", *Art/Text*, Los Angeles, 66, August-October, p. 83.
MacAdam, B.A., "Julião Sarmento", *Artnews*, 98, 3, March, p. 135.
Risatti, H., "Julião Sarmento", *Artforum*, XXXVII, 8, April, pp. 126-127.
Sardo, D., "De Reojo", *Arte y Parte*, Santander, 23, October-November, pp. 82-92.
Benezra, N., *Julião Sarmento: Fundamental Accuracy*, Washington D.C., Hishhorn Museum and Sculpture Garden, [1-4].

Chillida, A., "A Julião Sarmento", "To Julião Sarmento", *Julião Sarmento: Flashback*, Madrid, Palacio de Velázquez, Museo Nacional Centro de Arte Reina Sofia, p. 203.
Lingwood, J., "Flashback", *Julião Sarmento: Flashback*, Madrid, Palacio de Velázquez, Museo Nacional Centro de Arte Reina Sofia, pp. 15-19, 147-151.
Netta, I., "Julião Sarmento", *Das Gedächtnis öffnet seine Tore*, München, Städtische Galerie im Lenbachhaus, p. 190.
Sardo, D., "Augenblick", *Tage der Dunkelheit und des Lichts: zeitgenössische Kunst aus Portugal*, Bonn, Kunstmuseum Bonn, pp. 122-132.
Sardo, D., "Flashback", *Arte Ibérica*, Lisbon, 3, 28, October, pp. 9-14.
Searle, A., "El Observador Observado", "The Watcher Watched", *Julião Sarmento: Flashback*, Madrid, Palacio de Velázquez, Museo Nacional Centro de Arte Reina Sofia, pp. 91-99, 111-119.
O Livro da Arte do Século XX, Cacém, Texto Editora.
Melo, A., *Panorama Arte Portuguesa no Século XX*, edited by P. Pernes, BPI / Fundação Serralves / Campo das Letras, Porto.
Molder, M.F., *Matérias sensíveis*, Relógio d'Água, Lisbon.

1998
Godfrey, T., "John Murphy, Julião Sarmento", *Untitled*, London, 17, Autumn, p. 22.
Green, D., "A Conversation Piece: John Murphy / Julião Sarmento", *Contemporary Visual Arts*, 20, pp. 72-73.
Mehta, M., "John Murphy, Julião Sarmento: a Conversation Piece", *Art Monthly*, 219, September, pp. 36-38.
Sardo, D., "Le bât qui blesse: le travail de Julião Sarmento", *Parachute*, January-March, pp. 4-9.
Wakefield, N., "Julião Sarmento Works that Elegantly Turn Contradiction into Paradox", *Elle Deco*, 9, 1, February-March, pp. 60, 62 e 64.
Nakamura, N., Miyake, A., *Let's Talk About Art*, Kitakyushu, 1998, Center for Contemporary Art and Korinsha Press, pp. 47, 49, 51, 53, 55, 57, 59, 61.
Macri, T., "Idiosincrasie di una Alternativa: intervista a Julião Sarmento", exhibition catalogue, *Alternativa zero: tendenze polemiche dell'arte portoghese nella democrazia*, Galleria Bianca, Cantieri Culturali alla Zisa, Palermo; Charta, Milan, pp. 47-49.
Tarantino, M., "A Conversation Piece", *John Murphy-Julião Sarmento: a Conversation Piece*, Museum of Modern Art, Oxford, pp. 2-3.

Morgan, S.,"'Just a Song at Twilight' - The House With the Upstairs in it: Themes and Variations", *The House With the Upstairs in it*, London Projects, London.
Macrì, T., *Cinemacchine del desiderio*, Costa & Nolan, Genoa-Milan.
Melo, A., *Artes plásticas em Portugal dos anos 70 aos nossos dias*, Difel, Lisboa.
Lima Pinharanda, J., *Alguns corpos: imagens da arte portuguesa entre 1960 e 1990*, EDP, Lisboa.

1997
Blase, C., "Julião Sarmento", *Noëma: Art Magazine*, 10, February-March, p. 70.
Blase, C., "Julião Sarmento, Bernd Klüser", *Noëma: Art Magazine*, 11, April-May, pp. 40-41.
Cameron, D., "47th Venice Biennale", *Artforum*, XXXVI, 1, September, pp. 118-120.
Greenberg, S., "Sarmento Goes to Venice", *The Art Newspaper* ("Suplement I & II"), VIII, 68, March, pp. I e VII.
Melo, A., "Border Crossing", *Artforum*, XXXVI, 6, February, pp. 33-35.
Patrick, K., "Julião Sarmento & Rachel Whiteread at the 47th Venice Biennale", *Contemporary Visual Arts*, 16, July-September, pp. 70-71.
Sikoronja, R., "Portugal: Julião Sarmento", *Noëma*, 44, June-July, p. 92.
Vetrocq, M.E., "The 1997 Venice Biennale: a Space Odissey", *Art in America*, 85, 9, September, pp. 66-77.
Garcia, A., "En la piel de toro", "On the Hide of the Bull", *En la piel de toro*, Madrid, Palacio de Velázquez, Museo Nacional Centro de Arte Reina Sofia, pp. 19-38, 218-227.
Gassner, H., "Wo der Schmerz regiert", "Where Pain Rules", *Julião Sarmento: Werke 1981-1986*, Munich, Haus der Kunst, Cantz, pp. 9-43, 44-74. Reprinted in *Julião Sarmento*, Bologna, 1998, Galleria d'Arte Moderna / Editrice Compositori, pp. 9-43 / 44-74.
Melo, A., "Territory of Desire", "Il territorio del desiderio", *Julião Sarmento*, Lisboa, La Biennale di Venezia, XLVII Esposizione Internazionale d'Arte, Padiglione Portoghese / Instituto de Arte Contemporânea, pp. 10-17.
Spector, N., "Julião Sarmentos 'White paintings': das Gesehene ungesehen machen", "Julião Sarmento's 'White paintings': Unseeing the Seen", *Julião Sarmento: Werke 1981-1986*, Munich, Haus der Kunst / Cantz, pp. 167-172, 173-178. Reprinted in *Julião Sarmento*, Galleria d'Arte Moderna / Editrice Compositori, Bologna, 1998, pp. 167-172, 173-178.
Tarantino, M., "I Don't Want to See Landscape", "Ég vil ekki sjá landslag", *Absense / Presence: Christine Borland,*

Kristján Gudmundsson, Julião Sarmento, Kópavogur Art Museum, Reykjavík, pp. 4-7, 32-35.

Tarantino, M., "Eyes Without a Face", *Julião Sarmento: Casanova*, New York, Sean Kelly Gallery, [7-11].

Melo, A., "The Territory of Desire", *Julião Sarmento*, Electa, Milan, pp. 9-44; "O território do desejo", *Julião Sarmento*, Lisboa, Assírio & Alvim, pp. 9-44.

Celant, G., "Julião Sarmento: a Sensuous Revelation (Essay/Interview)", *Julião Sarmento*, Electa, Milan, pp. 45-53, 83-87, 105-109, 147-151, 185-191; "Julião Sarmento: una rivelazione sensuale (Essay/Interview)", *Julião Sarmento*, Assírio & Alvim, Lisboa, pp. 45-53, 83-87, 105-109, 147-151, 185-191.

Ene-Liis Semper
1969, born in Tallinn.
Lives and works in Tallinn.

Solo Exhibitions

2001
Oasis, solo exhibition, Begane Grond, Utrecht.
Bac-Présence Balte, The Human Project, Visby, Athens, Barcelona.
The Baltic Times, Museum of Contemporary Art, Zagreb.

2000/2001
Grosse Kunstausstellung Düsseldorf, Verein zur Veranstaltung von Kunstausstellungen e.V., Messe Düsseldorf.

2000
Inverse Perspectives, EDSVIK Gallery, Sweden.
He and She (with Raoul Kurvitz), Gallery Noas, Riga, Latvia.
10 Paar, art from Estonia and Flanders, Castle of Kuressaare, Estonia; Hoeve Vandewalle – Kuurne, Flanders.
Borderline Syndrome. Manifesta 3, European Biennial of Contemporary Art, Ljubljana.
PICAF, Seoul.
Here, (with Marko Laimre), the Art Museum of Estonia, Rotermann Salt Storage Arts Center, Tallinn.

1999
New video installations (with KIWA), Sebra Gallery, Tartu.
Private Views, Budapest.

1998
Solo exhibition with Mark Raidpere, the Estonian Museum of Arts, Rotermann Salt Storage Arts Centre, Tallinn.
ArtGenda, Kulturhuset, Stockholm.

Distant Lighthouses, Fabrica Porto Brandao, Lissabon, Portugal; EDSVIK Gallery, Sweden.
Art from Estonia, Latvia, Lithuania, Sarajevo.
Breathing Circle (with KIWA), Sebra Gallery, Tartu.

1997
Video installations, Vaal Gallery, Tallinn.

1996
Group T – 10, the Art Museum of Estonia, Tallinn.

1995
Wait We're Loading, group exhibition of Estonian artists, Gothenburg Art Museum, Sweden.
Biotopia, 3rd annual exhibition of the Soros Center for Contemporary Arts, Tallinn.

1994
Unexistent Art, the 2nd annual exhibition of the Soros Center for Contemporary Arts, Tallinn.
1993, 1994, 1995 French – Baltic Video Art Festival, Riga – Tallinn – Vilnius.

1992
Exhibition of Estonian theatre designers, Ugala Theatre, Viljandi.
New Generation, international young theatre designers' exhibition, Maarjamäe Castle, Tallinn.

1991
Exhibition of Estonian theatre designers, Estonian Theatre Association, Tallinn.

Videography

2000
Untitled I
Untitled II
Into New Home
Sleeping Man
Licked Room
Stairs

1999
Oasis

1998
Natural Law
Come!
Endspiel
FF/Rew

1997
Fundamental

1996
Untitled

1995/96
Home I – II

1995
10 Seconds

1994
Ultra
Femina I
Femina II

1993
Fashion

Performances
2000
Happy Birthday, PC Department Store, Tallinn.
Va Banque, Estonian National Library, Tallinn.

1999
Strong Union, Bank of Estonia, Tallinn.

1998
Treasure Island, Rotermann Salt Storage Arts Centre, Tallinn.
God Number xxx, Club Hollywood, Tallinn.
Untitled – Jancis, Kurvitz and Semper Live, Rotermann Salt Storage Arts Center, Tallinn.

1997
Painting Venice, with R. Kurvitz, opening of Estonian exhibition at the 47th Venice Bienniale, Venice.

1995
Myra Factory, music club Pilot, Moscow.

1994
Myra Factory, M/F Kronborg, Tallinn.

Bibliography

2000
Borderline Syndrome. Manifesta3, *European Biennial of Contemporary Art,* Ljubljana.
10Paar. *Art from Estonia and Flanders. Eesti ja Flaami kunst. Kunst uit Estland en Vlaanderen,* Tallinn.
"Has The Title Stolen The Show? Three Views Of Manifesta 3 From Three Different European Ports", NU: The Nordic Art Review, II, 5/00.

1998
Distant Lighthouses, Fabrica Porto Brandao, Lisboa.
Art from Estonia, Latvia, Lithuania in Sarajevo.

Richard Serra
1935, born in California.
Lives and works in New York and Cape Breton, Nova Scotia.

Solo Exhibitions

2000
Richard Serra: Mostra di sculture, Area archeologica dei Mercati di Traiano, Rome.

1999
Richard Serra Sculpture, Museo Guggenheim Bilbao, Bilbao.
Richard Serra, The Geffen Contemporary at The Museum of Contemporary Art, Los Angeles.

1998
Richard Serra: Torqued Ellipses, Dia Center for the Arts, New York.

1994
Richard Serra: Props, Wilhelm Lehmbruck Museum, Duisburg; travelled to National Gallery of Contemporary Art - Zacheta, Warsaw.

1993
Richard Serra: Weight and Measure, Tate Gallery, London.

1992
Richard Serra: Running Arcs, For John Cage, Kunstsammlung Nordrhein-Westfalen, Dusseldorf.
Richard Serra: The Drowned and the Saved, Synagoge Stommeln, Pulheim.
Richard Serra, Museo Nacional Centro de Arte Reina Sofía, Madrid.

1991
Richard Serra: Skulptur, Malmö Konsthall, Malmö.

1990
Richard Serra: Threats of Hell, capc Musée d'Art Contemporain, Bordeaux.
Richard Serra: The Hours of the Day, Kunsthaus Zürich, Zurich.

1988
Richard Serra: 10 Sculptures for the Van Abbe, Stedelijk Van Abbemuseum, Eindhoven.
Richard Serra: 7 Spaces,7 Sculptures, Städtische Galerie im Lenbachhaus, Munich.

1986
Richard Serra: Sculpture, The Museum of Modern Art, New York.

1984
Richard Serra, Musée nationale d'art moderne, Centre Georges Pompidou, Paris.

1980
Richard Serra: Elevator 1980; The Hudson River Museum, Yonkers, NewYork.
Museum Boymans-van Beuningen, Rotterdam.

1979
Richard Serra: Sculpture, Films 1966-1978, Staatliche Kunsthalle Baden-Baden.

1978
Richard Serra: Arbeiten/Works 66-77, Kunsthalle Tübingen, traveled to Staatliche Kunsthalle Baden-Baden.

1970
Pasadena Art Museum, Pasadena.
Leo Castelli Warehouse, New York.

Group Exhibitions

2001
The Global Guggenheim, Selections from the Extended Collection, Solomon R Guggenheim Museum, New York.
Changing Perceptions: The Panza Collection at the Guggenheim Museum, Guggenheim Museum Bilbao.
moving / in MUSEUM WORKS, Hamburger Kunsthalle, Hamburg.

2000
Age of Influence: Reflections in the Mirror of American Culture, Museum of Contemporary Art, Chicago.

1999
Casa de la Escultura (exposicion organizaza por el Modern Art Museum Fort Worth, Texas), El Museo de Arte Contemporaneo de Monterey.
Ausgestellt - Vorgestellt, Richard Serra for Susan Hartnett, Skulpturenmuseum Glaskasten, Marl.
Circa 1968, Museu Serralves, Museu de Arte Contempornea, Porto.
Collections paralleles, capc Musée d'art contemporain, Bordeaux.
Rendezvous, Masterpieces from Centre Georges Pompidou and the Guggenheim Museums, Solomon R. Guggenheim Museum.

1997
Overholland in het Kroller-Muller Museum, Kröller-Müller Museum, Otterlo.
Skulptur Projekte in Munster, City of Munster.
The 20th Century - The Age of Modern Art, Martin Gropius Bau, Berlin.
4th Biennale de Lyon, Halle Tony Garnier, Lyon, France.

1996
Abstraction in the Twentieth Century: Total

Risk, Freedom, Discipline, Solomon R.Guggenheim Museum, New York.

1995
1995 Biennial Exhibition, Whitney Museum of American Art, New York.

1993
Amerikanische Kunst im 20.Jahrhundert (Malerei und Plastik 1913-1993), Martin Gropius Bau, Berlin; travelled to Royal Academie of the Arts, London.
Gravity and Grace: The Changing Condition of Sculpture 1965-1975, Hayward Gallery, London.

1992
transForm; Bild Object Skulptur im 20 Jahrhundert, Kunstmuseum Basel, Kunsthalle Basel, Basel.
Schwerpunkt Skulptur, Krefelder Kunstmuseum, Krefeld.

1991-1992
Schwerelos (Weightless), Berlinische Galerie, Grosse Orangerie, Schloss Scharlottenburg, Berlin.

1989-1990
Geometric Abstraction and Minimalism in America, The Solomon R.Guggenheim Museum, New York.
The New Sculpture 1965-75: Between Geometry and Gesture, Whitney Museum of American Art, New York; traveled to The Museum of Contemporary Art, Los Angeles.

1988
Positions of Present Day Art: Merz, Stella, Kounellis, Paik, Serra, Nationalegalerie, Berlin.
Zeitlos, Hamburger Bahnhoff, Berlin.
Australian Biannual, Sidney.

1987
Documenta 8, Kassel.
Der unverbrauchte Blick, Martin Gropius-Bau, Berlin.

1986
Kiefer and Serra, Saatchi Foundation, London.
Qu'est-ce que La Sculpture Moderne?, Musée National d'Art Moderne, Centre Georges Pompidou, Paris.
Referencias, Centro de Arte Reina Sofia, Madrid.
Entre la geometria y el Gesto: North American Sculpture 1965-75, Palacio Velasquez, Madrid.

1985-1986
Transformations in Sculpture: Four Decades of American and European Art,

Solomon R. Guggenheim Museum, New York.

1985
Carnegie International, Museum of Art, Carnegie Institute, Pittsburgh.
Chicago Content: A Contemporary Focus 1974-1984, Hirshhorn Museum and Sculpture Garden, Smithsonian Institution, Washington.

1984
ROSC, Dublin, Ireland.
La Biennale di Venezia, Venice.
American Art Since 1970, Whitney Museum of American Art, New York; circulating exhibition.
Skulptur im 20.Jahrhundert, Merain-Park, Basel.

1983
Ars 83 Helsinki, The Art Museum of the Ateneum, Helsinki.
Kunst wird Material, Nationalgalerie, Berlin.

1982
Correspondencias: 5 Arquitectos, 5 Escultores, Palacio de las Alhajas, Madrid.
The New York School: Four Decades, The Solomon R.Guggenheim Museum, New York.
Documenta 7, Kassel.
'60-'80: Attitudes/Concepts/Images, Stedelijk Museum, Amsterdam.
"Arte Povera", Antiform, Sculptures 1966-69, Centre d'Arts Plastiques Contemporains de Bordeaux.

1981
Artists and Architects: Collaboration, The Architectural League, New York.
Westkunst, Museen der Stadt Köln, Cologne.
Kounellis, Merz, Nauman, Serra, Museum Haus Lange, Krefeld.
1981 Biennial Exhibition, Whitney Museum of American Art, New York.

1980
Mel Bochner/Richard Serra, Hayden Gallery, Massachusetts Institute of Technology, Cambridge.
La Biennale di Venezia, Venice.
Skulptur im 20. Jahrhundert, Wenkenpark, Riehen/Basel.
Pier + Ocean, Hayward Gallery, London; travelled to Rijksmuseum Kröller Müller, Otterlo.
Reliefs, Westfälisches Landesmuseum für Kunst und Kulturgeschichte, Münster; traveled to Kunsthaus Zürich.

1979
1979 Biennial Exhibition, Whitney Museum

of American Art, New York.
Z.B. Skulptur, Städelisches Kunstinstitut, Frankfurt.
Structures for Behavior, Art Gallery of Ontario, Toronto.

1976
Skulptur Ausstellung in Munster, Westfalisches Landesmuseum fur Kunst und Kulturgeschichte, Munster.
Documenta 6, Kassel.
Paris-New York, Musee national d'art moderne, Centre georges Pompidou, Paris.
Amerikanische Kunst von 1945 bis Heute, Nationalgalerie, Berlin.
Rooms, Institute for Art and Urban Resources, PS 1, Long Island.
200 Years of American Sculpture, Whitney Museum of American Art, New York.

1975
Sculpture: American Directions 1945-1975, National Collection of Fine Arts, Smithsonian Institution, Washington.
The Condition of Sculpture: A Selection of Recent Sculpture by Younger British and Foreign Artists, Hayward Gallery, London.

1973
1973 Biennial Exhibition, Contemporary American Art, Whitney Museum of American Art, New York.

1972
Documenta 5, Kassel.
Spoleto Arts Festival, Spoleto.

1971
Art & Technology, Los Angeles County Museum of Art.
Prospect 71-Projection, Stadtische Kunsthalle, Dusseldorf.
Amerikanst Kunst 1950-70, Louisiana Museum, Humlebaeck.
Il Triennale India, Lalit Kala Akademi, New Delhi, (organized by the International Council of the Museum of Modern Art, New York).

1970
Conceptual Art/Arte Povera/Land Art, Galleria Civica d'Arte Moderna, Turin.
Tokyo Biennale '70 (Between Man and Matter), Tokyo Metropolitan Art Gallery, Tokyo (10th International Art Exhibition of Japan).

1969
Five Sculptors, University of California, Irvine.
Anti-Form, Museum of Contemporary Art, Chicago.
Anti-Illusion:Procedures/Materials, Whitney Museum of American Art, New York.

When Attitude Becomes Form, Kunsthalle Bern; traveled to Haus Lange, Krefeld, Institute of Contemporary Art, London.
Op Losse Schroeven, situaties en cryptostructuren (Square Pegs in Round Holes), Stedelijk Museum, Amsterdam.
Kunst der sechziger Jahre, Wallraf-Richartz Museum, Cologne.

1968
1968 Annual Exhibition: Contemporary American Sculpture, Whitney Museum of American Art, New York.
Three Sculptors (with Mark di Suvero and Walter de Maria), Noah Goldowsky Gallery, New York.

1966
From Arp to Artschwager 1, Noah Goldowsky Gallery, New York.

Bibliography

2000
Richard Serra, edited by H. Foster, The MIT Press, Cambridge, Massachusetts and London.

1998
Richard Serra Sculpture 1985 - 1998, exhibition catalogue, The Museum of Contemporary Art, Los Angeles.

1994
Serra, R., *Writings Interviews,* The University of Chicago Press, Chicago and London.

1986
Richard Serra: Sculpture, exhibition catalogue, The Museum of Modern Art, New York.

Santiago Sierra
1966, born in Madrid.
He lives and works in Mexico City.

Solo Exhibitions

2000
Kunst Werke, Berlin.
P.S.1., New York.
Proyecto Zapopan, Zapopan, Jal. México.
Acceso A, Mexico D.F.
ACE Gallery, New York.
ACE Gallery, México D.F.
Belia De Vico Arte Contemporáneo, Guatemala

1999
Espancio Aglutinador, La Habana, Cuba
Museo Rufino Tamayo. Sala 7. México D.F.
ACE Gallery, Los Angeles.

1998
La Torre de los Vientos. Arte in Situ. México D.F.

1997
Galería BF15. Monterrey, N.L.
Galería Art & Idea. México D.F.

1996
Museo Carrillo Gil. México D.F.

1994
Galería Angel Romero, Madrid.
Espacio "P", Madrid.

Group Exhibitions

2000
Pervitiendo el Minimalismo. Museo de Arte Centro Nacional Reina Sofía. Madrid.
Ewtramuros. Havana.
IX Muestra Internacional de Perfomance, X–Teresa Arte Actual, México D.F.
P.R.00, San Juan de Puerto Rico
Living the Islands, PICAF, Pusan.
Documentos. ACE Gallery, Los Angeles.
A shot in a head, Lisson Gallery, London.
Friends and Neighbors, EV.A 2000, invited by the 4th Biennial, Limerik.

1999
FIAC '99, Galería BF15. Paris.
Plaza G & T, Guatemala.
Representar / Intervenir, X–Teresa Arte Actual, Méxi co D.F.
México Nuevo, Centre d'Arts Plastiques de Villefranche-sur-Saone.
Mèxico Nuevo, Museé de la Vallé de Barcelonnette.
Paradas Continuas, Museo Carrillo Gil, México D.F.

1998
Made in Mexico-Made in Venezuela, Art Metropol Gallery, Toronto
Cambio II, Museo Universitario del Chopo, México, D.F.
Cambio I, Sandra Gehring Gallery, New York.

1997
Shopping, Galería Art & Idea, México, D.F.
Opening, Galería Art Deposit, México, D.F.
New Text from Mexico, Art Deposit Gallery, New York.

1996
A otro lugar muy lejos de aquí. Instituto Cultural Cabañas, Guadalajara, Jal., México
1995
Fundaciòn Joan Mirò, Barcelona.

1993
El ojo Atómico, Madrid.

Trabajos de los 80, Galería Angel Romero, Madrid.

1992
Atelier del Sur. Islas Canarias.
Dibujos Laborales, Galería Angel Romero, Madrid.

1991
Sala K3 de Kampnagel. Hamburg.
VII Muestra de Arte Joven, Museo Español de Arte Contemporáneo, Madrid, Spain St. Petri zu Lübeck, Lübeck.

Bibliography

2000
Medina, C., "Recent Political Forms. Radical Pursuits in Mexico", *Trans,* Autumn.
Medina C., "They work for it", *Untitled,* Summer.
Pedrosa, A., "Santiago Sierra", *Art Forum,* January.
Zamudio, V., "Arte, Violencia y agresión", *Atlantica,* January.
Jiménez, C., "Turbulencias en el Panóptico. Promovidas por Santiago Sierra y expuestas a continuación", *Lapiz,* Autum.

1999
Antliff, A., "Hecho en México/hecho en Venezuela", *Poliester,* Spring-Summer.
Castro, F., *Heterotopias,* edited by IVAM, Valencia.
Crux Villegas, A., "Rapresentar/Intervenir", *Art Nexus,* October.
Flores, J., "Jeunes muntants et artistes de fin de siècle", *Art Press,* February.
Knight, C., "Busted Blocks", *Los Angeles Times,* July.

1998
Cicna, M., "Santiago Sierra", *Movimiento Actual,* November, Monterrey.

1997
Jusidnam, J., "Santiago Sierra", *Art Forum,* September.
Ruíz, T., "Santiago Sierra", *Curare,* September.

1993
Jiménez, C., Brea J.L., *Cambio de marcha en el Arte Español,* edited by J. Mordó, Madrid.

Lars Siltberg
1968, born in Stockolm.
Lives and works in Göteborg.

Solo Exhibitions

2000
Margarete Harvey Gallery, St Albans.

Zinc Gallery, Stockholm.

1999
Galleri Ping Pong, Malmö.
Galleri 60, Umeå.

1998
Galleri Signal, Malmö.

Group exhibtions

2000
UH-galleries, Hatfield.
Rauma Biennale Balticum, Rauman Taidemuseo.
Some parts of this world, Galleri Bakkeliti Bambi, Helsinki.
Frankfurt Art Fair - ArtCinema 2000, Frankfurt.
Stockholm Art Fair – Zinc Gallery, Stockholm

1999
Galleri Box – Boxoffice, Göteborg.
Hasselblad Center, Göteborg.
Galleri 54 – Loop, Göteborg.

1998
Galleri Rotor - FF-videobar, Göteborg.
Galleri Box – BoxEdition, Göteborg.
Galleri 54 – Fotografi, Göteborg.
stART – Art in the streets, Stockholm.

1996
City Galleriet, Stockholm.
Art Genda, Konsthallen, Göteborg.
Art Genda, Öxnehallen, Copenhagen.

Bibliography

2000
Face, exhibition catalogue, text by E. van der Heeg.
Our friends from the north, exhibition catalogue, text by K. Kubicki.
Rauma Biennale Balticum, exhibtion catalogue, text by L. Siltberg.
ZOO Magazine, # 5, with attached DVD.
ZOO Magazine, # 7, with attached DVD.

1999
Some parts of this world, exhibition catalogue, text by N. Olsson.

1998
stART'98: Art in the streets, exhibition catalogue, text by M. Castenfors.

Nedko Solakov

1957, born in Cherven Briag.
Lives and works in Sofia.

Solo Exhibitions

2001
Chat, The Royal Academy of Free Arts / IASPIS, Stockholm.
A (Not So) White Cube, P.S.1 Center for Contemporary Art, New York.
Anywhere, Tanya Rumpff Gallery, Haarlem.

2000
Stories 1, Center for Contemporary Art, Ujazdowski Castle, Warsaw.
Squared Baroque - Baroqued Square, Ikonen-Museum / Portikus, Frankfurt am Main.

1999
"........" #2, Galerija Dante Marino Cettina, Umag.
Announcement, as the official participation of Bulgaria, La Biennale di Venezia, Venice.
".......", ATA Center for Contemporary Art, Sofia.

1998
A Christmas Show, Galerie ars Futura, Zurich.
Silly, Galerie Arndt & Partner, Berlin.
Sea Show, with Slava Nakovska, Ted Gallery, Varna.
A Quiz, De Vleeshal, Middelburg.
Thirteen (maybe), Musee Nationale d'Historie et d'Art, Luxembourg.

1997
The Paranoid Man, Galerie Georges-Philippe & Nathalie Vallois.
The Absent-Minded Man, FRAC Languedoc-Roussillon, Montpellier.
Wars, Galerie Erna Hecey, Luxembourg.
Somewhere (under the tree), Deitch Projects, New York.

1996
Semipoor-Semirich, The Swiss Ambassador's residence, Sofia.
Desires, Galerie Arndt & Partner, Berlin.
Doodles, National Museum of Fine Arts' mirrors, Sofia.

1995
To Touch the Antiquity, Ata-Ray Gallery, Sofia.
Mr. Curator, please..., Künstlerhaus Bethanien, Berlin.

1994
The Superstitious Man, MCA, Skopje; CCS, Bard College, Annandale-on-Hudson.
The Collector of Art, Ludwig Museum, Budapest.

1993
Their Mythological Highnesses, Ata-Ray Gallery, Sofia.
Lessedra Gallery, with Mitjo Solakov, Sofia.
Good Luck, Medizinhistorisches Museum, Zurich.

1992
Just Imagine, BINZ 39 / Artest, Zurich.
Neue Arche Noah, ifa Galerie, Berlin.
Nine Objects, National Museum of History, Sofia.

Group Exhibitions

2001
Marking the Territory, Irish Museum of Modern Art, Dublin.
Loop - Alles auf Anfang, Hypovereinsbank Kunsthalle, Munich; P.S. 1, New York.
A World within a Space, Kunsthalle Zurich, Zurich.
4th International Cetinje Biennale, Cetinje.
Locus / Focus, Sonsbeek 9, Arnhem.

2000
The Last Drawing of the Century (A Window onto Venus), Zerynthia, 6th Biennale of Havana, Havana.
Partage d'exotismes, 5e Biennale de Lyon, Lyon.
3 Räume - 3 Flüsse, Hann. Münden.
Drawing on the Figure: Works on Paper of the 1990s from the Manilow Collection, MCA Chicago.
L'Autre moitie de l'Europe, Jeu de Paume, Paris.

1999
Zeitwenden, Kunstmuseum Bonn, Bonn; Museum Moderner Kunst Stiftung Ludwig Wien, Vienna.
Locally Interested, ICA / National Gallery for Foreign Art, Sofia.
After the Wall, Moderna Museet, Stockholm; Ludwig Museum, Budapest; Hamburger Bahnhof, Berlin.
Faiseurs d'histoires, Casino Luxembourg - Forum d'art Contemporain, Luxembourg.

1998
Revolution - Terror, ISEA'98, Liverpool / Manchester.
Kräftemessen 2: Bulgariaavantgarde, Künstlerwerkstatt Lothringerstrasse, Munich.
A Century of Artistic Freedom, Wiener Secession, Vienna; Helsinki City Art Museum, Helsinki.

1997
Heaven - Private View, P.S. 1, New York.
Unmapping the Earth, Kwangju Biennale'97, Kwangju.

1996

Enclosures, The New Museum of Contemporary Art, New York.
The Scream / Borealis 8, Arken Museum of Modern Art, Copenhagen.
Inklusion: Exklusion, Künstlerhaus Graz, Steirischer Herbst '96, Graz.
Manifesta I, Natuur Museum, Rotterdam.

1995
Orient/ation, 4th Istanbul Biennial, Istanbul.
Beyond Belief, MCA Chicago; ICA Philadelphia.
Caravanseray of Contemporary Art, Fuori Uso / Aurum, Pescara.
Club Berlin - Kunst Werke, 46 Esposizione Internazionale d'Arte, La Biennale di Venezia, Venice.

1994
22 Bienal, San Paulo.

1993
Aperto'93, La Biennale di Venezia, 45. Esposizione Internazionale d'Arte, Venice.

1992
3rd Istanbul Biennial, Istanbul.

Bibliography

2000
Levin, K., *Nedko Solakov - Stories 1*, solo exhibition catalogue, Center for Contemporary Art, Ujazdowski Castle, Warsaw.
Volk, G., "Nedko Solakov", *Art in America*, 12.
FRESH CREAM - Contemporary Art in Culture, Phaidon Press, London.
Locally Interested, exhibition catalogue, ICA Sofia.
Martinez, R., "Who Doesn't Like Stories? On Nedko Solakov", *ARCO Noticias*, 18.
Partage d'exotismes - 5e Biennale d'art contemporain de Lyon, exhibition catalogue, Reunion des Musees Nationaux.
Brown, N., Nedkova, I., Bleakley, A., Esche, C., *Essays on Solakov's The Right One CD-ROM*, AVRE / FACT, Liverpool.
L'autre moitie de l'Europe, exhibition CD-ROM catalogue, Jeu de Paume, Paris.

1999
Zeitwenden - Ausblick, exhibition catalogue, Kunsmuseum Bonn / Dumont.
After the Wall, exhibition catalogue, Moderna Museet Stockholm.
La Biennale di Venezia, 48. Esposizione Internazionale d'arte, exhibition catalogue, Marsilio.
Nedko Solakov - Some Stories, Vlasblom & Partners, Hoorn.

1998

Dannatt, A., "Nedko Solakov - Global Art", *Flash Art*, 201.
Bulgariaavantgarde. Kräftemessen II, exhibition catalogue, Salon, Cologne.
A Century of Artistic Freedom. 100 years Vienna Secession, exhibition catalogue, Prestel, Munich/New York.

1997
Phillips, C., "Report from Sofia - The View from Europe's Lower East Side", *Art in America*, 10.
Unmapping the Earth, exhibition catalogue, 97 Kwangju Biennale, Kwangju.

1996
Inklusion: Exklusion, exhibition catalogue, Steirischer Herbst 96, Dumont.
Levin, K., *The Scream*, exhibition catalogue, The Nordic Arts Centre, Helsinki.
Manifesta 1, exhibition catalogue, Foundation European Art Manifestation, Rotterdam.
The Sense of Order, exhibition catalogue, Moderna Galerija, Ljubljana.

1995
Fricke, H., "Nedko Solakov", *Artforum*, 4.
Beyond Belief, exhibition catalogue, Museum of Contemporary Art, Chicago.
Herbstreuth, P., "Nedko Solakov", *Kunstforum International*, 131.
Nedko Solakov - "Mr. Curator, please....", solo exhibition catalogue, Künstlerhaus Bethanien, Berlin.

1994
22 Bienal Internacional San Paulo, exhibition catalogue, Fundacao Bienal de San Paulo, San Paulo.
Neray, K., *Nedko Solakov - The Collector of Art*, solo exhibition catalogue, Ludwig Museum, Budapest.
Bubnova, J., Abadzieva, S., *Nedko Solakov - The Superstitious Man*, solo exhibition catalogue, MCA, Skopje.

1993
La Biennale di Venezia, 45. Esposizione internazionale d'arte, exhibition catalogue, Marsilio.

1992
3-rd International Istanbul Biennial, exhibition catalogue, Istanbul Foundation for Culture and Arts.

Eliezer Sonnenschein

1967, born in Haifa.
Lives and works in Tel-Aviv.

Unofficial / Unauthorized Exhibitions

1998
90 Years of Israeli Art, The Phoenix Collection, Tel-Aviv Museum of Art, Tel-Aviv.

1996
Virtual Reality, Tel-Aviv Museum of Art, Tel-Aviv.

1994
Anxiety, Museum of Israeli Art, Ramat Gan.
90-70-90, Tel-Aviv Museum of Art, Tel-Aviv.
Bograshov - Street-Project, Tel-Aviv.
Separate Worlds, Tel-Aviv Museum of Art, Tel-Aviv.
A Fence of Cyprus Fruit of Time Mr. Sweety, Tel-Aviv Museum of Art, Tel-Aviv.

1987
Friends in Arms, self initiated exhibition during Military service in 'Shakif El Hardum', Lebanon.

Official exhibitions

2001
Biennial of Venice, Venice, cdited by H. Szeemann.

2000
Seventh Biennial of Havana.
LISTE 2000, Basel.
Fondazione Sandretto Re Rebaudengo per l'arte, Turin, cdited by F. Bonami.
Drawings, Martin Kudlek Gallery, Cologne.
Platforma, Sommer Contemporary Art, Tel-Aviv.

1999
Baby Demo Test Space, Herzlyia Museum of Art.
ACP, Sommer Contemporary Art, Tel-Aviv.
Explosive Drawing, Hamumche, Alternative Space, Tel-Aviv.

1998
Spring at the end of Summer, Young Contemporary Israeli Art, Tel-Aviv Museum of Art, Tel-Aviv.
Jewish Urban Dimensions, Gallerie des Kunstvereins, Heidelberg.

1997
Young Israeli Artists, The Israel Congress Center, Tel-Aviv.
Israeli Art, a historical display from the Museum collections including works from the '20s through the '90s, and works by recipients of the 1997 Museum Prizes, Tel-Aviv Museum of Art, Tel-Aviv.

1996
Virtual Reality, Tel-Aviv Museum of Art, Tel-Aviv.

1993
The America-Israel Cultural Foundation Scholarship Recipients, The Genia Schreiber University Art Gallery, Tel-Aviv University.

Georgina Starr

1968, born in Leeds.
Lives and works in London.

Solo Exhibitions

2001
The Bunny Lake Collection, Anthony Reynolds Gallery, London.

2000
Pinksummer, Genoa.
The Bunny Lakes are Coming, Anthony Reynolds Gallery, London.
Hawerkamp, Munster.

1998
Galerie Brigitte Trotha, Franfurt am Main.
Tuberama, IKON Gallery, Birmingham.

1997
Galerie Philippe Rizzo, Paris.

1996
Barbara Gladstone Gallery, New York.
Hypnodreamdruff, Art Now, Tate Gallery, London.

1995
The Party, with Elise Tak, Bloom Gallery, Amsterdam.
Rooseum, Center of Contemporary Arts, Malmö.
Visit to a Small Planet, Kunsthalle Zurich.

1994
Crying, Galerie Krinzinger, Vienna.
The Nine Collections of the Seventh Museum, Stroom.
(Un)Controlling, Stedelijk Museum Bureau, Amsterdam.
Getting to Know You, Anthony Reynolds Gallery, London.

1992
Mentioning, Anthony Reynolds Gallery, London.

Group Exhibitions

2001
Tokyo TV, Palais de Tokyo, Paris.
"dai, dai, dai, where do we go from here?", Montevideo, Amsterdam.
Science et Cité: La vérité est ailleurs, Centre pour l'image contemporaine, saint-gervais, Geneva.
ART/MUSIC: rock, pop and techno, Museum of Contemporary Art, Sydney

2000
Anyone could be anyone else in most ways, Galerie Brigitte Trotha, Frankfurt.
On the Edge of the Western World, Yerba Buena Center for the Arts, San Francisco (and tour).
VideoVibe – Art, Music and Video in the UK, edited by C. Perrella and D. Cascella, British School at Rome and tour.
Magic/Object/Action, Sheffield.
Unhoused, Antiguo Colegio de San Ildefonso, Mexico City.
On Stage, South London Gallery.
Kunstcontainer, touring in Germany.
Doppelganger, Shed im Eisenwerk, Frauernfeld.
Strange Paradise, Casino de Luxembourg.
Diary, Cornerhouse, Manchester, edited by M. Heller.
Présumés innocents, capcMusée d'art contemporain, Bordeaux.

1999
Make/Believe, The Fabric Workshop and Museum, Philadelphia.
Self Portrait, Mercer Union, Toronto.
Hypertronix, Espai d'art contemporani, Castello.
The Order of Things, Ramapo College, New Jersey.
The Degree Show, Leeds 13, Leeds.
Landscape Memories, Rosamund Felsen Gallery, Los Angeles.
Dial M for..., Kunstverein Munich.
Out of Site, BüroFriedrich, Berlin.
Popping Up in Oostellingwerf, Oostellingwerf, Holland.
Ainsi de suite 3, Centre Régional d'Art Contemporain, Sète.
Sweetie, British School of Rome, Rome and tour.
Act I. Stage Design and The Visual Arts, Kunstforeningen, Copenhagen.
Festival Ricione TTV, Riccione.
Visions of the Body: Fashion or Invisible Corset, The National Museum of Modern Art, Kyoto/ Museum of Contemporary Art, Tokyo.
Natural Reality, Ludwig Forum für Internationale Kunst, Aachen.

1998
Critical Elegance, Museum Dhondt-Dhaenens, Deurle.
Malos Habitos, Galeria Soledad Lorenzo. Madrid.

Family, Inverleith House, Edinburgh.
U.K Maximum Diversity, Benger Areal, Bregenz.
Made In London, Museu de Electricidade, Lisbon.
REAL/LIFE, Tochigi Prefectural Museum of Fine Arts and tour.
Galerie der Stadt Schwaz, Schwaz, Tirol.
I'm still in love with you, Twentieth Century Women's Club, Eagle Rock, California (publication and record album).
English Rose, The Ginza Artspace, Tokyo.
Infra-slim, The Soros Center for Contemporary Art, Kyiv.
Beige and Sneakers, Buro Friedrich, Berlin.
A Night with Pony, Halle fur Kunst, Luneburg.
In (Between) the Images, Neues Forum, Graz, Austria.
New British Video Programme, Museum of Modern Art, New York.

1997
Screen, Anne Faggionato, London.
Heaven, P.S.1, New York.
Het Eigen Gezicht, Museum Beelden ann Zee in Scheveningen, The Hague.
Private Face-Public Space, Gasworks, Athens; L. Kanakakis Municipal Gallery of Rethymnon, Crete.
Tales from the city, Stills Gallery, Edinburgh.
619 KBB 75, Mobile, Paris.
7th Kwangiu Biennale, Kwangiu, Korea.
Camping, Neueraachen Kunstverein, Aachen.
Pictura Britannica, Museum of Contemporary Art, Sydney, Art Gallery of South Australia, Adelaide, Te Papa, New Zealand.
Package Holiday, The Hydra Workshop, Hydra, Greece.
Särkyneen Sydämen Hotelli, Hotel Otava, Pori.
Strangely Familiar, Ladywood Health and Community Centre, Birmingham.
Tales from the City, Stills Gallery, Edinburgh.
Ein Stück vom Himmel, Kunsthalle, Nürnberg and South London Gallery.
Hypermnesiac Fabulations, The Power Plant, Toronto.

1996
Up Close and Personal, Philadelphia Museum of Art, Philadelphia.
Supastore de Luxe, UP & Co, New York.
Full House, Kunstmuseum Wolfsburg, Wolfsburg.
'ID' an international survey of the notion of identity in contemporary art, Van Abbemuseum, Eindhoven.
Galerie Tanja Grunert, Cologne.
New Photography 12, Museum of Modern Art, New York.
Rational Behaviour, The Tannery, London.

Bart College, Annandale on Hudson, New York.
On a Clear Day, Cambridge Darkroom, First Site, Focal John Hansard Gallery, ICA, Middlesborough Art Gallery, Oldham Art Gallery.
Fernbedienung, Grazer Kunstverein, Graz.
Ferens Art Gallery, Kingston upon Hull.
Electronics Undercurrents, Statens Museum for Kunst, Copenhagen.
Roslyn Oxley Gallery, Sydney.
Elsewhere, Galerie Froment Putman, Paris.
The Cauldron, Deanclough,Henry Moore Institute, Halifax.
No10, Rhona Hoffman Gallery, Chicago.

1995
The British Art Show, Manchester and tour.
Troisième Biennale de Lyon, Lyon.
Brill, Montgomerie Glasoe Fine Art, Minneapolis.
Brilliant, Walker Art Center, Mineapolis, Contemporary Arts Museum, Houston.
Night and Day, Anthony Reynolds Gallery.
Ateliers d'Artistes de la Ville de Marseille, Marseilles.
Wild Walls, Stedelijk Museum, Amsterdam.
Here and Now, Serpentine Gallery, London.
Campo, La Biennale di Venezia, Venice.
Auto Reverse, Saint Gervais Genève.
Couldn't get ahead, I.A.S, London.
La Valise du Celibataire, Maastricht.
Everytime I See You, Malmö, (Nicolai Wallner).
In Search of the Miraculous, Starkmann Ltd, London.
Hopeless, Center for Contemporary Art, Glasgow.
Anthony Reynolds Gallery, London.
Kunstforeningen, Copenghagen.

1994
It's how you play the game, Exit Art, New York.
Use Your Allusion; Recent Video Art, Museum of Contemporary Art, Chicago.
Points de vue (Images d'Europe), Centre Georges Pompidou, Paris.
Electric Ladyland, Jousse Seguin, Paris.
Schipper & Krome, Cologne.
Le Shuttle, Kunstlerhaus Bethanien, Berlin.
Untitled Streamer Eddy Monkey Full Stop Etcetera, Anthony Reynolds Gallery, London.
Europa 94, Munich.
WM Karaoke, Portikus, Frankfurt.
Without Walls, The Face magazine.
Looking at Words: Reading Pictures, Elms Lester, London and touring.
Andrea Rosen Gallery, New York.
high fidelity, The Rontgen Kunst Institut, Tokyo.

1993
Open Atellerdagen, Rijksakademie, Amsterdam.

high fidelity, Kohji Ogura Gallery, Nagoya.
Restaurant, La Bocca, Paris.
Wonderful Life, Lisson Gallery, London.
Ha - Ha, Killerton House, Devon.
Aperto, Venice Biennale, Venice.
Barclays Young Artists, Serpentine Gallery, London.

1992
Through View, Diorama Gallery, London.
P.G.6, Slade Gallery, London.

1991
A.V.E. 91, Filmuis, Arnhem.

1990
A.V.E. 90, Gemeente Museum, Arnhem.

Bibliography

2001
Rota, E., "Georgina Starr", *Flash Art (Italy)*, February – March.
Bertola, C.C., "Georgina Starr", *Tema celeste*, 83.

2000
Starr, G., *The Bunny Lakes* (vinyl record).
Strange Paradise, exhibition catalogue, Casino de Luxembourg.
Beasley, M., "Georgina Starr", *Untitled*, Autumn/Winter.
Beech, D., "Georgina Starr", *Art Monthly*, October.
Buck, L., *Moving Targets 2 A User's Guide to British Art Now*, Tate Publishing.
Diary, exhibition catalogue, Cornerhouse, Manchester.

1999
Starr, G., *Popping Up in Ooststellingwerf* (CD).
Act I. Stage Design and The Visual Arts, exhibition catalogue, Kunstforeningen, Copenhagen.
Visions of the Body: Fashion or Invisible Corset, exhibition catalogue, The National Museum of Modern Art, Kyoto/ Museum of Contemporary Art, Tokyo.
Puvogel, R., "Georgina Starr, Starrwood", *Kunstforum*, January – February.
Kuni, V., "Georgina Starr", *Frieze*, January – February.

1998
Tuberama, exhibition catalogue, IKON Gallery, Birmingham.
Starr, G., *Tuberama* (CD).
Starr, G., *Pony* (CD).

1997
Starr, G., *Starvision*, 1.
Private Face-Public Space, exhibition catalogue, Gasworks, Athens; L. Kanakakis Municipal Gallery of Rethymnon, Crete.

Tales from the city, exhibition catalogue, Stills Gallery, Edinburgh.
Pictura Britannica, exhibition catalogue, Museum of Contemporary Art, Sydney, Art Gallery of South Australia, Adelaide, Te Papa, New Zealand.
Package Holiday, exhibition catalogue,The Hydra Workshop, Hydra, Greece.
Ein Stück vom Himmel, exhibition catalogue, Kunsthalle, Nürnberg and South London Gallery.
Hypermnesiac Fabulations, exhibition catalogue, The Power Plant, Toronto.

1996
'ID' an international survey of the notion of identity in contemporary art, exhibition catalogue, Van Abbemuseum, Eindhoven.
On a Clear Day, Cambridge Darkroom, First Site, Focal John Hansard Gallery, ICA, Middlesborough Art Gallery, Oldham Art Gallery.
Frankel, D., "Now you see it, now you don't", *Artforum*, October.
Davies, P., "Georgina Starr", *Flash Art*, October.
Leturcq, A., "Georgina Starr, The Perfect Party", interview, *Blocnotes*.
Chodzko, A., "Georgina Starr", interview, *Tate The Art Magazine*, Spring.

1995
Starr, G., *Visit to a Small Planet* (book).
Wild Walls, exhibition catalogue, Stedelijk Museum, Amsterdam.
Gibbs, M., *Art Monthly*, November.
Régnier, P., "Georgina Starr", *Blocnotes*, 9, Summer.
Bangma, A., "Wild Walls", *Frieze*, 25.
Flood, R., "Smashing", *Frieze*, 25.
Russo, A., "A Body of Works", *Art Monthly*, April.
Corvi Mora, T., "Georgina Starr", *Purple Prose*, Spring.

1994
Grant, S., "World Cup Football Karaoke", *Art Monthly*, September.
Leturcq, A., "Georgina Starr", *Blocnotes*, 6, Summer.
van den Boogerd, D., "(Un)Controlling", *Flash Art*, Summer.
Renton, A., "Georgina Starr", *Flash Art*, June.
Gibbs, M., "(Un)Controlling", *Art Monthly*, April.

1993
Starr, G., *So I Said* (book).
Starr, G., *Mentioning* (tape, book and musical score).
high fidelity, Kohji Ogura Gallery, Nagoya.
Ha - Ha, exhibition catalogue, Killerton House, Devon.
Aperto, exhibition catalogue, Venice Biennale.

Barclays Young Artists, exhibition catalogue, Serpentine Gallery, London.
Muir, G., "Yesterday", *Frieze*, November-December.
Kunstforum International, Bd. 123.
Cottingham, L., "Wonderful Life", *Frieze*, 12, September/October.
Wilson, A., "Ha Ha and Over the Limit", *Art Monthly*, September.
Roberts, J., "Twins Peak", *Frieze*, 9, March-April.

1992
Starr, G., *Static Steps* (book).
Starr, G., *Whistle* (vinyl record).

Do-Ho Suh
1962, born in Seoul.
Lives and works in New York and Seoul.

Solo Exhibitions

2001
Do-Ho Suh: Some/One, Whitney Museum of American Art at Philip Morris, New York, New York.

2000
Do-Ho Suh, Lehmann Maupin Gallery, New York, New York.

1999
Seoul Home / L. A. Home, Korean Cultural Center, Los Angeles, California.
Sight-Seeing, NTT InterCommunication Center, Tokyo, Japan.

Group Exhibitions

2001
Uniform, Order and Disorder, P.S.1 Contemporary Art Center, Long Island.
Made in Asia, Duke University Art Museum, Durham.
Subject Plural: Crowds in Contemporay Art, Contemporay Art Museum Houston, Houston.
BodySpace, The Baltimore Museum of Art, Baltimore.
Uniform, Order and Disorder, Stazione Leopolda, Florence.

2000
Currents in Korean Contemporary Art, Taipei Fine Arts Museum, Taipei, Taiwan.
My Home is Yours. Your Home is Mine, *Rodin Gallery/Samsung Museum*, Seoul, Korea.
Open Ends, The Museum of Modern Art, New York, New York.
Koreamericakorea, Art Center Sonje, Seoul, Korea / Sonje Art Museum, Kyungjoo, Korea.
Greater New York, P.S.1 Contemporary Art Center, Long Island City, New York.

1999
Trippy World, Baron/Boisante, New York, New York.
The Self, Absorbed, Bellevue Art Museum, Bellevue, Washington.
Uniform, Center for Curatorial Studies, Bard College, Annandale-on-Hudson, New York.

1998
Beyond the Monument, Metrotech Center Commons, Brooklyn, New York.

1997
Do-Ho Suh / Royce Weatherly, Gavin Brown's Enterprise, New York.
Promenade in Asia 1997, Shiseido Gallery, Tokyo.
Techno/Seduction, The Cooper Union, New York, New York.

1996
Arcos da Lapa Project, Arcos da Lapa, Rio de Janeiro.

1995
6 Artists Now, Gallery Hyundai, Seoul.

1994
Invitational Exhibition, Woods-Gerry Gallery, Rhode Island School of Design, Providence.
Picture Him, Picture Her, 105 Dyer Gallery, Providence.

1993
Open Door, Sol Koffler Gallery, Rhode Island School of Design, Providence.

1990
Light from the East-II, Kyiv City Museum, Kyiv.
Korean Contemporary Painting Exhibition, Hoam Gallery, Seoul.
The Groping Youth 1990, The National Museum of Contemporary Art, Kwachon.

1989
20th São Paulo International Biennial, Fundaçao Bienal de São Paulo, São Paulo.

Bibliography

2001
Molesworth, H., Bodyspace, exhibition catalogue, Baltimore.
Liu, J., "Do-Ho Suh," *Frieze,* January/February, p. 118.
Bonami, F., "Uniforms and Signs. Art as Desertion", *Uniform, Order and Disorder,* exhibition catalogue, Florence, January, pp. 236-240.
Malhotra, P., "Do-Ho Suh", *Tema Celeste,* 83, January/February, pp. 52-55.
Harper, G., "Do-Ho Suh at Lehmann

Maupin", *Sculpture,* January/February, pp. 62-63.

2000
Nahas, D., "smocktalksizematters: Lost in Space, disorientation is a sliding scale", *Smock,* November, p. 36.
Leffingwell, E., "Do-Ho Suh at Lehmann Maupin", *Art in America,* November, p. 162.
Cotter, H., "Do-Ho Suh", *The New York Times,* September 29, p. E31.
Levine, K., "Short List: Do-Ho Suh", *The Village Voice Choices,* September 19, p. 78.
Dannatt, A., "Little People at Lehmann Maupin", *The Art Newspaper,* 106, September, p. 78.
Dailey, M., "Greater New York", *Art Press,* 259, July/August, pp. 66-67.
Canning, S., "You can't always get what you want: sifting through the Whitney Biennial 2000 plus: 'Greater New York' bucks the biennial", *Art Papers Magazine,* July/August, pp. 20.
Kino, C., "Surveying the Scene II: The Emergent Factor", *Art in America,* July, pp. 44-49.
Joo, E., "Why Korean-American Art?", *Wolgan Misool,* June, pp. 90-95.
Won, H.-J., "Special Feature: Korean-American Artists", *Wolgan Misool,* June, pp. 72-73.
Ross, D., "KOREAMERICAKOREA", *KORE-AMERICAKOREA,* exhibition catalogue, May, pp. 10-16, pp.32-35, Seoul.
Ahn, M.-H., "Greater New York: 144 faces of New York Contemporary Art," *Misul Segae,* May, pp. 120-121.
Saltz, J., "Greater Expectations-The First Offspring of an Art World Marriage", *The Village Voice,* March 14, p. 67.
Cotter, H., "New York Contemporary, Defined 150 Ways", *The New York Times,* March 6, pp. E1, E5.

1999
Yoon, N.-J., "Emerging Artist: Do-Ho Suh-Wearing thin and opaque clothing," *Art,* December, pp. 74-77, Seoul, Korea.
Lazar, J., "Emerging Artist: Do-Ho Suh-Seoul Home/L.A. Home", *Art,* December, p. 8.
Song, M.-A., "Next Generation: Do-Ho Suh", *Wolgan Misool,* November, 1999, p. 30.
"Public Art 1998 in Review," *Art in America,* Septembe, pp. 50-51.
Johnson, K., "A fertile Garden of Sculptures," *The New York Times,* August 13, pp. E-33, 35.
Komatsuzaki, T., *Do-Ho Suh's Latest Challenge: Sight-Seeing,* exhibition catalogue, Tokyo.
Fehrenkamp, A., "Commissions: Chakaia Booker, Tony Matelli, Valeska Soares, and

Do-Ho Suh", *Sculpture,* March, 18, 2, pp. 14-15.
Bennett, P., "Public Spaces: Vexing the Monument", *Landscape Architecture,* February, p. 12.
Park, Y.M., "Uplifting Asian Artists-The Story of Exile, Migration, and The Third World," *Wolgan Misool,* February, pp. 86-92.

1998
Gibson, A., "Asian American Cross-Cultural Vision: The Task at Hand", *Cross-Cultural Voices,* exhibition catalogue, pp. 9-13, Stony Brook, New York.
Reichardt, J., "Electronically Yours", *Electronically Yours,* exhibition catalogue, July, Tokyo, pp. 25-26, 37.
Kwon, M., "Uniform Appearance", *Frieze,* January/February, London, pp. 68-69.

1997
Levin, K., "Do-Ho Suh", *The Village Voice Choices,* June 3, p. 18.
Baik, J.-S., "Promenade in Asia 1997", *Wolgan Misool,* April, pp. 98-101.
Cotter, H., "Techno Seduction", *The New York Times,* February 7, p. B28.

1996
Chun, S.-B., "Artist at Work: Do-Ho Suh", *Gana Art,* March, pp. 104-105.
Yoon, N.-J., "Young Artist of the Month: Do-Ho Suh", *Space,* March, pp. 95-99.
Kim, Y.-D., "Review-6 Artist Now", *Wolgan Misool,* January, pp. 154-155.

1989
Yoon, Y.-S., "Sketches from the 20th São Paulo International Biennial", *Space,* December, pp. 136-141.

1987
Tchae, C.-S., "Artist of the Month: Do-ho Suh", *Auditorium,* May, pp. 44-45.

Fiona Tan
1996, born in Pekan Baru.
Lives and works in Amsterdam and Berlin.

Solo Exhibitions

2001
Fiona Tan, Wako Works of Art, Tokyo.
Matrix 145, Wadsworth Atheneum Museum of Art, Hartford.
Fiona Tan – recent works, Galerie Michel Rein, Paris.

2000
Lift, Galerie Paul Andriesse, Amsterdam.
Carwreck Cinema, Aussendienst Hamburg.
Facing Forward, Galerie Massimo de Carlo, Mailand.
Scenario, Kunstverein Hamburg.

1999
Roll I & II, Museum De Pont, Tilburg.
Cradle, Galerie Paul Andriesse, Amsterdam.
Elsewhere .., Begane Grond, Utrecht.

1998
J.C. Van Lanschot Prize, Stedelijk Museum voor Aktuele Kunst, Gent.
Linnaeus' Flower Clock, Stedelijk Museum Het Domein, Sittard.

1997
Open Studio, Rijksakademie van beeldende kunsten, Amsterdam.

Group Exhibitions

2001
Yokohama Triennale, Japan.
Endtroducing, Villa Arson, Nice.
Berlin Biennale 2, Berlin.
Mobile Walls, recent acquisitions 1996, Museum Boijmans van Beuningen, Rotterdam.

2000
Shanghai Biennale, Shanghai Art Museum, Shanghai.
<hers> Video as a Female Terrain, Steirischer Herbst 2000, Graz.
Still/Moving, Museum of Modern Art, Kyoto.
Powersources, FRI-Art, Centre d'Art Contemporain, Fribourg.
Art Unlimited, Art, Basel.
Biennale de Lyon, Institut d'Art contemporain, Villeurbanne.
Exploding Cinema, Museum Boijmans van Beuningen, Rotterdam.

1999
Stimuli, Witte de With Centre for Contemporary Art, Rotterdam.
8e Biennale de l'Image en mouvement, Centre pour l'Image Contemporaine, Geneve.
Life Cycles, Galerie für Zeitgenössische Kunst, Leipzig.
The Power of Beauty, Gemeentemuseum Helmond.
International Biennale of Photography, Centro de la Imagen, Mexico City.
Zug(luft), Museum Kurhaus, Kleve.
Go Away, Royal College of Art, London.

1998
Power Up, Gemeentemuseum Arnhem.
World Wide Video Festival, Stedelijk Museum Amsterdam/De Melkweg.
Traces of Science in Art, Het Trippenhuis KNAW, Amsterdam.
Biennale de l'Image Paris 98, E.N.S.B.A., Paris.
Entrè-fiction, Centre d'Art Contemporaine Rueil-Malmaison.
Kunst nu - Rineke Dijkstra/Tracey Moffatt/

Fiona Tan, VMHK, Gent.
unlimited.nl, De Appel, Amsterdam.

1997
2nd Johannesburg Biennale, Johannesburg.
Cities on the Move, Wiener Secession, Vienna, CAPC Bordeaux, PS1, New York and tour.
The Second, Stedelijk Museum Amsterdam and tour.

Bibliography

2000
Scenario - Fiona Tan, Amsterdam, essays and texts by L. Cooke, J. Berger, O. van den Boogaard, H. Honigmann, S. Schmidt-Wulffen, F. Tan, NAi publishers, Rotterdam.
<hers> Video as a Female Terrain, Steirisc[:her:]bst, Springer Verlag, Vienna.
Monshouwer, S., "Een kinderdroom - Tijdloze beelden en existentiële inzichten", *Kunstbeeld,* 9.
Lütticken, S., "Fiona Tan - Paul Andriesse", *Artforum,* December.
From #3, #4, Witte de With Center for Contemporary Art, Rotterdam .
[Scenario]- Fiona Tan, texts by S. Schmidt-Wulffen, F. Tan, Kunstverein, Hamburg.

1999
8e Biennale de L'Image en Movement, catalogue Centre pour l'Image Contemporaine, Geneva .
Zug(luft), catalogue Museum Kurhaus Kleve, Rotation vandenberg&wallroth inv.
International Biennale of Photography, Centro de la Imagen, Mexico City.
Tan, F., "Uit 't zicht", *De Filmkrant,* 203, September.
Moukhtar, E., "Smoke Screen - Tussen beeld en blik", *Skrien,* 236.
Steevensz, B., "Het absolute bestaat niet", *Metropolis M,* 1.

1998
Cream - Contemporary Art in Culture, Phaidon Press, London, .
Bos, S., *Framing is a choice, J.C. van Lanschotprize 1998,* S.M.A.K., Gent.
ter Borg, L., *Fiona Tan, Linnaeus' Flower Clock, Traces of Science in Art,* catalogue Het Trippenhuis KNAW, Edita Amsterdam.
Dercon, C., Tan F., *The choice of the experts, 11 museum directors choose a young artist,* International Press Centre Nieuwspoort, The Hague.

1997
Cities on the Move, edited by H. Hanru and H. Ulrich Obrist, Wiener Secession and capc Musée d'Art Contemporain de Bordeaux, Verlag Hatje.
Tan, F., *Collecting Presents,* Hong Kong, RABK, Amsterdam.

Trade Routes, History and Geography, 2nd Johannesburg Biennale.
The Second - Time Based Art from The Netherlands, Stedelijk Museum Amsterdam, Montevideo/TBA.

Javier Téllez
1969, born in Venezuela.
Lives and works in New York.

Solo Exhibitions

2001
Bedlam, Museo Rufino Tamayo, Sala 7, Mexico City.

2000
Bounced, Serge Ziegler Gallery, Zurich.

1999
I am Happy Because Everyone Loves Me, Gasworks Gallery, London.

1997
The Ship of Fools, Sala Mendoza, Caracas.

1996
The Cure of Folly, Museo de Bellas Artes, Caracas and Museo Arturo Michelena, Valencia, Venezuela.

Group Exhibitions

2001
False Start, Center for Curatorial Studies Bard College, New York.

2000
Kwangju Biennale, Korea.
Greater New York: New Art in New York Now, P.S1 & MOMA Museums, New York.
SOS:Scenes of Sounds, Tang Museum, Saratoga.
The End, Exit Art, New York.
Demostration Räume, Or Gallery, Vancouver.

1998
III Bienal Barro de América, Paço das Artes, San Paulo, Brazil.
IX Premio Mendoza, Sala Mendoza, Caracas.
Longuitud de Onda: Videos-Fotografía, Museo Alejandro Otero. Caracas.

1997
Así Está la Cosa, Centro Cultural Arte Contemporáneo, Mexico City.
Primera Bienal de Artes Visuales MercoSur, Porto Alegre.
Kiosk, Public Art Project, Downtown Arts Festival, New York.
Norte del Sur: Venezuelan Art Today, Philbrook Museum of Art, Tulsa.

1996
Video Faz, Art & Idea, Mexico City and Museo de Guadalajara, Mexico.
Sweat, Exit Art, New York.

1995
Imaginary Beings, Exit Art, New York.
Una Visión del Arte Venezolano, Museo de Arte Contemporáneo Sofía Imber, Caracas.
Il Salón Pirelli, Museo de Arte Contemporáneo Sofía Imber, Caracas.

1994
Insane Asylum, I.S.P. PS1 Museum, New York.
Courage, New Museum of Contemporary Art, New York.
Let the Artists Live, Exit Art, New York.
Projects, Franklin Furnace Archive, New York.
It's How You Play the Game, Exit Art, New York.
The Next Generation, Christinerose Gallery, New York.

Bibliography

2000
Kim, Y.Y., *Exotica Incognita. Man + Space,* Kwangju Biennale, Korea.
Siegel, K., "Greater New York", *Art Forum,* May.
Zamudio, R., "Plato's Cave, Alberti's Window and Benthams Panopticum: Notes on Javier Tellez's I am Happy Because Everyone Loves Me", *NY Arts,* 5, May.

1999
Fajardo-Hill, C., *IX Salón Mendoza,* Sala Mendoza, Caracas.
Fuenmayor, J., *Longuitud de Onda,* Museo Alejandro Otero, Venezuela.
Sichel, B., "Bienal Mercosul", *Flash Art,* XXXI, 198, January-February.
Haber, A., *First Mercosur Biennial, Art Nexus,* 27, January-March.
Jouannais, J.I., *1ere Biennale do Mercosud, Art Press,* 232, February.
Zamudio, R., "Penalty", *Estilo,* 9, 33.
Kent, S., "Javier Tellez", *TimeOut,* 1529, December 8-15.
Negrotti, R., "Javier Tellez in Gasworks", *What's On in London,* December 1-8.
Téllez, J., "Mimetismo y Anamorfosis en los Rostros de Messerschmidt", *Zona Tórrida,* Universidad de Carabobo, p. 155-172 .

1998
Hernández, C., "El artista trickster o de como el hospital se metió dentro del museo", *Arte y Locura: Espacios de Creación,* Serie Reflexiones en el Museo, 3, Museo de Bellas Artes, Caracas.
Téllez, J., "Los palimpsestos de la identi-

dad", *Estilo,* 34.
"Sobre las estrategias de exhibición", *El Nacional. Papel Literario,* November 29.

1997
Fuenmayor, J., *Así está la cosa: Nada más latinoamericano que temer parecerlo,* Centro Cultural Arte Contemporáneo, Mexico City.
Gallo, R., *La Nave de los Locos,* Fundación Mendoza, Caracas.
Morais, F., Guevara, R., Primera Bienal de Artes Visuales MercoSur, Porto Alegre.
Tuchman, P. and Duque, L., *Norte del Sur: Venezuelan Art Today,* Philbrook Museum, Tulsa.
Gallo, R., "Javier Téllez", *Poliester,* Fall.
Krebs, V., *Del Alma y el Arte,* Serie Reflexiones en el Museo, 2, Museo de Bellas Artes, Caracas.
Palenzuela, J.C., *50 Obras del Salón Michelena,* Colección El Tiempo Derramado, Tierra de Gracia Editores, Caracas.

1996
Gallo, R., *Video Faz. Art & Idea,* Mexico City.
Hernández, C., *La Extracción de la Piedra de la Locura,* Museo de Bellas Artes, Caracas.
Sichel, B. *Arco Latino,* Madrid.
Gallo, R., "Javier Téllez, Silverstein Gallery", *ArtNexus,* September.
Costa, E., "Javier Téllez at Silverstein Gallery", *Art in America,* November.
Hernández, C., "Javier Téllez: Arqueólogo Trickster", *Estilo,* December.
Téllez, J., "De un Hospital dentro del Museo", *La Extracción de la Piedra de la Locura,* exhibition catalogue, Museo de Bellas Artes, Caracas.

1995
Cárdenas, M., *Il Salón Pirelli,* Museo de Arte Contemporáneo Sofía Imber, Caracas.
Duque, L.A., *Una Visión del Arte Venezolano,* Colección Ignacio y Valentina Oberto, Museo de Arte Contemporáneo Sofía Imber, Caracas.

1994
Avgikos, J., *International Studio Program,* P.S.1 Museum, New York.

Alessandra Tesi

1969, born in Bologna.
Lives and works in Bologna and Paris.

Solo Exhibitions

2000
Prove Generali, Museo d'Arte Moderna e Contemporanea, Palazzo delle Albere, Trento.

1999
Interference Pearl, Un progetto per il Castello, Castello di Rivoli, Musée d'Art Contemporain, Rivoli, Turin.
Boxe d'or, Emporio Armani Saint Germain, Paris.
Opale 00, Galerie Massimo Minini, Brescia.

1998
La Croce Verde, Santa Maria della Scala, Sienne.

1997
Spazio Aperto, Galerie d'Art Moderna, Bologna.
Le danger gluant de l'ordinaire, Musée du Papier Peint, Rixheim. (Projet realisé avec le concours du Ministère de la Culture, Drac Alsace et de l'Institut Culturel Italien, Strasbourg)
Tic de l'esprit, Galerie Neon, Bologna.
Rosso D-R, Institute of Visual Arts, University Art Museum of Wisconsin, Milwaukee.

1996
Castello di Rivara, Rivara, Turin.
Galerie Paolo Vitolo, Milan.

Group Exhibitions

2000
Che c'è di nuovo, Casina Pompeiana, Naples.
L'altra metà del cielo. Una nuova generazione di artisti italiani, Musée d'Art Moderne et Contemporain Rupertinum, Salzbourg; Musée d'Art Moderne et Contemporain, Chemnitz; Schirn Kunsthalle, Frankfurt.
L'ombra della ragione. L'idea del sacro nell'identità europea, Galleria D'Arte Moderna et Villa delle Rose, Bologna.

1999
Côté Sud... Entschuldigung, La Ferme du Buisson, Centre d'Art Contemporain, Noisiel.
Insight Out-Landscape and Interior in contemporary photography, Kunstraum Innsbruck; Kunsthaus Hamburg; Kunsthaus Basel.
Clues, The Netherlands Media Art Institute, MonteVideo/TBA, Amsterdam.

Effetto Notte, Associazione Culturale Napoli Sotterranea, Naples.
Selezione Italiana per il PS1, Fondazione Pistoletto, Biella.

1998
Subway, métro et espaces publiques, Milan.
The Measure of All Things, Fondation Ursula Blickle, Kraichtal; Galerie im Traklhaus, Salzburg.
Fuori Uso '98/Opera Nuova, ex-Mercato Ortofrutticolo, Pescara.
Liberamente, Palazzo del Capitano et Spazio ex-Arrigoni, Cesena.
Côté Sud... Entschuldigung, Institut d'Art Contemporain, FRAC Rhône Alpes-Nouveau Musée, Villeurbanne.

1997
Giro d'Italia dell'Arte..., L'Attico, Rome.
Des histoires en formes, Le Magasin, Centre d'Art Contemporain, Grenoble.
Officina Italia, Chiostri di San Domenico, Imola.
Fatto in Italia, *Films and Videos*, Centre d'Art Contemporain, Geneva; Institute of Contemporary Arts, London.
1968-1998 Fotografia e Arte in Italia, Palazzo Santa Margherita et Galleria Civica, Modena.
Da Bologna, La Chaufferie, Galerie de l'Ecole des Arts Decoratifs, Strasbourg.

1996
Prospect '96, Frankfurter Kunstverein, Schirn Kunsthalle Frankfurt, Frankfurt
Carte Italiane, Art Center Eleftherias Park, Athens.
Panorama Italiano 1, Trevi Flash Art Museum, Perugia.
Ultime Generazioni, XII Esposizione Nazionale Quadriennale d'Arte di Roma, Palazzo delle Esposizioni, Stazione Termini, Rome.
Jahresgaben 1996, Frankfurter Kunstverein, Frankfurt.

1995
Aperto '95/Out of order, Ga1erie d'Art Moderne, Bologna.
Il giovane ospite, Casa di Giorgione, Castelfranco Veneto.

1994
Equinozio d'autunno 1994, Castello di Rivara, Rivara, Turin.
Biennale Giovani Artisti dell'Europa Mediterranea, Corderie Nationale, Lisbon; Moderna Galerie, Rijeka.
We are moving, Viafarini, Milan.

Jaime-David Tischler

1960, born in San José.
Lives and works in San José.

Solo Exhibitions

1999
Memoria Ingrávida y Síntomas de Identidad (Weightless Memory and Symptoms of Identity), part of the show Cuatro Visiones, Museo de Arte y Diseño Contemporáneo, San José.

1998
Threads of Desire, Intar Latin American Gallery, New York.

1997
Pies de Barro (Feet of Clay), Galería H2O, Barcelona.
Fragmentos de un Deseo Mendicante (Fragments of a Mendicant Desire), Instituto Tecnológico de Costa Rica, Cartago.
Sendas Equívocas (Equivocal Paths), Galería Nacional de Arte Contemporáneo (GANAC), Museo de Arte Costarricense, San José.

1996
False Sequences, Homerion Theater Gallery, Isle of Kyos.
Bajar al Cielo (Descent into Heaven), Biennale Primavera Fotográfica de Cataluña, Centro Cívico de La Barceloneta, Barcelona.

1995
Descent into Heaven, Fotofeis International Festival of Photography, Bonhonga Gallery, Unst, Isle of Shetland.
En el Cielo se Baila Merengue (Merengue is Danced In Heaven), Casa de la Cultura de Puntarenas, Puntarenas.
Fragmentos de un Deseo Mendicante, Galería Manuel de la Cruz González, San José.
Bajar al Cielo, Café del Teatro Nacional, San José.

1994
Frammenti di un Desiderio Dimenticato (Fragments of a Forgotten Desire), Photogrammatica Festival of Photography, Galería Studio Córdoba, Rome.
Del Azar y Otros Eclipses (On Chance and other Eclipses), Café del Sol, Barcelona.
En el Cielo se Baila Merengue, Escola de Fotografia GirsArt, Barcelona.
Tindra Fe (To Have Faith), Café de la Virreina, Barcelona.

Group shows

2000
Ex3: El Peso de lo Ausente (The Weight of Absence), Instalación, Museo de Arte y Diseño Contemporáneo, San José.

Imágenes de Hombres: En el Pecado llevarás la Penitencia (Images of Men. In Sin you shall carry your Penitence), Instalación, Museos del Banco Central, San José.
Fotoseptiembre, Festival Internacional de Fotografía, Tribunal Supremo de Elecciones, San José.
Latent: Contemporary Latino American Art in New York, Il Gallery, New York.

1999
La Envoltura del Alma (The Wrapping of the Soul), Museo de Arte y Diseño Contemporáneo, San José.

1998
A Photographer's Tale, The Lessie Lohmann Gay Art Foundation, New York.
Itinerario Español: Plástica Costarricense (Spanish Journey: Costa Rican Plastic Art), Centro Cultural de Españo, San José.
El Cuerpo en/ de la Fotografía (The Body in/of Photography), Museo de Arte y Diseño Contemporáneo, San José.

1997
Selecciones de la Colección Permanente (Selections from the Permanent Collection), Museo de Arte y Diseño Contemporáneo, San José.

1995
Finalistas del Concurso Brasil 95 (Finalist of the Brazil 95 Contest), Museo de Arte y Diseño Contemporáneo, San José.
Cuarta Bienal de Artistas Judíos Costarricenses (Fourth Biennale of Costa Rican Jewish Artists), Centro Israelita de Costa Rica, San José.
Selecciones de la Colección Permanente (Selections from the Permanent Collection), Museo de Arte y Diseño Contemporáneo, San José.
L'Imatge Gay & Lesbica (The Gay and Lesbian Image), Casal Lambda, Barcelona.

Bibliography

2001
Alvarado, Ileana y Hernández, E., "Imágenes de Hombres", exhibition calogue, Museos del Banco Central de Costa Rica, p. 1.

2000
Ardón, J., "Mirar a Jaime" (Personal Interview), *La Nación*, February 20, p. 1.
Muñoz, Kattia, "Autorretrato al Desnudo" (Art Critique), Semanario Universidad, Costa Rica, Cultura, p. 12, September 13.
Collado, Adriana y Monge, M.J., "El devenir de un autorretrato al desnudo" (Art Critique), Quadrivium, Universidad de Costa Rica, p. 9, October.
Díaz, T., "Todo por Abarcar" (Art Critique), *La Nación*, November 20, p. 12.

1999
Díaz, T., "Caminos al Andar" (Art Critique), *La Nación*, November 28, p. 4.
Ponce, B., "Cuatro Instalaciones" (Art Critique), *La Nación*, Culturales, December 14, p. 8.

1997
Hernández, E., *Sendas Equívocas*, exhibition catalogue, Museo de Arte Costarricense, April, p. 1.
Ponce, B., "Los Cuatro Mundos de Tischler" (Art Critique), *La Nación*, Culturales, April 30, p. 11.
Tischler, J.-D., "Arte Amordazado" (National Debate on Art and Pornography), *La Nación*, Foro/Replica, October 3, p. 14A.
Lobo, T., "Cangrejos Dos" (National Debate on Art and Pornography), *La Nación*, Foro, October 15, p. 14A.
Molina, Á., "Jaime-David Tischler" (Art Critique), *ABC Cataluña*, Arte, October 27, p. 11.
Tischler, J.-D., "Pies de Barro", La Nación, Costa Rica, Ancora, November 2, p. 2.
Sánchez, M., "Jaime-David Tischler: Vanguardia hecha Fotografía" (Personal Interview), Gayness, Costa Rica, Personaje del Mes, August, p. 14.

1996
Bufill, J., "Y Además" (Art Critique), *La Vanguardia*, Cultura Arte, May 10, p. 46.
Pérez, D., *La Herida Narcisista* (El Espíritu de una Colección), exhibition catalogue, Museo de Arte y Diseño Contemporáneo, San José, p. 87.

1995
González, L., *Bajar al Cielo*, exhibition catalogue, Editorial GrisArt, Barcelona, counter leaf.
Ponce, B., "Gris y Negro" (Art Critique), *La Nación*, Culturales, June 26, p. 10.
Mata, Á., "En las Habitaciones de la Soledad" (Art Critique), *La República*, Ventana, July 7, p. 2C.
Büchler, P., *Jaime-David Tischler: Descent into Heaven*, Fotofeis Catalogue, Fotofeis Ltd, Scotland, p. 101.
Soto, R., *Jaime-David Tischler* (Costa Rican Art Anuarium), Editorial Arte y Cultura de Costa Rica, p. 122.

Niele Toroni
1937 born in Muralto.
Lives and works in Paris.

Solo Exhibitions

2001
Niele Toroni, Musée d'Art Moderne de la Ville, Paris.

2000
Niele Toroni, Museum Dhondt-Dhaenens Deurle.
Peinture en cage no 2, Musée d'Art Contemporain, Lyon.
Intervention, Fondation Belgacom, Bruxelles.
Intervention, Gemeentemuseum, The Hague.
Niele Toroni, Galerie Yvon Lambert, Paris.

1999
Itinere 2, Centro Arte Contemporanea, Spolèto.
Niele Toroni, Base, Florence.
Niele Toroni–Für Rimbaud, Für Heine, Galerie Barbara Weiss, Berlin.
Niele Toroni, Galerie Shimada, Tokyo.

1998
Interventention, Schweizer Rück, Zürich, Adliswil.
Eight people from Europe, Museum of Mordern Art, Gunma.
Intervention, Fachhochschule, Ulm.
Niele Toroni, Galleria Artiaco–Pozzuoli, Naples.

1997
Niele Toroni, Marian Goodmann Gallery, New York.
Hommage aux hirondelles, Galeri Yvon Lambert, Paris.
La Roulotte de chantier, with P. Marietan, musique 1ère fête des arts en Suisse, Lucerne.
Niele Toroni, Capc, Musée D'Art Contemporain, Bordeaux.

1996
Niele Toroni, City Museum of Art, Chiba.
Intervention, Kunst in der Neunen Messe, Leipzig.
Niele Toroni, Museum der Bildenden Künste, Leipzig.
Intervention, Palais del Congrès, Shimonoseki.
Intervention , Fachhochschule, Ulm.

Group Exhibitions

2001
Assumer les lieux comme ils sont, École Supérieure des Beaux-Arts, Nîmes.
Intervention, La Biennale di Venezia, Venice.

2000
Intervention, La Beauté, Avignon.
Intervention, Collection Lambert, Avignon.
Tela–Muro, Museo Cantonale d'Arte, Lugano.

1999
Intervention, Centro Arte Contemporaneo, Bellinzona.

1998
La collection Y.Lambert – œuvres sur papier, Museum of Art, Yokohama.
Intervention, Musée d'Art Moderne, Strasburg.

1997
L'empreinte, Musée National d'Art Moderne, Centre Georges Pompidou, Paris.
Coton and paper, Galerie Nächst St. Stephan, Vienna.
La rayure, l'intervalle, le jour..., Frac Nord-Pas de Calais, Dunkerque.
97 Kwangju Biennale, Kwangju.

1996
Chaos, Wahnsinn, Kunsthalle, Krems.

Gavin Turk
1967, born in Guildford.
Lives and works In London.

Solo Exhibitions

2001
The Che Guevara Story, Residence in the East End of London.

2000
More Stuff, Centre d'Art Contemporain, Geneva.
Gavin Turk, fig-1, London.

1999
The Importance of Being Ernesto, Galerie Krinzinger, Vienna.
The Stuff Show, South London Gallery, London.

1997
Gavin Turk, Charing Cross Road, London.

1996
Unoriginal Signature, Habitat, Kings Road, London.
Gavin Turk, (Part of British Art in Rome) Galleria D'Arte De Crescenzo & Viesti, Rome.

1995
Turkish, Aurel Schiebler, Cologne.

1993
Collected Works 1989-1993, Jay Jopling, Denmark Street, London.

A Marvellous Force of Nature, Jay Jopling/White Cube, London.
A Night out with Gavin Turk, Victoria Public House, Bapisha Gosh, London and Schiefer Haus, Cologne.

1992
Signature, Bipasha Ghosh/Jay Jopling, London.

Group Exhibition

2001
Dead, The Roundhouse, London.
Century City, Tate Modern, London.

2000
In Memoriam, The New Art Gallery, Walsall.
Conversation, Milton Keynes Gallery, Milton Keynes.
Out There, White Cube^2, Hoxton Square, London.
Ant Noises, Saatchi Gallery, London.

1999
The Self Absorbed, Bellevue Art Museum, Bellevue, Washington.
6th International Istanbul Biennial, Istanbul.
Officina Europa, Galleria d'Arte Moderna di Bologna, Bologna.
Now It's My Turn to Scream. Works bv ContemDorarv British Artists from the Loagan Colllection, Haines Gallery, San Francisco.
Skin Deep, The Israel Museum, Jerusalem.
Mode of Art, Kunstverein, Dusseldorf.

1998
Dinstinctive Elements: Contemporary British Art Exhibition, National Museum of Contemporary Art, Korea.
Camouflage 2000, Galerie Praz-Delavallade, Paris.

1997
Sensation. Young British Artists from the Saatchi Collection, Royal Academy of Arts, London; Hamburger Bahnhof, Berlin.
Material Culture, Hayward Gallery, London.

1996
Private View, The Bowes Museum/Henry Moore Institute, Leeds.
Museum Vitale, Museum Schloß Morsbroich, Leverkusen.
Sex & Crime, Sprengel Museum, Hannover.
Works on Paper, Irish Museum of Modern Art, Dublin.

1995
Young British Artists III, Saatchi Collection, London.

Contemporary British Art in Print, Scottish National Gallery of Modem Art, Edinburgh; Yale Center for British Art, New Haven.
Seventeen, Greenwich Street, New York.

Bibliography

2001
Lewison, C., "In Memorium: The New Art Gallery, Walsall", *Flash Art*, January/ February, p. 66.
Turk, G., "You ask the questions", *The Independent*, January 31, p. 7.
Turk, G., "The Che Guevara diary", *The Times*, January 22, p. 23.
Jones, J., "Glad to be Che", *The Guardian*, January 22, p. 11.
McLaren, D., "The Revolution will not be televised", *The Independent on Sunday*, January 21.

2000
Darwent, C., "Dying is an art and they do it very well", *The Independent on Sunday*, December 10.
Sutcliffe, T., "No smoking in the art room", *The Independent*, November 25, p. 4.
Chiswick, L., "Creatures of Habit", *The Independent Magazine*, November.
Grandiean, E., "Gavin Turk joue avec le faux au Centre d'art contemporain", *Tribune de Geneve*, October 10.
Bennett, O., "Hip to be Square", *The Independent (Magazine)*, April 1, p. 8-15.
Vendrame, S., "Der unsterbliche Körper und dessen Vergänglichkeit", *Frame Magazine*, p. 57-61.
Jenkinson, P., Burstow, R., Robinson, D., *In Memorium*, The New Art Gallery Warsall.

1999
Mikhail, K., "Come to the aid of the arty", *The Independent*, August 6, p. 10.
Salaman, N., "Still Dancing", *COIL*, 8.
Bevan, R., *Now It's My Turn to Scream. Works bv Contemporary British Artists from the Logan Collection*, San Francisco Museum of Modern Art.
Backhaus, C., *Mode of Art*, Kunstverein, Dusseldorf.
Erdemci, F., [Director]. *6th International Istanbul Biennale*.
Collings, M., *This is Modern Art*, Weidenfeld & Nicolson, London.
Mickelborg, F. *Gronningen*, Charlottenbrog, Copenhagen.

1998
Buck, L., "Best of 1998", *Artforum*, December, p. 112-13.
Lillington, D., "Beroemd en berucht", *Metropolis M*, 6, p. 18-22.
Withers, R., "Gavin Turk: South London Gallery", *Freize Magazine*, 43, p. 88-87.

Burrows, D., "Exquisite Corpses", *Art Monthly*, November, p. 24-25.
Freedman, C. and Turk, G., "Making Omelettes", *Modern Painters*, Autumn, p. 99-101.
Buck, L., "UK artist Q & A", *The Art Newspaper*, 84, September, p. 55.
Burrows, D. (ed.), *Who's Afraid of Red White & Blue. Attitudes to popular and mass culture, celebrity, alternative and critical cultical practice and identity politics in recent British art*, Article Press and UCE.
Muller, B., *UK Maximum Diversity*, Galerie Krinzinger, Vienna.
Farquhason, A., Compston, J., *Gavin Turk. Collected Works 1994-98*, Jay Jopling, London and South London Gallery.
Farquharson, A., *Distinctive Elements*, Contemporary British Art Exhibition, National Museum of Contemporary Art, Korea.
Hepworth, S., Wood, K., *Feeringbury VIII. Cultivated*, Feeringbury Manor, Feering and Firstsite, Colechester (in Association with Curtain Road Arts).

1997
Buck, L., *Moving Target: A Users Guide to British Art Now*, Tate Gallery Publications.
Marshall, C. (ed.), *Breaking the Mould. British Art of the 1980s and 1990s. (The Weltkunst Collection)*, essays by R. Cork, P. Curtis, Lund Humphries Publishers, London and the Irish Museum of Modern Art.
Rosenthal, N., Shone, R., Malony, M., and Jardin, L., *Sensation. Young British Artists from the Saatchi Collection*, Royal Academy of Arts, London.
Collins, M., *Blimey! From Bohemia to Britpop: The London Artworld from Francis Bacon to Damien Hirst*, 21, London.

1996
Roberts, J., "Last of England", *Frieze*,

1996.
Codognato, M., *Artisti Britannici a Roma*, Umberto Allemandi & c., Rome.
Private View, Henry Moore Institute, Leeds.

1995
Collings, M., "Transformer man", *The Guardian*, October 18.
Sanders, M., "Ever Get the Feeling You're Being Elvis?", *Dazed & Confused*, 12, p. 85-87.
Gamett, R., "Young British Artists IV", *Art Monthly*, June, 187.
Operat 95, Mito, Edizioni del Girasole, Ravenna.
Elliott, P., *Contemporary British Art in Print*, Scottish National Gallery of Modem Art, Edinburgh / Paragon Press, London.

Wilson, A. and Bill, S., *Collected Works 1989-1993*, Gavin Turk / Jay Jopling, London.
Seventeen, Greenwich Street, New York.

1993
Bernard, K., "Art mart", *Harpers & Queen*, October.

1992
Wilson, A., "London Summer Round-Up", *Art Monthly*, September, 159, p. 18-19.
Eshun, E. "Art attack", *The Face*, July, p. 89-93.
Marconi, G., *Group Exhibition*, Giò Marconi Gallery, Milan.

1991
"Gavin Turk : Great Expectations", *G-Spot*, Winter Edition, 1, p. 28.

Richard Tuttle
1941, born in Rahway (New Jersey).
Lives and works in New York and Abiqui.

Solo Exhibitions
2000
TwoWith Any To, Sperone Westwater, New York.
Richard Tuttle: Reservations, BAWAG Foundation, Vienna.
RichardTuttle, Perceived Obstacles, Stiftung Schleswig-Holsteinische Landesmuseum, Schloss Gottorf, Schleswig; Westfälisches Landesmuseum für Kunst und Kulturgeschichte, Münster.

1999
Richard Tuttle, The Arts Club of Chicago.

1998-99
Richard Tuttle, Die Konjunktion der Farbe, Ludwig Forum für Internationale Kunst, Aachen.
Richard Tuttle: Replace the Abstract Picture Plane, Books and New Works, The Kamm Collection of the Kunsthaus: A Selection by the Artist, Kunsthaus Zug, Switzerland.

1998
Richard Tuttle: New Mexico, New York, Sperone Westwater, New York.

1996-97
Richard Tuttle: Books and Prints, Widener Gallery, Trinity College, Hartford; The New York Public Library.

1996
Richard Tuttle: Replace the Abstract Picture Plane, Kunsthaus Zug, Switzerland.
Richard Tuttle: New and Early Work, Sperone Westwater, New York.

1995
Richard Tuttle, Selected Works: 1964-1994, Sezon Museum of Art, Tokyo.

1992-1995
The Poetry of Form: Richard Tuttle, Drawings from the Vogel Collection, Instituto Valenciano de Arte Moderno, Spain; Indianapolis Museum of Art, 1992; Museum of Fine Arts, Santa Fe,1995.

1991
Twenty Floor Drawings, Richard Tuttle, Institute of Contemporary Art, Amsterdam.

1990
Richard Tuttle, Sprengel Museum, Hannover.

1987
Nîmes au printemps, Richard Tuttle, Galerie des Arènes, Musée d'Art Contemporain, Carrée d'art, Nîmes.

1986
Richard Tuttle: Wire Pieces, CAPC Musée d'Art Contemporain de Bordeaux.

1983-84
Richard Tuttle: Zeichnungen, 1968-1974, Städtisches Museum Abteiberg Mönchengladbach.

1979
Richard Tuttle, CAPC Centre d'Arts Plastiques Contemporains de Bordeaux.

1978
Richard Tuttle: Title 1-6, Title I-IV, Title A-N, Title 11-16,Titre 1-8,Titolo 1-8, Stedelijk Museum, Amsterdam.

1977
Richard Tuttle/New York: 100 Zeichnungen und Aquarelle, 1968-1976, Kunsthalle Basel.
Zwei mit Zwei: Two With Any Two, Kunstraum Munchen.

1975-1976
Whitney Museum of American Art, New York; Otis Art Institute Gallery of Los Angeles County, 1976.

1974
Annemarie Verna Galerie, Zurich.

1973
Richard Tuttle: Das 11. Papierachteck und Wandmalereien/The 11th Paper Octagonal and Paintings for the Wall, Kunstraum München.

1972
Projects: Richard Tuttle, The Museum of Modern Art, New York.

1971
Richard Tuttle, Dallas Museum of Fine Arts.

1969
Nicholas Wilder Gallery, New York.

1968
Richard Tuttle, Galerie Schmela, Dusseldorf.

1965
Richard Tuttle: Constructed Paintings, Betty Parsons Gallery, New York.

Group Exhibitions

2000
Whitney Biennial, Whitney Museum of American Art, New York.
Cosmologies, Sperone Westwater, New York.

1999-2000
The American Century; Art & Culture 1900-2000, Whitney Museum of American Art, New York.

1999
Circa 1968, Museu de Serralves, Museu de Arte Contemporânea, Porto, Portugal.

1998
Agnes Martin/Richard Tuttle, Modern Art Museum of Fort Worth; SITE Santa Fe.

1997
La Biennale di Venezia, XLVII Esposizione Internazionale d'Arte, Venice.

1995–96
52nd Carnegie International, The Carnegie Museum of Art, Pittsburgh.

1994
From Minimal to Conceptual Art/Works from the Dorothy and Herbert Vogel Collection, National Gallery of Art, Washington.

1990
The New Sculpture 1965-75: Between Geometry and Gesture, Whitney Museum of American, New York.

1987
Skulptur Projekte Munster, Westfalische Landesmuseum, Munster.

1985
Wasserfarbenblatter von Joseph Beuys, Nicola De Maria, Gerhard Richter, Richard Tuttle, Westfalischer Kunstverein Munster, Munster.
Drawings and Acquisitions: 1981-1985, Whitney Museum of American Art, New York.

1983
Documenta 7, Kassel.
60-80: attitudes/concepts/images, Stedelijk Museum, Amsterdam.

1980
Pier + Ocean, Hayward Gallery, London; Rijkmuseum Kroller-Muller, Otterlo.

1977
Documenta 6, Orangerie, Kassel.

1976
Rooms P.S. 1, Biennale di Venezia, 1976, The Institute for Art and Urban Resources, New York.

1974
Cut, Folded, Pasted & Torn, Museum of Modern Art, New York 1975.
"Selections from the Collection of Dorothy and Herbert Vogel," The Clocktower, Institute for Art and Urban Resources, New York.

1973
Contemporanea, Parcheggio di Villa Borghese, Rome.
A Selection of American and European Paintings from the Richard Brown Baker Collection, San Francisco Museum of Art, San Francisco.
Bilder, Objekte, Filme, Konzepte, Städtische Galerie im Lenbachhaus, Munich.

1972
Documenta 5: Befragung der Realitat: Bildwelten heute, Museum Fridericianum, Kassel.
Actualite d'un Bilan, Galerie Yvon Lambert, Paris.

1969
Live in Your Head: When Attitudes Become Form: Works, Concepts, Processes, Situations, Informations, Kunsthalle, Bern; Museum Haus Lange, Krefeld; Institute of Contemporary Arts, London.

Bibliography

2000
Kimmelman, M., "Richard Tuttle; Two With Any To", *The New York Times*, January 28.

1998
Agnes Martin/ Richard Tuttle, exhibition catalogue by M. Auping, texts by A. Martin, R. Tuttle, Modern Art Museum of Fort Worth, FortWorth.

1997
Biennale di Venezia, XLVII Esposizione Internazionale d'Arte, *Future, Present, Past*, exhibition catalogue by G. Celant, text by the artist, Electa, Milan.

Storr, R., "*Just* Exquisite? The Art of Richard Tuttle", *Artforum*, 36, 3, November, pp. 87-93 and cover.

1996
Kimmelman, M., "Art in Review: Richard Tuttle," *The New York Times*, Friday, September 20.

1992
The Poetry of Form: Richard Tuttle, Drawings from the Vogel Collection, exhibition catalogue, with essays by J. Cowart, H.T. Day, S. Harris, B. Waller, Institute of Contemporary Art, Amsterdam; Valencia, IVAM.

1991
Richard Tuttle, exhibition catalogue, with foreword by E. Lipschutz-Villa, essays by S. Harris and D. Schwarz, interview by R. Marshall, Institute of Contemporary Art, Amsterdam; Sdu Publishers, The Hague.

1987
Richard Tuttle: Wire Pieces, exhibition catalogue by J.-L. Froment, with essays by G. Celant, J. Glaesemer, H. Kern, E. Lubell, F. Pluchart, M. Tucker, interview by S. Couderc, texts by the artist, Musée d'art contemporain de Bordeaux, Bordeaux.

1979
Verna, G., "List of Drawing Material of Richard Tuttle & Appendices",, *Gianfranco & Annemarie Verna, Robert Krauthammer, Alfred Gutzwiller and Richard Tuttle*, Zurich.

1975
Tucker, M., *Richard Tuttle*, exhibition catalogue, Whitney Museum of American Art, New York.

1971
Richard Tuttle, exhibition catalogue, text by R.M. Murdock, Dallas Museum of Fine Arts, Dallas.

1970
Pincus-Witten, R., "The Art of Richard Tuttle", *Artforum*, 8, February, pp. 62–67 and cover.

1969
Monte, J., Tucker, M., *Anti-Illusion: Procedures/Materials*, exhibition catalogue, Whitney Museum of American Art, New York.
Szeeman, H., *Live in Your Head: When Attitudes Become Form: Works, Concepts, Processes, Situation, Information*, exhibition catalogue, Kunsthalle Bern, Bern.

Cy Twombly
1928, born in Lexington, Virginia.
Lives and works in Virginia and Rome.

Solo Exhibitions

2000
Cy Twombly: Coronation of Sesostris, Gagosian Gallery, New York.

1998
Eight Sculptures, American Academy, Rome.

1997
Cy Twombly, Cheim & Read, New York.
Ten Sculptures, Gagosian Gallery, New York.

1996
Photographs, Gagosian Gallery, Beverly Hills.

1995
Untitled Painting, The Museum of Fine Arts, Houston.

1994
Cy Twombly, A Retrospective, The Museum of Modern Art, New York; traveled to: The Menil Collection, Houston; The Museum of Contemporary Art, Los Angeles; "Cy Twombly, Retrospektive", Neue Nationalgalerie, Berlin.
Untitled Painting, Gagosian Gallery, New York.
Cy Twombly, C & M Arts, New York, in association with Galerie Karsten Greve, Cologne/Paris/Milan.

1993
Peintures. Oeuvres sur papier et Sculpture, Galerie Karsten Greve, Paris.
Cy Twombly - Octavio Paz, Kunstmuseum Bonn, Bonn.

1992
Cy Twombly - oeuvres gravées, Galerie Vidal - Saint Phalle, Paris.

1990
Drawings and 8 Sculptures, Thomas Ammann Fine Art, Zurich.

1989
Paintings and Sculptures 1951 and 1953, Sperone Westwater, New York.
Paintings of Cy Twombly, Galerie Karsten Greve, Cologne.
Cy Twombly, The Menil Collection, Houston; traveled to Des Moines Art Center, Des Moines.
Bolsena, Gagosian Gallery, New York.

1988

Poems to the Sea, Dia Art Foundation, Bridgehampton.

1987
Bilder, Arbeiten auf Papier, Skulpturen, Kunsthaus, Zurich; travelling to: "Cuadros, trabajos sobre papel, esculturas", Palacio de Velásquez/Palacio de Cristal, Madrid; "Paintings, Works on Paper, Sculpture", Whitechapel Art Gallery, London; "Bilder, Arbeiten auf Papier, Skulpturen", Städtische Kunsthalle, Düsseldorf; "Peintures, Oeuvres sur papier, Sculptures", Musée national d'art moderne, Galeries contemporaines, Centre Georges Pompidou, Paris, 1988.
Serin auf Papier 1957-1987, Städtisches Kunstmuseum, Bonn; travelling to: "Sèries sobre paper 1959-1987", Centre Cultural de la Fundació Caixa de Pensions, Barcelona.
Cy Twombly, Städtische Galerie Haus Seel, Siegen.

1986
Drawings, Collages and Paintings on Paper: 1955-1985, Gagosian Gallery, New York.
Paintings, Galerie Karsten Greve, Cologne.

1985-1986
Paintings and Drawings, Dia Art Foundation, New York.

1984
Cy Twombly, Galerie Karsten Greve, Cologne; travelling to: The Mayor Gallery, London; Galerie Ulysses, Vienna.
Cy Twombly. Oeuvres de 1973-1983, capc Musée d'art contemporain, Bordeaux.
Cy Twombly, Staatliche Kunsthalle, Baden-Baden.
Paintings and Drawings: 1952-1984, Hirschl & Adler Modern, New York.
Sculpture, Galleria Gian Enzo Sperone, Rome.

1982
XI Recent Works, Sperone Westwater Fischer, New York.
Arbeiten auf Papier, Galerie Karsten Greve, Cologne.
An Exhibition of Paintings, The Mayor Gallery, London.
Cy Twombly, Galerie Yvon Lambert, Paris.

1981
Skulpturen, 23 Arbeiten aus den Jahren 1955 bis 1981, Museum Haus Lange, Krefeld.
Works on Paper 1954-1976, Harbor Art Museum, Newport Beach; travelling to: Elvehejem Museum of Art, Madison; Virginia Museum of Fine Arts, Richmond, 1982; Art Gallery of Ontario, Toronto, 1982.

1980
Paintings and Drawings 1959-1976,

Mayor Gallery, London.
Cy Twombly, Galerie Yvon Lambert, Paris.
50 disegni 1953-1980, Padiglione d'Arte Contemporanea, Milan.

1979
Paintings and Drawings 1954-1977, Whitney Museum of American Art, New York.
Bilder 1957-1968, Galerie Karsten Greve, Cologne.

1978
"Cy Twombly", Artline, *The Hague*.

1977
Cy Twombly: Paintings, Visual Arts Museum, New York.
Three Dialogues, Galerie Yvon Lambert, Paris.
Bilder und Zeichnungen, Galerie Karsten Greve, Cologne.

1976
Bilder und Gouchen, Galerie Art in Progress, Düsseldorf.
Cy Twombly, Kenstner-Gesellschaft, Hanover.
Dessins 1954-1976, Musée d'art moderne de la Ville de Paris, Paris.
Cy Twombly, Galleria Gian Enzo Sperone, Rome.

1975
Bilder und Zeichnungen, Galerie Karsten Greve, Cologne.
Paintings, Drawings, Constructions 1951-1974, Institute of Contemporary Art, University of Pennsylvania, Philadelphia; travelling to: San Francisco Museum of Art, San Francisco.

1974
Roman Notes, Gouachen 1970, Galerie Heiner Friedrich, Munich.
Cy Twombly, Galleria Gian Enzo Sperone, Turin.
Cy Twombly, Galerie Yvon Lambert, Paris.

1973
Cy Twombly, Galleria Gian Enzo Sperone, Turin.
Bilder 1953-1972, Kunsthalle, Bern; travelling to: Städtische Galerie im Lenbachhaus, Munich.
Zeichnungen 1953-1973, Kunstmuseum, Basel.

1972
Cy Twombly, Leo Castelli Gallery, New York.
Cy Twombly, Galleria dell'Ariete, Milan.

1971
Cy Twombly, Galleria Sperone, Turin, Italy.

Bilder, Zeichnungen, Galerie Möllenhoff, Cologne.
Cy Twombly, Galerie Yvon Lambert, Paris.

1970
Cy Twombly, Galleria La Tartaruga, Rome.
'Roman Notes,' 24 neue Arbeiten, Galerie Neuendorf, Cologne.

1969
Cy Twombly, Galerie Rudolf Zwirner, Cologne.

1968
Disegni e collages di CY TWOMBLY 1954-1968, Galleria La Tartaruga, Rome.
Paintings, Leo Castelli Gallery, New York.

1967
Cy Twombly, Galleria Notizie, Turin, Italy.
Cy Twombly, Leo Castelli Gallery, New York.

1966
Drawings, Leo Castelli Gallery, New York.

1965
Cy Twombly, Museum Haus Lange, Krefeld; travelling to: Palais des Beaux-Arts, Brussels; Stedelijk Museum, Amsterdam.

1964
Peintures récentes, Galerie Bonnier, Lausanne; travelling to: Basel, Galerie Handschin.
Nine Discourses on Commodus by Cy Twombly, Leo Castelli Gallery, New York.

1963
Dipinti di Cy Twombly, Galleria Notizie, Turin.

1961
Cy Twombly, Galerie Rudolf Zwirner, Essen.

1960
Cy Twombly, Galleria La Tartaruga, Rome.
Cy Twombly, Leo Castelli Gallery, New York.

1957
Cy Twombly, The Stable Gallery, New York.

Group Exhibitions

1995
1995 Biennial Exhibition, Whitney Museum of American Art, New York.

1988
Oggetto: Beuys, Broodthaers, Duchamp (...), Twombly, Warhol, Lucio Amelio, Naples.
Zeitlos - Kunst von heute (The Still Presence of the Absent), Hamburger Bahnhof, Berlin.

Positionen Heutiger Kunst - Positions of Present-Day Art, Nationalgalerie, Berlin.
La Biennale di Venezia, XLIII Esposizione Internazionale d'Arte, Venice.
Baselitz, Kounellis, Twombly, Lucio Amelio, Naples.

1987
About Sculpture, Anthony d'Offay, London.
Individuals: A Selected History of Contemporary Art, 1945-1986, Museum of Contemporary Art, Los Angeles.
Three Decades of Exploration - Homage to Leo Castelli, Museum of Art, Fort Lauderdale.
Yae Asano/Cy Twombly - Paintings, Akira Ikeda Gallery, Tokyo.

1986
L'Aventure Delle Differenze, Galleria Chisel, Genoa.
Kunsthaus, Zurich.
De Sculptura, Wiener Fest Wochen, U-Halle des Messepalastes, Vienna.
Centro de Arte Reina Sofia, Madrid.
Biennale of Sydney, Sydney.

1985
Italia Aperta, Fundacion Caja de Pensiones, Madrid.
Bilder Fur Frankfurt, Museum fur Moderne Kunst, Frankfurt.
Ouverture, Castello di Rivoli, Turin.
Kunsthaus Zurich, Zurich.

1984
Sculpture in the 20th Century, Burlinger Park, Basel.
La grande Parade, Stedelijk Museum, Amsterdam.
Sperone Westwater, New York.

1983
1983 20th Century American Art: Hightlights of the Permanent Collection, Whitney Museum of American Art, New York.
The Historic and the Avantgarde, Trans/Form, New York.

1982
Balthus and Twombly, Thomas Ammann Fine Art, Zurich.
The New York School: Four Decades, The Solomon R, Guggenheim Museum, New York.
Documenta 7, Kassel.
Avanguardia Transavanguardia 68, 77, Mura Aureliane, Rome.
Zeitgeist," Internationalle Kunstaustellung, Berlin.
Chia, Cucci, Lichtenstein, Twombly, Sperone Westwater Fischer, New York.

1981

A New Spirit in Painting, Royal Academy of Arts, London.

1980
Artemisia, Institute of Contemporary Arts, London.

1977
Drawing Now - Zeichnung Heute, Staatliche Kunsthalle Baden-Baden, Baden-Baden; Graphische Sammling Albertina, Vienna.
Formen und Funktionen der Zetichnung in der sechziger und siebziger Jahren, Documenta 6, Kassel Galerie Art In Progress, Dusseldorf.

1976
Drawing Now, The Museum of Modern Art, New York.
Twentieth-Century American Drawing: Three Avant- Garde Generations, The Solomon R, Guggenheim Museum, New York.

1975
American Art Since 1945, Museum of Modern Art, New York, traveling exhibition.

1974
Contemporanea, Parcheggio di Villa Borghese, Rome.
Surrealitat-Bildrealitat 1924-1974, Stadtische Kunsthalle, Dusseldorf; Staatliche Kunsthalle Baden-Baden, Baden-Baden.

1973
Biennial Exhibition of Contemporary American Painting and Sculpture, Whitney Museum of American Art, New York.
American Drawings 1963-1973, Whitney Museum of American Art, New York.
New York Collection for Stockholm, Moderna Museet, Stockholm.

1971
The Structure of Color, Whitney Museum of American Art, New York.

1970
Contemporary Drawing Show, Fort Worth Art Center, Fort Worth.
Due Decenni di Eventi Artistici in Italia 1950-1970, Palazzo Pretorio, Prato.

1969
Annual Exhibition of Contemporary American Painting and Sculpture, Whitney Museum of American Art, New York.
Painting and Sculpture Today - 1969, Indianapolis Museum of Art, Finch College Museum of Art, New York.

American Painting: The 1960's, American Federation of Arts (travelling exhibitions).

1968
Sammlung Hahn, Wallraf-Richartz-Museum, Cologne.
Italienische Kunst des 20 Jahrhunderts, Kunsthalle Koln and Museum Bockum.
Sammlung 1968 Karl Stroher, Kunstverein Hamburg, Hamburg; Neue Nationalgalerie, Berlin; Kunsthalle Dusseldorf, Dusseldorf; Kunsthalle Bern, Bern.

1967
Annual Exhibition of Contemporary American Painting and Sculpture, Whitney Museum of American Art, New York.
Ten Years Leo Castelli, Leo Castelli Gallery, New York.

1966
Two Decades of American Painting, organized under the auspices of International Council of the Museum of Modern Art, New York.

1964
La Biennale di Venezia, XXXII Esposizione Internazionale d'Arte, Venice.
Galleria Nazionale d'Arte Moderna, Rome.
Contemporary Drawings, The Solomon R, Guggenheim Museum, New York.
Leo Castelli Gallery, New York.

1963
9 Europeische Kunstler, Haus am Waldsee, Berlin.
Schrift und Bild, Stedelijk Museum, Amsterdam.
Staatliche Kunsthalle Baden-Baden, Baden-Baden.
Leo Castelli Gallery, New York.

1962
Primio Marzotto, Marzotto.

Bibliography

2001
Johnson, K., "Coronation of Sesostris", review of Cy Twombly, *The New York Times*, January 19.
Saltz, J., "Solar Power", *Village Voice*, January 23, p 69.
Schwabsky, B.,"Coronation of Sesostris", review of Cy Twombly, *Artforum*, March, p. 142.

2000
"Twombly/Turner", *The New York Times Magazine*, May 28, p 42.
Catalogue Exhibition, *Cy Twombly – Coronation of Sesostris*, text by D. Shapiro, Gagosian Gallery, New York.

1999
Turner, J., review of Cy Twombly at the American Academy, *ARTnews*, January.

1998
Kuspit, D., review of Cy Twombly at Gagosian Gallery, *Artforum*, March, p. 96.

1997
Cy Twombly – Ten Sculptures, introduction by D. Sylvester, Gagosian Gallery, New York.
Catalogue Raisonné of Sculpture, *Cy Twombly (Volume I, 1946-1997)*, edited by N. Del Roscio, text by A. Danto.
Johnson, K., review of Cy Twombly at Gagosian Gallery, *The New York Times*, November 21.

1994
Schwab, C., "Returning to his Lexington Roots", *The News Gazette*, Lexington, October 12.
"Cy Twombly: A Retrospective", *Flash Art*, November - December, p. 31.
MacAdam, B.A., "Cy Twombly: Museum of Modern Art, Gagosian, C & M", *ARTnews*, December.

1989
Plagens, P., "Under Western Eyes", *Art in America*, January, pp. 33-41.
Schwabsky, B., "The Carnegie International", *Arts Magazine*, February, p. 10.
Baker, K., "Carnegie International", *Artforum*, March, pp. 138-139.
Rubinstein, M.R., review of Cy Twombly at Sperone Westwater, *ARTnews*, May, p. 158.
Yau, J., review of Cy Twombly at Sperone Westwater, *Contemporanea*, May, p 92.
Cy Twombly - Bolsena, introduction by H. Bastian, Gagosian Gallery, New York.

1988
Smith, R., "Art: Cy Twombly at Pace", *The New York Times*, Friday, January 22.
Gooding, M., "Cy Twombly – Whitemanesque Plenitude and Capacity for Self-Contradiction", *Flash Art International*, 139, March-April, p. 102-103.
Albertazzi, L., "Cy Twombly", *Contemporanea International*, May/June, p. 123.
Catalogue, La Biennale di Venezia, XLIII Esposizione Internazionale d'Arte, edited by Simonetta Rasponi, Gruppo Editoriale Fabbri, Venice, pp. 84-87.
Lewis, J., book review, "Cy Twombly - Paintings, Works on Paper, Sculpture", *Contemporanea International*, 1, 2, July-August, p. 117.
"Cy Twombly," *Bijutsu Techo*, October, 40, 600, pp. 218-219.

Madoff, S.H., "Venice Biennale: Calm Waters", *ARTnews*, 87, 7, September.
Templon, D., interviewed in *Flash Art News*, supplement to *Flash Art International*, October, 142.

1987
Szeeman, H., "Cy Twombly, Frank O'Hara and others", *Cy Twombly*, Zurich.
Schmidt, K., *Cy Twombly*, exhibition catalogue, Galerie Haus Seel, Kornmart, Seigen.

1986
Schwabsky, B., *Arts,.* 61, 1, September, p. 118.
Waterlow, N., *The Biennale of Sydney*, Sydney, 1986.
Museum of Contemporary Art, *Individuals, A Selected History of Contemporary Art 1945-1986*, essays by K. Linker, D. Kuspit, H. Foster, R.J. Onorato, G. Celant, A. Bonito Oliva, J.C. Welchman, T. Lawson, Los Angeles.

1985
Feinstein, R., "Cy Twombly's Eloquent Voice", *Arts*, January, 59, 5, cover and pp. 90-92.
Museum fur Moderne Kunst, *Bilder fur Frankfurt*, Frankfurt.
Bastian, H., *7000 Eichen*, Berlin.
Fuchs, R., *Ouverture*, Castello di Rivoli, Turin.
Bastian, H., *The Printed Graphic Work of Cy Twombly*, Munich and New York.

1984
Brenson, M., "Artists Choose Artists", *The New York Times*, June 15, p. 21.
C.A.P.C. Musee d'Art Contemporain de Bordeaux, *Cy Twombly*, Bordeaux.
Castello, M., "Il Tempo della foce", *Tema Celeste*, 2, year II, June, pp. 17-22.
Rosenblum, R., "Cy Twombly", *The Art of Our Time, The Saatchi Collection*, 2, London.

1983
Welish, M., essay "Cy Twombly", Stephen Mazoh Gallery, New York.
Lawson, C., review, *The New York Times*, April 22, p. 23.
Smith, R., "Backward versus Forward", *The Village Voice*, XXVIII, 21, May 24, p. 83.
Kuspit, D., "Zeitgeist: Art's attempt to give a spirit to the Times", *Vanguard*, 12, 4, May 12, pp. 20-23.
Glueck, G., "The Met Makes Room For the 20th Century", *The New York Times*, Sunday, September 18, Section 2, pp. 27, 30.

1982
Meyers, J.B., "Marks: Cy Twombly",

Artforum, XX, 8, April, pp. 50-57.
Groot, P., "The Spirit of Documenta 7", *FlashArt*, 109, International, Summer, pp. 20-25.
Cy Twombly; catalogue, Sperone Westwater Fischer, New York.
Cocuccioni, E., "Avantgarde-Transavantgarde", *FlashArt*, 109, November, pp. 70-71.
Fuchs, R.H., foreward, *Documenta 7*, Paul Dierichs GmbH & Co., Kassel.
Frackman, N., Kaufmann, "Documenta 7: The Dialogue and a Few Asides", *Arts Magazine*, 57, 2, October, pp. 91-97.
Ohff, H., "Sammlung Dr. Erich Marx: Beuys, Rauschenberg, Twombly, Warhol", Kunstwerk, 35, June, pp. 77-78.

1981
Joachimedes, C., Rosenthal, N., Serota, N., editors, *A New Spirit in Painting*, Royal Academy of Art, London.
Morgan, S., "Cold Turkey: 'A New Spirit in Painting,'at the Royal Academy of Art, London", *Artforum*, 19, 8, April, pp. 46-47.
Pohlen, A., "Review: Cy Twombly: Museum Haus Lange/Krefeld", *FlashArt*, 105, December - January, p. 59.
Storck, G., Introduction, *Cy Twombly: Skulpturen*, Museum Haus Lange, Krefeld.

1979
Blistene, B., "Cy Twombly: 'Fifty Days at Iliam'", *FlashArt*, 88-89, March-April, p. 31.
Barthes, R., catalogue, *Cy Twombly: Paintings and Drawings 1954-1977*, Whitney Museum of American Art, New York.
Lambert, Y., editor, *Cy Twombly: catalogue raissone des oeuvres sur papier, 1973-1976*, Multhipla, Milan.
Sheffield, M., "Cy Twombly: Major Changes in Space, Idea, Line", *Artforum*, May, pp. 40- 45.
Welish, M., "A Discourse on Twombly", *Art in America*, 67, 5, September, pp. 80-83.
Young, G., "The Cy Twombly Story", *The Figures*, Berkeley.
MacWilliam, D., "A Union of Sex and Sea: Cy Twombly", *Vanguard*, 8, 5, June/July, pp. 11-14.
Russell, J., "Art: Twombly Writ on Whitney Walls", *The New York Times*, April 13.

1978
Bastian, H., *Cy Twombly Bilder Paintings 1952-1976*, I, Propylaen, Berlin.

1977
Catalogue, Galerie Karsten Greve, Cologne, 1977.
Brundage, S., Reiring, J., editors, *Leo Castelli: Twenty Years*, Leo Castelli Gallery, New York.

1976
Pleynet, M., *Cy Twombly, Dessins 1954-1976*, Musee d'Art Moderne de la Ville de Paris. Bastian, H., *Cy Twombly*, Introduction by C.-A. Haenlein, Kestner-Gesellschaft Hannover.
Waldman, D., *Twentieth Century American Drawing: Three Avant-Garde Generations*, The Solomon Guggenheim Museum, New York.
Rose, B., *Drawing Now*, The Museum of Modern Art, New York; Kunsthaus Zurich; Staatliche Kunsthalle Baden-Baden.

1975
Cy Twombly: Paintings, Drawings, Constructions,1951-1974, essays by S. Delehanty and H. Bastian, Institute of Contemporary Art, University of Pennsylvania, and San Francisco Museum of Modern Art.
Bastian, H., *Cy Twombly - Grey Paintings*, Galerie Art in Progress, Munich.
Bastian, H., catalogue, Galerie Karsten Greve, Cologne.

1974
Pincus-Witten, R., "Cy Twombly", *Artforum*, April 1974, pp. 60-64.

1973
Bastian, H., *Cy Twombly Zeichnungen 1953-1973*, Propylaen Verlag, Berlin.
Huber, C., *Cy Twombly Bilder 1953-1972* (Forward by Carlo Huber and Michael Petzet),
Meyer, Franz and Heiner Bastian, *Cy Twombly Zeichnungen 1953-1973*, Kunstmuseum Basel.
Solomon, E.M., *American Drawings 1963-1973*, Whitney Museum of American Art, New York.
Contemporanea, essays by A. Bonito Oliva and others, Incontri Internazionali d'Arte, Rome.
de la Motte, M., "Cy Twombly", *Kunstforum*, 4/5, pp. 112-123.
"Zweischen Kunst und Leben: Cy Twombly im Basler Kunstmuseum", *Basler Volksblatt*, May 11.

1972
Baker, K., review of exhibition at Leo Castelli Gallery, *Artforum*, April, pp. 81-82.
Ratcliff, C., "The Whitney Annual", *Artforum*, April, pp. 28-32.
Robertson, B., "Cy Twombly at Castelli", *Art in America*, March - April, pp. 119-120.

1971
Kunst um 1970 - Art Around 1970, introduction by Wolfgang Becker, interview with Peter Ludwig, Sammlung Ludwig in Aachen; Neue Galerie der Stadt Aachen.

1970
Catalogue, Galerie Bonnier, Geneva.
Bott, G., Stroher, K., *Bildnerische Aukdrucksformen 1960-1970: Sammlung Karl Stroher*, catalogue, 4, Hessisches Landesmuseum, Darmstadt.

1969
Last, M., review of exhibition at Leo Castelli Gallery, *ARTnews*, January, p. 64.
Reuther, H., "Cy Twombly", *Das Kunstwerk*, February, pp. 42-45.

1968
Pincus-Witten, R., catalogue, *Learning to Write*, Milwaukee Art Center, Milwaukee.

1967
Whitney, D., editor, *Leo Castelli: Ten Years*, Leo Castelli Gallery, New York.
Catalogue, Galleria Notizie, Turin.

1966
Wember, P., catalogue, Stedelijk Museum, Amsterdam.
Brose, S., catalogue, Kunstverein Frieberg im Briesgau.
Gollin, J., review of exhibition at Leo Castelli Gallery, *ARTnews*, April, pp. 164-165.

1965
de la Motte, M., "Cy Twombly", *Art International*, June, pp. 32-35.

1964
Restany, P., excerpt from "Twombly, La Revolution du Signe", Catalogo 1, Galleria la Tartaruga, Rome.
Campbell, L., review of exhibition at Leo Castelli Gallery, *ARTnews*, May, p. 13.
Judd, D., review of exhibition at Leo Castelli Gallery, *Arts Magazine*, May, p. 38.

1963
Lonzi, C., catalogue, Galleria Notizie, Turin.
Catalogue, essays by F. O'Hara, P. Buccarelli, E. Villa, F. Marino, C. Vivaldi, M. de la Motte, G. Dorfles, P. Resany, Galleria la Tartaruga, Rome.
Mahlow, B., essay "Schrift und Bild", Stedelijk Museum, Amsterdam and Staatliche Kunsthalle Baden-Baden.

1962
Restany, P., essay, "Twombly, La Revolution du Signe", *Sculpture di Nevelson*.
Dorfles, G., "Le Immagini Scritte de Cy Twombly/Written images of Cy Twombly", *Metro*, 6, pp. 62-71.

1961
Restany, P., catalogue, *Twombly, La Revolution du Signe*, Galerie J., Paris.
Catalogue, Galerie Rudolf Zwirner, Cologne.
Vivaldi, C., "Cy Twombly: between irony and lyricism", *La Tartaruga*, February.

1960
Hayes, R., review of exhibition at Leo Castelli Gallery, *ARTnews*, December, p. 15.
Leonhard, K., "Stuttgarter Kunstbrief", *Das Kunstwerk*, July, p. 78.
Sawin, M., review of exhibition at Leo Castelli Gallery, *Arts Magazine*, November, p. 59.

1959
Gendel, M., "Recent Exhibition in Milan", *ARTnews*, January, p. 52.

1957
Sawin, M., review of exhibition at Stable Gallery, *Arts Magazine*, February, p. 57.

1953
Campbell, L., "Rauschenberg and Twombly", *ARTnews*, September, p. 50.

1951
Motherwell, R., *Notes on Cy Twombly*, catalogue, The Seven Stairs Gallery, Chicago.
Read, Prudence B., review of exhibition at Kootz Gallery, *ARTnews*, December, p. 48.

Salla Tykkä
1973, born in Helsinki.
Lives and works in Helsinki.

Solo Exhibitions
2001
Lasso, Delfina Project Space, London.

1999
Power, Studio Mezzo, Helsinki.

1997
Healthy Young Female, Helsinki.

Group Exhibitions

2001
Trans Sexual Express Barcelona, Barcelona.
La Biennale di Venezia, Venice.
Bida, Valencia.

2000
Master Degree Show, Helsinki.

1999
Beauty queens, Art Center Ahjo, Joensuu.

1998
ArtGenda Retro, Stadtgallerie Kiel, Kiel.
Intimacies, Rethymnon Centre for Contemporary Art, Greece

The Nude and the Masked, Helsinki City Art Museum, Helsinki.
ArtGenda, Kulturhuset Stockholm, Stockholm.

Bibliography

"Taru Elfving - Salla Tykkä - a healthy young female?", *Make - the magazine of women's art*, 90.
La Biennale di Venezia, Leevi Haapala, Vertical Loops and Propassions in Salla Tykkä's Lasso.
BIDA, Salla Tykkä, On Power and Control.

Keith Tyson
1969, born in Ulverston, Cumbria.
Lives and works in London.

Solo Exhibitions

2000
One of Each, Galerie Ursula Krinzinger, Vienna.
Studio Wall Drawings, Anthony Reynolds Gallery, London.

1999
Molecular Compound 4, Kleineshelmhaus, Zurich.
Delfina, London.

1997
ICA/Toshiba Art and innovation Award Exhibition.
Galerie Georges Philippe Vallois, Paris.
Anthony Reynolds Gallery, London.

1996
David Zwirner Gallery, New York.

1995
From the Artmachine, Anthony Reynolds Gallery, London.

Group Exhibitions

2001
2nd Berlin Biennale, Berlin.
The Fantastic Recurrence of Certain Situations: Recent British Art and Photography, Sala De Exposiciones Del Canal De Isabel II, Madrid.
Makeshift, University of Brighton Gallery, Brighton.
Out of Line, Arts Council Touring exhibition, UK.
A B See D, Anthony Reynolds Gallery, London.

2000
Media_city Seoul 2000, Seoul.
The British Art Show (national touring exhibition organised by the Hayward Gallery), Edinburgh and tour to Southampton, Cardiff and Birmingham.
Domestic Pairs Projects, Kunsthaus, Glarus.
Over the Edges, Stedelijk Museum voor Actuele Kunst, Ghent.
Dream Machines, National Touring Exhibition Programme (Hayward Gallery) and tour to Dundee Contemporary Arts, Dundee.

1999
Seeing Time: Selections from the Pamela and Richard Kramlich Collection of Media Art, San Francisco Museum of Modern Art.

1998
Nerve, Nash Room, ICA, London.
Il luogo degli angeli, San Michele and Museo Laboratorio, San Angelo touring to Lucca.
Holding Court, Entwistle Gallery, London.
It's a curse, it's a burden, The approach, London.
Klink Klank, H.M.S. Plymouth, Birkenhead.
Diving for Pearls, H.M.S. Onyx, Birkenhead.
U.K Maximum Diversity, Bregenz.
Show me the money, 8 Dukes Mews, London.
Bad Faith, 3 months gallery, Liverpool.
What's in a Name?, Anthony Reynolds Gallery, London.

1997
Sarah Stone's Truly Supastore, Cornerhouse, Manchester.
Municipal Gallery of Rethymnon, Crete.
Private Face-Urban Space, Gasworks, Athens; L. Kanakakis.
Fondazione Sandretto Re Rebaudengo per l'Arte, Turin.
Low Maintenace & High Precision, Hales and 127 Deptford High Street, Lewisham.
Dissolution, Laurent Delaye, London.

1996
Art and Innovation Shortlist Exhibition, Institute of Contemporary Arts, London.
Superstore Deluxe, UP & Co., New York.
Monsieur ma conscience, Friche Belle de Mai, Marseilles.
On a Clear Day..., Cambridge Dark Room, First Site, Focal Point,
John Hansard Gallery, ICA, Middlesborough Art Gallery.
Replicators, http:// adaweb.com.
Madame ma conscience, Galerie Georges-Philippe Vallois, Paris.
In Passing, The Tannery, London.
Disneyland After Dark, Kunstamt Kreuzberg/Bethanien.
White Hysteria, Contemporary Art Centre of South Australia.
Surfing Systems, Kasseler Kunstverein, Kassel and tour.
Pandemonium, Institute of Contemporary Art, London.

1995
Night and Day, Anthony Reynolds Gallery, London.
Disneyland After Dark, Uppsala Konstmuseum, Uppsala.
Institute of Cultural Anxiety, Institute of Contemporary Art, London.

1994
Streamer Mute, Pilot Edition, p IV, V, Winter.
Anthony Reynolds Gallery, London.
Untitled Streamer Eddy Monkey FullStop Etcetera.

1993
Spit in the Ocean, Anthony Reynolds Gallery, London.
The Observatory, Anthony Reynolds Gallery, London.
The Space Between, Gallery Fortlaan 17, Gent.

1990
Passive Voyeurs, Stanwicks Theatre Complex, Carlisle.

Bibliography

2001
Withers, R., "Keith Tyson", *Artforum*, April.
2nd Berlin Biennale, text by K. Tyson, Berlin.
Makeshift, text by D. Green, University of Brighton Gallery.

1999
Spellbook: describing the creation of magic items, by K. Tyson.
Media_city Seoul 2000, text by J. Millar.
Buck, L, *Moving Targets 2: A User's Guide to British Art Now*, Tate Publishing.
One of Each, text by K. Tyson, Galerie Ursula Krinzinger, Vienna.
The British Art Show, exhibition catalogue.
Over the Edges, Stedelijk Museum voor Actuele Kunst, Ghent.
Dream Machines, exhibition catalogue, text by S. Hiller and J. Fisher.
Keith Tyson, exhibition catalogue, text by J. Millar and K. Bush, Delfina, London.
Molecular Compound 4, text by K. Tyson.
Seeing Time: Selections from the Pamela and Richard Kramlich Collection of Media Art, text by C. Iles, Museum of Modern Art, San Francisco.
Archer, M., "Keith Tyson", *Art Monthly*, 230, October.
Craddock, S., "Decisions, Decisions", *Untitled*, 19, Summer.
Hall, J., "Keith Tyson", *Artforum*, Summer.
Morrissey, S., "Keith Tyson", *Contemporary Visual Arts*, 23.
Gellatly, A., "It's a curse, it's a burden", *Frieze*, 45, March-April.

1998
Il luogo degli angeli, San Michele and Museo Laboratorio, San Angelo.
Beech, D., "AnotherTyson Ear Bending", *everything*, 2:3.

1997
Private Face-Urban Space, Gasworks, Athens; L. Kanakakis.
Fondazione Sandretto Re Rebaudengo per l'Arte, Turin.
Bush, K., "Keith Tyson", published in *Guarene Arte 97* catalogue, Ed. Fondazione Sandretto Re Rebaudengo per l'Arte.
Burrows, D., "Low Maintenance & High Precision", *Art Monthly*, September.
Beech, D., "Keith Tyson", *Art Monthly*, June.

1996
On a Clear Day..., Cambridge Darkroom.
Surfing Systems, Kasseler Kunstverein, Kassel.
Buck, L., "Silver Scene", *Artforum*.

1995
Disneyland After Dark, Uppsala Konstmuseum, Uppsala.
Morgan, S., "the future's not what it used to be", *Frieze*, March/April, 21.
Grant, S., "Institute of Cultural Anxiety", *Art Monthly*, February.
"Around the Compendium in 54 Aphorisms, (Including Jokers)", *Mute*, 1. Spring.

1993
"Streamer" - continuous text and illustration sequence running through exhibitions, magazines, internet, etc.

Eulàlia Valldosera
1963, born in Vilafranca del Penedès, Barcelona.
Lives and works in Barcellona.

Solo Exhibitions

2001
EulàliaValldosera. Obres 1990-2000, Fundació Antoni Tàpies, Barcelona.

2000
EulàliaValldosera, Works 1990-2000, Witte de With, Rotterdam.
Still Life, Galeria Joan Prats, Barcelona.
Arco '00, Still Life, Project Rooms, Galería Helga de Alvear (Madrid), Galeria Joan Prats (Barcelona), Madrid.

1999
Provisional Home, Kusthalle Lophem, Bruges.

Eulàlia Valldosera, Musee d'Art Contemporain de Montreal, Montreal.
Les Demoiselles de Valence, Musee de Valence and Art 3, Valence.

1998
Habitación, Galería Helga de Alvear, Madrid.
Aparences, Visions de Futur '98, Aliança Francesa, Sabadell.
Eulàlia Valldosera, Galería Visor, Valencia.
Artl29, Relationships, Statements, Galería Helga de Alvear (Madrid), Basel.

1997
La caiguda, Metrònom, Barcelona.

1996
Aparences, El Roser, Lleida.

1995
Apparenze, Galleria Gentili, Florence.

1994
Palma 19, Galería Palma Dotze, Vilafranca del Penedès, Barcelona.

1992
Vendajes, Cicle Tangents. Entorn a la performance. Sala Montcada, Fundació "la Caixa", Barcelona.
Burns, Bandages, Galerie van Rijsbergen, Rotterdam.

1991
Et melic del món, Galería Antoni Estrany, Barcelona.

Group Exhibitions

2000
Scéne de la vie conjugale, Ville Arson, Nice.
Expo Hannover 2000, Arte en el Pabellòn, Pabellòn de España, Hannover.
Col.lecció, Noves incorporacions, Museu d'Art Contemporani de Barcelona (MACBA), Barcelona.

1999
Zetwenden, Ausblick. Künstler blicken ins nächtste Jahrtausend, Kunstmuseum, Bonn.
Cuerpos contaminados, Fundación Alejandro Otero, Caracas.
Futuropresente, Pràcticas artísticas en el cambio de milenio, Sala de Exposiciones de la Plaza de España, Madrid.
La casa, il corpo, il cuore, Konstruktion der Identitäten, *Museum moderner Kunst Stiftung Ludwig*, Vienna.

1998
Transgenéric@s Koldo Mitxelena, San Sebastián.
El punto ciego, Spanische Kunst der 90er,

Kunstraum Innsbruck, Innsbruck.
Scattered Affinities, Apex Art C.P., New York.
Biennale de l'image Paris 98: De très court-sespaces de temps, Centre National de la Photographie (CNP), École Nationale Supérieure des Beux-Arts (Ensba), Paris.
Côté Sud... Entschuldigung, Institut d'Art Contemporain/Nouveau Musée, Villeurbanne, Lyon.
The Campaign Against Living Miserably, Royal College of Art Galleries, London.
Places in Gothenburg, Göteborgs stads kulturförvalthing, Gothenburg.

1997
2nd Johannesburg Biennale, Trade Routes, Newton, Johannesburg.
5th Biennale of Istanbul, On Life, Beauty, Translations and other difficulties, Istanbul.
Connexiones Implicites, École Nationale Supérieure des Beaux-Arts (Ensba), Paris.
Truce: Echoes of Art in an Age of Endless Conclusions, SITE, Santa Fe.
Skulptur Projekte in Münster 1997, Münster.

1996
10th Biennale of Sydney, Jurassic Technologies Revenant, Sydney.
Manifesta 1, Kunsthal, Rotterdam.

1995
1rst Kwang-ju Biennale '95, Beyond the Borders, Museum of Contemporary Art, Kwang-ju, South Korea.
Herejías/Heresies: Crítica de los mecanismos, Centro Atlántico de Arte Moderno (CAAM), Las Palmas de Gran Canaria.

1994
Mudanzas, Whitechapel Art Gallery, London.
Anys 90. Distància Zero, Centre d'Art Santa Mònica, Barcelona.

1993
Di volta in volta, Castello di Rivara, Turin.

1992
Hospital: Human Material, *W'139*, Amsterdam.
Interferenzen IV: Performance-intermedia, Museum moderner Kunst Stiftung Ludwig, Vienna.
In Vitro, KRTU, Fundaciò Joan Miró, Barcelona.

1991
Historias de Amor, Fragmentos de un discurso artístico, Ateneo Mercantil, Valencia.

Bibliography

2001

Eulàlia Valldosera. Obres 1990-2000, Rotterdam: Witte de With; Barcelona: Fundació Antoni Tàpies.
Eulàlia Valldosera. Works 1990-2000, Rotterdam: Witte de With; Barcelona: Fundació Antoni Tàpies.

2000
"Eulàlia Valldosera", *Zoo*, 7, London.
ArteVisión. Una historia del arte elecrónico en España (CD-Rom Español-English), ed. C. Giannetti, MECAD (Media Centre d'Art i Disseny), Sabadell, Barcelona.
Eulàlia Valldosera, On mirrors, control and trust, 4 práticas delante del espejo, Art 3 and Galeria Joan Prats, Barcelona.
Still Life, Eulàlia Valldosera, Una intervención en la Galeria Joan Prats, edited by E. Valldosera, H. Tatay Huici, Galeria Joan Prats, Barcelona.
Valldosera, E., "Provisional Home", *Quaderns d'arquitectura i urbanisme: L'íntim, L'intime*, 226, Col.legi d'Arquitectes de Catalunya, Barcelona.
Pérez, L.F., "Eulàlia Valldosera", *Lápiz*, 162.
Lorés, M., "Still Life, Eulàlia Valldosera: an intervention in the Galeria Joan Prats", *Contemporary Visual Arts*, 29.

1999
Zeitwenden-Ausblick, Global Art Rheinland 2000, ed. Ronte, D., DuMont Buchverlag and Kunstmuseum Bonn, Cologne.
La casa, il corpo, il cuore. Konstruktion der Identitäten, Museum moderner Kunst. Stiftung Ludwig, Vienna.
Valldosera, E., *Changing the System? Artists talk about their practice. A Discussion Event in Rotterdam, April 1999*, ed. NIFCA, Helsinki.
Transportable, ed. Chantal Grander, Tinglado 2, Tarragona.
Alvarez-Reyes, J.A., "Eulalia Valldosera, Iluminar habitando las esquinas", *El punto ciego, arte español de los años 90*, Universidad de Salamanca, Kunstraum Innsbruck, Junta de Castilla y León.
Reindl, U.M., "Eulalia Valldosera", *Mode of Art*, Verlag des Kunstvereins fur die Rheinlande und Westfalen, Düsseldorf.
Fora de camp, Set itineraris per l'audiovisual català dels anys 60 als 90, ed. Corominas, A., Espelt, R., KRTU and Generalitat de Catalunya, Departament de Cultura.
Valldosera, E., "El tocador (The Dressing Table)", *Nuevas visiones/Nuevas pasiones, Seis artistas de la colección Helga de Alvear en Villa Iris*, Fundación Marcelino Botín, Santander.
Vonna, K., "Eulàlia Valldosera", *Manifesto - Côté Sud... Entschuldigung*, Institut d'Art Contemporain/Nouveau Musée, Villeurbanne.

Engulta Mayo, N., "Afinidades dispersas. Ciencia-ficción, fantasía y otros desplazamientos", *Afinidades dispersas*, ed. Benlloch P., Enguita, N., Fundación Telefónica, Madrid.
Grant Marchand, S., *Eulalia Valldosera*, Musee d'Art Contemporain de Montreal, Montreal.
Lamarche, B., "Effet cinéma. L'espagnole Valldosera et ses projections lumineuses", *Le Devoir*, February 27.

1998
Martínez, R., "Entrevista con Eulàlia Valldosera", *Atlántica*, 2, Centro Atlántica de Arte Moderno, Las Palmas de Gran Canaria.
Ribalta, J., "Fotografische Schau-Stücke", *Zetgenössische Fotografie aus Spanien. Contemporary Photography from Spain, Canogar, Fontcuberta, Palacín, Valldosera, Vallhonrat*, Galería Helga de Alvear, Galerie Wolfgang Gmyrek, Madrid-Düsseldorf.
Martínez, R., "Eulàlia Valldosera", *Cream. 10 curators, 10 writers, 100 artists. Contemporary art in culture*, Phaidon Press Limited, London.
Transgenéric@s, ed. Juan Aliaga, Mar Villaespesa, Gipuzkoako Foru Aldundia, Disputación Foral de Gipuzkoa.
Cómo nos vemos. Imágenes y arquetipos femeninos, ed. Victoria Combalia, Tecla Sala, Ajuntament de l'Hospitalet, Barcelona.
De la Nuez, I., "Eulàlia Valldosera, El mapa, els somnis, les ombres i el cos del món", *Mar de Fondo*, ed. Rosa Martínez, Direcció General de Promoció Cultural, Museus i Belles Arts, Valencia.
González-Alegre, A., "Pasar quien sabe si tranquilamente, por un muro de pronombres, por un barullo de banderas", *Fisuras na Percepción*, 25 *Biennal de Arte de Pontevedra*, Deputacion Provincial de Pontevedra, Pontevedra.
Impasse. Art, poder i societat a l'Estat Espanyol, Biennal d'Art Leandre Cristòfol, Centre d'Art La Panera, Lleida.
Llorca, P., "La cicatriz interior", *La cicatriz interior*, Consejería de Educación y Cultura de la Comunidad de Madrid, Madrid.
Valldosera, E., "The Room", *Places in Gothenburg*, Göteborgs stads kulturförvaltning, Gothenburg.
Ashtey-Miller, B., "Eulàlia Valldosera", *The Campaign against living miserably*, Royal College of Art, London.
Pérez, L.F., "Estrategias del deseo", *Lápiz*, 145.
Bourne, C., "Eulalia Valldosera", *De tres courts espaces de temps. Biennale de l'image Paris 98*, Centre National de la Photographie, Paris; Actes Sud, Aries.
Daho, M., *De imagen y soportes. 45 Salón*

Internacional de fotografía, Caja de Asturias - Palacio de Revillagigedo, Oviedo.
Huesca imagen, Caja de Asturias, Oviedo.
Miquel Garcia, J., "Eulàlia Valldosera", *Coincidències*, Museum Dhondt-Dhaenens, Deurle.
Valldosera, E., "A symbolic action", *5th International Istanbul Biennial*, Istanbul Foundation for Culture and Arts, Istanbul.
Brignone, P., "Les madones au liquide vaiselle: Eulàlia Valldosera", *Omnibus Journal d'Art*, 23.

1997
Marzo J.-L., "Eulàlia Valldosera", *5th International Istanbul Biennial*, 1, edited by Rosa Martínez, Istanbul Foundation for Culture and Arts, Istanbul.
Trade Routes, History and Geography, 2nd Johannesburg Biennial, ed. Matthew Debord.
Valldosera, E., "La calguda", *Metronom (1997-1998)*, Fundació Rafael Tous d'Art Contemporani, Barcelona.
Valldosera, E., "Aparences", *Metronom (1996-1997)*, Fundació Rafael Tous d'Art Contemporani, Barcelona.
As large as life, ed. Anton Lederer, Margarethe Makovec, Raum für Kunst, Kunstforderungsverein.
Lamaison, P., "Des trous dans le reel", *Connexions implicites*, Ecole Nationale Superieure des Beaux-Arts, Paris.
Leandre Cristòfol, Biennal d'Art Lleida, ed. Glòria Picazo, Ajuntament de Lleida, Centre d'Art de la Panera, Lleida.
Valldosera, E., "Twilight zone", *Sculpture. Projects in Münster 1997*, ed. Klaus Bußmann, Kasper König, Florian Matzner, Verlag Gerd Hatje, Stuttgart.
Luces, camara, acción (...) ¡Corten! Videoacción: el cuerpo y sus fronteras, IVAM, Valencia.
TRUCE: Echoes of Art in an Age of Endless Conclusions, SITE, Santa Fe.
La imagen convincente, Estudio Helga de Alvear, Madrid.
Martínez, R., "Eulàlia Valldosera", *Flash Art*, 30, 196.
Valldosera, E., "Arrivals... Fondness for the phone", *Zingmagazine*, Summer.
Llorca, P., "Eulàlia Valldosera: El Roser", *Artforum*, 36, 9.

1996
Art Espanyol per a la fi de segle, ed. Victoria Combalia, Tecla Sala, Ajuntament d'Hospitalet, Barcelona.
Valldosera, E., "Projection, The Fall. Two linked projects for manifests", *Manifesta 1*, Foundation European Art Manifestation, Rotterdam.
Cooke, L., "Embodiments", and Bobka, V., "Eulalia Valldosera", *10th Biennale of*

Sydney: Jurassic Technologies Revenant, Biennale of Sydney, Sidney.
Aparences / Appearances, Jorge-Luis Marzo, Eulàlia Valldosera, J. Lebrero Stals, Lynne Cooke, Rosa Martínez. Ed. Eulàlia Valldosera, El Roser, Ajuntament de Lleida, Lleida.
Sin número Arte de Acción, Círculo de Bellas Artes, Madrid.
Martínez, R., *Thinking of you. A selection of contemporary art*, Konsthallen Göteborg, Gothenburg.

1995
Enguita, N., *Estación de Transito*, Club Diario Levante, Institut Valencià de la Dona, Valencia.
Apariencias, ed. E. Valldosera, Gentili, Florence.
Valldosera, E., "Palma 19", *La Llum*, Palma Dotze, Ajuntament de Vilafranca, Barcelona.
Montornès, F., *Grønne Gnister, Journeys from a common place*, Charlottenborg, Copenhagen.
Valldosera, E., "Dominios", *Herejías / Heresies, Crítica de los mecanismos*, ed. Jorge-Luis Marzo, Centro Atlántico de Arte Moderno, Las Palmas de Gran Canaria.
Allen, J., "El yo multiple. Visiones multimedia de la representación", *Atlántica. Revista de las Artes*, 11, Centro Atlántico de Arte Moderno, Las Palmas de Gran Canaria.
Beyond the Borders. Kwang-ju Biennale, Kwang-ju Biennale Foundation, Seoul.
Biennale Mladih - Rijeka 1995, Rijeka: Moderna galerija Rijeka, 1995.
Scarpini, A., "Eulàlia Valldosera", *Flash Art*, 193.
Combalia, V., "Eulàlia Valldosera. Corps indigne et trascendant", *Art Press*, 201.
Picazo, G., "Die fotografische Dimension. Inszenierungsstrategien I: Das Subjekt, Das Objekt. Fotografie als Mittel der Selbstdarstellung in der Spanischen Kunst", *Kunstforum International*, 129.

1994
Perez, L.F., "Los silencios del cuerpo", *Los 90: Cambio de marcha en el arte español*, ed. J.L. Brea, Galerfa Juana Mordó, Madrid.
Marzo, J.-L., "Ventriloquías", *Anys noranta. Distància 0.*, Centre d'Art Santa Monica, Generalitat de Catalunya, Barcelona.
Biennal 1994. Jovens criadores da Europa e do Mediterraneo, Clube Portugues Artes e Ideias, Lisbon.
Territorios indefinidos, Museo de Arte Contemporáneo, Elche; Institut de Cultura Juan-Gil Albert, Alicante.
Valldosera, E., "Tres objetos para un lavabo y una foto", Jan Sennema, "La marca de la

bestia", *Becas de creación artística Banesto*, Fundación Cultural Banesto, Madrid.
Combalia, V., Valldosera, E., "Eulàlia Valldosera", *3a Biennal Martínez Guerricabeitia*, Servei d'Extensió Universitaria. Universitat de València, València.

1993
Valldosera, E., "La mirada vertical", *El Blanc Negre*, Balmes 21, Universidad de Barcelona, Barcelona.
Members only, ed. Ruth Turner and Lola Estrany, Galeria Caries Poy, Barcelona.

1992
Valldosera, E., "Embenatges (Bandages)", *7 performances*, videocatalogue, min. 17.55-25.30. Ciclo Tangents. Sala Montcada, Fundación "La Caixa", Barcelona.
Valldosera, E., "Bandagen", *Interferenzen IV. Performance-intermedia*, Museum Moderner Kunst Stiftung Ludwig, Vienna.
Valldosera, E., "Fotograffas", *Muestra de Arte Joven*, Ministerio de Cultura, Madrid.
Combalía, V., "1992: la nouvelle generation espagnole", *Art Press*, 166.
Perez, L.F., "Eulàlia Valldosera: Estrany, Barcelona", *Flash Art*, 25, 162.

1991
Valldosera, E., "El ombligo del mundo", Combalía, V., "Eulàlia Valldosera: el cuerpo como metáfora", *Historias de Amor. Fragmentos para un discurso artístico*, Instituto de la Juventud, Generalitat Valenciana, Valencia.
Biennal de Joves Creadors '91, Ajuntament de Barcelona, Barcelona.
Valldosera, "El melic del món", *In Vitro*, Fundación Joan Miró, KRTU, Generalitat de Catalunya, Barcelona.

Minnette Vári
1968, brn in Pretoria.
Lives and works in Johannesburg, South Africa.

Solo Exhibitions

2001
Minnette Vári, Serge Ziegler Galerie, Zurich.

1998
Beyond the Pale, Invited and supported by the French Institute of South Africa, Galerie d'Alliance Française, Johannesburg.

1994
Minnette Vári, Centurion Art Gallery, Centurion, South Africa.

1992
Painting and Language, FIG Gallery, Johannesburg.

Group Exhibitions

2001
Rest and Motion, cdited by K. Smith, Oudtshoorn National Arts Festival, Oudtshoorn, South Africa.
Short Stories, cdited by R. Pinto and curatorial team: V. Kortun, A. Poshyananda, A. Pasternak, E. Valdés Figueroa, La fabbrica del vapore, Milan.
In and Around, cdited by E. Valdés Figueroa, MAK Center, Los Angeles.

2000
Memórias Intimas Marcas, cdited by F. Alvim, Museum van Hedendaagse Kunst Antwerpen (MUHKA); Museu da Cidade, Lisbon, Portugal.
South Meets West, cdited by B. Fibicher, Y. Konaté, Y. Vera, Kunsthalle Bern; National Museum, Accra.
Johannesburg, cdited by C. Kellner for *Atmosfere Metropolitane*, co-ordinated by R. Pinto, Openspace, Milan.

1999
Towards-Transit, cdited by R. Fischer, S. Ziegler Gallery, Zurich.
FNB Vita Art Prize exhibition, Sandton Civic Art Gallery, Johannesburg.
Channel, cdited by R. Weinek and G. Smith, Association of Visual Arts, Cape Town.
Dialog 1: Vice Verses, residency with S. Jirkuff, E. Raidel and T. Rose, cdited by C. Kellner, O.K. Centre of Contemporary Art, Linz.

1998
Demokratins Bilder / Democracy's Images: Photography And Visual Art After Apartheid, cdited by R. Bester, K. Pierre, J.-E. Lundström, Bildmuseet, Umeå.

1997
Transversions, cdited by Y. Yeon Kim for *Trade Routes: History and Geography, the 1997 Johannesburg Biennale*, Museum Africa, Newtown, Johannesburg.
Purple and Green, cdited by A. Fourie, The Pretoria Art Museum.
Photosynthesis: Contemporary South African Photography, cdited by K. Grundling, Standard Bank National Arts Festival, Grahamstown; Standard Bank Gallery, Johannesburg; The South African National Gallery, Cape Town.
Purity and Danger, cdited by P. Siopis, Wits Art Gallery, Johannesburg.
Zone, With J. Brundrit, J. Ractliffe and M. Tosoni, The Generator Art Space, Africus

Institute of Contemporary Art, Newtown, Johannesburg.

1996
Hitch-Hiker, cdited by C. Kellner, The Generator Art Space, Africus Institute of Contemporary Art, Newtown, Johannesburg.
Colours: Kunst aus Sudafrika, cdited by S. Vogel, A. Hug, The House of World Cultures, Berlin.
FNB Vita Art Now 1995 award exhibition, Johannesburg Art Gallery.
The Way West, Two person show with Anton Karstel, Newtown Galleries, Newtown, Johannesburg.
Unplugged, Project initiated by K. Geers, The Rembrandt van Rijn Gallery, Newtown, Johannesburg.

1995
Primavera en Chile / Springtime in Chile, Museo de Arte Contemporaneo, Santiago.
The Laager, Fringe exhibition at *Africus Biennial*, Newtown Cultural Precinct, Johannesburg.
Uncommon Thread, Five artists from South Africa, Britain and Zimbabwe, Fringe exhibition at Africus Biennial, The Civic Gallery, Johannesburg.

1994
FNB Vita Art Now 1993 award exhibition, Johannesburg Art Gallery.

Bibliography

2001
El Arte Que Viene / The Art To Come, Paco Barragán, Subastas, Madrid.

2000
Kerkham, R., "A deadly explosive on her tongue", *Thrird Text*, Spring.

1999
Grey Areas, Representation, Identity and Politics in Contemporary South African Art, edited by B. Atkinson and C. Breitz, Chalkham Hill Press, Johannesburg.

1998
Atkinson, B., "Morphing Minnette", *Electronic Mail & Guardian*, http://www.artthrob. co.za, November 24.
Williamson, S., "Artbio", *Artthrob*, 7, http://www.artthrob.co.za.

1997
Gendered Visions, The Art of Contemporary Africana Women Artists, edited by S.M. Hassan, Africa World Press, Trenton, New York.

1996
Art in South Africa, The Future Present, Sue

Williamson and Ashraf Jamal, David Philip Publishers, Cape Town.

1992
GIF 1, book of original prints, The Artists' Press and FIG Gallery, Johannesburg.

Francesco Vezzoli
1971, born in Brescia.
Lives and works in Milan.

Solo Exhibitions

2001
Francesco Vezzoli, cdited by D. Cameron, New Museum of Contemporary Art, New York.

2000
Francesco Vezzoli: A Love Trilogy, cdited by D. Eccher, Modern Art Gallery, Bologna.

1999
Francesco Vezzoli, Anthony d'Offay Gallery, Londra.
Francesco Vezzoli: An Embroidered Trilogy, cdited by P. Colombo, Centre d'Art Contemporain, Geneva.
Francesco Vezzoli: An Embroidered Trilogy, cdited by C. Perrella, The British School at Rome.
Francesco Vezzoli: An Embroidered Trilogy, Gio' Marconi Galleria, Milan.

Group Exhibitions

2001
SurFace, cdited by P. Kyande, Lunds Konsthall, Lund.
Squatters, cdited by Vincente Todoli, Museum Serralves, Porto.
La Biennale di Venezia, 49. Esposizione Internazionale d'Arte, Venice. cdited by H. Szeemann.
The Tirana Biennal, cdited by H. Kontova. Tirana.
Magic and Loss Contemporary Italian Video, cdited by C. Perrella, LUX Center, London.
Remedy for Melancholy, Edsvic Art, Sollentuna - Baltic Art Center, Visby, Sweden.

2000
Migrazioni e Multiculturalità cdited by P. Colombo, Premio per la Giovane Arte Italiana, New Temporary Contemporary Art Center, Rome.
Group Show, Anthony d'Offay Gallery, London.
Art & Facts, Franco Noero Galleria, Turin. Curata da Mariuccia Casadio.

1999
EXIT, Chisenhale Gallery, Londra.

6th International Istanbul Biennal, cdited by P. Colombo, Istanbul, Turkey. *Videodrome*, cdited by D. Cameron, New Museum of Contemporary Art, New York.

1998
Fast Forward: Indipendent Italian Films and Videos, Brown University, Providence - ICA, Boston.

1997
Made in Italy (Video program), cdited by P. Colombo, Centre d'Art Contemporain, Geneva - ICA, London.

Bibliography

2000
Corbetta, C., "Francesco Vezzoli", *NU: The Nordic art Review*, II, 6/2000.
Casadio, M., "A matter of needle point", *Vogue Italia*, 604, 12/2000.
Gioni, M., Kontova, H., "Francesco Vezzoli: Foto di Gruppo con Signora" (In conversation), *Flash Art*, 224, October-November. (cover)
Maraniello, G., "Mani di Fata: Francesco Vezzoli e l'Arte del Ricamo", *Flash Art*, 224, October-November.
O'Neill, L., "Francesco Vezzoli", *Vogue Hommes International*, 8, Fall-Winter.
Maraniello, G., "Francesco Vezzoli", *Espresso: Art Now in Italy*, Electa.
Casadio, M., "Golden & Sour", *Vogue Italia*, January.
Casadio, M., "Embroidered", *Vogue Italia*, February.
Flood, R., "Opening: Francesco Vezzoli", *Artforum*, March.

1999
Perrella, C., "Francesco Vezzoli", *6th International Istanbul Biennal*, exhibition catalogue.
Beatrice, L., "Ouverture: Francesco Vezzoli", *Flash Art International*, October.
Vallora, M., "Tra Zanicchi e Valeri, gli scherzi di Vezzoli", *La Stampa*, June 7.
Guiliani, F., "Un Superkolossal in dieci Minuti", *La Repubblica*, May 25.
Cravel, P.F., "Divine & Divani", *L'Uomo Vogue*, Autumn.

Bill Viola
1951, born in New York.
Lives and works in Long Beach (California).

Solo Exhibitions

2001
Bill Viola: Five Angels for the Millennium, Anthony d'Offay Gallery, London.

2000

The World of Appearances, Helaba Main Tower, Frankfurt (permanent installation).
Bill Viola: New Work, James Cohan Gallery, New York.

1997
Bill Viola: Fire, Water, Breath, Guggenheim Museum (SoHo), New York.
Bill Viola: A 25-Year Survey, organized by the Whitney Museum of American Art. Travelling to Los Angeles County Museum of Art; Whitney Museum of American Art, New York (1998) ; Stedelijk Museum, Amsterdam (1998) (catalogue); Museum für Moderne Kunst, Frankfurt, (1999); San Francisco Museum of Modern Art, California (1999); Art Institute of Chicago, Illinois (1999-2000).

1996
Bill Viola: New Work, Savannah College of Art and Design, Savannah, Georgia (installation).
Bill Viola: The Messenger, Durham Cathedral, *Visual Arts UK 1996*, Durham. Travelling to South London Gallery, London (1996); Video Positiva-Moviola, Liverpool; The Fruitmarket Gallery, Edinburgh; Oriel Mostyn, Gwynedd; The Douglas Hyde Gallery, Trinity College, Dublin (1997).

1995
Buried Secrets, United States Pavilion, The Venice Biennale, 46th Esposizione Internazionale d'Arte, Venice. Travelling to Kestner-Gesellschaft, Hannover.

Group Exhibitions

2001
Bill Viola: Five Angels for the Millennium, Anthony d'Offay Gallery, London.

2000
The World of Appearances, Helaba Main Tower, Frankfurt (permanent installation).
Bill Viola: New Work, James Cohan Gallery, New York.

1997
Bill Viola: Fire, Water, Breath, Guggenheim Museum (SoHo), New York.
Bill Viola: A 25-Year Survey, organized by the Whitney Museum of American Art (catalogue). Travelling to Los Angeles County Museum of Art; Whitney Museum of American Art, New York (1998) ; Stedelijk Museum, Amsterdam (1998) (catalogue); Museum für Moderne Kunst, Frankfurt, (1999); San Francisco Museum of Modern Art, California (1999); Art Institute of Chicago, Illinois (1999-2000).

1996
Bill Viola: New Work, Savannah College of

Art and Design, Savannah, Georgia (installation).
Bill Viola: The Messenger, Durham Cathedral, *Visual Arts UK*, Durham. Travelling to South London Gallery, London (1996); Video Positiva-Moviola, Liverpool; The Fruitmarket Gallery, Edinburgh; Oriel Mostyn, Gwynedd; The Douglas Hyde Gallery, Trinity College, Dublin (1997).

1995
Buried Secrets, United States Pavilion, La Biennale di Venezia, 46. Esposizione Internazionale d'Arte, Venice, travelling to Kestner-Gesellschaft, Hannover, Germany (1995); University Art.

Screening

2000
Déserts, music by Edgard Varèse, performed live by the BBC Symphony Orchestra at the Barbican Centre, London, England.

1999
Déserts, music by Edgard Varèse, performed live by Los Angeles Philharmonic conducted by E.-P. Salonen at the Hollywood Bowl, Los Angeles, California.

1994
Premier screening of 35 mm film *Déserts*, at *Wien Modern*, with live performance of composition Déserts by Edgard Varèse, performed by Ensemble Modern, conductor Peter Eötvös, October 23, Konzerthaus Wien, Vienna.

Bibliography

1997
Bill Viola, exhibition catalogue with contributions by L. Hyde, K. Perov, D.A. Ross, B. Viola, Whitney Museum of American Art, in association with Flammarion, Paris. New York; German Language edition, Cantz.

1995
Bill Viola: Buried Secrets, exhibition catalogue edited by M. Zeitlin, with texts by C. Haenlein, S. Kalil, B. Viola, Arizona University Art Museum, Tempe, Arizona. Viola, B., *Reasons for Knocking at an Empty House: Writings 1973-1994*, edited by R. Violette with B. Viola, The MIT Press, Cambridge, Massachusetts, and Thames & Hudson, London, in association with Anthony d'Offay, Gallery, London.

1985
Bill Viola: Statements by the Artist, exhibition catalogue with introduction by J. Brown, The Museum of Contemporary Art, Los Angeles.

Not Vital
*1948, born in Sent, Engadine
Lives and works in New York, Sent and Agadez (Niger).*

Solo Exhibitions

2001
de Pury & Luxembourg, Zurich.
Galerie Thaddaeus Ropac, Salzburg, also

2000
Galerie Luciano Fasciati, Chur, also 1996.
Galerie Nils Staerk, Copenhagen.

1999
Sperone/Westwater, New York, also 1997 and 1995.
Baron/Boisante, New York, also 1994, 1993, 1990 and 1988.

1998
Galerie Nordenhake, Stockholm.

1997
Kunsthalle, Bielefeld.
Konsthall, Malmö.
Galleria Milleventi, Milan and 1995 in Turin.

1995
Galleria Gian Enzo Sperone, Rome.
Galerie Lehmann, Lausanne, also 1993.

1994
Galerie Edith Wahlandt, Stuttgart.
Berggruen & Zevi Limited, London.

1992
Studio Guenzani, Milan.
Galerie Thaddaeus Ropac, Paris.
Galleria Cardi, Milan.

1991
Bündner Kunstmuseum, Chur, and 1979.

1990
PS Gallery, Tokyo.
Musee Rath, Geneva.
Curt Marcus Gallery, New York, also 1988.
Galerie Ascan Crone, Hamburg, also 1988.

1989
Akhneton Centre of Arts, Cairo.
Galerie Montenay, Paris.

1988
Kunstmuseum, Luzern.

1987
Gallery Nature Morte, New York also 1986 and 1984.
Galerie Rudolf Zwirner, Cologne.

1986
Margo Leavin Gallery, Los Angeles.

1985
Willard Gallery, New York.
Galerie Barbara Farber, Amsterdam.

1982
Kunsthaus, Glarus.

1980
Mendelson Gallery, Pittsburgh.

1972
Galleria Diagramma, Milan.

Group Exhibitions

2000
Bündner Kunstmuseum, Chur, also 1996, 1991, 1990, 1989 and 1976.
Cosmologies, Sperone/Westwater, New York.
And away we go, Baron/Boisante, New York.

1999
Head to Toe, Fine Arts Center, University of Massachusetts, Amherst.

1998
Galerie Thaddaeus Ropac, Salzburg "The Erotic Sublime"

1997
Anselmo, Boetti, Laib, Merz, Nauman, Paolini, Pistoletto, Vital, Zorio, Sperone/Westwater, New York.
Animals, Baron/Boisante, New York.
Animeaux et animeaux, Museum zu Allerheiligen, Schaffhausen (catalogue).

1996
Thinking Print: Books to Billboards, The Museum of Modern Art, New York.
The Material Imagination, Untitled, Guggenheim Museum, New York.

1995
Hong Kong Museum of Art, Hong Kong (catalogue).

1994
A Century of Artists Books, The Museum of Modern Art, New York.
Drawings in Black and White: A Selection of Contemporary Works from the Collection, The Museum of Modern Art, New York.
Natur – Kultur, Projekt Schweiz II, Kunsthalle, Basel.

1993
Self-Evidence, Self-Portraits in Prints & Photographie, New York Public Library, New York.

1992
Drawn in the Nineties, Katonah Museum of Art, Katonah; Fine Art Gallery, Indiana University, Bloomington; Illingworth Kerr Gallery, Calgary, Alberta; Huntsville Museum of Art, Huntsville; Worcester Art Museum, Worcester; Lamont Gallery, Phillips Exeter Academy, Exeter; University Art Gallery, San Diego.

1989
Monochrome, Barbara Krakow Gallery, Boston.
Projects and Portofolios, Brooklyn Museum, Brooklyn, and 1986.
The 1980's: Prints from the Collection of Joshua Smith, National Gallery of Art, Washington, D.C.

1988
Kaldeway Press, Metropolitan Museum of Art, New York (catalogue).
Recent Acquisitions, The Museum of Modern Art, New York.
Blow up, Kunstmuseum, Luzern.

1987
Similia/Dissimilia, Städtische Kunsthalle, Düsseldorf; Wallach Art Gallery, Columbia University,
New York; Leo Castelli Gallery, New York; Sonnabend Gallery, New York.
Drawings Since 1940, The Museum of Modern Art, New York.
The Antique Future, Massimo Audiello Gallery, New York.

1985
Large Drawings, The Museum of Modern Art, New York.
American Paintings 1975-1985, Aspen Art Museum, Aspen CO.
Time after Time, Diane Brown Gallery, New York.

1982
Anoimals ans Archetypes, P.S. 122, New York.

Bibliography

1999
Not Vital, catalogue, Sperone/Westwater.
Albert, M., Szeemann, H., *Allianz und Kunst*, catalogue.

1998
Iannacci, A., Nordal, B., *Not Vital*, Malmö Konsthall.
Steegmann, M., *Animeaux et animeaux*, Museum zu Allerheiligen, Schaffhausen.

1996
Kellein, T., *Not Vital*, D.A.P.

1995

Upshaw, R., "Not Vital at Sperone/ Westwater", *Art in America*, November.
Iannacci, A., "Not Vital at Sperone/ Westwater", *Artforum*, September.
Tsang, G.C., *Beyond Switzerland*, exhibition catalogue, Hong Kong Museum of Art.
"Carte Blanche", *Artis*, December.

1994
Kellein, T., *Projekt Schweiz II*, exhibition catalogue, Kunsthalle, Basel.

1992
Neri, L., "Not Vital: Common Currency", *Parkett*, 33.

1991
Vital, N., *Auost 1991*, photos by F. Puenter.
Beat Stutzepr "Not Vital, Druckgrafik und Multiples", exhibition catalogue, Bündner Kunstmuseum, Chur.
Ripely, D., "What is etched is etched", *Artscribe*, January.

1990
Ritschard, C., *Le veau d'or ou la sculpture conceptuelle de Not Vital*, exhibition catalogue, Musée Rath, Geneva.
Kuspit, D., *Union of Primitivism and Nonobjectivity*, exhibition catalogue, PS Gallery, Tokyo.
Kimmelman, M., "Not Vital", *The New York Times*, April 27.

1989
Kuspit, D., "Relics of the Present", *Artforum*, January.
Andre von, "Graffenried and Mohamed Taha Hussien", *Not Vital at Akhneton*, exhibition catalogue, Cairo.
Iannacci, A., "Arcaico", *Vanity*, May.

1988
McEvilly, T., *Art Presse*, November.
Cotter, H., *Art in America*, October.
Kunz, M., *Not Vital*, exhibition catalogue, Kunstmuseum, Luzern.
Guenzani, C., Stutzer, B., *Bigger than you*, exhibition catalogue.
de Weck, Z., *Not Vital*, exhibition catalogue, Swiss Institute, New York.
Vital N., *Che vosch far cunter il vent nu posch pischar*, Galleria Sperone, Rome (book) sd.
Garvey, E.M., *The Kaldewey Press at the Metropolitan Museum of Art*, exhibition catalogue, New York.

1987
Collins and Milazzo, "Tropical Codes", *Kunstforum*, March.
Jones, M., *Similia/Dissimilia*, exhibition catalogue.

1984
Stutzer, B., *Aspekte aktueller Bündner*

Kunst, exhibition catalogue, Bündner Kunstmuseum, Chur.
Schwabsky, B., "Invitational", *Arts Magazine*.
K., Larsen, "The Cooked and The Raw", *New York Magazine*, September 24, 198 sd.

1982
M., Huggler, "Not Vital", *DU*, November 11.

Massimo Vitali
1944, born in Como.
Lives and works in Lucca.

Solo Exhibitions

2001
Arndt & Partner, Berlin.
Serieuse Zaken, Amsterdam.
Crown Gallery, Brussels.
Gallery Hotel Art, Florence.

2000
Fotohof, Salzburg, May.
Hotel Des Arts, Commission, Toulon.
Espace Malraux, Commission, Chambery.

1999
Galerie du Jour Agnes B, Paris.

1998
Marianne Boesky Gallery, New York.
Recontres Internationales de la Photo, Arles.
Photographer's Gallery, London.

1997
Studio Guenzani, Milan, November.
Spiagge Italiane, Galleria ConsArc, Chiasso.

Group Exhibitions

2001
Mutamenti+Analogie, Centro Trevi, Bolzen.
Biozones, Forum Culturel Blanc-Mesnil, Bobigny.

2000
Tempo!, Palazzo delle Esposizioni, Rome.
Arte y Tiempo, Centre de Cultura Contemporanea, Barcelona.
Toi, Paris,tu m'as pris dans tes bras, Galerie du Jour Agnes B., Paris.
PS1, New York.
Le Temps Vite, Centre George Pompidou, Paris, Reopening Exibition.
In Uso, Museo Michetti, Francavilla al Mare.

1999
Farniente, Maison de la Culture, Amiens.
Photography from the Martin z. Margulies Collection, The Art Museum at Florida International University, Miami.

The Big Picture: Large Format Photography, Middlebury College Museum of Art, Middlebury.

Bibliography

2001
Heidenreich, S., *Frankfurter Allgemeine Zeitung*, "Berliner Seiten", February 23.
Jonkers, G., *Het Parool*, February 17.
de Klerck, H., *De De Volkskrant*, February 20.
Daniels, C., *Die Welt*, March 22.
Bers, M., *Tema celeste*, March-April.

2000
Rossi, L., *Specchio della Stampa*, April.
Alpago-Novello, C., *Il Diario*, May 5.
Aletti, V., *Village Voice*, July 18.
Messina, D., *Corriere della Sera*, August 20.
Kottman, P., *NRC Handelsblad*, Cultureel Supplement, November 17.
Beach & Disco, Steidl Verlag , Goettingen, January.
Les plages du Var. Les pieds dans l'eau, exhibition catalogue, Toulon.
Pique-Nique, Binome, Paris, October.

1999
Guerrin, M., *Le Monde*, February 28.
Rosen, M., "Massimo Vitali at Galerie du Jour Agnes B.", *Artforum*, Paris, Summer.
Arena, September.
Photography from the Martin Z. Margulies Collection, The Art Museum At Florida, International University Press.
Farniente, Maison de la Culture d'Amiens, September.

1998
Redmond, P., *The Face*, January.
Tatley, R., *Dazed and Confused*, March.
Double Take, Summer.
Bouzet, A.-D., *Liberation*, (cover story, culture), July 28.
Il Giornale dell'Arte, July-August.
Connaissance des Arts, July-August.
Art in America, October.

Jeff Wall
1946, born in Vancouver.
Lives and works in Vancouver.

Solo Exhibitions

2001
Marian Goodman Gallery, New York.
Galerie Rüdiger Schöttle, Munich.
Galerie Johnen & Schöttle, Cologne.
Museum für Moderne Kunst, Frankfurt.

2000
Galeria Helga de Alvear, Madrid.

1999

Galerie Johnen & Schöttle, Cologne.
Odradek, Mies van der Rohe Foundation, Barcelona, Brochure.
Jeff Wall/Pepe Espaliu: Suspended Time, EAC, Castellon, Spain. Catalogue.
Jeff Wall:Oeuvres 1990-1998, Musée d'art contemporain de Montréal.

1998
Here and Now II: Jeff Wall, Henry Moore Institute, Leeds.
Jeff Wall: Photographs of Modern Life, Museum für Gegenwartskunst, Basel, Works from 1978 to 1997 in the Basel Public Art Collection and the Emanuel-Hoffmann Foundation.
Marian Goodman Gallery, New York.
Galerie Rüdiger Schöttle, Munich.
Galerie Johnen & Schöttle, Cologne.

1997
The Hirshhorn Museum and Sculpture Garden, Washington; The Museum of Contemporary Art, Los Angeles; Art Tower Mito, Mito; travelling, organized by the Museum of Contemporary Art, Los Angeles.

1996
Museum of Contemporary Art, Helsinki, travelling to the Whitechapel Gallery, London (continuation of 1995 exhibition touring Chicago - Paris).
Jeff Wall: Landscapes and Other Pictures, Kunstmuseum Wolfsburg, Wolfsburg, Catalogue.
Jeff Wall: Space and Vision, Munich Art Prize exhibition, Städtische Galerie im Lenbachhaus, Munich.

1995
Museum of Contemporary Art, Chicago, travelling to the Musée Nationale du Jeu de Paume, Paris, Catalogue.
Marian Goodman Gallery, New York.
1994
The White Cube, London. Deichtorhallen, Hamburg.
Stadtische Kunsthalle Dusseldorf, Dusseldorf.
Galerie Rüdiger Schöttle, Munich.
Neue Gesellschaft fur Bildende Kunst, Berlin.
Centro d'Arte Reina Sofia, Madrid.
Galerie Johnen & Schottle, Cologne.
De Pont Foundation for Contemporary Art, Tilburg.

1993
Kunstmuseum Luzern, Lucerne. Travelling to The Irish Museum of Modern Art, Dublin.
Galerie Roger Pailhas, Marseille.
Fondation Cartier pour l'art contemporain, Jouy-en-Josas.

1992
Louisiana Museum, Humlebaek.
Palais des Beaux-Arts, Brussels
Marian Goodman Gallery , New York.

Group Exhibitions

2001
The Museum of Modern Art, New York, collaborations with Parkett, 1984 to now.
Settings and Players: Theatrical Ambiguity in American Photography, White Cube, London, Catalogue.
Uniform: Order and Disorder, Stazione Leopolda, Florence.

2000
Voici, 100 ans d'art contemporain, Palais des Beaux Arts, Brussels.
Hypermental: Rampant Reality 1950 2000, from Salvador Dali to Jeff Koons, Kunsthaus, Zurich. Travelling to the Hamburger Kunsthalle, Hamburg, 2001.
La forma del mondo/La fine del mondo, Padiglione d'Arte Contemporanea di Milano, Milan.
Mixing Memory and Desire/Wunsch und Erinnerung, Neues Kunstmusem Luzern, Lucerne.
Encounters: New Art from Old, The National Gallery, London, Catalogue.
Biennale of Sydney, Sydney.
La Beauté, Mission for the Year 2000, Avignon, France.
Icon + Grid + Void: Art of the Americas from The Chase Manhattan Collection, The Americas Society, New York.
Around 1984: A Look at Art in the Eighties, P.S.1 Contemporary Art Center, New York.
Art at Work: Forty Years of the Chase Manhattan Collection, Queens Museum of Art, New York.
Staged, Bonakdar Jancou Gallery, New York.
Home, Art Gallery of Western Australia, Perth.
Architecture without Shadow, Centro Andaluz de Arte Contemporaneo, Seville, Travelling to Centre de Cultura Contemporania de Barcelona, Barcelona.

1999
am Horizont, Kaiser Wilhelm Museum, Krefeld.
Carnegie International 1999, Carnegie Museum of Art, Pittsburgh.
Seeing Time: Selections from the Pamela and Richard Kramlich Collection of Media Art, San Francisco Museum of Modern Art. Travelling to the Centre for Art and Media Technology, Karlsruhe, 2000.
Foul Play, Thread Waxing Space, New York.
Warten, Kunst - Werke, Berlin (details)

The Time of Our Lives, New Museum of Contemporary Art, New York.
Gesammelte Werke 1: Zeitgenössiche Kunst seit 1968, Kunstmuseum Wolfsburg, Wolfsburg.
Plain Air, Barbara Gladstone Gallery, New York.
Flashes: Collection Fondation Cartier pour l'art contemporain, Centro Cultural de Belem, Portugal. Catalogue.
From Beuys to Cindy Sherman: the Lothar Schirmer Collection, Kunsthalle Bremen, Bremen, Catalogue. Travelling to the Staatliche Galerie im Lenbachhaus, Munich.
So Faraway, So Close, encore... bruxelles, Brussels.
The Museum as Muse: Artists Reflect, The Museum of Modern Art, New York.
August Sander: Landschaftsphotograhien/Jeff Wall: Bilder von Landschaften, Die Photografische Sammlung/SK Stiftung Kultur, Cologne. Catalogue. Travelling to the Nederlands Foto Instituut, Rotterdam.
Art at Work: Forty Years of the Chase Manhattan Collection, Museum of Fine Arts & Museum of Contemporary Art, Houston.

1998
Under/Exposed: The World's Greatest Photo Exhibition, Stockholm Metro, Stockholm, the Underground of Stockholm.
Aspen Museum of Art. (details)
The Parkett Artists' Editions at the Museum Ludwig, Museum Ludwig, Cologne.
Auf der Spur: Kunst der 90er Jahre im Spiegel von Schweizer Sammlungen, Kunsthalle, Zurich.
Breaking Ground, Marian Goodman Gallery, New York.
Roteiros, Roteiros, Roteiros, Roteiros, Roteiros, Roteiros, Roteiros, Bienal de Sal Paulo, San Paulo, Brazil. Catalogue.
Odradek, Center for Curatorial Studies, Bard College, Annandale-on-Hudson.
Museum of Contemporary Art, Helsinki, Opening exhibition for the new Museum.
The Art of the 80s, exhibition of contemporary art for the Lisbon World Expostion 1998, Culturgest, Lisbon.
Inner Eye: Contemporary Art from the Marc and Livia Straus Collection, The Harn Museum of Art, University of Florida, Gainesville. Travelling to the Neuberger Museum of Art, 2000.
Tuning Up #5: Selections from the Permanent Collection, Kunstmuseum Wolfsburg, Wolfsburg.
Extenuating Circumstances, wall hangings for the Law Courts at 's-Hertogenbosch, Museum Boijmans Van Beuningen, Rotterdam.

Bibliography

2000
Lowry, J., "History, allegory, technologies of vision", *History Painting Reassessed*, ed. David Green and Peter Seddon, Manchester University Press, London and New York, pp. 97-111.

1999
Cortès, J. M., "Temps Suspés: Fragilitat I Dramatisme en l'Obra de Jeff Wall I Pepe Espaliù", *Jeff Wall, Pepe Espaliù: Temps Suspés/Tiempo Suspendido*, Espai d'Art Contemporani de Castello, Castellón, Spain, pp. 22-57. English translated (uncredited) pp. 215-225.
Ganteführer, A., Lange, S., Wiesenhöfer, M., "Ein Gespräch über die Landschaften im Werk von Jeff Wall", *Jeff Wall: Bilder von Landschaften*, The Photographic Collection/SK Culture Foundation, Cologne, pp. 25-30.
Gingras, N., "De l'invisible et d'autres préoccupations photographiques/On the Invisible and Other Photographic Concerns", *Jeff Wall: Oeuvres 1990 - 1998*, The Musée de l'art contemporain de Montréa, pp. 15-21, 86-91. English translation by K. Fleming.
Lussier, R., "Regard sur les années 90/A Survey of the 90s", *Jeff Wall: Oeuvres 1990 - 1998*, The Musée de l'art contemporain de Montréal, pp. 9-14, 81-85. English translation by R. McGee.

1998
Roberts, J., "Jeff Wall: the social pathology of everyday life", *The Art of Interruption: Realism, Photography and the Everyday*, Manchester University Press, Manchester and New York, pp. 184-198.

1997
Stemmrich, G., "Vorwart", *Jeff Wall, Szenarien in Bildraum der Wirklichkeit: Essays und Interviews*, Verlag der Kunst, Fundus Books, pp. 7-31.
Brougher, K., "The Photographer of Modern Life", *Jeff Wall*, The Museum of Contemporary Art/Scalo Verlag, Los Angeles and Zurich, pp. 13-41.

1996
De Duve, T., "The Mainstream and the Crooked Path", *Jeff Wall*, Phaidon Books, London, pp. 26-55.
Groys, B., "Life Without Shadows", *Jeff Wall*, Phaidon Books, London, pp. 56-69.
Ammann, J.-C., *Jeff Wall: Odradek, Taboritskà 8*, Prag, 18. Juli 1994, brochure, Museum für Moderne Kunst, Frankfurt.
Chevrier, J.-F., "Die dunkle Seite einer Glücksverheißung", German translation by W. Grommes of French original text, "Le versant sombre d'une promesse de bon-

heur", *in Jeff Wall: Space and Vision*, catalogue for the Munich Art Prize exhibition at the Städtische Galerie im Lenbachhaus, Munich, Schirmer/Mosel, Munich, pp. 25-32.
Chevrier, J.-F., "Spiel, Drama, Rätsel", German translation by W. Grommes of French original text, "Jeu, drame, énigme", in *Jeff Wall: Space and Vision*, catalogue for the Munich Art Prize exhibition at the Städtische Galerie im Lenbachhaus, Munich, Schirmer/Mosel, Munich, pp. 13-24.

1995
Migayrou, F., *Jeff Wall, Simple indication, la lettre volée*, Singularités, collection directed by M.-A. Brayer, Brussels.
Chevrier, J.- F., "Jeu, drame, énigme", *Jeff Wall*, The Museum of Contemporary Art, Chicago; Galerie Nationale du Jeu de Paume, Paris; Helsinki Museum of Contemporary Art, Helsinki; Whitechapel Art Gallery, London, pp. 16-21. English translation by B. Holmes, "Play, Drama, Enigma", in same publication, pp. 11-16.
Fer, B., "The Space of Anxiety", *Jeff Wall*, The Museum of Contemorary Art, Chicago; Galerie Nationale du Jeu de Paume, Paris; Helsinki Museum of Contemporary Art, Helsinki; Whitechapel Art Gallery, London, pp. 23-26. French translation by B. Alcala, "L'espace de l'anxiété", in same publication, pp. 28-32.

1994
Pelenc, A., "The Uncanny", English version of French original, "Cette 'Inquietante Etrangete", *Restoration*, Kunstmuseum Luzern, Kunsthalle Dusseldorf.

1993
Atkinson, T., "Dead Troops Talk", *Dead Troops Talk*, Kunstmuseum Luzern, The Irish Museum of Modern Art, Deichtorhallen, Hamburg.

1992
Auffermann, V., "Triangular Relationships in an Unwritten Novel", *Jeff Wall; The Storyteller*, Schriften zur Sammlung des Museums für Moderne Kunst, Frankfurt.
Linsley, R., "Jeff Wall: The Storyteller", *Jeff Wall; The Storyteller*, Schriften zur Sammlung des Museums für Moderne Kunst, Frankfurt.
Fischer - Jonge, I., "The Repressed Encounter: Pictures by Jeff Wall", *Jeff Wall*, The Louisiana Museum, Humlebaek, pp. 16-23.

1990
Grynstejn, M., *Notes on a Work by Jeff Wall*, brochure, Museum of Contemporary Art, San Diego, np.

1988
Migayrou, F., "Transfiguration des types", *Jeff Wall*, Le Nouveau Musée, Villeurbanne, pp. 12-28.

1986
Barents, E., "Typology, Luminescence, Freedom: Selections from a conversation with Jeff Wall", *Jeff Wall: Transparencies*, exhibition catalogue, Schirmer/Mosel, Munich; Rizzoli, New York, 1987. Reprinted in French in Jeff Wall (trans. M. Hugonnet and J.-L. Maubant, Le Nouveau Musée, Villeurbanne, 1988.

Magnus Wallin
1965, born in Kaseberga.
Lives and work in Malmö.

Solo Exhibitions

2001
Physical Sightseeing, Borås Konstmuseum, Borås.

2000
Physical Sightseeing, Uppsala Konstmuseum, Uppsala.
Skyline, Moderna Museet, Stockholm.

1999
Nordiska Klassiker, Bergens Kunstförening, Bergen.

1998
Non-Stop, ART space 1%, Köpenhamn.
Exit/Non-Stop, Akershus kunstnerssenter, Lillestrøm, Norge.

1997-98
Check in Check out/Non-Stop, Malmö Konstmuseum (F-rummet), Malmö.

1997
Watch Out, Fri. Art Centre D'Art Contemporain Kunsthalle, Schweiz.
Drive in, Zoolounge, Oslo.

1996
Take Two, Centraal Museum in Utrecht, Nederländerna.
Fan, Down Town, Köpenhamn.

1995
Pick me up, Krognoshuset, Lund.
Mary..., Galleri Isidor, Malmö.

1994
Watch Out, Galleri Nicolai Wallner, Köpenhamn.

1991
Tapko, Köpenhamn.

Group Exhibitions

2001
7th International Istanbul Biennial, Istanbul.

2000
Exit & Limbo, Prize Guarene Arte 2000, Turin.
Millenium Risk, Trafó Kotárs Müvészetek Háza of Contemporary Arts, Budapest.

1999
End of the World & Principle Hope, Kunsthaus Zürich, Zurich.
Bangkok 1%, Navin Gallery, Bangkok.
Detox, Kunstnerernes Hus, Olso.
Zoom, National Art Gallery, Kuala Lumpor, Malaysia.
Edstrandska Priset, Rooseum, Malmö.
Eksenter, Våghallen, Svolvær, Norge.
A Window, Kvangju City Art Museum-Biennale i Syd Korea.
Euro-Ride, Transmission Gallery, Glasgow.
New Life, Scandinavian Art Show, Tokyo.
Nasubi Gallery (Cities on the Move 4) Louisiana, Humlebæk.

1998
Arkipelag, Swedish Mess, Nordiska Museet, Stockholm.
Out of the North, Wüettembergischer Kunstverein, Stuttgart.
Bind Date, Gallery W139, World Wide Video Festival, Amsterdam.
Momentum,The Nordic Biennial, Pakkhus, Moss.
Brytningstider, Norrköpings Konstmuseum.

1997
The Louisiana Exhibition 1997, Louisiana, Humlebæk.
Funny versus Bizzare, Contemporary Art Centre, Vilnius.
1996 27 680 000, Contemporary Art in Swedish Television.
When the Shit Hits the Fan, Overgaden, Köpenhamn.
Nordic natives in Global Village, Offside, Bergen.
Uppdate, Turbinhallen, Köpenhamn.

1995
Oslo one night stand, Kunstnerernes Hus, Oslo.
Deadline, Uppsala Konstmuseum, Uppsala.

1993
ICA, Malmborgs, Malmö.
Galleri Nicolai Wallner, Köpenhamn.

1991-92
About Art and (mass)Media, Norrköpings Konstmuseum.

Bibliography

2001
Stiernstedt, M., "Magnus Wallin", *Art Forum*, March-April.
Nielsen, T.O., *Skyline or the commercialization of...*, Moderna Museet Projekt, Stockholm.

2000
Nilsson, J.P., *Priset för Bekvämlighet och Tystnad*, Guarene Arte, Turin.

1999
"New Life", *Flash Art* (group shows), 207, Summer.
Allerholm, M., "I paradiset finns inga handikappade", *Dagens Nyheter*, 01/08.
Arrhenius, S., Body Contact Hungering for the Real, Like virginity, once lost, five views on nordic art now.
Wallenstein, S.-O., Magnus Wallin, Physical Paradise, IASPIS-galleriet, Stockholm, pp. 2-99.
Magnus Wallin, Physical Paradise, Neste Stopp, Lofoten, Norge.
A Window Inside Outside, Kwangju City Art Museum – Biennale South Korea.
"New Life", *BT5 Monthly*, Art Magazine Bijutsu Techo, 51, 770, May.

1998
Gjesvik, T., och Kaminka, I., Border-Line Traffic, 12 Netter, Bergen.
Produced: W139, Magnus Wallin, Blind Date, 16th World Wide Video Festival.
M., Nishihara, "New Life Scandinavian Art", *Studio* (Voice multi-media mix magazine), 273, September.
Sandberg, L., "Lotte Sandberg on going beyond the local context", *Siksi. The Nordic Art Review*, 13.
Nielsen, T.O., *EXIT-or the Comfort of Sameness and Other Cultural Mythologies*, Out of the North.
Artist Index, PAKKHUS, MOMENTUM Nordic festival of contemporary art.
Warr, T., *In the Dark about Art*, Sutemos/Twilight.
Hultman, K., *Magnus Wallin EXIT*, Brytningstider.
Jørgensen, J.N., "Non-Stop", *KUNSTmagasinet 1%*, #1.

1997
Nielsen, T.O., "The Individual's Exposure", *Siksi. The Nordic Art Review*, 3.
The Louisiana Exhibition 1997, new art from Denmark and Scania.

1995
Nilsson, J.P., "TILT", *Siksi. The Nordic Art Review*, 3.
Jönsson, D., "Magnus Wallin", *90-tal*, 16.

1994
Nacking, Å., "Magnus Wallin", *Siksi. The Nordic Art Review*, 2.

Nick Waplington
1965, born in Pitcairnisland.
Lives and workes in London.

Solo Exhibitions

2001
Americanhusband.com, Deitch Projects, New York.

2000
Nothing, The Lux, London.

1999
Crimes & Suicides, Gilles Peyroulet & Cie, Paris.
The Indicisive Memento, Holly Solomon Gallery, New York.
Smokie Motels for the Baby Jesus, Dorothee de Pauw Gallery, Brussels.

1998
Safety in Numbers, Parco Gallery, Tokyo.
New Work, Underwood Street Gallery, London.

1997
Safety in Numbers, Holly Solomon Gallery, New York.
The Wedding, Burden Gallery, New York.

1996
Weddings, Parties, Anything, National Museum of Film, Photography & Television, Bradford.
Living Room – New Work, Cambridge Darkroom Gallery, Cambridge.
The Wedding, Stadt Museum, Stockholm.

1995
The Wedding, Galerie Fotohof, Salzburg.

1994
Other Edens, The Photographers Gallery, London.
Living Room 1987-1994, Norton Museum, Palm Springs.

1993
Living Room 2/Documentary, The Museum for Photography, Braunscheweig.
Half Lives, Royal Photographic Society, Bath.

1992
Nick Waplington, Philadelphia Museum of Art, Philadelphia.

1991
Living Room, Burden Gallery, New York.

1990
Family Pictures, Pomeroy Purdy Gallery, London.

Group Exhibitions

1999
Past Forward, Holly Solomon Gallery, New York.
Home, Stephen Bulger Gallery, Toronto.
Emerging Images: Selected Contemporary Photography, Susquehanna Art Museum, Harrisburg (Guest edited by Andrew Bale).

1998
Remix, Holly Solomon Gallery, New York.

1996
Offside, Manchester Art Galleries, Manchester.
Offside, Sunderland City Art Gallery, Sunderland.
Offside, Firstsite Colchester, Colchester.
The Dead, National Museum of Film, Photography & Television, Bradford.
The Dead, Horsens Museum, Denmark.
The 90's - Family of Man, Casino Luxembourg, Luxembourg.
On the Bright Side of Life, N.G.B.K., Berlin.

1995
After the Sublime, Cambridge Darkroom, Cambridge.

1995
After the Sublime, Harewood House, Leeds.

1994
Present/Future, Jakobson Fine Art, Atlanta.
Three Photographers, Forum Stadtpark, Graz.
Who's Looking at the Family?, Barbican Art Gallery, London.

1993
Mesiac Fotografie, Bratislava.
Kreig, Neue Galerie, Gratz.
Air Alexander, Kunsthalle, Rotterdam.
Uber die Grossen Stadte, Neue Gasellshaft fur Bildende Kunst, Berlin.
Aperture 40th Anniversary Exhibition, Burden Gallery, New York (Catalogue).

1992
Our Town, Burden Gallery, New York.
Enter the Others, The French Institute, Lisbon.
Neno's, The Vigo Photo Centre, Vigo.

1990
Relative Values, Centre for Creative Photography, Houston (Catalogue).
Colour Work, Photographer's Gallery, London.

Bibliography

2001
Waplington, N., *Truth or Consequences*, Phaidon, London/New York.

Waplington, N., *Nothing*, DVD Film, BBC, London.

1999
Waplington, N., *Smokie Motels for the Baby Jesus*, Artist's Publication, London.
"Which Picture is Erotic, Beautiful, Soothing, Moving, Disturbing?", *Marie Claire*, Guest Editor, Susan Sarandon, p. 40-44.
Aletti, V., "Radar: Nothing Happens", *Out*, March, p. 40.
Aletti, V., "Voice Choices: Photo", *The Village Voice*, March 9, p. 89.
Bradley, A., "The Indecisive Memento", 21, p. 68-69.
Hastreiter, K., "Intimate Portraits: Encounters & Estrangements", *Paper*, March, p. 126.
Leffingwell, E., "Nick Waplington at Holly Solomon", *Art in America*, November, p. 144,145.
Pinchbeck, D., "Art Market: Our Choice of New York Contemporary Galleries", *The Art Newspaper*, 92, May, p. 70.
Sanders, M., "The Cult of Creativity", *Flash Art International*, March/April, p. 76-80.
Slyce, J., Review, *Flash Art International*.
Van Dyke, J., "The Emerging Image, Selected Contemporary Photography", *Exhibition Brochure*, Susequhanna Art Museum.

1998
Strauss, D. L., Review, *Art forum*, March, p. 98.
Slyce, J., "The Photographer Stripped Bare by His Subjects, Even", *Creative Camera*, May.
Templado, L., "The Moment of Youth", *Asahi Evening News*, July 7th.
Waplington, N., *The Indecisive Momento*, Booth Clibbom Editions, London.

1997
Aletti, V., "Art: Nick Waplington", *The Village Voice*, December 9th, Voice Choices, p. 3.
Johnson, K., Art in Review, *The New York Times*, December 19th, p. 40.

1996
Waplington, N., *Safety in Numbers*, Booth Clibbom Editions, London.

1995
Waplington, N., *Weddings, Parties, Anything*, Aperture, New York.

1995
Waplington, N., *Other Edens*, Aperture, New York.

1991
Waplington, N., *Living Room*, Aperture, New York.

Maaria Wirkkala
1954, born in Helsinki.
Lives and works in Espoo.

Solo Exhibitions

2001
A void me, Museum of Architecture, Helsinki.
Researcher´s Cells, Statens Konstråd, Stockholm.

1996
Working Year, 3-days gallery, Helsinki.

1991-92
Archive of Moments, Ars Fennica, exhibition, Turku Art Museum, Kouvola Art Museum; Aine Art Museum, Finland.

1989
Meanwhile in Another Place, passing-by places near Helsinki airport and harbour, Finland.

1987
Departure, March 7, 20:30 on frozen sea near Helsinki.

1985
Moving Pictures, August 26, 21:30, Suomenlinna Helsinki.

1984
Space of Mind, Galleria Bronda, Helsinki.

1983
Fragment of a Journey, Galleria Bronda, Helsinki.

Group Exhibitions

2000
Edstrand Foundation Art Prize, Rooseum Malmö, Sweden.

1999-2000
Dreams 1900-2000, Equitable Gallery, New York; Vienna Historisches Museum, Vienna.

1999
Under the Same Sky, Contemporary Art Museum Kiasma, Helsinki.

1997
5th Istanbul Biennial, Istanbul.

1996
Ostsee-Biennal, Kunsthalle Rostock, Germany.

1995
4th Istanbul Biennial, Istanbul.
Tirami su, project for FRAME, La Biennale di Venezia, Venice.

1993
Baltic Sculpture 93, Gotland Art Museum, Sweden.
Borealis 6, Reykjavik Art Museum, Reykjavik.

1991
Entrance to Exit, Daad gallery, Berlin.

1990
Charcoal on the Wall, Helsinki Art Hall, Helsinki.

Bibliography

2001
Dream Screen, works by Maaria Wirkkala, Johansson Hanna ed. Jack in the Box, Helsinki.
Forskarcellerna, Statens Konstråd, Sweden.

2000
Blind Wall, documentation of the urban project for Contemporary Art Museum Kiasma, Helsinki.

1997
5th Istanbul Biennial catalogue.

1996
Ostsee Biennale catalogue.

1995
L'art urbain en Europe, ISELP.
Maaria Wirkkala, Finnish Fund for Art Exchange, catalogue for the Venice Biennale.

1991
Maaria Wirkkala, Ars Fennica Art Prize catalogue.

1989
Meanwhile in Another Place, documentation of urban art project.

Xiao Yu

1965, in Mongolia.
Lives and work in Beijing.

2000
Fuck off, Shanghai.
Documentary Show of Chinese Avant-garde Art in the 1990s, Fukuoka, Japan.
The 5th Lyon Biennale, Lyon.
Hurt: Works by Wang Yin, Xiao Yu and Yang Maoyuan, Beijing.
Obsession with Harm, Beijing.
CCAA, Chinese Contemporary Art Award.

1999
Post-sense Sensibility: Alien Bodies and Delusion, Beijing.

1998
Counter-Perspective: The Self and the Environment, Beijing.

1996
Union – CAFA Graduates Show (Mostra dei diplomati presso l'Accademia Centrale di Belle Arti), Beijing.

1994
Xiao Yu '94 Performance – Partner-hunting.

Xu Zhen

1977, born in Shanghai.
Lives and works in Shanghai.

Group Exhibitions

2001
Developing Time, Shanghai.
Mantic Ecstasy–Photography and Video, Shanghai.

2000
Useful life, Shanghai.
Fuck off, Shanghai.
Inertia & Mask – Works on Paper, Shanghai.
Big Torino 2000, Turin.
EXIT, London Chisenhale Gallery.
Video-circle, Hong Kong – Berlin.

1999
Love, Tokyo Art Festival, Japan.
Food for Thought, MU Art Foundation, Eindhoven.
The Same but also Changed, Shanghai.
Ideas and Concepts, Shanghai.
BM 99, Bienal de Maya, Maya, Portugal.
Xchange, Paris.
Art for Sale, Shanghai.

1998
Jin Yuan Lu 310, Shanghai.

Vadim Zakharov

1959, born in Duschanbe.
Lives and works in Moskow and Cologne.

Solo Exhibitions

1999
Psychedelics of Choose, Project for the Academy of Fine Art in Odense, Danmark.

1998
Letzter Punkt des Verlegers Pastor Zond, Verlegerstatigkeit 1992-98, Galerie Hohenthal und Bergen, Berlin.

1997
Japanisches Heft N° 3, Begegnung mit einem Rocker auf dem Christusgrab im Dorf Schingo (Provinz Aomori), Galerie Carla Stützer, Cologne.
Deadend of Our Time (with S.Anufriev), ICA Moscow, Obskuri Viri, TV Gallery, Moscow.

1996
Stories of the Black Widow, Project for the National Academy of Fine Art in Oslo.
Funny and sad adventures of Foolish Pastor, Project for Atopic Site, Tokio, Japan.

1995
Der letzte Spaziergang durch die Elysischen Felder, Kunstverein Köln, Cologne.

1994
Typographische Erhebung, Galerie Sophia Ungers, Cologne.
A. Krupp von Bohlen und Halbach Stiftung, Katalogförderung.

1992
Alexander Puschkin the Bookpublischer, Galerie "L", Moscow.
Provincial bubbles of Cologne Pastor, Deweer Art Gallery, Otegem.

1991
Das Weissanstreichen von Peter und dem Wolf auf dem Territorium der Garnitur von Madame Schleuse, Galerie Walcheturm, Zürich.

1990
Brother`s Karamazoff, with Viktor Skersis, Galerie Sophia Ungers, Cologne.

1989
Kunstverein, Freiburg im Breisgau.
Galerie Peter Pakesch, Vienna.

1984
APTART Gallerie, Moscow.

1983
SZ (Skersis/Zakharov) APTART, Moscow.

Group Exhibitions

2001
Milano-Europa 2000, The seeds for the Future, Padiglione d'Arte Contemporanea, Milan.

2000-2001
Amnesia, New Museum Weserburg, Bremen.

2000
L'Auture Moitiè de l'Europe, Musée Nationale du Jeu de Paume, Paris.

1999-2000
Zeitwenden: Rückblick und Ausblick, Kunstmuseum Bonn; Museum Moderner Kunst, Vienna.

1998
vollkommen gewönlich, Kunstverein Freiburg im Marienbad.
Germanische Nationalmuseum Nürnberg, Kunstverein Braunschweig, Kunsthalle Kiel.
Präprintium. Moskauer Bücher aus dem Samizdat, Staatsbibliothek Berlin; New Museum Weserburg Bremen.

1997
Fort! Da! Cooperations, Villa Merkel Galerie der Stadt Esslingen.
2000 minus 3, ArtSpace plus Interface, Steirischer Herbst, Graz.

1996
Ostsee Biennale-96. Bekannt(-)Machung, Kunsthalle Rostock.

1995-96
Flug, entfernung, verschwinden, Konzeptuelle moskauer Kunst, Galerie hlavniho mesta prahy, Prag; Haus am Waldsee, Berlin; Stadtgalerie im Sophienhof, Kiel.

1995
Heart of darkness, Kröller-Müller Museum, De Hoge Veluwe.
No Man's Land, Copenhagen Contemporary Art Center, Kopenhagen.
Kräftmesse. Privatisierungen, Kunstlerwerkstatt Lothinger Straße 13, Munich.

1994
Fluchtpunkt Moskau, Ludwig Forum, Aachen.
I.Kabakov, I.Chuikov, V.Zakharov, Galerie Deweer Art, Ottegem.
Ritratto Autoritratto, Trevi Flash Art Museum, Trevi.

1993

1983
Exchange 2, Shedhalle, Zurich.
Trade Routes, The New Museum, New York.
Die Sprache der Kunst, Kunsthalle Vienna, Vienna/Kunstverein, Frankfurt.

1992
Kunst Heimat Kunst, Steirischer Herbst, Graz, Schloßpark Eybesfeld.

1991
Mani Museum - 40 Moskauer Künstler im Frankfurter Karmeliterkloster, Frankfurt.
Perspectives of Conceptualism, Clocktower Gallery, New York.
BiNationale, (Israelische - Sowjetische Kunst um 1900), Kunsthalle Düsseldorf; The Israel Museum.
Metropolis, Internationale Kunstausstellung, Martin Gropius Bau, Berlin.

1990
Contemporary Russian artists, Museo d'Arte contemporanea Luigi Pecci, Prato.
Between Spring and Summer, ICA Boston; TAM, Tacoma.
Von der Revolution zur Perestrojka, Sammlung Ludwig, Kunstmuseum, Luzern.
In the USSR and Beyond, Stedelijk Museum, Amsterdam.
A la Bibliothek, Salzburger Kunstverein.

1989
Vienna - Moskau - New York, Messepalast Vienna.
100 years of Russian art - from private collections in the USSR, Barbican Gallery, London.

1989-90
10 + 10, MAM, Fort Worth; MOMA, San Francisco; Albright Knox Gallery, Buffalo; Museum of Modern Art, Washington; Krimskij Val, Moscow.

1988
I live, I see, Kunstmuseum, Bern.
8 Artists from USSR, Gallery de France, Paris.

1987
First Exhibition in Avantgardist´club (KLAVA), Moscow.
Retrospektive der Arbeiten von Moskauer Künstlern 195-87, Ermitage-Galerie, Moscow.
In der Hölle, (Klava), Moscow.

1986
APTART, The New Museum of Contemporary Art, New York.

1983
Come Yesterday and you´ll be first, City without walls, New York.

1978-1982
Exhibitions in der APTART Gallerie, Moskow.

Bibliography

2000-2001
Amnesia, New Museum Weserburg, Bremen.

2000
L'Auture Moitiė de l'Europe, Musée Nationale du Jeu de Paume (catalogue-CD-ROM), Paris.

1999-2000
Zeitwenden rückblick und ausblick, Kunstmuseum Bonn

1998
Someone else with my Fingerprints, Salon Verlag, Cologne.
vollkommen gewönlich, Kunstverein Freiburg im Marienbad, Germanische Nationalmuseum Nürnberg, Kunstverein Braunschweig,Kunsthalle Kiel, Kunstfonds e. V., Wienand, Cologne.
Präprintium. Moskauer Bücher aus dem Samizdat, Edition Temmen, Bremen.

1997
Ford! Da! Cooperations, Cantz Verlag, Stuttgart.
2000 minus 3. ArtSpace plus Interface, Steirischer Herbst, Graz.
Mystical Correct, Salon Verlag, Cologne.

1996
Paper Art 6. Dekonstruktivische Tendenzen, Cantz Verlag, Stuttgart.

1995
No Man's Land. Art from the Near Abroad, Copenhagen Contemporary Art Center-Nikolaj.
M.Broodthaers. Korrespondrnzen, Oktagon Verlag, Stuttgart.
Der letzte Spaziergang durch Elysischer Felder.
Kölnischer Kunstverein, Cantz, Stuttgart.
Catoir, B., "Träumen auf der roten Luftmatratze...", *Frankfurter Allgemeine Zeitung*, June 25.
Bode, U., "Garten der Vergeblichekeiten...", *Süddeuche Zeitung*, July 24.
Flug - Entfernung - Verschwinden. Konzeptuelle Moskauer Kunst, Cantz, Stuttgart.
Kräftemesse, Cantz.
Heart of darkness, Kröller-Müller Museum, Oterlo.

1994
Fluchtpunkt Moskau, Katalog. Werke der Sammlung Ludwig und Arbeiten für Aachen, Cantz.

1993
Agosta, S., *Balkon*, 10.
Die Sprache der Kunst, catalogue, Kunsthalle Vienna.
Ilya Kabakov: NOMA oder Der Kreis der Moskauer Konzeptualisten, Cantz.
Schreibheft, 42, Rigodon Verlag, Essen.

1992
Jolles, C., *Kunstbulletin*, 3.
Malsch, F., "Aptart", *Kunstforum*, Bd. 114.

1991
Mani Museum - 40 Moskauer Künstler im Frankfurter Karmeliterkloster, Frankfurt am Main.
Perspectives of Conceptualism, Clocktower Gallery, New York.
Kittelmann, U., *À la Bibliothek*, Salzburger Kunstverein.
Jolles, C., *Züricher Woche*, 31. 01. 91, Zurich.
Solomon, A., *The Irony Tower*, Knopf.
Fama & Fortune Bulletin.
Groys, B., *Zeitgenössische Kunst aus Moskau*, Klienhardt & Biermann, Munich.
Ostkunst - Westkunst, Ludwig Forum Aachen.
Binationale 1991, Sowjetische Kunst um 1990, DuMont Buchverlag, Cologne.
Metropolis, International art exhibition Berlin, Martin-Gropius-Bau. Rizzoli, New-York.

1990
Contemporary Russians Artists, exhibition catalogue, Museo d´arte contemporanea Luigi Pecci, Prato.
Between Spring and Summer (Soviet Conceptual Art in the Era of Late Communism), Boston, exhibition catalogue, in Tacoma und Washington.
Von der Revolution zur Perestrojka, Sammlung Ludwig, Kunstmuseum Luzern.
In the USSR and Beyond, Stedelijk Museum, Amsterdam.

1989
"Victor Misiamo", *Contemporanea*, September.
Vienna - Moskau - New York, Wiener Messepalast, Vienna.
100 years of Russian art - from private collections in the USSR, Barbican Gallery, London.
Kunstverein Freiburg, exhibition catalogue, Januar/Februar.
Galerie Peter Pakesch, exhibition catalogue, Vienna.
Momentaufnahme - Junge Kunst aus Moskau, Katalog Städt. Museum Münster.
Sowjetkunst heute, exhibition catalogue, Museum Ludwig, Cologne.
10 + 10, MAM, Fort Worth.
Jolles, C., *Moscou Années 80.*

Mosca: Terza Roma. Sala I, Katalog ´89, Rom.
Spazio Umano, 2/89.
Tupitsyn, Margarita, *Margins of Soviet Art*, Giancarlo Politi Editore.
Smolek, N., *Artforum*, Oktober.

1988
Sowjetkunst heute, exhibition catalogue, Museum Ludwig, Cologne.
IC Kunst BO, Westbahnhof Berlin.
Moskau, Moskau, Videotape, S-Press.
Ich Lebe - Ich Sehe, exhibition catalogue, Kunstmuseum Bern.
Künstler in Moskau, Edition Stemmle, Zurich.
Sotheby's, Russian Avantgarde and Soviet Contemporary Art, Moskow, July.

1987
Flash Art International Magazine, 137, October/November.
"Elephanten stören das Leben", *Durch*, Kunstbulletin, Graz.
Moskau, Moskau, Videotape, S-Press.

1983
Come Yesterday And You´ll Be First, Newark. Apt-Art-Galerie, exhibition catalogue, New York.

Heimo Zobernig
1958, born in Mauthen.
Lives and works in Vienna.

Solo Exhibitions

2000
Galerie Meyer Kainer, Vienna.
CCB Projectroom, Centro Cultural de Belém, Lisboa.

1999
Kunstverein Munich.
Der Katalog, MAK (with Ernst Stouhal), Vienna; Portikus, Frankfurt am Main.

1998
Galerie für Zeitgenössische Kunst Leipzig, Leipzig.
Galerie Meyer Kainer, Vienna.
Init. Kunst-Halle Berlin, Berlin.
Bonner Kunstverein, Bonn.

1997
Centre for Contemporary Art, Ujazdowski Castle, Warszawa.
Villa Merkel, Esslingen.

1996
The Renaissance Society at The University of Chicago.

1995

Richard Foncke Gallery, Gent.
Wiener Secession, Vienna.

1994
Kunsthalle Bern, Bern.
Kláster sv. Anezky Ceské, Národní galerie v Praze, Prague.

1993
Salzburger Kunstverein, Salzburg.
Neue Galerie, Graz.
Kunsthalle Luzern, Luzern.

1992
Amerikaner, steirischer herbst 92, Forum Stadtpark, Graz.
Galerie Achim Kubinski, Cologne.

1991
Hôtel des Arts, Fondation nationale des arts, Paris.
EA-Generali Foundation, Vienna.
Andrea Rosen Gallery, New York.
Villa Arson, Nice.

1990
Galerie Christian Nagel, Cologne.
Richard Kuhlenschmidt Gallery, Los Angeles
Galerie hlavního mesta Prahy (with Franz West), Prague.

1989
Galerie Sylvana Lorenz, Paris.

1988
Galerie Juana de Aizpuru, Madrid.

1986
Galerie Borgmann-Capitain,Cologne.

1985
Galerie Peter Pakesch, Vienna.

1983
Musikgalerie Villach.

1980
Dramatisches Zentrum (with Alfons Egger), Vienna.

Group Exhibitions

2001
Museum as Subjects . . ., The National Museum of Art, Osaka.
La Biennale di Venezia, Esposizione Internazionale d'Arte, Venice.
Vom Eindruck zu Ausdruck. Grässlin Collection, Deichtorhallen, Hamburg.

2000
Rembrandt oder nicht/Räumen, Kunsthalle Hamburg.
Re-Play, Generali Foundation, Vienna.

1999
Get Together. Kunst als Teamwork, Kunsthalle Vienna.
dCONSTRUCTIVISM: life into art, Queensland Art Gallery, Brisbane.

1998
Minimalisms, Akademie der Künste, Berlin.
Mai 98 - Positionen zeitgenössicher Kunst seit den 60er Jahren, Kunsthalle Köln, Köln.
Das Jahrhundert der künstlerischen Freiheit - 100 Jahre Secession, Secession, Vienna.

1997
check in, Museum für Gegenwartskunst, Basel.
Skulptur. Projekte Münster 1997, Westfälisches Landesmuseum, Münster.
Documenta X, Kassel.

1996
Wunderkammer Österreich, Kunsthaus, Zurich.

Kunst in der neuen Messe Leipzig, Leipzig.

1994
Temporary Translation(s), Sammlung Schürmann, Deichtorhallen, Hamburg.
Jetztzeit, Kunsthalle Vienna; De Appel, Amsterdam.

1993
Kontext Kunst, Trigon '93, steirischer herbst 93, Neue Galerie, Graz.
Backstage, Topologie zeitgenössischer Kunst, Kunstverein in Hamburg.
Project Unité, Art, Architecture, Design, Le Corbusier's Unité d'Habitation, Firminy.
Parallax View: New York-Köln, PS 1, New York.

1992
3rd International Istanbul Biennal, Istanbul.
Documenta IX, Kassel.

1991
Apt Art International, Mosow.

1990
Le désenchantement du monde, Villa Arson, Nice.

1989
Wittgenstein, Das Spiel des Unsagbaren, Wiener Secession.

1988
Graz 1988, steirischer herbst 88, Grazer Kunstverein, Stadtmuseum, Graz.
Aperto 88, La Biennale di Venezia, Esposizione Internazionale d'Arte, Venice.

1987
Aktuelle Kunst in Österreich, Europalia 87, Museum van Hedendaagse Kunst, Gent.

1986
Tableaux Abstraits, Villa Arson, Nice.
Sonsbeek '86, Arnheim.
De Sculptura, Messepalast, Vienna.

1984
Zeichen, Fluten, Signale - neukonstruktiv und parallel, Galerie nächst St. Stephan, Vienna.

Bibliography

2000
Farbenlehre. Heimo Zobernig, Galerie & Edition Artelier, Graz.

1999
Der Katalog, Hans Petschar/Ernst Strouhal/Heimo Zobernig, Springer-Verlag Vienna New York.

1998
Text und Kunst, Bonner Kunstverein, Bonn, Texte: I. Graw, A. Pohlen, D. Snauwaert, J. Winkelmann, H. Zobernig.
Heimo Zobernig, texts by P. Pakesch, A. M. Potocka, M. Slizinska, Centre for Contemporary Art, Ujazdowski Castle, Warszawa.

1997
Formalismus, texts by C. Höller, T. Trummer, Österreichische Galerie Belvedere, Vienna.
Heimo Zobernig, texts by R. Damsch-Wiehager, R. Metzger, Villa Merkel, Esslingen, Cantz Verlag.

1996
Heimo Zobernig, Galeria Potocka, Kraków, Texte: M. Dusini, M. A. Potocka.
Heimo Zobernig, texts by J. Decter, A. Goldstein, H. Walker, M. Wigley, ua., The Renaissance Society at The University of Chicago, Chicago.

1995
Farbenlehre, Ferdinand Schmatz / Heimo Zobernig, Springer-Verlag Vienna New York.
Heimo Zobernig, Wiener Secession, Vienna, Texte: J. Decter, P. Tscherkassky.

1994
Heimo Zobernig, text by U. Loock, Kunsthalle Bern, Bern.

1993
Galerie Peter Pakesch 1981-1993, Vienna.
Heimo Zobernig, text by H. Amanshauser, W. Fenz, I. Graw, F. Schmatz, P. Weibel, Neue Galerie Graz/Salzburger Kunstverein, Graz/Salzburg.
Jahresmuseum 1993, text by O. Rychlik, Kunsthaus Mürzzuschlag.

1992
Lexikon der Kunst 1992, Ferdinand Schmatz / Heimo Zobernig, Edition Patricia Schwarz, Stuttgart.
Amerikaner, steirischer herbst 92, Forum Stadtpark, Graz, Mitarbeit: M. Poledna.
Heimo Zobernig, text by I. Graw, Galerie Achim Kubinski, Cologne.

1991
Heimo Zobernig, text by S. Breitwieser, H. Draxler, R. Zettl, EA-Generali Foundation, Vienna.
Heimo Zobernig, text by K. Gräßlin, Kunstraum Daxer, Munich.
Heimo Zobernig, text by H. Draxler, I. Graw, F. Perrin, F. Schmatz, O. Zahm, Villa Arson, Nice.

1990
Multiple choice, text by H. Draxler, Jänner Galerie, Vienna.
Freiherr Knigge, A., *Über den Umgang mit Menschen*, Heimo Zobernig, *Über den Umgang mit Büchern*, Edition Forum Stadtpark, Graz.
Heimo Zobernig, Forum Stadtpark, Graz, Plakat/Text: Fareed Armaly.
Franz West, Heimo Zobernig, text by D. Bogner, u.a., Galerie hlavního mestra, Prag.
Heimo Zobernig, Galerie Achim Kubinski, Köln, Text: M. Prinzhorn.

1989
Heimo Zobernig, Galerie Peter Pakesch, Vienna.

1988
Die Kunst der Enzyklopädie, Ferdinand Schmatz / Heimo Zobernig, edited by Galerie P. Pakesch, Vienna; Edition Artelier, Graz.

1987
Heimo Zobernig, Galerie Ralf Wernicke, Stuttgart.
Heimo Zobernig, Galerie Peter Pakesch, Vienna, Text: A. Oehlen.

1986
Franz West, Heimo Zobernig texts by P. Pakesch, F. Schmatz, H. Zobernig, G. Schöllhammer, F. West., Galerie Christoph Dürr, Munich.
Heimo Zobernig, text by P. Pakesch, Galerie CC, Graz.

1985
Heimo Zobernig, Galerie Peter Pakesch, Vienna.

1982
documenta Urbana, Kassel, Katalogbeitrag: M. Geiger, R. Labak, H. Zobernig.

Special Projects

Bunker Poetico

Marco Nereo Rotelli
1955, born in Venice.
Lives and works in Casal Maggiore (Cremona) and Milan.

A project in three phases:

1. Orsogril

1000 poems donated by poets and non-poets from all over the world will be hung to the iron gate designated by the sign "limite invalicabile" ("insurmountable limit") that separates the area of the Corderie from the military Arsenal creating a mobile and mental wall of poetry.

2. Bunker
On the surface of the bunker will be affixed together with a poem by Pier Paolo Pasolini the final judgements by the Tribunal of Rome against the author when he was accused of offences deriving from his film Rogopag. The question is: "Can we re-construct, through poetry, a free mental dimension open to the Other, that is to say a dimension 'ulterior' with regards to the unilateral thinking of power?"

3. Incontri
I propose this time a "space for voice and thinking" that needs to be understood as an integral part of the project, that is, a work of visual art that also takes advantage of the contribution and of the multiple layers of meaning that poetico-philosophic material can give. A cycle of three conferences will offer both the possibility of essaying "the state of things" and of letting the poetic word of poetry interact with its natural counter-melody: philosophical logos.

Chen Zhen Hommage
Chen Zhen
1955, born in Shanghai.
He died in Paris in 2000.

Solo Exhibitions

2000
GNAM, Turin.

Galleria Arte Continua, San Gimignano.

1999
ADDC-Espace Culturel François Mitterrand, Périgueux.

1998
National Maritime Museum, Stockholm.
Tel Aviv Museum of Art, Tel Aviv.

1996
Centre international d'art contemporain de Montréal and Deitch Projects, New York.
New Museum of Contemporary Art, New York.

Group Exhibitions

1999
3rd Asia-Pacific Triennial of Contemporary Art, Queensland Art Gallery, Brisbane.
dAPERTutto, La Biennale di Venezia, 48. Esposizione Internazionale d'Arte, Venice.

1998
1998 Taipei Biennal: Site of Desire, Taipei Fine Arts Museum.
Global Vision: New Art from the '90s, Deste Foundation, Athens.
Cities on the Move, Louisiana Museum of Modern Art, Humlebæk.
La Biennale di Venezia, 48. Esposizione Internazionale d'Arte.

1997
Biennale d'Art Contemporain de Lyon.
97 Kwangju Biennale: Unmapping the Earth.
Trade Routes: History and Geography. 2nd Johannesburg Biennale.

1996
First Shanghai Biennial, Shanghai Art Museum.

Bibliography

1998
Chen Zhen, Xian Zhu, Chen Zhen: Transexperiences, Kitakyushu, Japan, Center for Contemporary Art, CCA Kitakyushu, and Korinsha Press & Co., Ltd.
Global Vision: New Art from the '90s, Part II, exhibition brochure, text by K. Gregos, Deste Foundation, Athens, Greece.
Chen Zhen: Jue Chang/Fifty Strokes to Each, exhibition catalogue, texts by N. Guralnik, M. Omer; correspondence between N. Guralnik, Chen Zhen, Tel Aviv Museum of Art, Israel.

1997
Pujo, A.,Chen Zhen: Les Pas Silencieux/ Silent Paces, 5 Projets aux ftats-Unis 1994-

1997, Paris, L'Association Française d'Action Artistique, Ministère des Affaires Étrangères. Published on the occasion of Chen Zhen's installation in Artists Projects, the re-opening show at P.S. 1 Contemporary Art Center, Long Island City, New York, 1998.

1996
Chen Zhen, exhibition catalogue, texts by C. Gosselin, Hou Hanru, Centre international d'art contemporain de Montréal.

Heli Global Art Tour
Michael Schmitz
1963, born in Burscheid (Colonia).
Lives and works in Rome.
www.europedentist.org/globalheliarttour

Human Condition
Anur
1971, born in Sarajevo, Bosnia-Herzegovina.
Lives and works in Sarajevo and in Milan.

Solo Exhibitions
1998
Human Condition II, Centro Arte Contemporanea, Spazio Umano, Milan.

1995
Human Condition, Istituto Europeo di Design, Milan.

Group Exhibitions

2000
Made in Bosnia, McCann Erickson – Milan.
Made in Bosnia, Galerija Bosne i Hercegovine.
1999
Biennale dei Giovani artisti, Rome.
Maxumim II, Collegium artisticum.
Maxumim III, Collegium artisticum.

1998
Maxumim I, Collegium artisticum.

Bibliography

2000
Made in Bosnia, exhibition catalogue.

1998
Maxumim, exhibition catalogue.

Museum in progress
www.mip.at

Ken Lum
1956, born in Vanouver, Canada.
Lives and work in Vienna.

Billboard projects (at 2,500 locations in Vienna)
Gerwald Rockenschaub 1991/92, Bernard Bazile 1992/93, Felix Gonzalez-Torres 1993/94, Hans-Peter Feldmann 1994/95, Rosemarie Trockel 1995/96, Beat Streuli 1996/97, Navin Rawanchaikul/Rirkrit Tiravanija, Rudi Molacek 1997/98, Jeremy Deller 1998, Martine Aballéa 1998/99, Markus Schinwald 1999/00, Thomas Bayrle 2000/01.

Large scale picture series
Large Scale Picture, on the facade of the Kunsthalle Vienna.
Ed Ruscha 1993, Walter Obholzer 1994, Gerhard Richter 1995/96, Douglas Gordon 1996, Ken Lum 2000/01.
Safety Curtain (large scale picture series in the Vienna State Opera).
Kara Walker 1998/99, Christine und Irene Hohenbüchler 1999/00, Matthew Barney 2000/01.

Electronic media
"Do it"-TV Version 1995 (series of video clips produced for the Austrian Broadcasting Corporation).
Shere Hite, Dave Stewart, Gilbert & George, Michelangelo Pistoletto, Steven Pippin, Yoko Ono, Erwin Wurm, Leon Golub, Nancy Spero, Lawrence Weiner, Eileen Myles, Rirkrit Tiravanija, Jonas Mekas, Ilya Kabakov, Michael Smith, Damien Hirst, Robert Jelinek.

Portraits of Artists 1992 – 2000 (video series)
Vito Acconci, Philip Akkerman, Donald Baechler, John Baldessari, Robert Barry, Georg Baselitz, Thomas Bayrle, Dara Birnbaum, Christian Boltanski, Günter Brus, Chris Burden, Clegg & Guttmann, Helmut Federle, Hans-Peter Feldmann, Andrea Fraser, Gilbert & George, Heinz Gappmayr, Bruno Gironcoli, Felix Gonzalez-Torres, Douglas Gordon, Dan Graham, Mary Heilmann, Georg Herold, Carsten Höller, Jenny Holzer, Mike Kelley, Jan Knap, Jeff Koons, Joseph Kosuth, Elke Krystufek, Maria Lassnig, Paul Mc Carthy, Matt Mullican, Hermann Nitsch, Oswald Oberhuber, Tony Oursler, Raymond Pettibon, Michelangelo Pistoletto, Arnulf Rainer, Jim Rosenquist, Hubert Schmalix, Jim Shaw, Nancy Spero, Haim Steinbach, Philip Taaffe, Rirkrit Tiravanija, Niele Toroni, Lawrence Weiner, Franz West, Christopher Wool, Heimo Zobernig.

Stealing eyeballs 2001
Richard Fenwick, Fork Unstable Media, Imaginary Forces, Reed Kram, Reala, Stefan Sagmeister, Spin, Alexei Tylevic, Vectorama.org, Marius Watz.

Exhibitions in Austrian newspapers and magazines
The Message as Medium 1990/91
Fareed Armaly, Werner Büttner, Clegg & Guttmann, Mark Dion, Andrea Fraser, Michael Krebber, Thomas Locher, Christian Philipp Müller, Stephen Prina, Heimo Zobernig.

Travelling Eye 1995/96
Nobuyoshi Araki, John Baldessari, Peter Fischli/David Weiss, Bernhard Fuchs, Nan Goldin, Felix Gonzalez-Torres, Richard Hoeck, Roni Horn, Jean-Luc Moulène, Gabriel Orozco, Jack Pierson, Gerhard Richter

Global Positions 1999/00/01
Alexander & Susan Maris, Roberto Cuoghi, Adrian Jones, Dolores Zinny & Juan Maidagan, Bülent Sangar, Annika Eriksson, Nathan Coley, Paola Pivi, Lois Weinberger, Hüseyin Bahri Alptekin, Marcel Dzama, Jeroen de Rijke/Willem de Rooij, Daniel Jewsbury, Vincent Leow, Claude Closky, ...

Interventions 1995 – 2000
Michelangelo Pistoletto, Hans-Peter Feldmann, Noritoshi Hirakawa, Chris Marker, Dan Graham, Lloyd de Mause, Jonas Mekas, Christian Boltanski, Mona Hatoum, Jun Yang, Susan Hiller, Joan Brossa, Paul Virilio, Joseph Grigely, Martin Walde, Matt Mullican, Christian Marclay, Ayse Erkmen, Critical Art Ensemble, Lawrence Weiner, Hoy Cheong, Christine und Irene Hohenbüchler, Heimo Zobernig, Marlene Streeruwitz, Oswald Oberhuber, Kara Walker, Aleksandar Battista Ili_, Heimo Zobernig, Markus Schinwald, Cameron Jamie ...

Vital Use 1994/95
Fabrice Hybert, Hans-Peter Feldmann, Wolfgang Tillmans, Jef Geys, Frédéric Bruly-Bouabré, Andrea Zittel/Rudi Molacek, Michelangelo Pistoletto, Carsten Höller, Rosemarie Trockel, John Lennon/Yoko Ono, John Latham

Signs of Trouble 1998/99
David Crow, The Designers Republic, Mevis & van Deursen, Anne Burdick, J. Abbott Miller, Tomato, Cornel Windlin & M/M, 2 x 4, Michael Rock & Susan Sellers, Jonathan Barnbrook

TransAct I – Transnational Activities in the Cultural Field (2000/2001)
Martin Adel, Eleanor Antin, Neal Ascherson, Autonomer Feministischer Widerstandsrat/Autonomous Feminist Resistance Council, Zeigam Azizov, John Baldessari, Bella Ban, Hermann Beil, Fritz Bergler, Ellen Berkenblit, Patricia Bickers,

Michael Blum, Anna & Bernhard Blume, Christian Boltanski, Ecke Bonk/the typosophic society, Saskia Bos, Pierre Bourdieu, Sabine Breitwieser, Günter Brus, Roger M. Buergel, Pavel Büchler, Georg Chaimowicz, Alice Creischer, Arthur C. Danto, demonstate/links gegen Rechts, Chris Dercon, Ines Doujak, Philippe Duboy, Jimmie Durham, Harun Farocki, Marina Faust, Hans-Peter Feldmann, Pia Gazzola, Jochen Gerz, get to attack, Leon Golub, Douglas Gordon, Richard Gordon, Franz Graf, Daniela Hammer-Tugendhat, Andreas Hapkemeyer, Bodo Hell, Richard Hoeck, Werner Hofmann, Christine & Irene Hohenbüchler, Horáková & Maurer, Stephan von Huene, Ann Veronica Janssens, Johanna Kandl, Helmut Kandl, Alexander Kluge, Kasper König, Christian Kravagna, Gregor Kri_tof, Gerhard Lang, Augustine Leisch, Hans Peter Litscher, Martin Löw-Beer, Sylvère Lotringer, Iñigo Manglano-Ovalle, Christian Marclay, Stephen Mathewson, Nina Menkes, Cornelia Mittendorfer, Petr Nedoma, Max Neuhaus, Ruth Noack, Oswald Oberhuber, Walter Obholzer, Klaus Ottomeyer, Haga-Roch Paillet, Simon Patterson, Edith Payer, Cathrin Pichler, Lisl Ponger, Stephen Prina, Martin Prinzhorn, Projektteam Namentliche Erfassung der österreichischen Holocaustopfer/Project team Recording of the names of the Austrian victims of the Holocaust, Doron Rabinovici, L.A. Raeven, Alejandra Riera, Bernhard Riff, Viktor Rogy, August Ruhs, Naomi Tereza Salmon, Peter Sandbichler, Heribert Schiedel, Ferdinand Schmatz, Walter Schmögner, Tim Sharp, Wolf Singer, Nancy Spero, Isa Stech, Theo Steiner, Helmut Stockhammer, Ernst Strouhal, Beatrix Sunkovsky, Yehuda Emmanuel Szafran, Harald Szeemann, Emmerich Tálos, Lidwien van de Ven, Lawrence Weiner, Barbara Westman, Ulf Wuggenig, Slavoj Žižek, Heimo Zobernig

An open letter to Federal President Klestil signed by American scientists
David Abraham, Christopher S. Allen, Steven Beller, Seyla Benhabib, Guenter Bischof, John W. Boyer, Christine Day, Istvan Deak, Robert Dupont, Geoff Eley, Thomas C. Ertman, David Good, Helmut Gruber, Peter Hall, Julia Hell, Jeffrey Herf, Michael G. Huelshoff, Tony R. Judt, John J. Kulczycki, David Large, Richard S. Levy, Charles Maier, Andrei S. Markovits, Richard Mitten, Johannes von Moltke, Regina Morantz-Sanchez, Beth Simone Noveck, Peter Pulzer, Anson Rabinbach, Jonathan Steinberg, George Steinmetz, Vladimir Tismaneanu, Liliane Weissberg, Steven Whiting, Jack Zipes

Statement signed by American historians

Leon Botstein, Helmut Gruber, Klemens von Klemperer, William G. McGrath, Richard Mitten, Anson Rabinbach, Richard L. Rudolph, Carl E. Schorske, Stephen Toulmin, Michael P. Steinberg

imprint
museum in progress
concept: Kathrin Messner, Joseph Ortner
team: Roman Berka, Sabine Dreher

Refreshing

Artists
Massimo Bartolini
1962, born in Cecina (LI).
Lives and works in Cecina (LI).

Cai Guo Qiang
1957, born in Quanzhou City, Fujian Province.

Olafur Eliasson
1967, born in Reykjavik.
Lives and works in Copenaghen and Berlin.

Tobias Rehberger
1966, born in Esslingen.
Lives and works in Frankfurt am Main.

Rirkrit Tiravanija
1961, born in Buenos Aires.
Lives and works in New York and Berlin.

Intervention by
Massimo Bartolini, *Rot bostane*, bar, Arsenale, Giardini delle Bombarde.
Olafur Eliasson, Tobias Rehberger, Rirkrit Tiravanija, *Do not use rusty brown, please*, caffé ristorante, Arsenale, Isola delle Vergini.
Cai Guo Qiang, *Senza titolo*, carretti ambulanti (*wheelbarrow*), varie sedi della Biennale.

Curatori
Pier Luigi Tazzi, Fabio Cavallucci

Realizzazione
Sitin e Orange Expo

Produzione e gestione
Attiva

SECESSION Project Facade
www.secession.at

Participating Artists
Franz West, John Baldessari, Dorit Margreiter, Günter Brus, Jochen Gerz, Peter Land, Richard Prince, Markus Geiger, Joseph Kosuth, Werner Reiterer, Louise Bourgeois, Renée Green, David Shrigley,

Paul McCarthy, Extra Territoria, Heimo Zobernig, Monica Bonvicini.

Concept and Organisation
Matthias Herrmann, Sylvie Liska, Eleonore Louis.

The Platform of Thought

Seni Camara
1945, born in Bignona (Senegal), where she lives and works.

Ousmane Ndiaye Dago
1951, born in Ndiobene (Senegal). Lives and works in Dakar.

Gilberto De La Nuez
1913, born in Cuba, where he died in1993

John Goba
1944, born in Marru Jong (Sierra Leone). Lives and work in Mountain Cut.

Ettore Jelmorini
1909, born in Intragna (Switzerland), where he died in 1968.

Cheff Mway
1931, born in Nkuene-Meru (South Imenti, Kenya). Lives and works in Timau.

Jean Baptiste Ngnetchopa
1953, born in Nkongsamba (Cameroun). Lives and works in Bafoussam.

Auguste Rodine
1840, born in Paris (France), where he died in 1917.

Hans Schmitt
1912, born in Frankfurt/Sachsenhausen (Germany). Died in 1998.

Peter Wanjau
(Kenya)

Anonymous sculptor Giriama

Exhibited works

A1 – 53167
30 de Junio
2000
25 colour photographs

Chantal Akerman
Woman sitting after killing
2001
video projection

Sunday Jack Akpan
Portrait of a seated chief
2001
sculpture

Francis Alÿs
Mr. Peacock will represent Mr. Alÿs at the 49th Venice Biennale
2001
performance

Tiong Ang
School
1999
digital video projection

Gustavo Artigas
Las reglas del juego - The rules of the game
2000-2001
installation

Atelier Van Lieshout
A-Portable
2001
installation

Vanessa Beecroft
The Sister Project (January)
2000
chibacrome print

The Sister Project (February)
2000
chibacrome print

The Sister Project (March)
2000
chibacrome print

The Sister Project (April)
2000
chibacrome print

The Sister Project (May)
2000
chibacrome print

The Sister Project (June)

2000
chibacrome print

The Sister Project (July)
2000
chibacrome print

The Sister Project (August)
2000
chibacrome print

The Sister Project (September)
2000
chibacrome print

The Sister Project (October)
2000
chibacrome print

The Sister Project (November)
2000
chibacrome print

The Sister Project (December)
2000
chibacrome print

Joseph Beuys
La fine del XX secolo (Das Ende des 20 Jahrunderts)
1982-1983
installation

Olivestone
1984
installation

Voglio vedere i miei montagne (Ich will meine Berge schen)
1950-1971
installation

Richard Billingham
Playstation
1999
dvd video, continuous loop

Liz smoking
1998
DVD video projection, continuous loop

Untitled (BWO)
1990
black & white photograph on alluminium (triptych)

Untitled (BW1)
1990

black & white photograph on alluminium

Untitled (BW2)
1990
black & white photograph on alluminium

Untitled (BC25)
1997
colour photograph

Pierre Bismuth
From Humanity to Something Else and Vice Versa
2001
text on wall

From Green to Something Else
2001
work in progress, painted walls

Botto & Bruno
House where nobody lives
2001
installation
wallpaper, walk-over pvc

Martin Bruch
Photographic installation on 43 m
304 colour photographs

Tania Bruguera
La Isla en Peso
2001
video installation

Roderick Buchanan
Endless column
2000
video installation

Deadweight
2000
installation

Chris Burden
The Flying Steamroller
1996
installation

Maurizio Cattelan
La nona ora
2000
installation

Loris Cecchini
Bbbreathless
2001
installation

COM & COM
C-Files: Tell Saga, The Trailer
2000
Video Beta, 4'

C-Files: Tell Saga, Installation
2001
installazione/installation

Cracking Art Group
Turtles in Venice - S.O.S. world
2001
installation

Chris Cunningham
Flex
2000
video, 12' 13"

All is Full of Love
1999
video DVD, 4' 9"

Monkey Drummer
2001
video DVD, 2' 24"

Josef Dabernig
Wisla
1996
black and white 16 mm film to DVD
8'

Max Dean – Raffaello D'Andrea
The table: Generation A
1984-2001
interactive installation

Lucinda Devlin
Gas Chamber, Maryland State Penitentiary, Baltimore, Maryland (The Omega Suites)
1991
colour photograph

Electric Chair, Indiana State Prison, Michigan City, Indiana (The Omega Suites)
1991
colour photograph

Final Holding Cell, Indiana State Prison, Michigan City, Indiana (The Omega Suites)
1991
colour photograph

Electric Chair, Broad River Correctional Facility, Columbia, South Carolina (The Omega Suites)
1991
colour photograph

Electric Chair, Holman Unit, Atmore, Alabama (The Omega Suites)
1991
colour photograph

Lethal Injection Chamber, Nevada State
Prison, Carson City, Nevada
(The Omega Suites)
1991
colour photograph

Electric Chair, Greensville Correctional
Facility, Jarratt, Virginia
(The Omega Suites)
1991
colour photograph

Final Holding Cell, Greensville
Correctional Facility, Jarratt, Virginia
(The Omega Suites)
1991
colour photograph

Lethal Injection Chamber, Petosi
Correctional Center, Petosi, Missouri
(The Omega Suites)
1991
colour photograph

Witness Room, Petosi Correctional
Center, Petosi, Missouri
(The Omega Suites)
1991
colour photograph

Electric Chair From Witness Room,
Diagnostic and Processing Center,
Jackson, Georgia (The Omega Suites)
1991
colour photograph

Autopsy Room, Diagnostic and
Processing Center, Jackson, Georgia
(The Omega Suites)
1991
colour photograph

Lethal Injection Chamber, Louisiana
State Prison, Angola, Louisiana
(The Omega Suites)
1992
colour photograph

Electric Chair, Somers Correctional
Institution, Somers, Connecticut
(The Omega Suites)
1991
colour photograph

Lethal Injection Chamber, Territorial
Correctional Facility, Canon City,
(The Omega Suites)
1991
colour photograph

Lethal Injection Chamber, Texas State
Prison, Huntsville, Texas
(The Omega Suites)
1992
colour photograph

Final Holding Cell, Texas State Prison,
Huntsville, Texas
(The Omega Suites)
1992
colour photograph

Gas Chamber, Central Prison, Raleigh,
North Carolina
(The Omega Suites)
1991
colour photograph

Gallows, Department of Corrections,
Smyrna, Delaware
(The Omega Suites)
1991
colour photograph

Lethal Injection Chamber, Stateville
Correctional Center, Jollet, Illinois
(The Omega Suites)
1991
colour photograph

Lethal Injection Chamber from Witness
Room, Cummins Unit, Grady, Arkansas
(The Omega Suites)
1991
colour photograph

Rostrum, Lethal Injection Chamber,
Cummins Unit, Grady, Arkansas
(The Omega Suites)
1991
colour photograph

Gas Chamber, Arizona State Prison,
Florence, Arizona
(The Omega Suites)
1992
colour photograph

Electric Chair, Greenhaven Correctional
Facility, Greenhaven, New York
(The Omega Suites)
1991
colour photograph

Lethal Injection Chamber, Idaho State
Penitentiary, Boise, Idaho
(The Omega Suites)
1997
colour photograph

Witness Room, Broad River Correctional
Facility, Columbia,
South Carolina
(The Omega Suites)
1991
colour photograph

Executioner's Room, Greenhaven
Correctional Facility, Greenhaven,
New York
(The Omega Suites)

1991
colour photograph

Lethal Injection Chamber from Family
Whitness Room, Parchman State,
Penitentiary, Parchman, Mississippi
(The Omega Suites)
1998
colour photograph

Witness Room, Territorial Correctional
Facility, Canon City, Colorado
(The Omega Suites)
1991
colour photograph

View from Witness Room, Stateville
Correctional Center, Jollet, Illinois
(The Omega Suites)
1991
colour photograph

Rineke Dijkstra
Omri
Givatti Brigade Rotern Regiment
The Golan Heights, Israel
29 marzo 2000
C-print photograph

Maya
Induction Center, Tel-Hashomer, Israel
12 aprile 1999
C-print photograph

Abigail
Herzilia, Israel
10 aprile 1999
C-print photograph

Omri
Kiryat Shmonah, Israel
25 settembre 2000
C-print photograph

Maya
Herzilya, Israel
21 novembre 1999
C-print photograph

Abigail
Palmahim Israeli Air Force Base, Israel
18 dicembre 2000
C-print photograph

Amit
Golani Brigade, Orev Unit
Elyakim, Israel
26 maggio 1999
C-print photograph

Itamar
Golani Brigade, Orev Unit
Elyakim Israel
26 maggio 1999
C-print photograph

Erez
Golani Brigade, Orev Unit
Elyakim Israel
26 maggio 1999
C-print photograph

Stan Douglas
Le Détroit
1999-2000
proiezione bifocale di film 35 mm/ 35
mm film installation for two 35 mm
film projectors

Atom Egoyan
Julião Sarmento
Close
2000-2001
DVD projection
11', loop

Helmut Federle
El Omrane
2000
acrylic on canvas

Legion XVI
1997
oil, acrylic on canvas

Secondary Determination
2000
resin, oil on canvas

Regina Galindo
El dolor en un pañuelo
1999
video

Lo voy agritar al viento
1999
video

Cristina Garcia Rodero
Haïti, Rites vaudous
2000
17 black and white photographs

**Yervant Gianikian – Angela Ricci
Lucchi**
La marcia dell'uomo
2001
video installation

Luis González Palma
Sin titulo I
1998
coloured black and white photograph

80 mm f5.6 1/30 seg.
1998
coloured black and white photograph

La imagen del mundo
1998
coloured black and white photograph

Time out
2000
coloured black and white photograph

Destino
2000
coloured black and white photograph

La Mirada critica
1998
coloured black and white photograph

Reciclaje
2000
coloured black and white photograph

Ausencias
1997
coloured black and white photograph

LGP
2000
coloured black and white photograph

Entre raices y aire
1997
coloured black and
white photograph

Paul Graham
Untitled no. 1
(Paintings)
1999
colour photograph

Untitled no. 2
(Paintings)
1999
colour photograph

Untitled no. 3
(Paintings)
1999
colour photograph

Untitled no. 4
(Paintings)
1999
colour photograph

Untitled no. 5
(Paintings)
1999
colour photograph

Untitled no. 7
(Paintings)
1999
colour photograph

Untitled no. 8
(Paintings)
1999
fotografia a colori /
colour photograph

Untitled no. 10
(Paintings)
1999
colour photograph

Untitled no. 11
(Paintings)
1999
colour photograph

Untitled no. 12
(Paintings)
1999
colour photograph

Untitled no. 13
(Paintings)
1999
colour photograph

Untitled no. 14
(Paintings)
1999
colour photograph

Untitled no. 15
(Paintings)
1999
colour photograph

Untitled no. 16
(Paintings)
1999
colour photograph

Untitled no. 17
(Paintings)
1999
colour photograph

Untitled no. 18
(Paintings)
1999
colour photograph

Untitled no. 19
(Paintings)
1999
colour photograph

Veli Granö
Pentti Hauhiala
(Tangible Cosmologies)
1994
colour print and slide

Ilmari Joronen
(Tangible Cosmologies)
1994
colour print and slide

Vainö Heikkinen
(Tangible Cosmologies)
1993
slide

Pentti Parvio
(Tangible Cosmologies)
1994
colour print and 2 slides

Timo Lehtonen
(Tangible Cosmologies)
1994
colour print

Esko Rahkonen
(Tangible Cosmologies)
1996
colour print and slide

Esko Pessi
(Tangible Cosmologies)
1994
colour print and slide

Mauri Perkonoja
(Onnela – a trip to Paradise)
1987
colour print and slide

Veijo Rönkkönen
(Onnela – a trip to Paradise)
1996
colour print and slide

Arto Ali-Eskola
(Onnela – a trip to Paradise)
1986
colour print and slide

Juuso Peltomäki
(Diy Lives)
1999
colour print and slide

Hai Bo
They no. 3 (soldiers)
1998-2000
Dyptich
Photographs

They no. 5 (Han Yu)
1998-2000
photograph

They no. 6 (Woman)
1998-2000
Dyptich
Photographs

The three sisters
1998-2000
Dyptich
Fotografie /Photographs

Bridge
1998-2000
Dyptich
Photographs

Winter
1998-2000
Dyptich
Photographs

Federico Herrero
Elena Ocallaghan 1 Dutch
2000
mixed media on canvas

Otro tipo de sapercida
2000
mixed media on canvas

Head
2000
mixed media on canvas

Barna vi Jones en Lacsante Astoria
2000
mixed media on canvas

El tal y el señor Climent
2000
mixed media on canvas

No habeis estado nunca en Puig Cerdà?
2000
mixed media on canvas

El, Ella y Mixeta
2000
mixed media on canvas

Grüen-ac
2000
mixed media on canvas

Soelve dies
2000
mixed media on canvas

Gary Hill
Wallpiece
2000
video sound installation

Laura Horelli
Courrent Female Presidents
2001
installation, 6 portrait prints on
alluminium

Yishai Jusidman
Sumo VI
1995-1996
oil on wood

Sumo X
1996
oil on wood

Sumo XII
1996
oil on wood

Sumo XIX
1997
oil on wood

Sumo XX
1997
oil on wood

Sumo XXIV
1997-1998
oil on wood

F.A. Mexico City
2000-2001
mixed media

M.T.
1998
oil and egg tempera on wood

P.R.
1998
oil and egg tempera on wood

Mutatis Mutandis: B.T.
1999
installation

Mutatis Mutandis: A.M.
1999
installation

Mutatis Mutandis: Sumo XXV
1999
installation

J.P.
1998
oil and egg tempera on wood (dyptich)

Ilya e Emilia Kabakov
Not everyone will be taken into the future
2001
installation

Marin Karmitz –
Samuel Beckett
Comèdie
1966
35 mm film on DVD
18'43"

Abbas Kiarostami
Au travers de la fenêtre
2001
video DVD
1 h 40'

Susan Kleinberg
Fear not
2001
audio video installation

Matthieu Laurette
Vivons remboursés!

1997
travelling showroom in a display truck

Other Countries Pavillion/Citizenship
Project
2001
work in progress

Marko Lehanka
Wilderer
2000-2001
mixed media

Bauernsaule
2001
mixed media

Kachelbrunnen
1999
mixed media

High Voltage Hirsch
1999
mixed media

Bank
1998-2001
mixed media

Bacchus
1993
mixed media

Galerie-Fussboden
2001
mixed media

Blauer Brunnen-Fussboden
2001
mixed media

Christiane Löhr
Kleiner Turn
1999
sculpture, ivy seeds

Ingeborg Lüscher
Fusion
2001
video projection

Mark Manders
Reduced Nightscene
with one Beautiful Stone
(reduced to 88%)
2000
installation

Tuomo Manninen
Midwives
1996
Chromogenic colour print

Foilosmen and anéféist - University
Fencing Association

1997
Chromogenic colour print

Dancers - The National Ballett
2000
Chromogenic colour print

Taxidermists
1999
Chromogenic colour print

Association of Wives of Professors
2000
Chromogenic colour print

Ice Swimmers Club
1996
Chromogenic colour print

Helsinki Association of the Unemployed
1995
Chromogenic colour print

Non Fighting Generation
2000
Chromogenic colour print

Ten Step Group Salvation Army Men's Shelter
2000
Chromogenic colour print

Male Choir-Amici Cantus
1997
Chromogenic colour print

Balloon Sales People
2000
Chromogenic colour print

Hell's Angels MC Finland
1999
Chromogenic colour print

Lazimpat Fitness Center
1995
Chromogenic colour print

LAP Kindergarten
1995
Chromogenic colour print

Scouts
1995
Chromogenic colour print

Monks
Chromogenic colour print

Little Angels Boarding School
1995
Chromogenic colour print

Lorry Drivers
1995
Chromogenic colour print

The Newars
1995
Chromogenic colour print

Firemen
1995
Chromogenic colour print

Zoo Staff
1995
Chromogenic colour print

Hare Krishnas
1997
Chromogenic colour print

Eva Marisaldi
Senza fine
200025 plaster bas-reliefs

Viktor Maruščenko
Chernobyl
1991
27 black and white photographs

Barry McGee
Stephen Powers
Todd James
Street Market
2001
installation, mixed media,
variable dimensions

Marisa Merz
Tête rose
1989
polychrome clay

Testa
1982
polychrome clay

Chantal Michel
Weisses Rauschen
1997
video projection
on the floor

Priscilla Monge
Room
2001
installation

Another Tempest
2000
engraved marble

Ron Mueck
Untitled (Boy)
1999
sculpture

Untitled (Baby)
2000
sculpture

Untitled (Shawed Head)
1998
sculpture

Marco Neri
Quadro Mondiale
2000
egg tempera on linen
192 pieces 35×50 cm each

Ernesto Neto
O Bicho
2001
installation
textile and spices

Carsten Nicolai
Frozen water
1999-2001
installation

Olaf Nicolai
Untitled (Blutstropfen)
2000
3200 posters (each 68×98 cm),
wall paper

Maze (The Dukes of Hazzard)
2001
installation

Manuel Ocampo
*Paradigms Following Their Adherents
To The Grave (zombie guitarist)*
2000
acrylic on canvas

*Moral Exorcism Meaningless Outside
A Ritualistic Heroism (zombie painter
kids)*
2000
acrylic on canvas

*The Absolute Other of the In-Place
Paradigm of Practice*
2000
acrylic on canvas

*An Absolutized Extreme form
of Emblematic Abstraction*
2000
acrylic on canvas

*The Failure to Express
is Its Expression*
2000
acrylic on canvas

*The Unseen Power
of the Monochrome*
2000
acrylic on canvas

Arnold Odermatt
Stans

1953
black and white photograph

Hergiswil
1964
black and white photograph

Stansstad
1963
black and white photograph

Beckenried
1954
black and white photograph

Wolfenschiessen
1970
black and white photograph

Stansstad
1953
black and white photograph

Stansstad
1967
black and white photograph

Stansstad
1969
black and white photograph

Buochs
1965
black and white photograph

Stansstad
1967
black and white photograph

Stans
1953
black and white photograph

Hergiswil
1961
black and white photograph

Stans
1964
black and white photograph

Hergiswil
1961
black and white photograph

Hergiswil
1967
black and white photograph

Stansstad
1969
black and white photograph

Buochs
1966

black and white
photograph

Stansstad
1949
black and white photograph

Wolfenschiessen
1952
black and white photograph

Stansstad
1957
black and white photograph

Buochs
1958
black and white photograph

Stansstad
1968
black and white photograph

Beckenried
1969
black and white photograph

Buochs
1956
black and white photograph

Stansstad
1967
black and white photograph

Ennetmoos
1978
black and white photograph

Stansstad
1958
black and white photograph

Stansstad
1964
black and white photograph

Stansstad
1950
black and white photograph

Stansstad
1952
black and white photograph

Dallenwil
1977
black and white photograph

Oberdorf
1964
black and white photograph

João Onofre
Casting

2000
DVD video projection
12'59"
*"Che io abbia la forza, la convinzione
e il coraggio (...)" tratto dalla
sceneggiatura di* Stromboli *di Roberto
Rossellini, 1949 /based upon Roberto
Rossellini's (et all) screenplay
of* Stromboli, *1949*

Tatsumi Orimoto
Art-Mama
1996-2000
installation

Tanja Ostojić
Black square on white (on my Venus Hill)
1996-2001
body art performance

I'll be your Angel
2001
performance

Manfred Pernice
Untitled
2001
installation

Paul Pfeiffer
Untitled as of yet
2001
Mixed media

Self-Portrait as a fountain
2000
installation

The Long Count (Rumble in the Jungle)
2000
video installation

Sex Machine
2001
video projection

Poltergeist (Fork)
2001
installation

Poltergeist (Spoon)
2001
installation

John Pilson
Mr. Pickup
2000-2001
video

A la claire fontaine
2001
video

Alexandra Ranner
Midnight

2000
model of installation

Aprèslude
2001
installation

Neo Rauch
Weid
2001
oil on paper

Tank
1999
oil on paper

Nerv
2001
oil on paper

Tabu
2001
oil on paper

Ubung
1998
oil on paper

Regel
2000
oil on paper

Heli Rekula
Landscape n. 5 "American Star"
1998
colour print mounted on alluminium

Fantasy of devotion
1996/1998/2001
16 mm film transfered on DVD, 3'

Untitled (from theme Pilgrimage)
1996
colour print mounted on alluminium

Gerhard Richter
Abstract painting (Rhombus) 851 – 1
1998
oil on canvas

Abstract painting (Rhombus) 851 – 2
1998
oil on canvas

Abstract painting (Rhombus) 851 – 3
1998
oil on canvas

Abstract painting (Rhombus) 851 – 4
1998
oil on canvas

Abstract painting (Rhombus) 851 – 5
1998
oil on canvas

Abstract painting (Rhombus) 851 – 6
1998
oil on canvas

Gerd Rohling
Wasser und Wein
1984-2001
installation

Alexander Roitburd
Psychedelic invasion of the battleship "Potemkin" into Sergey Eisensteyn's tautological hallucinations
1998
video installation

Tracey Rose
Ciao Bella
2001
video installation on DVD

Mimmo Rotella
Islam
1999
décollage and painting
on canvas

Blank (Blank Fessure)
1980
collage

Blank (Brown Blank)
1980
collage

Violet Blank Cynar
1980
collage

La Noix Jaune
1973
plastified print

Performance
1973
plastified print

Segreto
1966
plastified print

Lina Orfei
(Lina la domatrice)
1986
décollage on canvas

Anri Sala
Uomoduomo
2000
DVD video projection

Charles Sandison
Living Rooms
2001
installation

City Halls
2001
site specific data
installation

Sarenco l'Africano
Sarenco l'Africano
1990-2001
variable size installation

Ene-Liis Semper
ff/rew
1998
video installation, 7'

Richard Serra
Four
2001
weatherproof steel sculpture
weatherproof steel

Left/Right
2001
weatherproof steel sculpture
weatherproof steel

In/Out/Left/Right
2001
weatherproof steel sculpture
weatherproof steel

Santiago Sierra
200 Personas remuneradas para se Tenidas de Rubio
2001
Performance, video installation

Lars Siltberg
Man with balls on hands and feet containing: man on ice, man on water, man on art
1998-2001
DVD video projection

Nedko Solakov
A Life (Black & White)
1999-2001
black and white paint; 2
workers/painters constantly
repainting in black and white
the space walls for the entire
duration of the exhibition

Eliezer Sonnenschein
Port
2001
installazione

Georgina Starr
The Bunny Lake Collection
2000
mixed media
Catwalk
2001
Performance

Do-Ho Suh
Floor
1997-2000
installation

Who am We ?
1996-2000
wallpaper

Fiona Tan
Smoke Screen
1997
16 mm film installation (silent)

Facing Forward
1999
video projection

Javier Téllez
Choreutics
2001
video installation

Alessandra Tesi
Opale 00
1999-2001
video projection on screen with glass
microspheres. Installation in daylight

Zenit
2001
Composition-videoprojection
on screen with glass microspheres.
Installation in daylight

Jaime David Tischler
*La Sagrada Familia
(Bajar al Cielo)*
1994
Gelatin silver print. Gold toned

*Nienteme una Eternidad
(Bajar al Cielo)*
1994
Gelatin silver print. Gold toned

*No fui el primero que tu finca surco
(Bajar al Cielo)*
1994
Gelatin silver print. Gold toned

*Falso auto-retrato
(Bajar al Cielo)*
1994
Gelatin silver print. Gold toned

*Las bañistas
(Bajar al Cielo)*
1994
Gelatin silver print. Gold toned
*Auto-retrato come Parmenides mirando
las aguas pasar
(Bajar al Cielo)*
1995
Gelatin silver print. Gold toned

Ausencia
(Bajar al Cielo)
1995
Gelatin silver print. Gold toned

Amatorius
(Fragmentos de un Deseo Mendicante)
1995
Gelatin silver print. Gold toned

Ave Mundi
(Fragmentos de un Deseo Mendicante)
1995
Gelatin silver print. Gold toned

La Ley del Desseo I – II
(Fragmentos de un Deseo Mendicante)
1995
Gelatin silver print. Gold toned (dyptic)

Yo soy la Medida Ultima de tu caida
(Pies de Barro)
1996
Gelatin silver print. Gold toned

El Precario Equilibrio de mi Desseo
(Pies de Barro)
1996
Gelatin silver print. Gold toned

El Contorno de tu Existencia
(Hilos del Desseo)
1998
Gelatin silver print. Gold toned

La Circumcision
(Hilos del Desseo)
1998
Gelatin silver print. Gold toned

El deslumbriamento
(Hilos del Desseo)
1998
Gelatin silver print. Gold toned

El Lenguache de las fuentes I-II-III
(Hilos del Desseo)
1998
Gelatin silver print. Gold toned (tryptic)

Retorno y Ausencia
1998
Gelatin silver print. Gold toned (tryptic)

Niele Toroni
Intervention in Padiglione Italia
2001
imprints of paint brush no. 80 at
regular space intervals

Gavin Turk
Bin Bag
2000-2001
sculpture
painted bronze

Richard Tuttle
Ten, C
2000
Acrylic on plywood

Ten, B
2000
Acrylic on plywood

New Mexico, New York, E no. 1
1998
Acrylic on plywood

New Mexico, New York, E no. 3
1998
Acrylic on plywood

New Mexico, New York, E no. 4
1998
Acrylic on plywood

Waferboard 6
1996
Acrylic on plywood

Waferboard 9
1996
Acrylic on plywood

Cy Twombly
Lepanto
2001
series of 12 paintings, acrylic
on canvas

Untitled
Sculpture

Salla Tykkä
Lasso
2000
video, 3' 48" loop

Keith Tyson
Studio wall drawing:
Monument for the present
state of things
2000-2001
mixed media on paper,
series of 68

The Thinker
2000
sculpture

Eulalia Valldossera
Provisional Home
1999
installation

Minnette Vári
Mirage
1999
video projection
1' 40", looped

Oracle
1999
video projection
Video 2', audio 6', looped

Rem
2001
video projection
7' 18", looped

Francesco Vezzoli
Embroidery of a Book:
Young at any Age
2000
laser prints on canvas with metallic
embroidery, 18 parts

Joan Crawford was an embroiderer
2000
laser prints on canvas with metallic
embroidery, 18 parts

Bill Viola
The Quiet of the Unseen
2000
video installation

Surrender
2001
video on plasma flat panel display
(dyptic)

Not Vital
70 Camels in and above Water
2001
installation

Massimo Vitali
Riccione - Agosto 1997
1997
colour photograph on plexiglass
(dipthyc)

Pic Nic Allé
colour photograph on plexiglass
(4 pieces)

Sun park Kempense Meren no. 0775
colour photograph on plexiglass
(dipthyc)

Jeff Wall
Blind Window no. 1
2000
lightbox

Blind Window no. 2
2000
lightbox
Diagonal composition no. 3
2000
lightbox

Sunken Wall
1996

scultura/ sculpture
lightbox

Magnus Wallin
Exit
1997
3D animation

Skyline
2000
3D animation

Nick Waplington
Private Fantasy/Public Domain
2000
computer grafic with photography &
image manipulation
37 images

Maaria Wirkkala
Dream Screen Prime Time
2000
video installation

Found a mental connection
1998
installation

Xiao Yu
Ruan
1999
installation

Xu Zhen
Rainbow
2000
video projection, 4'

Vadim Zakharov
Theology Conversation
1996-2000
7 photographs

Heimo Zobernig
Nr. 18
2000
video installation
13' loop

PIATTAFORMA DEL PENSIERO / THE PLATFORM OF THOUGHT

Erich Bödeker
Apollo 0
1970
sculpture
mixed media
Heilige Barbara
1970
sculpture
mixed media

Schwarze Stürzende
1969
sculpture
mixed media

Seni Camara
Untitled
1998
sculpture
ceramic

Untitled
1998
sculpture
ceramic

Untitled
1998
sculpture
ceramic

Ousmane Ndiaye Dago
La Femme-Terre
1998
photograph on plastic

Gilberto De La Nuez
Los No Alineados
1979
oil on canvas

John Goba
Untitled
1997
sculpture
coloured wood and porcupinr prickle

Ettore Jelmorini
Mazzo di fiori
1960
marble sculpture

Madonna
1960
marble sculpture

Musicista
1960
marble sculpture

Cheff Mway
Column of indipendence

1998
sculpture
tecnica mista

Jean Baptiste Ngnetchopa
Untitled
1999
sculpture

Auguste Rodin
Homme qui marche sur colonne
1900
sculpture
bronze

Le penseur (le poète élèment de la port de l'enfer)
1896
bronze sculpture

Hans Schmitt
Adam und Eva
1975
sculptures
mixed media

Mutter mit Kind
1969
sculpture
mixed media

Mann mit seinem Hund auf einer Bank
1975
sculpture
mixed media

Peter Wanjau
AIDS killing
1998
sculpture
acrylics and wood

One man can fill the world
1998
sculpture
acrylics and wood

Swollen imagination and stomach
1998
acrylics and wood

Football madness
1998
acrylics and wood

Scultore Giriama
Grave stele
1930
sculpture, engraved wood

Anonymus
Standing Regal Bodhisvatta
Gujarat – Pratihara
X-XI century
Stone sculpture

Anonymous
Buddha: Monumental gilded head
Siam
XIV century
Bronze

Anonymous
Two Standing Cāmarādhariṇī
Gujarat – Pratihara
X-XI century
Stone sculpture

Anonymous
Mithuna, tantric yoga exercices
Templar Erotic Frieze
(man with six women)
Tanjore – District
XVII-XVIII century
Engraved wood

Anonymous
Narasiñha with 8 arm (templrelief)
Kerala, South India
XV-XVI century
Coloured teak wood

Anonymous
Śiva Naṭarāja
Mysore, Hassan District (Belur Region)
XII century
black basalt

Anonymous
Tirthaṅkara Pārśavanātha (large size stele with 78 Jina e 32 figures)
India del Nord, Gujarat
XI-XIII century
Bronze

Anonymous
Mask for ritual dances
Painting, wool and wood

Anonymous
African totem
Engraved wood

Anonymous
U.S. Navy Diving Helmet

SPECIAL PROJECTS

Bunker Poetico
Marco Nereo Rotelli
Bunker Poetico
2001
work in progress with hundreds of Poems

Hommage to Chen Zhen
Chen Zenh
colour photograph

Chen Zhen
documentary video
on monitor display

Heli Global Art Tour
Michael Schmitz
Kinderbaum
2001
found raising project for a children's home in South Africa

Human Condition
Peace brothers
1999
C-print

With God on Our Side
1999
C-print

Sarajevo Humor
1999
C-print

Buy five get one free
1999
C-print

Made in Bosnia
1999
C-print

Museum In Progress

Ken Lum
There is no place like home
2001
poster

refreshing_

Massimo Bartolini
Rot bostane
2001
café

Olaffur Eliasson
Tobias Reheberger
Rirkrit Tiravanija
Do not use rusty brown, please
2001
Café and restaurant

Cai Guo-Qiang
Untitled
2001
wheelbarrows

Secession

Franz West
Haider haidert
2000
poster

John Baldessarri
Smile (with hair and moustache)
2000
poster

Dorit Margreiter
*Rüktritt der Bundesregierung
als voraussetzung für eine
antirassistische politike*
2000
poster

Jochen Gerz
Der Eintrag
1993-1999
poster

Richard Prince
Untitled (joke)
2000
poster

Markus Geiger
Ohne Titel
2000
poster

Joseph Kossuth
Ballade for midgest no. 1
2000
poster

Luise Bourgeois
Untitled
2000
poster

Rène Green
*Normalization is seized
by imaginatiom*
2000
poster

EXTRATERRITORIA
Untitled
2000
poster

Monica Bonvicini
One title
2000
poster

Illustrated works

A1 – 53167
30 de Junio, June 30th
2000
Colour print, 75 × 100 cm
Courtesy Contexto
p. 175

Chantal Akerman
Women sitting after killing
2001
Beta sp + 7 monitors + sound
& magnetoscope player MPEG,
still from film
p. 89

Sunday Jack Akpan
Chief
2001
Concrete, acrylic paints and flatting
p. 49

Francis Alÿs
*Mr. Peacock will represent Mr Alÿs
at the 49th Venice Biennale*
2 peacocks, 2 guardians, postcards
p. 115

Tiong Ang
School
1999
Videoprojection, still from video
p. 137

Anonymous
Standing Cāmarādhariṇī
Gujarat, Pratihara
X-XI century
Stone sculpture, 94 × 41 × 33 cm
p. 8

Anonymous
*Templar Erotic Frieze
(man with six women)*
Tanjore, District
XVII-XVIII century
Wood frieze, 54 × 25 × 10 cm
p. 8

Anonymous
Standing Cāmarādhariṇī
Gujarat, Pratihara
X-XI century
Stone sculpture, 95 × 40 × 32 cm
p. 8

Anonymous
Tirthaṅkara Pārśavanātha (Large-sized
Stele with 78 Jina and 32 figures)
North India, Gujarat
XI-XIII century
Bronze, 73 × 39 × 13 cm
p. 6

Anonymous
Śiva Naṭarāja

Mysore, Hassan District
(Belur Region)
XII century
Black basalt, 70 × 51 × 19 cm
p. 10

Anonymous
Buddah: larged-sized gilded-head
Siam
XIV century
Bronze, 42 × 32 × 31 cm
p. 11

Anur
Buy five, get one free
From the project *Human Condition*
1999
C-print, 130 × 180 cm
p. 302

With God On Our Side
From the project *Human Condition*
1999
C-print, 130 × 180 cm
p. 303

Gustavo Artigas
*Las reglas del juego
The rules of the game*
2000-2001
Video and photo documentation,
files and sport props, variable size,
still from video
p. 259

Atelier Van Lieshout
Women on waves
2000
Project
p. 159

Massimo Bartolini
Rot Bostane
2001
Project for *Refreshing*
p. 306

Samuel Beckett-Marin Karmitz
Comédie, 1966
35 mm film, 18' 43"
(film still)
p. 15, 43

Vanessa Beecroft
The Sister Project (November)
2000
C-print, 182,9 × 315 cm
Photo: Todd Eberle
p. 241

Joseph Beuys
*Voglio vedere i miei montagne
(Ich will meine Berge sehen)*
1950-71
Installation of 29 elements,

4,2 × 5,8 × 7,82 cm
p. 19

*La fine del XX secolo
(Das Ende des 20. Jahrhunderts)*
1983
21 basaltstones in different sizes, felt,
clay, wheel-barrow, squared wood,
installation, 4,7 × 12 × 9 cm
p. 20

Olivestones
1984
Limestone, olive oil, installation,
variable size
Kunsthaus Zurich
Photo Buby Durini
p. 21

Richard Billingham
Untitled
1990
Black and white print on aluminium,
98 × 147 cm, editions of 5 plus 1 AP
p. 261

Pierre Bismuth
*From Humanity to Something Else
From Something Else to Humanity*
2001
Vinyl letters on wall, project for
installation at the Italian Pavilion
p. 177

A new face
2001
Collage on newspaper
(Guardian May 3th)
Private collection
p. 178

Upping the tempo
2001
Collage on newspaper
(Guardian May 2th)
Private collection
p. 179

Erich Bödeker
Schwarze Stürzende
1969
Cocrete on wooden painted board,
128 × 70 × 40 cm
p. 8

*Apollo 0
(birds drinking trough)*
1970
Concrete, painting,
metal handle, 87 × 39 × 40 cm
p. 8

Heilige Barbara
1970
Wood (mine stamp), wood piece,

painting miner lamp, 190 × 28 cm
p. 8

Botto & Bruno
Under my red sky
2000
Wall paper e pvc, 800 × 900 × 330 cm
Photo: Ela Bialkowska
Palazzo delle Esposizioni Roma
p. 161

Martin Bruch
*Wien Maria Ilfestraße
89/36*
10.02.87, 21:23
C-print
p. 139

*Wien Margaretestraße
108/15, store room*
07.08.98.09:43
C-print

Tania Bruguera
La isla en peso, Virgilio Piñuera, 1943
p. 219

Roderick Buchanan
Deadweight + Peloton (video)
2000
Installation view
p. 185

Chris Burden
The Flying Steamroller
1996
Steel, concrete, 1968 Huber road
grader
p. 65

Cau Quo Quiag

Seni Camara
Untitled
1998
Terra-cotta, h 30 cm
p. 5

Maurizio Cattelan
*La rivoluzione siamo noi
We are the Revolution*
2000
Polyester resin figure, felt suit,
metal coat rack, puppet:
124,9 × 32,8 × 23 cm; wardrobe rack:
188,8 × 46,9 × 52 cm
Courtesy Marian Goodman Gallery,
New York
p. 123

Loris Cecchini
BBBreathless
2001
Model Urethanic rubber
Courtesy Galleria Continua,

Galérie Yvon Lambert,
Paris 1979
Photo: G. Cima
p. 41

Guvin Turk
Bin Bag 3
2000, 2001
Painted bronze, 55 × 56 × 58 cm
Courtesy Jay Jopling, London
p. 217

Richard Tuttle
Ten, C
2000
Acrilic on fit ply wood, 10 panels, each
25.4 × 25.4 cm, overall 101.6 × 101.6 cm
SW 01028
p. 53

Cy Twombly
Lepanto
2001
Acrilic on canvas, 216 × 334 cm
Private collection
Courtesy Gagosian Gallery
p. 27

Lepanto
2001
Acrilic on canvas, 216,5 × 334,5 cm
Private collection
p. 28

Lepanto
2001
Acrilic on canvas, 216,5 × 303,5 cm
Private collection
Courtesy Gagosian Gallery
p. 29

Salla Tykka
Lasso
2000
Video, stills from video
p. 277

From the series *Pain, Pleasure, Guilt*
2000
C-print, 1000 × 1200 mm
Courtesy of the artist
p. 278

From the series *Pain, Pleasure, Guilt*
2000
C-print, 1000 × 1200 mm
Courtesy of the artist
p. 279

Keith Tyson
*The thinker (After Rodin) –
Technicals/notes*
2001
Mixed media on paper, 157 × 127 cm

framed
p. 255

*Section of an Infinitive Dam holding
Back the Terrible Weight of the Abyss*
Mixed media on paper, 157 × 126 m
framed
p. 256

*Lecture about current problems with
Beatrix Ruf*
Mixed media on paper, 157 × 126 m
framed
Private collection, Basel
Courtesy Anthony Reynolds Gallery,
London
p. 257

Eulàlia Valldosera
*Provisional Home
(Provisional Living #1)*
1999
Installation with slide projection,
installation view, variable size
©Eulàlia Valldosera / S.I.A.E.
p. 171

*Provisional Home
(Provisional Living # 1)*
1999
Installation with slide projection,
installation view, variable size
©Eulàlia Valldosera / S.I.A.E.
p. 172

*Provisional Home
(Provisional Living # 1)*
1999
Installation with slide projection,
installation view, variable size
©Eulàlia Valldosera / S.I.A.E.
p. 173

Minnette Vàri
Mirage
Miraggio
1999
Video animation, 40', looped
indefinitely, 100', variable size,
stills from video
p. 237

REM
2001
Video animation, 18' looped
indefinitely, variable size,
stills from video
p. 238

Oracle
1999
Video animation, video 2', audio 6',
looped indefinitely, variable size,
stills from video
p. 239

Francesco Vezzoli
*Embroidery of a Book:
Young at Any Age*
2000
33 parts, 33 × 43,2 cm each,
detail
p. 271

*Embroidery of a Book:
Young at Any Age*
2000
33 parts, 33 × 43,2 cm each,
detail
p. 272

*Embroidery of a Book: Young
at Any Age*
2000
33 parts, 33 × 43,2 cm each, detail
p. 273

Bill Viola
The Quintet of the unseen
2000
Video installation, still from video
Photo: Kira Perov
p. 93

Not Vital
70 camel's head
2001
Sculpture, 60 m long
p. 81

Massimo Vitali
De Haan-Kiss-# 0756
2001
Color Print on plexiglass, aluminium
frame, edition 1/3, 370 × 150 × 2 cm
p. 59

Riccione Diptych
1997
Color Print on plexiglass, aluminium
frame, edition 4/9, 150 × 180 × 2 cm
p. 60-61

Jeff Wall
Sunken Area
Trasparency in lightbox,
219 × 274 cm
p. 75

Magnus Wallin
Exit
1997
3D animation, stills from video
Courtesy Antenna
p. 193

Exit
1997
3D animation, stills from video
Courtesy Antenna
p. 194

Skyline
2000
3D animation, stills from video
Courtesy Antenna
p. 195

Peter Wanjau
One man can fill the world
1998
Painted wood, h. 54 cm
Photo: Maurizio Brenzoni
p. 6

Aids Killing
1998
h. 63 cm
Photo: Maurizio Brenzoni
p. 6

Nick Waplington
www.dwarfswop.com
2000
©Nick Waplington
p. 197

www.extramaritalrelations.com
2000
Copyright Nick Waplington
p. 197

Maaria Wirkkala
Dream screen/prime time
2000
Mixed media installation, 50 × 70 cm
Photo: Timo Torikka, 2000
p. 94

Found a mental connection
1998
Installation, variable size
Photographed by R. Träskelin 1998
p. 95

Xiao Yu
Ruan
1999
Holograph of installation, 70 × 50 cm
p. 199

Xu Zhen
Rainbow
Body part being slapped - graduately
turning red, video, 4', still from video
p. 291

Vadim Zakharov
Theology Conversation
1996-2000
Mixed media installation, variable size
p. 121

Heimo Zobernig
Nr. 18
2000
Video installation, site specific,

mixed media, still from video
p. 111

Nr. 18
2000
Video installation, site specific,
mixed media, still from video
p.112

Nr. 18
2000
Video installation, site specific,
mixed media, still from video
p. 113

Artists Index

Questo volume è stato stampato per conto della Elemond Spa
presso lo stabilimento di Martellago Mondadori Printing Spa
Via Castellana, 98, Martellago (Venezia) nell'anno 2001